INTRICATE
ETHICS

OXFORD ETHICS SERIES
Series Editor: Derek Parfit, All Souls College, Oxford

The Limits of Morality
Shelly Kagan

Perfectionism
Thomas Hurka

Inequality
Larry S. Temkin

Morality, Mortality, Volume I
Death and Whom to Save from It
F. M. Kamm

Morality, Mortality, Volume II
Rights, Duties, and Status
F. M. Kamm

Suffering and Moral Responsibility
Jamie Mayerfeld

Moral Demands in Nonideal Theory
Liam B. Murphy

The Ethics of Killing
Problems at the Margins of Life
Jeff McMahan

Intricate Ethics
Rights, Responsibilities, and Permissible Harm
F. M. Kamm

F. M. KAMM

INTRICATE ETHICS

Rights, Responsibilities, and Permissible Harm

OXFORD
UNIVERSITY PRESS

2007

OXFORD
UNIVERSITY PRESS

Oxford University Press, Inc., publishes works that further
Oxford University's objective of excellence
in research, scholarship, and education.

Oxford   New York
Auckland   Cape Town   Dar es Salaam   Hong Kong   Karachi
Kuala Lumpur   Madrid   Melbourne   Mexico City   Nairobi
New Delhi   Shanghai   Taipei   Toronto

With offices in
Argentina   Austria   Brazil   Chile   Czech Republic   France   Greece
Guatemala   Hungary   Italy   Japan   Poland   Portugal   Singapore
South Korea   Switzerland   Thailand   Turkey   Ukraine   Vietnam

Published by Oxford University Press, Inc.
198 Madison Avenue, New York, New York 10016

www.oup.com

Oxford is a registered trademark of Oxford University Press

Library of Congress Cataloging-in-Publication Data
Kamm, F. M. (Frances Myrna)
Intricate ethics: Rights, responsibilities, and permissible harm / F. M. Kamm.
    p.   cm. — (Oxford ethics series)
Includes bibliographical references and index.
ISBN-13 978-0-19-518969-8
ISBN 0-19-518969-8
1. Consequentialism (Ethics)   2. Ethics.   3. Responsibility.   I. Title.   II. Series.
BJ1031.K36 2006
171'.5—dc22   2005047341

9 8 7 6 5 4 3 2 1

Printed in the United States of America
on acid-free paper

In memory of my dearest parents,
Mala Schlussel Kamm and Solomon Kamm,
loving souls, gifted people

ACKNOWLEDGMENTS

A very different version of this book was begun in 1998–1999. I am grateful to New York University for its sabbatical year support and to the Guggenheim Foundation for the fellowship that helped make possible time for writing. The book was originally meant to contain work on normative theory and practical ethics, but by the end of that sabbatical year the normative and practical writings had been separated into different books.

I next received support from a fellowship from the National Endowment for the Humanities (for May 2001–January 2002) and was in residence at the Center for Advanced Studies in the Behavioral Sciences at Stanford (supported by a Mellon grant) from September 2001 to January 2002. It was there that I finished the first complete draft of the present book. I am very grateful to the center for its supportive atmosphere. I submitted the draft to Derek Parfit, the editor of the Oxford Ethics Series. Unbelievably, in a matter of days, I was the beneficiary of fifty-five single-spaced pages of comments on both intellectual substance and style. At that time, I also received many helpful comments on the book from Peter Graham and Ryan Preston. There was obviously still work to be done.

In January 2003, after many years at New York University, I accepted the generous offer (coordinated by the academic dean of the Kennedy School of Government, Frederick Schauer) from the Kennedy School of Government and the Department of Philosophy at Harvard University. Thanks to the current academic dean of the Kennedy School, Stephen Walt, I was provided with financial support in the spring of 2003 that allowed me time to make much further progress on the manuscript. This was followed by new comments on the revised manuscript from Parfit, and on parts of it from students in my Harvard Philosophy Department seminar, and Ruth Chang, Liam Murphy, Shelly Kagan, and Larry Temkin. My sabbatical leave in the fall of 2004, also supported by the Kennedy School, made possible the submission of the manuscript for publication in Winter 2004. In Spring 2005, while I had the privilege of being a Visiting Fellow at All-Souls College, I also benefited from discussions with Derek Parfit and comments by others (noted in the text) that led to further revisions. In the summer of 2005, as I went over the manuscript copyedited by Oxford University Press, I was fortunate to be in residence at the New York University School of Law, thanks to Profs. Liam Murphy and Clayton Gillette as well as Dean Richard Revesz.

In addition to those who have funded and commented on my work, I am greatly indebted to the many talented and patient people who have helped me by editing and typing my manuscripts. Carrie-Ann Biondi, now herself a professor of philosophy, edited in detail a version of the entire manuscript in 2002–2003. She was enormously helpful and superbly efficient. Several typists have, incredibly, been able to follow the ins and outs of directions on my (often handwritten) manuscripts. Lynne Meyer Gay and Mandy Plodek, who have done most of the work, have been unfailing in their support and the excellence of their work. I am also grateful to Ann Lai and Ann Sawka for excellent typing on several chapters. Deborah Bula at New York University and my assistants over the years at Harvard—Aaron Jette, Greg Dorchak, Mary Naus and currently the excellent Camiliakumari Wankaner—have helped with typing, faxing, mailing, and payments, all necessary to completing the book. I admire their professionalism and appreciate their help. Samuel Pigott, Kate Tighe and Paula Maute proofread, and Harry Dolan prepared the index.

I am grateful to my family (especially Ruth and Gerard Klein, Frances and John Martin, Vivian Oster, Denise Kamm, Lea Schlussel, Ben Zion Schlussel, Esther Schlussel, and Philippe Markiewicz) and my friends and colleagues (especially Thomas Scanlon, John Sexton, Gertrude Ezorsky, Lewis Kornhauser, Rosemund Rhodes, and the late Robert Nozick) for their support. Derek Parfit's comments and encouragement have been of the greatest import. Maria Twarog and Agnes and Hubert Mosezjuk have been kind and steadfast helpers in many aspects of daily life (including the care of a dear cat, Lalka). I believe this is, in part, due to their devotion to my mother, Mala Kamm, the memory of whom (along with that of my father, Solomon Kamm, my uncle, Samuel Kamm, and my aunt, Zella Oster) has sustained and enriched me.

CONTENTS

Introduction   3

SECTION I: NONCONSEQUENTIALISM AND THE TROLLEY PROBLEM

1 Nonconsequentialism   11
2 Aggregation and Two Moral Methods   48
3 Intention, Harm, and the Possibility of a Unified Theory   78
4 The Doctrines of Double and Triple Effect and Why a Rational Agent Need Not Intend the Means to His End   91
5 Toward the Essence of Nonconsequentialist Constraints on Harming: Modality, Productive Purity, and the Greater Good Working Itself Out   130
6 Harming People in Peter Unger's *Living High and Letting Die*   190

SECTION II: RIGHTS

7 Moral Status   227
8 Rights beyond Interests   237
9 Conflicts of Rights: A Typology   285

SECTION III: RESPONSIBILITIES

10 Responsibility and Collaboration   305
11 Does Distance Matter Morally to the Duty to Rescue?   345
12 The New Problem of Distance in Morality   368

SECTION IV: OTHERS' ETHICS

13 Peter Singer's Ethical Theory   401
14 Moral Intuitions, Cognitive Psychology, and the Harming/Not-Aiding
    Distinction   422
15 Harms, Losses, and Evils in Gert's Moral Theory   450
16 Owing, Justifying, and Rejecting   455

Bibliography   491

Index   499

INTRICATE
ETHICS

INTRODUCTION

This book is about nonconsequentialist ethical theory—its methods and content as I see them—and some alternatives to it, either substantive or methodological. Many of the chapters are based on essays of mine on normative theory published since 1996.[1] However, even these chapters significantly revise and expand the substance of the articles on which they are based.

Section I, "Nonconsequentialism and the Trolley problem," consists of chapters that first provide a general introduction to my past work and then present more detailed discussion of particular aspects of nonconsequentialist theory pertaining to harming persons. The section begins with "Nonconsequentialism" (chapter 1), which is, to a large extent, a summary of two of my previous books and to some degree an introduction to new discussions that follow in later chapters. The first seven parts of chapter 1 include summaries of my *Morality, Mortality*, volume 2, on the topics of prerogatives, constraints, inviolability, and the significance of status, also adding some new points. The last part includes summaries of chapters 5–12 of my *Morality, Mortality*, volume 1, on a nonconsequentialist theory of aggregation and the distribution of scarce goods, also adding some new points.[2] It provides those who have not read these books with a background to my thinking and a sense of the project I am trying to carry forward in this book. Hence, while chapter 1 introduces problems and views, the more detailed discussion of many of these occurs in later chapters. There follows a chapter that reexamines the question of whether the numbers of people who would be saved or killed makes a difference to what we should do. As later chapters will assume that there is reason to do what saves a greater number of people, it is appropriate that this question should be dealt with first. I contrast two subcategories of a method known as pairwise comparison—confrontation and substitution—by which conflicts might be resolved in a non-consequentialist theory. I argue that substitution is permissible. Chapter 3, "Intention, Harm, and the Possibility of a Unified Theory," examines how another philosopher, Warren Quinn, dealt with some of the issues I discuss in "Non-consequentialism." While critical of the significance for permissibility of the intention/foresight distinction, it also presents my attempt to see how far we can offer a unified account of the moral foundations of the harming/not-aiding and the intention/foresight distinctions.

The next three chapters make use of the Trolley Problem (to which the reader was introduced in chapter 1) for the purpose of unearthing principles of permissible harm. Chapter 4, "The Doctrines of Double and Triple Effect and Why a Rational Agent Need Not Intend the Means to His End" is concerned with the Doctrine of Double Effect and an addition to it that I call the Doctrine of Triple Effect. The chapter introduces and explains a second distinction, besides intending versus foreseeing; this is the distinction between acting because of an effect that one's act will have and acting in order to produce the effect. This distinction supports my claim that very common notions of what it is to intend an effect are wrong. The chapter also focuses on the bearing that the "because of" relation has on a theory of instrumental rationality. The question is asked: Must a rational agent, insofar as he is rational, intend what he believes is the means to his end? I argue that the possibility of acting because of an effect we will produce without intending to produce the effect helps to show that a rational agent, insofar as he is rational, need not intend the means to his end. In conclusion, I consider some practical implications of these points.

The next chapter, "Toward the Essence of Nonconsequentialist Constraints on Harming: Modality, Productive Purity, and the Greater Good Working Itself Out," briefly reviews several proposals that have been made to account for when it is permissible to harm innocent bystanders, including the Doctrine of Triple Effect. Problems that seem to arise for each of these proposals are considered, and then two new proposals—the Doctrine of Initial Justification and the Doctrine of Productive Purity—are introduced. Having argued for substitution rather than confrontation of persons in chapter 2, in this chapter I argue for substitution rather than subordination of persons as a way of dealing with conflicts between people. In addition, I draw connections between what we learn from considering the Trolley Problem and what are known as innocent threat cases, I consider when a principle of permissible harm may be overridden, and finally draw a practical implication from my discussion.

This chapter, more than others, makes clear that I believe that finding a principle of permissible harm (if there is one) is, in part, like a rigorous scientific or technical enterprise. It involves *very* intricate ethics. Thomas Nagel, in discussing his views about a principle of permissible harm (based on the Doctrine of Double Effect) says: "I won't try to draw the exact boundaries of the principle. Though I say it with trepidation, I believe that for my purposes they don't matter too much, and I suspect they can't be drawn more than roughly: my deontological intuitions, at least, begin to fail above a certain level of complexity."[3] My approach to finding a principle of permissible harm (as well as my views about what the principle is) is very different. I think that the principle can be drawn more than roughly, and that in doing this, we should, if we can, rely on intuitions even at great levels of complexity.

In general, the approach to deriving moral principles that I adopt may be described as follows: Consider as many case-based judgments of yours as prove necessary. Do not ignore some case-based judgments, assuming they are errors, just because they conflict with simple or intuitively plausible principles that account for some subset of your case-based judgments. Work on the assumption that a different principle can account for all of the judgments. Be prepared to be surprised at what this principle is. Remember that this principle can be simple, even though it is discovered by considering many complex cases. (If the principle is complex, this would not undermine the claim that people have intuitive judgments in accord with it, since people need not be conscious of the principle to have case-based intuitive judgments.) Then, consider the principle on its own, to see if it expresses some plausible value or conception of the person or relations between persons. This is necessary to justify it as a *correct* principle, one that has normative weight, not merely one that makes all of the case judgments cohere. (In this book, I spend less time on this last step than on the earlier ones.) Since the principle that is justifiable may be surprising, be prepared to be surprised at what the point of non-consequentialism turns out to be. This is only a working method, and it remains possible that some case judgments are simply errors. (However, more caution in drawing this conclusion is involved with the method I employ than seems to be common when others use other variants of the method known as *reflective equilibrium*.) I say, consider your case-based judgments, rather than do a survey of everyone's judgments. This is because I believe that much more is accomplished when one person considers her judgments and then tries to analyze and justify their grounds than if we do mere surveys.[4]

The last chapter in this section, "Harming People in Peter Unger's *Living High and Letting Die*," examines Peter Unger's views on the permissibility of harming innocent bystanders and the duty to harm ourselves in order to aid others. It also considers his views on the method of using intuitive judgments about cases in order to discuss moral principles. (In section IV, in a chapter titled "Peter Singer's Ethical Theory," I argue that Singer underestimates how extreme the implications of his consequentialist views are and that, in fact, they imply something like Unger's principles of permissible harm. Hence, my criticism of Unger implicitly begins a criticism of Singer's views that continues at several other places throughout these chapters.) Since Unger makes heavy use of the Trolley Problem in discussing these issues, it is appropriate for this chapter to follow on my detailed discussion of that problem.

Section II, "Rights," begins with "Moral Status," a basic discussion of different forms of moral significance that entities may have, culminating in being the subject of a right. The next chapter, "Rights beyond Interests," includes an overview of theories of rights and an attempt to show how certain other elements of nonconsequentialist theory (already discussed in section I) may help us to better understand the foundation and content of rights. Some ideas discussed in earlier chapters—for example, inviolability, the distinction between harming and not-aiding, and distinctions among ways of harming people—appear again. But now the purpose is to see how they function in the new context of rights theory. An important thesis of this chapter is that we should not think of rights as only protecting and promoting interests, but also as reflecting someone's status and worth simply as a person. I try to show that this thesis may help explain why the very same interest is protected in some ways and not in others. The next chapter, "Conflicts of Rights: A Typology," adds more detail to the discussion of conflicts of rights in "Rights beyond Interests." It also shows how questions about aggregation that arose in section 8 of chapter 1 and in chapter 2 appear in a new guise as part of the theory of rights.

Section III, "Responsibilities," discusses issues that, I believe, are newer to recent nonconsequentialist theory: responsibility and collaboration, and new ways in which physical distance might bear on our duty to aid. The discussion of collaboration in "Responsibility and Collaboration" grows directly out of reconsidering one of the most famous cases in the literature of modern ethics, Jim and the Indians, used by Bernard Williams to criticize consequentialism. This case would require someone to kill, in a way ordinarily thought to be impermissible, a person who would otherwise soon die anyway. It is appropriate to consider it after our earlier discussion in section I of a principle of permissible harm that would ordinarily rule out killing in such a way. This chapter also revisits another issue introduced by Williams, namely, "agent regret."

Both consequentialists and nonconsequentialists have a hard time believing that mere physical distance between people could affect the strength of our duty to aid, even though it seems to play a role in intuitive judgments, at least at first blush. The first chapter on the topic, "Does Distance Matter Morally to the Duty to Rescue?" harks back to the methodological issues discussed in chapter 1 in connection with determining whether killing is morally equivalent to letting die. So it applies what was said there about determining whether a set of contrasting factors is a morally relevant distinction to the issue of whether physically near versus far is a morally relevant distinction. This chapter also includes detailed discussions of Peter Singer's and Peter Unger's arguments concerning our duty to aid and its independence from distance. The second chapter on the topic, "The New Problem of Distance in Morality,"[5] argues in detail that, whether or not distance is morally significant, the problem of distance in morality has been misunderstood. It offers a reconception of the problem and tries to answer some of the new questions to which this revised problem gives rise.

Section IV, "Others' Ethics," is devoted to the views of others within the consequentialist and nonconsequentialist camps. The section begins with "Peter Singer's Ethical Theory," an examination of the ethical theory to which Singer subscribes, on topics other than harming some to aid others and the significance of distance. (His views [and views to which, I believe, he is committed] on the latter issues were discussed in previous chapters.) As a follow-up to Singer's (and Unger's) criticism of the use of intuitive judgments about cases, the next chapter, "Moral Intuitions, Cognitive Psychology, and the Harming/Not-Aiding Distinction," considers empirical work by Daniel Kahneman and Amos Tversky on the use of intuitive judgments and framing effects. Their work precedes but is similar in spirit to Peter Unger's, I believe, and could be useful in supporting consequentialism. My main claim in this chapter is that the harming/not-aiding distinction is neither captured by the loss/no-gain distinction that is employed by these psychologists nor is it undermined by the same framing effects. (The primary argument for this is that *losses* can come about by not-aiding and so can also be distinct from harming.) A brief discussion of the moral theory of Bernard Gert, "Harms, Losses, and Evils in Gert's Moral Theory," which follows is pertinent given the discussion of Kahneman and Tversky, for I argue that Gert is a nonconsequentialist who does not distinguish the role that a harming/not-aiding distinction rather than a loss/no-gain distinction plays in his own theory.

Contractualism (also known as contractarianism)[6] is a metatheory that is theoretically compatible with consequentialism as the favored normative principle of contractors. However, in Thomas Scanlon's theory, contractualism is proposed as a foundation for nonconsequentialist principles. The first half of the next chapter, "Owing, Justifying, and Rejecting," which is my discussion of parts of his book *What We Owe to Each Other*, is concerned with Scanlon's account of wrongness and his view of the value of human life. I argue that Scanlon's theory is best understood not as an account of "wrongness" (as he claims) but as an account of "wronging" and that, in this regard, it has connections with the theory of rights (discussed in chapter 8). The second half of the chapter begins by comparing Scanlon's contractualism with the type of method used in this book and then examines the particular reasons that might be given by contractors in rejecting or accepting proposed moral principles, such as the probability of harm, giving priority to the worst off, and aggregating harms and benefits.

One might summarize a good deal of the plot line of this book as follows: Nonconsequentialists argue for the moral importance of many distinctions in how we bring about states of affairs. I try to present and consider the elements of some of these distinctions. A good deal of section I focuses on providing a replacement for a simple harming/not-aiding distinction and revising and even jettisoning the significance for permissibility of conduct of the intention/foresight distinction.[7] A good deal of section III is concerned with examining the possible moral significance of other distinctions (collaboration versus independent action; near versus far). Some moral philosophers (such as Singer and Unger) think that many nonconsequentialist distinctions have no moral importance, and other philosophers (such as Gert) employ distinctions other than harming/not-aiding and intending/foreseeing. The work of yet others (Kahneman) could be used to argue that the distinctions that some nonconsequentialists emphasize are reducible to distinctions (loss/no-gain) that are suspect. Some of the chapters examine these alternative views. Finally, some philosophers hold foundational theories, like contractualism, that could be used to derive and justify the nonconsequentialist distinctions by an alternative method from the heavily case-based ones I employ. I examine this alternative foundational approach and defend a case-based approach.

NOTES

1. I hope that a companion volume will be based on my articles since 1996 on practical ethical issues.

2. These books were published in 1996 and 1993, respectively, by Oxford University Press.

3. Thomas Nagel, *The View from Nowhere* (New York: Oxford University Press, 1986), pp. 179–80.

4. For more on my method of working, see the introductions to Kamm, Creation and Abortion, and *Morality, Mortality*, vols. 1 and 2 (New York: Oxford University Press, 1992, 1993 and 1996). In those introductions, I suggested that people who have responses to cases are a natural source of data from which we can isolate the reasons and principles underlying their responses. The idea was that the responses come from and reveal some underlying psychologically real structure, a structure that was always (unconsciously) part of the thought processes of some people. Such people embody the reasoning and principles (which may be thought of as an internal program) that generates these responses. The point is to make the reasons and principles explicit. (Unlike the deep structure of the grammar of a language, at least one level of the deep structure of moral intuitions about cases seems to be accessible upon reflection by those who have the intuitive judgements. An alternative model is that the responses commit people to principles that, however, were not in fact really psychologically present and generating their judgements.) If the same "deep structure" is present in all persons—and there is growing psychological evidence that this is true (as in the work of Professor Marc Hauser)—this would be another reason why considering the intuitive judgements of one person would be sufficient, for each person would give the same response.

5. Originally I called it the "Problem of Moral Distance," but it now seems to me that "moral distance" suggests something other than the moral relevance of mere physical distance.

6. I am reminded of Thomas Scanlon's Berlinesque quip about the use of these slightly different terms by different people to refer to the same thing: "Let's call the whole thing off."

7. Much more attention is paid to this latter distinction in this book than in *Morality, Mortality*, vol. 2.

SECTION I

Nonconsequentialism and
the Trolley Problem

1

NONCONSEQUENTIALISM

I. INTRODUCTION: DEFINITION AND ROOTS

Nonconsequentialism is a type of normative ethical theory that denies that the rightness or wrongness of our conduct is determined *solely* by the goodness or badness of the consequences of our acts or of the rules to which those acts conform. Nonconsequentialism does not deny that consequences can be a factor in determining the rightness of an act. It does insist that even when the consequences of two acts or act-types are the same, one might be wrong and the other right. Hence, nonconsequentialism denies the truth of both act and rule consequentialism, which are understood as holding that the right act or system of rules is the one that maximizes the balance of good consequences over bad ones as determined by an impartial calculation of goods and bads.[1] (Henceforth, I shall refer to this as "maximizing the good.") This sort of consequentialist calculation requires that we have a theory of what is good and bad; it may be an extremely liberal theory, holding that killings are bad or that autonomy is good, but we are still required to maximize the good.[2]

Despite the name "consequentialism," some consequentialists think that certain actions have value or disvalue in themselves. Some also think that acts and consequences can have different moral significance depending on their historical context. These theorists would think that we always ought to maximize the goodness of states of affairs where this could include the act itself, its consequences and the historical context of these. Strictly, this would make them also be nonconsequentialists. But in addition to denying pure consequentialism, typical nonconsequentialists also deny that we always ought to maximize the goodness of states of affairs. Because of the possibility of this alternative contrast, instead of speaking of consequentialism versus nonconsequentialism, we could contrast teleology, in which we decide what to do solely by considering what state of affairs we will bring about, with deontology, in which what we do is not determined solely by what we will bring about. I shall henceforth use "nonconsequentialism" to mean a theory that denies that the rightness or wrongness of our conduct (or rules governing our conduct) is determined solely by the goodness or badness of the state of affairs we would bring about.

Contemporary nonconsequentialism finds its spiritual roots in the work of Immanuel Kant and W. D. Ross. Some nonconsequentialists are especially drawn to Kant's second formulation of the Categorical Imperative, which specifies that we should always treat rational humanity in oneself and in others as an end-in-itself and never merely as a means, and to his distinction between perfect and imperfect duties. Persons are said to have a special kind of unconditional value—value independent of serving anyone's (even their own) ends and independent of their being in a particular context—that makes them worthy of respect. Merely counting each person's interests in a consequentialist calculation of overall good, while it seems to literally distinguish persons from mechanical tools, is not enough to ensure that we treat someone as an end-in-itself in the Kantian sense. Rather, it is thought, if I am an end-in-myself then this fact can constrain even conduct that would maximize overall good.

Furthermore, suppose that for my sake someone does or would (counterfactually) constrain his behavior toward me in a given context in some way even if this is contrary to his interests or to maximizing the good (e.g., he will not kill me to save his own life). This does not ensure that when he still uses me against my interests in that context (e.g., cuts off my leg) without my consent, when I do not deserve such treatment nor am liable to it in virtue of what I have done, but only because this is instrumentally useful to him, that he is not treating me as a mere means. Hence, I think that it can be appropriate to say that someone is treating me as a mere means in the absence of any knowledge about whether he does or would constrain himself in some way for my sake. I do not have to have such knowledge before I can conclude that he is treating me merely as a means.[3]

On this view, how I *treat* you—as a mere means or not—is not determined by and should not be identified with something else, namely, my overall attitude toward you or belief about you. My overall attitude toward you may be that you are not a mere means and so I would not treat you in all ways as a mere means in a particular circumstance even if this is useful to me. That does not, according to the interpretation I am presenting, make it conceptually impossible for me to treat you as a mere means in this particular circumstance. (Possibly, one might say that insofar as I cut off your leg when this only serves my interests, I treat you as a mere means. However, insofar as I restrain myself from doing even worse things to you, for your sake and against my own interests, I do not treat you as a mere means.)[4]

Perhaps the following principle is roughly true: If someone's behavior toward you and the reasons for it could be used as *evidence* for the claim that she has the overall attitude toward you that you are a mere means, then even if this evidence is not proof of the particular *attitude* (because in this or other circumstances she would have constrained her behavior for your sake), then this behavior constitutes *an instance of treatment as a mere means.*[5]

Some nonconsequentialists suggest that we divide this Categorical Imperative into two components: (a) Treat persons as ends-in-themselves, and (b) do not treat them as mere means.[6] If we treat people as mere means, then we fail to treat them as ends-in-themselves. Nonetheless, we might fail to treat people as ends-in-themselves, even though we do not treat them as mere means, such as when we act without their consent in a way that does not involve (or even evaluate) them as causally efficacious tools but that is merely foreseen to harm them against their interests (when this act had no chance of being in their interests). An example is when we decide not to stop ourselves from running over someone because our doing so would interfere with our rushing sick people to the hospital.

Despite the importance of Kantian-theory to nonconsequentialists, some question whether an act is impermissible just because the agent treats someone as a mere means or not as an end-in-himself in doing the act. For suppose I do an act that is justified by its great good consequences despite some foreseen side effect harm to a few people. However, I do the act not for its good consequences, but only in order to produce the harm to the people as an end in itself (and I would not in any other way constrain myself for their sakes). Presumably, this still does not make my doing the act impermissible.[7]

The second element of Kant's legacy that appeals to some contemporary nonconsequentialists is his distinction between perfect and imperfect duties. The perfect duties describe specifically what we must do and they take precedence over the imperfect duties, which give us leeway in how or when we fulfill them. Thus, in Kant's view, I may not kill one person in order to fulfill a duty to save others. Contemporary nonconsequentialists, however, often diverge from Kant's absolutist conception of perfect duties (i.e., that such duties always take precedence over imperfect duties), and some claim merely that the class of negative duties (e.g., not to harm) is more stringent than the class of positive duties (e.g., to aid). Some contemporary interpreters of Kant have argued that his theory is not absolutist and does not imply, for example, that lying to someone in order to stop him from committing a murder is wrong.[8] (It is not clear, however, that this interpretation, which seems to rely on the view that people's bad acts can lead to their forfeiting a right not to be lied to, can also yield the truth that it is permissible to lie to *an innocent bystander*, if this is necessary to stop a murderer.)

W. D. Ross is another major inspiration for contemporary nonconsequentialism. Although Ross thought that there was a prima facie duty of beneficence, he also thought that there are numerous other prima facie duties, for example, a duty not to harm, a duty of gratitude, and a duty to do justice. If these prima facie duties conflict, as he thought they might, we have no single scale on which to weigh them or rule by which to order them so as to determine what our actual duty is. In this sense, the duties are incommensurable, but that need not mean that conflicts be-tween them cannot be correctly decided by the exercise of judgment.[9] Some con-temporary nonconsequentialists have tried to modify Ross's view by more precisely determining the relative weights or ordering of prima facie duties, or by more precisely characterizing the prima facie duties, so that it becomes clearer which takes precedence. This latter endeavor might require stating duties so that they specify their own limits or finding more basic duties than the ones Ross described that do not as easily come into conflict with each other.

II. CONTEMPORARY NONCONSEQUENTIALISM OUTLINED

Nonconsequentialism is now typically thought to include prerogatives not to maximize the good and constraints on producing the good. A prerogative denies that agents must always maximize good consequences. Hence, it allows for the possibility that some acts are supererogatory, these being acts that, though they are not morally required, are morally valuable, sometimes in virtue of producing better consequences. Constraints limit what we may do in pursuit of our own, or even the impartial, good. The most commonly proposed constraints are a strong duty not to harm (contrasted with a weaker duty to aid) and/or a strong duty not to intend harm (contrasted with a weaker duty not to cause or allow harm that is merely foreseen). Those who are only partially nonconsequentialists might advocate prerogatives but no constraints[10] or constraints but no prerogatives.[11]

However, commonly proposed constraints ignore important moral complex-ities. Consider, for example, the constraint on harming. In the Trolley Case, a runaway trolley will kill five people, if a bystander does not divert it onto another track where, he foresees, it will kill one person. Nonconsequentialists typically think that the bystander may divert the trolley—killing one person to save the five—although, in other cases, they oppose killing one person to save five.[12] An appropriate constraint might better capture nonconsequentialist judgments of cases. If it does, it will capture the precise way in which an individual is thought to be inviolable and protected by a negative right not to be harmed, even if the harm would help to maximize the good. (Saying that someone is inviolable is a bit stronger than just saying that he has a right not to be harmed, as some rights might be permissibly infringed and then a person with such an infringeable right would not be inviolable to the same degree.)

Many nonconsequentialists employ a distinctive methodology. They test and develop theories or principles by means of intuitive judgments about cases. They compare the implications that proposed principles of permissible conduct have for hypothetical cases (such as the Trolley Case) with their considered judgments about what can permissibly be done in such cases. If the implications of the principles and judgments conflict, they may develop alternative principles. If the implications of the principles and judgments are compatible, the nonconsequen-tialist must still offer a theory identifying the fundamental, morally significant factors that underlie the principles in order for those principles to be fully justified.

If the principles cannot be fully justified, she may have to treat her initial judgment of cases as errors and ignore them in developing principles. She might also seek an error theory to account for her mistaken judgments.

Nonconsequentialism is not merely concerned with using this methodology to characterize and justify prerogatives and constraints, although they have been the focus of contemporary discussion. For example, the nonconsequentialist may also propose that there are distinctive ways of distributing aid among people that do not merely try to maximize the good.

In the remainder of this chapter, I shall explore these issues in more detail. Hopefully, this chapter will serve as an introduction to many topics and to my past work on them. But this will only be an introduction, for some positions taken (e.g., on intention and impermissibility) will be clarified, revised, and applied in new contexts in later chapters. When complex matters are discussed too briefly in this chapter, it is because we will return to them again in later chapters.

III. PREROGATIVES

Moral prerogatives permit an agent (1) to act in ways that do not maximize the impartial good (even when the impartial good would involve maximizing the number who get to act on such prerogatives), and (2) to act for reasons that stem from his personal perspective rather than from the perspective of an impartial judge. But how should we describe these prerogatives more precisely? Suppose that they permit us to assign a constant by which each agent can multiply the weight of his personal concerns, so that his concerns can outweigh an impartial good. A problem is that the results of such weighting could sometimes conflict with our intuitive judgments. For example, even if we assign a large multiplicative factor, we can envision some disaster whose prevention would, in principle, be required at the cost of an agent sacrificing his most significant projects. Yet, intuitively, we might not think that he is morally obligated to make the sacrifice. On the other hand, it seems morally wrong for agents to multiply their insignificant projects by this same large factor so that the pursuit of these projects often outweighs the more vital needs of others.

Here is an example of how the first problem might arise. Derek Parfit says[13] that surely it could be reasonable to give some weight to others at least to the degree of one-millionth of the weight one gives to oneself. He also says, one would have sufficient reason to give up one's life to save at least a million people. Parfit does not explicitly connect the two claims or say that it would be morally wrong not to sacrifice one's life. But a multiplicative-factor approach to explaining the prerogative might do these things, if it endorses the appropriateness of aggregating the small weight that is initially being assumed reasonable for one to give to each person. But this aggregation seems illicit. Here is an analogy: Surely it could be reasonable for me to give some weight to the welfare of birds, so that I care for a bird at least one-billionth of how much I care for myself. Does this imply that it would be reasonable or required of me to sacrifice my life to save a billion birds? I do not think so. It seems to me that to say that it is reasonable to care about a bird a bit (by comparison to how much one cares about oneself) implies that it is reasonable to protect its welfare when this involves no big imposition on one to do so. This is compatible with there being an upper limit on what it is reasonable for me to do for birds no matter how many of them could be saved. (Furthermore, if it is reasonable to give any of them much greater weight than one-billionth of how much one cares for oneself, that is also compatible with an upper limit on what it is reasonable to do for a great number of them.)

It seems more reasonable for the multiplicative factor to depend on the relative importance of the project to the agent, and even to permit agents to give some fundamental projects lexical priority relative to some impartial goods. Even this reasonable qualification of prerogatives seems to be an imperfect characterization, since a true prerogative gives the agent the option to care *less* for the pursuit of his projects than for the needs of others, and this does not seem to be captured by a multiplicative factor greater than one. This is a reason to think that the prerogative represents a concern for one's autonomy rather than for the importance of one's own interest, from one's own perspective, relative to the interests of others.

Some justify prerogatives by claiming that humans are psychologically pre-disposed to be most concerned about their own projects. Hence, if people are mor-ally permitted to pursue their nonoptimal projects for personal reasons, they will not be alienated from their fundamental psychological natures.[14] Notice that such a justification does not preclude person Z from interfering with someone else in Z's quest to maximize impartial good; it only says that someone need not always act of his own accord to promote the impartial good for impartial reasons. If we could show why someone's acting on a prerogative should be protected from interference by Z acting to maximize the good, we would have connected someone's prerogative with constraints on others, as part of a theory of individual rights to do and to not be interfered with. Further, the justification described also suggests that agents should be permitted to try to control that about which they care most. However, I should not be able to try to control someone else's life merely because that is what I care about most. Hence, a theory of prerogatives should specify from an impartial per-spective what we are entitled to try to control from a partial perspective.

Others justify prerogatives by claiming that consequentialist morality is too demanding, for it could require an agent to sacrifice everything to maximize the impartial good. This justification, though, is troublesome, for nonconsequentialism also can be very demanding: We may have to make enormous sacrifices in respecting constraints on interfering with others. Why should agents have to sacrifice projects to avoid violating constraints, but not to promote the impartial good? To adequately address this question, I believe, we also need a theory of what individuals are entitled to control, as we shall see below.

Still others ground prerogatives in the idea that people are ends-in-themselves. Since we should not view people—either ourselves or others—as mere means by which to promote the greater good, each of us can sometimes justifiably pursue nonoptimal goals. On this view, the foundation of prerogatives can also be the foundation of constraints on interferences, as both are connected to the idea of personal sovereignty. Even more fundamentally, prerogatives can be seen as a by-product of the fact that moral obligation is not about producing as much good as possible; rather, it is about respect for persons and doing as much good as that requires.

IV. CONSTRAINTS

I have suggested that the theory of prerogatives should be connected to a theory of constraints and negative rights.[15] By understanding constraints, we will better understand why we must suffer greater losses in order to avoid violating constraints than to maximize the good.

A. Harming versus Not-Aiding

Some nonconsequentialists claim that there is a strong moral constraint against harming people. Consequentialists argue that there is no intrinsic moral difference between harming and not-aiding (call this the Equivalence Thesis). Hence, consequentialists believe that we may generally harm in order to aid if this does more good overall. Consequentialists sometimes employ the methodology of intuitive judgments about cases to support the Equivalence Thesis. They identify seemingly comparable cases of harming and not-aiding, that is, cases where contextual factors, such as intention, foresight, consequences, motive, and effort, are equal. They claim that in such cases, we judge that harming and not-aiding are morally equivalent. However, to prove a universal claim like the Equivalence Thesis, one set of comparable cases will not suffice. For it may be that in some equalized contexts, a harming and a not-aiding will be judged as being morally equivalent, yet in other equalized contexts, they will not be. What I call the Principle of Contextual Interaction accounts for this possible phenomenon: A property can behave differently in one context than in another. However, if we can find even one set of comparable cases in which a harming is morally worse than a not-aiding, we rebut the Equivalence Thesis, for while a single positive instance cannot prove a universal claim, a single negative instance can defeat it.

    For example, James Rachels uses cases like the following pair of Bathtub cases in an attempt to prove the Equivalence Thesis: (1) Smith will inherit a fortune if his little cousin dies. One evening, while the child is taking his bath, Smith drowns him. (2) Jones will inherit a fortune if his little cousin dies. As Jones enters the bathroom, the child slips and falls face down in the bathwater. Although Jones could easily save the child, he does nothing, intending that the child die.[16] Rachels, and others following him, claim that in the Bathtub cases, a killing and a letting die are morally equivalent and, further, that this shows that killing and letting die are morally equivalent per se. But is even the first claim true? A test of its truth is to see if it would be permissible to impose the same losses on Jones and Smith, if these losses were to bring their victims back to life. I do not think it would. Although it might be permissible to kill Smith, it would not be permissible to kill Jones. So perhaps there really is a moral difference between the killing and the letting die in these cases, even though both of them are morally wrong.

The same point can be made about killing and letting die in other cases, if we ask how much effort an agent must expend to avoid killing someone and to save someone, where death is equally foreseen or intended. Here is a pair of Road cases: (1) We know that if we drive down one road, we will kill someone who cannot move out of the way. The only alternative is to go down a side road, where we risk hurting ourselves. (2) We know that to save someone from drowning, we must go down a side road, where we risk hurting ourselves. I think that an agent is obligated to face a larger personal risk to avoid killing than to avoid letting die. If this is right, then there is a fundamental moral difference between killing and letting die.

These cases suggest that killing and letting die are morally different per se, but they do not tell us *why* they differ. We might be able to determine why if we focus on differences that remain *in these cases*, after equalizing the contexts: (1) In killing, we introduce a threat that was not previously present; in letting die, we do not interfere with a currently present threat. (2) In killing, we act; in letting die, we fail to act. Presumably, the nonaction is not a mere omission but a refraining. For example, we are not asleep while someone dies, but we consciously choose not to aid. (3) (i) In killing, we cause someone to lose a life that he would have had independently of our efforts at that time; (ii) in letting die, someone loses a life that he would have had only with our help at that time. (4) In killing, we initiate an interference with the victim;[17] in letting die, we avoid being interfered with (by having to aid).

These four differences might explain the fundamental moral difference between killing and letting die, if they were essential (or conceptual) differences between killing and letting die and not just differences in some cases. Are they? Consider (2). Suppose that we actively terminate (e.g., pull a plug on) life-saving assistance we are providing to save Michael from a threat that we did not produce, and we do so in order to avoid the substantial effort involved in continuing aid (Terminate Aid Case). We foresee that Michael will die. In this case, I believe that we let Michael die, even though we *act* to stop the aid and not merely omit to provide it. The letting die by removing the aid is as acceptable (or unacceptable) as not starting the aid to begin with. Moreover, we are partial *causes* of Michael's death even if action is thought to be necessary for causation; after all, it resulted because we acted. Hence, we cannot distinguish between killing and letting die simply by saying that the latter always involves no action and does not cause death. Still, in the Terminate Aid Case, we do not introduce a cause that induces death. If we did, we would be killing. That is, only killings can have the property of inducing death, although perhaps some killings do not.[18]

The fact that we do not induce death seems connected to (1) a threat already being present. Let us consider whether (1) is an essential difference between killing and letting die. If someone has been using my life-support machine since his birth, was there ever a threat already present to him, such that if I pull the plug he dies of it? To help answer this question, consider that most of us have never been under threat of starvation, because we have always been provided with the food that is a defense against starvation. If the person supplying our food should stop, I suggest that he lets us die, but we face the threat of starvation for the first time. What has been already present is a need or vulnerability that would, without help, have led to a threat. Let us then say that letting die involves, at least, a *potential threat already present*. Even revised in this way, (1) implies that, as I have put it elsewhere, letting die always needs an "accomplice" to achieve death in the way that killing does not.[19] That is, without a (potential) threat, refraining from aiding someone will not lead to death, but introducing a threat which induces death can lead to death even if another (potential) threat is absent.[20] In the Terminate Aid Case, we also stop our being interfered with by discontinuing aid (4), and the victim loses only what he would have had if we had continued aid (3)(ii). I suggest that revised (1), (3)(ii), and (4) are definitional or essential properties of letting die, but not killing and, hence, are essential differences between the two.[21]

We must be careful in speaking of essential differences, for there are two types: (a) differences that are essentially true of either killing or letting die per se and also necessarily excluded from cases involving the other, and (b) those that are essentially true of only one but not necessarily excluded from cases involving the other. The first type is the most obvious difference; the second type is still a vital difference, even though such an essential difference is "exportable" to an instance of the contrasting behavior. Thus, some *cases* of killing (though not all cases of killing and hence not killing per se) could contain what is an essential property only of letting die, and vice versa. For example, this is true when we induce death in someone who is receiving life support from us, for this killing case has two of the essential properties of letting die, namely (3)(ii) and (4).[22] Nonetheless, these exportable essential properties could still explain the moral difference between killing and letting die per se. Indeed, rather than compare equalized cases of killing and letting die, we could compare two cases of killing that are alike in all respects except that only the second case has an essential exportable property of letting die. (I call this "cross-definitional equalization.") For example, killing someone who is independent of our aid is compared with killing someone who is receiving life-saving aid from us. If the killing in the second case is less morally problematic than the killing in the first, then we have strong evidence that the relevant essential exportable property of letting die is morally significant.

If the property involved in the previous example functions in the same way on its home ground (i.e., in letting die), and killing has no essential property that can make the act of killing less bad than letting die, then letting die would have at least one more morally improving essential property than killing has, and hence letting die would be morally better per se in virtue of that property.

Exportable properties could account for one way that defenders of the Equivalence Thesis might find cases in which a killing and a letting die were morally equivalent: They could find examples of killing and letting die in which essential properties of one of the behaviors were exported to the case involving the other. Then, as long as other morally relevant properties were equivalent in the cases, we would have identified a killing and a letting die that were morally equivalent. But that would not show that killing and letting die per se were morally equivalent; it would show just the reverse, since it would show that one of the behaviors (but not the other) has this particular morally significant exportable essential property.

I have argued[23] that letting die essentially has properties that can make those acts morally more acceptable than acts of killing. These properties are that the "victim" loses only life that he would have had with the agent's help at that time,[24] and that the agent avoids his being interfered with.[25] But these properties could be morally important only if one has a stronger claim relative to another person to what one has independently of the current aid of that other person than he has to it, and this applies both to one's life and to the efforts we as aiders could make on behalf of others. The moral distinction between killing and letting die, hence, is connected to the idea of separate persons with entitlements (relative to certain pertinent others at least) to what makes them separate persons.

Hence, we might have to make great efforts to avoid being the first to interfere with others,[26] especially with what they are caused to have independently of our current aid, while legitimately making fewer efforts to prevent someone from going without only what he would have had by our providing aid. This helps us to understand that being morally obligated to make great efforts not to kill others, at least when the case does not share certain essential properties of letting die, is consistent with a prerogative not to maximize the good by aiding others. However, if we explain the moral distinction between killing and letting die as I have, we must do more work to explain why killing one person to save five in the Trolley Case is permissible—a task I take up in subsequent sections.

Notice that the account of the difference between killing and letting die I have given is in one important way "victim focused"—that is, it looks to whether the victim loses only what he would have had via help of the person who kills or lets die. This is by contrast with an approach that focuses on whether an agent acts or does not act. However, the approach does also focus on the agent in respect of what happens to him, that is, whether he would be imposed on first (if he acts by aiding) or whether he imposes first on another person (if he acts by harming).

There are certain things we should remember in applying our conclusions about killing and letting die to the more general moral distinction between harming and not-aiding: (1) When we kill or let someone die, we might reasonably think that she has some right to her life. But when we harm or do not aid someone in cases involving something other than her life, what she loses—or fails to get—may be something to which she has no right. (2) Generally, when someone kills, he interferes with another's body in ways he does not do when he lets that person die. However, if we harm someone in non-life-and-death contexts, we may not necessarily interfere with her body any more than if we do not aid her. Suppose that we combine these two factors and construct a set of harming and not-aiding cases:[27] (a) Some money that does not belong to anyone is accidentally transferred to my bank account, and you harm me by transferring it out by computer. (b) You fail to transfer some money that belongs to no one into my account. There may be no great moral difference between harming and not-aiding in these cases, though in the first, you deprive someone of what he had independently of your aid, while in the second, you fail to improve his condition. This is consistent with my earlier claim that properties which account for the moral difference between killing and letting die are important only if one has a greater claim than another to what one would have independently of that other person.

B. Intending versus Foreseeing Harm

The *Doctrine of Double Effect* (DDE) is historically the most important formulation of the supposed moral distinction between intending and foreseeing harm. This doctrine states that there is a moral constraint on intending evil (such as harm), even when the evil will be a means to a greater good. Nonetheless, we may be permitted to employ neutral or good means to promote a greater good, even though we foresee the same evil side effects, if (a) the good is proportionate to the evil, and (b) there is no better way to achieve this good. If we intend an evil (even as a means), bringing about the evil would give us a reason for action, and this is thought to be wrong.[28] Thus, it is said to be impermissible to end a just war by intentionally killing ten civilians (Terror Bombing Case), but it could be permissible to end the war by intentionally bombing munitions factories, even foreseeing that twenty other civilians will certainly die as an unintended side effect (Tactical Bombing Case). The DDE does not claim that when (a) and (b) are satisfied, we may always proceed. There may be other reasons that our act would be impermissible (e.g., we promised not to harm the civilians). It is just that the occurrence of the lesser evil as a side effect will not by itself make the act impermissible.

The supposed moral distinction between intending and foreseeing bad effects applies to omissions as well as to actions and so is independent of the harming/not-aiding distinction (though not all not-aiding involves an omission).[29] Some nonconsequentialists embrace the moral significance of only one of these distinctions; others embrace both. Moreover, some nonconsequentialists wish to revise the DDE so that it is a nonabsolute constraint. For example, they revise the DDE so that it does not apply at all in situations of self-defense, and so that in other situations, it only implies that we must tolerate worse consequences before intending bad effects than we have to tolerate before acting in ways in which bad effects are merely foreseen.

Many object to the DDE because we can typically describe behavior it supposedly rules out so that the agent does not strictly intend any evil and so see it as a reason for action. For example, the terror bomber might intend only that the civilians appear dead until peace is declared. Of course, he foresees with certainty that civilians will die, since the only way to make them appear dead until the war ends also leads to their death. But the tactical bomber also foresees with certainty the deaths of civilians.[30] The terror bomber, then, has here been redescribed so that he does not differ from the tactical bomber. We might try to recapture the moral distinction between these two cases by revising the DDE. The revised version could prohibit intending evil and also prohibit intending even minor intrusions on, or involvement of, persons[31] when the agent foresees that these others will suffer significant harm to which they did not consent. This is a significant revision to the doctrine. The original DDE barred agents from aiming at evil as a means or an end. The revision prohibits agents from intentionally treating persons as tools whenever the results would be foreseeably bad for those persons, even though there is no intention that evil occur as a means or an end.

The traditional DDE also seems problematic because it does not rule out producing a greater good by necessary means just because they have lesser bad side effects. As Philippa Foot notes, it does not rule out using a gas to save five people, even if we foresee that the gas will seep next door and kill one person (Gas Case). It does not rule out rushing to the hospital to save five people, foreseeing (but not intending) that we will run over and kill one person on the road (Car Case).[32] Yet, Foot claims, intuitively we think that it is impermissible to do these things because of the evil side effects. Only if we combine the DDE with a constraint on harming do we avoid the counterintuitive results.

In certain ways, the DDE is also too strong. It seems to rule out the intrapersonal case of intentionally harming someone as a means to promoting that person's overall good, and it rules out intentionally harming someone to help others, even when that person will be no worse off than he would have been otherwise (though he becomes worse off than he was).

A further complexity exists.[33] The DDE suggests that the *greater* good against which the bad side effect is compared must be *intended*. But can the greater good not be a mere foreseen side effect of what was intended? For example, in the Massacre Case, a tactical bomber targets one portion of a munitions factory for destruction. He intends to bring about this small good but foresees two side effects: (1) killing ten innocent civilians and (2) stopping a massacre of twenty other civilians. The side effect in (1) is too large an evil to be outweighed by the small intended good of eliminating a few bombs. The side effect in (2) seems to be a great enough good in traditional DDE reasoning to outweigh (1), but its occurrence is not currently necessary to the war effort and it is not intended. (The bomber may want the massacre to stop, but this does not mean that he will do [or omit to do] something in order to have it stop.) Hence, if the DDE were a necessary condition for moral permissibility, it might block the attack on the munitions factory, even if such an attack would be permissible were the greater good intended.

Notice that if the tactical bomber in this case proceeds only *because* (2) will occur, this need not imply that he intended to produce that good. This is a case in which his bringing about something can give him reason to act without his intending to bring it about.[34] This suggests that the Counterfactual Test for detecting intention (rather than mere foresight) is flawed. This test states that if we would not proceed with our act had a particular effect *not* occurred—assuming that everything else is held constant—then in acting, we intend that effect as a means or as an end. However, as the Massacre Case suggests, in some cases we might proceed only because an effect such as (2) will occur and would not act if it did not, yet still not intend its occurrence. This distinction between doing something *because* an effect will occur and doing it *in order that* it occurs also suggests that there is a third type of case in-between the Tactical Bombing and the Terror Bombing cases: Suppose that it is militarily valuable to bomb a munitions factory only if it is not immediately rebuilt. The factory will be rebuilt unless the population is grieving as a consequence of the deaths of civilians in the bombing. Hence, we carry out the tactical bombing of the factory only because we foresee that civilians will die, even though we do not intend that they die (Munitions Grief Case). I believe that if it were permissible to bomb the factory when the deaths are merely foreseen, it is permissible to bomb in this case, even if terror bombing is impermissible. Because of this third type of relation between an act and its effects—acting because the effects will occur, though not intending that they occur—it might be more inclusive to adopt what I call the *Doctrine of Triple Effect* (DTE).[35]

Might the DDE and the view that the distinction between harming and not-aiding is morally significant have a common foundation? Perhaps the former is also connected with the idea of separate persons and their entitlement, relative to a particular agent, to what makes them separate? When we intend that some event cause someone to lose what he has independently of us (even if not independently of others), we take the fact that someone will be interfered with as a factor in favor of a state of affairs, even if we do not cause the loss. This can show disrespect for the person's having what he is entitled to (at least relative to us). (Though, as we shall see below and in chapter 3, sometimes taking the fact that someone will be interfered with as a reason to favor a state of affairs does not show such disrespect, and does not even involve intending the interference.) When we merely foresee the fact that someone will be interfered with, we can take this as a factor against a state of affairs, even if the badness of its occurring is overridden by other considerations. However, when we let someone die, with the intention that some event we do not cause deprive him of what he has independently of us, what the person actually loses is still only what he would have had if we had helped him. By contrast, when we harm, even without intending to, the person can lose what he would have had independently of us. Hence, the disrespect for entitlements is once removed when it relies solely on intentions—as in a case of letting someone die intending his death—rather than on actions that cause harm.[36]

V. COMPLICATIONS ON THE CONSTRAINTS

As I noted earlier, many contemporary nonconsequentialists want to develop W. D. Ross's conception of prima facie duties. Ross thought that when these duties conflict, we have no rule or principle for ranking them. Hence, some non-consequentialists have tried to develop more complex accounts that describe duties that are less frequently in conflict with other duties. For example, the Trolley Case suggests how we might more precisely characterize the duty not to harm so that it does not conflict with a duty (or mere desire) to aid. We want something more helpful than a principle that merely says, sometimes the duty to not harm takes precedence over aiding and sometimes it does not. We are looking for a principle and its justification that explains why it is permissible to help some people by redirecting a fatal threat so that it kills one other person, and yet it would be impermissible to kill one person in order to harvest his organs to save others (Transplant Case). The principle and its justification must also explain why some things we could do to stop the trolley (e.g., pushing an innocent bystander into its path) are as impermissible as harvesting someone's organs to save others.[37]

Philosophers have offered many ways of explaining these intuitive judgments. One way is as follows: When (a) we redirect the trolley, we merely foresee the death of the one person; when (b) we harvest the organs for transplant, we intend the one person's death; and when (c) we push the innocent bystander into the trolley's path, we intend his involvement and foresee his death. Hence, (a) is permissible and (b) and (c) are not. However, this DDE-inspired explanation suggests that we could legitimately detonate a bomb to stop the trolley, even though we foresee, but do not intend, that the bomb will kill an innocent bystander. However, I believe that this is impermissible.

Another way of explaining these intuitive judgments is as follows: In the Trolley Case, we do not initiate a new threat. We merely redistribute a preexisting threat so that a greater number of people are saved. But this, even in combination with the previous explanation, cannot be a sufficient condition for acting permissibly. If a trolley is headed toward one person (and so a preexisting threat exists), we may not redirect it, foreseeing that it will kill five people, even if we do this because redirecting the trolley also causes a rock to move that saves twenty people from another threat. Neither does this second explanation offer a necessary condition for acting permissibly. Suppose that a trolley is headed toward five people who are seated on a large swivel table. Although we physically cannot redirect the trolley, we can swivel the table and save the five people. However, we thereby start a rock slide that will kill one innocent bystander (Lazy Susan Case). Here we start a new threat, rather than redistribute an existing one, and it kills someone. Nonetheless, I believe that it is permissible to swivel the table, and for the same reason that it is permissible to redirect the trolley. The problem, though, is explaining why.

One proposal to solve this problem is the *Principle of Permissible Harm* (PPH).[38] The basic idea of the PPH is that an act is permissible if (i) a greater good or (ii) a means that has a greater good as its noncausal flip side causes a lesser evil. However, it is not permissible for an act (iii) to require lesser evil (or someone's involvement leading to lesser evil) as a means to a greater good or (iv) to directly cause a lesser evil as a side effect when it has a greater good as a mere causal effect unmediated by (ii).[39] By "noncausal flip side" is meant that the description of the occurrence of the means to the good (i.e., the turning of the trolley) in a context where there are no other threats to the five is also a description of the five being saved and hence a description of the occurrence of the greater good.[40] The PPH denies that we may never harm someone in order to aid another. For example, when harm is a side effect of the achievement of a greater good, we may permissibly do what harms. Suppose that by directing gas into a room, we can save five people. However, their breathing when they would otherwise be dead alters the air flow in the room, redirecting germs that then kill an innocent person. In this case (unlike Foot's Gas Case described above), it is permissible to use the gas to save the five people, because it is the greater good itself—the people being alive—that causes the death.[41]

The PPH explains why we may permissibly redirect the trolley. The trolley moving away, which kills the one person, is a means to saving the five, and this greater good is its noncausal flip side. That is, given that the trolley moving away occurs in a context where no other fatal threat faces the five, the absence of threats and the five's being saved just is the trolley moving away. Further, our act of pressing a button that causes the redirection of the trolley, an act that ultimately leads to harm, is permissible by (iv), because it produces the harm only by pro-ducing a means (the redirecting of the trolley) that has a greater good as its non-causal flip side. By contrast, suppose we set off a bomb to stop the trolley, but the bomb kills an innocent bystander. The bomb's exploding has a *causal effect* of moving the trolley away from the five. Hence, in this sort of case, the absence of threats to the five and the saving of the five is not a *noncausal* flip side of the bomb's exploding. According to the PPH, the act that sets the bomb off is impermissible.

A problem for the PPH is to explain the Loop Case. Here a trolley is headed toward five people, and it can be redirected onto another track where one person sits. However, the track loops back toward the five.[42] The trolley will either kill the five in its original direction, or if we redirect it, it would kill the five after it loops, were it not that the trolley hits the one person (thereby killing him) and grinds to a halt. I believe that it is permissible to redirect the trolley in this case. Yet, hitting the one person is a causal link to saving the five; it is not merely a foreseen side effect, of no use to stopping the trolley. Does this mean that if we redirect the trolley, we intend the hitting of the one person as a means to our goal? Presumably, we would refuse to redirect the trolley unless the person were hit, for if the trolley did not hit him, five people would die anyway, and it would be a waste of effort to turn the trolley if the five would not be saved. In short, we redirect the trolley *because* we believe that the one person will be hit (and we foresee he will certainly die).[43] However, as I said above when discussing the Counterfactual Test, this does not necessarily imply that we intend to hit him. Consequently, our judgment in the Loop Case is consistent with the PPH (iii). The judgment also shows that a rational agent can pursue a goal (saving the five) that he knows is achievable only by his causing a certain event, and do so without intending to cause that event.[44] That is—contrary to what is commonly believed—a rational agent can continue to intend something without intending the means to it.

However, the Loop Case is a problem for the PPH even if hitting the one need not be intended. This is because the hitting of the one person is causally necessary to produce the greater good (saving the five), so how can the greater good, or a means that has the greater good as its noncausal flip side, be producing the lesser evil? We might revise the PPH as follows: When the trolley heads away from the five people, we are left with what I call the *structurally equivalent component of the greater good* (*structural equivalent*, for short). This is what would be the greater good if only no new problems, such as looping, arose from what we have done to deal with the original problem of the trolley coming at the five in one way. We are left with a structural equivalent because the only threat that the five still face—the trolley coming at them from another direction—*arises* only because we removed the initial threat (the trolley coming from a different direction). The structural equivalent of the greater good, or a means that has it as its noncausal flip side, produces this new problem as well as a harmful means for eliminating that new problem (the hitting of the person), and this makes redirecting the trolley permissible, I believe.[45] So the PPH should be revised to allow that a structural equivalent of the greater good or a means that has it as a noncausal flip side may produce a lesser evil, even when the lesser evil is necessary to sustain the greater good (by defusing new problems that arise from permissible remedies for the original threat).[46]

VI. INVIOLABILITY

The PPH, or a principle like it, implies that persons have rights not to be treated in certain ways simply in order to save more lives. These rights protect persons against some ways of maximizing the good; they give them some inviolability. The inviolability is not absolute. It is limited *qualitatively*. That is, the PPH itself permits some ways of harming. The inviolability may also be limited *quantitatively*. For example, the PPH might be overridden in order to save a great many people. The former limitation is internal to the PPH; the latter is an external restriction of it. One particular way in which the PPH may be limited is by what I call the *Principle of Secondary Permissibility* (PSP). For example, in the first instance, it is impermissible to push an innocent bystander into a trolley that will crush his leg in order to save five other people from the trolley's killing them. However, suppose the alternative is to redirect the trolley away from the five and toward that very same person, thereby killing him. Redirecting it toward him would ordinarily be permissible and is, suppose, something we would do if we could do nothing else. However, since it is in his interest to have his leg crushed rather than to be killed, *secondarily* it becomes permissible, I think, to push him into the trolley, an action that was not, in the first instance, permissible.

Are people so inviolable that agents may also not violate the PPH restrictions on harming one person, even if that is the only way of minimizing comparable violations of the PPH itself? The claim that we may not violate someone's rights in order to minimize violations of comparable rights is sometimes called the "paradox of deontology." Some claim that if we really care about rights, we should minimize their violation, even if this requires us to violate comparable rights. Those who agree with this say that they cannot see how one person's right could stand in the way of minimizing the violation of the comparable rights of others. If they, nevertheless, think that we should not violate the restrictions of the PPH, it is because, they say, we are concerned with the agent who would act rather than with the rights of the potential victim per se. This model derives any constraint on violating rights in order to minimize comparable rights violations from "inside (the agent) out (to the victim)" rather than from "outside the agent (in the victim's right) in (to the agent)."[47]

The agent-focused explanation of the constraint on minimizing rights violations has frequently employed the idea of agent-relative duties. *Agent-relative duties* are ones whose content makes essential reference to the particular agent whose duty it is. For example, agent A has the following duty: to see to it that agent A not kill someone. By contrast, an agent-neutral duty might say the following: Agent A has a duty to see to it that a killing not take place.

Some argue that both consequentialist and nonconsequentialist theories can embrace forms of agent relativity. For example, Amartya Sen argues that although each agent has the same agent-neutral duty to produce the best state of affairs, from each agent's perspective, the state of affairs in which he kills one person is worse than one in which another agent kills more people.[48] Hence, each individual has a duty to avoid *his* killing. This is an agent-relative consequentialist system, since there are multiple agent-relative best outcomes, not just one agent-neutral best outcome that different people are in different positions to forward. But how can this approach explain a constraint (which I believe does exist) on my killing one person in order to save a greater number of people whose rights I either have or will *myself* endanger? For suppose, if I do not kill the one person, the consequence will be a world in which I am the killer of a greater number of people, and this is the worse world of the two from my perspective. If, according to this approach, I must produce the best world, I should kill the one person. But this is the wrong conclusion, I believe.

A nonconsequentialist agent-relativist might argue that we have special responsibilities to the person who would be our victim (who is the person we will kill, not the ones we let die), even if killing him would promote better agent-neutral consequences. That is, our victim's interests are magnified from our perspective.[49] However, if the only way to save a greater number of people, whose rights we ourselves have endangered or will endanger, is by killing one person, why should our responsibility to our many victims not dictate that we kill the one? Yet, this is the wrong conclusion.

In order to avoid these problems, both consequentialist and nonconsequentialist agent relativists might give special weight to an agent's present acts. They might claim that we should be especially responsible for what we do and what we produce *now*, by contrast with our past and future acts. But why should our current actions and consequences take moral precedence over our past or future ones? Why should *now* be so important (at least if we are now the same person that we were and will be)? In addition, in an agent-relative consequentialist system that puts highest negative value on the outcome in which the agent now kills someone, it seems the agent should prefer states of affairs to come about that ensure that he does not kill someone. He should, therefore, prefer that it be impossible for him to kill the one person because, for example, someone else will kill that one person first or because the many others who might be saved if the one is killed are rapidly killed so that there is no reason that could tempt him to kill the one person. But it is wrong to prefer such states of the world as a means to ensuring that one will not kill someone now (even if such states are the consequences of one not killing someone now).

There are, I believe, agent-focused views that do not essentially involve an agent's attending to himself in acting. While they focus on the quality of an agent's act or state of mind to derive his duty, rather than on a victim's right, they do not take note of the "agent's mark" on the act, victim, or outcome. For example, the quality of the act or state of mind in which an agent must engage if he kills the one person, even in order to save five, is found to be repellent. The act would be the agent's if he did it, but it is not essentially its being *his* rather than what it is in itself that repels the agent.[50] Advocates of this view might claim that it explains why someone should not kill one person to save a greater number of people even from her *own* wrong acts. But notice that the explanatory structure of this duty-based constraint is essentially the same as a rights-based constraint. In both, one instance of either an act-type or a right-type stands in the way of minimizing misconduct involving many instances of the same act-type or right-type. If the logic of concern for the duty does not require that we minimize its violation but simply not violate it, why does the logic of the concern for the right require that we minimize its violation or else fall prey to a so-called paradox of deontology?

Now consider the Art Works Case: If someone loves beauty, she will be disposed to preserve and not destroy art works. What should this person do if she must destroy one art work to preserve several equally good ones? Presumably, it is permissible for her to destroy one art work in order to save the five. This is so despite the fact that the act of destruction is repellent. This suggests that the constraint on harming persons, as opposed to art works, is not derived from inside the agent outward, but from *outside* her inward, because the constraint reflects the kind of entity upon which she would act—a person, not a work of art.

Consequently, I advocate a victim-focused, rights-based account of constraints and claim that it can be shown not to be paradoxical after all. Suppose that the only way we can prevent five people from being killed in violation of the PPH is to kill one person, A, in violation of the PPH. Does it make sense to express concern for the inviolability of the five by treating A as *violable* for their sakes? If so, then morality would say that sometimes it is permissible to treat people inconsistently with PPH restrictions, and this just means that people are less inviolable than they would be if it were impermissible to do this. By contrast, although it is true that if we do not kill A, more people will be seriously violated, this does not mean that their *inviolability* is less. Inviolability is a status. It defines what we can permissibly do to people rather than what actually happens to them. If the five people are killed because A is not killed, morality does not endorse (that is, make permissible) their being killed. By contrast, if it were permissible to kill A to save the five, the *inviolability of all six*—and of every person—would be less. After all, for it to be permissible to kill A implies that we may kill anyone else in similar circumstances and that morality *endorses* killing people in this way.[51]

In discussing the moral significance of the killing/letting die distinction, I said that my approach was victim-focused: It considered whether what the victim lost was what he would have had independently of the agent. Now, in considering whether we may minimize losses to victims of what they would have had independently of the agents who act on them, I have extended the victim-focused approach, rejecting the permissibility of minimizing in this way because of what it implies about the status of the victim and of all persons.

The explanation I have offered for why it might be impermissible to kill A in order to save others from being killed puts emphasis on what it is permissible to do to people—(roughly) their status—rather than on what happens to them. Unlike an agent-focused account, this explanation does not focus on what *I* do rather than what others do. The fact that if I kill someone, *I* would be acting *now* and the victim would be *mine* does not play a pivotal role in explaining why I must not kill him even though my duty is an agent-relative duty. We explain why I must not kill him by focusing on each person's inviolability. His right, not my agency, constitutes the moral constraint. The fact that the other five people have this same right does not diminish the constraint against violating the one person's rights that I come up against.

Thus, my account highlights an *agent-neutral value*: the high degree of inviolability of persons that lies at the base even of an agent-relative duty (that I not kill rather than that there not be killings). Each agent must protect this value and does so in being constrained by the rights of the first person he encounters, even though the identity of this person will differ for each agent. This agent-neutral value is not a consequentialist value that we promote by bringing about something through action or omission. The value already resides *in* persons and we act in the light of it.

If a person has a high degree of inviolability, she will have a strong right protecting her. Hence, another way to put the argument I have given for not killing the one person to minimize violations of comparable rights is that the importance of persons can be expressed by rights being strong, rather than by their being so weak as to allow that we may minimize violations of them by transgressing them. Indeed, if the right itself claims that someone should not be used in order to stop rights violations, morality would be *self-defeating*, if it allowed us to violate such a strong right.

If people are inviolable in a certain way, then, I believe, they have a *higher*—and not merely a different—status. It might be argued that a creature also has a higher status if we must harm one of them to prevent harm to many. But we must remember that if the one person may be sacrificed, then those others may, in the appropriate circumstances, also be sacrificed, and this lowers their status. Furthermore, if the fact that a greater number of people can be saved makes the sacrifice of one permissible, this does not speak to the status of any person as an individual.

Suppose that people have a right not to be harmed, even if harming them would be in order to minimize the violation of comparable rights of others. From behind a veil of ignorance (the *ex ante* perspective), no one knows whether she would be the single person sacrificed or one of the many whose rights would be protected. However, everyone would know that her chances of being one of the many who would be saved is greater than the chances of being the one who is sacrificed. Why would it not be permissible for each to agree, *ex ante*, to forgo a right not to be sacrificed for others, even when at the time of the sacrifice she refuses to consent to be sacrificed? After all, this would reduce the chances that her own right not to be harmed would be violated.

Moral theories that permit in this way the maximization of each person's *ex ante* probability of not being killed or of surviving would justify killing in many cases. Suppose that the members of a community consider purchasing an ambulance. They know that they will save more lives if they have one, but they also foresee that in speeding through town, the ambulance will kill a few people. Now, imagine that we can save still more lives by attaching a device to the ambulance that prevents the driver from swerving to miss a pedestrian whenever swerving would result in more people dying as a result of not getting to the hospital. Using this device would maximize the *ex ante* probability of survival of each person (Ambulance Case). Nonetheless, I believe that an agreement to use the device would not make its use morally legitimate. In general, we cannot permissibly bargain away our moral status not to be treated in certain ways in order to increase our life prospects nor to minimize overall rights violations. In part, this may be because it is person's having this high status that makes it reasonable to be concerned about the life prospects and rights violations of persons in the first place.[52]

VII. NONABSOLUTENESS OF CONSTRAINTS

As I have already noted, even constraints, such as the PPH, that make clearer when harming does and does not take precedence over aiding, might not be absolute. Those nonconsequentialists who think constraints have thresholds beyond which they may be overridden are called "threshold deontologists." Although such nonconsequentialists must explain when the constraints may be overridden and what it means that they may, I shall not attempt to do that here.[53] Instead, the point I wish to make is that even if the constraints may be permissibly overridden to achieve some greater goods (including avoiding great harms), this need not imply that the constraints may permissibly be overridden in pursuit of personal goals—not even if the pursuit of those same personal goals makes it permissible to fail to pursue these greater goods. The relationship among the constraints, the greater good, and personal goals, at least, seems to be intransitive. Suppose that G stands for "greater good," P for "personal interests and goals," C for "duty to respect a constraint," and > means "may permissibly override." P > G and G > C may both be true, and yet P > C may not be true. Suppose that someone insists on transitivity. Then she would need to deny that P > G (i.e., deny prerogatives), or hold that constraints are absolute (i.e., deny that G > C) in order to avoid P > C, unless there is some other explanation of the apparent intransitivity.

Let us assume that there is an adequate defense of why P > G, and let us try to show that sometimes G > C. Ordinarily, promises morally constrain us. Yet it might sometimes be permissible to break even an important promise (e.g., a bodyguard's promise to protect her employer's life) in order to save thousands of people. We might permissibly break the promise in order to save the thousands, even if saving thousands of people requires a great personal sacrifice that is supererogatory. This supports the claim that G > C, even if P > G.[54] Nevertheless, we might be required to suffer a grave personal loss in order to respect the constraint created by the promise (e.g., the bodyguard might have to endanger her own life in order to keep her promise). Hence, −(P > C). We now see that there are two ways to measure the moral significance of acts: (1) how great a personal loss we are required to suffer in order to perform them, and (2) the capacity of one type of act to take precedence over another. Producing the greater good may be more important by measure (2), but not by measure (1); abiding by constraints may be more important by measure (1) and not by (2).

How can we explain the apparent intransitivity without denying that G > C or that P > G? How can we explain the conflict between measures (1) and (2)? Constraints are minimum standards that we must all meet. We may be required to sacrifice our personal goals to meet, but not go beyond, these standards. This explains P > G, even if −(P > C). Someone might suggest that G > C if the loss to the agent of not achieving G exceeds the amount she would have to sacrifice in order to respect C. But someone might violate C for G, even though she cares more about C than G, and hence would not lose more personally if G did not come about than if C did not. The evidence for this is that she would suffer a greater personal loss in order to do C than to bring about G. In short, the proper solution is not to "personalize" the loss of G. Rather, the agent understands that promoting the greater good is, from an impartial perspective, morally more important than doing what the constraint calls for.

In essence, my account explains the apparent intransitivity in the relation among prerogatives, constraints, and the pursuit of the greater good in a nonconsequentialist theory by noting that the precedence relation in each premise is based on a different factor: P > G reflects the entitlement of each individual as an end-in-herself not to sacrifice her personal interests and goals for the greater good; G > C reflects the impartial weight of the good; while −(P > C) reflects the greater moral importance of minimal standards than the greater good in relation to personal interests. We should not expect transitivity if different factors account for precedence relations.[55]

VIII. NONCONSEQUENTIALIST PRINCIPLES FOR AIDING AND AGGREGATING

That nonconsequentialism may distinguish between the stringency of a duty not to harm and a duty to aid (other things being equal) does not mean that it cannot endorse duties to aid and positive rights to be aided. Nonconsequentialism might not only imply duties to aid; it might also offer distinctive principles for *how* to aid, whether we aid because we are duty-bound to do so or not. These principles may conflict with the goal of maximizing the good. It could also provide distinctive reasons for doing what maximizes the good. In this section, I shall describe what I believe some of these principles and reasons are. We have already implicitly relied on some of these in previous sections. For example, when we assumed that it would be better if fewer rather than more people were killed by a trolley, we also implicitly assumed the more general claim that it would be better if more people survived than if fewer did, other things being equal. This is one of the principles we should now consider in more detail.

A. Suppose that we cannot help everyone in need because each person needs some scarce resource (that does not belong to him). Different principles exist for different situations: (a) There may be true scarcity so that more of the resource will not appear; (b) there may be temporary scarcity, so we can eventually help everyone; or (c) we may be uncertain whether we are in (a) or (b). I shall focus on (a).

Suppose that we are dealing with two-way conflict cases between potential recipients of a scarce resource. When there are an equal number of people in conflict who stand to lose the same thing if they are not aided and to gain the same thing if they are aided (and all other morally relevant factors are the same), fairness and concern for each dictate giving each side a (maximal) equal chance for the resource by using a random decision procedure. But there may be a conflict situation in which *different* numbers of relevantly similar people are on either side, and they stand to lose and gain the same thing. This latter conflict situation raises the question of whether nonconsequentialism permits and even requires us to give each person an equal chance to be helped, or permits and even requires us to aggregate and help the greater number of people.

Some, like John Taurek, have argued that in conflicts like this latter one, it is worse *for* the greater number but better *for* the lesser number, if the greater number die, and there is no impersonal sense of "worse" in which it is worse if more die.[56] However, the following Argument for Best Outcomes suggests how we might argue that it is worse if more people die: (1) Using Pareto optimality,[57] we see that it is worse if both B and C die than if only B dies, even though it is not worse for B. That is $B + C < B$. (Notice that it is worse, to a still greater degree, if B, C, and D die. Our judgment that the world is worse to a greater degree, although it is also only worse for one additional person by comparison to what is true if B and C die, may be made from a point of view outside that of any person. This would go beyond Pareto optimality and support the idea of an impartial point of view.)[58] (2) A world in which A dies and B survives is just as bad as a world in which B dies and A survives. This is true from an impartial point of view, even though the worlds are not equally good for A and B. (3) Given (2), we can substitute A for B on the right side of the moral equation in (1) and get that it is worse if B and C die than if A dies. Hence, nonconsequentialists, as well as consequentialists, can evaluate states of affairs from an impartial point of view.

Although it would be worse that B and C die than that A dies, this does not necessarily mean that it is right for us to save B and C rather than A. As nonconsequentialists, we cannot automatically assume that it is morally permissible to maximize the good, for this may violate justice or fairness. Some might claim that if we save B and C on the basis of (3), we abandon A to save the greater number without giving him a chance, and not giving equal chances is unfair. They might object that where ">" means "clearly ought to be saved," and "=" means "equally permissible to save," $B + C > B$, $A = B$, but $-(B + C > A)$ because it could be unfair to deprive someone of his equal chance to be saved, a factor not necessarily required by the first two premises.

Hence, it is important to see if it is really wrong to produce the best outcome in conflict cases involving different numbers of people because not giving equal chances is wrong. It is also important to see if someone is wronged if one takes giving equal chances as a possible reason on which one may act. Here are two arguments against its being wrong not to give equal chances, the second of which also implies that it is wrong to give equal chances (unless the greater number request this). The Consistency Argument *in*directly shows that in saving the greater number of people, we need not be overriding fairness or justice: In many other cases, nonconsequentialists will not violate justice in order to save the greater number. For example, they will not ordinarily kill one person in order to save five. Moreover, they (arguably) would not deprive a teacher of a chance for an organ transplant simply because a doctor who alone can save the lives of four others also needs the organ. Why would nonconsequentialists refuse to sacrifice justice or fairness in order to save more lives in these other cases, but override justice or fairness to save even two lives rather than save one in ordinary conflict cases? It is most reasonable to believe that they would choose to save the greater number rather than the one because fairness is not being overridden in this case. That is, those who are sensitive to issues of fairness do not think fairness requires that we give A a chance against B and C.

Second, the Balancing Argument claims that in conflict situations such as we have been considering where each stands to lose and gain the same thing, justice demands that each person on one side should have her interests balanced against those of one person on the opposing side; those whose interests are not balanced out in the larger group help determine that the larger group should be saved.[59] If we instead toss a coin between one person and any number on the other side, giving each person an equal chance, we would behave no differently than if it were a contest between one and one, where equipose can be resolved by the coin toss. If the presence of each additional person would make no difference, this seems to deny the equal significance of each person. If this is so, then justice does not con- flict with producing the best outcome.[60] The Balancing Argument claims that any individual who remains unbalanced can complain that he, as an individual, is wronged, if his presence does not make a difference to the outcome when this is in his interest. Hence, this argument also implies that it would be wrong to say that one may take giving equal chances as a possible reason on which to act, for this would conflict with what we owe each person. In sum, aggregating the interests of many people, thereby producing the greatest good, might be required, but for the distinctly nonconsequentialist reason that what we owe to each individual is to weigh him against an opposing equal, rather than because we have a duty to produce the greatest good.[61]

How might we extend nonconsequentialist principles to conflicts when the individuals are not equally needy and stand to gain the same thing? Consider a case where the interests of two people conflict with the interests of one. The potential loss and gain of the one is equal to the potential loss and gain of one of the other two. The potential loss and gain of the second of the pair is less than that of the others. A consequentialist claims that we must maximize the good and therefore choose to help the pair. A contractarian arguing behind the veil of ignorance might agree to this if she were trying to maximize the *ex ante* expected good of each person. Must a nonconsequentialist, who is committed to balancing equals when what each stands to lose and gain is the same also do what maximizes the good?

No, at least not always. Suppose that the potential lesser loss is a sore throat, and the greater loss is death rather than living for ten years (Sore Throat Case). To take away someone's chance to live in order to gain a small good of preventing a sore throat in a person who is otherwise fine fails to show adequate respect for the person whose life is at stake, since from her partial point of view, she is not indifferent between her survival and the survival of one of the pair. In short, although helping the pair is better than helping only one of the pair, and helping one dying person is as good as helping the other dying person, helping the pair is not necessarily better than helping the single person in this case.

This nonconsequentialist form of reasoning gives equal consideration to each individual's partial point of view from an impartial point of view, so it combines subjective and objective perspectives. Hence, I call this type of reasoning *sobjectivity*. It underlies even the requirement of fairness to toss a coin between one person and another. For though saving one person is as good as saving another from an impartial perspective, it is not as good from the partial perspectives of each, and concern for these partial perspectives leads us to give each an equal chance in cases involving a conflict between two people who stand to lose and gain the same thing. Sobjectivity implies that certain extra goods (like the throat cure) can be morally irrelevant. I call the principle underlying this latter claim the Principle of Irrelevant Goods. Whether a good is irrelevant is context-dependent. Curing a sore throat is morally irrelevant when others' lives are at stake, but not when others' earaches are. This Sore Throat Case shows that the principle underlying the Balancing Argument is not merely that what we owe to each person is to balance her interests against the equal interests of an opposing person and let the remaining individuals' interests (whatever they are) help to determine the outcome.[62]

We might expand on this conclusion by suggesting that any loss or gain X that is significantly less than N, and so could not by itself make it the case that someone is a contestant for a scarce resource against someone with N, cannot legitimately determine any distribution in combination with N.[63] But suppose that X is saving someone's legs. We should save one person's life rather than someone else's legs when these are the only morally relevant considerations. Perhaps, though, it is right to automatically save one person's life and a second person's legs rather than to give a third person an equal chance at having his life saved (Legs Case).

We might try to explain this latter judgment as consistent with our judgment in the Sore Throat Case in the following way: According to nonconsequentialists, each of us who is otherwise fine has a duty to suffer (at least) a relatively minimal loss (e.g., a sore throat) in order to save another person's life. So long as suffering the small loss is a duty for any given person, no number of the small losses can be aggregated to outweigh saving the life. Further, if it matters to each person from his partial point of view that his be the life saved in a conflict situation, we each also have a duty to suffer a minimal loss in order to give someone else a significant chance at life. So long as suffering the small loss in order to give someone a significant chance at life is a duty for any given person, no number of the smaller losses can be aggregated and combined with another's life to outweigh someone's significant chance to live. However, when the loss X is greater than the loss we each have a duty to suffer in order to save the life (e.g., if X is losing legs), then we should prevent $N + X$ rather than give someone else an equal chance to avoid N.[64]

By contrast, according to a consequentialist, what an individual has a duty to suffer has nothing to do with what may or may not be aggregated, and an aggregate of small losses could outweigh a greater individual loss. (At least, this is true if the consequentialist does not think that the goodness of an outcome is affected by the distribution of losses and gains over individuals. Some have argued that consequentialists need not necessarily deny that distribution can affect the goodness of outcomes. Let me put this possibility aside here.) Further, the consequentialist may say that an individual also has a duty to suffer the large loss of a leg to save someone's life. So while the consequentialist principle requires individuals to give up more than sobjectivity does, it could require *groups* of individuals each to give up less, because the aggregate of losses could count against a larger loss to an individual. Hence, even if he thought that one had a duty to give up legs to save a life, this might not stop a consequentialist from preventing the loss of legs in many individuals rather than saving a life. In sum, according to consequentialists, what an individual has a duty to do has nothing to do with what may or may not be aggregated, and the sum of what may be aggregated might permissibly outweigh a greater individual loss.

A problem for the version of sobjectivity that relies on a duty-based theory of relevant and irrelevant goods is raised by the following cases. Suppose that, according to a nonconsequentialist, one has no duty to lose three fingers in order to save a life. From an impartial point of view, we might still think that giving one person an equal chance at life is more important than automatically saving another's three fingers in combination with saving a third person's life. If so, we should revise our reasoning to allow us to take account of the point of view of an individual from an impartial perspective without limiting ourselves to considering whether he has a duty to sacrifice something in order that someone else's life be saved. We might instead try to decide which additional losses that we could prevent are relevant or irrelevant to our decision about which of two people to save from death in the following way: (1) Producing a certain additional good would be relevant in a choice between two lives in the sense of making the side to which it is added deserve a greater proportional chance of being aided, if producing an aggregation of many instances of the additional good alone could have proportional weight against saving a life. (2) A certain additional good could be relevant in a choice between two lives, in the sense of being determinative of our choice when it is conjoined with one life against another life, if either (a) the good on its own in some circumstances merits a proportional chance against a life when the choice is about whom to aid, or (b) an aggregation of many instances of it alone could in some circumstances directly outweigh saving a life.[65]

It is possible that we should employ one of the forms of sobjectivity that we have just discussed only to choose whom to aid here and now (e.g., in an emergency room) and adopt yet another form of sobjective reasoning in order to make macro decisions, for example, whether to invest in research to cure a disease that will kill a few people or in research to cure a disease that will only wither an arm in many. This form of sobjectivity, employed in the macro context, would permit the aggregation of lesser losses and gains to many people, who are not among the worst off, all by itself, without the addition of anyone who is one of the worst off and who faces a greater loss and gain, to outweigh greater losses and gains to a few who are among the worst off. It might also be employed here and now when the loss to each of the many is significant even by comparison to the greater loss to each of a few of the worst off. Since aggregation would be permitted sometimes when *no individual person in the larger group would be as badly off as any individual in the smaller group would be*, this form of sobjectivity is in conflict with theories that insist on helping the worst off first and that employ pairwise comparison of individuals on opposing sides in a conflict. (This method requires that the side we help have at least as many worst off people who will suffer as great a loss [and possibly get as great a gain] individually as those on the other side.)[66]

This form of sobjectivity does not imply that many lesser losses (e.g., paralyses) are the *equivalent* of a life they can outweigh, in the way that one life is the equivalent of another life. Rather, this form of sobjectivity implies that we will not bear the *cost* of many paralyses to instead save a life by providing aid. This Nonequivalence Thesis is supported by the fact that this form of sobjectivity (unlike the previous forms described) should not be used to decide whether to harm (by contrast to not-aid) someone rather than bear the cost of paralysis to many others. For example, if a trolley were headed toward harming a thousand people, who would each be paralyzed, it would be wrong, I think, to redirect the trolley toward one person who would be killed (even if it were permissible to save the thousand from paralysis rather than save the one person from a trolley headed toward him). This contrasts with the permissibility of redirecting the trolley away from even two people who would be killed and toward one who will be killed.

Can this form of sobjectivity, which sometimes allows an aggregate of lesser losses and gains to those not worst off, all by itself, to outweigh greater individual losses and gains to the worst off, be defended by arguing as follows: Just as it would be rational for each individual to bear a small risk of death (e.g., from taking a medicine) in order for him to avoid paralysis, so when each faces a high probability of paralysis (since many people will be paralyzed), it would be rational for each to accept a low probability of dying without care (as only a few will die), in order to prevent paralysis? But in the latter multiperson case, by contrast with the first single-person scenario, we know with certainty that some people will die and others will live. Is this not a morally significant difference between the two types of scenarios?[67] Perhaps this means that we should look elsewhere for our argument to defend this version of sobjectivity.

Finally, suppose that we did argue even for the permissibility of investing in cures for truly minor problems affecting many, such as headaches, rather than in a cure of a rare fatal disease, on the ground that it is reasonable for each person to take a small risk of being the one who will die in order to have headache cures at hand for his many, certain-to-occur headaches. This does not imply that here and now we should not save someone from dying from the rare fatal disease, if we could, rather than cure millions of headaches. For example, suppose that, sur-prisingly, giving someone who develops the fatal disease all of the aspirin that has been produced to cure headaches could still now save him. It could be wrong to leave him to die on the grounds that it was reasonable *ex ante*, in order to produce the aspirin for headaches, for each person to take a small risk of dying because no help for him would be available when he fell fatally ill.[68] It is here and now that the irrelevant utilities of headache cures do not aggregate to override saving the life.

B. A nonconsequentialist theory must also consider, in deciding how to dis-tribute scarce goods or resources that lead to goods, whether certain characteristics that one candidate has to a greater degree than another are morally relevant for deciding who gets the resource. I call this the Problem of Interpersonal Allocation with *Intrapersonal Aggregation* because one candidate has all of the characteristics the other has and more. Principles that I described above that apply when the additional goods produced by helping one side in a conflict would be distributed over more people may have to be revised so as to apply when additional goods would be concentrated in one person rather than another, for example, in a two-person conflict.

A system I suggest for evaluating candidates for a resource starts off with only three factors—urgency, need, and outcome—but it could add other factors later. *Urgency* is here defined (atypically) as how badly off someone will be if he is not helped.[69] *Need* is here defined as how badly someone's life will have gone as a whole if he is not helped, when this includes how bad his future will be and how bad his past has been. *Outcome* is defined as the difference in expected outcome produced by the resource relative to the expected outcome if someone is not helped.

The neediest candidate for resources may not be the most urgent. Suppose that A will die in a month at age sixty-five unless helped now, and B will die in a year at age twenty unless helped now. I suggest that B is less urgent (since his future will be less bad due to having one year rather than one month of life remaining) but he is needier, since one's life will be worse as a whole (other things being equal) if one dies at twenty rather than at sixty-five.[70] To consider how much weight to give to need, we hold the two other factors (outcome and urgency) constant and imagine two candidates who differ only in neediness. A utilitarian consequentialist argu-ment for taking differential need into account in cases where life is at stake could be that there is something like diminishing marginal utility of life (i.e., even if the outcome is numerically the same in both people, a better outcome is provided if we give a unit of life to those who have had less life). I do not think that this sort of argument is necessarily correct.

A different argument for taking differential need into account is fairness: Give to those who, if not helped, will have had less of the good (e.g., life worth living) that our resource can provide before giving to those who will have had more even if they are not helped. Fairness is a value that depends on comparisons between people. But even if we do not compare candidates, it can simply be of greater moral value to give a certain unit of life worth living to a person who has had less of such life.[71]

But need will matter more the more absolutely and comparatively needy a candidate is, and some differences in need may be governed by a Principle of Irrelevant Need. For example, additional need may be morally irrelevant when each candidate is absolutely needy, a big gain for each is at stake, and, possibly, if the needier person is helped he will wind up having more of the good (e.g., a longer life) than the person who was originally less needy than he.

Suppose that there is a conflict between helping the neediest and helping the most urgent (where the outcomes are the same). I claim that when there is true scarcity, it is more important to help the neediest than the most urgent, but if scarcity is only temporary, the most urgent can be helped first, if this is necessary (because he has to be treated sooner). This is because the neediest will be helped eventually anyway.

Still, there are constraints on the relevance of need in a nonconsequentialist theory of distribution. Giving a resource to the person who will have had less overall of the good that the resource can provide may be impermissible if it fails to respect the rights of each person. For example, consider another context: If two people have a human right to free speech, how long someone's right has already been respected may be irrelevant in deciding whom to help to retain free speech. Similarly, if having health or life for a certain number of years were a human right, it might not be appropriate to ration resources on the basis of the degree to which people's rights have already been met. If this is true, it implies that we should be very careful to determine whether people have rights to certain goods (rather than just an interest in having them). For it could have a big impact on which distributive principles we should use.

Now we come to the factor of outcome. A consequentialist might consider all of the effects of providing a resource in considering its outcome. I suggest that for nonconsequentialists, at least in micro allocation contexts, (1) effects on parties who do not directly need the resource (e.g., a patient would live because his doctor acquires the resource) should be given less weight than effects on people who directly need the resource; (2) some differences in outcome between candidates may be irrelevant because achieving them is not the goal of the particular sphere which controls the resource (e.g., that one potential recipient of resources in the health care sphere will write a novel if he receives a scarce drug should not count in favor of his getting it); and (3) other differences in expected outcomes between candidates may be covered by the Principle of Irrelevant Goods, even if they are relevant to the sphere. For example, relative to the fact that each person stands to avoid death and live for ten more years, that one person can get a somewhat better quality of life or an additional year of life should not determine who is helped, given that each wants what she can get. One explanation for this is that what both are capable of achieving (ten years of life worth living) is the part of the outcome about which each reasonably cares most in the context, and each wants to be the one to survive.[72] The extra good is frosting on the cake. The fact that someone might accept an additional risk of death (as in surgery) to achieve the cake plus frosting for himself does not mean that he should accept an additional risk of death so that another person who stands to get the greater good has a greater chance to live. For these reasons, all forms of sobjectivity require that in allocating the resource, we ignore the extra good that is small relative to the good of which each candidate is capable, even if consequentialism and theories of *ex ante* maximization of individual expected good would decide otherwise.

However, in life-and-death decisions, any *significant* difference between two people in the number of life years we can expect in the outcome may play a role in selecting whom to help. This result follows from the form of sobjectivity that permitted saving one person's life plus another's leg rather than giving a third person an equal chance to have his life saved. This is because it allows context-relative significant differences to help determine outcomes. Still, when the large additional benefit would be *concentrated* in the same person, who would already be benefited by having her life saved for at least the same period as the other candidate, it should count for less in determining who gets the resource than if the additional benefit were distributed to a third person. This is on account of fairness (which suggests giving priority to providing each candidate with a chance for the more basic good before providing any with additional goods) and the diminishing moral value of providing an additional benefit to someone who would already be greatly benefited (by contrast to affecting positively in a significant way yet another person).[73] Large differences in the expected quality of life among candidates for a resource should count in situations where improving the quality of life, rather than saving life, is the point of the resource.

What if taking care of the neediest or most urgent candidates for resources conflicts with producing the best difference in outcome? Rather than always favoring the worst off, we might assign multiplicative factors in accord with need and urgency by which we multiply the expected outcome of the neediest and most urgent. These factors represent the greater moral significance of a given outcome going to the neediest (or most urgent), but the nonneediest (less urgent) candidate could still get a resource if her outcome would be very large.

We can summarize these views concerning the distribution of scarce resources or goods quantitatively in what I call an *outcome modification procedure for allocation*. If we first assign points for each candidate's differential expected outcome, we then assign multiplicative factors for need and urgency in accordance with their importance relative to each other and to the outcomes. We multiply the outcome points by these factors. The candidate with the highest points gets the resource or good.

Sometimes the conflict between helping different people can be reduced because it is possible to help everyone to some extent, even though not completely. For example, imagine the following case where each stands to lose or gain the same thing, all other things are equal among individuals, and we can either (a) certainly save five lives on one island, (b) certainly save one life on another island, or (c) reduce the chances of saving the five in such a way that all six now share the same reduced chance of being saved together. I argued above that a nonconsequentialist should prefer (a) to (b), but it is still possible for her to prefer (c) to (a) or (b). In particular, the suggestion is that we may reduce the chance of saving the majority by the proportional weight (1/6) of the minority if all will then have a 5/6 change of being saved. I believe that (c) should be preferred over (a), even though the expected utility of these two outcomes is the same, because all will now have a chance to share the same fate.

Finally, we should be aware that many real-life cases in which we can help everyone to some degree are even more complicated. For example, a nonconsequentialist theory must deal with dividing resources among individuals who stand to lose and gain to different degrees, where the probability of satisfying the needs is different, and where the number of people who fall into different need/gain categories differs.[74]

NOTES

This chapter, to a large extent, summarizes core elements of two of my books, *Morality, Mortality*, vols. 1 and 2 (New York: Oxford University Press, 1993 and 1996). Section 8 deals with volume 1, sections 1–7 deal with volume 2. It should acquaint the reader with my starting point in developing my view further from those two books. While some new points are added in this chapter, most of the further development is in later chapters. It is based on "Nonconsequentialism," in Blackwell's *Guide to Ethical Theory*, ed. Hugh Lafollette (Oxford: Blackwell's) (2000).

1. Consequentialism can also be joined with a nonimpartial conception of the good; for example, the right act is the one that maximizes *my* good. I shall not deal with such forms of consequentialism in the text.

2. Some consequentialists allow for "satisficing" the good. That is, producing enough but not maximizing. I shall not consider this view in the text. Satisficing theories can also conflict with nonconsequentialist principles, since the latter can deny that the rightness of conduct is solely a function of producing enough of a balance of good consequences over bad.

3. Perhaps, we can treat someone as a mere means even if we do not use him as a causal means. For example, suppose we were to decide between two candidates for a life-saving resource on the basis of their ability to save other lives. The person who is denied the resource solely because he is not useful, might thereby be treated as a mere means because he is evaluated (but not used) merely instrumentally. (I discuss this case in my *Morality, Mortality*, vol 1.)

4. An analogy may help make my view clearer: If someone only puts me in a cage, feeds me monkey food, harms me in an experiment along with the monkeys, speaks to me as she speaks to the monkeys, pets me as she pets the monkeys, and so on only in order to do her experiment, when this is against my interests and I have not consented, I believe that she is treating me as a mere monkey. Could she answer my complaint by pointing out that, for my sake, she would never have shocked me during this very experiment had I rebelled, the way she would have shocked the monkeys? I do not think that the fact that she would have abided by this constraint is relevant to the question of whether she was actually during the experiment treating me as a mere monkey. The same, I believe, is true about whether she is now treating me as a mere means.

5. These remarks are a response to a different view presented by Derek Parfit in his Tanner Lectures (the basis for his forthcoming book, *Climbing the Mountain*). According to Parfit (in written communcation to the author from which all subsequent Parfit quotations are taken), we treat someone "as a means when we make use of the person's abilities, activities, or body." We treat someone "merely as a means if we also regard this person as a mere instrument or tool: someone whose well-being and moral claims we ignore, and whom we would treat in whatever way would best achieve our aims." Parfit's view implies that if we are actually benefiting

someone in accordance with his wishes, we could still be treating him as a mere means, if we act in this beneficial way only because it suits us. And if we would, even counterfactually, constrain our use of someone in a very minor way for his sake, though this were against our interests, we would not be treating him merely as a means whatever we actually do. Hence, suppose I enslave and kill someone solely for my goals, but would not have deprived him of water as he died (were there any water around) for his sake, though this interfered with my goals. Then I would not be treating him as a mere means when I enslave and kill him to achieve my goals, on Parfit's account.

However, it is also part of Parfit's account that we are open to the same moral objection if we are close to treating someone merely as a means. He further claims that "we do not treat someone merely as a means, nor are we even close to doing that, if either (1) our treatment of this person is governed in sufficiently important ways by some relevant moral belief, or (2) we do or would relevantly choose to bear some great burden for this person's sake. Hence, Parfit's account implies that (while I might be acting impermissibly), I would not treat someone merely as a means or be even close to doing that in the following case: The only way to stop a trolley from killing five people is to push someone over a bridge in such a way that his legs will be crushed under the trolley. I push the person over to accomplish this. If it were possible to run under the bridge and, at the cost of my own life, pull the person out once his crushed legs have stopped the trolley, solely in order to prevent him from dying, I would do so. Unfortunately, this is not possible. My account, by contrast, implies that one would have treated the person merely as a means simply in throwing him over so that his crushed legs stop the trolley, regardless of the fact that one's attitude toward this person is that he is not just a tool and one would have made big sacrifices for his sake.

Thomas Scanlon (in his "Means and Ends" (unpublished)) argues that sometimes whether we treat someone merely as a means is a function of the meaning of our act which is, in turn, a function of the attitude underlying it (p. 15). So sometimes we might have to know about someone's attitude to know whether he is treating us as a mere means. He gives as an example A inviting B to a dance merely in order to associate with the in-crowd who accept B as a member. B might reasonably complain that he was just being used (i.e., treated merely as a means) because A's purpose in asking B to the dance had nothing to do with concern for him (p. 14). It is important to notice that on Parfit's account of treating merely as a means (by contrast with Scanlon's), this information we have about A's attitude would not yet be enough for us to know whether A is treating B merely as a means in the circumstances described. For suppose that A would have given up on her goal of taking B to the dance, despite her loss of social status, if going to the dance would have damaged A's health, and she would do this out of concern for A. Then, on Parfit's account of treating merely as a means, A would not be treating B merely as a means because she takes him to the dance just in order to be with the in-crowd (when A's health is not jeopardized).

By contrast, Scanlon's conclusion that B is being treated merely as a means would not be affected by the additional piece of information about A's willingness to constrain herself, nor need he wait upon it before deciding that B is being treated merely as a means. While on Scanlon's account, deciding whether someone is treating another merely as a means sometimes requires knowledge of an agent's attitude, a very particular attitude of A's is enough to settle the issue of whether A is treating B merely as a means, independent of A's other attitude that would lead to her sacrificing herself so that no health damage comes to A. In this way, Scanlon's view and my view overlap.

Parfit and Scanlon, however, agree in rejecting Kant's view that if one is treating someone merely as a means (on their differing view of what that is), one's act is, therefore, impermissble. I shall return to this point.

6. For example, see Warren Quinn, "Actions, Intentions, and Consequences: The Doctrine of Double Effect," in his *Morality and Action* (Cambridge: Cambridge University Press, 1993), 192.

7. We shall return to discuss this issue in more detail in later chapters.

8. See Christine Korsgaard, "The Right to Lie: Kant on Dealing with Evil," *Philosophy & Public Affairs* 15 (1986): 325–49.

9. W. D. Ross, *The Right and the Good* (Oxford: Clarendon Press, 1930).

10. For example, Samuel Scheffler, *The Rejection of Consequentialism* (New York: Oxford University Press, 1982).

11. For example, Shelly Kagan, *The Limits of Morality* (New York: Oxford University Press, 1989).

12. For example, Philippa Foot, "The Problem of Abortion and the Doctrine of Double Effect," in her *Virtues and Vices and Other Essays* (Berkeley: University of California Press; and Oxford: Blackwell, 1978), 23–24.

13. In "Climbing the Mountain" (unpublished manuscript).

14. See Scheffler, *The Rejection of Consequentialism.*

15. Strictly, one can be constrained by a duty that has no correlative right or by someone's positive rather than negative right. Furthermore, saying that someone has a right does not necessarily imply that we are constrained by it, since it may be possible to infringe a right (i.e., the right may be permissibly overridden without its failing to exist). Similarly, constraints need not be absolute. For more on these issues, see chapters 8 and 9 (this volume).

16. James Rachels, "Active and Passive Euthanasia," *New England Journal of Medicine* 292, no. 2 (January 9, 1975): 78–80.

17. If the killing were in the interest of the person killed, she would not be a victim.

18. For example, if I terminate life-saving assistance that neither I am nor an institution I represent is providing *without permission from the recipient of aid*, I kill. This is true even though the patient dies of an underlying threat I did not introduce.

19. See *Morality, Mortality*, vol. 2, pp. 92–93.

20. This, however, does not by itself *morally* distinguish what someone does when he collaborates with a threat by letting die from what someone does when he adds a completing part of a threat to another part already present but not sufficient to kill.

21. Judith Jarvis Thomson argues (in "Physician-Assisted Suicide: Two Moral Arguments," *Ethics* 109 [April 1999]: 497–518) that an agent not inducing the cause of death by terminating aid, and the victim losing only what he would have had from the agent's continuing aid, are not sufficient to make not beginning or terminating aid a letting die. If the aidee has a right to the aid and he does not by his consent give the agent a liberty right to terminate or not begin aid, the agent's terminating aid (and even not beginning aid) will be a killing. I disagree with Thomson, as I think these would be prima facie impermissible lettings die.

22. This case shows that (3)(i) (as described on p. 18) concerned with killing does not involve an essential characteristic of killing. This is also shown by the possibility of killing someone who would have been killed at the same time by someone else, if we had not killed him. Hence it is not always true that in a killing, the victim loses a life he would have continued to have independently of our efforts at that time.

23. In more detail in *Morality, Mortality*, vol. 2.

24. This also should apply in cases where the "victim" and "agent" are the same individual, so when someone disconnects life support he is providing to himself, he lets himself die. But what shall we say about a case in which a doctor is providing a patient with life support, and the patient unplugs himself? Does the patient kill himself (even permissibly) rather than let himself die merely because he is stopping aid that he is not providing? I believe not, and that

this is because the patient's continued consent (or even mere nonresistance) to the provision of aid is part of what is involved in the provision of aid. When he withdraws his consent or non-resistance, he withdraws what he is providing that helps him to live. Hence, he lets himself die.

25. I have not claimed that inducing death, which is essentially absent from letting die, or the presence of a (potential) threat already, which is essential to letting die, are morally significant. This is because (a) killings that do not involve inducing may be as bad and as prohibitable as those that do, and (b) inducings that involve someone losing only what he would get from the support of the person who induces death may be no worse than letting die. An example of (a) is when I remove someone's protective blanket in the middle of a fire without his consent and so the fire consumes him.

26. "First" is intended to contrast with responding to interference with interference, for example, in self-defense.

27. Suggested by Bruce Ackerman.

28. I shall argue in chapter 3 that bringing about an evil can give us a reason for action without our intending the evil. Hence, I argue there (and below) that the fact that something gives us a reason to act is not a sufficient condition for saying that we intend it. (When we act merely foreseeing the evil, we can still see it as a reason *not* to act, but may decide that this reason is overridden and so act despite the occurrence of evil.)

29. Hence, there are four possible combinations: harming while foreseeing harm, harming while intending harm, not-aiding while foreseeing harm, and not-aiding while intending harm.

30. Jonathan Bennett, "Morality and Consequences," in *The Tanner Lectures on Human Values*, vol. II, ed. S. McMurrin (Salt Lake City: University of Utah Press, 1981). Of course, if their deaths are the means to make them appear dead, the terror bomber will be intending their deaths.

31. Warren Quinn, "Actions, Intentions, and Consequences: The Doctrine of Double Effect," in his *Morality and Action* (Cambridge: Cambridge University Press, 1993).

32. Foot, "The Problem of Abortion and the Doctrine of Double Effect," and "Killing and Letting Die," in *Abortion: Moral and Legal Perspectives*, ed. Jay Garfield and Patricia Hennessey, pp. 177–85 (Amherst: University of Massachusetts Press, 1984).

33. This and the next few paragraphs anticipate very briefly the discussion in chapter 4.

34. This possibility, as well as other points raised in this paragraph, are discussed in detail in chapter 4.

35. For more on this, see chapter 4. Additional problems with the DDE are discussed in chapters 3 and 5. For example, the DDE and the DTE both try to determine the impermissibility of acts (or omissions) based on the intentions of the agent. In discussing a version of Kant's Categorical Imperative above, we noted that this whole approach may be flawed.

36. For more on the possibility of a unified account underlying the harming/not-aiding distinction and the intending/foreseeing distinction, see chapter 3.

37. Recently, psychologists have suggested that people distinguish among these cases because they think it is *impersonal* to merely redirect a piece of machinery, but it requires *personal* intrusion on someone to cut him up or push him in the way of a trolley. The personal is disfavored relative to the impersonal. (See Sandra Blakeslee, "Watching How the Brain Works as It Weighs a Moral Dilemma," *New York Times*, September 25, 2001 Section F, p. 3. reporting on the work of Joshua Greene.) However, this distinction cannot account for the moral distinctions between cases. For suppose that we push someone into the trolley by pressing a button that redirects a second (previously nonthreatening) trolley toward the person. The second trolley pushes him into the path of the first trolley. This "impersonal" way of pushing someone is, intuitively, no more permissible than the personal way.

38. As described in Kamm, *Morality, Mortality*, vol. 2.

39. For modifications and elaboration of the PPH, see chapter 5.

40. I take it that whenever we do something that will save a greater number of people (even in the Transplant Case), we think of ourselves as pursuing the greater good, which is the greater number living for a significant period of time beyond what they would otherwise have lived. When we save people from threats such as the trolley or from a disease, and they thereby live a bit longer, this is a necessary component in producing the greater good, which is their living significantly longer. We would not produce the component unless we thought it would lead to the greater good. Strictly, it is such a component of the greater good—the first stage of their living longer—that is the flip side of turning the trolley away. I shall continue to speak of the greater good being the flip side of means when I assume that we are correct in our expectation that a first temporal stage is the beginning of an actual greater good.

41. Again, strictly speaking, it is the first temporal component of an expected greater good that causes the death.

42. Judith Jarvis Thomson, "The Trolley Problem," in *Rights, Restitution and Risk*, ed. William Parent (Cambridge, MA: Harvard University Press, 1986), pp. 94–116.

43. In another variant of the case, it is the crushing of the person to death that is causally necessary to stop the trolley. I believe it is permissible to redirect the trolley in this case too, even though we redirect the trolley, in part, *because* we believe that he will be crushed to death.

44. For more on this, see chapter 4.

45. Even if the structural equivalent, or means having it as a noncausal flip side, did not produce all that is necessary to get rid of the new problem, turning the trolley could be permissible according to the PPH. It is quite all right for us to do something else (besides redirecting the trolley) that is morally innocent and also helps to stop the trolley, so long as it does not help to cause a bad effect, such as one person being hit. For example, suppose we know that the one person will be hit if we redirect the trolley, but this will only slow the trolley, and we must pour sand on the tracks farther down the line to stop it entirely. Pouring the sand is permissible.

46. Notice that I say "sustaining the greater good" rather than "sustaining the structural equivalent of the greater good." I think that it is appropriate to speak of only the structural equivalent when we see that what we have done to remove a threat will cause another equally serious problem for the same people. For five people subject to a looping trolley is not the greater good. However, when we know that the threat of a looping trolley leads to its own defusing (by hitting the one), we have, I think, the right to say more. We can say that in the presence of the threat defused, what was initially referred to as the structural equivalent of the greater good *is* the greater good, and it is sustained, rather than produced, by the defusing of the further threat to it. The description given of the PPH here is very brief and meant only as a summary of my earlier work and an introduction to certain distinctions. For clarification and elaboration of this discussion of the Trolley Case, the PPH, and another account of when it is permissible to harm in order to aid, see chapters 5 and 6.

47. This approach is favored by Stephen L. Darwall, "Agent-Centered Restrictions from the Inside Out," *Philosophical Studies* 50 (1986): 291–319; and Elizabeth Anderson, *Value in Ethics and Economics* (Cambridge, MA: Harvard University Press, 1993).

48. Amartya Sen, "Rights and Agency," *Philosophy & Public Affairs* 11 (1982): 3–39, reprinted in *Consequentialism and Its Critics*, ed. Samuel Scheffler, 187–223 (Oxford: Oxford University Press, 1988).

49. Charles Fried, *Right and Wrong* (Cambridge, MA: Harvard University Press, 1978); and Thomas Nagel, *The View from Nowhere* (New York: Oxford University Press, 1986).

50. Nagel, *The View from Nowhere*; and Bernard Williams, "Utilitarianism and Moral Self-Indulgence," in his *Moral Luck* (Berkeley: University of California Press, 1981).

51. The relation between status and permissibility is actually more complicated than is represented here. For if it is sometimes permissible to do what wrongs a person, then it is whether we wrong him rather than act permissibly without wronging him, as well as whether what we do is permissible, that reflects his status. I discuss this below and again in chapter 7. Furthermore, if we think of the PPH as giving rights, and rights as sometimes permissibly infringed, protections given by rights would not always express one's status, even if status were a function only of permissibility.

52. Note that I also do not think it would be permissible to agree *ex ante* for purely altruistic reasons that one should be sacrificed for the sake of others when one knows one might refuse to consent at the time of the sacrifice due to weakness of will. (That is, it is not only if the agreement were prompted by a desire to increase one's own chances of being saved that I am objecting to it.) Yet this is consistent with the permissibility of waiving one's rights at the time of one's voluntarily sacrificing oneself (or at the conscious point nearest to that time) in order to save others. For more discussion of the issue of *ex ante* agreements, see chapter 8.

53. For a bit more on this, see chapters 7 and 8.

54. I do not mean this to be understood as implying that, in a situation where an agent will do G instead of C and G requires great personal sacrifice, P may always take precedence over G. That is, an agent may not fail in a duty in order to instead produce good that he knows will require much sacrifice of him, never intending to make the sacrifice. (Derek Parfit originally raised this point.) Yet I also do not think that once someone fails to do his duty for the sake of G, he cannot later change his mind about bringing about G because of great costs to himself, even though it is too late to do C. I also do not think that an agent who fails to do a duty that could require cost x of him must, in doing what aims to bring about G instead, do as much as x if this is necessary to produce G. However, I am primarily concerned with the fact that P > G, G > C, and −(P > C), when each premise is thought of as a separable item, in a different context, not as a relation between P and G once one has allowed G to dominate C. That is, one could require a great deal of effort from an agent to abide by a constraint, even though one could not require the same effort to bring about a greater good. Hence, to the extent that when someone fails to do his duty in order to instead do what will clearly require a supererogatory sacrifice, he must then make great efforts to promote G, this will not be because there is something about G that commits him to make these efforts. Rather it is because in these circumstances, there is something about the importance of C that makes it obligatory for him to be doing what he knew was necessary for G (even if it is P), if he is not to be at fault in not doing C.

55. Even if the same factors explained the precedence relations in the first two premises, intransitivity could arise due to the Principle of Contextual Interaction: The interaction of P and C could produce a new factor not present when P and G and G and C interact, and this could account for the apparent intransitivity. For more on this, see *Morality, Mortality*, vol. 2.

56. See John Taurek, "Should the Numbers Count?" *Philosophy & Public Affairs*, 6 (1977), 293–316. I discuss Taurek's views in detail in my *Morality, Mortality*, vol. 1.

57. According to which, if one of two outcomes would be worse for someone and better for no one, this outcome would be worse, period. And if it would be better for someone and no worse for anyone, this outcome would be better, period. Nonconsequentialists can, I believe, reject Pareto optimality as a general principle. For example, one can argue that it will be better if someone gets punishment he deserves even if it is better for no one and worse for him. Still, in the context with which I am concerned in (l), involving innocent people, Pareto optimality seems to hold.

58. For the possibility of understanding this in a different way, see chapter 16.

59. Of course, justice demands something different, according to nonconsequentialists, when we would have to take something from one person to give help to the others.

60. Some might suggest that we should give chances in proportion to the numbers of people in each group, but I think that this is a mistake. For discussion, see *Morality, Mortality*, vol. 1.

61. For more detailed discussion of the Balancing Argument, see my "Equal Treatment and Equal Chances," *Philosophy & Public Affairs* 14 (1985): 177–94; *Morality, Mortality*, vol. 1; and chapter 2, this volume.

62. I argue that Thomas Scanlon's use of what he calls the Tiebreaker Argument fails to deal with this issue. See chapters 2 and 16.

63. I call the form of subjective reasoning leading to this conclusion sobjectivity 1. It is discussed in detail in *Morality, Mortality*, vol. 1.

64. I call the form of subjective reasoning leading to this conclusion sobjectivity 2. It is discussed in detail in *Morality, Mortality*, vol. 1.

65. I call the form of subjective reasoning leading to this conclusion sobjectivity 3. It is discussed in detail in *Morality, Mortality*, vol. 1. Clause (b) raises the possibility, discussed below, that an aggregate of lesser losses may override a greater loss to an individual.

66. I call this form of subjective reasoning sobjectivity 4. It is discussed in detail in *Morality, Mortality*, vol. 1. Dan Brock objects to my claim that we can morally distinguish between (1) a procedure for choosing whom to help of those people before us here and now, and (2) a procedure for deciding how to invest funds for research and facilities to cope with various illnesses. He argues that if we must act according to procedure (1) when people come to us, then we will be obligated to do research and develop facilities so that we can best behave as procedure (1) tells us when the time comes. This amounts to the view that we had duty at t_1 (when doing research and development) to make it possible for us to fulfill the duties we will have at t_2 (in the emergency room). On the other hand, he claims that if we are permitted to fund research and development in manner (2), this must be because we may or must distribute among those before us by using procedure (2). (See his "Aggregating Costs and Benefits," *Philosophy and Phenomenological Research* 51 [1998]: 963–67.)

I disagree with both of these claims. Suppose that I have a car, and a seriously ill person asks me to take him to the hospital. I have a duty to do so. But I do not have a duty to buy a car so that when I face a seriously ill person, I will be able to take him to the hospital. (Indeed, I might permissibly refrain from buying a car just so that I will not be put in the position of having to take people to the hospital when they confront me.) Likewise, I believe that we may have a duty to behave in a certain way if we have a resource, but not necessarily to see to it that we have that resource. Furthermore, it might be permissible (or even required) that we invest our money so as to favor people A over people B, but when we have money left over and people B confront us, we might have a duty to help them rather than people A. For example, I might have to invest in music CDs to keep my friends happy rather than in a car that could take a stranger to the hospital. Yet, if I wind up with some money and confront a poor stranger who needs it to go to the hospital, I should give it to him rather than to my friends who want more CDs.

What I would like to insist on is that even if one form of sobjectivity represents the principle of public investment, it would not on that account be the principle that should govern how we distribute aid in an emergency room, for example, if 100 people come in with arms falling off at the same time as one person comes in with a fatal condition. In part, this is because if a policy allocates some money to an institution like an emergency room, this might just be a way of saying that in some areas of life, however small, a different principle than is involved elsewhere governs distribution.

67. For more on this difference between these scenarios, see chapter 8, "Rights beyond Interests," and my "Health and Equity," in *Summary Measures of Population Health* (WHO, 2002), pp. 685–706.

68. I think John Broome fails to take this into account when he argues for aggregating small benefits on the basis of macro allocation decisions. See his "All Goods Are Relevant," in *Summary Measures of Population Health* (WHO, 2002), pp. 727–729.

69. The more common notion of urgency is how soon someone will need help.

70. Note that in the ordinary sense of "urgency"—how soon someone must be treated—A and B are equally urgent.

71. Dennis McKerlie, "Priority and Time," *Canadian Journal of Philosophy* 27 (1997): 287–309, makes this point.

72. This implies that use of QALYs (Quality Adjusted Life Years) should be limited in life-and-death contexts for the purpose of selecting candidates for scarce life-sustaining resources.

73. For more on the independent value of affecting different people, see chapter 16, "Owing, Justifying, and Rejecting."

74. Furthermore, it may be permissible not to exclude even the most trivial concerns from receiving some of our resources, when the resources are *divisible*. So, if we do not face the choice of either giving all of our money to curing a fatal disease that hits a few people or saving many from headaches or withered arms, we could give some to each cause. In the earlier cases for which I suggested principles, I imagined that the resources were not divisible. Problems may receive divisible resources in proportion to the importance of solving them, but also in proportion to the probability of our resources' successfully dealing with the problem. In my earlier discussion, I imagined that we could as successfully treat a fatal disease as a nonfatal one, but that may not be true. Numbers of people affected by choices may also enter in. Even with divisible resources it is possible that we should require a much greater number of people experiencing headaches, and a much higher probability of curing them, to appropriately invest as much in headache cures as in cures for fatal diseases that deprive a few people of much of their lives.

2

AGGREGATION AND TWO MORAL METHODS

In chapter 1, we considered briefly whether the number of people we can help counts morally in deciding what to do in conflict situations when we cannot help everyone. In this chapter, I shall revisit this question at greater length, for as noted in chapter 1, the claim that the number of people does count has been and will be presupposed in later chapters on harming and aiding persons.[1] I begin by reconsidering the arguments of John Taurek and Elizabeth Anscombe as to whether the number of people we can help counts morally. I then consider arguments that numbers should count given by the present author elsewhere and by Thomas Scanlon and criticism of them by Michael Otsuka. I examine how different conceptions of the moral method known as *pairwise comparison* are at work in these different arguments and what the ideas of balancing and tiebreaking signify for decision making in various types of cases. I conclude by considering how another moral method, which I call "virtual divisibility," functions and what it helps to reveal about an argument by Otsuka against those who do not think that numbers count.

I

Among those who argue that numbers do not count is John Taurek. He claims that if we can save either A or a group of B, C, D, E, and F, there is no reason to save the greater number per se. (I shall assume, unless noted otherwise, that there are no morally relevant differences between individuals in the cases to be discussed and that groups between which we must choose have no overlapping members.) Two major premises in his argument are that (1) no one of the people in the larger group will suffer a greater loss than the one person would; and (2)(a) it is not true that we produce a better outcome if the greater number survive, (b) as there is no impartial perspective from which to judge this issue; it is better for the one for him to survive and better for the five for them to survive. (Presumably, it is only better for each of the five that the five survive as this is a way to his own survival, assuming they are strangers.) His conclusion is: If we wish to show equal concern and respect for each person, we should give everyone a (maximal) equal chance to survive by, for example, tossing a coin.

Among the implications of Taurek's view that numbers do not count that have not, to my knowledge, been emphasized are the following:

a. Suppose a trolley is headed toward killing five people, and it is possible for a bystander to turn it away from them and toward a track where one person will be killed instead. If numbers do not count, this should be treated as if it were a case of one person on each track. If we do not favor letting die over killing, we might then toss a coin to determine if we let five die or turn the trolley to one. Similarly, if we do not favor letting die over killing, it should be just as permissible to toss a coin and, if called for, turn a trolley that is headed toward one person away from him and onto a track where five will be killed. Those who think that numbers do not count may, of course, combine that view with a moral distinction between killing and letting die and then avoid these results. But suppose a trolley is at a crossroads, and if it stays there it will set off a nuclear weapon that will destroy civilization. We could avoid this by turning the trolley onto a track where one person will be killed or onto a track where five people will be killed. Those who do not think mere numbers of people dead count could still think a qualitative difference, such as the destruction of civilization, should be avoided. Hence, it seems they should toss a coin to decide whether to kill one or to kill five if the trolley were at a crossroads.[2]

While those who think that numbers count would say that someone would make the morally wrong decision if she saved one person instead of a different group of five, I do not think that they would necessarily say that we must force such a person to save the five just because she is going to be saving someone anyway. However, I believe that those who think that numbers count would say that we should interfere, even by force, with someone who is about to turn a trolley away from killing one person toward killing five instead or about to send a trolley to kill five when she could send it to kill one instead, even if in doing this, she is carrying out a fair toss of a coin. Dealing with numbers in the context of killing rather than saving may make clearer the contrast between the numbers count and anti-numbers count camps.[3]

b. Suppose that in one part of the country, someone is about to save a group of five people rather than save one different person when it is impossible to save everyone, and he does this without giving both groups an equal chance. He merely counts the numbers. In another part of the country, someone is about to save a group of five people rather than save two different persons when it is impossible to save everyone, and he does this without giving both groups an equal chance. He merely counts the numbers.

Suppose numbers should not count in these two circumstances. Then these two decision makers each behave incorrectly. Suppose we can go only to one but not to both of them in time to reason with him so that he gives everyone with whom he is dealing an equal chance. If the first decision maker does not give an equal chance, one person will have been treated unfairly in a way that is possibly bad for him. If the second decision maker does not give an equal chance, two people will have been treated unfairly in a way that is possibly bad for them. But if numbers do not count, this cannot be a reason to go to the second decision maker. Rather we should toss a coin to decide where to go to try to bring about fairness.

I do not raise these points as arguments against those who do not think numbers count, only to point out some implications of their position that I think are striking.

Now, let us evaluate Taurek's argument. Taurek's premise (2) should be eliminated as a premise in an anti-numbers count argument, I believe. One reason is that the part of it, (2)(b), that claims that there is no impartial perspective from which to judge outcomes yields results that even many of those who reject counting numbers would find unacceptable. For, as Taurek notes, premise (2)(b) also implies that from A's perspective, the saving of his leg (or fingernail) could be a better state of affairs than the saving of B's life. Yet, I think, even those who think that numbers do not count would not committ themselves to tossing a coin between saving A's leg and B's life.[4] This implies that an antinumbers advocate could impose, from some impartial perspective, at least some objective (or intersubjective) comparison of what A and B stand to lose and so of the outcome in which A does not lose a leg versus the one in which B's life is saved.[5] The antinumbers advocate could hold that it is only if A and B stand to lose something equal or comparable (and perhaps attain something equal or comparable) that a coin should be tossed, other things being equal. We can all still recognize that from A's perspective it is not as good for A if B survives as if A does, and this is part of what leads us to want to give A his equal chance when comparable losses and perhaps gains are at stake. I have called such a mixing of objective and subjective perspectives "sobjectivity."[6] I think it is part of the moral point of view.

Indeed, Taurek's own premise (1) suggests that we are engaging in a pairwise comparison, individual by individual, to see whether anyone will suffer a loss much greater than anyone else, because if someone will, then we would not toss a coin. This presupposes the more objective view of losses I have just described and is compatible with the rejection of premise (2)(b).

However, this degree of commitment to an impartial comparison does not (at least at first glance) by itself, commit one to the rejection of component (a) of premise (2) (that it is not true that we produce a better outcome if the greater number survive). As noted, taking into account whether one person will suffer a loss greater than another is consistent with taking to heart that when the losses are equal, A still prefers that he not suffer his loss rather than that B not suffer his equal loss and vice versa. For this reason, one might toss a coin between them. And if no one of a greater number will suffer a greater loss than A would, then we cannot say that the outcome is worse if they die because someone will suffer a greater loss or refuse to toss the coin on the ground that A's loss would be much less than anyone else's.[7]

However, the following Argument for Best Outcomes (already presented in chapter 1)[8] suggests how we might argue that it is worse if more people die and so it allows us to reject premise (2) in its entirety. Consider states of the world independently of how they come about. Imagine that one of them already exists necessarily but we do not know which it is and we are merely expressing an opinion as to which state it would be better (or worse) to be in existence. (1) Using Pareto optimality, we see that it is worse if both B and C die than if only B dies, even though it is not worse for B, that is, $B + C < B$. (2) A world in which A dies and B survives is just as bad as a world in which B dies and A survives. This is true from an impartial point of view, even though the worlds are not equally good for A and B. That is, there is moral equivalence in the death of A or B. (3) Given (2), we should be permitted to substitute A for B on the right side of the moral equation in (1) and get that it is worse if B and C die than if A dies. That is, if $B + C < B$ and $A = B$, then $B + C < A$. Alternatively, we can substitute A for B on the left side of the moral equation in (1) and get that $A + C < B$.[9] Notice that the substitution of, for example, A for B on the left side of the equation really means that A is being saved as a substitute for B. The permissibility of substituting people for one another in the situations with which we are dealing is a further step beyond the moral equivalence of saving A or B; it is a way of employing that moral equivalence.

Even if Taurek's premise (2) is wrong, and it would be worse that B and C die than that A dies, this does not necessarily mean that it is right for us to produce the first state of affairs by automatically saving B and C rather than A. As noted in chapter 1, we cannot assume that it is morally permissible to produce the best state of affairs, for this may violate justice or fairness. Some might claim that if we save B and C on the basis of (3), then we abandon A to save the greater number without giving him a chance, and not giving equal chances is unfair. Giving an equal chance recognizes that each person, from his personal point of view, is not indifferent to who survives, even if from an impartial perspective (employed in determining which outcome is better) one is indifferent. By contrast, we do not deprive B of any chance to be saved if we save B and C rather than just B.[10]

II

Unlike Taurek, Elizabeth Anscombe argued that numbers can be a reason for saving some people rather than other people but not a reason upon which one must act. We may save A rather than B and C without wronging anyone, or we may save B and C rather than A without wronging anyone. She believes that A's need gives us a reason to save him, and saving the greater number can also give one a reason to save B and C. But, she claims, when one has a reason to do X and a reason to do Y, one need not have a further reason to do X rather than Y in order to be justified in doing X.

Let us consider Anscombe's argument more carefully. The claim that one need not have a reason to do X rather than Y (or vice versa) when one has a reason to do X and a reason to do Y, suggests that when someone could save A and B rather than just save A alone, he does nothing wrong and wrongs no one if he just saves A, as he has a good reason (satisfying need) to do that. This seems clearly wrong. It is not merely that satisfying need implies that it is wrong to save no one. It also implies that it is wrong to save A alone when one could also save B. But nothing Anscombe says explains this, and what she does say, literally, suggests that one does not need a justification for ignoring all of the reasons that there are so long as one has some reason to act. Further, the reason of satisfying need is present for both saving A and for saving the greater number. But if this reason is present for saving either side, someone might ask, why not satisfy it along with a reason (even if it is not a conclusive reason) for saving the greater number?

This brings me to the next point. Anscombe's view that taking numbers into account is a possible reason for choice implies that it is not unfair (or otherwise wronging) to A not to give him an equal chance when there is more than one person on the other side in a conflict. Anscombe explicitly says that she thinks that no individual considered as an individual in the larger group is wronged if we save A instead of him. We now also see that she must think that A is not wronged if we do not give him an equal chance when we save the greater number. (This contrasts with the view that we have already examined that the reason numbers might not be any reason at all in conflict situations is that taking numbers into account is inconsistent with giving everyone an equal chance.)

If it is wrong to save only A when one can save A and B, this implies that satisfying more need is better, other things being equal. But, as argued above, if numbers can be a possible reason in conflict cases, this implies that a failure to give equal chances (at least in cases of unequal numbers) is not a wrong-making feature. When these two claims are combined, do they imply that we ought to save the greater number because satisfying more need is better and no wrong would stand in the way of producing the better outcome? Not necessarily, for if Anscombe thought that giving someone an equal chance were at least another possible reason for action, one would still have permission to save the one if he wins a coin toss rather than the greater number, on her view.

III

Given our discussion of Taurek and Anscombe, we see that it is not only important to decide if it is wrong to produce the best outcome in conflict cases because someone is wronged in not being given an equal chance. It is also important to see if at least someone in groups with more people is wronged if one does give equal chances. Recall (from chapter 1) that there are (at least) two arguments against its being wrong not to give equal chances, the second of which also implies that it is wrong to give equal chances (unless the greater number requests this) because someone in the group with more people will be wronged.

i. The Consistency Argument indirectly shows that in saving the greater number of people, we need not be overriding fairness or justice: In many other cases, nonconsequentialists who think that numbers count will not violate justice in order to save the greater number. For example, they will not ordinarily kill one person even in order to save a thousand. Why would such nonconsequentialists, who refuse to sacrifice justice or fairness in order to save more lives in these other cases, override justice or fairness in order to save merely two people rather than one? It is most reasonable to believe that they would choose to save the two rather than the one because fairness or justice is not being overridden in such a case. That is, those who are sensitive to issues of fairness and justice do not think fairness or justice require that we give A a chance in a conflict with B and C.

ii. Second, the Balancing Argument claims that in a conflict case involving unequal numbers each of whose life is at stake, justice demands that each person on one side should have her interests balanced against those of one person on the opposing side; those whose interests are not balanced out in the larger group help to determine that the larger group should be saved. Those who are balanced out in the larger group are saved instead of those in the smaller group. In this sense, they are substituted for those in the smaller group. This is consistent with the view that from the moral perspective it is as worthwhile to save one person as to save another.

If we instead were to toss a coin in order to choose between one person on one side and any number on the other side, giving each person an equal chance, we would behave no differently than if it were a contest between one and one. In the contest between one and one, when the equipoise is broken by giving equal chances, this takes seriously the fact that each person, from his point of view, is not indifferent as to who is saved and this also does not ignore the weight of any other person. Suppose that we continue to use a random decision procedure when additional people are added, but each person is on a separate island and only one can be saved no matter what we do. In this case, giving each an equal chance does not ignore the presence of the additional people. It is appropriate that each gets an equal chance when no one who can be saved is accompanied by someone else whose also being saved can substitute for saving a person on another island who is alone.[11] But if such a substitution is possible and yet makes no difference to what we do, then this would seem to deny the equal significance of each person.

Taking account of the equal significance of each person takes precedence over accommodating the personal perspective that would lead to a random choice, just as saving someone who will die rather than someone who will just lose a leg takes precedence over accommodating the personal perspective from which someone may not unreasonably care more about his not losing a leg than about someone else dying. Might one way of understanding why helping the worse off individual takes precedence over accommodating the personal perspective be that it involves a form of substitution of equals, that is substitution of equal parts of a loss? For suppose that A will lose one leg if we do not help him and B will lose two legs if we do not help him. Losing a leg is part of losing two legs. (Losing use of a leg is also part of losing a life.) Preventing the loss of one leg can be achieved by either helping A or helping B. If we prevent the loss of a leg by helping B, we achieve as much (judged from an impartial point of view) as if we did this by helping A, but we also prevent more bad in helping B. According to this analysis, it is because we can achieve in B at least all that we would achieve in A that we should help B avoid a worse fate. But this analysis puts the emphasis in the wrong place, I think. Those who are concerned with helping the person who would be much worse off are concerned that he would be without two legs rather than just without one. They are, therefore, most concerned that he keep a leg that prevents him from being without two. This leg has greater value—having it keeps him from falling to the worst point—than A's leg whose loss would mean that he still had at least one leg. Hence, what is most important is not that the value we would get from saving A's leg can be achieved in helping B. Rather, it is that something of greater value can be achieved if we help B: saving a leg that prevents the worst outcome of having no legs. This implies that those concerned with preventing the worst outcome would help B rather than A whether they could save both his legs or just one (as in A). (What of those who would only help B if both his legs could be saved? They, indeed, would seem to equate, and be willing to substitute, the achievement of normality in A with normality in B.)

On the basis of this analysis, we can see that at least those anitnumbers theorists who think that we should not toss a coin in order to choose between preventing the loss of a leg and the loss of a life (or two legs) are committed to overriding the weight of the personal point of view (though not by engaging in substitution of at least some things that are considered to be equal only from an impartial perspective). They do this when someone would be much worse off. Hence, if they are opposed to the substitution of equals interpersonally—as when B is substituted for A in the Balancing Argument—then it must be for some reason besides the overriding weight of the personal point of view. What could this factor be? Perhaps it is what is referred to as the "separateness of persons." They may think that it is only when losses are aggregated intrapersonally rather than interpersonally (as when we add up numbers of separate lives that will be lost) that we respect the separateness of persons though we employ substitution. This point connects with Taurek's premise (1), for it emphasizes that if many people are not saved, then there is still no one who suffers a greater loss than the one person would suffer if he were not saved. He seeks to emphasize that there is something wrong with thinking that adding up losses over people speaks to the loss that one individual will face. Hence, he thinks that it is a mistake to add millions of headaches, each suffered by a different person, and conclude that the sum involves a greater loss than a thousand headaches suffered by one person.

A possible response to this argument based on the separateness of persons is to note that when someone suffers the same loss as someone else, rescuing him is, from an impartial view, equivalent to rescuing the other person. There is no such equivalence when we rescue someone from one headache rather than save someone else's life. It is this equivalence from the impartial view of individuals who are balanced that makes it consistent with the separateness of persons to then count the lives of the other people we might save and favor saving the greater number. For we can do this without thinking that we are merely summing losses over different people while forgetting what any individual as an individual will lose, and without forgetting that the badness of the loss of a life is fundamentally a matter of how bad it is for the person who suffers the loss rather than of how bad it is for others to lose the person.

It seems then that one conclusion we can assert is that neither the importance of the personal point of view nor the importance of the separateness of persons justifies not counting numbers, once we accept the correctness of straightforwardly saving an individual who will lose a life rather than a limb. This is a negative conclusion, casting doubt on an argument for numbers not counting. Another negative conclusion is that it is not always wrong in moral argument to substitute preventing a loss to one person for preventing an equal loss to another person. A positive conclusion is that numbers should count (at least) when what is at stake is preventing equal losses in people because: (i) We can produce a better outcome, if we save the greater number (from the Argument for Better Outcomes), and (ii) we only give appropriate weight to the equal loss that each person will suffer when we give great enough weight to each additional life so that saving it overrides the personal point of view of those who can be balanced and substituted for by their equal and opposite number (from the Balancing Argument). (We shall add to this positive conclusion below.)

Hence, justice and fairness do not conflict with producing the best outcome when different numbers of lives are at stake. Justice also does not require always giving equal chances in this circumstance; it requires not giving equal chances. Nor does justice conflict with merely substituting saving some people for saving others in cases of unequal numbers when preventing equal losses is at stake. The Balancing Argument also implies that any individual who remains unbalanced in cases where preventing equal losses to each is at stake can complain that he, as an individual, is wronged if his presence does not make a difference to the outcome (when this is in his interest). (This would be the answer to Anscombe's question "who is wronged?") This argument also implies that Anscombe would be wrong to say that one may take giving equal chances as a possible reason on which to act in the cases where numbers differ and preventing equal losses to each is at stake, for this would conflict with the balancing that we owe to each person. Hence, aggregating the interests of many people, thereby producing the greatest good, might be required, but for the distinctly nonconsequentialist reason that what we owe to each individual in cases where preventing equal losses to each is at stake is to weigh him against an opposing equal and allow the remaining person's weight to count as well, rather than because we have a duty to produce the greatest good.

IV

Thomas Scanlon is a contractualist.[12] In his version of contractualism, he insists on what he calls the Individualist Restriction (IR), namely, that only an individual, on behalf of himself or another individual, can register complaints (which I shall use as interchangeable with "objections") to a principle that is proposed for governing our relations with each other. However, he wants to be able to argue that when we have a choice between saving a smaller group of people and saving a larger group of people whose members do not overlap, we should save the larger group, other things being equal. (While Scanlon rejects Taurek's second premise—that we would not produce the better outcome in saving the greater number in a conflict situation—he does not wish to rely on the fact that the outcome is better, within a contractualist framework, as an argument for saving the greater number. Similarly, my Balancing Argument was supposed to work independently of considering that we produce the best outcome in saving the greater number.) Scanlon claims that he can adhere to the IR and still count numbers of people because the justification for counting numbers need not involve considering the complaints that a *group*, rather than an individual, lodges against a principle that ignores numbers. Rather, the justification for counting numbers is what he calls the Tiebreaker Argument.

Consider a conflict between saving A and saving B and C, each of whom would otherwise lose his life and is otherwise equal in morally relevant respects. Scanlon claims that if A were alone, A's weight would be recognized by saving A. If he were in conflict only with B, we would have to recognize B's weight as well and hence modify our decision procedure. We could do this by tossing a coin. When C is present with B, if we still only tossed a coin, giving everyone an equal chance, C's presence would make no difference to what we do. But, Scanlon thinks, C as an individual could complain about this on his own behalf. This is because the weight of A and B could be recognized and fully taken account of, if we allow them to balance each other, and C's weight as another person needing to be saved could be taken account of by making him the tiebreaker between A and B.

The Tiebreaker Argument is in some ways like the Balancing Argument (as Scanlon has acknowledged). However, Kristi Olson has pointed out a significant difference between the two arguments.[13] This difference arises because Scanlon does not accept a presupposition of the Balancing Argument. This presupposition is that fairness and equal concern require us to give each person in a two-person conflict case a maximal equal chance, as can be done in a coin toss. Scanlon's view, by contrast, seems to be that we may choose to help either person in a two-person conflict, so long as we do not have a morally illicit reason for helping one rather than another (for example, his race). Olson argues that if Scanlon thinks we may simply pick B rather than A and save him, then when we can also save C if we save B (but not if we save A), this just gives us another nonillicit reason to do what it was permissible to do anyway, namely, to choose B to be saved. On Scanlon's account, therefore, counting numbers does not requires us to omit doing something that we were required to do in a two-person conflict, namely, to give everyone an equal chance. On Scanlon's view, giving equal chances is not something we were ever required to do. Hence, Olson concludes, Scanlon's answer to why numbers may or should be counted is in one way easier to generate than a comparable answer that the Balancing Argument tries to generate. This is because the

Balancing Argument is trying to justify not giving equal chances against a background presupposition that in a conflict involving only two people, one should give equal chances.

Notice also that in Scanlon's argument, because A's presence is said to be dealt with if it is balanced against B's (even though A gets no chance of having his life saved), it turns out that in the context of A's tying with B, it is C (and not A or B) who would ultimately have an objection in Scanlon's contractualist system, if C did not affect the outcome. Though B would be another beneficiary of the satisfaction of C's complaint, he could not directly complain on his own behalf, if C does not affect the outcome when it is in C's interest to do so.

If we think that the Balancing and Tiebreaker arguments show that numbers count, then we still need not think that, in all situations when life and death are at stake for everyone and we have to choose between nonoverlapping smaller and larger groups, we should choose the larger group. For example, suppose that we have a scarce organ to distribute. The organ is necessary in order for either transplantation to save the life of a teacher or to create a serum that alone can cure a doctor's terrible headache. The latter is a much less important direct use of the organ. However, the doctor is the only one who can do surgery to save four patients and he cannot operate with the headache. We thus face a choice of doing what will save four lives or doing what will save only one. Still, the fact that the teacher would be excluded on instrumental grounds (i.e., he cannot do surgery) unrelated to the best *direct* use of the particular scarce resource we have and the doctor would be selected even though helping him is not the best *direct* use of the resource might be reasons not to do what saves the greater number.[14]

V

Scanlon's IR is a descendant of a moral method known as *pairwise comparison*,[15] which is used by many nonconsequentialists and is also suggested by Taurek's premise (1). They all compare individuals one at a time to see who has the biggest concern and potential complaint against a proposed principle or action. However, there seem to be different understandings of how pairwise comparison should operate, though this is not commonly noticed. In examining these differences we will get another perspective on Balancing and Tiebreaker arguments, as well as a better understanding of Scanlon's IR. One view suggests that in conflict scenarios we should compare individuals on opposing sides, one at a time, to see how badly off they would be if not aided and also how big would be the benefit each would get if aided. Another view claims that in doing pairwise comparisons we should compare only baselines (i.e., here understood as how badly off someone would be if not aided) and not consider how big a benefit is at stake for each person who would be at the same baseline. On the former view, if A will die without aid and live for five years if aided, and B will die without aid and live for ten years if aided, then it might be correct to save B. Indeed, it might be said that B's fate would be worse if he is not aided because, though A would also die without aid, B would lose out on more (i.e., ten years) than A. On the second view, A and B would be equals and we should thus toss a coin in order to decide who will receive aid. This is one difference in views about pairwise comparison. Let us suppose (at least for now) that both baseline and benefit should be compared pairwise, one person at a time, in conflict situations.

According to the next view of pairwise comparison, which I shall call the Context-Aware View (for reasons to be explained below), once we find a match of baseline and benefit in one person with another, the person on one side for whose match we were searching is no longer compared with anyone else. He has met his match and is, in a sense, silenced relative to others. (The person with whom he is matched is likewise silenced relative to others on the other side.) An alternative view, which I shall call the Blinder View, involves pairwise comparing a person from one side until we find someone on the other side who will be worse off if not aided and/or get a bigger benefit if aided.[15] It is only when we find *more* than someone's match that he is no longer pairwise compared with individuals on the other side. The Context-Aware and Blinder views represent the second difference in views about pairwise comparison. On the Blinder View, if one is equal to anyone on the other side, and all on the other side are equal, one is equal to everyone on the other side. Hence, a coin should be tossed. When there are four equal persons (same baselines, same benefits), two on each side, the Context-Aware View of pairwise comparison tells us to toss a coin because each is matched with an equal and opposite number. The Blinder View also tells us to toss a coin in this situation, but only because at least one person (and, in fact, each person) on one side should have an equal chance against *both* of those on the other side.[17] I think that the Context-Aware View of pairwise comparison is involved in the Tiebreaker and Balancing arguments and that the Blinder View is involved in Michael Otsuka's criticism of these two arguments.[18]

Let us consider these two views in more detail. This should make clear why they bear these names.

Imagine a group of 1,000 individuals who are in competition with another group of 900 individuals for an education, where all are equally needy and capable of as good an outcome. We pair off each of the 900 on one side with each of the 900 on the other. There are people on one side with no matches on the other, each as needy and capable of benefit as the original 900. Because of this, according to the Balancing and Tiebreaker arguments, we should balance the two sets of 900 individuals and break the tie between them not by tossing a coin, but by doing what, in addition to helping the 900 on one side, will help 100 more people. Notice that in this way of doing pairwise comparison, when we are comparing any two equal sets of individuals, we allow ourselves to be aware of the context in which they are situated, hence the title Context-Aware View. That is, we are aware that there are further people on one side as well. Indeed, this is what leads us to just balance out the equal members of a set rather than proceed to make a random choice (e.g., toss a coin) between them. Balancing "silences" the people balanced relative to others; they are not further compared with any other individuals.

Contrast this understanding of pairwise comparison with the interpretation of how to do pairwise comparison offered by the Blinder View. We take individual A from one side and pairwise compare him with someone on the other side, but we do so "with blinders on" as to the context of these two individuals. If they are equal in all morally relevant respects, we would see no reason not to toss a coin to decide between them. We then take the blinders off before tossing the coin, becoming aware of the context, and if we find another individual on the side opposite to A's with whom to compare A, we again compare the two with blinders on as to their context.[19] If they are equal in all morally relevant respects, we still see no reason not to toss a coin between them. We follow this procedure until A himself is compared with all individuals on the opposite side. A is not balanced and silenced by having met his match. He would only be silenced by meeting more than his match, that is, someone needier or more likely to produce a better outcome. Then we compare anyone else on A's side with all of the same individuals on the opposite side in the same way, putting blinders on and off. This way of doing pairwise comparison would eventually result in our having to toss a coin between a smaller group and a larger group of persons of equal need and outcome, because each person on one side would be owed an equal chance against any number of other individuals on the other side.

We might say that this blinder form of pairwise comparison involves the *confrontation* of persons rather than the *substitution* of persons that is involved in balancing. (Confrontation of persons rather than substitution most obviously occurs when we toss a coin between two people.)[20] I believe that this form of pairwise comparison is not what respect for persons requires. It is sometimes said that nonconsequentialism takes seriously the separateness of persons and does not permit us to consider a benefit in one person a sufficient substitute for a loss in another person.[21] But strictly speaking, I do not think this is true. As I argued in section III(ii), I think substitution can be permitted in a theory that is still nonconsequentialist, most obviously in cases involving choosing whom to aid. (It is something else—subordination—that is hard to justify.[22])

As I said above, balancing that silences occurs as the result of a pairwise comparison match only when we are aware of a context in which there are individuals who could be helped in addition to those who would be balanced. Given that the Tiebreaker Argument makes use of balancing that silences, this affects, I believe, how we should understand Scanlon's IR. It should be understood as implying: (1) Several individuals' concerns or complaints together cannot create a tie with another individual's concern or complaint; only an individual's concern or complaint can do that. (For example, several people with headaches cannot create a tie with someone who will lose an arm.) (2) But individuals' concerns or complaints may be evaluated in the context of another individual's concern or complaint, and this may change the relation between the individuals' concerns or complaints. (3) The flip side of (2) is that an individual concern or complaint may be evaluated in the context of how other individuals' concerns or complaints relate to each other. It may also be evaluated in order to see how it relates to and changes the relation of those other individual concerns or complaints.

Scanlon clearly enunciates (1). However, I believe that his presentation of IR conceals (2) and (3). This is because he emphasizes comparing the concerns or complaints *only* of individuals, and this may suggest comparing each individual's concern or complaint with blinders on.

To make clearer the role of (2) and (3) in a Tiebreaker Argument, consider the following Three Islands Case. Suppose that we could save the life of either (1) A on one island, or (2) B on another island, or (3) C on a third island. It would be a mistake to think that the first two people balance and silence each other and then conclude that we should help C. Rather, we should give each person a maximal equal chance to be saved (e.g., pick one by using the three-straws method); all three confront each other. It is only if C will be saved along with A or B that balancing which silences those balanced is allowed to occur, and the Tiebreaker Argument can be employed. In the latter sort of case, proponents of the Tiebreaker or Balancing arguments not only pairwise compare A and B, but they see what I would call a dynamic relation among the concerns of A, B, and C. That is, they see that B balances and silences A only when C, for example, joins B. (This is an instance of [2]. The change in the relation of A and B's concerns in the presence of C is that they are balanced and silenced, rather than involved in what I called a confrontation.) Further, C's concern is an individual (versus group) concern in sense (1), but not in the sense of the significance it would have in isolation (as in the Three Islands Case) or when pairwise compared with A's life with blinders on as to the presence of B. Rather, C's concern is considered with blinders off, in a context where not only does A match B (the relation between other individuals' concerns), but B would be saved if C is (involving B's relation to another individual's concern). (These are instances of [3].)

But if all of this is true, it may be said, do not the Balancing and Tiebreaker arguments, which are meant to lead to the conclusion that numbers count, assume that numbers count? For they assume that a person (like C) being helped *as well* (that is, in addition to B) makes a difference (that is, leads to balancing which silences rather than giving equal chances). Are not the two arguments for numbers counting, therefore, circular?

I believe that one of Michael Otsuka's criticisms of the Balancing and Tie-breaker arguments[23] is that to work as arguments for numbers counting, they must already assume that numbers do count. I think his point is based on noticing that, according to these two arguments, someone like C has a complaint if numbers are not counted not when he is in isolation, as in the Three Islands Case, but only in the context where B *in addition* has a life that would be saved when C's is.

An answer to this challenge is as follows: Pairwise comparison, combined with an impartial perspective on the individual's losses and gains, implies that there is equal moral value in helping either person of two who are equal in morally relevant respects. We recognize that the satisfaction of B's concern (i.e., he would lose his life if he is not saved) morally speaking gives all that would have been gotten by the satisfaction of A's similar concern.[24] This grounds the permissibility of sometimes substituting the satisfaction of A's concern with that of B's instead, for example, when the life of C overrides the personal perspective of A that would interfere with just substituting B for A. Of course, for the antinumbers advocate, substitution is a controversial step in the argument. But if we accept substitution, this implies that at the point where we consider that C will be saved *in addition* to B, the counting of numbers and the saving of B and C rather than A alone are no more controversial than the claims that we get the better outcome if we save B (= A) and C rather than B (= A) alone (Pareto Optimality) and also the separate claim that we should save B (= A) and C rather than B (= A) alone.[25] Those who object to counting numbers do not reject the view that it is better if B and C are saved than if B alone is and the view that we ought to save B and C rather than B alone. So, the Balancing and Tiebreaker arguments for counting numbers do not assume that numbers count in the controversial sense that in conflict situations we should help the greater number. The arguments try to prove this, without assuming it, and it is both the appropriateness of the impartial perspective from which we see the moral equivalence of saving A and saving B and the possibility of substitution based on this that are bearing most of the weight of the argument.

VI

Now, suppose we can save either A's life or B's life but not both, and also save C's legs only if we save B. (We call this the Legs Case).[26] If we just pairwise compare the potential loss and gain of every individual with blinders on, it is not unreasonable to think that losing or gaining legs pales before losing or gaining a life in the sense that we would save someone's life rather than someone else's legs, other things being equal. Yet, proponents of the Tiebreaker and Balancing arguments could (correctly, I think) treat the legs as a tiebreaker, given the way they do pairwise comparison with context awareness. This is a case in which a tiebreaker between two lives is less than another life. Let us consider how such cases shed light on the idea of tie-breaking and balancing.

Typically, when we think of breaking a tie, (a) our focus is on the individuals who are tied and (b) how to settle things between *them*. Factor (b) emphasizes that we must find a way to break the tie, but does not yet tell us to use balancing that silences, as opposed to tossing a coin to do it. Factor (a) implies that we do *not* focus on how it would be wrong to forego consideration of *that* which would break the tie for its own sake. Taking the perspective involving (a) and (b), if A ties B when lives are at stake and we could also cure a sore throat in C (who is otherwise fine) only if we save B, it might be said that it would be permissible to use the good achieved in curing C's sore throat as a tiebreaker. (We call this the Sore Throat Case).[27] That part of Scanlon's argument which focuses on how A's weight has been taken account of by requiring that someone who has as strong a concern, such as B, balance him out, would lead one to conclude that A could have no complaint if C's sore throat was used to break the tie. After all, A's concern has been given all of the recognition it deserves, it might be said, when it is balanced against B's equal concern. But unlike the additional person who needs his life saved, C with the sore throat cannot do what Scanlon says C could do if his life were also at stake. He cannot equate himself to B and say to A that just as the decision procedure was changed in recognition of B's weighty concern (by including B as a possible candidate for being saved), so it should be changed in recognition of C's comparably weighty concern. If the sore throat were used as a tiebreaker, because we understand the Tiebreaking Argument as focusing on those in the tie and settling things between them, then it seems that someone who has a much smaller concern could have an effect on the procedures used to settle a tie as great as would be had by someone who has an equally weighty concern. That is, the outcome will be no different in a Tiebreaking Argument whether C has a sore throat or whether C's life is at stake. We will no longer toss a coin or possibly pick A to be saved.

Consideration of the Sore Throat Case shows that there are (at least) two separate issues in a Tiebreaking Argument: (i) Is A in a tie with B? (ii) Would the tiebreaker have a complaint for his own sake, based on the seriousness of his own need, if he does not break the tie? My own view is that only if the answer to the latter question is yes should we proceed to engage in balancing and silencing as opposed to tossing a coin as a way of breaking the tie. Hence, my own view is that, in the Sore Throat Case, concern to also cure the sore throat should not be a tiebreaker. It is what I call an "irrelevant good" in this context. I believe that it is inappropriate for A to lose his 50 percent chance of being saved if we toss a coin in order to choose between him and B simply for the sake of getting the additional gain of curing C's sore throat. If we did balance and silence, then A could complain, even though his weight has been balanced by B's.[28]

Of course, even if a sore throat is irrelevant to deciding whose life should be saved in the choice between A and B, it may still be relevant in deciding whose earache should be treated. This raises the following problem.[29] Suppose that we could either save A's life and prevent B's earache, or save C's life and prevent D's earache and cure E's sore throat. E's sore throat could help to select saving D over B, were these people's problems all that was at stake. Should the sore throat then have a role in deciding in our actual case? I believe not, for lives are at stake, and it should play no role in depriving someone of getting his chance to live given what else is true of the case. (What if the sore throat cure were relevant to deciding whose problem we should take care of when the latter problem itself was relevant to deciding whose life should be saved [as an earache is not]? We shall consider such a case below.)

So, sometimes treating each person appropriately *will* stand in the way of producing the best outcome, as I assume that saving a (B's) life and curing a (C's) sore throat is a better outcome than just saving a (A's) life. Hence, Scanlon's Tiebreaker Argument is too simple, if it implies that we should *not* give A and B equal chances in the Sore Throat Case. Of course, as was noted above, Scanlon does not think that we owe A and B alone equal chances; rather we may just pick one or the other to help. If this is so, then perhaps we could still say that his argument is too simple, if it implies that the sore throat may play a role in picking between A and B. (Suppose it would be wrong to use the sore throat cure as a grounds for picking between A and B, even though it is not an illicit reason in itself [unlike race]. Would this not be because, contrary to Scanlon, we owe A a fair chance against B? Possibly not, for it might be that we are permitted to pick between items of a certain sort but not on certain grounds, even if the grounds are not intrinsically illicit.) On the other hand, if Scanlon's argument in some way takes seriously whether there is a complaint on his own behalf of the individual who is to be a tiebreaker, then it may here give the right result, but only because it is more than a simple tiebreaker argument. It would then be misleading for Scanlon to describe his argument as a tiebreaker argument. For when we must break a tie, our focus is on the individuals tied, not on how the refusal to use someone else's need as a tiebreaker will wrong the potential tiebreaking individual.

The Sore Throat Case also suggests that the Balancing Argument, according to which we owe each individual to pairwise balance and silence him with an equal, does not apply to all cases where there are unequal numbers of people who need help. Namely, we should balance and silence each with his equal only when the nature of the need of any additional person on one side is serious enough relative to the most important needs of those in the tie. This really means that those who are balanced and silenced will have no complaint only when the additional people on one side would themselves have a complaint as individuals if balancing and silencing were *not* done. (We shall amplify on this below.)

Now, return to the Legs Case, where saving C's legs is what would be a tiebreaker between A's or B's life. If A should not complain if C's legs are a tiebreaker, then it is presumably because C, in the context where B will be saved when C is helped, is appropriately asking us to focus on his complaint if he loses his legs as well as on the fact that B can balance A. He does not just say that we need some way to break the tie. But it is still true that he cannot say to A (as Scanlon emphasizes that C could do if his life were at stake) that just as the decision procedure was changed when B arrived on the scene, it should be changed now that he, C, is on the scene. For he cannot claim that his loss and gain are anywhere as important as B's, given that he would not be anywhere as badly off or stand to gain as much, nor can he claim that he could stand in the same pairwise relation to A as B did. The argument for unfairness to C in not considering his legs, which I think is correct, can neither be based on the mere fact that he can break a tie between two people where the focus is on them, nor on the fact that he has the same standing based on his substantive concern as they have (and for this reason his should be the focus when they create a tie). In the Legs Case, as in the Sore Throat Case, someone with less of a concern than A would be allowed to determine an outcome just as much as if his life were at stake. Hence, the Legs Case shows that the additional people on one side can themselves have a complaint as individuals if we do not balance and silence even when they would not be as badly off as those who will be balanced and silenced. This is another case where it becomes clear that an individual can complain on his own behalf only because of his relation to another person (B), as I emphasized in components (2) and (3) of how to understand Scanlon's IR (p. 59). A Three-Island Case involving A, B, and C's legs would leave C with no complaint if we just tossed a coin in order to choose between A and B.[30]

In sum, "tiebreaking" is a somewhat misleading title if it leads us to think only of the equal weight of those between whom the tie exists. But the remedy of focusing on the complaint of the tiebreaker on his own behalf (which leads to balancing and silencing as a way to break the tie) is also misleading if it requires that the tiebreaker must say that he is another person with a concern equal to that of those tied. Morally appropriate consideration of the good of another in tiebreaking is both narrower than the first approach and broader than the second approach.

We have been arguing that C's legs are not an irrelevant good when compared with A's getting a fifty percent chance at life, when B would be saved along with C's legs. Now imagine a conflict between saving C's legs or D's legs. Would the fact that only if we help D could we also save E's arm be a good reason to forgo giving C a fifty percent chance to be helped? Suppose that the answer is yes, even though saving E's arm along with B's life would not be enough reason to deprive A of his fifty per cent chance to live. Could saving E's arm then be a tiebreaker between saving either A's life and D's legs or B's life and C's legs?

I believe so, for the following reasons. I have suggested that the tie between A and B can be broken by C's legs. If D accompanies A, then A's being entitled to an equal chance is a side effect of D's having a right to an equal chance against C; it is not the result of A's weight per se, for that weight has already been overridden by B and C's legs. Hence, the weight of E's arm should be judged only relative to what C and D stand to lose rather than to what A stands to lose. And we have already assumed that an arm is relevant to legs even if not to lives.

An implication of this analysis is that a sore throat could appropriately result in A's losing a fifty percent chance to be saved in cases where (i) a sore throat is important enough relative to what is at stake for those who are in a certain tie to break the tie, and (ii) that tie is the one on account of which a random decision procedure would have been called for in a case where lives were also at stake. A further implication of this analysis (and the idea of irrelevant goods) bears on how we do Context-Aware pairwise comparison. Suppose that certain goods are irrelevant to a tie because there is a big qualitative gap between what individuals in a tie stand to lose and gain and what anybody accompanying them stands to lose and gain in conflict cases. Then, once we find a match between those who will suffer most and/or gain most, we need not proceed to see if there are other matches among those whose losses and/or gains are irrelevant to deciding what to do. But this will not be so when the additional matches are of losses and/or gains that are relevant to what is at stake in other ties.[31]

So far, I have been considering the bearing on the idea of tiebreaking of cases where what is at stake for an additional individual is less than what is at stake for the people who create the tie. But the Sore Throat Case also bears on the claim, made above in answering the circularity objection, that taking account of another person in the Balancing and Tiebreaker arguments for saving the greater number of people's lives employs a form of aggregation that is no more controversial than the claim that we ought to save B and C rather than B alone.[32] I said, that if A and B are tied, from an impartial view saving each is of equal moral value. So from that point of view saving B is like saving A. Furthermore, it is clear that we ought to save A and C instead of just A. So if we may substitute B for A, we ought to save B and C instead of just A. But the Sore Throat Case may seem to present a challenge to this simple view. For while we ought to save A and cure C's sore throat rather than just save A, I have claimed that it is *not* true that we ought to save B and cure C's sore throat rather than toss a coin between A and B, and if A wins, save him. (This is consistent with it still being true that we would produce a better outcome if we save B and cure C's sore throat than if we save A.) Hence, for purposes of deciding what we ought to do (rather than whether we produce the best outcome), it is not true that once we get to the stage in arguments like the Balancing or Tiebreaker arguments of considering B and C together versus A, the aggregation of B and C is always no more controversial than the aggregation of A and C.

But this, no more than the earlier circularity objection, should lead us to doubt the Balancing and Tiebreaker arguments for saving the greater number of lives, I think. For the objection to directly saving B and curing C's sore throat rather than tossing a coin between A and B accompanied by C with his sore throat does not stem from an objection to the moral equivalence of saving A or B or to balancing them where this involves substituting B for A. Rather it stems from a concern about when balancing (rather than tossing a coin) is triggered. It is a concern over when the interests of the additional person are great enough so that the case should be treated as one involving anyone besides A and B at all. And if the case should be treated as if only A and B are involved, their moral equivalence does not imply directly saving B, but, I think, implies tossing a coin to give each an equal chance. Presumably, however, what plays a part in determining whether the interests of the other person are relevant is the fact that A is not indifferent as to whether he or B is saved. If we were choosing between saving objects with no such personal perspectives, then C's sore throat might well be relevant and C could complain if his sore throat did not trigger substitution. In a sense then, someone's personal point of view can make a consideration disappear. The moral point of view, I believe, takes account of the personal, as well as the impartial, perspective, but it need not accord the personal perspective enough weight to let it stand in the way of saving B and C's legs.

VII

Above, I noted that in Scanlon's view only individuals can be tie makers. (This was [(1)] in my analysis of how we should understand Scanlon's IR.) It has been pointed out by Derek Parfit[33] that if Scanlon also accepts that in pairwise comparison we should compare not only baselines (of how badly off someone would be if not aided), but also degrees of benefit (of how well off someone would be if aided), then his views will have highly implausible implications. For example, suppose we can either help one person, A, who would otherwise die, to live twenty years or help two people, B and C, who would otherwise die, to live twelve years and eight years, respectively. If only individuals can create ties, and pairwise comparison is for baseline and benefit, then there is no tie in this scenario, for we would not toss a coin in order to choose between A and any of the others on their own in deciding whom to aid. Hence, we should not save the greater number according to the Tiebreaker Argument. Not saving the greater number here, however, seems wrong.

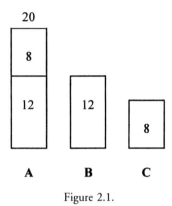

Figure 2.1.

How might Scanlon deal with this problem that Parfit raises for him?[34] It may help in thinking about Parfit-type cases to consider what we would do if the good we could give to A were, counterfactually, divisible. So imagine that A could first get a portion of it that another person, B, might get instead, if we tossed a coin in order to choose between them. For example, A and B could be tied with respect to how badly off they will be if not helped and also with respect to the *possibility* (dependent on winning the toss) of getting a benefit of living up to twelve years. There would be two ways to break the tie between A and B to decide whom to help. One way is vertically (as I call it), by imagining that if A gets the first benefit (of twelve years), he could also get another benefit of eight more years, which B cannot have. A second way to break the tie is horizontally (as I call it), by imagining that if B gets the first benefit, another person C, who would be as badly off as A and B if not helped, will benefit to the degree of getting eight years of life. If we give greater weight to tiebreaking on the horizontal dimension, it could be because it is morally more important to help another person who will be as badly off as the others (so long as he will be helped significantly) than it is to provide someone (such as A) with an additional eight years on top of twelve.[35] (I think this could be true even if the benefit given to C did not, when combined with that given to B, amount to twenty years.)

In the actual case, of course, we cannot divide the potential benefit to A in this way and decide where to put the parts of it. But the reasoning we have just used could, it might be argued, still be used to justify saving the greater number in our actual case. In essence, we can reason in the actual case with a moral method that I shall call the Method of Virtual Divisibility (see figure 2.1). That is, when we must choose between saving A, who would receive twenty years, or B, who would get twelve, and C, who would get eight, we imagine creating the possibility of a tie between A and B by marking off the point (twelve years) to which they could each be benefited, if the benefit to be awarded were divisible, and then see whether the additional eight years we can produce would be better placed in saving C or in saving A for additional years. If helping the worst off takes priority and there is "virtual" tying between A and B at twelve years, we should actually give the twelve years to B and the eight years to C. I call this Balancing Argument II because it involves balancing the *parts* that A and B could each have and substituting B's part for A's, if C accompanies B. So, the idea is that if Scanlon would distribute an actually divisible benefit in a certain way, then he should be committed to saving the greater number even when it is a choice between giving a greater benefit to one person or smaller benefits to others (who would otherwise be as badly off as that one person).

But the use of the Balancing Argument II and the Method of Virtual Divisibility can be extended, and their extension casts doubt on Scanlon's insistence on (1) in the IR, namely, that only an individual with a concern or complaint confronting another individual can create a tie. (This is also a point that Parfit emphasizes.) Suppose that A could be saved for twenty more years of life, or we could save B for only three years and C for only three years. It might indeed not make sense to break the virtual tie between A and B at three years by giving C three years instead of achieving in A an additional seventeen years. That is, the concern of another worst-off person to be taken care of to a significant degree when B could be helped as much as A up to the virtual tie point of three years might be trumped by the size of the additional benefit possible for A after we awarded the three years to him instead of to B. Helping another worst-off person to a significant degree might not always have priority.

But suppose that we add ten other people (D, E, etc.) to the side of B and C, and each of those people need as badly to be saved and each can live for three years. Now it seems more reasonable to save the greater number, who would each be as badly off as A would be if not helped. Here it becomes clear that if there is any tiebreaking that justifies doing this, it is neither a tie created by A and one person who is actually equal to him in baseline and benefit nor a tie created by any one person with another via virtual divisibility at a high enough level of benefit so that a smaller benefit to another person at the same baseline can break the tie. At best, it is a tie created by a *group* of people via virtual divisibility. That is, A and B are virtually tied for three years, A and C are virtually tied for the second three years that A might have (in addition to the first three), A and D are virtually tied for the third three years that A might have (on top of six years), etc. Only once we are (imaginatively) left with a much smaller additional gain possible to A, can one person accompanying the others complain that helping another worst-off person is more important than giving this additional gain to A. (Perhaps it is even best not to speak of Scanlon-type tiebreaking at all as occurring in such scenarios where numbers count, if what is really going on is that components of a group of people rather than any individuals per se are creating ties.)

Hence, a method that helps Scanlon avoid implausible conclusions also eliminates a part of his IR. As Parfit notes, in formulating the IR, Scanlon seems to have in mind not allowing an aggregate of benefits over many people who are better off than another person to outweigh a benefit to the worse-off person. But when all people face equally bad prospects, it seems that an aggregate of interpersonal benefits should sometimes be allowed to count against someone else's greater benefit.

Let us now consider possible problems with the Method of Virtual Divisibility. The first problem is that it is potentially misleading. Recall the case where either A gets twenty years or B gets twelve and C gets eight. We may be misled in using the method into thinking that one of our options is giving (a) additional resources (b) in multiple acts of aid to A in order to move him first to twelve years and then beyond to twenty. We may think that these are resources and attention that go beyond A's fair share and might otherwise go to a greater number of people. But, in fact, if we help A, then it is just in helping him once, and possibly with no more resources going to him than are needed to help *each* one of B and C, that we will produce a bigger benefit in him than in others. (This could occur if we had enough resources to help everyone but the problem is that A is located else- where than B and C and we cannot go in two directions at once to distribute resources.) Indeed, if we wanted to help A live *only* to the twelve-year level, we might have to give him fewer resources than would be given to each of B and C on the other side, as he is such an efficient user of resources (i.e., generates bigger benefits from the same resources others would get).

We must be careful, therefore, not to commit what might be called the "allocation fallacy," when concluding by the Method of Virtual Divisibility that we should help the greater number each to a lesser degree rather than help a smaller number each to a greater degree (when everyone is equally needy).[36] The allocation fallacy involves thinking that because we should not produce benefits to one person by allocating all parts of a divided resource to him, we are thereby committed to not producing the same benefits in him when a single part of that resource is to be allocated to him, if it means not helping others with the rest of the resources. That is, we must not think that we would be undertaking multiple acts of allocation of greater resources to A and, therefore, *unfairly* helping him with a lot of resources, when we would really only be undertaking one allocative act to A with no more than his fair share of resources but producing a much bigger benefit in him rather than in others. In general, we must distinguish two things: (a) aiding a person with resources that amount to, for example, twenty times his fair share, and (b) helping one person with his fair share of resources even when this results in our not being able to give each of nineteen others her fair share of resources because, for example, the nineteen are located elsewhere. The former behavior (a) has a consideration against it from the point of view of fairness that the latter (b) lacks.

But now let us consider a possible deeper problem: Suppose the Method of Virtual Divisibility avoids the allocation fallacy because it allows us to imagina- tively divide and distribute the benefits that can be achieved themselves without any commitment as to resources necessary to achieve this. This alone does not avoid a similar fallacy, I think, for the fact that we should and would allocate a divisible benefit itself over several people, rather than give it all to one, does not, by itself, imply that we should not save one person because we thereby produce in him a greater benefit than we could produce in the lives of each of many others.

Consider other imaginary cases like this. I might choose to distribute intelli- gence genes in a conflict case so that many have adequate intelligence, leaving one person with nothing, rather than make the one a genius by giving him all of the genes. But this alone (all by itself) does not prove that I have a reason to save several people of normal intelligence rather than someone who is already a genius (just because he is a genius). I might also choose to give several people each reasonable life-spans leaving someone else with no further life rather than provide him with a very long life-span. But this alone does not imply that, if I can save either someone who already has long-life-span genes or else several with shorter-life-span genes, my first choice by itself rationally commits me to saving the greater number rather than the single person. The deep fallacy in deducing whom to save from how we should allocate resources or benefits is that it attempts to reduce *production* to *allocation*, for one can produce an end state without allocating anything, and unfair allocation need not imply unfair production.[37]

Hence, if we should aid a greater number of people when each benefits less than one other person would benefit, it must be for a different reason than that is how we should allocate a resource or a benefit. One possible reason is that achieving a greater good in one person—even through no unfair allocation of resources, attention, or benefits—is not morally as important as helping more people, who would be equally badly off if not aided, to achieve the most significant part of the good. The most significant part of a good is that which, to a significant extent, lifts someone up from the lowest baseline. Goods in addition to that, it might be said, have diminishing marginal value. On this view, one is actually giving a smaller benefit to A, if one gives him a second three year period of life than if one gives C his first three year period of life. But perhaps life does not have diminishing marginal value. A second reason to aid the greater number of people when each benefits less than one other person would benefit is that it is morally more valuable to give even an equal benefit to someone who is worse off than to someone who is already better off. Producing this has more moral value than producing the goods that lift someone up who has already moved beyond the lowest baseline. There is "diminishing moral value" in giving such an equal benefit to those who already have some of the good at issue. It is true that A, in our example, faces death just as much as each of the other people. Hence, helping him is not obviously a case of helping someone who is better off. He too needs to be lifted from the lowest baseline, and this will be the concomitant of lifting him far above it to twenty years of life. But, if we assume that numbers count, then it is more important to help more of the worst off. And the Method of Virtual Divisibility, in allowing us to virtually divide benefits, shows us to which baseline each component of a benefit will be added, and hence how morally significant giving it is. For example, in the case presented above, if A and B are virtually tied at three years, the next three years we can produce would move A from a baseline of three years to six, but it would move C from a baseline of zero to three years. Hence, if the additional three years went to A, they would not go to a person at the lowest baseline, but they would go to a person at the lowest baseline, if they went to C.[38] This is the method's real use, I believe. This use also shows that (1) in Scanlon's IR is not correct: In the absence of a tiebreaking argument, a group of people can lodge a complaint in virtue of the group's concerns.

VIII

Those who deny that numbers count reject, unlike Scanlon, the idea of dealing with ties between people in the following way: We morally get everything we would have gotten if we had saved A if we instead save B, so we may sometimes balance A and B (in the sense that involves substituting B for A), and save B and C. Balancing Argument II involving virtual divisibility, which I gave in section VII to deal with a problem Parfit raises for Scanlon, might not be acceptable to them (even if it were to Scanlon). This is for the same reason that the original Balancing Argument is not acceptable to them: It depends on the permissibility of giving A zero if we achieve just as much moral value in helping someone else as we would get in helping A, when we can thus also significantly help other people who are as badly off. If there were a tie between individuals, then some who reject counting numbers would only toss a coin in order to choose between them. And this would be true whether the two were actually tied or tied in the sense that involves virtual divisibility, even when one person is accompanied by someone who can also be helped.

Michael Otsuka, however, would appear to have developed an argument against numbers not counting that does not rely on any type of balancing-of-equals step, a step which numbers opponents find problematic.[39] He seems to give an argument for counting numbers that bypasses the issue of how to deal with ties, real or virtual. However, I do not think that his argument does bypass the need for some sort of tiebreaker or balancing style argument in order to justify numbers counting, as I hope to show. Further, I see a relation between both Balancing Argument II and the Method of Virtual Divisibility just described and Otsuka's argument, and so I shall present his argument in a way that highlights that relation.[40] (I do not mean to, thereby, deny his originality.) Like one version of the argument involving virtual divisibility, his argument also works by imagining what someone would do when a resource is divisible and then claiming that this has implications about what one must do when a resource is not, in fact, divisible. But he makes novel use of the assumption that those who think that numbers do not count accept pairwise comparison that checks for both baselines and (crucially) degrees of benefit, so that they would not toss a coin between people who are at the same baseline but get very different benefits.[41]

Otsuka asks us to imagine that four people will be completely paralyzed if we do nothing. We have three pills. In three of the people, one pill will relieve paralysis in two limbs to a maximum of two unparalyzed limbs per person. In the fourth person, one pill will relieve paralysis in one limb, but recovery can be achieved to a maximum of three limbs (with three pills).

Otsuka claims that in distributing the pills, the antinumbers person can reject option (1) which involves giving all three pills to the person who would thereby get three working limbs. Instead of doing this, he would prefer (in increasing order) to (2) give two pills that provide two working limbs in the fourth person and one pill that provides two limbs in one of the three; (3) give one pill that gives one working limb to the fourth person and two pills that each give two working limbs to two of the three; or (4) (best of all) give three pills that each provide two limbs in three people and give nothing to the fourth. The reasoning here relies on the fact that even an antinumbers theorist can believe that we should put each pill where it can produce the bigger benefit, given that each person would be as badly off if not helped. Because the pill will produce more good in each of the first three people than it will in the fourth person, pairwise comparison (of the sort that involves baseline and benefit) never yields a tie between any of the three who can get bigger benefits and the lone fourth person. Hence, we need not toss a coin between the greater and the lesser number, if we want to show equal concern for each person. Pairwise comparison in Otsuka's case, with his assumptions, therefore, results in the willingness of an antinumbers theorist to leave one person with zero and help the greater number of people seemingly without relying on the idea that in a tie we get as much moral value if we save one person or another and so we may balance, substitute and count numbers.

But then, Otsuka asks, if the antinumbers theorist *dis*favors option (1) (i.e., distributing the three pills so as to help one person get three limbs), will it not be inconsistent for him (given his antinumbers position) to favor helping one person in the following case? A fourth person will get three working limbs, if he is helped, while if three people are helped, each of them will get two working limbs. The antinumbers position seems to commit the theorist to helping the single person on the following grounds: As numbers of people do not count, the situation is the same as if only two people were in conflict. We should *not* toss a coin between only two people who would be at the same baseline when one will get a significantly bigger benefit than the other, and three limbs working is a significantly bigger benefit than two limbs working. But if the antinumbers theorist would make choices stepwise in the first Pill Distribution Case that lead to someone who could have had three working limbs having none, preferring (4) to (3), (3) to (2), and (2) to (1), how can he, in essence, now prefer (1) to (4)?[42] Consistency with the first Pill Distribution Case seems to require helping three people to each have two working limbs instead of helping one person to have three, but doing this seems to require deciding to give smaller benefits to each of several people simply on the basis of counting numbers of people. Hence, Otsuka concludes, the view that numbers of people do not count leads to inconsistent choices in cases, and this is a ground for rejecting the view.

Notice that the Method of Virtual Divisibility can be used to provide an argument for preferring (4) to (1) that is like the argument based on actual divisibility provided by Otsuka's three different pills. We could treat each of the working limbs that would be present in the fourth person in (1) separately, comparing each with the two limbs that could instead be provided to each of the three people. In these three comparisons, one limb would not tie with nor dominate two limbs. (Suppose, however, that one thinks that the difference between getting two limbs and getting one is not significant enough to interfere with a tie between them, and so we should toss a coin to decide to whom to give a pill. Then one could create another example, perhaps using years of life, where each pill will provide a year in a candidate who will live for three years if he gets three pills compared, via virtual divisibility, with twenty years in each of three other candidates that could be gotten instead if each of the three receives a pill. It is harder to deny a significant difference between getting one year and twenty years if one accepts pairwise comparison involving baselines and benefits.)

Does Otsuka's argument succeed against the antinumbers theorist and does it bypass the need for a judgment about the moral equivalence of saving one person or another, tying, and balancing that involves substitution? Here are some reasons to think it does not:

(A). Otsuka's argument may only show that those who are against counting numbers must be committed to a form of pairwise comparison that does not compare the amount of benefit to be gotten. That is, they must not refuse to toss a coin between a person who avoids total paralysis by getting three working limbs and one who avoids total paralysis by getting two or one working limb(s), or between a person who avoids paralysis by getting one limb from a pill and a person who avoids paralysis by getting two limbs from a pill. Why should they be committed to this? Because, I shall argue, pairwise comparison of degree of benefit depends on a hidden form of tying that involves balancing and substitution of morally equivalent benefits in different people, and this is problematic for antinumbers theorists. And if pairwise comparison of benefits depends on such substitution of equivalents, then Otsuka's argument, appearances to the contrary, does not provide an argument against the antinumbers theorist that does not rely on the sort of balancing and substitution that is at the heart of the Balancing and Tiebreaker arguments.

To see why all this might be true, consider in a conflict case the part of a greater good that a person A could potentially get which B, who is at the same baseline, could also potentially get. This may be the most crucial part of the good, as it is the part that lifts a person from his lowest baseline. Consider this from the point of view of someone who rejects the position that balancing is permissible. He rejects the position that merely because it is just as good if A or B gets that most crucial part of the good, therefore, A's getting it can be substituted for B's getting it. From this perspective, it is morally inappropriate to take the fact that A could *also* get an additional unit of good that B would not get as a reason to favor A. We must first settle whether A or B will get the first part of the good, and that would require tossing a coin. So, where A stands to get two working limbs if not totally paralyzed, and B stands to get only one working limb, we must first settle who gets at least one limb. A's winding up with two limbs if he wins the toss is only a result of his not being deprived of a chance to get one limb. In other words, if we let the greater benefit that one person can achieve decide who gets the pill in Otsuka's Pill Distribution Cases, we will have assumed that it is equally good whether A or B gets the first unit of good (one limb), so that A's getting it can be substituted for B's getting it. Only that assumption allows us to decide things by considering the additional unit of good that A would get. Hence, Otsuka's argument relies on virtual divisibility and balancing at the level of one limb and virtual breaking of the tie with an additional working limb that will be present in one person and not in another. If the opponent of numbers accedes to this, then he should also accede to helping a person who will be totally paralyzed rather than one who would only be paralyzed in one limb, without tossing a coin. This is so even if he only helps the worse-off person to the extent of saving one of his limbs. And, I have argued, if he accepts all of this, then he may as well use the original Balancing and Tiebreaker arguments given by the present author and by Scanlon and accede to counting numbers of lives saved.

Hence, Otsuka seems to have shown, at most, that those who reject counting numbers because they reject a Balancing or Tiebreaking argument are committed to what many would also think is another implausible view, namely, do not select among those who share a baseline merely because some can achieve significantly greater benefits. (I shall consider next whether he does, in fact, show this.)

(B). How does Otsuka's argument relate to the allocation fallacy? In Otsuka's first case, in order to produce three working limbs in someone, we would have to give him three pills, pills that could individually help others to a greater degree. It may be this *method* of bringing about the person with three working limbs that the antinumbers theorist could reject. This is because it involves giving the person more than his fair share of resources. Hence, when Otsuka imagines the antinumbers theorist being committed to helping someone who will get three working limbs rather than helping each of three people who will get two limbs, it is possible that helping there be a three-limbed person could involve giving the fourth person only one pill, the same number any one of the three would get. This is possible because, for example, his system could employ the pill more efficiently than any of the three. As noted above, in discussing Scanlon and the way we may be misled by the Method of Virtual Divisibility, it is not inconsistent with refusing to give someone multiple portions of a resource when others could use portions of the total, to give someone a single portion of a resource because we thereby produce a bigger benefit in him, even if doing this means that we are not able to give the rest of the multiple portions of the resource to other people.

Suppose that the numbers skeptic might in this way distinguish different methods by which we help there to be a person with three working limbs. Then Otsuka's inconsistency argument fails. If so, then Otsuka's inconsistency argument does not—contra (A) above—show that the numbers skeptic is committed to the form of pairwise comparison that does not compare benefits but only baselines. For the numbers skeptic can avoid inconsistency by distinguishing two different ways in which (1) can come about: favoring (1) over (4) when one method is employed and (4) over (1) when the other method is employed. Another argument, such as I have tried to give in (A), would be needed to show that if one is anti-numbers, one will also have problems with comparing benefits and baselines.

What if the benefit to be gotten by each person were equal (e.g., if no one could get more than one limb from a pill), but only one person could benefit to the extent of getting three working limbs? In such a variant of Otsuka's case, one could straightforwardly give one person rather than another a pill on the grounds of helping a worst-off person before helping a better-off person (i.e., helping someone who had not already gotten one pill). Therefore, one could prefer that three people each get one pill than that one person gets three. One could pick straws from a set of four, giving each person an equal chance to get a pill, leaving one without anything. If (contrary to what I have argued), an anti-numbers theorist can still decide to straightforwardly help someone who will be significantly worse off than someone else (even though this seems to involve a form of balancing via virtual divisibility), then this is what he too should do.

But suppose that for some reason a pill given to three of the people (A, B, and C) only works if all three take it. D's pill will work if he alone takes it. Then the antinumbers theorist faces a choice of giving D a pill or giving A, B, and C one each. Giving it outright to the three would deprive D of his equal chance. So, the antinumbers theorist should toss a coin between D and the three. If D wins, he gets his pill. But because two other pills will now go to waste if D is given only one pill, it becomes permissible for the anti-numbers theorist to give D all three pills rather than give one to each of the other three people.

NOTES

Material on which this chapter is based was first presented at the conference on Thomas Scanlon's *What We Owe to Each Other*, University College, London, June 2004, and subsequently published as "Aggregation and Two Moral Methods," in *Utilitas* 17 (March 2004), pp. 1–23. I am grateful to Professor Veronique Munoz for inviting me to speak. For comments, I am grateful to members of the audience at UCL, at the Georgetown University Philosophy Department, and at the University of Delaware Philosophy Department, and to Alexander Friedman, Roger Crisp, Michael Otsuka, and Thomas Scanlon.

   1. I first discussed the question in "Equal Treatment and Equal Chances," *Philosophy & Public Affairs* 14 (1985: 177–194). See also "The Choice between People, 'Common Sense' Morality, and Doctors," *Bioethics* 1 (1987): 255–71; and *Morality, Mortality*, vol. 1 (New York: Oxford University Press, 1993).

   2. I am grateful for discussion of my cases to Michael Otsuka.

   3. As we shall see, Elizabeth Anscombe thinks that numbers can be a reason to save one group over another, but not a reason upon which one *must* act, so long as one will save someone in a nonoverlapping group. (See her "Who Is Wronged?" *Oxford Review* 5 [1967]: 16.) Would she also think that there is no definitive reason to harm fewer people so long as one will harm someone in a nonoverlapping group?

   4. It is possible that Taurek himself would be willing to do this, however.

   5. By "objective" might be meant some true theory of the importance of any given loss to a person, independent of his view of the matter. By contrast, two people may each agree that it would be much worse for him to lose his life than for him to lose his leg, even if this were not objectively true. On the basis of this interpersonal agreement, I would claim that we could also say that, from an impartial point of view, it is worse if B loses his life than if A loses his leg. This is because B loses an item that, they agree, is of greater concern to a person. Suppose someone claimed that there was no impartial point of view, but only various personal perspectives. Then he would say that even though it would be worse from each person's personal perspective to lose his life than to lose his leg, there is no point of view from which one can make the interpersonal comparison that it is worse if B loses his life than if A loses his leg. Hence, when I say that we can make judgments from an impartial perspective, my denial of what the person who claims that there are only personal perspectives says does not strictly depend on accepting that there are objective judgments. The dispute between us remains if we just consider subjective rankings and he denies interpersonal comparisons that I think we can make. This is all I require for my argument to proceed. Hence, though I will say that someone who accepts an impartial view is making objective judgements, this could be translated as the view that he is making interpersonal judgements. I discuss this issue in response to a question raised by Larry Temkin.

   6. I first described sobjectivity in 1987 ("The Choice between People, 'Common Sense' Morality, and Doctors," p. 255), and again in more detail in *Morality, Mortality*, vol. 1.

7. Below I shall reconsider whether the degree of commitment to the impartiality involved in thinking that saving someone's life should take precedence over saving someone else's leg implies a commitment to its being a better outcome if the greater number survive.

8. In *Morality, Mortality*, vol. 1, I called it the Aggregation Argument.

9. But is it true that if the state of affairs in which A survives is morally equivalent to the state of affairs in which B survives, then they necessarily relate in the same way to the combination of B and C? Perhaps A interacts with C in a way that B does not, so that saving C counts for nothing in comparison with A, resulting in B + C = A. (For example, suppose that A is C's mother and B is C's father. Saving a mother could be the moral equivalent of saving a father, and saving a son could add something to saving either a father or a mother. But it is still possible that it is a worse state of affairs in which a child survives instead of the person who procreated him.) This possibility, however, depends on its not being morally equivalent whether one saves A or C, and this is contrary to an assumption in our cases that each person counts as much as any other person. But even with this assumption in place, why could it not be that the combination of two equals produces a better state relative to one equal but not to another equal? If such an interaction effect were possible, however, there would also be no reason to assume that the survival of B and C is a better state of affairs than the survival of B. If we do not worry about this in premise (1), then why worry about any other interaction effect?

10. It might also be objected that we could generate an intransitivity where ">" means "clearly ought to be saved," and "=" means "equally permissible to save": (i) B + C > B, (ii) A = B, but (iii) −(B + C > A) (or −[A + C > B]), because it could be unfair to deprive someone of his equal chance to be saved, a factor not present if we act on B + C > B or toss a coin because A = B. But notice a problem with this analysis. Premise (ii) says that it would be equally permissible to save either A or B. It does not say that we should toss a coin between A and B. That is why we are tempted to derive the conclusion that A + C > B (i.e., -(iii)). But if this is not derivable, because we should give equal chances, then (ii) is not correct either, for we must give A and B alone equal chances. But once this becomes a premise, there is no longer any temptation to derive the conclusion that A + C > B.

11. For more on this sort of case, see below in the discussion of the Three Islands Case.

12. Scanlon's complete theory is laid out in his *What We Owe to Each Other* (Cambridge, MA: Harvard University Press, 1998).

13. In her "Scanlon's Precarious Balancing Act" (unpublished).

14. By "direct" I mean for the sake of the good that the resource itself can provide. So suppose that I could give a drug either (a) to save two people or (b) to save one person who (having used his share) could distribute the rest of it to save three other people who also need that very drug but whom I cannot reach. Giving the drug to the one person would still lead to the best direct use of the drug.

15. I believe the name is due to Thomas Nagel, who employed it in his paper "Equality," reprinted in his *Mortal Questions* (New York: Cambridge University Press, 1979).

16. I believe the British word for "blinder" is "blinker."

17. On the Blinder View, once a person on one side finds a match on the other side and finds no one who is more than his match, we know that we must toss a coin regardless of who else is with these people. On the Context Aware View, finding a match and no one who is more than a match does not yet tell us what to do. I owe this point to Shelly Kagan.

18. See his "Scanlon and the Claims of the Many versus the One," *Analysis* 60 (2000): 288.

19. Michael Otsuka believes that the fact that we do take the blinders off after one comparison and make sure to compare A with any other individual on the other side means that the decision procedure is affected by the presence of another person. (And, if we found

someone whose loss or gain would be greater, we might not toss the coin, thereby also showing sensitivity to the presence of another person.) Hence, it is not true, he says, that we decide in the same way as we would if it were a contest between A and just one other person. See his "Scanlon and the Claims of the Many," p. 288.

20. The Blinder View is a form of confrontation that gives maximal equal chances to each person. But there are other forms of confrontation, for example, a series of individual tosses between A and however many people are on the other side, so long as A keeps on winning those tosses. Here, A's chances of winning are much less than those of the members of the group that he confronts. I discuss this in "Equal Treatment and Equal Chances," and in *Morality, Mortality*, vol. 1.

21. This phrasing recalls what John Rawls says in *A Theory of Justice* (Cambridge, MA: Harvard University Press, 1971).

22. The nonsubstitution thesis is certainly true insofar as there is, in general, no compensation to a person if he is killed just because we replace him with another person. I discuss the contrast between substitution and sub-ordination in chapter 5.

23. In "Scanlon and the Claims of the Many," p. 288.

24. Though, of course, it does not give A all of the satisfaction of A's concern which saving him would have given him. It also does not give to the fact that A's concern would not be as well satisfied when B survives as when A does the recognition that giving equal chances does. Thus, a premise in these arguments caters even less to the subjective perspective of each person than a procedure that refuses to toss a coin between A's leg and B's life. For though A may care more about his leg than about B's life, he cares even more about his life than about B's life, given that he cares more about his life than about his leg.

25. I shall reexamine this below.

26. I discussed a similar case involving one leg in *Morality, Mortality*, vol. 1 and also discussed the Legs Case in chapter 1.

27. This is a case that I discuss at length in *Morality, Mortality*, vol. 1 and referred to chapter 1.

28. Suppose someone thinks of "whom the sore throat is next to" as itself a randomizing device to select between A and B. (This is on the assumption that A and B had an equal chance to be the one next to someone with a sore throat.) This way of thinking still is concerned with giving A and B an equal chance. (Similarly, we might choose between two coins to use in a fair toss in order to choose between A and B on the grounds that one of the coins was magic and would also cure C's sore throat.) By contrast, the view to which I am objecting is one that sees C's sore throat as a good with whose achievement we should not allow giving equal chances to A and B to interfere. Not everyone would agree with my objection. Some think that the justification for tossing a coin is that it ensures that no invidious discrimination leads us to pick one person rather than another (As I noted above, Scanlon seems to think this.) Producing a sore throat cure in another is not a reason for a selection that violates this nondiscrimination condition. Notice that what I have said so far is consistent with it not being true that whenever lives are at stake, we should not break ties with a minor concern such as a sore throat. For suppose there are a billion (or more, if necessary for argumentative purposes) individuals on a billion separate islands waiting to be saved, and we can save only one, and with one of them is someone whose sore throat would also be cured. Here, each person has only a very small chance of being saved. Might it be that the loss to him of a one-in-a-billion chance of being saved can be outweighed by saving someone and also curing someone else's sore throat? I suspect not. Consider an analogy: Each holder of a lottery ticket has a vanishingly small chance of winning, but this does not make it appropriate to just award the prize to the person who is next to someone whom we can then also benefit in a small way.

29. Posed to me by Larry Temkin.

30. Because someone with less of a concern than those in the tie might determine the outcome, some of those who think that numbers of lives should count may want to move back from tie breaking and balancing in the Legs Case. Instead, they may wish to give only a higher proportional chance to the side with B and C. I myself do not think that this is correct. For more on this see my *Morality, Mortality* vol. 1, and Scanlon's *What We Owe to Each Other*.

31. I owe to Shelly Kagan this last point. The discussion in this paragraph was prompted by questions raised by Kagan and Larry Temkin.

32. As Michael Otsuka emphasized to me.

33. In *Climbing the Mountain* (unpublished); and in "Justifiability to Each Person," *Ratio* 16 (2003): 368.

34. I first dealt with this issue in "Owing, Justifying, and Rejecting," *Mind* 111 (2002): 323.

35. I argued for the greater moral value of distributed rather than concentrated benefits in *Morality, Mortality*, vol. 1.

36. I originally referred to the allocation fallacy as the divisive fallacy in "Aggregation and Two Moral Methods."

37. The Method of Virtual Divisibility can also mislead if one mistakenly thinks that A in our example will actually get at least twelve years of life regardless of our decision about whether to give him or C eight additional years. This is not true, of course.

38. I am not claiming that giving any small good that does practically nothing to ameliorate someone's low baseline has more moral value than a bigger good located at someone else's higher baseline. Hence, I do not think we are committed by my argument to distribute one extra second of life to each of billions of people who will soon die rather than save one person, who will then live for twenty years. But how do we decide when a good is significant relative to the baseline at which all are and also relative to the larger good someone else can achieve? This is a different problem from the earlier one discussed, of the relevance of the small good of a sore throat cure to our decision of whose life to save. In that case, the person who would get the sore throat cure was not at the same low baseline (i.e., facing death).

39. See his "Skepticism about Saving the Greater Number," *Philosophy & Public Affairs* 32 (2004): 413.

40. My published discussion of these issues in "Owing, Justifying, and Rejecting" was independent of his argument.

41. It is possible that this assumption is not true of all who reject counting numbers, just as some might toss a coin to decide between saving someone's leg and saving another person's life.

42. Otsuka notes that Scanlon faces the same problem even though he thinks numbers do count, for he would respond to Otsuka's two pill distribution cases in the same way as the antinumbers theorist, given that he considers both baseline and benefit in deciding whether there is a tie.

3

INTENTION, HARM, AND THE POSSIBILITY OF A UNIFIED THEORY

One of Warren Quinn's primary aims in his writings on normative theory is to justify revisionist versions of nonconsequentialist doctrines that draw moral distinctions between doing and allowing harm (which he calls the Doctrine of Doing and Allowing [DDA]) and between intending and merely foreseeing harm (the Doctrine of Double Effect [DDE]). In this chapter, I will examine and raise objections to Quinn's revisions, building on my discussion of nonconsequentialism in chapter 1. This is the next step in further refining some claims made there and will raise issues that will be discussed in greater detail in the next two chapters.

I

a. Let us start with an examination of the DDA. One of Quinn's revisions to the traditional view is that *omitting to act* because one intends that an object *move*, though one foresees that its movement will harm someone, is to be classed with acting as a second form of what he calls "positive agency." Other omissions are classed as "negative agency." (Intending that an object move, of course, is different from intending the harm or involvement of a person.) This revision is Quinn's attempt to retain the connection between all *doings* and *action* by linking doing, sometimes, not to the action of the agent but to the action of an object that could have been—but was not—prevented by the agent.

This revision of the DDA raises several problems. First, there is an oddity in focusing on omitting to act because one intends the *movement* of an object; this sort of intention implies that there is an important moral distinction between (1) a case in which someone refuses to remove water from a tub when he sees that this is the way to save a child from drowning, because he *intends that the water remain* at a certain high level, and (2) a case in which someone omits to aid the child whom he sees is about to be drowned if water rises because he *intends the water level to move upward*. Drawing a moral distinction here seems odd, because, in both cases, one intends some state of the world—whether it is a moving object or not, the action of an object or its inaction—that causes a death.

Second, cases in which someone begins his life in a position which involves his imposing on someone (so that there is no movement toward imposition) should, I believe, be treated like cases involving someone's doing harm (perhaps unknowingly), even though these cases involve no action. Quinn's revision of the DDA, with the focus on the action of an agent or object, has no way of capturing this intuition.

Third, Quinn's inclusion of some omissions along with actions under positive agency has a counterintuitive implication for the Trolley Case, in which the trolley is headed toward killing five people but may be redirected so that it kills only one other person. Quinn says that refusing to redirect the trolley from killing the five toward killing the one involves intending that the trolley be away from the one. But this, he says, this involves intending the movement of the trolley in a way which we foresee will harm five people. Hence, omitting to redirect the trolley is, on Quinn's view of positive agency, morally equivalent to *directing* a trolley toward killing five people. But killing one person is better than killing five, and hence, Quinn argues, his theory of positive agency explains why we may redirect a trolley toward one rather than let it kill five. It is like a choice between killing one or killing five, rather than a choice between killing one and letting five die.

I believe his solution to the Trolley Case is flawed, for it implies that if a trolley were headed toward one person and we redirected it toward five, we would be doing something no worse than if we let a trolley hit five rather than redirect it toward one. This is because actively redirecting toward five and omitting to redirect away from five are in the Trolley Case, he claims, both forms of positive agency and he draws no moral distinction between them. Yet, I think, these choices are not morally equivalent. For example, we are not obligated to redirect a trolley from five toward one, but (I believe) we are obligated *not* to redirect it from one toward five. Another indication that there is a morally significant difference between these choices is that I might permissibly kill someone in order to prevent him from redirecting the trolley from one toward five, but I should not kill someone if this alone would prevent him from omitting to aid the five because he intends that the trolley be away from the one.[1] (It is also possible that Quinn is wrong in claiming that an agent intends that the trolley be away from the one just because he does not want to be involved in killing him by redirecting the trolley from the five. If so, the failure of Quinn's solution to the Trolley Case would not be evidence against his claim that his two forms of positive agency are morally equivalent. This is because not redirecting the trolley away from the five would not involve intending its movement in a way that the agent foresees will kill the five.)

Fourth, it seems wrong to think that the intentions of the agent give rise to the impermissibility of his omission, yet Quinn's analysis seems to commit him to this. For example, Quinn claims that if we must rush five people to the hospital but see someone ahead on the road, we should not continue driving when this will kill the person even if we do not intend to kill him. However, he says, suppose the car is not being driven by us but was set to go automatically by others. It would also be wrong, he thinks, for us to omit to brake when we intend the car to continue on its way to the hospital with the five people, even when we do not intend but only foresee the hitting of the person on the road (Rescue Case I). Nevertheless, he thinks it *is* permissible for us to attend to the needs of the five people in the back of the car when they will die without such attention, even though this means we cannot also step on the brake and we foresee that the car will then hit the one person. Unlike the previous case, we do not here intend the car continuing on, and Quinn thinks this makes for the difference in the permissibility of not braking (Rescue Case II).

To show this is not correct, consider a variant on Quinn's Rescue cases. Suppose we go to the back of the car to provide the five with aid they need to survive. However, we do this only because we intend that we not be available to prevent the car continuing on the road because we intend that it continue. (That is, in Rescue Variant I, we would not go back to help the five, if doing so did not interfere with our braking the car.) Does the fact that we intend the event of the car continuing on even though it will hurt the one person on the road imply that it is impermissible for us to go and provide needed aid to the five? I do not think it does. I suspect (on the basis of what he says in his discussion of the DDE, as we will see in the following sections) that Quinn would agree. But then, it is wrong to claim that intending versus merely foreseeing an event that will cause harm accounts for differences in permissibility of behavior in his own two Rescue cases.

It might be suggested that Quinn's view should be replaced with one that emphasizes not an agent's intention that an object move but rather the actual causal role in producing good of an event that will lead to harm to others. That is, it might be said that if the car's continuing on the road to the hospital will have a causal role in saving the five, it is wrong to fail to brake. (This suggestion is prompted by noticing that the car continuing to the hospital is causally useful to saving the five in Quinn's Rescue Case I, but in Rescue Variant I it is not useful for saving the five. Rather, our ministering to the five in the back of the car is what is saving them.) This proposal is also flawed, I believe. For imagine that we have to stay with the five to give them resuscitation that keeps them alive and can eventually save them. Hence, we do not brake and the car continues on the road to the hospital, killing the one. But we foresee that once we are at the hospital, there will be much faster techniques than our continuing resuscitation to save the five, and those techniques will be what actually saves them. Then the car's going over the road would, in fact, have played a causal role in the five surviving, and it will also cause the death of the one (Rescue Variant II). Yet this does not show that we should not engage in resuscitation without which the five would die right away.

Now, it might be said, in Rescue Variant II, although going over the road *actually* has a causal role in saving the five, it is not *necessary* for it to occur in order that the five be saved, as our slow and continued resuscitation would eventually have saved them anyway. So, it may be thought, what we need is the introduction of a modal notion—the *necessity* of the causal role of the event that will harm—in order to rule an omission to stop the event as impermissible. But this further proposal would also not be quite right. To see this, consider Rescue Variant III: If we stay with the five to provide necessary resuscitation, we cannot brake the car and so the one will be hit and die. We also know that as a result of our giving the five the resuscitation, they will develop another life-threatening problem as we will transmit to them a quick-acting deadly virus. However, the car's continuing on to the hospital means that the cure for the virus will also be available for them. In this case, there would be no point in our resuscitating the five were it not that the car does not brake, for if they did not get to the hospital, the virus would soon kill them anyway. Here the movement of the car that harms the person on the road is a necessary, not merely actual, causal route to the five being saved for a significant period of time. Does this make it impermissible to resuscitate the five? I do not think so.

b. Let us now examine Quinn's views about the foundations of the moral significance of the DDA. He relates the primacy of not doing harm over preventing harm to the fact that persons have special authority over themselves and so have negative rights not to be interfered with. But how does this explanation fit with his view (examined in section (a)) that part of positive agency involves omissions in which we intend an event despite the fact that we foresee that it will cause harm? Quinn does not explain how omissions combined with intentions concerning moving objects can conflict with respecting the fact that people have special authority over themselves and have negative rights. It is possible that a person exhibits an attitude inconsistent with respect for another's having special authority over himself when he intends that something (even if not himself) interfere with that person or with that person's having what is rightfully his.[2] However, intending an event that one foresees will interfere with someone is not the same as intending that an event interfere with someone, and it is the former that plays a role in Quinn's new notion of positive agency.

Unlike Quinn, I think that the unwillingness to forgo a benefit from an event that foreseeably will harm someone and to make an effort to stop the event seems less morally offensive than the unwillingness to forego a benefit from and make an effort to *stop one's causing* such an event. For example, suppose a bomb going off will stop a trolley headed toward killing five people but part of the bomb will also directly hit and kill a bystander as a side effect. It is impermissible, I believe, to set such a bomb. But is it also impermissible to refrain from stopping (by minor effort) a bomb that will go off of its own accord when one knows that its going off will redirect the trolley from killing five, despite foreseeing (but not intending) that parts of the bomb will as a side effect directly hit and kill a bystander? I suspect it is not impermissible to refrain.

Finally, at crucial points, Quinn's foundational argument seems incomplete and also to involve equivocation between normative and nonnormative senses of terms. He says, for example: "A person is constituted by his body and mind.... For that very reason, it is fitting that he have primary say over what may be done to them . . . because any arrangement that denied him that say would be a grave indignity."[3] But a cat is constituted by its body and mind, and such constitution does not make it fitting that it have such primary say, nor would denial of such a say be a grave indignity. What is it about persons in particular such that they must have primary say over that of which they are constituted, if this is indeed so?

Quinn continues: "In giving him this authority, morality recognizes his existence as an individual with ends of his own—an independent being. Since that is what he is, he deserves this recognition."[4] If being an independent being just means having ends of one's own, then can we not recognize this as true of someone in a nonnormative sense, without necessarily having to give someone authority over the mind and body that generates and promotes these ends? Why does having ends of one's own make one deserve not only nonnormative recognition of this fact, but also the moral authority to resist others' interference with one's body and mind?[5] Quinn claims that without such authority we would be cells in a collective whole, not beings in our own right. This claim makes it seem as though we would have to deny the incontestable *nonnormative* truth that we are independent beings with ends of our own. But we can, without logical contradiction, say that an independent being ought to be subordinated for the good of the whole.

Quinn means, I think, that it would be undignified for a person to have the moral status of a cell in a collective whole, and that moral individualism (not just any morality) is the only condition under which people can have dignity. But, as noted above, I do not believe that he fully explains why. Finally, it is not clear that negative rights which prevent interference are enough to give one authority over one's own mind and body. Suppose that we had a positive moral duty to aid others whenever this would be for the greater good; then, even if we had a negative right that others not interfere with us to enforce such a duty, our authority over our mind and body would be insufficient to make us not be "moral cells". In order to show that we are not moral cells, we also need an argument showing that we have a prerogative (i.e., that it is morally permissible) not to always sacrifice ourselves for the greater good.[6] Oddly enough, Quinn never discusses the issue of such a prerogative.

II

Now let us consider Quinn on the DDE. Quinn describes the DDE as disfavoring *direct* over *indirect agency* with respect to harm or other evils. His major revision of the DDE is to alter its traditional requirement that one not intend *harm* to also include the requirement that one not intend the *involvement* of a person that will foreseeably cause that person harm (without his consent). This revision is Quinn's attempt to deal with the objection to the DDE that it does not rule out many objectionable acts (or omissions), if we can truly describe our intentions very narrowly. For example, suppose we intend to chop up someone for an experiment, but if he managed to recombine and survive unharmed after the experiment, we do not intend otherwise. (Of course, we foresee that this outcome will not happen.) Should the DDE not be a ground for ruling out this act just because we do not intend harm? In these cases of narrow intention, Quinn claims that it is still true that we intend involvement of the person and we foresee the harm. Given this revision, Quinn locates the DDE's foundation in a thesis related to that of the special authority someone has over himself raised in connection with the DDA, namely, that what is one's own should not be used without one's permission, when this will lead to one's being harmed, and so someone else should not intend the employment of what is one's own without one's permission, when this will lead to one's being harmed.

Authority over oneself can fail to be taken seriously in two ways in Quinn's view. First, as we have seen in section 1, by causing harm (or, on his view of positive agency, by omitting to stop while intending the event that causes harm) without intending involvement of a person or harm. Here, we act despite the harmful involvement of others and so we may not treat people as ends-in-themselves because we do not constrain our actions in the light of their interests and goals. Second, we can fail to take the special authority seriously by using a person as a mere means to our ends (or aiming against his good as an end in itself). We do this if we cause his involvement intending it or, instead, omit to aid, intending either his involvement that leads to harm or harm itself. This proposal dovetails with the view (presented in chapter 1) that when one intends (and not merely foresees) an involvement of the person one takes his being involved as a factor in favor of a state of affairs. It is a factor in favor of a state of affairs because his being involved lets us use him for our ends.

The revision of the DDE and the foundation for it that Quinn suggests should not satisfy traditional supporters of the DDE (or modern ones like Thomas Nagel),[7] who emphasize the impermissibility of intending or pursuing *evil itself* (such as harm). For on Quinn's view, it is no worse to intend harm than to intend a minor intrusion on a person that one foresees will lead to harm. If one wishes to argue that intending harm is still worse, one will have to take a different route in order to deal with the "narrow intention" objection to the DDE. Indeed, I surmise that one would have to try again to explain why sometimes the line between an intended event and its foreseen harm is too close for the two to be sensibly pulled apart for moral purposes.[8] Therefore, while I find the alternative doctrine that Quinn suggests to be sensible, it is really very different from the traditional DDE.

In section I, I raised an objection to Quinn's view that we can distinguish between permissible and impermissible omissions on the basis of whether an agent intends an event that she foresees will harm someone. Can a similar sort of objection be raised against his view that the intention of the agent to involve someone in a harmful way can distinguish between permissible and impermissible behavior? There are several points to be considered in this connection. The first is whether Quinn characterizes intending involvement in a way that divides the permissible from the impermissible cases. Consider the contrast Quinn draws between what he calls the Guinea Pig Case and the Scarce Resources Case. In the Guinea Pig Case, a doctor leaves a patient to die in order to learn about the course of the patient's disease as it kills him. In this way, she will have more knowledge with which to help five other patients with the same disease. In the Scarce Resources Case, a doctor leaves a patient to die because she uses the limited resources she has to save five other people. Only what the doctor does in the first case is wrong, and in that case, according to Quinn, what matters is that the effect of the omission to aid serves the doctor's ends precisely because it involves the patient in a way foreseen to be bad for him.

But now consider Scarce Resources Variant I: The doctor knows that if she gives the scarce resources to the five, they will soon develop another disease as a result of the treatment. They will then need organ transplants to survive. She knows that these organs would only be available because they can be taken from the one patient who dies as a result of not getting the resources. In this case, it would make no sense for the doctor to help the five rather than the one unless the one patient did die, so here too the effect of omitting to aid the one patient serves the doctor's end of saving the five precisely because it involves the patient in a way foreseen to be bad for him. Yet in this case, I believe, the doctor *does not intend* the single patient's death, even though she only saves the five because that death will occur. Hence Quinn's objection to *intending* the involvement of the patient in the Guinea Pig Case is not captured by the claim that the effect of the omission serves the doctor's end precisely because it involves the patient in a way foreseen to be bad for him. (Furthermore, it is permissible for the doctor to give the scarce resources to the five patients in Scarce Resources Variant I.)

Scarce Resources Variant I shows that there is a difference between (i) acting or omitting so as to deliberately involve someone to further our purposes and (ii) acting or omitting only because someone's involvement and harm will occur and further our purposes. Quinn says that the DDE "distinguishes between agency in which harm comes to some victims, at least in part, from the agent's deliberately involving them in something in order to further his purpose precisely by way of their being so involved."[9] The Scarce Resources Variant I shows that this statement has two separate components. That is, a distinction should be drawn between an agent doing something "in order to further his purposes precisely by way of" someone's being negatively involved and an agent's "deliberately involving" such a person. This is because in Scarce Resources Variant I, arguably, one does not deliberately involve the single patient, as his dying is a mere side effect of helping the five, but one does something (help the five) only because one will further one's purposes precisely by way of the single patient being negatively involved. Being "incidentally (versus deliberately) affected" as a result of pursuing a particular purpose and being "usefully affected" for that purpose are, it seems, not necessarily contrasting notions.

Now that we have considered complications in how Quinn characterizes intending someone's involvement, the second point is to note that Quinn himself in his discussion of the DDE rejects the view that the agent's bad intention in acting always determines that the act (here including omission) is impermissible. For he says that when the person affected had no positive or negative right pertaining to the act to begin with, an agent's having a bad intention in acting does not make his act impermissible.[10] For example, suppose that a certain form of life-saving aid is su-pererogatory, but the only reason the agent refuses to give it is that he intends that someone die. This alone does not make it impermissible for him not to aid, ac-cording to Quinn. Further, Quinn says that in his Scarce Resources Case, a single patient's right to be aided by a doctor does not stand if the doctor would aid five instead. This means that Quinn should agree that if a bad doctor decides to aid the five only because she intends the death of the one patient as an end, her not-aiding the one is still permissible. The DDE, as traditionally understood, is a prin-ciple that aims to derive the impermissibility of an act from the intention of the agent. Hence, his rejection of this component of the DDE, at least when other factors are present that could justify the act or omission whether or not they are concerns of the agent, is also a significant revision of the DDE, though not one that Quinn emphasized.

Given this revision, it should also be permissible to aid the five in the following case. A bad doctor decides to aid the five with the scarce resources only in order that the one die. He does this because he knows that the resources work very slowly and before they save the patients, he will have learned enough from the death of the one whom he does not treat to develop a new, fast cure for the five and win a prize. Here the doctor only aids these five with available resources because he intends to use the one patient's death to get a new cure and win a prize. Quinn should, I think, agree that any right of the one to be treated still yields to the rights of the five, and therefore the doctor's intentions are irrelevant both as to whether he actually fulfills the rights of the five (which he does despite not caring to) and as to whether there is a right in the one to receive the resources (which there is not). The fact that not aiding the single patient plays a causal role in developing a treatment that actually saves the five before the scarce resources do so also does not affect permissibility of the doctor's behavior.

It is still true that the doctor acts badly in acting permissibly for the wrong reason he has, even if he fulfills his duty to the five in acting for the wrong rea-son.[11] But, I would emphasize, it is not true that someone acts badly whenever his intention in acting does not focus on a property of the act that helps to make the act permissible. For example, the fact that he would go and raise money for Oxfam is not a factor that justifies a doctor in omitting to fulfill his duty to help a patient. But suppose a doctor has worked a hard day and is about to permissibly go off duty after treating one more patient. Then five patients come in to be treated. Given how much time it will take, it would be supererogatory of him to treat them. If he does, however, he would not be able to go to help the single patient. The only reason he decides to save the five is that a big contribution will be made to Oxfam if he does so. In this case, the doctor acts to produce an effect (money to Oxfam) that would not alone make it permissible to leave the one patient, but I do not think he acts badly (even toward the one patient). This is because helping Oxfam is a worthy aim and he also acts permissibly (in helping five people rather than one person), even though it is not his helping Oxfam that makes the act permissible.

Given what Quinn says about bad intentions not necessarily making an act impermissible, we can conclude that his view that intending harm or the involvement of persons leading to harm can affect permissibility applies only to cases where the act that harms or the omission that leads to harm infringes a right in a way that cannot already be justified for some other reason. In such cases, his claim could be that it is harder to justify the harmful involvement of a person when it is deliberately brought about in order to serve our purposes than when it is a side effect of our pursuing our purposes. By contrast, as we saw in discussing his second form of positive agency, which involves intending an event that harms but not necessarily intending the harmful involvement, he is not as careful in limiting his claim. That is (as variants on Rescue Cases showed), he overlooks the fact that omitting to stop an event whose harmfulness one foresees because one intends the event's occurrence does not affect the permissibility of an omission when omitting to stop the event is already justified by other factors. (So, suppose that someone intends that the car he did not start continue on the road solely because he will win a prize if it does. This does not make his not braking impermissible if his desire for the prize leads him to go back to minister to the five who would otherwise die, just because going back will make him unable to brake the car.)

Hence, it seems that Quinn thinks that when all else is the same, sometimes the fact that one intends a harmful involvement will, by itself, make an act impermissible. Suppose that someone rejects Quinn's view. She could still hold that an act that is already impermissible for reasons other than an agent's intention is a more serious wrong because of the agent's intention. For example, suppose that one doctor does not give a patient ordinary treatment simply in order that the patient, who is his enemy, die. Another doctor does not give a patient ordinary treatment because the doctor is lazy and does not care about the patient. Both doctors act wrongly in failing to give that to which the patient has a right in the circumstances. It can be argued that the first wrong act is a more serious wrong than the other.[12] Therefore, an account of why the intention that there be harmful involvement makes a moral difference will be relevant even to those who reject the view that it plays a role in determining permissibility. We will consider some such accounts in the next section.

III

Suppose that we combine Quinn's revisions of the DDA and the DDE but we do not limit his addition of a second form of positive agency to intending the movement (rather than the status quo position) of objects. Is it then true that all cases that violate the DDE by involving direct agency will also involve what Quinn considers to be cases of positive agency, because they also involve intending events (whether movements or not) that lead to the intended involvement of people in harmful ways? This will be true only if an agent, insofar as he is rational, must intend the means to his end of involving people. But even if this latter claim is not true,[13] we can argue that insofar as an agent does intend the events that bring about the harmful involvement of persons, all cases running afoul of the DDE will also run afoul of Quinn's version of the DDA (which includes some omissions as

	I(ntend)	F(oresee)
D(o)	DI	DF
A(llow)	AI	AF

Figure 3.1.

positive agency). By contrast, on standard views, the DDA and the DDE cut across each other, as in figure 3.1. (Quinn's view implies that AI involves DI.) Quinn did not seem to realize that his view has this implication, because he says that "the DDE therefore cuts across the distinction between harming and allowing harm."[14] But this latter claim is true only if we reject Quinn's second form of positive agency.

Furthermore, if all cases that run afoul of the DDE also run afoul of the DDA, Quinn's analysis might yield the following result: Omitting to stop some threat because we intend the involvement of someone, though we foresee that this leads to his harm, is worse than doing what causes this merely foreseen harm. This is because the former but not the latter already involves *both* kinds of disfavored agency, that is, (the second form of) positive agency and direct agency (and a summing of wrongs can make things worse). In this sense, violating the DDE would be a more serious wrong than violating the DDA. Of course, if we reject Quinn's account of the second form of positive agency (involving omissions) or its application to cases beyond those involving movement of an object, this general result will not follow.

I suggested in chapter 1 that there might be a different form of unity between the DDA and the DDE, and Quinn's account also seems consistent with this: If intending the involvement of someone when we foresee harm to him is wrong because it is inconsistent with respect for his special authority over himself, and the foundation of the DDA also lies in its relation to such authority over the self, then both the DDA and the DDE would have the same foundation.[15] Call this the Unified Theory. To be more precise, when someone harms, even without intending harm or involvement, he still interferes with claims to noninterference derived from the authority over the self, and this is a prime facie ground of disrespect for such authority.[16] Someone who does not aid, while intending harm or involvement leading to harm, shows a lack of respect for authority over the self by taking it as a factor in favor of a state of affairs that it involves interference with, or other harmful involvement of, someone without his consent. This is by contrast with taking someone's being interfered with as a factor against a state of affairs that may, nevertheless, be overridden by other considerations.[17] When someone does not aid but does not intend harm or involvement, he does not show a lack of respect for authority over the self by taking it as a factor in favor of a state of affairs that it involves interference with someone. (This does not exclude that what he does

Intend (Involvement/Harm)	Foresee
Harm — Disrespect/Disrespect	Disrespect/No Disrespect
Not-Aid — No Disrespect/Disrespect	No Disrespect/No Disrespect

Figure 3.2.

might be wrong for some other reason.)[18] When someone harms and also intends harm or involvement leading to harm, he is *doubly* guilty of disrespect for authority over the self. Hence, this form of harming could be worse than harming with no such intentions (if a summing of wrongs is correct) *without* this implying that the foundation of the DDE (i.e., the wrong of intending involvement or harm) is different from the foundation of the DDA (i.e., the wrong of harming).[19] In order for not-aiding to show disrespect for authority over the self, someone who is not aiding must also violate some version of the DDE. In the case of harming, this additional condition is not necessary for someone to show (a different form of) a lack of respect for authority over the self. Figure 3.2 summarizes these claims.

Suppose we reject Quinn's view that his first and second types of positive agency are morally equivalent; that is, we reject the view that omitting to stop an event because one intends it's occurrence despite the fact that it causes involvement leading to harm is morally the same as causing such an event. Then we need not hold that showing disrespect for authority over the self is involved in that form of not-aiding as it is in harming. But why should we treat not-aiding when one does have a disrespectful intention (e.g., one intends that harm occur) differently from harming that does not have a disrespectful intention (e.g., one merely foresees the harm), even though each involves a form of disrespect for authority over the self? Because typically (though not necessarily), when I intend the loss of what someone is entitled to (at least relative to me), I intend the loss of what he now has quite independently of me and independently of whatever (or whomever) will cause the loss. Nevertheless, when I do not aid him to prevent the loss, he still does not lose anything he would have had quite independently of me. Rather, he loses out on only what he would have had with my aid. That is, even though an event causes the loss of what he now has independently of me and independently of whoever causes his loss, my not stopping that event leads to his losing out on only what he would have had through his dependence on me. By contrast, when I do what harms him, he typically loses out on what he would have had independently of me. Hence, in the not-aiding case, my involvement with the actual attack on his authority over himself (or other forms of personal entitlement) is at one remove; in the harming case, it is immediate. (I use "immediate" and "at one remove" here rather than "direct" and "indirect" only so as not to confuse them with Quinn's direct and indirect agency, which refer to a different contrast.) Furthermore, in the not-aiding case the one remove involves deciding whether there will be involvement of, or interference with, that over which the agent who would aid has special authority (i.e., his resources or efforts).

Hence, despite a unified foundation for the DDA and the DDE, we can treat different failures differently. Quinn's account of the difference between (a) intending involvement leading to harm or harm itself and (b) doing an act despite the involvement and harm it causes also emphasizes a difference, despite (what I claim is) foundational unity stemming from special authority over oneself. According to Quinn, only (a) treats people as available for our purposes, in particular, available to be used for our profit.[20] In (b), we pursue goals by, intrinsically legitimate means but refuse to be constrained by their effects on others' purposes and interests. Only the former, he claims, treats people as mere means (which includes not treating them as ends-in-themselves). Quinn thinks the former is more insulting treatment than the latter, holding effects on welfare constant.

I would add that intending the harmful involvement of others to further our ends signals that one needs the presence of the person for one's purposes. Because one is dependent on the availability of the person, his rightful independence from oneself is not permitted. (In the case in which the person is a threat to us and it becomes our goal to use him to eliminate his threat—what Quinn calls "eliminative" agency—one would also have no objection to the independence of the person. This is because his independence would eliminate his being a threat and hence the need to use him, at the same time as it eliminates our being able to use him. This analysis can help account for Quinn's sense that eliminative agency is not as bad as using to profit, which he calls "opportunistic" agency.)

By contrast, acting despite the effects on the person signals that the existence of the person is a potential hindrance by which one refuses to be limited when one has otherwise legitimate ways of achieving one's goals. But the person's independence from oneself is quite permissible, if only it would happen. This accounts for the special insult involved in intending harmful opportunistic involvement within a Unified Theory based on respect for special authority over oneself. Hence, the Unified Theory can account for the more insulting nature of the mere-means form of disrespect even as it also distinguishes what is done when people immediately (i.e., through causing), rather than at one remove (i.e., through not-aiding), are involved with a loss to others. It not only doubles the sources of disrespect for authority over the self when intending harmful involvement and harming are combined, it helps to mark the difference in the two things that are combined.

Among the issues raised in this chapter are (1) when a certain effect one will cause gives one a reason to act, it is not necessarily true that one intends to bring about that effect; (2) an agent's intention (and, more generally, his reasons for action) may not affect the permissibility of his act; and (3) correct moral principles concerning harm might have a modal form. These are issues with which we shall continue to deal in chapters 4 and 5.

NOTES

This chapter is a revised and expanded version of part of my review of Warren Quinn's *Morality and Action* (New York: Cambridge University Press, 1993), in *Journal of Philosophy* 93, no. 11 (1996): 578–84.

    1. What I have in mind is that, if I kill him, his body would fall on a lever redirecting the trolley away from the five. Quinn responds to this objection in *Morality and Action*, p. 197, and I respond to Quinn in turn in my *Morality, Mortality*, vol. 2 (New York: Oxford University Press, 1996), p. 85.

    2. As I argued in chapter 1.

    3. *Morality and Action* p. 170.

    4. Ibid p. 170.

    5. This is a question that Shelly Kagan also asks in his *The Limits of Morality* (New York: Oxford University Press, 1989).

    6. Prerogatives are described in chapter 1.

    7. Thomas Nagel, *The View from Nowhere* (New York: Oxford University Press, 1986).

    8. Discussion in chapter 5 may bear on this issue.

    9. *Morality and Action*, p. 184.

    10. Ibid, p. 188.

    11. This is the way Judith Thomson puts it in discussing a similar case in her "Physician-Assisted Suicide: Two Moral Arguments," *Ethics* 109 (April 1999): 497–518.

    12. I discuss this issue in more detail in my "Terrorism and Several Moral Distinctions," *Legal Theory*, 12 (2006), 19–69.

    13. In chapter 4, I will argue that this claim is, in fact, not true.

    14. *Morality and Action*, p. 187.

    15. I first suggested this in *Morality, Mortality*, vol. 2.

    16. Some cases of harming may not involve such prima-facie disrespect even in the absence of consent. For more on this possibility, see the discussion of forms of harming permitted by constraints in chapters 4 and 5.

    17. In chapter 4, we shall consider in more detail cases in which it is not prima facie disrespectful to take it as a factor in favor of a state of affairs that it involves interference with someone. Hence, we shall see that this characterization of what is disrespectful about intending unconsented-to harm or involvement is too broad. From the perspective of the DDE, this is because not all cases where we take interference with another as a reason to bring about a state of affairs or as a reason to omit stopping another's interference involve intending such interferences. In this chapter, the Scarce Resources Variant I was given as an example of this. There may be other ways of characterizing such cases as well that do not rely on the intending/not-intending distinction. This is discussed in chapter 5.

    18. This assumes that not-aiding because one intends the movement or location of an object that we foresee will harm does not, per se, offend against someone's authority over himself.

    19. In *Morality, Mortality*, vol. 2, I concluded the *reverse* from the fact that harming while intending harm is worse than harming while foreseeing harm. That conclusion now seems to me poorly argued.

    20. But it does not always do so, he says. For example, suppose we intend harm to someone as a way of stopping his doing us harm. Then we do not profit from his availability—as in what Quinn calls "direct opportunistic agency"—because he causes the problem that we must use him to stop. Hence, harming him is "direct eliminative agency," Quinn says.

4

THE DOCTRINES OF DOUBLE AND TRIPLE EFFECT AND WHY A RATIONAL AGENT NEED NOT INTEND THE MEANS TO HIS END

I. INTRODUCTION

In previous chapters, we have mentioned that one tempting way to distinguish between intending and merely foreseeing harm (or involvement leading to it) is that in the former but not the latter the fact that harm will occur gives us a reason to do the act that causes the harm (or to omit to do what would stop the harm). However, we also noted that it is sometimes true that when we do *not* intend harm, its occurring still gives us reason to do the act that causes it, and not just because it is a sign of other things that are causally useful. In this chapter, I will investigate this issue in detail and argue that when an act we have some reason to do causes harm as a side effect, that side effect can contribute to giving us a sufficient reason to do the act that causes the harm because of the causal role of the harm, and yet we need not intend the harm. Sometimes in these cases it is permissible to act even if it would not be permissible to do an act while intending the harm. This point, I believe, will help us better to understand some of the variations of the Trolley Problem.

Investigating the distinction between doing something *intending* to bring something else about and doing something *because* we will bring something else about also enables us to derive two very general results. First, common conceptions of intention (accepted by such philosophers as Jonathan Bennett and Judith Thomson) are problematic. Second, contrary to what is usually thought about instrumental rationality, a rational agent, insofar as he is rational, *need not* intend a means that he knows is necessary to an end that he continues to intend. In discussing the latter point, I shall examine the work of Christine Korsgaard on instrumental rationality.[1] In investigating these issues, I will temporarily put to one side the other points made in chapter 3 that suggest that we need not consider an agent's intentions (or any other state of mind) in deciding on the permissibility of his act.

In her 1985 article "The Trolley Problem,"[2] Judith Jarvis Thomson introduced a variation on the so-called Trolley Case. As pointed out in chapter 1, it is known as the Loop Case. To review some of what we know already, the standard Trolley Case involves, let us say, five people on a track toward which an out-of-control trolley is heading. If it continues, it will kill them. However, if we redirect it away from them, it will go down another track where it will kill someone who is unable to be removed. Even many nonconsequentialists intuitively think that we may redirect the trolley in this case, thereby saving five and foreseeably killing one. Another way to stop the trolley from hitting the five is to push an innocent bystander in front of it.[3] Its hitting him stops it, but we foresee that he will die as a consequence (Bystander Case). Nonconsequentialists intuitively think that this is impermissible. One account of why it is permissible to act in the way described in the Trolley Case but not in the way described in the Bystander Case is that, in the former, we merely foresee the hitting and death of the one person but do not causally require or intend either consequence in order to save the five. By contrast, in the Bystander Case, the hitting is causally required, and we intend it in order to save the five, even if we only foresee that being hit will certainly lead to the bystander's death.

In Thomson's Loop Case, everything is as it is in the Trolley Case, except that the track to which we can redirect the trolley away from the five loops back toward them. Were it not for the presence of the one person on the side track whose being hit stops the trolley, it would go around to kill the five shortly. Hence, in this case, the hitting of the one (which will cause his death) is causally required to stop the trolley and save the five, as it is in the Bystander Case. Yet Thomson claims that it strikes many nonconsequentialists that it is permissible to redirect the trolley in the Loop Case.[4]

The problem is to explain why it is permissible to redirect the trolley in the Loop Case, but pushing the one person in the way of the trolley in the Bystander Case is not permissible. Providing such an explanation is one focus of this chapter. I shall be especially concerned to examine the Loop Case in the light of the Doctrine of Double Effect (DDE). My main point here will be to distinguish between doing something *in order* (or *intending*) *to* bring about something else and doing something *because of* something else that will thus be brought about. I hope to show that in the Loop Case, we do not intend to hit the one. Hence, while Thomson may be right that the person in the Loop Case is a mere means, we do not *intend* his being a mere means. By contrast, in the Bystander Case, we do intend this. This difference (or a related difference that does not depend on considering the intentions or other attitudes of agents) may be morally significant.[5] The distinction between "in order to" and "because of" forms the basis for my introducing the Doctrine of Triple Effect (DTE), which sometimes permits an agent to do something, when he does it because he will bring about an evil or involvement leading to evil (that he does not intend). It also permits an agent to do something that has a bad side effect when he does it because he will bring about a great good though he does not intend the good.

II. EVIL AS A CAUSE OF GOOD

A traditional formulation of the DDE says that we must not intend evil as an end or as a means to a greater good.[6] However, we are sometimes permitted to use neutral or good means to achieve a good, even if the same evil is foreseen as a certain-to-occur consequence, so long as the intended good is greater than (or proportional to) the evil and there is no better way to achieve the good.

Let us consider cases in which death is an evil. Neither the Bystander nor the Loop cases, as I have described them, involve intending the death of the person; at most, they involve intending his being hit. Is this an evil in itself, independent of its consequences? Perhaps not. But a revision to the DDE (call it DDE[R])[7] is more plausible than it, I think. It says that we must not intend evil, and we also must not intend the involvement of a person without his consent when foreseeably this will lead to an evil to him. (Call evil and/or such involvement evil*.) This would rule out the permissibility of action in the Bystander Case because the innocent bystander's involvement, and hence evil*, is intended. One question is whether it also would rule out the permissibility of action in the Loop Case. I shall mostly be concerned with the DDE(R) rather than the DDE, henceforth, while addressing this question.

Note that "something being intended as a means" is not the same as "something playing a causal role." The DDE and DDE(R) do not rule out that the good which is to justify bringing an evil* into existence is, in fact, caused by evil*. A version of the Trolley Case helps to make this clear. In the Track Trolley Case,[8] the trolley is headed toward killing five people and it can be redirected in a direction where one person will be hit, though his being hit is not necessary to stop the trolley. However, the mechanism that redirects works as follows: We now push a button that will redirect the trolley (when it later gets to a crosspoint) toward where one person presently sits. This very same button also controls the track on which the one person sits and pressing it has the effect of moving that track down so that the one person is pushed into the path of the trolley as it heads toward the five *before* the trolley reaches the crosspoint. The weight of the one person is in fact what stops the trolley. However, we know that if he were not there to stop it, the trolley would be redirected once it gets to the crosspoint, and it is in order to achieve this that we press the button. In this case, if we redirect the trolley, we do so without running afoul of the DDE or the DDE(R). For although we foresee that on account of what we do, the person's being hit will be the cause of the trolley's not hitting the five, we need not intend either this or his death that follows in order to stop the trolley. This is because there is another way to stop the trolley that we act to bring about; that is, stopping the trolley in another way is causable by our act.

It is possible that Thomson could have intended for her Loop Case to be like the Track Trolley Case in one important way: In the Track Trolley Case, I would redirect the trolley even if the person were not moved into the path of the trolley. Possibly, we should redirect the trolley in the Loop Case even if we knew (contrary to fact) that the one would not get hit. This is because the five would be no worse off being killed by the looped than by the nonlooped trolley. If so, we need not be redirecting the trolley because we believe that the one will be hit. However, the permissibility of redirecting the trolley in the Loop Case does not depend on this possibility, I believe. To make this clear, let us assume that it would make no sense to redirect the trolley if I did not think that it had at least a chance of hitting the one, since redirecting requires much effort. Hence, I redirect the trolley that causes the one to be hit *because* I believe that there is some chance (to the point of certainty) that I will cause the one to be hit. I would not redirect the trolley *unless* I believed this. This is not true in the Track Trolley Case. (Of course, it is assumed that hitting the one in the Loop Case actually stops the trolley. I certainly should not redirect the trolley if I know that it will hit and kill the one and the trolley will not be stopped by this, for then six would die instead of five.)

Does all this mean that I intend to hit the person in the Loop Case (as I have now redescribed it) and thus redirecting in this case violates the DDE(R)? I suggest that no is the answer to both questions. To support these claims, it will help to first make clear how I (intuitively) see the structure of the Loop Case. The only threat that faces the five that prompts my act to help them is the trolley heading toward them from one direction. This is the first problem. If this threat is not taken care of, they will die in the near future; to save them for a long enough life, it must be taken care of, though this does not mean that taking care of it is sufficient to save them. The problem that would exist (if the one on the side track were not there to stop it) of the trolley coming at the five from a different direction—perhaps even faster than from its initial direction—*only arises* because I redirect the trolley away from the five. One way to see this new problem is as a *second threat* facing the five because I have taken care of the only threat that faced them to begin with.

It may be thought that this cannot be true, since it is the same trolley and in that sense the same, rather than a second, threat that faces them when it loops toward them. But it might be argued that the fact that the device that threatens them (namely, the trolley) is the same is irrelevant. The case in which the same trolley comes at them in a new way has the same structure as a case in which a *different* device comes to threaten the five as a result of my removing the initial trolley threat. Consider the Wagon Case: The trolley is headed toward killing the five. We divert it and, as it goes on the side track, it stops. But we know that it will stop on a button whose depression will cause a wagon on the side track to be set in motion. The wagon will head around the loop toward killing the five, but it will be stopped by hitting one person on the side track. The wagon is a new threat in the obvious sense that it is a new threatening device that was threatening no one previously. Nevertheless, the case is (intuitively) the same, for moral purposes, as the Loop Case. It does not matter for moral evaluation whether a new threatening entity is created or the trolley hits from a different direction.[9]

Still, it may seem odd to say that when I divert the trolley in the original Loop Case, so that it threatens the one person and potentially the five, that I have created a new threat. After all, we say that I have *diverted the threat* in diverting the trolley, and this implies that it is the same threat. Instead of worrying about this point, I will just say that in diverting the trolley in the Loop Case, I have created a *new problem* (that is, the trolley directed toward the one and potentially looping toward the five if the one does not stop it). The cases should be morally the same, whether I create the new problem by setting the wagon in motion in the Wagon Case or by diverting the trolley toward one person and potentially toward the five from a new direction in the Loop Case.

III. THE COUNTERFACTUAL TEST

I claim that doing something *because this will cause* the hitting of an innocent bystander does not imply that one *intends to cause* the hitting or that one does anything in order to hit.[10] This is because there is a general conceptual distinction between doing something because it will have an effect and doing it in order to produce an effect. As a case where it should be clear that there is a conceptual difference between acting because I will thereby cause an effect and acting intending to cause the effect, consider the Party Case.[11] I intend to give a party in order for me and my friends to have fun. However, I foresee that this will leave a big mess, and I do not want to have a party if I will be left to clean it up. I also foresee a further effect of the party: If my friends have fun, they will feel indebted to me and help me clean up. I assume that a feeling of indebtedness is something of a negative for a person to have. I give the party because I believe that my friends will feel indebted and (so) because I will not have a mess to clean up. These expectations are conditions of my action. I would not act unless I had them. The fact that they will feel indebted is a reason for my acting. But I do not give the party even in part in order to make my friends feel indebted nor in order to not have a mess. To be more precise, it is not a goal of my action of giving the party to do either of these things. I may have it as a background goal in my life not to have messes, but not producing a mess is not an aim of my giving the party. Further, if I see that my friends are feeling indebted, as a good host I may try to rescue them from these feelings (while expecting that I may not succeed). I might do this because I do not want to omit to help them only because I *intend* something negative for them, their feeling indebted. This would not be inconsistent with giving the party *because of* my belief that they will, as a side effect, feel indebted.

The Party Case shows that there is a conceptual difference between acting because I believe I will have a certain effect and acting in order to bring about (intending) the effect, even though in both cases that the effect will occur is a reason for my acting. Hence, the idea (common since Elizabeth Anscombe's *Intention*)[12] that if we find a reason why someone acted, we find what he intended is wrong. Jonathan Bennett says that "one's intentions in acting are defined by which of one's beliefs about consequences explains one's acting in that way."[13] But I have argued that in the Party Case my belief that my acting will cause feelings of indebtedness in my friends helps explain my acting, and yet I do not intend this consequence. Hence, a common way of defining what one intends seems to be incorrect.[14]

Further, the Party Case shows that a common test for the presence of an intention, known as the Counterfactual Test, is inadequate. This test asks us to consider an effect, such as the hitting of the bystander, and imagine that (contrary to the laws of nature) it would not occur if we performed the act that we wish to perform, but everything else would remain the same. Would we still continue to perform the act? If we decline to perform the act because the act would not bring about the effect, it is said that this shows that we intended to produce the effect.[15] But if, as I claim, one can do an act (e.g., give the party) because one believes that it has a certain effect (e.g., feelings of indebtedness), and not do it because one believes that it does not have that effect—that is, one's act is conditional on the belief that one will produce the effect—and yet not intend that effect, then the Counterfactual Test for the presence of intention is inadequate. This test fails to distinguish effects the belief in which is a condition of action from effects that are intended. Hence, this test cannot be used to show that we intend to hit the bystander in the Loop Case just because we act on condition of our hitting him.[16, 17]

This conclusion holds even though the Party Case as I have imagined it is not intended to be exactly analogous to the Loop Case. In the Party Case, I would refuse to do something that would be an overall good (have the party) unless something bad did not happen to me (a mess). Here the negative to others (feeling indebted and cleaning-up efforts) is not needed to keep the party itself going on. Also, those who suffer feelings of indebtedness and have to clean up are overall still better off because the party more than compensates them. But in the Loop Case, the hitting of the one person is needed to help the five go on living, and the one who is hit does not directly benefit from the five others being alive. (Hence, Party Case II is a better, if not perfect, analog to the Loop Case: I will not have a party unless this produces feelings of indebtedness leading to cleaning-up efforts by some of my guests because the party itself will not continue on long enough to be a success unless a mess is not allowed to accumulate during it.)

To further consider the plausibility of the claim that one need not intend an effect that one produces and on condition of which one acts, we should now consider other tests for intention that may be better than the Counterfactual Test.

IV. BRATMAN'S TEST FOR INTENTION

Michael Bratman's test for intention has three components,[18] and we will use them to test redirecting the trolley away from the five in the Loop Case.

1. *If we intend to bring about x, we seek means to accomplish the end of bringing it about.* But, in the Loop Case, we do not survey the field for any way to hit the one. Rather, we notice that what we must do to accomplish one of our aims, that is, stopping the trolley from hitting the five from the first direction (that is, from the

front), will also, *without our doing anything extra*, cause the one to be hit. (This does not mean that we notice that something we *will do anyway* has this effect, since we may not do what will accomplish one of our aims unless it has this other effect.)

2. *If we intend to bring x about, we pursue x. That is, if one way fails to produce x, we adopt another way.* But if we act because we notice that our doing only what needs to be done in order to stop the trolley from hitting the five from the front will thereby also cause the one to be hit, we need not, as rational agents, be committed to hitting the one by other means if the hitting fails to come about. For example, suppose the redirected trolley would jump over the one person on the track. We need not be committed to giving the trolley an extra push that is unnecessary to get it away from hitting the five from the front but necessary to get it to hit the one person, when hitting the person is what is causally necessary to prevent the jump over him (Extra Push Case). We also need not be committed to *making it* true that redirecting the trolley without any extra push causes the hitting.

Why would someone who redirects the trolley not be committed to doing these things? Here is a possible explanation: In redirecting the trolley, the agent merely foresees that an act he must undertake to stop the threat from coming from the front will cause a hitting that stops the threat from returning around the back. If he gives the extra push in the Extra Push Case as described, he will do something that is undertaken especially to accomplish the hitting that is not necessary for stopping the threat from coming from the front. Doing something extra in this case would certainly involve intending the hitting. If he thinks that it is wrong to intend the hitting, he should not do something extra in order to make it happen. If he is unwilling to do something extra because it involves intending, but not unwilling to redirect the trolley on condition that it will hit, this suggests that in doing the latter he is not already intending the hit.

Notice, however, that there is another type of extra push that would be permissible for him.[19] Suppose that an extra push is unnecessary to get the trolley away from its first hit. However, an extra push would cause vibrations that stop the trolley from jumping over the person on the track and heading around the loop to the five. As a side effect of not jumping over the one person, the trolley hits him, however, in this case, the one person's being hit is not causally necessary to stopping the looping at all. The vibrations alone do that. The extra push in this case essentially redirects the trolley a second time away from its route toward the five around the loop, and that leads it to hit the one person as a side effect.

In other cases as well, undertaking an extra act to save the five would not indicate an intention to hit the one, even if hitting the one is a means (i.e., what we must do) to save the five.[20] Consider the Two Loop Case. Suppose that after being redirected from its initial hit, the trolley will go around a looping track toward the five, unless it is redirected again—by an extra push not needed to get it away from its initial hit. If it is redirected again, it will go onto a track that loops to the five too but on which a person sits. The person will be hit and this will stop the trolley. Nothing I have said about the extra push in the Extra Push Case implies that some-one opposed to intending the hit may not give the extra push in the Two Loop

Case. For in the latter case, the extra push is just like the first redirection in the regular Loop Case: We redirect the trolley again to save the five from the second way in which it would hit them, but we do this only because the one will be hit and stop any further looping.

Let us return to the original Extra Push Case and consider an objection to the use I have made of it. Is there another possible reason that someone may not do the extra act to hit the one in the Extra Push Case, consistent with his intending the hit when he redirects the trolley initially? Suppose that doing something extra in this case is wrong independently of its being the expression of an intention to hit someone. That is, suppose that the only act it is permissible to do, for reasons having nothing to do with intending a hit, is the act necessary to redirect the trolley away from its first hit at the five. Then it remains possible that even if an agent, insofar as he is rational, had to intend the hit when doing this permissible act, he would not do anything extra to accomplish the hit if the permissible act failed. But are all extra acts he could do that would cause a hit impermissible per se? In fact, for reasons that will be presented more fully in chapter 5, I think that such acts are impermissible. However, what makes them impermissible is, I believe, that they are mere means to the hit. An act being a mere means to the hit can be distinguished from any state of mind, such as an intention to hit, that brings it about. But acts that are mere means to some end are commonly intended for that end, whether or not it is the intention that makes the act impermissible. (Recall that I said I would not in this chapter attack the view that intention can be relevant to permissibility.) But then, if turning the trolley away initially is permissible, this must be, in part, because it is not a mere means to causing the hit, and acts that are not mere means to causing the hit are acts that, prima facie, one need not do because one intends the hit. This is a further reason for believing that turning the trolley away from its initial hit need not involve intending the hit of the one.

3. *If we intend x, and our intentions should be consistent insofar as we are rational, then we will filter out intentions that conflict with intending x.* But, I believe, it is consistent for someone who redirects the trolley because he believes that it will hit the one to then try to rescue the one from being hit.[21] If intending the rescue is inconsistent with intending the hit, this would show that the agent, insofar as he is rational, did not intend the hit. Call this the Rescue Test.[22] (It is purely hypothetical: We ask ourselves whether we, as rational agents, could will rescuing consistent with other things we will. No actual rescue need be possible.) The person who redirects the trolley in the Rescue Variant of the Loop Case may think:

> I will redirect the trolley and then try to push the one out of the way. For if I have an opportunity to save him and do not do so merely because he would then be hit, I would intend his being hit. This I must not do whether by action or omission. If I fail in my rescue efforts, I get the advantage of the five's being saved because the one will be hit. If I succeed in the rescue, the five are no worse off and they had some chance of being saved (for I might have been unsuccessful in the rescue). I still only bother to do something else necessary to save the five (i.e., redirect the trolley) because the one can be hit.

(The occurrence of this internal monologue is not necessary if the person is not to intend the hit. It is only meant to make plain what dispositions to act he has that are inconsistent with intending the hit.)[23]

Suppose that the rescue is consistent with what prompts one to do only what is necessary to redirect the trolley from its initial hit in the Loop Case. Michael Bratman has suggested that one could *aim* to hit the person while still *aiming* to rescue him, as it is possible for a rational agent to have two inconsistent aims even if not two inconsistent intentions.[24] However, I also wish to deny that the agent aims to hit the one. So this is a problem for the definitiveness of the Rescue Test. Note also that it would be consistent with retaining the clear intention to hit the one in the Extra Push Case (where giving an extra push exhibits an intention to hit) to then try to rescue the one from being hit, for there is this possibility: I gave the extra push only intending that there be *some chance* that the one will be hit. The object of *that* intention is not defeated when I try a rescue that may fail. Then is not the Rescue Test also consistent with *intending* that there be a chance that the one is hit in the Loop Case? Admittedly, it is highly implausible to attribute such a limited intention (to produce a mere chance of a hit) to an agent in this case. Let us allow the supposition, nevertheless.

Of course, in the Extra Push Case, I would do something extra for no reason but that there be (at minimum) some chance of the one being hit. By contrast, in the Loop Case, I already have some reason to redirect the trolley, that is, to stop it from hitting the five from the front. (This is what I have described in discussing Bratman's condition [1] on intention.) However, might it be that I have two aims in redirecting the trolley in the Loop Case, that is, to stop the trolley from hitting the five from the front *and* to create a chance of the one being hit? Here is a possible analogy to that supposition: I will not go to the store to fulfill my aim of buying shoes unless I can also fulfill my aim of getting a hat (in order to give it as a present) without doing anything extra. This is because the effort in getting to the store is too great to be justified just by the shoe purchase, and I do not have extra money for a hat. I learn that the store is giving away a free hat with every shoe purchase, so I go to the store (Store Case I).

I do not think that this case is analogous to the Loop Case, however. I do not think that the Loop Case involves two aims, not even a second aim to create some chance of the one being hit, which aim could be consistent with trying to rescue the one. Before explaining why, let me say that I assume that if I aim to hit the one, and I would not be willing to do anything else in order to bring about the hitting besides redirecting the trolley, then it has to be claimed that I redirect the trolley, at least in part, in order to hit the one. I assume further that if I did redirect the trolley in order to hit the one, I aim at his being hit not for its own sake but in order to accomplish my further aim, namely, that the trolley be prevented from looping. It follows, I think, that I would also have to redirect the trolley, at least in part, in order to stop it from looping. But the threat that the trolley will loop around only comes into existence because I redirect the trolley initially. I claim that because this is so, it makes no sense to say in the Loop Case that I redirected the trolley *in order to* keep the trolley from looping. For this reason, the Store Case I is not the proper analogy to the Loop Case, for it assumes that I intend to get the hat, as well as the shoes, because I intend to give a present.

Hence, the better analogy to the Loop Case is as follows: I will not go to the store to get the shoes I want unless I am reimbursed for the gas expenses I incur in getting there, since the trip is expensive and I am so poor that I have just enough for the shoes. If I do not get reimbursed for the expenses I incur, I will not have the shoes for long, as I will have to sell them to pay the gas bill, and my aim is to get shoes that I can keep. The store offers to reimburse my gas bill by mail if I buy the shoes I want. (I am proud and would not do anything extra to get the reimbursement, beyond buying the shoes that I want.) Hence, without doing anything extra beyond what I do to get shoes, I avoid the threat of the gas bill and I can keep the shoes (Store Case II). But would we say that I went to the store not only in order to get shoes but also in order to get my gas bill reimbursed? If I were someone who particularly desired that a store do something for me, as an end, we might say this. But I am only interested in not spending more money. Given that there would be no gas bill threatening to undermine my purchase if I did not go to the store for shoes (just as there would be no looping trolley threatening to undermine what I have already achieved for the five, if I did not initially redirect the trolley to save the five), and I do not want a store to repay me per se (as I do not per se want the hit on the one person that defuses the threat of a looping trolley), it makes no sense to say that I go to the store, in part, *in order to* get my gas reimbursed (i.e., to get what eliminates the financial threat in order to keep my shoes). For the same reason, it makes no sense to say that I redirect the trolley, in part, in order to hit the one (i.e., to do what eliminates the looping trolley threat, so the five stay okay).

There is an important conclusion to draw from Store Case II. When one reason (going to buy shoes) does not alone justify our acting (because of an interfering effect that will mean that we do not retain the shoes for long), another effect of our act (getting reimbursed for gas) can help to justify our act without this effect being something we act in order to bring about. In these cases, we act because of the effect but need not aim at it as a goal in action. The same is true of hitting the one: Redirecting the trolley to stop the five from being hit from the front would not suffice to justify redirecting it in the context where redirecting it can lead to the looping; some other effect (the hitting) that prevents the looping can cause what justifies our redirecting (i.e., saving the five, all things considered, analogous to keeping the shoes, all things considered, in Store Case II). We act *because* of that other effect that we will produce, but not *in order to* bring it about. Hence, our behavior in the Loop Case is consistent with the DDE(R) and the DDE.

Consider further the set of aims I have attributed to the person in discussing the Rescue Test. Are they best described as his having a primary intention that the one not be hit and a subsidiary intention to save the five if, despite his best efforts, he fails to save the one? No, because, in the Loop Case, he is in control of whether a threat ever faces the one person at all, and a primary intention not to hit the one would imply never redirecting the trolley at all. Here we come to a crux of the

matter: The DDE(R) in essence says that we may redirect the trolley if the good
we seek is great enough to justify the lesser evil *and* we do not intend (or aim at) the
lesser evil or involvement leading to it as an end or a means to that good. Hence,
redirecting the trolley is permitted if we will save five from the trolley coming at
them from *both* directions (i.e., save the five, all things considered) by doing what
causes the one to be hit so long as we do not intend this hit. The DDE(R) does not
require that we intend *not* to hit him (nor that our primary intention be that he not
be hit), and only this would also rule out redirecting the trolley while merely
foreseeing the hit.[25] (Put another way, it is permissible for us to be willing to hit
him, without our thereby willing to hit him.) We redirect the trolley *because* the five
can benefit in case we cannot rescue the one; it need not be our aim to hit the one in
order to stop the looping, but we also need not aim *not* to hit him. (We might
redirect the trolley with the aim to create an opportunity to benefit the five. But we
could aim to create an opportunity to benefit the five without aiming to create a
chance of hitting the one, because this chance will occur without our aiming at it.)

We conjectured that satisfying the Rescue Test might show too little, because
satisfying it might be compatible with intending some chance of a hit. But the
Rescue Test also shows more than is needed, since it shows that we may be willing
to *aim*, at a later point in time (i.e., after we have redirected the trolley), that the hit
of the one not occur, even if when we redirect the trolley, we do not aim that the
hit not occur. Are *these* aim and non-aim compatible? They can be if it is permissible *not* to aim at the one *not* being hit, when he would be hit *as a result* of my
removing one of the problems facing the five (i.e., the trolley coming from the first
direction), but impermissible to *not* aim at his *not* being hit, when this implies that
I refuse to rescue him because I am aiming at his being hit. Hence, sometimes I
might have to aim at his not being hit as the alternative to this would be my aiming
at his being hit.

I have also said that the Rescue Test is hypothetical; it need not be possible
that the trolley can be prevented from hitting someone. Hence, everything I have
said should also show that we may redirect the trolley when and because the trolley
will *definitely*—not just possibly—hit the one, without our intending or even
aiming that the hit take place. I conclude that in the Loop Case, I need not intend
or even aim at a chance of the one being hit, and it need not be the case that I
redirect the trolley, in part, in order to hit the one and in order to keep the trolley
from looping.

V. MORAL SIGNIFICANCE OF THE "BECAUSE OF"/"IN ORDER TO" DISTINCTION

What is the *moral* significance of the distinction between intending that something
evil* occur and acting only because one believes that one's act will cause evil* to
occur? If I intend something bad, as a rational agent I am committed to doing other
things to bring it about (if there is nothing per se objectionable about doing those

other things). But if I do an act for the sake of another of its properties only because I can also take advantage of one of its bad effects, this does not commit me to doing anything else to bring the bad effect about nor to make it the case that my act brings the bad effect about. In this way, it is like merely foreseeing the evil*. Furthermore, I will have some other reason (even if not a sufficient one) besides producing the bad effect for doing the act that has the bad effect. For example, in the Party Case, giving the party will lead to fun. In the Party Case, though this reason is not sufficient, it is my *primary reason* for acting, in the sense that it is the goal—either a final goal or an intermediate goal, such as a means that I intend to my final goal—that originally motivates me to think of giving a party, and this reason *would be sufficient* for action if no problems, such as a mess, arose. The *secondary reason* for giving the party is that the undesirable effect of giving the party that would ordinarily be an objection to giving it (despite the primary reason for acting) can be taken care of by the foreseen evil* (guilt in my friends) that I produce. The bad effect, we might say, *defeats the defeaters* of my primary reason, and so maintains the sufficiency of my primary (goal) reason. It is not, however, my goal in action to produce what will defeat the defeaters of my goal.[26] (This is another way of understanding the cases I discussed in section III.)

Recall Party Case II, a closer analogy to the Loop Case. There, my primary reason for acting is to give a successful party, and this would be defeated by a mess accumulating *during the party*. The guests' guilt defeats this defeater of my reason for action. Notice that in the Party Case, the defeater would defeat my pursuing my goal, but a mess occurring after the party, had it occurred, could not defeat the goodness of the party. By contrast, in Party Case II, the defeater threatens not only my having the party at all, but it would also threaten the continuing existence of the party to the point of success had I started the party.

These Party cases are different from a case in which I act only because I expect that a bad effect of my act will produce something else, say, my winning a prize for having the neatest house once my guests clean it up (Prize Party Case). In this case, without the impetus of achieving the additional good of a prize, I would not have a sufficient reason to have a party. That is, the fun and the prize are sufficient for acting, but the fun alone (and anything the fun leads to, in case *it* is just my means to something else) would not be sufficient. It may be that acting because of the evil* in this sort of case will have a different moral character from acting because of evil* in the first sort of case. (This is so even though the tests for intending of evil*, for example, the Rescue Test, would give the same negative results in the Prize Party Case as in the Party cases. That is, the host in the Prize Party Case could think it wrong to omit relieving his guests of a feeling of indebtedness if he could.) Hence, the distinction between intending evil* and acting merely because of it need not alone imply that acting because of evil* is permissible even if acting intending evil* is not. We shall discuss this issue further in chapter 5.[27]

As discussed in chapter 3, Warren Quinn offered a moral explanation for distinguishing intending evil* from acting with mere foresight to its occurrence. The former, he said, was objectionable because (and when) it involved treating other people as available to be used for our profit when it was seriously harmful to them and they did not consent; it involved treating people as mere means in an objectionable sense. Acting with mere foresight to such harm involved not being willing to constrain the pursuit of our goals by legitimate means simply because of the harm to others that would result. It could involve objectionably failing to treat people as ends in themselves by not taking seriously enough their interests as constraints on our goals. Objectionably treating as a mere means to our profit involves not treating as an end, but not necessarily vice versa. He thought that treatment as a mere means adds an additional objectionable element to merely acting despite uncompensated harm to others, holding constant harm done in the two cases.

How does Quinn's explanation of the additional bad element added by intending evil* fare in the light of the distinction between acting because of an evil* one will produce but not intending it? Do we treat people as available for our purposes so that we may profit in the Loop or Party cases? We certainly do the act that harms them, in part, because evil* to them will advantage us. We are more than not constrained by the evil* to others; the evil* provides a reason to do the act that causes it, yet it is, I believe, permissible to act. If Quinn's explanation predicts these acts are wrong, I suggest that would show that his explanation is wrong. However, I do not think that what we do in these cases constitutes treating people as available for our purposes.[28]

There are two points to make; one concerns "profit" and the other "availability." In the Party Case, my guests would make me worse off than I would be without the party (as the mess they produce overrides the fun for me). Hence, when they serve my interests, they merely eliminate the threat of the mess they themselves present to me. This is unlike improving my position from what it would be without their presence.[29] But I do not think this a crucial point, for in the Loop Case, hitting the bystander is the only thing that can improve the position of the five over what it would be without the presence of the bystander, yet I do not think that makes turning in the Loop Case violate Quinn's explanation of the moral significance of intending evil*. This is because we do not treat the person as "available" for our purposes. This is shown by the fact that we need not be willing to give the extra push in the Extra Push Case, if that were necessary in order to hit the bystander. It is only because he would be hit as a mere side effect of getting the trolley away from its initial hit that we allow ourselves to consider the further causal role that his involvement could play and how this could help justify our turning the trolley. This contrasts with the availability of a person for our purposes when we would do other things that need to be done in order to hit him. In chapter 3, I made this same point by trying to separate two thoughts that Quinn seems to run together: (a) deliberately bringing about someone's harmful involvement (not present in the Loop or Party cases) and (b) causing harmful involvement that is useful to us because it is harmful involvement.[30]

The trouble is not, I think, that the Loop Case cannot cohere with a more precise version of Quinn's explanation of the problem with acting while intending evil*. Rather, the problem is that if the Loop Case coheres, then the Prize Party Case (and other cases with the same structure)[31] will also cohere with Quinn's explanation. Yet causing the lesser evil* in these cases may be, I believe, imper-missible. Admittedly, it may be not impermissible because evil* is intended, since evil* need not be intended in such cases. Yet, I think that the reason it is imper-missible is closely connected to why acting while intending evil* is thought to be impermissible (when it is). If this is so, and Quinn's explanation does not capture this connection, his explanation may not correctly explain why intending evil* is thought to be impermissible (when it is).[32]

So far, all we have seen, morally speaking, is that we can not explain what is morally wrong with acting while intending evil* by showing that it involves taking the fact that one will produce evil* as a reason for action (rather than acting despite evil*). This is because we do this as well in acting only because of the evil*, and yet we do not thereby always act wrongly, even if we would act wrongly in a com-parable case in which we must be intending evil*. It seems crucial, if one wants to engage in the project of explaining the wrongness of an act by referring to the agent's reasons for it at all, to determine whether causing evil* is a primary (goal-type) or only a secondary reason (as described on pp. 102)[33]

VI. WHY A RATIONAL AGENT NEED NOT INTEND THE MEANS TO HIS END

A. Intending an End and Acting Because One Will Produce the Means

But now, a further question about intending (or aiming at) hitting the one person in the Loop Case arises. In the Loop Case, do I redirect the trolley while having the goal that it *stay away* from the five rather than just be away from them in one direction? Suppose I do. I also believe that my hitting the one is necessary in order that the trolley stay away from the five. Can we not show that I intend to hit the one because, insofar as I am rational, I must intend what I believe to be the means to my end? Or can I, insofar as I am rational, intend an end (the trolley staying away from the five) without intending what I believe is a necessary means to it when I believe that I will bring about the means without intending to do so? I think that this is possible. I could have a goal, see that it would be wrong to intend the means to it, but act because I foresee that I will bring about my means as a side effect of doing something else that I have at least *some* (justifying) reason to do. We now see that showing that we need not intend to hit the one in the Loop Case may help to show that, contrary to what is usually called the Principle of Instrumental Rationality, a rational agent, insofar as he is rational, can continue to intend an end without intending what he believes are the means (within his power) to it. Let me expand on this point.

It is commonly thought that if a rational agent intends an end and believes that his doing something is a means necessary to that end, then insofar as he is rational and does not abandon the end, it follows that he intends that means to his end. Call this the Claim.[34] This is the part of practical reason referred to as "instrumental rationality." It is taken to be a normative requirement or even a truth analytic to intending an end.[35] I shall argue that the Claim is not true. A rational agent, insofar as he is rational, is not required to intend what he believes (even correctly) are the means (within his power) necessary to his intended end. He can continue to intend the end without intending the means he believes necessary to attain it. It has been said that "most philosophers think it is both uncontroversial and unproblematic that practical reason requires us to take the means to our ends."[36] I shall argue that "take" should not be understood to mean or imply "intend."

Suppose that an agent intends an end x, and that he believes (correctly) that z is a means necessary to this end. Nothing can be substituted for z. The means necessary to an end is (or are) something that an agent must do or omit to do if the end is to come about. (Rather than keep on repeating "means (within his power) necessary to his end," I shall assume, unless otherwise noted, that this is meant by "the means." [This is in contrast to there being alternative ways of achieving the end, no one of which is necessary.] If I speak of "a means," I shall be referring, unless otherwise noted, to one of the things necessary for achieving an end rather than one of alternative possible ways of achieving an end.) The means is not just whatever must occur in order for an end to come about. No one thinks that an agent, insofar as he is rational, must intend everything that he believes must occur, but not as a result of his acts, in order that his end come about. Suppose, for example, that I know that lightning must strike someone if my end is to be achieved, and lightning will strike him unavoidably regardless of what I do, allowing me to pursue my end. This does not mean that I must intend that lightning strike someone, insofar as I intend the end and am a rational agent. Furthermore, the means is not *by definition* something that an agent must intend to do or omit to do if his end is to come about. If that were how means were defined, in saying "an agent must intend the means to his end," we would be saying "an agent must intend the things that he must intend (to do or omit to do)," and that would be redundant.[37]

It seems clear that the typical agent in the Loop Case is conceived as intending that the trolley stay away from the five. To make this clearer, imagine what the agent would do if he found out that he had to do other things in order to keep the trolley from looping. For example, suppose that hitting the one only makes the trolley slow down, and this alone makes it possible for him to throw stones at the trolley in order to stop it. Certainly, he would (and could permissibly) look for ways to throw stones, pursue another route of throwing them if the first one failed, and rule out plans that interfered with his throwing stones, all in order to keep the trolley away from the five. The fact that he would intentionally do these other things, innocent in themselves, solely for the purpose of stopping the trolley shows that he intends the trolley to stay away from the five. (Note that I am still *not* claiming that in the Loop Case he redirects the trolley in order that it not loop.)

We can conceive of the Loop Case, then, as one in which the agent has one goal—keeping the trolley away from the five—and there are at least two things necessary to achieve it: One is redirecting the trolley away from hitting the five from the front; a second is hitting the one. The first means produces as a foreseen side effect the second means. The agent only brings about the first means because he believes that he will thus bring about the second (with some probability), but, I have argued, this does not mean that he intends its occurrence or acts in order to bring it about, though his acting does bring it about.

Intending a goal (such as the five being free of threats) may require that an agent be willing to intend *some* means (whether a necessary one or just a possible alternative) in order to bring the goal about, on pain of just wanting and producing an event, but not intending it. The agent in the Loop Case does this when he redirects the trolley away from hitting the five *in order to* keep the five threat-free. However, he need not *intend* (or be willing to intend) everything that it is necessary for him to do in order that the goal come about, so long as he believes that he will do everything he must do whether he intends it or not. In sum, a rational agent, insofar as he is rational, need not intend—and may even refuse to intend—some of what he believes are the means to an end that he still intends. He may intend goal x, know that his bringing z about is necessary for x to come about, but not intend z. The reason this is possible is that while it is true that if an agent continues to intend an end, then insofar as he is rational, he must be willing to bring about what he believes are the means to it, he need not intend (or will) to bring about the means in order for him to (be willing to) bring about the means.

As noted above, it is recognized that a rational agent need not (and often cannot) intend things that he knows are necessary for his end, if they will occur in any case independently of him. My claim is that he also need not intend and may refuse to intend things that he knows are necessary for his end, even if they will occur only if he brings them about. Another way of putting this point is that while he must bring about the means in order *that* his end occur, he need not bring about the means in order *to* bring about his end. That is, he must do z in order *that* x come about, but he need not do z in order *to* bring x about.[38]

To take account of my objection to the Claim, we could revise it to say: If an agent intends an end, then insofar as he is rational, he must intend what he believes are the means to his end, *if he believes that intending them is necessary to bring about his end (perhaps because intending them is necessary to bringing them about), but not otherwise.*[39] Call this Claim*. Claim* is compatible with the claim that in order for an agent to be intending an end at all rather than just wanting it to come about and producing it, it is necessary that he be willing to bring about at least some of the things that will produce his end *in order to* bring about the end. Call this Claim**. This amounts to saying that he must *be willing* to intend a means, though he need not actually intend any means because he may bring about all of them without his intending to bring them about. However, notice that these means in Claim** may not be means in the sense of what is necessary to produce the end, since the agent may only have to be willing to bring about one of the options of a set of alternatives (each of which can help produce the end) *in order to* bring about the end. That is, Claim** says that there must be something that the agent is willing to intend to do (or omit) in order to bring about his end if he is to have this end. However, he need not intend or be willing to intend all or even any of the required means (i.e., intend something if it is a means in the sense of necessary to his end), unless this is necessary to bring about the end. (An implication of this is that where doing z is both necessary and the only thing that is sufficient in order that x occur, the agent must be willing to intend z on pain of only wanting and producing, but not intending, x.) Claim* and Claim** may be constitutive of instrumental rationality, but the Claim is not.

B. Some Types of Cases

Of the sorts of cases that can be counterexamples to the Claim, the Loop Case is one of a type that involves an agent who has only one goal x (saving five), the means to which are p (redirecting the trolley) and q (hitting one). This case involves, according to the DDE and DDE(R), someone being prohibited from intending a means q for moral reasons. Alternatively, we could suppose that there are nonmoral reasons for not intending means q (e.g., it is too costly given that our end is x). However, if one brings about means p, this has q as a side effect.

There are at least two versions of these "single-goal" types of cases. In one version, p, which leads to q, is itself a *very* great good and q is a lesser evil*. In this case, even though p is not intended as any more than a means to x (the good that is our goal), it might, I suggest, still justify the agent in causing q as a side effect. The DDE and even the DDE(R) as standardly interpreted, however, imply that if we intend a greater good *as a goal*, not merely as a means, the fact that a lesser evil* is a side effect will not be sufficient to make our act impermissible. Hence, I think that we should further revise these doctrines to allow that if our act will lead to a greater good, though we do not intend the good as any more than a means, then a lesser evil* that will be its side effect will not be sufficient to make the act impermissible.[40] In this sort of case, even if x does not occur, q (the lesser evil* or great cost) could be justified by p's occurrence. Thus, if it is impermissible to intend q as a means to x because it is a lesser evil* (or it is merely too costly to use q for x), I may still intend p as a means to x, and it can justify the lesser evil* q (or compensate for the cost of q).

The Loop Case exemplifies a second version of the single-goal case, in which the agent's only goal is x, and p (turning the trolley from its initial hit) is not itself a greater good that could justify the lesser evil* (or costly) q, independently of x.[41] Despite this difference between the two versions, it is true *in both of them* that an agent does p (whatever it is, given that he sees it as a means to x) *because* he believes that it will lead to q. If he did not believe that p would lead (at least with some probability) to q, he could not reasonably believe that he would achieve x (his goal) by doing p. Hence, he would not do p unless he believed it could lead to q; if he believed his doing p could not cause q, he would not do p. He does p in order to bring about x because p can lead to q.

(Is the following an example of a third version of the single-goal case? Suppose that we bomb a munitions plant in wartime as a means p to stopping a war x. We foresee that the munitions plant blowing up will cause the deaths of some children as a side effect. We also know that our causing the deaths of the children is another necessary condition q for the end of the war.[42] That is, we must cause the nation to lose both munitions and civilians in order that it surrender. Hence, if the deaths did not occur, there would be no point in bombing the munitions plant. In this Munitions and Civilians Case, q is necessary not to defeat something that is caused by our bombing and that threatens the success of the munitions operation, analogous to what happens in the Loop Case. Rather, q is an independent factor needed to bring the war to an end. This suggests that there are two intermediate goals in this case, even though ending war is presented as a broad, final goal. Hence, it is not really a third version of a single goal case. Nevertheless, let us consider it. The DDE and DDE(R) rule out our acting with the intention that the children be killed. They do not rule out dropping bombs when the deaths are merely a foreseen side effect. Let us assume [for the time being] that it would be permissible to cause such merely foreseen deaths. Then it is consistent with these doctrines to proceed to bomb the munitions plant in order to stop the war only *because* the children will also die as side effects, as this need not involve intending their involvement or deaths.)

I have claimed that doing p in order to produce x because q will happen does not show that we intend q, though q must also occur in order that x come about. We can do p because q will thus occur, but not in order to produce q. Hence, if it would be wrong to aim at the deaths of the children as a means of ending the war, this could not be raised as an objection to my case in which we drop the bomb on the factory because the children will die.[43] Hence, this bombing case would be another example in which a rational agent, insofar as he is rational, may cause but need not intend or be willing to intend an evil* that is a means to his end, even when that means is necessary to produce the very end whose existence might justify bringing about this evil*.[44] In the bombing case, it is some evidence that the agent need not intend the children's deaths, that he could, insofar as he is rational, refuse to do something, in itself innocent, to make it the case that his bombs are ones that also cause the children's deaths. That is, he could, consistent with doing p because q occurs, refuse to do anything at all to bring about his goal x if he had to establish the connection between p and q. This is so, even though using bombs that do not cause the children's deaths would be pointless, since the war cannot be won by destroying the munitions plant alone.

C. Another Way to Intend an End without Intending the Means

To argue against the Claim, I have used cases in which we must rely on the controversial claim that acting "because of" is different from acting "in order to." But there is an easier, less controversial way to argue against the standard claim about instrumental rationality. It will again also show that the objection to intending the means need not be a moral one, as we are supposing it is in the Loop Case.

Suppose that an agent is forbidden to intend z for either moral or nonmoral considerations, and z is a necessary means to x. A nonmoral reason that it would be impermissible to intend z as a means is that it is very expensive given that all we would achieve with it is x. Let us assume that for either of these two reasons, the agent will refuse to intentionally bring about z in order to bring about x. Does this mean that the agent, insofar as he is rational, must give up intending x? I do not think so.

Suppose that this agent also intends another goal, y, and z is a side effect either of the means to y or of the achievement of y itself. So long as y is a greater good and z a lesser evil*, the DDE and DDE(R) do not rule out z occuring as a side effect of pursuing y. Alternatively, imagine that y is such an important goal that it (if not x) is worth bearing the great cost of z as a side effect. In both of these cases, the fact that he will bring about z as a side effect does not make the agent's act impermissible. The important point is that if the agent knows that he will bring z about in pursuit of y, he can continue to intend x. Evidence that the agent does intend x (and not merely wants it to occur) is that once he knows that he will bring about z as a side effect of the pursuit of y, he may intentionally bring about something else, m, because it is also physically necessary in order to produce x, in addition to z.

Consider a specific example to illustrate this "double-goal" type of case. Suppose that I want to build a private home and I must create a hole in plot A in order to do this. However, creating the hole is too expensive just to build my house, so I must not aim to do it. However, I receive a contract to build an apartment complex on plot B, which is next to A. In order to clear the land for the apartment complex, I must use explosives that unavoidably make a hole in plot B but, as an unintended side effect, they also create a hole in plot A. The hole in plot A is an undesirable side effect from the point of view of building on B, since it makes it harder for me to move materials to B, but it is a tolerable cost relative to the goal of building on B. Given that I will produce the hole in plot A as a side effect, I can still pursue my goal of building my home. I do everything else (e.g., buying bricks) that I must do to build my house in order to build it (House Case).

In the House Case, I do not pursue the goal of building an apartment complex because of its side effect, let alone in order to achieve either the side effect or the other goal. What I may not bring about intentionally (for reasons of cost), I may permissibly bring about as a mere side effect of building the apartment complex; believing that this side effect will occur, I may continue to intend another goal, namely, building my private house. I do other things to build my own house *because* I will produce a hole, but I do not intend to produce the hole. In this case, the good that justifies the bad side effect is not caused by it. (By contrast, the Loop Case shows that it does not violate the DDE or DDE[R] for an evil* [hitting the one] to be necessary as a cause of the very good [the five saved at the end of the day] that is needed to justify it.)

In the case where z is a moral evil, the DDE does not rule out making use of side effects of our acts whose occurrence we did not intend. It does not exclude an evil z causing a good x which is not needed to justify the existence of that evil, especially when the evil's existence is already justified by y. For example, suppose it is permissible to bomb a munitions factory in wartime, even though some children will die as a side effect of the exploding factory, but it is impermissible to aim at the deaths of the children, even in order to bring their warring parents out into the open so that we may attack them. Nevertheless, if we know the children will die as a side effect of the permissible bombing, it is permissible to arrange to attack the parents when, as we know, they will come out from hiding to bury their children.

Further evidence that the agent does not intend z is that if there were a way to bring about y without producing z as a side effect, he would do so, consistent with taking advantage of his causing z as a side effect. Suppose that there were two ways to bring about y: one with z as a side effect and one without. For example, clearing plot B with or without making a hole in A. It would be consistent with taking advantage of z as a side effect for the agent not to choose the route to y that causes z, for if he did, he would be intending z. For example, if equally good explosives that did not cause a hole in A were available, the agent would be committed to using them, given that he must not spend more than is necessary to construct the apartment complex. The fact that he should bring about y without z if he could implies that he would, *in those circumstances*, have to stop intending x. This, however, does not show that, in the circumstances where z is unavoidably a side effect, he does not actually intend x.

I conclude that it is a quite general phenomenon—independent of moral considerations—that a rational agent, insofar as he is rational, need not intend what he believes is a (necessary) means to the end that he still intends.

D. Korsgaard and the Claim

A philosopher who seems to defend something like the Claim is Christine Korsgaard.[45] She begins by discussing the claim that "practical reason requires us to take the means to our ends" (p. 215). She then says: "[T]he instrumental principle . . . says that *if* you will an end, you must be prepared to take the means" (p. 237). Finally, she cites Kant's claim that "whoever wills the end wills (insofar as reason has decisive influence on his actions) also the means" (p. 235). (She says that these claims could only be true if the agent knows what the means are. Let us assume this as well, for the sake of argument.)

Putting together these three versions of the Principle of Instrumental Rationality suggests that she believes that "take the means" is equivalent to "will the means." "Will" in "will the means" should have the same meaning as "will" in "will the end." She says: "Suppose someone claims that she wills an end; she asserts that all things considered, she has decided to pursue this end" (p. 236). Hence, I conclude that for Korsgaard, to will the means is to decide to pursue the means. In sum, Korsgaard seems to believe that the Principle of Instrumental Rationality claims: If I decide to pursue an end, I decide to pursue the means to the end (insofar as reason has decisive influence on my actions and I know what the means are). Let us assume that the means are whatever I must do (or omit) to bring about my end. She would then seem to believe that the Principle of Instrumental Rationality says: If I decide to pursue an end, *I decide to pursue the thing I must do to bring about my end* (insofar as reason has decisive influence on my actions and I know what the means are).

What I have argued in the previous subsections implies that this principle is not true. I need not decide to pursue the things I must do to bring about my end, if I decide to pursue an end, any more than I need intend those means. This is so if I know that I will do the things I must do to bring about my end without deciding to pursue them. Consider again the House Case. I do not decide to pursue the making of a hole on plot A, and, in particular, I do not decide to pursue the making of a hole on plot A in order to build my private house. Yet I do decide to pursue as an end building my private house, and I know that making the hole on plot A is a necessary means to my end.

It might be said in objection to this that I do decide to pursue making the hole in A *as a sign* of there being a hole in B. After all, if there can be no hole in B without, as a side effect, the hole in A, then if there is no hole in A, this is a sign that there is no hole in B, and I intend to make a hole in B. But in response to this objection, the following can be said. First, if "pursue" is to have the same meaning in "pursue an end" and "pursue a means," it seems I must decide to pursue the hole in A as more than a sign of a hole in B. Second, it is certainly *not* true that if I decide to pursue an end (building my private house), I must decide to pursue a means to that end as a sign of the success of *another* end (building the apartment house). Third, it is not true that if I decide to pursue an end, then I must decide to pursue the signs of *that* end coming about.

Korsgaard makes some very strong claims in support of the Principle of Instrumental Rationality. Consider the following claims she makes to support this principle: (1) "To will an end just is to will or cause to realize the end,[46] hence to will to take the means to the end. This is the sense in which the principle is analytic. The instrumental principle is *constitutive* of an act of the will. If you do not follow it, you are not willing the end at all" (p. 244); (2) "[s]o, willing an end is equivalent to *committing yourself*, first personally, to taking the means to that end. In willing an end, just as Kant says, your causality—*the use of means*—is already thought. What is constitutive of willing the end is not the outward act of actually taking the means but rather the inward, volitional act of prescribing the end along with the means it requires to yourself" (p. 245); (3) "[a] commitment to taking the means is what makes a difference between willing an end and merely wishing for it or wanting it or thinking that it would be nice if it were realized" (p. 252); (4) "[a]nd if I am to constitute *myself* as the cause of an end, then I must be able to distinguish between *my* causing the end and some desire or impulse that is 'in me' causing my body to act" (p. 247); and (5) "a person who does not conform to the instrumental picture becomes a mere location for the play of desires and impulses, the field of their battle for dominance over the body through which they seek satisfaction" (p. 254).

Contrary to (1), I claim that in the House Case, I do will the end of my building my private house, but I do not will to take the means to the end. Contrary to (4) and (5), in the House Case, I, and not some impulse in me causing my body to act, causes the end of building my house. It may be true that in willing an end, I must *be willing to do what is a necessary means to* the end. If this is all that is meant by "commitment to take the means," then such commitment does not involve *willing the means.*

Much (though not all) of what Korsgaard wishes to say could be said better by Claim**, which may be constitutive to being a willing agent and hence the true version of the Principle of Instrumental Rationality. Recall that, according to

Claim**, I do not decide to pursue an end at all rather than merely wish for it (as [3] says), unless I am willing to pursue at least *one* of the means to it. However, as I have said above, I need only be *willing to intend* (i.e., be willing to will) a means, *not actually will* (or pursue) a means, because I may produce the means without willing them. Also the sense of "means" that makes this true is not "things it is necessary that I do for my end." This is because I can decide to pursue my end by deciding to pursue something that is one of a set of ways of producing my end. The crucial distinction can be made by attending to two parts of Korsgaard's claim (2) above: It may be true that "[i]n willing an end, just as Kant says, your causality— *the use of means*—is already thought," if we interpret "means" in the sense of *"some* ways of producing your end" and "thought" in the sense of "willing to intend." But this is not the same as "prescribing the end along with the means it requires," if prescribing the means implies willing them and "the means it requires" are *all* of the things that it is *necessary* for you to do for the end to come about.

VII. CASES WHERE WE INTEND TO HIT THE ONE?

A. The Problem of Two-Step Cases

Let us now return to other variants of the Trolley Case. There are cases, unlike the Loop Case, in which, even though the second problem (e.g., the trolley coming from the second direction) only exists because we redirect the trolley away from the five, it may seem that an agent must be redirecting the trolley, in part, *in order to* stop the second problem. Consider the Double Track Case:[47] The deadly trolley is coming at the five. If I redirect the trolley away onto track A, it will loop around and hit the five from the other direction, as there is no one on the track to stop it. If I redirect it away onto track B, the trolley will be stopped from looping back to the five by the presence of a person on track B whose being hit stops it. The person will die as a result of the hit. In this case, can it sensibly be said that if I choose to redirect the trolley down track B rather than A, it is in order that the trolley not loop back to kill the five? In the Double Track Case, the choice to go to track B is something more than what is necessary to get the trolley away from its initial hit on the five, for this could be done if we redirect the trolley onto track A. Deliberately going to track B rather than A, it might be said, is done in order to ensure that the second problem does not arise.

Could someone now claim that though we redirect the trolley toward track B intending to stop the second problem, we still do not intend to hit the one person, as it will be a side effect of only what we do in order to deal with the first problem of the initial hit? It is a means we need not intend to an end we do intend. We may send the trolley to B because it will hit the one, but not in order to hit the one. But is this believable? If we choose among tracks toward which to redirect the trolley on the basis of where we are more likely to produce that causally necessary hit, don't we intend to hit the one? After all, hitting is not a *necessary* side effect of doing only what we *need* to do in order to deal with the first problem, for we could direct the trolley to track A to deal with the first problem. Still, it also seems consistent with choosing track B that a rational agent, insofar as he is rational, not be willing to give the trolley an extra push if this were necessary to cause the hit. This suggests that he does not intend to hit the one (unless of course, an extra push is ruled out on grounds other than that we would intend the hit in doing it and unrelated to factors created with such an intention).

Certainly, if the trolley *had already been* sent to track A (when it could have been sent to B) and there were still some way to divert it to B, diverting it would clearly be permissible according to the views we have considered in this chapter. (Call this the Two-Step Case.) This is because the second step would involve diverting from the looping route A so that the five will not be hit, and because the one on B will be hit and so stop further looping. (This is the same exact reasoning as in the original Loop Case.) It would be odd that one could permissibly do in two steps something that would be impermissible if done in one step (i.e., directly go to B rather than A), and odd that the two-step procedure involves no intention to hit the one while the one-step choice does involve such an intention. Can we not understand redirecting the trolley onto track B rather than A immediately as, in one fell swoop, turning the trolley away from its initial hit of the five in the only way that does not loop back toward the five? Deliberately putting oneself in a two-step scenario, that is, going first to track A and then taking the *only* way of diverting the trolley from looping by turning it to B, seems like only a subterfuge for choosing B right away from among several options. I believe this is, in fact, the basis of the correct view about the Double Track Case.

B. Susceptibility to a Threat

The Two-Step Case raises an interesting question worth examining both in its own right and because it bears on the resolution of the Double Track Case. Suppose that in Two-Step Case II, one could proceed *only* by first redirecting the trolley onto track A headed toward the five and then onto B where a person blocks the loop to the five. That is, there is no direct route to track B that could have been taken. Would it really be permissible in this case to redirect the trolley away from its initial hit on the five and onto track A because one knew that the way would then be open to redirect it onto B? Might the person on track B say: "If the first act (redirecting onto A) would be without point if not followed by a second act initially unavailable (redirecting onto B), and that second act will foreseeably threaten someone, we cannot morally justify performing the second act."

Similarly, in another case that involves no loop, suppose that the trolley is headed toward five people. It cannot be redirected except toward six other people. Doing this in itself would be without point and wrong. But we know that by another act, we can redirect the trolley away from hitting the six in a direction where it will hit one person instead (see figure 4.1). Certainly, if the one person were not there, it would make sense to turn toward the six merely as a way of getting into a position to turn it away from them, onto an empty track. I call all of these multiple-step trolley cases, where the steps are only possible in sequential order (unlike the Two-Step Case), Tree Trolley cases.[48]

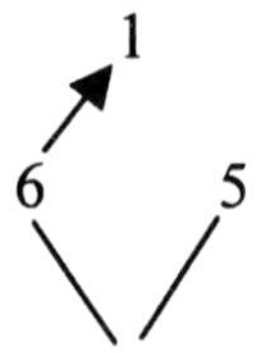

Figure 4.1.

Might the one person in both of these Tree Trolley cases revise his complaint somewhat? Could he complain that he has been made susceptible to the trolley threat *when he was not originally susceptible to it*—because there was no direct route from the five to the one—and that agents should not be permitted to act in a way that harms someone because of that newly *created* susceptibility? (The six were originally susceptible, since they could be harmed simply by diverting the trolley away from the five.) This revised objection (but not the first one) applies to the following case as well (see figure 4.2).

In this case, there *would* be a point in redirecting the trolley in the only way it can go, from the five toward the four, even if we could not then act to divert it from the four so as to cause less harm. If the revised complaint is justified, then it will be permissible to redirect the trolley away from the five toward the four, but not to proceed further to save *the four* by killing the one, at least when the original aim was to save *the five* and they have already been saved. It would still be permissible, though, to divert a different trolley away from the four people toward the one, assuming that this different trolley had not been diverted toward them from a greater number of people. Both the original and revised complaints, however, imply that a possibly unknown history—whether this trolley whose redirection we are now contemplating has been redirected away from other people already—could affect the permissibility of turning the trolley.

Suppose that it were not permissible to do a second threatening act in the Tree Trolley cases. Does this imply that we could not take advantage of the justification proposed in the Double Track Case above for redirecting the trolley onto track B rather than A, namely, that it would be permissible (if it were possible) to redirect toward A and then by a separate act redirect toward B (as in the Two-Step Case)? Not necessarily, because in the Double Track Case it was always physically possible to redirect toward B in one move; in this sense, the one person's susceptibility to

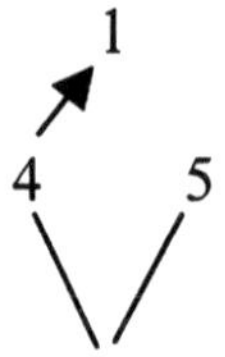

Figure 4.2.

being hit was not created by our first act. In addition, in that case, we would not have yet succeeded in saving the five.

Notice that nothing has been said in discussing Tree Trolley cases to imply that it is not permissible for an agent to do an act that he foresees will—without any further intervening act by him—lead to all of the consequences that in other cases we have considered require an intervening act. So, nothing has been said to imply that it would be impermissible in the Double Track Case to redirect the trolley away from the five toward track A, even if it could not have been immediately redirected to B, foreseeing that halfway around A, the trolley will move of its own accord to B and be stopped by hitting the one person.

An important moral can be drawn from this discussion. There are two senses of "susceptible to the threat." One is purely normative: If it is permissible to do the acts that lead to someone being threatened, then he is susceptible to the threat. A second sense is purely physical: By one redirection of the threat, someone can be threatened. If it is impermissible to redirect the trolley in some Tree Trolley cases though we would minimize lives lost, this shows that susceptibility in the normative sense sometimes depends on the physical sense of susceptibility.[49]

VIII. THE UNINTENDED GREATER GOOD AND INTENTION

An alternative analysis of the Loop Case (to that presented in Section VI) is that I do not *intend* the trolley to stay away from the five when I redirect it. It might be said (contrary to what has been argued) that if I will not intend a means that (I know) is necessary to the trolley staying away from the five (i.e., the hitting of the one), I do not intend its staying away. Rather, I intend to redirect the trolley away from its initial hit on the five and will do so only *because* I foresee that it will stay away, as I foresee the cause of its staying away (i.e., the hitting of the one). I act only because I foresee both of these things, but I do not act intending that either one occur.

Whether or not the Loop Case involves intending that the trolley stay away, it is certainly true that someone who did not intend that the trolley stay away could still act only *because* this would happen. For example, suppose that my goal is that the trolley not hit the five people from the front (the original direction of the trolley) because I do not want their faces damaged. However, I do not care if they are hit from behind by the looping trolley. I realize that my actual goal is not enough to justify the foreseen side effect of one innocent bystander dying. Then I learn that if the one is hit, this will stop the trolley entirely and save the five. I realize that this is a sufficiently large good that, *whether I intend it or not*, its occurrence would help justify the death of the one. Hence, I only now allow myself to redirect the trolley and cause the bad side effect (which in turn has the good effect of saving the five). Call this the Unintended Greater Good Case.

I believe that it is permissible to redirect the trolley in this case. This implies that the greater good, which justifies the bad side effect, *need not be intended* for the act to be permissible. The versions of the DDE and DDE(R) that I presented above claim that if we act by neutral or good means *in order to* produce a greater good, then the fact that a lesser evil* will be produced as a side effect does not interfere with the permissibility of the act.[50] Hence, redirecting the trolley in the Unintended Greater Good Case would be ruled out. An alternative moral doctrine that permitted us to redirect the trolley could be a doctrine that permitted us to act even when we act *because (we believe that)* we would bring about the greater good, not in order to bring about the greater good.

It might be said that once we find out that the occurrence of the greater good is necessary if we are to be able to pursue our goal, we come to intend the connection between our act and the occurrence of the greater good, as a means to our goal. The only problem, then, would be that the DDE and the DDE(R) should make it clear that we may permissibly be pursuing a greater good that can justify a lesser evil* *only as a means* to achieving a goal that does not justify the lesser evil* and not be pursuing this greater good as an end in itself.[51] However, even if this did not distort one point of the DDE and the DDE(R), which seems to be that our act be undertaken for the sake of the greater good as a final end, it would not be a correct description of a necessary condition for it being permissible to act when we cause evil*. For it could be permissible to act because the greater good will occur, even if we would not, or it were wrong for us to, intend the connection between our act and the greater good as a means to our actual end. For example, it might be open only to some and not to others to intend that particular greater good. The more fundamental point is, though, that I do not need to intend the connection between my act and the greater good, when the greater good already occurs as a side effect of my act and I can act *because* it does so.

The distinction between acting because I believe that my act will make a greater good occur and acting in order to produce a greater good shows that it is possible for someone to be concerned with justifying his behavior without being concerned per se with that which does the justifying, namely, the greater good. The reasons that justify his act are not his reasons for acting, though the fact that they justify his act is a reason for his acting. The alternative moral doctrine that I am describing insists that we be interested in justifying a lesser evil* with a greater good, but it does not insist that we be interested per se in producing the greater good that justifies our act.[52]

An agent who allows himself to act if he produces a greater good as an effect may actually do more good than someone who insists that intending the greater good for its own sake is a condition on acting with the foresight that a bad side effect will occur. Furthermore, if someone were to find in the expected existence of a greater good a mere opportunity for doing what he really intends to do, this may (though it need not) lead him to create new links between what he intends to do and a greater good where none previously existed, for the greater good can justify the evil* side effects of what he really intends to do. If he creates these links, he would be intending the greater good as a mere means to doing what he intends as an end. Though such agents may produce more good, they would also be seeking excuses for acting, and the facts that would justify their acts would not be their reasons for acting. These may be defects in agents' practical reasoning.

In the cases I have so far considered where the greater good is not intended, I said that the agent did not care about the greater good. However, it is also possible for an agent to want that greater good and act because it will occur, and yet not intend its occurrence. Consider the Massacre Case (first introduced in chapter 1). A tactical bomber targets for destruction one portion of a munitions factory. He intends to bring about (what he takes to be) this small good, but foresees two side effects: (1) killing ten innocent civilians and (2) stopping a massacre of twenty other civilians because the killers are distracted by the sound of bombing. Let us suppose that side effect (1) is too large an evil* to be outweighed by the small intended good. Side effect (2) is a great enough good to outweigh (1). Although the bomber cannot help but want the massacre to stop, stopping it is not intended, since this is not necessary to the war effort. Hence, if the DDE or DDE(R) as standardly understood were a necessary condition for moral permissibility, they would block the attack on the factory. Yet it could be permitted by another principle that allows the agent to act in part because he acts on condition of (2).

The Massacre Case also helps us to see a problem with another standard way of understanding intention. (Recall that Bennett's understanding of intention was criticized above.) Judith Jarvis Thomson says: "It is standard to take it that for a person to X, intending an event E, is for him to X because he thinks his doing so will cause E, and he wants E."[53] But I have argued that X-ing (e.g., bombing part of a munitions factory) because one thinks that doing so will cause E (e.g., the cessation of a massacre) and one wants E does not necessarily involve intending E. Further, a version of the Loop Case also shows that what Thomson says is the standard characterization of intention is not correct. Suppose in this new version of the Loop Case, I hate the man on the track whose being hit will stop the trolley, and I want him to be hit. Nevertheless, I can turn the trolley solely to save the five because I know the man will be hit and, thereby, stop its looping. I need not act intending that he be hit any more than someone who does not want his death need intend his being hit in the original Loop Case. Hence, I can act because I think that doing so will cause E and want E, and yet not intend it.

Our discussion of the unintended greater good also shows us that redirecting the trolley in the Loop Case may violate the DDE(R) and DDE not because we intend that the one be hit, but because we possibly *do not* intend the greater good (that the five be permanently saved from the trolley) that justifies the bad side effect. This is surprising, I think. So much discussion about the DDE has focused on whether we may intend a lesser evil that no attention has been paid to whether we must intend a greater good (as a goal or as a means).[54]

To sum up, on one interpretation of our relation to the end of the five being saved entirely from the trolley in the Loop Case, we do intend it but do not intend a means necessary to it. On another interpretation, we intend neither the end of the five being saved entirely from the trolley nor a means necessary to it. On neither interpretation do we intend that the one be hit. However, on the second interpretation, we may violate the DDE and DDE(R) in turning the trolley for a rather surprising reason, namely, that we do not intend the greater good.

It seems to me that in the Loop Case as standardly understood, we do intend that the five not be hit at all, and we intend this for its own sake. (Hence, I do not think that the Loop Case is, in fact, like the Unintended Greater Good Case.) Intending that the five not be hit at all may be our intention in redirecting the trolley away from hitting the five from the front. We see that this intention may be defeated (e.g., the trolley loops) but also see that there is a defeater of this defeater to our primary intention (i.e., the hitting of the one defeats the defeater). So, when we redirect the trolley, we intend the five to be saved at the end of the day. But we need not intend all of the means to it. We need not intend to hit the one, and we also need not intend that each of the particular ways in which the trolley could come back to the five not happen. I merely foresee that these things will or will not happen. I need not intend that the trolley not loop around and hit the five from the back in order to intend, when I first redirect the trolley, that the trolley move away and stay away from them. This is the interpretation of the Loop Case that seems to be most acceptable.

IX. THE DOCTRINE OF TRIPLE EFFECT

The Unintended Greater Good Case violates the DDE and the DDE(R) as they are standardly presented. In this case, I act because the greater good will occur, not in order that it does. In the Loop Case, I act because the hitting of the one will take place, not in order that it does. Hence, there is a third relation, in addition to intending and merely foreseeing, that I may have to a good or bad effect. Even if intending a bad effect were impermissible, acting because it will occur might not be. Interestingly, this same relation to an effect—acting because of it rather than merely foreseeing it or intending it—can, as we have seen, capture our relation to the greater good that justifies our act. In order to take account of this third relation to effects (both good and bad), I suggest a new doctrine; instead of the Doctrine of Double Effect, we may speak of the Doctrine of Triple Effect (DTE).[55] The DTE states: "A greater good that we cause and whose expected existence is a condition of our action, but which we do not necessarily intend, may justify a lesser evil* that we must not intend but may have as a condition of action."

If we need not intend nor aim to hit the one in the Loop Case—though, of course, we are not aiming *not* to hit him—we need not violate the no-intending evil* component of the DDE and DDE(R). Do we then need the DTE to explain the permissibility of redirecting the trolley in this case? Do we refer to the DTE *only* to help us see that acting "because of" is consistent with *not* acting "in order to," and thus does not violate the DDE(R)? Not quite, for another component of the DDE(R) says that an act that produces a lesser evil* that is foreseen as a side effect can be permissible if we use neutral or good means with the aim of achieving a greater good. But the lesser evil* we produce in the Loop Case is not a mere foreseen side effect; we act because we believe that we will produce it. The DTE makes it clear that evil* need not be a mere foreseen side effect. It also makes clear that we need not aim to achieve a greater good.

I stated in section I that one major focus of this chapter was to explain why it is impermissible to kill one person in the Bystander Case (where we would push someone in to stop the trolley) while it is permissible to kill one person in the Loop Case. One way to do so is to rely on the DTE. The Bystander Case violates the DTE because in it we intend that the one be hit. The Loop Case, for reasons discussed in this and the previous sections, does not violate the DTE.

X. FURTHER IMPLICATIONS OF THE DTE

A. The Munitions Grief Case

Consider some further implications of the DTE. The DDE has been used to distinguish morally between (1) terror bombing civilians in wartime and (2) tactically bombing military targets while foreseeing with certainty that civilians will be killed. The first, it is said, is impermissible; the second may be permissible. As noted in chapter 1, the DTE helps us see that there is an in-between type of case, an example of which is the Munitions Grief Case:[56] If we bomb military targets and the response to our bombing is that they are immediately rebuilt, it will be pointless to bomb. However, we know that civilians will be killed as an (unavoidable) side effect of our bombing, and this alone will make other citizens, consumed by grief, unable to rebuild. Hence, it would only be reasonable to bomb *because* we know that we will cause civilians to die. But this does not mean that when we bomb, we aim at their deaths. Though we take advantage of a bad side effect of our act (to provide us with a reason for that act), we need not be committed (as rational agents) to doing anything especially to make our act have that bad effect. I believe that bombing in the Munitions Grief Case can be permissible, even if terror bombing—where we intend that the deaths occur—is impermissible.[57]

B. The Secondary Transplant Case

Suppose that we have a choice between going to save five people from disease A in location X and going to save Joe from disease A in location Y. We cannot save all six, so either the one will die or the five will die. Ordinarily, it would be correct to save the five, I believe. However, the procedure we must use if we save the five (but not if we save Joe) will give them an infection that is rapidly fatal. If there were no way to stop the infection, we should save Joe instead. However, the one thing that can combat the fatal infection in the five is a transplant into each of them of one of the organs that would be available only from Joe if he dies (Secondary Transplant Case). This fact, I believe, would make it permissible not to save Joe, and instead to do what saves the five from disease A, only because we know that Joe's death will make it possible to deal with the new threat to the five that is a result of our dealing with the first problem they faced. Hence, it is not always impermissible to refuse to save someone because we expect to profit from his demise.

Note that the permissibility of acting in such a way in this case contrasts with the impermissibility of letting Joe die when we could save him from disease A, merely in order to acquire his organs to save the five. In the first case, we do something quite permissible (i.e., use a procedure to save five instead of one from disease A because we know that a defeater of the good consequences of this action (i.e., infection) will be defeated by an effect of our act (i.e., omitting to rescue Joe leads to the availability of his organs). In the second case, what we initially do to save the five involves deliberately refraining from helping Joe, not because helping him conflicts with doing something else that saves the five from at least one threat to them, but because we aim at Joe's death in order to help the five. In the Secondary Transplant Case, we aid the five *because* Joe will die and this will make his organs available, but we do nothing (act or omission) in order that he die as an end or means.[58] Further, suppose that once we started treating the five, it became possible to *also* give Joe another drug that can save him. We should not omit to give him this drug just because it puts in jeopardy ultimately saving the five. (This situation is in some ways like that in the Rescue Case discussed above, except that we do not cause the original threat to Joe's life as we do to the one person toward whom the trolley is redirected.)

The Secondary Transplant Case shows that there is a problem with Thomas Scanlon's claim that "[w]e all have special moral authority over our lives and bodies, and it is incompatible with this authority to allow the advantages to others of our dying sooner rather than later to count, in general, as justifying an exception to a principle" (such as one that tells us to save someone's life).[59] It is permissible to refrain from saving Joe because of the advantage of his dying even though we would save him if these advantages were not present. The Secondary Transplant Case is one of a type of case, and the type can form the basis for a general exception to a principle of saving a life. This is true, even if the advantages to others of our dying should not always be allowed to count. Put in terms of reasons for action, respect for authority over the self is offended if the fact that someone will die is what I have called a primary reason for our action. That is, it is a goal (either in the form of bringing about an end or a means) of our action. But respect for sovereignty is not always offended if the fact that someone will die is what I have called a secondary reason for our act (as when it defeats a defeater of our goal that our act produces). (Scanlon also ought not to say "intending his death, that is to say, taking the consequences of his dying sooner as considerations that justify refraining from saving him."[60] This is because "taking the consequences of his dying sooner as considerations that justify refraining from saving him" [i.e., seeing them as a justifying reason not to save him] is not, I have argued, the same as intending his death, for one can believe one's act is justified only because of its consequences without intending them.)

C. The Pain Case

A doctor has a terminally ill patient who is in terrible pain. She can give him a drug to relieve his pain. The drug has two possible foreseeable side effects. First, after it relieves the pain, it will cause the death of the patient. Second, were it not to cause the death of the patient, once the drug wore off, the pain would be as lengthy and many times worse than it was originally (Pain Case).[61] The doctor would be wrong to give the drug to her patient if it leads to much worse pain. Hence, if she gives the drug, with the patient's consent, it is *because* she believes that the drug will kill the patient *after* it provides pain relief and *before* the second effect of much worse pain can occur.

When a patient will die soon anyway, even if nothing is done, the greater good is often thought to be eliminating pain. Death is considered to be the lesser evil*. It is on these grounds that the DDE traditionally permits giving morphine to a termi- nally ill patient to stop his pain, even when it is foreseen with certainty that the morphine will shortly kill him. We may act, it says, despite the death. But the DTE says that it is permissible for the doctor to give the drug *because* the patient's death will occur, not despite its occurrence as in the DDE. According to the DTE, her behavior does not imply that she aims at the death nor that she is rationally com- mitted to seeking the patient's death (even if he consents) as a means to ending his pain or to establishing a connection between giving the drug and its causing death.[62]

The cases discussed in A, B, and C exhibit the same moral structure as the Loop Case. They involve acting because of a bad effect of one's act, and so are explicable by the DTE. In addition, they exhibit two particular features that are also present in the Loop Case: First, the bad effect defeats a defeater of a goal that would provide a sufficient reason for action. Second, they exhibit an additional feature that is intimately related to this last one, namely, the potential defeater of our goal is caused by the very act we must do to achieve our goal. As we have begun to see (in distinguishing the Party Case from the Prize Party Case and the Massacre Case from the Two Plants Case), cases explicable by the DTE (as we act because of the evil* but not intending it) need not always have these last two features.

XI. CONCLUSION

In this chapter, I have emphasized the distinction between acting in order to and acting because of. This has led to formulating the DTE and to reformulating our conception of instrumental rationality. In conclusion, I wish to note that the failure to distinguish between intending an effect and acting because of an effect might be present in legal as well as philosophical discussions. Chief Justice William Rehnquist, in *Vacco v. Quill*, 117 S.Ct. 2293 (1997), says, "The law distinguishes between actions taken because of a given end from actions taken in spite of their unintended but foreseen consequences." He here intends, I believe, to identify actions taken because of a given end with actions taken with the specific purpose (or intention) of achieving this end. Because he speaks of "end" rather than "effect," his meaning is clear. However, the law should also distinguish between actions taken because of a given effect and actions taken with the intention of achieving an end. If it does not, then it may be important to investigate the effects on legal decisions of the issues I have been discussing.

As interesting and fruitful as I find the issues and distinctions brought to the fore by the DTE, I do not think we should endorse the DTE as an adequate principle of permissible harm. One reason, as I have already suggested in discussing the Prize Party Case, is that there are acts that it incorrectly permits and cases that it does not correctly distinguish. Another reason as suggested in chapter 3, is the possible irrelevance of the agent's states or of mind or dispositions to the permissibility of an act. We will consider objections to the DTE and look further for a correct principle of permissible harm in chapter 5.

NOTES

This chapter is based on my "The Doctrine of Triple Effect and why a Rational Agent Need Not Intend the Means to His End," *Proceedings of the Aristotelian Society, 2000*, Supplement (74): 21–39, and "Why a Rational Agent Need Not Intend the Means to His End," in *From Liberal Values to Democratic Transition: Essays in Honor of JanosKis*, ed. R. W. Dworkin, pp. 15–27 (Budapest: Central European University Press, 2004).

   1. Readers who are interested only in my criticism of the standard principle of instrumental rationality and possible alternatives to it may read only section VI of this chapter.
   2. Judith Jarvis Thomson, "The Trolley Problem," in her *Rights, Restitution, and Risk* (Cambridge, MA: Harvard University Press, 1986), pp. 78–93.
   3. Note that we could push him in by directing another trolley (that is threatening no one) at him when it moves him in, rather than by our personally touching him. This too would be impermissible.
   4. I believe that the sense that it is permissible to redirect the trolley in the Loop Case need not be based on assuming that there is symmetry between the one and five, in that it would also be the five's being hit that would stop the trolley from looping around in the other direction and killing the one. To keep this point in mind, I wish to revise the Loop Case as Thomson presents it, so that there is a semipermeable brick wall behind the five. It is coated on one side, so that it would stop the trolley from looping toward the one if the five were not there, but not coated on the other side, so that if the one were not hit, the trolley would go through the wall toward the five. In my *Morality, Mortality*, vol. 2 (New York: Oxford University Press, 1996), I discussed the Prevented Return Case, in which a trolley redirected away from the five up a hill would come back down at them if it did not grind into one person. The case raises many of the same issues as the Loop Case, but it does not involve the trolley being headed toward the five even as we redirect it away from them, as does the Loop Case.
   5. When Thomson introduces the Loop Case in "The Trolley Problem," she compares it with the Transplant Case, in which we kill someone for his organs to transplant into five other people. Here is what Thomson says:

   Let us now imagine that the five on the straight track are thin, but thick enough so that although all five will be killed if the trolley goes straight, the bodies of the five will stop it, and it will therefore not reach the one. On the other hand, the one on the right-hand track is fat, so fat that his body will by itself stop the trolley, and the trolley will therefore not reach the five. May the agent redirect the trolley? . . . [W]e cannot really suppose that the presence or absence of that extra bit of track makes a major moral difference as to what an agent may do in these cases, and it really does seem right to think (despite the discomfort) that the agent may proceed.

   On the other hand, we should notice that the agent here needs the one (fat) track workman on the right-hand track if he is to save his five. If the one goes wholly out of existence just before the agent starts to redirect the trolley, then the agent cannot save his five—just as the surgeon in Transplant cannot save his five if the young man goes wholly out of existence just before the surgeon starts to operate.

Indeed, I should think that there is no plausible account of what is involved in, or what is necessary for, the application of the notions "treating a person as a means only" or "using one to save five" under which the surgeon would be doing this whereas the agent in this variant of Bystander at the Switch would not be. (p. 102)

However, if I am right, that we need not intend the involvement of the one person in the Loop Case but the surgeon does intend the involvement of the one in the Transplant Case, then either the one person in the Loop Case is not treated as a means only or else there is a plausible account of "treating a person as a means only" according to which the surgeon does and the agent in the Loop Case does not engage in such treatment.

Thomson says the following about the Loop problem in "The Trolley Problem":
There are two facts about what he does which seem to me to explain the moral difference between what he does and what the agent in Transplant would be doing if *he* proceeded. In the first place, the bystander [by the switch] saves his five by making something that threatens them threaten the one instead. Second, the bystander does not do that by means which themselves constitute an infringement of any right of the one's. (p. 103)

(Thomson repudiated this explanation in her *The Realm of Rights* [Cambridge, MA: Harvard University Press, 1990].)

I think that there are cases of permissible harming that do not satisfy these two conditions. For example, consider the Lazy Susan Case: A trolley is headed toward five people who are seated on a large swivel table. We are physically unable to redirect the trolley, but we can redirect the table so that the five are moved out of reach of the trolley. However, turning the swivel table causes it to bang into and kill a bystander who is near the table and cannot be moved. (Call this Lazy Susan Case 2, as it differs from the Lazy Susan Case presented in chapter 1, where the Lazy Susan causes a rock slide that kills a bystander.) Furthermore, imagine that the only way to turn the Lazy Susan involves our damaging (though not stopping) the out-of-control trolley, which is owned by the bystander who will be killed. (We must bounce a big rock off the trolley at an angle that releases the lock on the Lazy Susan.)

In Lazy Susan Case 2, we do *not* make something that threatens the five threaten the one instead. Rather, a new threat is created that threatens the one. (This is also true in Lazy Susan Case 1.) Arguably, we also infringe a property right of the one person in damaging his trolley. Yet it seems permissible to turn the Lazy Susan. So the two conditions that Thomson cites are not necessary for permissibly killing the bystander. Nor are they sufficient. For suppose that a bystander is on a public bridge. If we wiggle the bridge, this will cause a magnetic wave that turns the trolley away from the five. Unfortunately, the wiggling also topples the bystander off the bridge and in front of the already diverted trolley by which he is hit and killed. Though the two conditions that Thomson mentions seem to be present in this case, it is, I believe, impermissible to do what kills the bystander. So, I suggest, Thomson's earlier proposal still leaves the problem of distinguishing the Loop Case from the Transplant Case (without allowing or prohibiting too much) unresolved.

Thomson's subsequent proposal for the Trolley Problem, in her *The Realm of Rights*, would justify redirecting the trolley in the Loop Case if the following were true: It was to the advantage of each of the six—before they knew who would be among the five and who would be the one—that the trolley be redirected, even when it would not be to the advantage of the one that it be redirected when the time came for doing so. The problem is that this proposal could also justify pushing someone into the trolley to stop it in order to save the five. For example, suppose that all six were railroad workers (as Thomson imagines), and five will be assigned to work on the tracks and one to clean up the bridge over the track. It would be to the advantage of each, before they know their assignments, for someone to push the one off the bridge if this is the only way to stop the trolley from killing the other five. But this seems wrong. See my discussion of this proposal by Thomson in F. M. Kamm, "Nonconsequentialism; The Person as an End-in-Itself, and the Significance of Status," *Philosophy & Public Affairs* 21 (1992): 354–389.

6. I accept that there is a delicate distinction to be drawn between intending and aiming such that all intendings involve aimings, but not the reverse. I also accept that those who are against intending an evil should be against aiming at it even when this does not involve intending it. (I owe these points to Michael Bratman.) Hence, I shall consider aiming at an evil to violate the DDE even when it does not amount to intending. Nothing I say in this chapter, though, should depend on distinguishing intending from aiming.

7. As suggested by Warren Quinn, "Actions, Intentions, and Consequences: The Doctrine of Double Effect," in his *Morality and Action* (Cambridge: Cambridge University Press, 1993), and as discussed in more detail in chapter 3. This is a very significant revision, since one is no longer focusing on not aiming at evil per se.

8. This case, though not the following analysis, is owed to Keith DeRose.

9. The trolley need not even be coming from a different direction for there to be a new problem. We could imagine a Loop Case in which the diversion results in the trolley going in a perfect circle right back to where it was originally (A) and then heading toward the five. I still believe that it is proper to see the trolley's coming back to A and facing the five as a second problem that arises from what we did to take care of the first problem.

10. I first claimed this in *Morality, Mortality*, vol. 2.

11. I thank Sylvia, the cat at Rocco's Pastry Shop, for prompting the idea of this case.

12. *Intention* (Oxford: Blackwell, 1957).

13. In his "Morality and Consequences," in *The Tanner Lectures in Human Values*, vol. II, pp. 198–201 ed. S. McMurrin (Salt Lake City: University of Utah Press).

14. For criticism of yet another way of defining intention that is used by Judith Thomson, see below, p. 117.

15. If we do *not* decline to act in the absence of the effect, this does not necessarily show that we did *not* intend the effect, since the act may be overdetermined, that is, there may be several effects that we intend and the others would still occur and be sufficient for action. Note that the Counterfactual Test is supposed to be a test for what we strictly intend. It is not meant to deal with what some call "oblique intention," which holds that one intends what one foresees with certainty. Accepting that there is no conceptual difference between oblique intention and intention is just a way of denying the distinction that underlies the DDE and DDE(R). This seems wrong, for if I go into a bar for a drink to relax, foreseeing that I will certainly get a hangover tomorrow, this does not mean that I intended to get a hangover.

16. The Counterfactual Test would also fail to distinguish abiding by side constraints on action (that are not strictly effects of action) from intending effects (as Michael Bratman pointed out to me). For example, suppose that I will not drink some water if it would involve violating someone's right: Not violating the right is therefore a side constraint on my act. Hence, if I believed that, counterfactually, I would violate the side constraint, when all else would remain the same, I would not drink the water. According to the Counterfactual Test, this implies that I drink the water with the intention of not violating (in the sense of, in order not to violate) the side constraint. But this is wrong; it is not my aim in acting—though in a different situation it could be my aim—to do something which is an instance of not violating someone's right. My aim in acting is to quench my thirst. Rather, I take it as a condition on my acting in order to quench my thirst that I will not violate rights. Acting on condition that or because I believe that

I will not-x is not the same as acting in order to not-x. Admittedly, there may be a sense of intention other than acting "in order to." In this sense, when I refuse to do something if I will violate someone's right, it is true that I show my general background intention not to violate rights. But then my claim is that the distinction between these two senses of intention can be morally important and that it is the first sense ("in order to") with which the DDE, DDE(R), and theories of what one intends to do are concerned.

17. My counterargument shows that passing the Counterfactual Test is not sufficient for intention. It is still possible that passing this test is necessary for intention, as Peter Graham pointed out.

18. See Michael Bratman, *Intention, Plans, and Practical Reason* (Cambridge, MA: Harvard University Press, 1987), esp. chap. 10.

19. I owe this point to Lianne Young.

20. I am indebted for this point and the following case to Lianne Young.

21. Even if it is consistent to redirect the trolley and then try to rescue the one, one may ask whether it is morally permissible for anyone to rescue the one. After all, this will make things worse for the greater number. But consider an analogy: Someone being sick with serious disease A is what keeps five others from coming down with serious disease B, which is held in check by bacteria due to disease A. The five do not have a right that someone be sick with A to help them to avoid B. Now, we find a cure for disease A. It is wrong to deny someone that cure just so as to hold disease B in check in the five. Hence, it is morally permissible to rescue the one person on the side track in the Loop Case.

22. I owe the Rescue Test to Calvin and Gertrude Normore. My discussion of the Rescue Test owes much to a conversation with Calvin Normore.

23. Kristi Olson has argued that giving the extra push in the Extra Push Case and also deliberately not rescuing would redistribute a threat by means that do not infringe the right of the person on the side track. Hence they would satisfy Thomson's original proposal for the permissibility of redirecting the trolley. Nevertheless, they seem impermissible.

24. He suggested this in his comments on an earlier version of this chapter presented at the Chapel Hill Colloquium on Philosophy, October 1999. For example, he says, suppose that I know that I can only be accepted at one college, by the rules of college admission. Nevertheless, I send off applications to many colleges, aiming to win acceptance at each, though I do not intend to be accepted by many colleges, since I know that this is impossible.

25. This point bears on Michael Walzer's attempt to revise the DDE (for use in wartime). He says that the DDE will be mere sophistry if all it tells us to do is *not intend* harm to innocent noncombatants. It must be understood, he thinks, so that it also directs us to *intend not to* harm noncombatants. (See his *Just and Unjust Wars* [New York: Basic].) But if we must have this as an intention, it will rule out tactical bombing of munitions, in which we only foresee deaths, as well as terror bombing, where we intend deaths. Perhaps, Walzer means only that we must intend not to harm noncombatants to a degree that does not rule out bombing the munitions plant. For more on this view of Walzer's, see my "Failures of Just War Theory," *Ethics* 114, no. 4 (July 2004): 650–92.

26. I first attended to these distinctions between primary and secondary reasons in connection with a different principle (the Doctrine of Initial Justification [DIJ]), which I discussed in "Towards the Essence of Nonconsequentialism," in *Fact and Value: Essays on Ethics and Metaphysics for Judith Jarvis Thomson*, eds. A. Byrne, R. Stalnaker, R. Wedgwood, pp. 155–182 (Cambridge, MA: MIT Press, 2001). I discuss it again in chapter 5. It was Thomas Scanlon who made me see more clearly that these distinctions are pertinent here, too. Hence they connect the DIJ with the doctrine I will develop below based on the "because of"/"in order to" distinction, the Doctrine of Triple Effect (DTE). I say more about this in chapter 5.

27. It will turn out that it is also morally important in acting only because one will produce evil* that one have something that is *not* "produced" by the evil* but only sustained by it as a sufficient goal of action. This influences the moral standing of acting because of evil*. We shall not be able to be clearer about this until we further examine the idea of "producing" in chapter 5.

28. I discussed this issue in chapter 3 as well.

29. This makes it a case involving eliminative agency on my part, which Quinn differentiated from agency for profit. See chapter 3 on this.

30. Of course, turning the trolley in the Loop Case still differs from doing whatever needs to be done to make use of someone who will be hit, when this person will be hit because of an act we would undertake regardless of whether we would hit him. For example, suppose we knew that someone would be hit and killed as a mere side effect of what we do to save the five. We might then make plans to use his organs to save three other people. (This is ruled out neither by Quinn nor by the traditional DDE.)

31. Such as the Tractor Case discussed in chapter 5.

32. I shall discuss this issue further in chapter 5.

33. Of course, it may be wrong to try to explain the wrongness (in the sense of impermissibility) of an act by considering the agent's reasons for doing it. It may be better, in explaining the wrongness of an act, to think in terms of the "objective correlative" of a possible agent's reasons, that is, the properties of the act, its consequences or the relation between the two that an agent could point to as reasons for or against an act. This is what is attempted in chapter 5.

34. Of course, this is consistent with his giving up the end, once he sees what the means involve. The Claim can also be given a disjunctive form: An agent must either intend the necessary means or cease to intend the end.

35. For example, Kant says, "Whoever wills the end wills also (so far as reason decides his conduct) the means in his power which are indispensably necessary thereto. This proposition is, as regards the volition, analytical." Immanuel Kant, *Fundamental Principles of the Metaphysics of Morals*, trans. T. K. Abbott (Buffalo, N.Y.: Prometheus, 1990)., p. 45.

36. Christine Korsgaard, "The Normativity of Instrumental Reason," in *Ethics and Practical Reason*, ed. G. Cullity and B. Gaut, p. 215 (New York: Oxford University Press, 1997).

37. Those who believe that "intending the means" is analytic to "intending the end" do not thereby believe that "intending the means" is analytic to "the means." Without claiming that "means to his end" just are "things that the agent must intend to do or omit to do for his end," we could say: If an agent intends an end, then insofar as he is rational, he must intend some (of what are) means (i.e., things that the agent needs to do that can play a part in bringing about his end). I discuss this possibility in the text below, concluding that perhaps it would be better to say that the agent must be *willing to intend* such means.

38. John Broome (in his "Normative Requirements," a paper presented at the Conference on Moral Theory, L Lavandou, France, June 1999, p. 7) claimed that it is correct reasoning to derive the intention of fetching the corkscrew from your existing intention to open the wine and your belief that in order to open the wine, you must fetch the corkscrew. What I have said denies this. His argument for his claim is based on a comparison with theoretical reasoning: Suppose I believe that "Frances will open the wine," and that "in order for Frances to open the wine, Frances must fetch the corkscrew." Insofar as I am rational, I will then believe that "Frances will fetch the corkscrew." This is because the conclusion is derivable from the premises, and insofar as I am rational and I have the attitude of belief toward the premises, I should have the attitude of belief toward the conclusion. I agree with this. But Broome goes on to claim:

> The difference between the theoretical and practical reasoning is not in the propositions that constitute their content, but in the attitude you take toward these propositions. . . .

Because the conclusion is true if the premises are true; you cannot rationally set your-self (if you are Frances) to make the first premise true, and take the second as true without setting yourself to make the conclusion true. Your attitude toward the premises norma-tively requires you to set yourself to make the conclusion true. It requires you to intend it. ("Normative Requirements," p. 7)

Broome moves between using "setting yourself to" and "intending," but I think that this makes no real difference if what I have argued is correct. For the following is an implication of what I have argued: The fact that in Broome's case, if the premises are true, the conclu-sion must be true does not necessarily determine that a rational agent, insofar as he is ratio-nal, must have the same attitude toward the conclusion that he has toward the first premise. I do not have to intend, or set myself, to make the conclusion true, though I intend or set myself to make the first premise true and I believe the second premise, so long as I believe that I will make the conclusion true, even without intending, or setting myself, to make it true. For ex-ample, suppose I believe that I will, as a side effect of bringing in a tray of dessert, bring in a corkscrew that you have placed on it. Then I need not intend to bring in the corkscrew—indeed, I might refuse to make any even minimal extra effort necessary to get a corkscrew, believing it wrong to aim to get a corkscrew—consistent with my intending to open the wine and my belief that having the corkscrew is necessary for this.

39. I say "perhaps" because one might imagine that means z will come about without one intending it, but another means to bringing about one's goal just is intending means z (even though intending means z is not a means to bringing about means z.)

40. I will suggest in the text below an even more substantial revision of the DDE and DDE(R), i.e., that a greater good that is unintended can justify a lesser evil*.

41. In discussing the second of these cases, I shall not object to the DDE's and DDE(R)'s claim that it is permissible for a means that is not itself a greater good to cause a lesser evil* as a side effect, so long as the goal is a greater good. I do question the correctness of this aspect of these doctrines in my *Morality, Mortality*, vol. 2 (New York: Oxford University Press, 1996); in "Toward the Essence of Nonconsequentialism," in *Fact and Value: Essays for Judith Thomson*, ed. A. Byrne et al., pp. 155–182 (Cambridge, MA: MIT Press, 2001); and in chapters 1 and 5, this volume.

42. This particular case was first put to me for consideration by Thomas Nagel in 1999. I discuss similar cases in my *Morality, Mortality*, vol. 2.

43. This does not mean that I think that there is no objection to bombing in this case. One way to show that the DDE and DDE(R) are not adequate as principles of permissible conduct is to show that we do not intend the children's deaths and yet the bombing is wrong because of these side-effect deaths. I consider such an objection to the DDE in my "Failures of Just War Theory," and in this volume in chapters 1 and 5.

44. This case differs from one in which a rational agent causes, but need not intend, an evil* that is a means to his end, when that means is necessary to produce an end whose existence is *not* needed (and is even unable) to justify bringing about the evil*. For example, suppose I may permissibly cause a child's death as a side effect of achieving my end of bombing a muni-tions plant. I may have *another* end, that is, making the child's parents, who are the aggres-sors, miserable. I achieve this end by causing the child's death as a side effect. This is an instance of making good use of an evil* that will come about anyway and whose existence is (supposedly) already justified by some other end (bombing the munitions plant). See also n. 30.

45. Christine Korsgaard, "The Normativity of Instrumental Reason." All subsequent page citations to this article will be noted parenthetically in the text.

46. This also is puzzling for it is not true that causing to realize the end by itself requires willing its realization.

47. I owe this case to Michael Bratman and Gideon Jaffe.

48. I first discussed them in *Morality, Mortality,* vol. 2.

49. This discussion of the Double Track and Tree Trolley cases is introductory, as more details would be unnecessarily distracting at this point. For more on this issue, see chapter 5.

50. This, I believe, is the standard way in which the DDE is presented. Different philosophers, without drawing attention to the fact that they were doing this, have described the DDE differently from each other with respect to whether we are to intend the greater good. The traditional rendition requires aiming at a good that is greater than the evil side effect (and not just at any good). Here are three sample renditions: (1) "The agent acts with a good intention and seeks to realize a good end. . . . [T]he good end that the agent seeks to realize is not morally disproportionate to the bad consequence" (Nancy Davis, "The Doctrine of Double Effect: Problems of Interpretation," in *Ethics: Problems and Principles,* ed. J. Fischer and M. Ravissa [Fort Worth, TX: Harcourt Brace Jovanovich, 1992]), p. 201; (2) "(a) the intended final end must be good . . . and (d) the good end must be proportionate to the bad upshot" (Warren Quinn, "Actions, Intentions, and Consequences: The Doctrine of Double Effect," in Quinn, *Morality and Action),* p. 175; and (3) "the licit effect is the intended effect" (Baruch Brody, "Religion and Bioethics," in *A Companion to Bioethics,* ed. Helga Kuhse and Peter Singer, p. 44 [Oxford: Blackwell, 1998]). In (3), Brody is pointing to the fact that the intention/foresight distinction in the DDE's account of permissibility is meant to distinguish the two effects—the good one, which is intended, and the bad one, which is foreseen. If this is the correct way of understanding the "double effect" point of the DDE, then the doctrine does not so much distinguish intending a bad effect from foreseeing a bad effect, as it distinguishes intending a good effect from foreseeing a bad one. If this is so, and the good must be proportionate to the bad, this implies that according to the DDE we must intend the good.

One account of the DDE that does not point to an intended good says that the conditions that are to be met in order to permissibly produce a bad effect include: "(1) one's action also had a good effect . . . and (4) the good effect was important enough to outweigh the bad" (Robert Audi, ed., *Cambridge Dictionary of Philosophy,* s.v. "doctrine of double effect" [Cambridge: Cambridge University Press, 1995]). This entry also requires that one "did not produce the good effect through the bad," in addition to "not seeking the bad effect as an end or means." However, I have argued, the DDE does not require that the good that justifies the bad did not come about through the bad, only that we not intend that it do so. (See discussion of the Track Trolley Case, p. 93.) This version of the DDE, which I think is unrepresentative and inaccurate, only says that a greater good need occur; it is not necessary that the agent intend it. Of course, this account also does not state that the act could be permissible only if one acts *because* there was (expected to be) a greater good. For it is quite possible, according to this account, that one would have been willing to act even if a greater good would not have occurred, and yet one's act might still be permissible because a good greater than the bad side effect did in fact occur. Further, even if a nonstandard version of the DDE required that we *expect* a good effect that is great enough to outweigh the bad, this state of mind is not the same as acting *because of* that expectation. We might act, expecting a greater good, even if we would have acted without the expectation and so did not act because of it. (According to the nonstandard version of the DDE we are now examining, such an act might still be permissible.) This nonstandard account represents the DDE as a principle that makes no reference to the agent's intention for good. While such a principle may be correct, I do not think that it is the DDE.

51. For example, suppose that I want to achieve a small good of saving one friend about whom I care, but a side effect of doing this is that two strangers will be killed. My act would not be justified. Therefore, I seek a means of saving my friend that requires me to also save four other people. I intend this greater good merely as a means to saving my friend. This may

satisfy the DDE and DDE(R), because I do intend the greater good, but it is unlike standard ways of satisfying the DDE and DDE(R), because I intend the greater good not for its own sake but merely as a means so that I can accomplish another good that is insufficient to justify the lesser evil* of killing two people.

52. In the context of a contractualist theory such as the one that Thomas Scanlon lays out in his *What We Owe to Each Other* (Cambridge, MA: Harvard University Press, 1999), it is good to remember the difference between our having an interest in our act being justifiable to others and our having an interest in that which justifies the act, and the difference between the requirement that our act be justifiable to others and the requirement that we have an interest in that which justifies the act.

53. In her "Physician-Assisted Suicide: Two Moral Arguments," *Ethics* (1998): 512.

54. Of course, acting because of the greater good is still stronger than merely acting with foresight of it, and it might be suggested that the latter rather than the former is necessary for an agent to act permissibly when he will cause evil*.

55. Thomas Hurka suggested this name.

56. First presented in *Morality, Mortality*, vol. 2, and also discussed in my "Justifications for Killing Noncombatants in War," *Midwest Studies in Philosophy* 24 (2000): 219–28.

57. This case can be distinguished from a case where the threat to the success of our bombing mission is not a response to it (i.e., to rebuild) but the continuing functioning of another munitions plant and the deaths we cause interfere with the functioning of the other plant (Two Plants Case). (The latter case has a structure similar to that of the Munitions and Civilians Case and Prize Party Case discussed in this chapter and to the Tractor Case to be discussed in chapter 5.) I discuss the possible moral difference between actions in these two cases in my "Justifications for Killing Noncombatants in War" and will discuss the issue again in chapter 5.

58. The Secondary Transplant Case also differs morally, I believe, from a case in which we save the five because we know Joe's organs will be available to save them from a fatal infection that they have quite independently of our trying to save them. This case has the structure of the Prize Party Case and Tractor Case (that I discuss in chapter 5). More on this in chapter 5.

59. See his "Moral Assessment and the Agent's Point of View" (unpublished), p. 12, and his "Permissibility and Intention I," *Proceedings of the Aristotelian Society* Suppl. 74 (2000): 301–17. Scanlon himself recognizes that the Loop Case presents a problem for his view.

60. "Moral Assessment and the Agent's Point of View," p. 13.

61. I first discussed this case in "Physician-Assisted Suicide, Euthanasia, and Intending Death," in *Physician-Assisted Suicide: Expanding the Debate*, ed. M. Battin, R. Rhodes, and A. Silvers, pp. 28–62 (New York: Routledge, 1998).

62. However, if pain relief in someone who will die soon is a greater good and death is a lesser (or imminent) evil*, I believe that we can construct an argument for intentionally killing a terminally ill patient who is in much pain (with his consent). See, for example, my "A Right to Choose Death?" *Boston Review* 22 (1997): 20–23 (that expands on an argument briefly presented earlier in my *Creation and Abortion* [New York: Oxford University Press (1992)]).

5

TOWARD THE ESSENCE OF NONCONSEQUENTIALIST CONSTRAINTS ON HARMING

Modality, Productive Purity, and the Greater Good Working Itself Out

I. INTRODUCTION

In this chapter, I shall provide a much fuller account than I have provided in previous chapters of the nonconsequentialist constraint on harming (roughly) innocent, nonthreatening persons who would not otherwise be harmed, for whom further life is a good, and who have not consented to be harmed.[1] I begin by reexamining principles (taken to include doctrines) that have previously been proposed (and discussed in earlier chapters) to prohibit harming such people. I consider objections to these principles, ways to revise them, and objections to the revisions. I then develop the Doctrine of Initial Justification and an improvement on it, the Doctrine of Productive Purity, that reveal certain crucial distinctions between permissible and impermissible harm. I shall be engaging in a quasi-technical, intricate enterprise in drawing these distinctions more precisely.[2] In conclusion, I consider a practical application of the new principle, and exceptions to it, as well as the relevance of our discussion to the problem of innocent threats.

II. PRINCIPLES AND PROBLEMS

When may we significantly harm, without their consent, innocent, nonthreatening people who would not otherwise be comparably harmed, for whom further life is a good, and who have not consented to be harmed? In order to answer this question, let us begin by reexamining the Transplant Case. In this case, five people can be saved from dying of organ failure only if we kill one person to get his organs. The one person fits our description of an innocent, nonthreatening person, who is himself neither under any grave threat nor responsible for the problems of the five. Act consequentialists say that killing the one is permissible, given that there are no additional overriding bad consequences. Nonconsequentialists say that it is not permissible. Among the reasons that the latter have offered for the act's impermissibility is the priority of not-harming over aiding: We would harm the one if we kill him, but only not-aid the five if we did not give them the organs. Another reason that nonconsequentialists have given is the priority of not intending harm over merely foreseeing harm: We would intend harm to the one if we kill him, but only foresee harm to the five if we did not aid them. Some supporters of this intention/foresight distinction support the Doctrine of Double Effect (DDE). According to it, we may not intend evil as a means to a greater good nor as an end in itself, but if we pursue a greater good as an end by neutral or good means, a lesser evil that is a certain, foreseen side effect does not rule out our acting (as long as there is no other better way to achieve the greater good).[3]

Problems can be raised for the moral significance of both the harming/not-aiding distinction and the intending/foreseeing distinction, as we have seen. First, consider problems for the former:

a. In the Trolley Case, a trolley is headed toward killing five people, but a bystander can save them (only) by redirecting the trolley. However, if redirected, the trolley will go off in a direction where it will definitely kill one person. Typically, nonconsequentialists think that it is permissible (though not obligatory) to divert the trolley, even though this involves harming one in order to aid others.[4] This case suggests that not-harming does *not* always have priority over aiding.

b. In another case, five people are dying of organ failure. If we let one person who is suffering from pneumonia die by not giving him the easily provided penicillin he needs to be cured, we can use his organs to save the five (Penicillin Case). It seems impermissible to do this, even though it involves letting him die rather than harming him. Thus, the prohibition against harming does not exhaust the reasons that some acts are impermissible.

Now, consider problems for the moral significance of the intention/foresight distinction:

c. Suppose that a doctor is called and told that organs—innocently acquired—have arrived and must be transplanted quickly into his five patients. He drives to the hospital but on the road finds an immovable person in his path. If he takes a different route, he will be too late to do the transplants, and as he is the only one who can do them, the five will die. If he runs over the person on the road, he foresees, but does not intend, the death of the one and he knows that if he gets to the hospital, he will save the five (Car Case). It seems impermissible for him to proceed on this route, even though he does not intend to hit and kill the one person, and the greater good of saving the five would result.[5] In this case, the driver does intend to go over a spot in the road where the person is located. We could, however, imagine a variant where this is not so: Everything is as it is in the Car Case, except that no person is on the road. Instead, the driver can see that there is a puddle of deadly acid spilled on the road. If he drives through it, he knows that this will cause the acid to splash on and kill an immovable bystander at the side of the road (Splash Case). It seems impermissible for him to proceed on this route. Both the Car Case and the Splash Case reveal that the fact that we would cause lesser harms that are merely foreseen could rule out pursuing a greater good.

d. Consider again the Trolley Case. Suppose that it is a bad person who sees the trolley headed toward the five. He has no interest in saving the five per se, but he knows that it is his enemy who will be the one person killed if he redirects the trolley. He does not want to be accused of acting impermissibly, however, and so while he redirects the trolley in order to kill the one, he does so only *because* he believes that (i.e., on condition that) a greater good will balance out the death. Hence, he would not turn the trolley unless he expected the five to be saved (Bad Man Case). His redirecting the trolley is still permissible, I believe, though he does it in order to kill his enemy. This raises doubt about the correctness of principles such as the DDE, if they determine that an act is impermissible on the basis of the presence of bad intentions in the agent.[6]

e. Notice also that, in the Bad Man Case, the agent does *not* intend that the five be saved. He allows himself to act only because he believes that (i.e., on condition that) the greater good will outbalance the lesser evil, but he does not act with the ultimate aim of producing that greater good.[7] It is permissible, I believe, to redirect the trolley in the Bad Man Case, even though the agent does not aim at the greater good. (The same would be true if someone just wanted to redirect the trolley on a whim [and so had no intrinsically bad intention to kill his enemy], but allowed himself to act on the whim only because a greater good would outbalance the evil of the death.) But the DDE suggests that a lesser evil as a side effect does not rule out action *only if* we intend a greater good.[8]

f. Finally, as an objection to the DDE, it has been suggested that in many cases where an action is impermissible and the DDE tries to explain the impermissibility, we need not be intending harm, strictly speaking. We may have a much narrower intention. For example, although we must intend the removal of the organs in the Transplant Case, we need not intend the death or any other harm to the person, because if he survives the removal of his organs and is able to live well without his organs, this would not interfere with our saving the five. Of course, we foresee he will not survive and live well, but that does not mean that we intend that he not survive and live well.

III. THE DOCTRINE OF TRIPLE EFFECT

A great deal of contemporary nonconsequentialism has been concerned with revising moral principles that employ the harming/not-aiding distinction and/or the intending/foreseeing distinction in order to meet objections (a), (b), (c), and (f). Possibly objections (d) and (e) are newer. Let us first consider changes that might be made to a principle involving the intention/foresight distinction so that it can meet some of the objections to it. (We shall consider objections in reverse order from their presentation.)

In order to deal with the narrowness of the intention involved in objection (f), Warren Quinn suggested that we focus on the wrongness of intending the involvement of a person without his consent whether we intend or merely foresee that this involvement will lead to significant evil for him (e.g., harm to him).[9] This suggestion keeps us from focusing on the wrongness of intending the evil (e.g., harm to him), as the DDE has us do. Let us say (as we said in chapter 4) that Quinn's revision results in the DDE Revised (DDE[R]). When discussing the DDE(R), I shall (as in chapter 4) use evil* to mean "evil or involvement of a person without his consent when foreseeably this will lead to an evil to him."[10]

One way to deal with objection (e) (that is, not intending a greater good) is to revise the DDE or the DDE(R) so that the fact that one acts merely because one believes that a good greater than the evil* will occur, even if that greater good is not intended as an end (or even as a means), does not stand in the way of the act's permissibility. We can also distinguish between acting to produce a greater good while intending an evil* (as an end or means) and acting to produce a greater good because we expect to produce an evil*. Hence, even if intending an evil* is wrong (and even if, contrary to what the Bad Man Case suggests, it could make acts impermissible), acting because one believes that one will produce evil* may be neither wrong nor a ground for impermissibility of the act. On account of this third relation we can have to an effect, I have described the Doctrine of Triple Effect (DTE): A greater good that we cause and whose expected existence is a condition of our action, but which we do not necessarily intend, may justify a lesser evil* that we must not intend but the expectation of which we may have as a condition of action.[11] The DTE does not involve rejecting that part of the DDE and the DDE(R) that claims bad intentions make acts impermissible. It tries to distinguish carefully the cases where there are bad intentions.

I have argued that the DTE may help us with another version of the Trolley Case, known as the Loop Case, introduced by Judith Thomson.[12] Recall that in this case, the trolley is headed toward killing five people and can be redirected to a side track, but that side track loops around back toward the five. The trolley would kill the five from this other direction, but for the fact that there is one person on the side track toward whom we redirect the trolley and whose being hit by the trolley stops it from looping toward the five. In this case, one person being hit is causally necessary to the trolley stopping. I assume that we would not redirect the trolley unless we thought that the one would (with some probability up to certainty) be hit, for (let us suppose that) redirecting takes much effort and there would be no point in doing it if the five would shortly be killed anyway by the looping trolley. Does this mean that we intend to hit the one person, and thus that redirecting the trolley in the Loop Case violates the DDE or DDE(R) on account of our intending the hit that kills him?

I have suggested no to both parts of this question. To support these claims, I have tried to make clear how I (intuitively) see the structure of the Loop Case. The only threat that faces the five that prompts our act to help save them initially is the trolley heading toward them from one direction. This is the first problem. If this problem is not taken care of, they will die; to save them, it must be taken care of whatever else we do, though this does not mean that taking care of it is sufficient to save them. The problem that would exist (if the one on the side track were not there) of the trolley coming at the five again, from a somewhat different direction, *only arises* because we turn the trolley away from the five. I maintain that in re-directing the trolley in the Loop Case, we have created a new problem (the trolley redirected toward the one and, potentially, toward the five).[13]

A proponent of the DTE could argue that redirecting the trolley in the Loop Case is permissible for the following reasons: We redirect the trolley in order to save the five. To save the five, we must, at least, remove from them the only threat that faces them when we are prompted to act, that is, the trolley headed toward their front. We do this only because we believe that they will not die soon from another problem anyway, because we believe that the one person will be hit as a side effect of turning the trolley, thereby stopping the trolley. Because these other things will happen, the five will be saved from all threats. *This* makes redirecting the trolley in order to save them from the first problem it presents worth doing, but this is different from its being worth doing in order to hit the one. Although the ex-pectation of hitting the one as a side effect and the nonlooping of the trolley are conditions of our action, this does not mean that we redirect the trolley even in part *in order to* hit the one or even in part *in order to* stop the trolley from looping. (It even seems odd to say that we redirect the trolley in order to stop it from looping; this is because the threat of the trolley looping only arises because we redirect the trolley. However, I do not claim that this oddity of speech is definitive.)

As support for the claim that a rational agent who redirects the trolley because it will hit the one need not thereby have intended the hit, it might be argued that he need not be committed to doing anything extra (not in itself objectionable) in order to get the trolley to hit the one. For example, suppose that an extra push is not necessary to redirect the trolley from its original direction, but without it the trolley would jump *over* the one and head toward the five again. This is because it must hit the one if its jump is to be prevented (Extra Push Case). Unlike a person who aims at the hit as a means of saving the five, the agent I have in mind need not be committed to giving this extra push. (However, it is possible that there is something objectionable about giving an extra push in itself independent of in-tention. We shall consider this below.) Furthermore, he might even, consistent with redirecting the trolley because he believes that the one will be hit, try to rescue the one if this became possible rather than omit the rescue in order that the one be hit. The reasoning of an agent who does these things might be as follows: I may redirect the trolley so long as I am not aiming at hitting the one; I need not aim at *not* hitting him. I must not refuse to rescue the one if my only reason for not rescuing him would be that I aim at his being hit as a means to saving the five. But I might actually fail in my rescue or no rescue may be possible, and so long as this is true, it still makes sense to redirect the trolley, for then five will be saved (Rescue Case).[14]

We have been dealing with an implication of one way of meeting objection (e)—not intending the greater good does not rule out permissibility—to the DDE and DDE(R). Let us return now to how we might deal with objection (d) (as exhibited in the Bad Man Case). Perhaps we could rephrase the DDE or the DDE(R) so that it requires that we not do an act that *could only rationally have been done* by someone who intends evil*. Then acts (such as redirecting the trolley from five toward one) that could have been done by someone who does not intend evil* would be permissible, even when done by someone with an improper intention. This would imply that there is what I call a Principle of Alternate Reason, that is, when factors are present that could justify an act (or omission), and hence could be part of the justification of a rational agent, doing the act for an alternate reason is permissible, even when the reason does not point to factors that justify the act.

However, this revision suggests that what is important for permissibility are the characteristics of the act itself and its effects (or how they are related), as these are what make it possible for us to decide that a rational agent could have reasons to do the act without intending evil*. It is not that there need be no intention of evil* per se that matters for permissibility. Hence, this response to the objection just further reinforces the view that it is a mistake to try to find the source of the permissibility status of an act in the intention of the agent or a possible agent. When it is impermissible for an agent who intends evil* (as a means or end) to do an act, it will usually be because of some characteristics of the act or its effects (or their relation) independent of his intention.[15]

Objection (d) implies that revisions such as Quinn's that lead to the DDE(R) are misguided in that they still accept that a fundamental ground for the permissibility status of an act is the intention of the agent. Further, objection (d) can be raised to all "state-of-mind" principles. The DTE, used to respond to objection (e), like the DDE(R), is a state-of-mind principle. That is, it attempts to derive the permissibility of an act from the state of mind or dispositions of someone who does it. For example, suppose the bad person who redirects the trolley away from the five would have redirected it toward his enemy even if (counterfactually) the five had not been there. Then his behavior does not satisfy the DTE even when the five are there; this is because he does not redirect because, or on condition that, the five will be saved. Yet, I believe, contrary to what the DTE implies, that his act of redirecting the trolley when the five are there is still permissible.

As with the DDE and DDE(R), one might try to remedy this problem by revising the DTE so that it rules out acts that could *only* have been done by a rational agent who does not meet its requirements. For example, no such agent could have acted because of the greater good. Then acts that could rationally have been done because of the greater good will be permissible even if they are not actually done because of the greater good. However, this revision suggests that it is the characteristics of the act, its effects (it saves the five), or how they are related, not the state of mind or dispositions of the agent, that are important for permissibility or impermissibility. It is these facts that make it possible for a rational agent to act because they are present.

Despite this criticism of the DTE, we might still argue that the "because of" versus "in order to (or intending)" distinction is morally important. However, this will be because when acting "because one will produce evil*" is permissible and acting "in order to produce evil*" is not, the distinction in attitude will correspond to a distinction in the properties of the act, its effect, or the relation between them. That is, there will be an "objective correlative that accounts for permissibility or impermissibility." (I shall say more about this below.)

IV. OTHER POSSIBLE PROBLEMS WITH THE DTE

A second clear problem for the DTE is that, like the DDE(R), it would not rule out the doctor driving over the person in the Car Case and through the spill in the Splash Case, since it does not rule out a means to a greater good just because it has a lesser evil* as a mere side effect. This was objection (c).

A third problem is that there might be other cases in which the DTE gives the wrong results. Consider again the Double Track Case (introduced in chapter 4). The trolley is headed toward killing the five. We can redirect it onto track A, where it will loop back to kill the five because no one is on the track to stop the trolley, or onto track B, where one person being hit will stop the looping. One possible way to look at this case is that one has an *extra choice* to make between the two tracks that one did not have in the Loop Case. Everything one must do only to get the trolley away from its first hit on the five would be done if one redirected the trolley onto track A as well as onto B, but there would be no point in going onto A since the five would die from the redirected trolley. If one *picks* track B over A, is one not doing it in order to prevent the looping? Is one also, in part, aiming at hitting the one? If so, the DTE would say that one should not redirect the trolley at all in the Double Track Case. This seems puzzling, because it means that an irrelevant alternative (turning to track A) is ruling out something we would otherwise do if A were not there, namely, turn the trolley to B.

Of course (it was argued in chapter 4), the DTE also has the striking implication that a rational agent, insofar as he is rational, can intend a goal (i.e., not looping) without intending the means to it, when the means will be a side effect of something else he does (i.e., turning the trolley away from its first hit on the five). Hence, turning to track B could be done in order to accomplish the goal of not-looping that turning to A does not accomplish, without our also having to have the (intermediate) goal of hitting someone. This is one possible explanation of why someone who would choose track B could still reasonably refuse to do anything extra, if it were necessary just to hit the one, when his being hit is the only way of stopping the trolley from jumping over him, and then looping to the five.[16]

A still more accurate perspective on this case, I believe, shows us that the agent need not intend the not-looping in sending the trolley to B, only in not sending the trolley to A.[17] To begin with, recognizing that the trolley will hit the five unless something is done, the agent considers whether he should turn it to A. He intends that the trolley not loop to the five via A, as well as not continue in its original direction, however. The way to accomplish both of these aims is to send the trolley to B. He can do this without *intending* that the trolley not loop around B, but only because he knows it will not loop around B.[18]

Hence, turning the trolley to track B in the Double Track Case is not ruled out by the DTE after all. A more likely problem for the DTE is that it may fail to distinguish between the permissibility of redirecting the trolley in the Loop Case and (what I believe is) the impermissibility of redirecting the trolley in the following Tractor Case: The trolley is headed toward killing the five. It can be redirected and there is no way for it to loop back. However, there is another threat, a deadly tractor, also headed toward killing the five shortly. There is no point in making the big effort to turn the trolley if the five will then be hit by the tractor anyway. However, we know that if we redirect the trolley, it will gently hit and push (without hurting) one person into the path of the tractor. His being hit by the tractor stops it but also kills him. In this case, is it possible to say: We redirected the trolley in order to stop it from hitting the five from the first direction only because we knew that the one person would be pushed into the tractor and so stop it, but we did not redirect the trolley (even in part) in order to push him into the tractor?[19] If this were possible, then the DTE would not rule out redirecting the trolley in the Tractor Case. However, I believe that this act is impermissible. The Tractor Case and the Loop Case are I believe, morally different, and the DTE may not be able to explain this.

Staying within the terms of the DTE and its state-of-mind vocabulary and using the idea of primary and secondary reasons (introduced in chapter 4), let me say why I believe these cases are different. (This should also become clearer as a result of later discussion.) In the Tractor Case, a foreseen bad effect of our act will help us to achieve another goal besides keeping the trolley away from the five and dealing with any new problem that arises because of what we did to deal with the initial problem presented by the trolley. That is, it stops the tractor, a threat that is present independent of what we do to stop the trolley. If we did not set ourselves to achieve both goals, of keeping the trolley away and stopping the tractor, we would not have a sufficient *primary* reason to act. That is, we would not have a *goal* that was sufficient to justify action. (I include as a possible primary reason the goal of achieving the means to one's final goal.) By contrast, the bad effect of redirecting the trolley in the Loop Case just counteracts a new threat (the looping) that arose from our redirecting and that could undermine the achievement of the one goal that was a sufficient primary reason for our act (i.e., getting rid of the trolley threat that faced the five when we were called on to act). That the bad effect of redirection will defeat potential defeaters of our goal gives us a *secondary*, not a primary, reason to act. This is because defeating a defeater is not a goal of our acting, it is a condition of our acting. The permissibility of acting because of an act's bad effect seems to be related to already having a sufficient primary (goal) reason for action whose achievement is not produced by those bad effects, where "not produced" is consistent with the goal's achievement being sustained by those bad effects as they defeat potential defeaters of it. (I shall discuss the distinction between "produced" and "sustained" further below.)[20]

The DTE reminds us, however, that even if we act in order to achieve an additional goal that is produced by the bad effects, we need not intend the bad effects, because we will bring them about as a side effect of something else we do. So even if we act in part in order to remove the tractor threat, the DTE may allow redirecting the trolley in the Tractor Case because we do not intend the evil*. But if redirecting in the Tractor Case is not permissible—even if it does not involve intending evil*—this would show that only a subclass of cases in which we act (merely) because we will produce an evil* involves permissible acts. This provides another reason why the DTE is incomplete as a principle of permissible harm. The Tractor Case would also show that how we bring it about that evil* to someone is a means to our goal is not completely definitive as to whether he is treated permissibly or not. For we bring about evil* in the same way in the Loop and Tractor Cases, yet it also seems to matter whether evil* plays a sustaining or producing role relative to our goal.

V. TOWARD THE ESSENCE OF NONCONSEQUENTIALIST CONSTRAINTS ON HARMING

Given the problems with the simple harming/not-aiding distinction, the DDE, and the DTE, let us now try to inch our way by steps toward an alternative theory that may fare better. In a nutshell, this alternative theory is a variation on a downstream theory.[21] *Downstream theories* claim that lesser evil* must come downstream causally from the greater good. The alternative theory I will present, however, is different from a simple downstream theory, so it is only "downstreamish." It is merely downstreamish in two major ways: (a) in its understanding of what is necessary in order for evil* to be downstream, and (b) in the possibility that some evils* do not have to be downstream. This theory is intended to apply only to cases in which we will harm innocent, nonconsenting persons, for whom continued life would be a benefit, who are not threats or parts of threats, and who would not otherwise be comparably harmed. I believe that this theory can be represented as a non-state-of-mind theory, unlike the DDE, the DDE(R) and the DTE. That is, it neither rules out nor requires certain states of mind, or dispositions, such as intending evil or acting because of good, if acts are to be permissible or impermissible.[22] I believe that we can discover the key components of this theory by considering intuitive responses to cases and trying to explain their underlying deep structures. However, rather than strictly follow the order of discovery, in this section I shall propose components of the theory followed by a discussion of cases in which intuitions can be accounted for by that component and cases in which intuitions call for further refinements of the theory. Then, I shall offer a principle that captures the components. Finally, I shall consider what deeper ideas may underlie the principle and whether these ideas also figure in our idea of respect for persons.

A. The first thing we can show on the basis of intuitive judgments about cases is that it is permissible for a greater good already achieved to lead to a lesser evil*. Then the good that justifies the lesser evil* leads to it. For example, suppose that the trolley is headed toward five people for whom continued life is a good—an assumption I shall continue to make unless stated otherwise—and though we cannot redirect the trolley, we can move the five. Unfortunately, we know that we can only move them to land that is loosely packed and that their presence in this previously threat-free area will cause a landslide. We know that this landslide will kill one person below (Landslide Case). Intuitively, I believe that it is permissible to move the five, thereby causing the lesser evil*. It is permissible to aid the five even though our success causes harm. This is accounted for by the permissibility of the greater good (the five being saved) causing the lesser evil*.[23]

Suppose that when we move the five people away from the trolley, they themselves unavoidably tumble down the mountain and their bodyweight presents a lethal threat to the one person below (Tumble Case). We have here, I believe, generated a new variant on the sort of case that is often discussed by philosophers as "innocent threat" cases. (A famous early example is Robert Nozick's case of a morally innocent man fired out of a cannon who will land on another person killing him without himself being injured, unless the potential victim kills the threat.[24]) Standard innocent threat cases involve either a villain or a natural event endangering (or at least not improving the condition of) the innocent threat, endangering the potential victim of the threat, and producing a state of affairs—of the innocent threat imposing on the victim—that is not morally appropriate. But in our case a morally permissible act results in the improvement of the condition of those who become innocent threats, and the state of affairs of the innocent threat imposing on the victim is the preferred state and morally appropriate, in the sense that it constitutes the greater good causing the lesser evil*. Hence, the Tumble Case shows that it is permissible to turn five people into innocent threats to another person when this results from saving the five from some threat to them.

One focus of discussions about standard innocent threat cases is whether the person who is a threat has a responsibility to stop himself from threatening someone else, though he was not responsible for being a threat. Another focus of discussions is whether a person threatened with death may permissibly respond by harming the innocent threat who is not responsible for being a threat.[25]

With respect to the second focus, our case of the five tumbling down on the one could raise the same question about the victim's self defense but in a context where the person threatened would, in defending himself, eliminate a greater good. This is because he might have to kill the five people who threaten him as a result of their being saved from a threat to themselves.

With respect to the first focus, our case is especially interesting. For if it is permissible to move five people away from a threat to them despite the foreseen harm to another, why should the five be responsible for stopping themselves from being such a threat to another, if the cost of doing this is equivalent to what they would have suffered due to the trolley from which it was permissible to save them?

Furthermore, the Tumble Case raises new questions about responsibility. For suppose that there was no bystanding agent in the Trolley Case, but the five people could effect their own escape. For example, suppose that while they could not redirect the trolley, they could jump off the track and thus either start the landslide or begin tumbling down the mountain, threatening one person. If a bystanding agent could permissibly produce the greater good though it causes lesser evil*, the five may do this as well. They may not have disinterested motives, as a bystanding agent may have, but this does not make their act of producing the greater good impermissible. Hence, in addition to inquiring into whether one person may defend himself by attacking nonresponsible innocent threats, we can also inquire whether he may defend himself by attacking innocent threats who are responsible for permissibly becoming threats to him.

I will put off discussing the issue of whether and how a person threatened by the greater good may respond, in order to first discuss other cases where we may permissibly threaten others. Then we can discuss the possible responses of those threatened in all these different types of cases together.[26] The reason for raising this issue now is to show the connection between principles of permissible harm suggested by the Trolley Problem and the topic of innocent threats.[27]

If *only* a greater good may permissibly cause a lesser evil*, a principle of our morality would be that *the good that justifies the evil* should cause it.*[28] (Morally neutral acts that cause the greater good, which in turn causes the lesser evil*, are, of course, permitted.) This would be a strong version of nonconsequentialism, since the good is not allowed to be a causal consequence of evil* nor of means having evil* as a side effect. Nonconsequentialism is usually understood minimally as the denial that all that matters to the rightness or wrongness of acts is the goodness of the consequences of the acts. (It also denies that all that matters is the state of affairs produced, including *the act itself* and its consequences. For example, it claims that an act of killing A that will prevent more acts of killing B, C, and D may be impermissible, even if the state of affairs that would result, including that act and its consequences, would be better than the state of affairs without that act and its consequences.) Nonconsequentialism is typically described as focusing on *how* the greater good comes about; certain ways of bringing it about are wrong. (A) also shows that nonconsequentialism is concerned with the ways in which evil* can come about. If it were a requirement that the good that justifies an evil* cause the evil*, nonconsequentialism would involve a downstream principle, in that any evil* which must occur would have to be causally subsequent to the greater good.

B.i. We can go further, however. Although a greater good may permissibly cause, or lead to events that cause, lesser evil*, it is permissible that evil* come about in other ways. *Means that have a greater good as (what I will call) a noncausal flip side or aspect may permissibly cause, or lead to events that cause, a lesser evil*.* By "noncausal," I mean something tighter than causation—sometimes identity, sometimes constitution. Hence, on the view I am presenting, not all means to a greater good *cause* that greater good, as they can have a noncausal relation to it. Another way of putting this addition to (A) is that events that themselves cause lesser evil* should either (a) be means noncausally related to the greater good or (b) be caused by events that are means noncausally related to the greater good. Other events may permissibly lead to a lesser evil* only by way of such events.

These claims account for intuitions in several cases. In the Trolley Case, intuitively we think that we may redirect the trolley that causes the death of one. In the context where only the trolley threatens the five, the redirection of the trolley threat away from them—by which I mean the moving of the trolley itself away—is a means of saving them. It is the same event as their becoming free of threats, and this is the same event as their becoming saved. Put another way, in the context of the original Trolley Case, the five being free from threats is constituted by the trolley being away from them. Hence, there is a noncausal relation between the trolley turning away and the five being saved.[29] Because this is true, I will say that the five being saved, which is the greater good when continuing life is a good for the five, is the noncausal flip side of the redirection (in the sense of the moving away) of the trolley.[30] (Here is an analogy: When I raise my arm, the area under it is greater than it was. The relation between my arm going up and the increase in space under it is noncausal. The relation between the space becoming larger [an event] and the space being larger [a state of affairs] is also noncausal.)

I mean to distinguish this noncausal relation from a less "tight," ordinary causal relation that could connect the redirecting of the trolley and the saving of people, as in the following Van Case: A van is headed toward killing twenty people. If we redirect the trolley away from hitting five other people, then it will gently push into those twenty and move them away from the van. Here, whereas the saving of the five is a noncausal flip side of the redirection of the trolley, the saving of the twenty is a straightforward causal consequence of the redirecting of the trolley, for the moving trolley causes the movement of the twenty away from the van. This contrast, as slim as it seems, plays a crucial role from a downstreamish point of view, because it implies that in the Trolley Case what, in the circumstances, constitutes the greater good (i.e., the trolley moving [and so being] away from people for whom life is a good) is causing the lesser evil*. This links (B)(i) with (A).

The analysis I have provided of the Trolley Case shows that diverting a trolley that is headed toward five people is similar to directing a trolley at a crossroads toward one rather than five (when the trolley must be directed somehow for the sake of avoiding an even greater evil*). In the Crossroads Case, we face a choice between killing one and killing five, rather than between letting five die and killing one (as in the Trolley Case when it involves a bystander agent redirecting). But in both cases, the greater good of five being saved is a noncausal flip side of the trolley turning, when the context involves no other threats facing the five. However, redirecting in the Trolley Case is not exactly the same as directing in the Crossroads Case. For suppose that I must choose between sending a threat down track A, where one person will be killed, or down track B, where five people will be killed. The noncausal flip side of my sending the threat down track A is that I do not send it down B and that the five are saved. But sending the threat to A is *not a necessary means* to the greater good of the five people being saved, because the five could be saved simply by my not sending the threat to B, even if I do *not* send the threat to A. By contrast, redirecting the trolley that is already headed toward the five is a necessary means of saving the five, given the facts of the case. Of course, in the Crossroads Case, if I do not send the threat down B and I also do not send the threat down A, a greater evil*—the avoidance of which makes it the case that I "must" send the threat to A or B—will occur. (For example, suppose that if the threat remains at the crosspoint, then it will blow up one million people.) Sending the threat somewhere is a necessary means to the avoidance of *that* greater evil*— and so the greater good of one million people alive instead of dead is the noncausal flip side of the means that are necessary for it to come about.[31]

Intuitively, it is permissible to do acts (e.g., push a button that redirects the trolley) that cause the event that has greater good as a noncausal flip side and lesser evil* as an effect. We can explain this by noting that pushing the button—an event that does *not* have the greater good as a noncausal flip side (or aspect)[32]—also does not *itself* cause the death of the one. It causes the death of the one and the saving of the five *by* causing the trolley to be redirected. The moving away of the trolley causes the death and has the greater good as its noncausal flip side.

The relation between the existence of the greater good and the moving away of the trolley in the Trolley Case may also be compared with the relation between the five, for whom continuing life is a good, being saved and the moving of a Lazy-Susan-type device with them on it. In the Lazy Susan Case, we cannot redirect the trolley, but we can move the five away from the oncoming trolley by turning the Lazy Susan on which they sit. The relation of the movement of the Lazy Susan to the greater good here also seems noncausal (though different from that in the Trolley Case) insofar as, in the specific context where no other threats face them, the five being saved is not a separate event that is a causal consequence of the moving of the Lazy Susan. Rather, it is an *aspect* of it. (An analogy is: When I raise my arm, the wristwatch on my arm is raised as well, as an aspect of the event that is the raising of my arm.)

Suppose that another person is seated opposite the five on the Lazy Susan. When we turn it, he will be moved into, and be hit and killed by, the trolley as the five are moved away from it (Lazy Susan Case 3).[33] Intuitively, it is still permissible to turn the Lazy Susan. I believe that this is because means that have the greater good as an aspect may cause, or lead to the cause of, the lesser evil*. The fact that the greater good is an aspect of what leads to the death of the one person again creates a link to the condition described in (A). Notice that this Lazy Susan Case shows that it is not only permissible to turn a threat away from the five and to turn the five away from a threat. It shows that it is also sometimes permissible to *push a person* (on the other side of the Lazy Susan) *into a threat*.

Sometimes people say that nonconsequentialists are squeamish and that this is why they think that it is impermissible to push an innocent bystander into the trolley to stop it. But this will not explain why they think that it is permissible to turn the Lazy Susan in the Lazy Susan Case 3. (I would say, "Nonconsequentialists are not squeamish; they are downstreamish.") Nor is it just that a device (the Lazy Susan) stands between them and the bystander they push into the threat that makes pushing him in permissible. First, the intervening device is not necessary, for suppose I am, in essence, the Lazy Susan. Five people are tied on my (super-strong) right arm, toward which the nonredirectable trolley is heading. On my left arm is tied a single person. If I turn myself so that my right arm is away from the trolley, I thereby unavoidably put my left arm and the person attached to it in front of the trolley. Doing this is permissible. Second (as already noted in chapter 1), the intervening device is not sufficient for permissibility. We may not redirect a trolley (which was threatening no one) toward one bystander in order to push him into another trolley headed toward the five people so that he stops it, any more than we may personally push him in.[34]

Now consider Lazy Susan Case 4 in which the one victim stands beside the Lazy Susan as we turn it in order to remove the five from the trolley threat. Suppose that he is positioned so that the five people are turned into him and their combined impact on him is the lethal threat he faces. This will be another case in which the greater good (of the five saved) causes lesser evil*. It is also another case in which principles that justify turning the trolley and the lazy susan also justify making people into innocent threats to others. Here again, we see a connection between the Trolley Problem and the problem of innocent threats.

How does the Lazy Susan Case 3 differ from the following Bridge Case? A person is on a bridge over the track and cannot move off it. If we move a pole, then it will topple him gently into the trolley that is headed toward five people; his being hit will stop that trolley and kill him. Intuitively, it is impermissible to do this. I suggest that this is because, unlike what is true in the Lazy Susan Case 3, the one person being hit (which leads to his death) is causally necessary for producing the greater good; it is not the effect of the greater good or of means that have a non-causal relation to the greater good (as when the greater good is a flip side or aspect of the means). Evil* in the Bridge Case is a causally necessary means to producing the greater good. The same reasons that rule out acting in the Bridge Case explain the impermissibility of acting in the Transplant Case, where cutting up someone (leading to his death) is causally necessary to saving other people.

Suppose that evil* (caused by our act) *actually produces* the greater good, but evil* *is not necessary*, given our act, in order for our act to produce the greater good (i.e., if evil* had not come about from our act, something else quite innocent due to our act would have produced the greater good). Then acting to produce the greater good can still be permissible, I believe, even when this act leads to evil* actually producing the greater good. (Notice that evil* could be necessary to produce the greater good given our act, even if it is not necessary tout court because there are other acts we could have done. The fact that there are other acts we could have done that would not require evil* to bring about the greater good does not rule out that an act we actually do requires evil* to bring about the greater good.) This implies that the correct nonconsequentialist principle of permissible harm will require a *modal notion*; that is, it will determine permissibility on the basis of what is *necessary* given our act to produce a greater good or how it is *possible* given our act to produce a greater good. We can refer to this as the Modal Condition.

Here is an example. Suppose that it is permissible to bomb a munitions plant in wartime because this will end the war, even though our bombs will also kill a few children next door as a side effect. It turns out, however, that it is the deaths of these children that will actually lead their parents to surrender, even before we finish getting rid of all the munitions necessary to end the war.[35] Even if it is not permissible to bomb the children as our chosen means to end the war, it would be permissible to do what causes their deaths in this case even if we foresaw what the parents will do. This is because what we do could end the war by an independent route, and so the children's deaths are not necessary to end the war. (I do not think that the conclusion in this case depends on the fact that the surrender is due to an intervening voluntary act by other agents [i.e., the parents] in response to the children's deaths. For we might imagine another case in which it is foreseen that when the children are set aflame, as a side effect of our bombing the munitions plant, this will trigger a much larger explosion in a second munitions plant that we cannot otherwise reach. It is this explosion that destroys crucial weapons and puts an end to the war much more rapidly than it could be ended by the destruction of the plant that we directly attack. Nevertheless, our attacking the first plant is the only act we could do that would be useful, even without its side effects, to end the war. The fact that it is superseded in doing this by the second explosion in the actual course of events does not make the attack on the first plant impermissible.)[36]

In what follows, I shall assume that it is whether our act leads to evil* as a necessary cause of the greater good, rather than whether evil* is or is not, in fact, a cause that is morally important. For brevity's sake, I will, henceforth, take the Modal Condition of "necessity given our act" to be implied when evil* causes greater good, unless otherwise noted. (However, below I will consider some problems with formulating the Modal Condition.)

In sum, the idea that it is permissible to use means that have a noncausal relation (as explained above) to a greater good, even though the means cause or lead to events that cause a lesser evil*, is again nonconsequentialist, in the sense that it is concerned with *how* the good and evil* come about. First, it is permissible that the greater good be noncausally related to what causes (or leads to what causes) evil*. Second, the greater good may be caused by an event (such as our pushing the button that redirects the trolley) that indirectly causes evil* by way of events (or effects of events) that are noncausally related to that greater good. The first component of the theory ([A] above) permitted cases where the greater good itself causes a lesser evil*, and so evil* is downstream from the greater good. Evil* also lies causally downstream from the greater good (rather than from something that merely causes the greater good) when the greater good is the noncausal flip side or aspect of an event that causes, or leads to what causes, evil*. Finally, in virtue of the Modal Condition, an act may be permissible because it is *possible*, given the act, for evil* to lie causally downstream from the greater good in these ways.

B.ii. A complication for the permissibility of a greater good (or means having it as its noncausal flip side or aspect) causing an evil* is introduced by considerations arising from the Tree Trolley cases.[37] These are cases in which we redirect a threat more than once. Suppose that the trolley that is headed toward three people is a trolley we, as bystander agents, have already redirected away from five people. En route to the three, it can be redirected again to a track where one person will be hit. (It was not possible to redirect it to that track initially.) May we, the same bystander agents, redirect it toward the one person? Intuitively, I think not. Yet, at each redirection, the greater good is the noncausal flip side of the means that causes the lesser evil*.

Unlike the cases we have considered so far, in this case the one is made physically susceptible to harm in virtue of our initial redirection, as he was not physically susceptible to harm from redirecting the trolley initially. (The three toward whom we redirected were already susceptible.) Does this make the moral difference? Making someone physically susceptible to a threat is somewhat like being responsible for putting someone in harm's way (as when we invite one person to sit on the trolley track). The latter also can make it wrong to redirect the trolley. But making someone physically susceptible in this way is not always a barrier to action.

Consider the following Original Goal Tree Trolley Case: The machinery running a trolley headed toward killing the five is such that if the trolley is not redirected several times by a single agent, it will come back and kill the five. It so happens that there are immovable people on each side track toward which the trolley must be (multiply) redirected. (Indeed, all of the tracks *except the last one* have more people on them than were originally threatened by the trolley.) Intuitively, it is permissible to multiply redirect the trolley in this case, so long as one reasonably believes that one will complete all of the redirections. None of the people on any of the tracks but the last need die (though some might), but the last person who will be harmed was not originally physically susceptible to harm. That is, he was not reachable by means of a single redirection. I believe that it is permissible for a bystander agent to redirect the trolley many times in this case because it accomplishes, in a rationally justifiable way, *the original goal* of saving the five people initially threatened. (Saving the five by killing more than five is not rationally justifiable [unless those to be killed have consented while competent].)[38]

Intuitively, a moral problem seems to arise in Tree Trolley cases when our original goal (saving the five) has been achieved and we then add another goal, namely, to eliminate a problem that *we* have created for people (in the course of achieving our first goal) in a way that harms someone who is susceptible to harm only as a result of what we originally did. We can call these New Goal Tree Trolley Cases. In our example above, we supposed that if we redirect the trolley away from five toward three, the five are saved. Then we are physically able to redirect, on a route we could not originally have taken, the threat from the three for whom we created a problem onto a track where one person will be killed. If there is a moral problem with our redirecting the second time in such cases, then conditions described in (A) and (B(i)) will not always make for permissible harmings. (Note that this case should be distinguished from the following one: We mistakenly redirect the trolley away from five toward three when we could have redirected it toward a track with two on it. It is permissible, I believe, to correct our error and redirect toward the two as they were originally physically susceptible, even though the five have already been saved.)

How can we explain these intuitive judgments? One possibility is that they are an indication of distinctions I will come to emphasize below, namely, the distinction between *substitution* and *subordination*. Roughly, when we redirect, we substitute one set of people for another. If the groups of three and two in our last example are reachable by tracks going from the original five, they both stand in the same substitutable-for relation to the five. If the track with the two is chosen instead of the track with the three, the two bear the same relation to the five that the three would have borne had we redirected toward them. By contrast, if the two are substituted only for the three when they could not have been substituted for the five, they relate to the three rather than sharing a relation the three had to the five. This gives rise to the sense, I believe, that they are subordinated to the three rather than merely substituted for them in relation to something else. But it is puzzling why this should be so, as the two's relation to the three seems to be the same as the three's relation to the five, and (as we shall see) I wish to claim that when the three are substituted for the five they are not subordinated to them.

Does the moral problem that I believe sometimes exists with redirecting a threat toward someone not originally physically susceptible to a redirected threat *not* arise when we seek to help someone to avoid a problem that we did not create? For notice that a bystander agent coming upon a Trolley Case may not be aware of the history of the situation; he may never be sure whether he is dealing with a case in which a trolley now headed toward five people was already redirected toward them away from an even greater number by another agent. The current agent is also unsure whether the one person to whom he would redirect the trolley was originally susceptible to the trolley threat or only became so as a result of a previous redirection. Is this absence of historical knowledge a reason for inaction by the agent in the ordinary Trolley Case? If the agent knew that someone else had redirected the trolley toward the five away from a greater number of people, would this be a reason for inaction on his part? In order that it not be such a reason, the problem of harming someone who was made physically susceptible to a threat by a previous rescue would have to be *agent-relative*. That is, if bystander agent A's act made C physically susceptible to harm, there is no problem with agent B redirecting toward C when the original goal of A's act is accomplished, even if there is a problem with A's doing so.

An agent-relative analysis would imply that if a bystander agent actually endangers three people (by turning a trolley toward them and away from five other people), then he has less responsibility for helping those three by redirecting the trolley toward someone he has made physically susceptible (in virtue of redirecting) than another agent who was not involved in the three being faced with a lethal threat. Indeed, this analysis would imply that it is impermissible for the first agent to do on behalf of the three what the second agent may do. Of course, when a bystander agent comes upon the trolley headed toward the five and he turns the trolley toward the three, he is acting permissibly in threatening them, and this, surprisingly, plays some role in the limitations on his further redirecting. For these limits do not, I believe, apply to a villain who directed the trolley toward the five originally. He has a responsibility to diminish the threat he presents; he may turn the trolley from the five toward the three, and then from the three toward the one made physically susceptible to being hit by the trolley only as a result of the first redirection. But the villain is only doing lesser wrongs to substitute for the greater wrong he originally set in motion. None of his acts is truly permissible; they are at best lesser wrongs. By contrast, the bystander agent's original redirection was permissible and he must not substitute an impermissible act for it just because fewer people will die.[39]

I do not pretend to have settled the questions concerning the Tree Trolley cases. I only wish to note that avoiding the possible moral problems raised by the Tree Trolley cases should be considered a side constraint on the permissibility of acts that satisfy the principle of permissible harm that I am in the process of isolating in this chapter.

C. i. What about the cases in which means that are necessary, given one's act, to cause a greater good also (necessarily) cause a lesser evil* and not by way of means that have greater good as a noncausal flip side or aspect? (For example, one sets off a bomb, and this both pushes the trolley away from the five and kills a bystander.) Why cannot evil* in this case be downstream from the greater good? In the temporal sense, the greater good may indeed come about before the evil*, but the evil* and the greater good would both be *causally* downstream from an event that causes both. Hence, in this case, evil* seems to be causally parallel to the greater good rather than downstream from it. This is true even if there are more intermediate causal steps between the bomb going off and the greater good coming about than between the bomb and the evil.* (As we shall see below, though, the greater good and the lesser evil* being parallel is not necessarily a sign that it is impermissible to act.) These sorts of cases raise a very important issue and must be discussed in some detail. The Car Case and the Splash Case, in which it seemed impermissible to act, involve our means to the greater good causing death, but the means neither have a noncausal relation to the greater good nor are caused by means that have a noncausal relation to the greater good. However, I do not think that this shows that all cases of which this is true involve impermissible ways to produce a greater good and a lesser evil*. In order to reveal this, I believe that it is important to distinguish among several types of cases.

(1) The first type includes cases in which our means, *in the sense of what we must do in order to achieve the greater good*, directly causes the evil*, even by, in a sense, "overlapping" with the involvement-of-the-person part of evil*. This is true in the Car Case, because we must go over a particular spot in the road (our means), and this spot is, in fact, already occupied by a person. Going over him is not something we must do in order to achieve the greater good, so it is not a means to the greater good; if he moved, we could still achieve that good. But going over the spot, which is a spot he already occupies, is something we must do, and so we must involve him given that he is there, which directly causes him harm (the other part of evil*). The overlapping seems to involve a form of "constitution in the context," that is, in this context, though not in all contexts, going over the spot (a type of event) is constituted (at least in part, in this token event) by going over the person. And this is part of evil*.

In the Splash Case, what already occupies the spot we must go over is something that should not be disturbed (i.e., the acid) because of the harm it will cause. In this case, what we must do does not overlap with the evil* or directly cause the evil*, but it overlaps with involving the acid, and this will directly cause harm. Hence, in the Splash Case, what we must do is, in this context, constituted by triggering the direct cause of evil*.

These two cases, which involve either constitution by evil* or constitution by triggering the direct cause of evil*, may be contrasted (conceptually if not morally) with a case in which what we must do to achieve the greater good directly causes evil* but is not constituted by evil*. (It also does not trigger the direct cause of evil* because it *is* the direct cause.) Suppose, for example, that we must drive over the empty road up to point X in order to get to the hospital, but a part of the car extends over point X to point X + 1, and it crushes the person immovably seated at X + 1.

I claim that when what we must do (i) overlaps with evil* or with the direct cause of evil* or (ii) directly causes evil*, it would be permissible to act if the greater good were the noncausal flip side or aspect of what we must do, but not permissible if the greater good is a causal consequence of what we must do.[40,41] Hence, the principle I am now developing implies that sometimes we may not employ a neutral means that causes the greater good and also causes the lesser evil*. This implication distinguishes the present theory from the DTE, the DDE, and the DDE(R), because these doctrines do not rule out the use of a means to the greater good on account of the means directly causing lesser evil*.[42] This implication may also morally distinguish (i) the case in which people in a car escaping from a deadly threat run over someone on the road from both (ii) the case in which we rush people in a car to a hospital to be rescued from a deadly threat but in doing so run over someone on the road, and (iii) the case in which we rush to people to save them from a deadly threat in a car that runs over someone on the road. Only in (i) is the greater good of people escaping from a deadly threat an aspect of means that causes lesser evil*. Hence it may be permissible when (ii) and (iii) are not.[43]

(2) The second type of case in which our means cause both an evil* and the greater good consists of cases in which our means, *in the sense of some entity we must use in order to achieve the greater good*, directly causes the evil*, but not because of something we must do with the entity in order to achieve the greater good. Here is an example: Suppose we are rushing five people to the hospital to be saved. Our car will veer off course because the road is bumpy, and it will thus hit someone before getting back on course to the hospital. If we drive so as to prevent the car from veering, we will not get to the hospital in time to save lives (Veer Case). Here our means (in the second sense of an entity we must use) will cause a person's death. Indeed, its location will overlap with the person, but not (arguably) because being in the spot where the person stands is necessary to get to the hospital. I believe that it is required to drive so as to prevent the car from veering. What if we reverse the order of events? That is, we must drive to the hospital in a car, and we know that after we disembark at the hospital this car will unavoidably continue on its way and run over someone near the hospital. I believe that using this car is impermissible. In other words, whether evil* results from the means *before* or *after* the greater good is accomplished is not crucial.[44]

There can also be versions of this second type of case in which the location of our means overlaps with the direct cause of evil* (as when the car veers over the acid, a spot where we need not go in order to get to the hospital), and cases where our means directly cause evil* without overlapping with it.

In these cases, including the ones where the entity directly causes the lesser evil*, the entity also *causes* (directly or indirectly) the greater good. Further, the entity's movement is not caused by anything that has a noncausal relation to the greater good. This, I believe, makes use of the entity impermissible in these cases. By contrast, I claim, if use of the entity has the greater good as a noncausal flip side or aspect, use of the entity is permissible even when it directly causes the lesser evil*. This is what happens in the Trolley Case.[45]

(3) In the third type of case in which our means causes a greater good, something that our means (in either sense used above) brings along with it causes evil*, either directly or by overlapping with the direct cause of evil*. For example, suppose the car we must use to achieve the greater good carries in it a supply of acid. If we rush to the hospital, the acid will be ejected and splash on a person causing his death. Nothing we must do or use to achieve our goal causes the death (as we need not carry acid nor eject it in order to get to the hospital). Nevertheless, our means introduces something (acid) in a context where it directly harms someone it would otherwise not have harmed. This, I believe, makes it imper-missible to proceed, when our means does not have a noncausal relation to the greater good. In another case, we need to flip a switch to cause the electricity that stops the trolley, but the same switch starts a death ray that will kill a bystander. Here, something we must do to stop the trolley (flip the switch) introduces a direct cause of death (death ray), which is not needed to stop the trolley. Flipping the switch is, intuitively, also impermissible.[46]

(4) In the fourth type of case in which our means causes both an evil* and a greater good, either (a) what we must do to achieve a greater good, (b) an entity we must use to achieve a greater good, or (c) what they bring along with them *indirectly* causes a lesser evil* by causing, without overlapping with, a direct cause of the lesser evil*. For example, suppose that we must drive on a road to the hospital in order to save five people, but driving on this road will cause vibrations that cause rocks at the roadside to tumble, killing one person. May we proceed? I believe that it is permissible to proceed. This case can be contrasted with a case in which we must drive on another road which is made up of loosely packed rocks that are thereby dislodged and tumble, killing a person. In this case, what we must do to save the five—go over the road—overlaps with moving the rocks. Hence, even though what we must do will only indirectly cause the death (by triggering the cause of death), its overlapping with the triggering of the cause of death makes it impermissible. By contrast with cases in (3), in (4) our means do not bring with them the cause of death. Rather, the cause is already present in the context into which we introduce our means and what they bring with them.[47]

The result of differentiating these four types of cases may be stated as follows: (a) Use of means that have a causal relation (rather than a noncausal relation) to the greater good is impermissible when using the means involves our being responsible for introducing into a context either what directly causes evil* (even by overlapping in part with evil*) or what overlaps with the direct cause of evil*. (b) When our means have a causal relation to the greater good, what use of them introduces to a context may permissibly be a direct cause of (without overlapping with) the direct cause of evil.* In this limited sense, what we introduce into a context may permissibly be an indirect cause of evil.* If component (b) is true, this would also show that a downstream theory is not necessary in order to account for all permissible evil*. For in (b), evil* is not causally downstream from a greater good or what has a noncausal relation to it. So far we have argued that evil* brought about in cases of types (1), (2), and (3) (but not [4]) will be permissible only if they are downstream from the greater good (where this includes being caused by the greater good or by means that have the greater good as its noncausal flip side or aspect).[48]

C.ii. At this point, it is useful to make several clarifying remarks. First, putting together what I have said so far in (A), (B), and (C), it may *seem* that I am suggesting that when means have a very intimate (e.g., noncausal) relation to the greater good, they can have any degree of intimacy with lesser evil* and, in general, that there should be no more intimate causal relation to the lesser evil* than to the greater good. The latter claim would imply that once the causal relation of means to lesser evil* is indirect (in the sense described in [4] above), we may proceed even if there is an indirect causal relation of our means to the greater good. However, I do not believe this way of putting my points is correct.[49] For (A), (B), and (C) do not rule out acting when our means have an even *more* indirect causal relation to the greater good than they have to the lesser evil*. For example, there may be a much longer causal chain to the greater good than to the lesser evil* and yet if the link to evil* is indirect (as described in [4]), action should be permissible.

Second, the permissibility of using means to the greater good that indirectly cause evil* (as described in [4]) does not license the creation of "Rube Goldberg" devices[50] to make permissible what would otherwise be impermissible. For if one inserts indirect connections between one's means and evil*, one is responsible for *introducing* those extra links; they are not present in the context with which what one introduces interacts.

Third, it is sometimes difficult to get clear about whether means that directly cause lesser evil* have a causal or noncausal relation to the greater good. For example, if it is permissible for someone to turn the trolley from five toward one, is it permissible for him to turn a trolley not yet headed toward the five toward one, as a means of preventing a villain from sending the trolley toward the five? One issue in this case is whether there is a moral difference between acting to prevent a bad consequence of someone's act after he has done his act (as in the original Trolley Case) and acting to prevent his act.[51] The point I am interested in now, however, is whether the causal/noncausal relation to the greater good plays a role in permissibility.

In one variation of this case, if someone sends threat A in a direction where one person will be hit, this has the greater good as its *noncausal* flip side because the threat must then be away from the five who are in a different direction. But doing so is necessary only because otherwise the villain will send the threat toward the five. It is the necessity of doing it to stop his action that suggests that sending threat

A toward the one person is a means that *causes* the greater good by way of stopping the villain. In a second variation of this case, we must send the threat in a direction where one person will be hit as a way of calming a nervous villain who will otherwise send threat B toward the five.[52] Here it is clear that we are interested in the *causal* effects of sending the threat. This case does not seem to differ from one where we would set off a bomb to causally stop a threat to the five knowing that the bomb will kill one person as a side effect, and this is impermissible. (If anything, it is worse to calm the nervous villain, for if we set off the bomb, there is no interest in the bomb killing anyone, but it is natural to think that the villain will only be calmed if the one person is killed.)

Fourth, using means that indirectly cause evil* (as described in [4]) is only permissible when a greater good depends on the use of the means. Acting for no overriding good reason when this will indirectly cause evil* is impermissible even when one does *not* introduce the additional steps that make the bad effect indirect rather than direct; they are part of the context. It is important, and in need of explanation, that pursuit of a greater good that has a mere causal relation to our means can still narrow the range of effects that make an act impermissible. It seems to narrow them to directly caused evils* (with or without overlap) and evils* produced by means that overlap with the direct cause of evil*. An explanation of this is needed because it seems like quite a concession to consequentialist reasoning that eventual production of a greater good can narrow the range of evils* that make acts impermissible in this way. In fact, I think that an important non-consequentialist element is driving our intuitions, namely, a distinction (as drawn above) between what we introduce into a context and what is already in a context causing evil*.

Fifth, our discussion helps us explain the difference between so-called cross-road and certain noncrossroad cases. When one kills someone as the alternative to killing five (Crossroad Case), one's directing a threat that will harm someone has the greater good as its noncausal flip side. This, I believe, makes it permissible. By contrast, suppose that one had already sent a threat to five people and one could stop it only by harming one other person (Noncrossroad Case). One could either throw him on the threat or set off a bomb that interfered with the first threat but sent fragments killing the one person. In these cases, the means one would use would cause the greater good, not have it as a noncausal flip side. Throwing someone on the threat would also involve evil* as itself a means. These factors help account for the impermissibility of a person using certain means to stop a threat for which he is responsible.

This discussion of neutral means has been concerned with those that lead to harm. The same strictures that apply when we cause harm do not apply when we employ neutral means to a greater good that interfere with our preventing lesser harm. Hence the harming/not-aiding distinction has a role to play. For example, suppose that in order to save five people, I must go to the lab to prepare a serum and so cannot stop to save a person on my route. Here it is not the greater good (or means noncausally related to it) but a mere causal means (going to the lab) to the greater good that interferes with saving someone. Yet it is permissible to go to the lab. Furthermore, recall that some not-aidings can involve *causing* an evil*.[53] For example, suppose going to the lab requires me to first disconnect myself from a machine I am using to save one other person. If this is aid I did not have to provide, I believe it is permissible to disconnect myself to save the greater number of people. Yet, I believe, I also thereby cause the death of the one person. This is so even though I let him die (because I do not induce death). Hence, it is permissible to use means that cause evil* when one is thereby not-aiding, without concerning oneself with the strictures enumerated in our discussion that apply when one is causing evil* by harming. This may be because when ceasing aid causes evil*, it is never the direct cause of death as it does not induce death nor does it overlap with the direct cause of death.[54]

D. What if an evil* *itself* had a noncausal relation (in the sense of a tighter relation than causation—such as "aspect of" or "flip side of") to a greater good (or to means that have a noncausal relation to a greater good)? It would then not be causally downstream from the greater good. Would it then be impermissible to bring the good about? Here is a possible example that can help us answer this question: Suppose that the trolley that is redirected away from the five people might have reached but did not reach the one. Could we say that something bad has happened to the one nevertheless, namely, he was placed under a threat even if it was never fulfilled? Suppose that being under a threat is itself an evil*. Then *in the context of* the (original) Trolley Case where the one person cannot be moved, the means to the greater good of the five being saved (i.e., the trolley moving away from them) overlaps with the evil* of one person being threatened. Indeed, in this case the overlapping may be nothing more than the means having the evil* as its noncausal flip side as much as it has the greater good of the five not threatened as its noncausal flip side. This evil* is not causally downstream from the good (nor does it cause the good), but it is still permissible to act.

There is further support for denial of a downstream requirement: Evil* is not downstream when a greater good has evil* as one of its aspects. (This is also a case where an evil* has a greater good as one of its aspects.) Yet here, acts leading to evil* are permitted. Further, if means have evil* as an aspect and a greater good as an aspect or noncausal flip side, the evil* is also not causally downstream from the greater good. Yet, it seems permissible to act. (An example might be turning the Lazy Susan with the five on it so that they are away from the trolley, though one person is spread on the bottom side of the Lazy Susan and will be crushed by its turning.)

To avoid possible misunderstandings concerning what I am saying about cases where evil* has a greater good as a noncausal flip side, consider the evil* of pushing someone into a threat without his consent, when the alternative to this is pushing three other people into the threat without their consent. In this case, the greater good of three not being pushed in is the noncausal flip side of the lesser evil*. Does what I have said above imply that it is permissible to push the single person in? No, because in this case, unlike the ones we have been considering, the lesser evil* is not a *necessary* means noncausally related to producing the greater good. This is because simply not pushing in the three would save them; an agent need not push in the one person as the alternative to pushing in the three.

Nevertheless, if one were going to do the wrong act of pushing in A, B, and C, is it permissible to push in D instead, because it is a less bad alternative that has the nonperformance of the worse act as its flip side? This act is permissible only in the sense that it is permissible to do this lesser wrong as an alternative to doing a greater wrong. Because it would be wrong to push in A, B, and C to begin with, however, we still do a wrong act when we push in D instead. This is a true case of doing the lesser evil*. (That would also be true if the individual pushed in were a member of the original group of three.) So, now we see that there could be a case in which it *is* permissible to push a bystander (who would not otherwise be comparably harmed) into the trolley when this is a mere means to stop the trolley. Namely, it is permissible when we would otherwise *wrongfully* push in a greater number, and yet in doing it we would still be doing a wrong act. However, it would not necessarily be permissible to substitute a wrong act that is less harmful to one person for a *permissible* act (not wrong) that is more harmful to others. This implies that an act that is otherwise wrong does not become permissible just because it has the nonperformance of a more harmful but permissible act as its noncausal flip side.[55]

How do cases in which greater good and lesser evil* are aspects of one event compare with cases described in (C) in which greater good and lesser evil* are *causally* parallel? Though evil* and greater good may be parallel when they are two aspects of a single event, being an aspect is a *tighter* relation than a causal relation between each of them and the event whose aspects they are. The same is true when means have a noncausal relation to both greater good and evil*. In the cases where greater good and evil* are parallel causal effects of a means, they themselves are not wedded; rather they are separate, causal offshoots of some third event. Interestingly, (A), (B), (C), and (D) suggest that when the greater good is wedded to, or *tainted* by, evil*, it can be easier to justify evil* than when the two are separate events caused by a third event.

It seems that, rather than it being crucial that evil* be downstream, it is crucial that evil* *not* be causally upstream from a greater good (and not being causally upstream is *not* the same as being causally downstream). It is also crucial that when evil* is a direct effect of our means (or of that with which they overlap), that it and the greater good not be causally parallel relative to our means. This is, in part, why I call the theory I am presenting only a downstream*ish* one.[56]

E.i. The next proposal is that it is permissible for a lesser evil* that is an effect of a greater good (or of means noncausally related to it) to sustain that greater good. This is so even if it is not permissible for evil* *to produce* that greater good. If it *sustains* the greater good, the greater good is not *produced* by it. In this sense, it doesn't cause the greater good even if it *causes* it to be sustained. In this case, is the evil* causally downstream from the good? Not necessarily, because an evil* that sustained a greater good could also, for example, be an aspect or a flip side of that greater good or of means that have that greater good as a noncausal flip side. For example, suppose that being threatened with the redirected trolley is itself an evil*, and that having the one person threatened is what sustained the greater good by defeating potential defeaters of it. Then the evil* might be a flip side of the good it was needed to sustain, not causally downstream from that good. Once again, it seems that in nonconsequentialism, it is important that an evil* not be causally upstream from, in the sense of not *producing*, a greater good and, when the evil* is directly produced by our means (or that with which the means overlaps), that it not be causally parallel to a greater good relative to our means. This has priority over any supposed requirement that the evil* be downstream from the greater good.

To understand (E), consider the Loop Case. The second problem (i.e., the looping trolley) exists as a consequence of our redirecting the trolley, because the redirecting causes the looping of the trolley. Independent of this consequence of redirecting the trolley in the Loop Case, *the noncausal flip side* of turning the trolley exists, that is, the five people being rid of the first problem involving the trolley. (This is the problem of the trolley being headed toward them from one direction, and this is the only problem that existed for them independently of our doing anything to save them.)[57] Their being rid of the trolley headed toward them in one direction is their being free of the original problem that prompted our rescue to begin with, and in the context where no other threats existed to them originally, it leaves them free of all threats that existed independently of our rescue. This noncausal flip side would completely justify any bad effects for the one person on the side track *unless* some major new problem arose for the five as a consequence of our redirecting the trolley, and this *new* problem were not itself eliminated. That is, in redirecting the trolley, we have achieved a state that, when we abstract from further consequences for the five of moving the trolley from its initial course, would be the greater good. I shall call such a state the "structural equivalent of the greater good" ("structural equivalent" for short). It cannot be called the greater good, because another problem to the five potentially now exists due to our rescuing them from all problems preexisting our intervention. After all, the five subject to the possibility of a looping trolley is not yet the greater good.[58]

Hence, achieving the structural equivalent would not justify us in redirecting the trolley (and hitting the one) unless the five will not die shortly anyway. So justification for redirecting can depend on how the further consequences of redirecting are likely to affect the condition of the five. It is a prerequisite of being justified in redirecting that there be a prospect that the condition of the five as it is in the structural equivalent *will remain*, thus becoming the greater good that, all things considered, justifies the lesser evil*.

This continuity between the *structural equivalent of the greater good* and *the eventual greater good that ultimately justifies the evil** rules out a different greater good (call it greater good 2), which could be caused by redirecting the trolley, from justifying the harm done by redirecting the trolley. For example, suppose that redirecting the trolley away from the five caused the one to be hit and die, but this did not stop the trolley from looping back toward the five. However, on its way back toward the five, the trolley depresses a button that prevents another trolley from running over three other people. Intuitively, redirecting the trolley in such a case should be ruled out as impermissible. I think that what accounts for this intuition is that the structural equivalent of the greater good, the means to which leads to harm to the one person, cannot be sustained and become the greater good.

Redirecting the trolley, then, cannot be justified by its leading to *that* greater good (via a structural equivalent and something that sustains it). Further, in this case redirecting that kills one person is not a means that has the structural equivalent of the greater good 2 as its noncausal flip side. It is merely a means to causing that different greater good 2 (i.e., three other people being saved), and such a means is ruled out by the requirement that means that cause the greater good not directly cause lesser evil*. Here again, we see that, although the strict requirement of (A)—that the good that justifies the evil* should cause it—is dropped, something of it remains: A structural equivalent that either directly causes the evil* or is noncausally related to means that directly cause the evil* (or overlap with what does) must be the structural equivalent of the greater good that ultimately justifies the evil*.[59]

Furthermore, it is through the sustaining of the structural equivalent that the greater good should come about. To see this, consider the Miracle Case, which is like the Loop Case except that hitting the one person on the side track does not stop the trolley, which returns to hit the five.[60] However, the trolley passing over the side track miraculously produces a serum that can be used to resurrect the five who have been hit and killed. It seems to me that in this case the structural equivalent is not sustained. Rather, it is eliminated, but a side effect of its elimination allows us to produce the same greater good anyway. Here, turning the trolley away, which directly causes the death of the person on the side track, is a means to *producing*, rather than to *sustaining*, the greater good. I think it is not permissible to turn the trolley in this case.

The hitting of the one by the redirected trolley in the Loop Case does not *produce* the structural equivalent of the greater good. The structural equivalent exists prior to the hit, as it is the noncausal flip side of redirecting the trolley. The hitting of the one stands outside the structural equivalent and defeats threats to it that arise from what we have done to rescue the five. By defeating a threat to the five (i.e., the looping trolley) that arises from what we have done to save them from a threat that preexisted our act, the evil* turns the structural equivalent into the greater good itself. It does this not by adding anything positive to the structural equivalent, but by preventing its being undone. In this sense, the evil* sustains the greater good by preventing undoing of the good, rather than by bringing about or producing the good.[61]

Notice that I say "sustains the greater good" rather than "sustains the structural equivalent of the greater good." This is because I think that it is appropriate to speak of only the structural equivalent when what we have done to remove threats that are initially present will cause another problem for the five people. The five people subject to the trolley from another direction is not the greater good. However, when the threat of a looping trolley leads to its own defeat (by hitting the one), we have, I think, the right to say more. We can say that when any defeater of the structural equivalent will be defeated, what was initially referred to as the structural equivalent of the greater good *is* the greater good, and it is sustained, rather than produced, by the defeating of threats to it.

That the greater good is sustained rather than produced by evil* is a non-consequentialist feature connected with how the good can come about. It is a feature that distinguishes morally between evil* that is causally necessary to sustain a greater good and evil* that is causally necessary to produce a greater good (not yet available to be sustained). Hence, there is a sense in which evil* is downstream from the greater good, even in the Loop Case, though I have already said that this is not the crucial factor. (For all we know, much that we achieve in life may depend on the existence of defeaters of defeaters. They may operate unseen and unknown by us, the hidden dynamics necessary to keep in place what we refer to as "a good state that has been achieved.")

Notice that the evil* *causally sustains* the greater good, and the turning of the trolley from the five *noncausally produces* the structural equivalent of the greater good. Hence causation is not necessary or sufficient for production. The fact that there is sustaining (not producing) at a crucial point and a noncausal (rather than causal) relation at another point make turning in the Loop Case permissible.[62]

Consider by contrast the Tractor Case. In it, recall, in addition to the trolley, a tractor is independently headed toward killing the five. The tractor threat exists independently of the further consequences of redirecting the trolley.[63] Given the existence of the two threats initially, we have no structural equivalent of the greater good when we redirect the trolley away from its initial hit on the five. For when we redirect the trolley and abstract from any new problem for the five thereby created, the five are still subject to a fatal tractor threat. This state of affairs is not what, if it were sustained, would be the greater good. That is, the structural equivalent of the justifying good does not yet exist as a noncausal flip side of redirecting the trolley. In the Tractor Case, the structural equivalent only comes into existence (is produced) at the same time as the final greater good does,[64] and its production depends, in part, on the effects of the removal of the trolley, namely, the one being hit. This is because it is the moving and hitting of the one (evil*) that causes the tractor to stop from the direction of its initial hit. The absence of the structural equivalent as a noncausal flip side seems a likely candidate for what underlies the intuition that redirecting the trolley in the Tractor Case is problematic.[65] And this is because a link with (A)—which requires that the greater good cause the evil* that it justifies— is not present and because, therefore, evil* helps to produce (rather than sustain) the greater good.[66]

As it turns out, in the Tractor Case, the *ultimate* justifying good comes into being when the structural equivalent does, as no further problems for the continuing existence of the five people are produced by what we do to get rid of the trolley and tractor. But this fact, that our redirecting the trolley can lead to the justifying good, does not mean that we have produced the structural equivalent without a causal role for evil*. When some evil* is causally necessary for the structural equivalent to be produced, that structural equivalent (or means that have it as its noncausal flip side) cannot be what leads to the evil*, nor can evil* stand outside the structural equivalent of the greater good and merely prevent the greater good from being undone by problems that arise from our original intervention.

Let us take (A)–(E) as the components of the theory of permissible harm, at least tentatively. As such, it is a non-state-of-mind theory. Explicitly comparing it now with the DTE, which is a state-of-mind theory, may be useful.[67] Indeed, it may show us how to translate a state-of-mind theory (like the DTE and DDE) into a non-state-of-mind theory. The DTE distinguishes between doing something "because of" and doing something "in order to." If we act in order to bring about an effect, it is a goal that we try to achieve (even if it is just a means to a further goal) I have described this as a primary reason for action. If we act merely because we will have an effect, this effect need not be a goal of our action, but it can provide what I described as a secondary reason for action. For example, if we see that potential defeaters of our goal will be defeated, this gives us a secondary reason for action. The structural equivalent of the greater good in the non-state-of-mind theory could be described (in state-of-mind terms) as involving the achievement of our goal, which was our primary reason for action, when it is considered independently of the presence of defeaters and defeaters of defeaters. In the Tractor Case, because the structural equivalent of the greater good is not present until there is at least a structural equivalent of the tractor being stopped, our goal (to use the state-of-mind term) must be to get rid of both the trolley and the tractor threats as they existed prior to our intervening.

Hence, when the occurrence of evil* is causally necessary to *produce* the structural equivalent of the greater good, put in state-of-mind terms, the expected evil*'s occurrence is necessary in order for us to reasonably formulate a *primary* reason (a goal) for action. (This does not mean that we need to intend the evil*; we can act only because it will occur, as the DTE also shows us.)[68] This contrasts with cases in which the occurrence of the evil* is necessary to *sustain* (the structural equivalent of) the greater good and so, in state-of-mind terms, is necessary only to provide a *secondary* reason for action, namely, to ensure that a defeater of a defeater of our goal will occur.

We might also say in non-state-of-mind terms that the structural equivalent of the greater good provides an *initial* sufficient justification for the evil*, in that it has the structure of what sufficiently justifies the lesser evil*, but it is still dependent on further effects that ensure that it will not be defeated. (This makes it only an *initial* sufficient justification by comparison to the final greater good, which is a sufficient justification of the evil*.) Hence, we can say that the evil* that is produced by a structural equivalent (or means that have the structural equivalent as its noncausal flip side) is *initially* sufficiently justified.

In the Loop Case, the state of affairs that provides (at least) an initial sufficient justification for an evil* is what, in the terms of the DTE, we act *in order to* bring about. We act in order to bring it about because we foresee that it will be sustained and hence just be the greater good that ultimately justifies the evil*. (We do not act in order to sustain it.) In the Tractor Case, by contrast, we act *in order to* remove both the trolley and the tractor threats.[69] This, however, does not mean (I have argued)[70] that we need to intend the means to the joint removal, namely, evil* (or means having evil* as a direct effect). Suppose that the evil* needed to stop the tractor is not intended and so satisfies the DTE. Still, evil* would be causally *producing*, not merely stopping hindrances to, the state that is needed to justify (or initially sufficiently justify) this evil*, and this makes it impermissible, I think, to do the act that leads to it. This is another way in which the principle I am developing differs from the DTE, which would allow turning the trolley in the Tractor Case, as we need act only because the evil* will occur. (It also differs from the DTE in ruling out side effect evil* that is directly caused by [or whose direct cause overlaps with] means that produce the greater good. This was discussed in [C].)

For the same reason that we may not redirect the trolley in the Tractor Case, it would be impermissible to redirect the trolley away from five people each of whom is shortly going to die of organ failure (which is another fatal threat to them existing independently of what we do), even if the death of the one hit by the trolley would make available the organs needed to save the five from their organ failure (Trolley-Organs Case I). By contrast, it would be permissible to save the five from the trolley threat, though this kills the one, *when what we do* to save the five *will cause* them organ failure, but we can permissibly get the organs they will need from the one who gets killed by the trolley. In the latter case (which I shall call Trolley-Organs Case II),[71] there is a structural equivalent of the greater good that is sustained by the evil* in the face of a further problem (organ failure) which our helping intervention causes.[72] Here the evil* is caused by means that have a noncausal relation to the structural equivalent and so it is initially sufficiently justified. In the former case, the evil* is necessary to *produce* a structural equivalent (that comes into being simultaneous with the final greater good). Hence the evil* is not caused by means that have a noncausal relation to the structural equivalent and it is not initially sufficiently justified.[73]

Yet the fact that producing a structural equivalent requires an evil* does not always make acting impermissible. For example, an evil* E may permissibly be required to produce a structural equivalent of a good that justifies a different greater evil* H if E is caused by what at least initially sufficiently justifies *it*. This involves (at least) a structural equivalent of a good great enough to justify E, a structural equivalent that has some chance of being maintained.[74] For example, consider the Component Case in which a trolley is headed toward five people. We can only push the trolley to the right a bit. We know that this will save one of the five (a component of the greater good) and also cause a bystander to be hit by the trolley, paralyzing his leg. His being hit redirects the trolley from hitting the remaining four, but the trolley only finally comes to rest when it hits and kills one other person. Intuitively, acting in this case is permissible. The underlying structure is that the paralysis (E) is caused by means whose noncausal flip side is one person being saved. Hence, paralysis (and the act causing it) is (at least) initially sufficiently justified. The hit then helps produce the good of four being saved, which justifies the death of the other one person. In this case, no structural equivalent (or greater good) is *produced* by an evil* that has to be justified (or initially sufficiently justified) by that very good. The evil* that causes *another* greater good (four people being saved) is already justified (and, hence [at least] initially sufficiently justified) by a lesser good (one person being saved).[75]

In sum, (A)–(E) suggest that much can be said for the permissibility of a harmful act leading to evil* when (at least) the structural equivalent of a sufficient justification of that evil* need not be causally produced or sustained by evils* that are *not* themselves (at least) initially sufficiently justified. This seems to be a requirement for the *purity of causal chains* leading to a greater good. This requirement expresses a concern that the causal chain that leads to a greater good G, where G justifies evil* E, need not involve evils* that are not at least initially sufficiently justified already.

What about the evils* that are mere side effects and not involved in any causal chains leading to the good? Must they, too, be (at least) initially sufficiently justified? We have suggested that some need *not* be, namely, evils* that are indirect side effects of means that cause the greater good.[76] However, this leaves it open that it must be possible for direct side-effect evils* to be at least initially sufficiently justified.

If all this were true, then for those evils* that are direct side effects and also the ones that need to be causally involved in producing or sustaining a greater good, we would have derived the Doctrine of Initial Justification (DIJ) (omitting "sufficient" after "initial" for brevity's sake): Lesser evils* to innocent, nonthreatening people who would not face comparable threats, for whom continuing life is a good; and who have not consented to the evils* should be causable given our act either (a) by what (at least) initially sufficiently justifies these evils* (for example, a structural equivalent that can become the greater good that ultimately justifies them) or (b) by means (or effects of means) that have (at least) the structural equivalent of the greater good as their noncausal flip side or aspect.[77] The motto here is: "We must have the possibility of at least initial sufficient justification all the way down for evils* that cause, or that are directly caused by what causes, the greater good." The DIJ could be used in a rule-like fashion, like the DDE, the DDE(R) and the DTE, to test acts for permissibility and to supplant the DDE, the DDE(R) and the DTE for this purpose.[78]

In stating the DIJ, I say that lesser evils* should be "causable," rather than "caused." I also speak of evils* that are "needed" in a causal chain rather than merely occur in a causal chain. This is because, as I have said before, it is the necessity of having evil* (or means with evil* as direct effect, etc.) that is not (at least) sufficiently justified in a causal chain that is prohibited under the DIJ. To further emphasize the importance of thinking of the theory of permissibility as involving such a Modal Condition, consider how Judith Thomson, in the course of her criticism of the DDE, argues against the significance of causal structure for determining permissibility.[79] She says that some might suggest that we take the DDE as prohibiting evil from causing good (rather than prohibiting that one intend evil as a cause of good): "One possibility is to construe the doctrine as concerned, not with intendings, but with sheer causal order; I ignored this possibility in the text above, since I think it pretty obvious that the doctrine so construed has no future at all" (p. 295, n. 9). Her reason for thinking this is given when she discusses a war between Good and Bad, in which a Good pilot bombs a munitions factory and as a side effect destroys a children's hospital. She says:

> Suppose a Good pilot bombed a place in Bad that contained both a munitions factory and a children's hospital, and that the Bads therefore sued for peace— not because of the loss of the munitions factory, but because of the loss of the

children: the bombing terrorized the Bads, bringing home to them what war was going to have in store for them. It can hardly be thought that the fact that the causal route to the Goods' winning the war passed through Bad terror, rather than through Bad lack of munitions, shows that it was impermissible for the pilot to drop his bombs. (p. 297)

Suppose that bombing is permissible in Thomson's case, even if killing children who live far from a munitions plant as a means to causing surrender is not permissible. (Notice, however, that the DIJ would not endorse the permissibility of bombing if the children's deaths are a direct side effect of our means.)[80] The permissibility, I believe, would depend on the fact that bombing the munitions could be justified by its *possible* (even if not actual) causal role in bringing about peace independent of the deaths of children. This is an instance of the Modal Condition: That is, bombing the munitions plant could reasonably be undertaken even if *there were no possibility* that fear generated by the side effect bombing of the children would lead to peace. Indeed, even if one foresees that fear generated by the unavoidable deaths will actually cause the war to end, that does not mean that one cannot permissibly bomb the munitions plant that will cause the deaths, if one could bomb it when no fear was generated by the deaths. This is because (it is assumed) destroying the munitions plant was at least part of a reasonable alternative causal route to end the war. According to the DIJ, it is neither the state of mind of the agent nor the actual causal structure that matters. What matters is whether, if our act had not led to the actual causal structure, some other event would have come about due to that act, it would have conformed to the DIJ, and it would have helped to produce the greater good of peace. Hence, Thomson's argument against a theory of permissibility based on actual causal structure does not rule out the correctness of a modalized DIJ.[81]

It is time now to point out some difficulties with formulating the Modal Condition properly. To begin with, how can it even be truthfully said that a certain event's occurring is necessary as a means, given one's act? Is it not always possible that some completely unpredictable effect of one's act could and, in fact, will produce an outcome that it was only reasonable to think could be achieved by evil*? For example, suppose, completely unpredictably, that it is the color of our bombs that terrorize citizens into surrendering before the deaths indirectly caused by the bombs can terrorize them into surrendering, and the surrender justifies the deaths as indirect side effects.

Is it a solution to this problem of unpredictable causal relations to say that the deaths are, given our act, "probably necessary" to produce the surrender and this is what makes our act impermissible?[82] But it seems that there are cases in which it is also probably necessary that evil* cause an outcome, yet it is permissible to do what produces evil*. For example, suppose it is permissible to redirect a trolley away from many people, even though the trolley would then run into one person on another track. However, there is only a slight possibility of our succeeding in redirecting the trolley because it is very heavy. Further, if what we do in the attempt to redirect the trolley does not succeed in redirecting, it will have the indirect effect of pushing someone into the path of the trolley, and it will be his being hit that stops the trolley. Does it become impermissible to do the only thing that we could otherwise permissibly do—try to redirect the trolley—just because it is probably necessary that the person be hit if the trolley is to stop (in the manner described)? I do not think so. (Notice that this case differs from one in which what we do will certainly succeed in redirecting the trolley away from many people to a track where one person will be hit, but before such redirection can occur, what we do indirectly causes someone to be toppled in front of the trolley and this actually stops it. In this case, it is not true that the person being hit is probably necessary to save the many, as if he were not hit there is an alternative means that will certainly save the many.)

How can we distinguish the types of cases in which the probable necessity of evil* being a causal means to producing some good makes our acting impermissible from those cases in which it does not? One suggestion is that in some cases there is reason for an agent to believe that there is a small probability of success without evil* being a means (as is true in the case where we have a slim chance of re-directing). By contrast, in other cases there is no reason for an agent to believe that this is true (as in the case involving the color of the bombs). Notice that what is in question here is not whether any agent actually believes that he has, or does not have, a reason, but simply whether there is a reason to believe. Hence, we are still not concerned with the state of mind of an agent. And, further, it is facts in the world that account for there being a reason or not to believe something, so it is ultimately this factual difference that is crucial.

F. I do not believe that satisfying the DIJ is, in fact, necessary for permissi-bility. For the next step is to see that some evils* that are direct side effects of what we must do (or, more broadly, of our means) in order to achieve a particular greater good need not be initially sufficiently justified. That some sort of moral distinction between such direct bad side effects and evils* causally necessary to produce a greater good shows up is interesting, given the role that the distinction between evil* side effects and evils* intended as means plays in the DDE and DDE(R). (However, recall that evils* necessary to causally *produce* a greater good are not all the evils* that cause a greater good, if causally sustaining is distinguished from causally producing. And evils* that produce a greater good could be non-causally productive, and/or intended, for even in state-of-mind terms one may act merely because they will occur [as in the Tractor Case].)

(1) Consider Component Case II. A trolley is headed toward five people. Moving the trolley to the right has as its noncausal flip side the saving of one of the five and has several effects. It causes two bystanders to be hit and killed by the trolley, but their being hit plays no role in saving the four others. Moving the trolley also causes another bystander to be hit, paralyzing his leg. His being hit causes the trolley to stop, saving the four. Here there is no greater good or structural equivalent of it that (at least) initially sufficiently justifies the deaths of the two. Rather, the greater good (and structural equivalent of it) that could provide any justification for moving the trolley to the right (given that two people are thereby killed) only comes about when the five are saved.[83] This is because saving one person, which causes the death of two, neither justifies these two deaths nor is it a structural equivalent of

what would justify the deaths. But saving the five would (initially and finally) justify the two deaths, and saving the five is a consequence of hitting the one person (which causes his paralysis) that stops the trolley. Yet it is, intuitively, permissible to turn the trolley.

I think this is because, first, the bad consequence of a bystander being hit that causes the greater good is itself (at least) initially sufficiently justified by saving one life. That is, the causal chain to the greater good is pure (as explicated in [E] above), for saving one life can justify the paralysis. Second, saving one life is a component of the greater good of saving five and that greater good *is* great enough to justify the deaths of the two. Suppose that each component (or its structural equivalent) at least initially sufficiently justifies any evil* to which it leads *that is also required to produce the greater good*. Then, other directly caused evil* side effects that those components (or means noncausally related to those components) cause but do not (at least) initially sufficiently justify may, it is claimed, be justified by the greater good once it is achieved.[84]

Notice that on this analysis, there is a big moral difference between (a) a component of a greater good or the component's structural equivalent (or means having these as a noncausal flip side or aspect) directly causing an evil* side effect that the component itself cannot even initially sufficiently justify, and (b) a mere means to a greater good directly causing such an evil* side effect. The latter happens, for example, in the Wiggle-the-Bridge Case, when shaking the bridge topples the person as a direct side effect of what is needed to stop the trolley. It is being claimed that causing the evil* in (a) may be permissible; causing the evil* in (b) is not (contrary to the DDE, the DDE[R], and the DTE).[85]

It is for this reason that I am led to say that a greater good that is in the *process of working itself out* (or coming into being), and means having it as a noncausal flip side or aspect, may directly cause any evil* as a *mere side effect*, if that evil* can be justified by that greater good once achieved. However, those evils* that causally produce the very good that may be needed to ultimately justify them must be at least initially sufficiently justified. To this extent, the aspect of the DIJ concerned with the causal purity of the chain to the greater good is retained, though the treatment of direct side effects is altered. (We shall shortly introduce another alteration as well.)

All of this is consistent with a particular good, G1, having in the causal chain that produces it an evil* that is a direct side effect of a component of another greater good, G2, even though that component cannot (at least) initially sufficiently justify the evil*, when the greater good (G2) of which it is a part will justify it. For in this case, it is not G1 that would justify the existence of this evil*; G2 would do that. (So, for example, the deaths of two people in Component Case II may permissibly cause the defusing of a bomb threat to one different person even before the five being saved from the trolley justifies the deaths of the two.) Causal chains that produce a greater good need to be pure, in the sense of having no evils* that are not (at least) initially sufficiently justified only if we expect that particular greater good to ultimately justify these evils*.

(2) So far, I have discussed grounds for revising the DIJ when the causal production of the greater good is at issue. Now I will consider grounds for revising it when causally sustaining, in contrast to producing, the greater good is at issue. To do this, consider the Worse-than-Dead Case. This case is like the Loop Case except that the five toward whom the trolley are headed are so sick that if they are not cured, it would be better for them to die than to continue living. (We are here reversing our previous assumption, and the assumption of all discussions of the trolley cases of which I know, that continuing life is a benefit to those whom the trolley initially threatens.) If we turn the trolley away from them, therefore, and just consider the noncausal flip side of this, independent of further effects of our action, we see that the condition of the five is not a structural equivalent of the greater good. That is, the sick state the five are in when we turn the trolley is not such that, if only it were sustained, it would be a greater good than the death of one other person for whom life is a good. (It is not even a greater good than the five being killed by the trolley.) We also see that their being in a state that is worse than death is not enough of a good to even initially sufficiently justify the death of the one, which turning the trolley will cause.

We could even imagine a further variant, Worse-than-Dead Case II. In this case, the five would not merely remain in the same bad state (as a result of their sickness) when the trolley moves away as they were in when it was heading toward them. Rather, they are put in a *worse* state if we turn the trolley away than they were when it was heading toward them, for suppose that attached to the front of the trolley is a device that subdues pain somewhat by emitting vibrations. Then when we turn it away, the five are in even worse pain than they were when the trolley was headed toward them.[86]

Despite all of this being true, as I imagine the Worse-than-Dead cases, we could have a reason to turn the trolley even though it will kill one person who stops it from looping. This is true if we suppose that in these cases we know that a while after the trolley has stopped, an innocently acquired serum will arrive (independently of turning the trolley), and we can cure the five of their sickness. If we don't turn the trolley, they would be killed, and we could not save them to a life worth living.

I believe it is intuitively permissible to turn the trolley in the Worse-than-Dead cases with this added element. This is because (1) the five being alive (rather than dead from the trolley) is (at least the structural equivalent of) a *component* of the greater good which consists in their being alive for a long time and in a condition in which life is worth living for them; (2) this component is the non-causal flip side of turning the trolley that hits the one; (3) hitting the one sustains that component; and (4) the other means we use to bring about the greater good are quite innocent.[87]

Suppose that the Worse-than-Dead cases involve (a structural equivalent of) a component of the greater good and this, not a structural equivalent of the greater good, can justify turning the trolley. What should we say about the Tractor Case? I said that in the Tractor Case it is not permissible to turn the trolley. In discussing the DIJ, I emphasized that in this case, when we turn away the trolley, we do not have a structural equivalent of the greater good. (This is because another fatal threat to the five, for whom continued life is a good, is still present independent of any effect of what we do to remove the trolley.) But this is true in the Worse-than-Dead cases too (though not because there is another independent fatal threat). And if keeping the five alive (even in a condition worse than death) is a component of the greater good in the latter case, is not five being free of a trolley threat a component of the greater good of their being free of all threats in the Tractor Case?[88]

What distinguishes the two cases, and hence what distinguishes the intuitively permissible from the intuitively impermissible? I believe it is that in the Worse-than-Dead Case the *required* causal role (given our act) of a lesser evil* that is not at least initially sufficiently justified is to *sustain* a component of the greater good. By contrast, in the Tractor Case, the required causal role (given our act) of a lesser evil* that is not at least initially sufficiently justified is to *produce* another component of the greater good. That is, it stops the tractor from hitting the five and so makes the five be free of the tractor. Sustaining a component seems not to require causal purity in the way that production does. If the distinction drawn between these cases is correct, it shows that it is neither how we bring about the evil* that makes its causal role permissible (for this is the same in the two cases) nor the necessity, given our act, of a causal role for initially unjustified evil* that makes the act impermissible. Rather it is crucial whether the causal necessity, given our act, of initially unjustified evil* is to produce rather than sustain the greater good or its components.

I summarize the results of our discussion in (F) as follows for cases of harming (as opposed to not-aiding): (1) If an evil* cannot be at least initially sufficiently justified, it cannot be justified by the greater good that it is necessary (given our act) to causally *produce*. However, such an evil* can be justified by the greater good whose component(s) cause it, even if the evil* is causally necessary to help *sustain* the greater good or its components. (2) In order for an act to be permissible, it should be possible for any evil* side effect (except possibly indirect side effects) of what we do, or evil* causal means that we must use (given our act) to bring about the greater good, to be at least the effect of a good greater than it is working itself out (or the effect of means that are noncausally related to that greater good that is working itself out). I shall call these two conditions the Doctrine of Productive Purity (DPP), as it is especially concerned with the causes that produce the greater good and concomitant evil* side effects. The DPP, like the DIJ, employs modal notions of necessity and possibility. The DPP can be used in rule-like fashion, like the DDE, the DDE(R), DTE, and DIJ, to test acts for permissibility and can supplant them for this purpose.[89]

G. What could be the deeper meaning of the sort of inviolability that is provided by the DPP (and the nonconsequentialist principle of permissible harm, if the DPP represents a part of it accurately)? I take inviolability to be (roughly) a status expressed by what it is impermissible to do to people.[90] I believe that the key point in the deeper meaning of the DPP derives from the initial observation in (A) that fewer people have no right to complain when more people being saved will itself result in their great loss. When this is true, I think a form of substitution of persons is part of our reasoning: The loss to the fewer who are harmed is matched by the avoidance of such harm to their equal and opposite numbers in the larger group who are saved. Sometimes non-consequentialists say that people are not substitutable one for another. Indeed, some might say that we may not harm the single person in the Transplant Case because a person is not substitutable for others. But the underlying rationale of the DPP, I believe, implies that this is the wrong way to put the objection to killing in the Transplant Case. It would be better to say that in the Transplant Case, where evil* is a causal means to a greater good, a person is *subordinated* to the good of others. I believe that on the causal structures distinguished by the DPP supervenes a moral distinction between substituting one person for another and subordinating one person to another. If this distinction is an important part of respect for persons, then the necessity (given our act) of certain causal structures will be consistent with respect for persons, and the necessity of others will not be.

In chapter 2, we saw that substitution is often permissible in cases where we must choose whom to aid. There the pertinent contrast was with what I called confrontation (such as is involved in tossing a coin between people), which, I argued, is not always required in conflict cases where we cannot aid everyone. Hence, my all-encompassing conclusion is that, consistent with respect for persons, confrontation is not always required; substitution is often permissible; and subordination is prima facie wrong.

Let me clarify this a bit by moving beyond cases where greater good causes lesser evil. When we choose to send a threat to one person rather than another, one person occupies the very same position that another person would have occupied relative to the threat. (He could have occupied it even if there were no one else who might otherwise have been in that position.) This is substitution. It occurs when one person's not being threatened is the noncausal flip side of sending the threat elsewhere. By contrast, when we do something bad to someone as a causal means to save someone else from a threat, the first person occupies a different position than the second person would have in being threatened. The position he occupies involves subordination to that other person, because the position he occupies—as the means to the good of another—makes essential reference to his usefulness to achieving a good for that other person. (I emphasize, it is "that other person" versus "another person." This is because one may be put into a useful position making essential reference to the good of some person without being subordinated to another person who would otherwise have occupied that very same position. So A may be substituted for B in the position of being a means to the good of C. Then A is not subordinated to B even if each would be subordinated to C.)

How is someone subordinated to other people when we use means to help them that only harm the person as a direct side effect? (I am here only considering the means that produce the greater good causally. When the means have a non-causal productive relation to the greater good [as in the Trolley Case], I have argued, we are back to pure substitution of persons that occurs when the greater good causes lesser evil*.) One way to conceive of what is going on here[91] is that we have a choice between using a certain means to rescue people or refraining from using the means and not harming someone as a side effect. Ordinarily, if we had a choice between using a mere tool (which had no good effects for others) or not harming a person as a result of its use, we would not substitute harm to the person for not using the tool. Analogously, if a trolley were headed to a tool that would do no one any good, we would not redirect it away from the tool and toward a person. But suppose the tool were useful for saving many people. If a trolley is going to destroy this useful tool, should we send the threat instead in a direction where a person will be killed? (Call this the Trolley Tool Case.) I believe not, even if it means that one cannot help many people with the tool. If we chose to save the tool because it would be useful to save many, we would be treating the choice between the tool and the person who would be harmed by the redirected trolley in the way we treat the choice between a threat going to many people or it going to one. This implies that the many people are transmitting their importance to the tool; these people would have the power to change the value of the things in the world we all share, so that the nondestruction of the one person is less favored than the non-destruction of the tool. This elevation of the tool over a person, in virtue of its usefulness for others, results in a subordination of the one person to the other people, I believe. Hence, subordination is a broader category than using some-one as a mere means. (I am only dealing with cases where we would harm a per-son, if we save the tool, not ones where we are unable to help a person if we save the tool.)

Now consider a case that involves choosing to *use* a tool such as a bomb to help many (not saving the tool from a threat), even though as a side effect someone will be directly killed by the use of the tool. In this case, I believe we choose between the use of the tool and the life of the person, and if the tool wins, it is because the people who would be saved elevate the tool and subordinate a person to it. So while the person is not a tool (as when his involvement is necessary as a means to the good of others), he is subordinated to a tool and to the power of those others who endow the tool with a significance comparable to their own.

But there are many questions raised by this analysis. For one, why is it per-missible to use a means that will cause harm to a person indirectly? In discussing such cases above (in section D), we distinguished between our introducing some-thing that is, or overlaps with something that is, threatening and the threat coming about in virtue of something else in the context to which we introduce something. But the fact that we should not allow ourselves to do even the latter if a greater good were *not* at stake suggests that the weight of the greater good of many people saved is being transmitted so as to elevate the importance of the use of the means relative to the importance of not harming a person.

And why does subordination not occur when a person's not being killed is less important than a mere nonjustifying component of a greater good, as in the Component Case II? In that case, the component is allowed to stand for the greater good itself with respect to directly causing the evil* side effect of two deaths. Why does subordination not occur when an evil* that is the result of either a structural equivalent, or a nonjustifying component, of the greater good causally *sustains* either the greater good or a component of it? Yet subordination does occur when such an evil* causally produces the greater good or its component. According to the DPP, once the greater good starts to exist, it has enormous power to justify evil* but not enough power to justify (i.e., make nonsubordinating) evil* means to its own further causal production.

This all still has to be explained. Suppose that the distinction between substitution and subordination were not the right one to do the job. It would still be true, I believe, that a moral theory about how persons should be treated is expressed by the types of causal relations that it is impermissible to require and permissible to allow among goods, harms, and events leading to these goods and harms. It is not greater or lesser inviolability alone that is important (thought of quantitatively) but rather the structure of respectful violability. Furthermore, it will remain true that the methodology for dealing with this issue is to (1) consider the principle that describes appropriate causal relations (whether it is the DPP or something else), (2) find the morally important distinctions that supervene on these relations, and (3) see how they figure in our concept of respect for persons.[92]

H. The DPP may justify the permissibility of turning the trolley from five toward one. It does not justify turning the trolley from one toward five. A bystanding agent who turned a trolley headed to one toward five instead would be acting impermissibly, other things equal. Furthermore, if a trolley were originally headed toward one person and that person himself controlled the switch, it would not be permissible for him to redirect it toward five people. However, if the trolley is redirected from five toward one, then it is permissible (not merely excusable bad conduct), I believe, for the one person, if he controls the switch, to redirect the trolley although it then goes back to the five. (Call this the Sending-Back Case.) If this is true, then whether a person is threatened as a consequence of saving others or just threatened tout court can be morally significant.[93]

The permissibility of sending back the trolley is not explained by the DPP. It is also not explained by the impermissibility of redirecting the threat toward him, as it is not impermissible. It may be explained, in part, by his having a general right not to be harmed that would be infringed when the trolley is redirected toward him. That is, while he has no right that the trolley not be redirected toward him away from the five, his general right not to be harmed is (permissibly) infringed, and this could result in his being wronged even in the course of a permissible act.[94]

Suppose that the single person physically cannot send back the trolley. However, he is able to put a protective shield in front of himself, and when the trolley hits the shield it will travel back toward the five (Protective Shield Case). Even if it were impermissible for him to send back the trolley, it would be permissible (and not merely excusable bad conduct) to use the protective shield despite its effects.

In sending the trolley back from himself or using the shield, the one person is resisting an improvement in the world and returning things to the way they were for the five. This does not mean he is limited to sending back and shielding when he makes people no worse off than they would have been without the original redirection. For suppose that sending back the trolley also threatened, for the very first time, several bystanding agents who had permissibly redirected the trolley. The victim's sending back the trolley is still permissible, I think. The fact that even multiple agents who redirect are susceptible to being permissibly threatened by one person to save himself in this way suggests several things.

First, a bystanding agent's liability to being harmed in this way might (in part) explain why it is only permissible, but not obligatory, for a bystanding agent to turn the trolley. For such an act opens him up to permissibly being harmed (at least in certain ways) by a self-defending victim. (This will not explain why it is not obligatory to redirect the trolley when it is known that there is no risk of the trolley being sent back toward the bystanding agent.)

Second, if the five people redirect the trolley away from harming them, then they might become liable to a self-defending or self-protecting victim making them worse off than they originally would have been. The ground for believing this is that the bystanding agent becomes liable to being made worse off than he would otherwise have been, in virtue of his agency.

Third, recall that in cases such as Lazy Susan Case 4, the five people become the threat to the one person. We said that these are cases where the five are innocent threats. Suppose that the one victim can resist their impact on him, for example, by using the protective shield even if their hitting it sends the five back into the trolley. Then considering the trolley cases will have helped us derive a position on the permissibility of harming innocent threats, even when their being threats to someone, in an important sense, involves no improper transgression of the rights of the victim.

Compare Lazy Susan Case 4 with what might be said about standard innocent threat cases (as described in section V[A]. These are cases in which a person is, for example, hurled at someone else and his impact will kill the victim but not harm the threat, unless the victim kills the threat. It has been argued by some that the rights of the victim not to be imposed on in this way will be violated by the innocent threat (not just by a villain who hurls him), even though he is a nonactive, nonresponsible threat. This is said to be a ground for the permissibility of the victim killing the innocent threat.[95]

It is also said to be a ground for the duty of an innocent threat to redirect himself, if he can, from threatening his victim. Suppose that the threat had a button he could press that would send him into a wall rather than into his victim below. He would have a duty to do this, at least at some cost, to himself. (A bystander who could stop a threat's fall onto a victim by swerving himself into a wall would have no comparable duty.) If he would have had a duty to do this if he had had a button then, if he lacks a button, why cannot the victim or a bystanding agent also, at the same cost to the threat, do what will stop the threat falling on the victim?[96]

Are these claims also true when the five become innocent threats to the one, for example, in Lazy Susan Case 4? Unlike the standard cases, where a wrong act or an unfortunate natural event results in someone being a threat, the five become threats as the result of a permissible act whose permissibility is determined by taking into account the harm to the one person. As in the Trolley Case, it seems that there is no right of the one person not to have the Lazy Susan turned, though there may be an infringement of some right of his not to be harmed and also a wronging of him in the course of this permissible act. Yet the victim may harm the threat. Further, the five do not have a duty to prevent themselves from harming the one person at the cost of their lives, however, there might still be a duty of the five (or of an agent who turns them) to impose some cost on the five so that the one is not killed. A ground for thinking this is that it does not seem permissible to remove the five from a threat that would not cause any of them to die, if their removal will cause them to become lethal threats to the one person. Hence, even if they have been removed from a trolley that does threaten to kill them, why should they not pay a significant cost less than death to avoid killing the one person? This is the equivalent of not avoiding a lesser loss to themselves by becoming lethal threats to the one person.

May a third party assist the victim in harming the innocent threat in standard innocent threat cases? If there is a real asymmetry in the positions of the threat and his potential victim, because the innocent threat will be imposing in a way that he should not, then a third party should side with the victim. A third party, however, should not assist the potential victim in the Lazy Susan Case 4. This is because the asymmetry favors the five in that case, as their imposing is the preferred alternative to their being killed and results from a permissible act.

Despite this asymmetry that favors the five, we argued that the potential victim may send the trolley back or put up a protective shield, even if that sends the five back into the trolley. In the standard innocent threat case, where it seems that the asymmetry favors the one victim, would it be permissible for the innocent threat to also put up a protective shield against a permissible self defensive threat from the victim? That is, if the potential victim may permissibly try to kill the threat, when this is necessary to stop the threat's improper imposition, may the threat put up a protective shield to protect himself although this implies that his fall will not be interfered with and he will kill the victim? I believe that it is permissible for him to do this. (It would not in the same way be permissible for a responsible aggressor to protect himself against the threat that would stop his aggression.) Hence, the threat need not refrain from doing something that interferes with preventing his wrongful imposition, just as the victim in Lazy Susan Case 4 need not refrain from doing something that interferes with the rescue of the five. They may both stand in the way of the existence of the preferred state of affairs (i.e., no wrongful imposition or the five being saved, respectively).

This discussion suggests that whether an imposition is wrongful or rights violating has less bearing on what may or must be done by various parties than has been thought.

VI. SECONDARY PERMISSIBILITY

Let us suppose that the DPP is correct. That does not mean that the DPP is absolute in the sense that there is no greater good whose achievement could not override it. "Threshold deontologists hold that, at least, the avoidance of very great evils* might bring us to a threshold where moral constraints are overridden. Also, recall that the DPP is a principle that tells us when one might harm people not otherwise under comparable threats. I wish now to consider a way in which DPP constraints on harming do not apply when people are under comparable threats. I believe that our conduct toward such people is governed by the DPP combined with what I have called the Principle of Secondary Permissibility (PSP).

Consider a case in which causing evil* to A in violation of the DPP would lead to A avoiding a greater evil*. For example, suppose that it is impermissible to paralyze A's legs as a means to a greater good. It would still be permissible, to do this as the alternative to permissibly killing A as a mere indirect side effect. This is, in part, because it is much better for him to be paralyzed than to be killed. This is an instance of the PSP. It sometimes allows as an alternative an act that would not have been permitted if it were the only act one could perform, when this alternative act is the one, of all those that could reasonably be done, that minimizes the harm that would permissibly have been done to the same person. (The minimization condition rules out picking a somewhat less harmful act that could have been done, but not the least harmful one.) The PSP implies that sometimes we need to know that would actually have permissibly been done if we do not do an act of a certain type before we can decide whether an act of that type is permissible.

The PSP also reminds us that an act for which we are allowed to substitute another act was permissible, even though it would have caused more harm than the act that was originally impermissible, and so it is worse (if not a greater moral evil) in that sense. It is because of this that, in some cases, what was originally a greater moral evil can become permissible secondarily, because it involves less harm to the same people.

In another case, suppose it would be permissible according to the DPP to produce a great good by innocent means despite the foreseen evil* side effect of killing Joe and Jim. There is an alternative, however: We could bring about the great good by killing Joe as a means and without harming Jim. I believe that it is sometimes permissible to kill Joe as a means, in part because he will be no worse off than he would otherwise permissibly be, and Jim will be much better off. (It may be that when the victim would be better off, we could be obligated to do what is secondarily permissible, but not obligated when he will not be better off.)

What if those who would die shortly anyway would not die as a result of a permissible act but of an impermissible act? For example, during World War II, the Allies were asked to bomb trains carrying people to Nazi extermination camps. If it were certain that those people would soon die of wrongful Nazi acts and if our killing them would have been a means to saving others by ending the war, it would have been permissible to kill them, I believe. What if we are reformed Nazis and cannot stop our underlings at the concentration camps but wish to save lives? Then we too are permitted to bomb the trains, but we bear greater responsibility for the deaths as we created the original impermissible threat of extermination that called for the substituted act.[97]

Notice that the PSP, unlike a general consequentialist justification, does not imply that if the consequences will be the same or better, then it does not matter how we bring them about. For example, the PSP does not claim that if it would be permissible to let someone die, then it would also be permissible to kill him or paralyze him even when we are not actually in a position to leave him to die of other causes because he is under no threat. By contrast to a consequentialist justification, the PSP requires that the person we would kill or otherwise harm would actually otherwise have been harmed to as great an extent anyway.

Consider now how the PSP may be extended to show that people who are not under comparable threats may also be made much worse off than they otherwise would have been and by a route that is not usually permitted by the DPP.[98] Suppose that we have the capacity to permissibly bomb a munitions plant (in accord with the DPP) to achieve a great good despite foreseen deaths as indirect side effects, but we choose not to take advantage of this option because we do not want to cause so many deaths. Then we find out that we could achieve the same great good if we instead kill as a means one of the many people whom we can still permissibly kill as a side effect*. He is one of those whom we would have the capacity to permissibly kill as a means if doing this were the alternative to *actually* causing his and many more deaths as a mere side effect. This is what the PSP has already been shown to imply. Why should the fact that we decided *not* to actually exercise our capacity and moral option to harm many people as a side effect—and so the one person is not actually under a threat and would not otherwise have died—stand in the way of our permissibly killing him as a means? The only reason he will be worse off if we do this than he would otherwise have been is that we would refrain from doing what it is both permissible and within our capacity to do (i.e., kill many as a side effect). The permissibility of killing him as a means to achieving the same good in this case is an Extension of the Principle of Secondary Permissibility (EPSP). This is because it does not depend on considering what we or others would *actually* otherwise do. It depends on considering what we can (in the sense of what it is permissible and within our current capacity to) otherwise do.

The EPSP also differs from a general consequentialist justification. This is because it requires that at the time we harm the person as a means, we actually have the capacity to permissibly harm him to as great an extent (in accord with a nonconsequentialist principle such as the DPP), but we refrain from doing so.[99]

What if it would be permissible to cause the bystander deaths as indirect side effects but we have no capacity to do this (e.g., soldiers in the plant would shoot down our planes before we could bomb). Would some further extension of the PSP imply that it is permissible to bomb one of the bystanders as a means to achieve the same good result? I think the fact that we do not merely refrain from doing what we can permissibly do but actually cannot do what is permitted marks a moral difference. It is a reason against the permissibility of killing the one person in this case that he will be worse off than there was any possibility of his being. What if someone else has the capacity to permissibly do what would kill the bystander but chooses not to do this? Does this license us to do something otherwise impermissible to the bystander under the EPSP? I do not think so.

What if entirely different people will be killed as mere means than would have been, or can be, permissibly affected as indirect side effects by the bombing of the military facility? When entirely different people will be affected and their harm will be in the disfavored means role, it is quite likely that it will remain wrong to bomb a few people rather than the military facility that causes greater indirect side-effect deaths. For we cannot, in general, do equal or somewhat less harm to fewer people in an impermissible way in order to avoid doing equal or more harm to a greater number of entirely different people in a permissible way. (This assumes that the additional number of dead people is not enough of an evil* that preventing it moves us above the threshold for not killing some people as means.)

When people speak about doing the lesser evil, they sometimes speak as though they have in mind a choice between two acts that remain wrong whichever is done. But this model is not present in the cases we have so far discussed. When a threshold is reached and then an otherwise forbidden act is done, or when an act is covered by the PSP, the act can be not a lesser moral evil but permissible. This is true even though it involves evil* (e.g., harm or involvement leading to it) to a lesser degree than some other act. In that sense it is a lesser evil.* But evil* is a ground for deciding that an act that produces it is a moral evil (i.e., morally wrong); evil* is not identical with a moral evil, for it is just a description of something bad happening to someone, and sometimes bringing about such a bad is permissible and not a moral evil.

Though typically discussions involving threshold deontological reasoning result in a justification that makes an act permissible, we can extend such reasoning, combined with the idea of substituting one act for another, to apply to cases where the act we should do instead of some other act is still a wrong act (i.e., a moral evil). We can do this, if we imagine a variation on our bombing case in which an agent has no adequate goal to justify causing so much indirect collateral damage by bombing a military facility. Hence, his act is morally wrong. Furthermore, in this case a small subsection of the very same people who would have been killed if the military facility had been hit would die if he bombs them instead as a means to his goal. I suggest that if it were wrong to bomb the military facility causing side-effect deaths and also wrong to bomb people as a means, considered as individual acts, then it would be morally better if the wrong of bombing the few is done in place of doing the other wrong act. This can be true, even though this involves using the few people as means, and though we assume that this act requires a type of causal role for people that can sometimes make an act impermissible when other types of acts causing the same or somewhat greater indirect side-effect deaths would be permissible.

This case of an agent bombing a few people who would otherwise die by another wrong act of his would then be a true case of doing a lesser moral evil. This is because producing the lesser evil* is still a moral evil and does not become at all a permissible act. We can call it a secondary wrong, and we can call the principle covering its choice the Principle of Secondary Wrong (PSW). Here an act that would have been wrong to perform, if it were the only act available, should be substituted for another wrong act in the second place, but it is still a wrong act. At least part of the justification for the substitution is that the number of lives lost will be very greatly reduced and all those who die as a means would have been dead as a side effect in any case. Hence, no one is worse off than he would have been and some are better off. The underlying idea as with the PSP, is that the stronger moral constraint against causing harm as a necessary means is not as strong when the same harm will not be avoided by abiding by the constraint. This conclusion implies that the fact that an agent kills people as a means to his end of winning a conflict should not always be taken as evidence of his having the worst intentions for them. For in the scenario we are now considering, given the alternatives, it is the person who would choose to cause more deaths who could exhibit the worst intentions toward people. This is because, given that he is going to do some wrongful killing of a group of people, and given that he believes correctly that his killing fewer of the same people as a means to his end is the morally preferable alternative, he could only rationally choose the act that kills more people as a side effect because he intends their deaths as an end in itself.

Now suppose that bombing the military facility and thus causing many indirect deaths would have been impermissible because the agent lacks an adequate goal, and that bombing fewer different people as a means to his end would also have been impermissible. The fact that many more people would die in the former operation than in the latter, might still make bombing the fewer the lesser wrong (despite its use of the morally less favored means role for people). This is a further instance of the idea of a secondary wrong. However, here the justification for doing the lesser wrong would have to be a great difference in numbers of dead that could bring us above a threshold in selecting between wrong acts.

Hence, we cannot say whether an act of the type disallowed by the DPP should not be done until we know the numbers who will be similarly affected if another act is done, who those affected are, and whether the alternative act was permissible or impermissible according to the DPP. This is in addition to having to know whether a threshold on abiding by constraints on treating people in certain ways is reached because transgressing the constraints is the only way to avoid some great evil that there is no other way to avoid.

VII. APPLICATION

I wish to conclude by considering how the DPP deals with a moral problem typically discussed by supporters of the DDE and the DDE(R)—distinguishing the terror bombing of innocent civilians from tactical bombing.[100] In the standard tactical case, a munitions factory is the target, and bombing it kills innocent civilians as a side effect but also produces a greater good. (Both acts would be undertaken by those waging a war for just goals, let us assume.)

Traditionally, these terror and tactical bombings are distinguished by the DDE on the grounds that we *intend* deaths in terror bombing but only *foresee* them in tactical bombing. Hence, tactical bombing might be permissible and is not ruled out on account of side-effect deaths per se. But we have already seen that it is impermissible to act in many cases in which we can produce a greater good only if we use means that, as a side effect, cause an evil*, and the act can be impermissible because of the side-effect deaths. I believe that the features that make action impermissible in many cases we have examined are present in many versions of tactical bombing. (This includes the kind standardly presented as a contrast with terror bombing where our bombs themselves kill civilians.) Hence, it is a puzzle why it has been thought that side-effect lesser evil* does not make tactical bombing impermissible.[101]

To consider this issue further, we should consider some varieties of tactical bombing. In the standard case, the evil* is the deaths of innocent children. In all of the cases that I have seen discussed, it is the children of the enemy nation who die. It is possible that in these standard cases, it is the fact that the children belong to the enemy nation, combined with some distinctions drawn by the DDE or the DPP, that would account for the permissibility of some tactical bombing. In order to make sure that this fact is not influencing our judgment, I shall imagine that all of my cases involve deaths of children belonging to a neutral nation across the border from the enemy. The munitions factory we must bomb (in one type of case) is near this border. To hold this factor constant between tactical and terror bombing, I shall also assume that we would have to terror bomb (or intentionally bomb for some other reason) the neutral nation's children in order to stop the enemy country from waging war against us.[102] Hence, if tactical bombing is not ruled out because it satisfies the DDE or the DPP, the side-effect deaths should not rule out doing what kills the neutral nation's children as well as the enemy's children. If killing only the neutral nation's children is objectionable, this shows that it is the special status as the enemy's children that is doing work previously attributed (by the DDE) to the structure of action and or state of mind of the agent alone.

In sum, our aim is to see whether the conditions enumerated in a principle of harm, rather than the difference in nationality, determine whether and when we may kill civilians in a just war.

Now consider some cases. Tactical Case 1, unlike the tactical case traditionally discussed, involves our dropping bombs *into* a school on enemy territory where the neutral children are visiting students. We bomb the school because there is a tunnel (open only during school hours) leading from this building into an otherwise impenetrable munitions plant. Only bombs dropped into the school will have an impact on the munitions plant. In this case, what we must do (drop bombs *into* the school) to destroy the plant will overlap with the evil*, since the children occupy the area that our bomb will occupy, and they die from this. However, their deaths are not a means to destroying the plant nor are their deaths intended to terrorize. According to the DPP, bombing in this case should be impermissible.

In Tactical Case 2, we bomb the munitions plant, but we cannot target precisely enough, so our bombs also kill the children from the neutral country in a school building nearby across the border in the neutral country. This is a case where our means (the bomb), though not what we must do with it in order to achieve our end, directly kills. The DDE would permit such action; the DPP would rule it out.

In Tactical Case 3, we bomb the munitions plant, but vibrations from our bombs cause the roof of the school across the border to collapse. The collapse of the roof causes the deaths of the children. The DPP does not rule out an evil* that is the indirect effect of means (and anything else we introduce into a context) that lead to a greater good. If this is how the Tactical Bombing Case has traditionally been conceived in standard comparisons with the Terror Bombing Case, then this might account for why it was thought that tactical bombing can be permissible despite the creation of lesser evil*. (Notice that this case differs from one where pieces of our *bomb* also hit the schoolhouse roof. For this can be construed as our means [in the sense of an entity we must use] overlapping with and triggering the direct cause of death. The DPP would rule out this bombing.)

In Tactical Case 4, we bomb the munitions plant and its blowing up, not our bombs, kills some of the neutral children. The blowing up of the munitions also causes the roof of their schoolhouse to fall, and this kills yet other children. In this case, it is the achievement of our goal (the munitions being blown up) that causes the evil*, by contrast to our means to this goal causing the evil* in cases (1)–(3). If the blowing up of the munitions were a greater good, the DPP would permit us to bomb, for it is the greater good that would cause the lesser evil*. If this is how the Tactical Bombing Case has been conceived in standard comparison with the Terror Bombing Case, then this might account for why it was thought that the creation of lesser evil* does not rule out tactical bombing being permissible. But in what sense is getting rid of munitions itself a greater good, rather than a means to the greater good of there being no war? If it is only a means, then its exploding and directly causing the deaths of children will be ruled out by the DPP. (Notice that blowing up the munitions is a means in the sense that it is something we must do to achieve our goal. It is not a device that we introduce; it is something we must do to a device that is already present in a context.)

Here are two ways in which getting rid of munitions can be seen as more than a mere means that helps cause the greater good of no war, even if it is not the greater good itself.[103] First, in a context where there is a limited amount of munitions, getting rid of these munitions has, as its noncausal flip side, the inability to kill people who would otherwise be killed with these munitions. Their not being killed by the munitions is not a further causal consequence of getting rid of munitions. Hence, even if getting rid of the munitions were a means to a greater good, it would have that greater good as its noncausal flip side and so, according to the DPP, it may directly cause a lesser evil*—as when blowing up the factory incinerates a few children but eliminates weapons that would have killed many people.[104]

However, suppose that more children will be directly killed by the explosion of the munitions plant than are saved by the absence of the small stock of munitions in the plant. May we still bomb the munitions plant, even if the evil* is greater than the good? We may be helped in answering this question by conceiving of the explosion of the plant in another way. If a small number not killed by munitions is a *component* of a greater good (that is, no more people being killed in war), then bombing could still be justified according to the DPP, but only if the greater good is truly construable as having that smaller good as its component. This would be so in Tactical Case 5: We blow up a small bit of an enormous munitions plant. Lives saved from this itself would not justify the evil* it causes. However, the fire in this part of the plant causes the rest of the plant to be destroyed (causing no more deaths of children). Lives saved as a noncausal flip side of the destruction of the total plant could justify the evil*. In this case, we first take care of part of the threat presented by the munitions in the plant, and then the rest of that very threat is also eliminated. Hence, the good that is the flip side of taking care of part of the munitions threat is a component of the greater good that is a flip side of taking care of the rest of the threat. The DPP would not rule out bombing in this case.[105]

However, suppose that we believe that the bombing of an enemy that kills innocent members of the *enemy* nation is permissible in many cases that the DPP rules out. This will be evidence for the view that harming a member of an enemy nation is another factor that narrows the scope of the constraints of a general moral principle like the DPP. Even independent of consent, innocents in a nation at war might be liable to harm in a manner contrary to the DPP. Then theories of just conduct in war that do not take account of the fact that some of those innocent bystanders who get killed are members of the enemy nation, and that they may be treated differently from a neutral nation's innocent bystanders, would not be correct.[106]

NOTES

This chapter is a substantial revision of "Toward the Essence of Nonconsequentialism," in *Fact and Value: Essays on Ethics and Metaphysics for Judith Jarvis Thomson*, ed. Alex Byrne, Robert Stalnaker, and Ralph Wedgwood, pp. 155–182 (Cambridge, MA: MIT Press, 2001).

For comments on earlier versions of this chapter, I am grateful to Michael Bratman, Ruth Chang, Ronald Dworkin, Shelly Kagan, Niko Kolodny, Liam Murphy, Thomas Nagel, Derek Parfit, Larry Temkin, Ralph Wedgwood, Susan Wolf, and members of the NYU Colloquium on Law, Philosophy, and Political Theory; Philamore; the Chapel Hill Colloquium on Philosophy; audiences at the colloquia of the Philosophy Departments of Harvard University and City University Graduate Center; and my graduate class in the Philosophy Department, Harvard University.

1. I exclude from consideration persons who are shields (because they are part of threats). I also exclude from consideration cases in which one must harm someone as part of one's attempt to stop aiding that person, for example, cases where one must kill someone in order to be able to stop providing that person with life support. For further exclusions from the constraint, see my "Failures of Just War Theory," *Ethics* 114, no. 4 (July 2004): 650–92.

2. Some of the material in the first part of this chapter briefly summarizes points made in greater detail in chapters 1, 3, and 4. This material is repeated to aid in comprehension of what follows and to help in seeing how the ultimate theory develops out of earlier steps. It is probably presented too briefly to be of much assistance to those who have not read the earlier chapters.

3. As already noted (in chapter 4), I accept that there is a delicate distinction to be drawn between intending and aiming such that all intendings involve aimings but not the reverse. I shall consider aiming at an evil to violate the DDE, even when it does not amount to intending.

4. The one person is typically envisioned as on a sidetrack, but this is not necessary. He could be in another part of the country or on a bridge over the track, and the redirection of the trolley, for example, on to the bridge would still be permissible. It is for this reason that

I do not think that there is a "risk free zone," at least prior to an act of redirection. (For more on this, see VB.ii.)

5. This case is modeled on one described by Philippa Foot in her "Killing and Letting Die," in *Abortion: Moral and Legal Perspectives*, ed. J. Garfield and P. Hennessey, pp. 177–85 (Amherst: University of Massachusetts Press, 1984). It is also modeled on a case she uses as an objection to the DDE (in Philippa Foot, "The Problem of Abortion and the Doctrine of Double Effect," in her *Virtues and Vices* [Oxford: Blackwell, 1978]): We must operate on five people in order to save their lives, but doing so requires that we use a gas. The gas is harmless to the five, but we foresee that it will unavoidably seep into a neighboring room, where it will kill an immovable patient. We may not operate on the five, she concluded, though we do not intend the lesser evil (Gas Case).

6. Judith Thomson also raises objections to the DDE on the ground that someone's intentions are irrelevant to whether his act is permissible. See her "Self-Defense," *Philosophy & Public Affairs* 20 (1991): 283–310 and her "Physician-Assisted Suicide: Two Moral Arguments," *Ethics* 109 (1999): 497–518.

7. He does not even act intending to save the five as a means to his killing his enemy. He need not do this, as the five will be saved without his intending that they be saved, just as long as he does what must be done to kill his enemy. To say that he intends to save the five as a means to his killing his enemy suggests that if his act did not save the five, he would, as a rational agent, be committed to doing something (in itself unproblematic) in order to make it the case that his act would save the five. But, as a rational agent, he need not be committed to doing this just because he wishes to take advantage of a connection that already exists between doing what kills his enemy and bringing about a greater good.

8. I believe that this is the standard way in which the DDE is presented. For more on this, see n. 50 in chapter 4.

9. See Warren Quinn, "Actions, Intentions, and Consequences: The Doctrine of Double Effect," in his *Morality and Action* (New York: Cambridge University Press, 1993).

10. As noted in chapter 3, this revision is not unproblematic, as it radically changes the apparent point of the DDE. Those defenders of the DDE who focus on not aiming at evil per se should be reluctant to accept the DDE(R). For example, I believe it is inconsistent with Thomas Nagel's defense of the DDE in his *The View from Nowhere* (New York: Oxford University Press, 1986) as he emphasizes how we "go against the moral grain" by pursuing evil. (His account is also problematic in that we can also pursue evil merely as a sign of what we intend and so pursuit of evil does not delimit cases of intending evil. For example, suppose we intend to bomb a munitions factory and it is permissible to do so despite the fact that children will die as a side effect. Clouds cover the factory and our only sign that we have succeeded in destroying it is the dead children next door. So we might keep bombing the factory until we see that the children are dead.)

11. See chapter 4 for more on this.

12. See Judith Thomson, "The Trolley Problem," *Yale Law Journal* 94 (1985): 1395–1415. I discussed the DTE, its application to the Loop Case, and what it implies about instrumental rationality in more detail in chapter 4.

13. As I pointed out in chapter 4, the trolley need not even be coming from a different direction for there to be a new problem. We could imagine a Loop Case in which the redirection results in the trolley going in a perfect circle right back to where it was originally (A) and then heading toward the five. I still believe that it is proper to see the trolley's coming back to the original point (A) as a second problem that arises from what we did to take care of the first problem.

14. Apart from the consistency of redirecting the trolley and then trying to rescue the one, one may ask whether it is morally permissible for anyone to try to rescue the one? After all,

this will make things worse for the greater number. But consider an analogy that should convince us that it is morally permissible, and even required to do the rescue: Someone dying from disease A means that we will have his organs to keep five others alive. The five do not have a right that someone be sick with disease A in order to help them. Now we find a cure for disease A. It is wrong to deny someone that cure just because we foresee that this will mean there are no organs with which to save the five.

15. There may be exceptions to this. For example, suppose we legitimately prohibit someone from doing an otherwise permissible act (e.g., chewing gum) as a way of punishing him for having a bad intention in doing the act (e.g., to show off). Punishment can be a way of trying to eradicate the tendency to form the bad intention. Another possible exception can arise, according to Thomas Scanlon, when an act's meaning is crucial for its permissibility and its meaning is a function of the agent's intention. (See chapter 1, endnote 3). When an act is permissible even if the agent does it with an improper intention, this is consistent with hoping that someone does not do the permissible act (e.g., hoping that he sleeps through the opportunity to act), so as to avoid his exercising his capacity for having inappropriate intentions and so as to avoid bad intentions being efficacious. But if the act is not only permissible but one's duty, one should put doing the act before avoiding actualizing one's capacity for having efficacious inappropriate intentions that will lead to the act. If the act produces a supererogatory good, we will have to consider the loss of benefits to others in deciding whether we prefer that a permissible act not be prompted by a bad intention. Furthermore, to the extent that the law should prohibit attempts, it may be correct to punish someone who did a permissible act while attempting (and thereby intending) but failing to do an impermissible act. For example, suppose the bad man in the Bad Man Case did not even know that five people stood to be saved if he redirected the trolley. Arguably, he attempted but failed to do an impermissible act (turning the trolley toward someone when this would not save anyone else), and he could be punished for this. For more on this issue, see my "Baselines and Compensation," *San Diego Law Review* 40 (2003): 1367–1386.

16. I am here suggesting a solution to a problem left open in discussion of this case in chapter 4.

17. Discussion with Niko Kolodny helped me to see this, though I am not sure he would agree with the following analysis.

18. It is tempting to say that the reasoning not to go to A would be the same whether or not track B were present. That is, A is first eliminated and then the reasoning to go to B is the same as in the regular Loop Case. (Kolodny suggested this.) But I do not think this is right. For suppose the route to the five via A took much longer to traverse than the original route of the trolley to the five. Then if B were not present as an alternative, we should choose A. We could not eliminate A in this variation without knowing about B. The analogue of the Double Track Case in the realm of the Party cases (discussed in chapter 4) may be the following variant: Suppose that I must serve beverages at my party in order to have a party. I have a choice of one that will eliminate feelings of indebtedness to a host and one that will not. I would not have the party at all if I had to use the first one as my guests would not clean up the mess caused by the party and removal of the mess is necessary for having a party. Choosing the second beverage as the only condition under which a party will be held could be permissible, even if doing certain extra things that become necessary to fuel feelings of indebtedness were impermissible. The adequacy of the analogy is complicated by the fact that in the Trolley cases, the one person harmed does not benefit along with others from this harm, and there is no other way to save the five than a way that harms the one. By contrast, in the Party Case, those who clean up also benefit from the party and the good of the party is achievable if I don't refuse to clean up the mess as well as if others clean it up.

19. Notice that in this case, unlike the Double Track Case, there is no route that we must decide against taking that gets the trolley away from its initial hit but does not involve hitting the one.

20. The structure of the Tractor Case is like the structure of the Prize Party Case described in chapter 4. In that case, I give a party in order to have fun and also because the clean-up efforts of my guests, which are expected effects of the negative feeling of indebtedness that my party produces in them, will lead to my winning a neatness prize. The fun alone is not, for me, a sufficient primary reason (goal) to act, with the bad effect (feeling of indebtedness) merely helping to defeat a potential defeater (the mess) of my goal in acting. The Prize Party Case contrasts with the Party Case, just as the Tractor Case contrasts with the Loop Case. For in the Party Case, I will give a party to have fun, if I do not have to clean up the mess by myself. I foresee that my guests' feelings of indebtedness to me (which are a harm to them) will lead them to clean up the mess. (In Party Case II, even more like the Loop Case, their cleaning up the mess during the party helps to keep the party alive.) Hence, I give the party to have fun because I expect the feeling of indebtedness to lead to the clean-up. Here the bad effect defeats the potential defeater of my achieving the goal (that gives me my primary reason for action).

21. I believe that this term was introduced by Jonathan Bennett.

22. I leave open the possibility, however, that punishability could depend on the reasonableness of an agent's ignorance of consequences and on what an agent was attempting to do. On the debate concerning whether reference to all states of mind is eliminatable in a theory of permissibility, see Judith Thomson's *The Realm of Rights* (Cambridge, MA: Harvard University Press, 1990) and Thomas Scanlon's "Permissibility and Intention I," *Proceedings of the Aristotelian Society* Suppl. 74 (2000): 301–17. One issue on which they divide is whether the fact that someone *had no way of knowing* that his act would lead to harm is relevant (or irrelevant) to deciding whether he is acting impermissibly (even if excusably).

23. Strictly speaking, it is the first few minutes of the five being saved, which is a component of the greater good that consists in their long-term survival, that causes the lesser evil*. (Derek Parfit emphasized this to me.) I shall continue to speak of the greater good causing the lesser evil* when it is such a time-slice component of it that causes the lesser evil*, for we would not undertake to produce that time-slice and allow it to cause lesser evil* unless we thought that it would be a component of long-term survival. Only the latter would justify the evil*.

24. See his *Anarchy, State and Utopia* (New York: Basic Books, 1974).

25. For example, see my "The Insanity Defense, Innocent Threats, and Limited Alternatives," *Criminal Justice Ethics* 6 (1987): 61–76; and Judith Thomson, "Self Defense."

26. See below Section VH for a brief discussion of this complex topic.

27. Another class of cases, which I shall call Threats Incorporated, more doubtfully shows the connection between principles suggested by the Trolley Problem and the topic of innocent threats. In these cases, as well, a greater number of people are threatened. We (or the people threatened) can get rid of the threat by doing what redirects it to fewer people. But redirecting the threat also makes the greater number of people themselves into threats to others. This is because the threat is already incorporated into them. Consider the Already Sick Case. Suppose that five people have deadly germs in their bodies but if either (1) they cough, or (2) a doctor pumps the germs out, they will be saved from the threat. Unfortunately, there is someone near them who cannot be moved and who will be immediately killed by the deadly germs once they are brought out. When people cough out germs that will harm others, they are threats to others, even if they are also thereby redirecting a threat. (By contrast, if the germs were merely on their way to the five, redirecting them would not make the people themselves into threats, at least not in the sense involved in standard innocent threat cases.) If a doctor may pump the germs out,

then presumably the people may permissibly cough them out. Hence, it would be permissible for them to become threats.

Might the fact that a threat is already part of these people, however, stand in the way of redirecting it? To examine this question, we might consider the positive analogue to a threat, namely, a benefit. Judith Thomson argued (in her "Killing, Letting Die, and the Trolley Problem," *The Monist* 59 [1976]: 204–17) that if a benefit were headed toward a smaller number of people, then it would be permissible to turn it toward a larger number of people instead. But if the benefit had already reached the smaller number, is it less likely that we could not take it away from them in order to give to the greater number, for it would have already become theirs? If so, then here the fact that the benefit is incorporated would stand in the way of redirecting it. Of course, people wish to retain benefits but do not wish to retain threats. Nevertheless, if being incorporated made a benefit belong to someone, it might also make a threat belong to someone, so that it is no longer eligible for redistribution. Rather, those to whom it belongs must cope with it. I believe that this issue deserves further investigation and that an answer could even have practical importance for the ways in which we may treat medical problems.

28. In this section, this is the first of what I call principles (including doctrines) of permissible harm. Strictly speaking, however, satisfying these principles is not sufficient to ensure that an act will be permissible. There may always be other factors, such as promises, that make an act impermissible even though it satisfies a principle of permissible harm. Hence, these principles should be understood as accounting for prima facie permissibility.

29. I thank John Gibbons for discussion on these points.

30. Notice that the point raised in n. 23 is relevant here too: Strictly speaking, it is the first few minutes of the five saved, which is a component of the greater good that consists in their long-term survival, that is the noncausal flip side of a means that causes the lesser evil*. But we would not undertake to produce that time-slice and let means to it cause evil* unless we thought it would be a component of long-term survival. Only the latter would justify evil*.

31. For more on this issue and its role in understanding Peter Unger's method of multiple options, see chapter 6.

32. I shall say more about aspects immediately below.

33. I call this Lazy Susan 3 to distinguish it from the various Lazy Susan cases described in chapters 1 and 4. In Lazy Susan 1 in chapter 1, the turning Lazy Susan causes a rock slide that kills a bystander, and in Lazy Susan Case 2 in chapter 4, the turning Lazy Susan slams into the bystander. These two cases (but not Lazy Susan Case 3) show that it is permissible to create new threats that kill people. I imagine in all of these Lazy Susan cases that the Lazy Susan does not belong to the single person and that we turn the Lazy Susan by taking hold of it or the five people on it. This is by contrast with taking hold of the single person on the Lazy Susan in order to turn it. The latter seems impermissible. As we shall see, this is because (roughly) taking hold of him (or what belongs to him) without his consent when it leads to harm to him is an evil*, and it would be a means to producing the greater good and, for example, not caused by a greater good that justifies its existence.

34. I suspect that these cases make problems for some recent psychological experiments trying to determine what accounts for people's intuitions in the Trolley Case, as noted in chapter 1.

35. This case is presented by Judith Thomson in her "Self-Defense," though she does not draw the distinction between evil* actually causing our good and evil* being necessary to cause our good. For more on this in connection with just war theory, see my "Failures of Just War Theory."

36. The Track Trolley Case discussed in chapter 4 could also exemplify this point, if it were in fact permissible in that case to do what has the side effect of pushing someone into the

trolley. A case involving an omission (modeled on one developed by Warren Quinn and discussed in chapter 3) is as follows: Suppose A must go to the back of a truck to help keep C and D alive by running their dialysis machines. The truck has been set in motion by others but it needs someone to brake, if it is not to continue on down a road where it will run over B. Because A is busy with C and D, the truck runs over B, his kidneys become available for transplant into C and D, and so his death is actually the means to saving C and D. But his kidney was not necessary to save them, as our giving dialysis would also have kept them alive.

37. These cases were introduced in chapter 4 in the course of discussing the Double Track Case. This section continues that discussion and aims to answer some questions that were left open there.

38. Similarly, suppose a trolley is headed toward five people and the only way to redirect it is to build a new track. It will then go toward one person who was not previously reachable. We may still turn the trolley because it saves the people we were originally trying to save at the cost of fewer lives lost. I discussed this case in *Morality, Mortality*, vol. 2.

39. Still, even a villain may not do just any lesser wrong to diminish the wrongs he does. He may not push one bystander into the trolley that the villain started in order to stop its hitting the five.

40. Recall that, as stated above, this is to be understood with an implicit modal operator, so it is really "the greater good *must* be a causal consequence of what we must do." (But it is hard to see how something that actually causes the greater good could have had a noncausal relation to it as well if the causal relation had not come about.)

41. The act will not be permissible whether the greater good is an indirect or a direct effect of what we do. In the Car and Splash cases, the greater good is indirectly produced by rushing to the hospital, as this is necessary in order to do the life-saving surgery. However, we could imagine a case in which we must rush over the spot in the road where someone immovably lays so that our car can gently push five people away from a trolley headed toward them. Though the greater good is here, arguably, a direct causal effect of what we do, it would also, I think, be impermissible to drive over the spot.

42. However, supporters of these doctrines may try to distinguish morally between means that overlap with evil* and those that directly cause evil* without overlapping in this way. The overlapping means (as in driving over someone on the road) may be ruled out. Indeed, identifying a means that is intended with that with which it overlaps (or in other words, with what it is constituted by in the context) may be one answer to the narrowness-of-intention objection. This approach will not work in the Splash Case, however, where the means to the greater good is constituted in the context by the direct cause of evil*, That is because these doctriness do not rule out a means being a direct cause of evil*.

43. Here are some more cases in which the impermissibility of our act is, I believe, due to the overlapping characteristics of our means: (a) Suppose that we must operate on five patients in order to save them and this requires (for some reason) spraying a gas in an adjoining room. Already occupying the adjoining room is another person (whose presence is not necessary in order to save the five but who will die if moved) and he will die from the gas if it is sprayed in his room. It is impermissible to operate on the five. This case is a variant on (what I call) the Gas Case, presented by Foot in her "The Problem of Abortion and the Doctrine of Double Effect." (b) Consider the Wiggle the Bridge Case: The trolley is headed under a public bridge toward five people. We know that if we wiggle the bridge, this will stop the trolley via magnetic waves. However, there is someone on the bridge, and we also know that wiggling the bridge will, as a useless side effect, topple him over the bridge to his death. Intuitively, I think that wiggling the bridge is impermissible. On one view, wiggling the bridge directly causes an evil*, just as redirecting the trolley does, but unlike the moving trolley, the wiggling bridge

has only a causal relation to the greater good, since it leads to the greater good by causing (via magnetic waves) the trolley to move away from the five. On another view, something we must do (i.e., wiggle the bridge) is wiggling an area that is already occupied by a person; this produces the overlapping of our means in this context with the involvement-of-a-person part of evil*. Furthermore, wiggling the bridge is neither caused by an event with a noncausal relation to the greater good nor causes the death solely by way of causing such an event.

44. Suppose that we must drive our car so that it pushes five people out of the way of a trolley, thus (directly, not indirectly) causing the greater good. (Driving to the hospital only indirectly causes a greater good.) But the road is bumpy and the car will first veer off-route, killing someone. It is impermissible to perform the rescue, I believe. What if we reverse the order of events? That is, we must drive the car so that it pushes five people out of the way of a trolley, but we know that after doing this the car will unavoidably continue on its way (and not as an effect of having saved the five), running over someone in the road. Using this car to rescue the five is also, I believe, impermissible.

45. Here are other cases of this second type: (a) We must operate on five people in order to save their lives by using a gas that will also seep into the next room, killing a person who cannot be moved. In this case, the entity that is needed to cause the greater good (the gas) will directly cause the lesser evil*, even though it is someplace where it need not be in order that the greater good be achieved. It seems impermissible to use the gas. (b) The trolley is headed under a bridge toward killing five people. We can stop it by wiggling the bridge on which no one stands. Wiggling the bridge, however, will, as a useless side effect, cause parts of the bridge to fall on, and kill, a bystander. It is impermissible to wiggle the bridge, I believe. (c) If we flip a switch, this sends out electricity that goes down the track, stopping the movement of the trolley headed toward five. On the track is a person who will be electrocuted as the electricity travels down the track. So what we must do in order to cause the trolley to stop (i.e., send electricity) also directly causes the death of that person. I suggest that it is impermissible to flip the switch.

46. Notice that if flipping the switch in this case is impermissible, then flipping it in the Track Trolley Case (discussed in chapter 4) should also be impermissible, in virtue of what happens to the one person on the track as a side effect. This is contrary to what the DDE, the DDE(R), and the DTE imply.

47. Other cases of type (4) are (a) we must use a gas in an operation to save five lives. The gas will seep into an adjoining room that one person immovably occupies. The gas does not harm him, but we know that its presence will eventually displace germs in the air, moving them closer to the person, and the displaced germs will kill him. A case of type (4) and its implication that acting in this case is permissible help us see that the permissibility of acting in the variant on the Gas Case where five are rescued, breathe normally and, thereby, alter the position of lethal germs (given in chapter 1) is overdetermined. That is, it is not a good case to show that the greater good, but not a mere means, may cause lesser evil* because in it lesser evil* is caused very indirectly. Better cases to show that greater good, but not a mere means, may cause lesser evil* are Landslide and Lazy Susan Case 4, where the greater good more directly causes lesser evil* (b) A trolley is on its way under a bridge toward killing five people. If we wiggle the bridge on which no one stands, it will stop the trolley. The wiggling of the bridge will cause nearby rocks (not parts of the bridge) to slide, and this kills one person. Notice the difference between our wiggling a bridge that *introduces* a death ray, and both our wiggling a bridge that has an effect on rocks already present in the environment and our wiggling a bridge whose parts fall on and kill someone.

48. This will be modified below.

49. Though it is the way I once put my points. See my "Harming Some to Save Others," *Philosophical Studies* 57 (Fall 1989): 227–60. I also there suggested that we might require a *more* intimate causal relation to greater good than to lesser evil, not just *as* intimate a relation.

50. These are devices designed to have long causal chains to a specific effect.

51. This issue is discussed in chapter 10.

52. This case is reminiscent of ones that Peter Unger developed. See chapter 6 on this.

53. As discussed in chapter 1.

54. I noted at the beginning of this chapter that cases in which one harms (e.g., by inducing death) in order to end life-saving aid that one is providing sometimes may also fall outside the strictures that are now being discussed.

55. Peter Unger's "method of multiple options," described in his *Living High and Letting Die* (New York: Oxford University Press, 1996), depends, I believe, on the contrary view, namely, that it is permissible to cause an evil* whose flip side is the nonperformance of an act (such as redirection) that is permissible but would cause more harm. Hence, I believe that Unger is wrong to say that, in order to stop a trolley headed toward five people, we may push in a second trolley with two different people in it who will thereby be killed, as the alternative to redirecting the first trolley toward three different people. But given that he thinks it permissible to send the trolley with two people into the first trolley, it is no wonder that he thinks that an agent should instead push one different person into the first trolley to stop it. In my view, doing the latter would involve substituting a less-harmful *wrong* act for a more-harmful *wrong* act of sending in the second trolley. As further clarification of this point, suppose that someone else will push three people (without their consent) in front of the trolley headed toward the five in order to stop the trolley. I can prevent this from happening by pushing in one different person instead. In this case, my doing the evil* has the *causal effect* of stopping someone else from doing greater evil*. It is for this reason not licensed by the principle of permissible harm I am describing. (This is in contrast with what happens in the cases described in the text, where I do evil* and so, as a noncausal flip side, do not impermissibly bring about a greater evil*.) Suppose that I started a trolley threat to three people yesterday and now could stop it only by pushing one different person in front of the trolley. In this case too, because the second lesser threat causally stops the greater evil*, it is not merely a less seriously wrong alternative to causing the greater evil. Suppose that someone will push three people in front of the trolley in order to stop it. He will desist only if I push in two of those same three people. This is permissible, I believe, (in part), because it makes the two no worse off than they would have been and it saves one of the people who would otherwise die. This is an instance of what I call the Principle of Secondary Permissibility (PSP), according to which we may sometimes do in the second place something that could not have been done in the first place, because our act is a substitute for an act (permissible or not) that would be worse or just as bad for the same victim(s). However, the fact that it is permissible for me to do this does not mean that I may instead push in an innocent bystander, who would not otherwise have been threatened, to stop someone else pushing in the three others. This is so even though doing that evil* would have as its noncausal flip side my not pushing in two of the three who would have been wrongly threatened in the first instance. We may not substitute a less harmful wrong act for a more harmful permissible act, even when the latter act itself would be wrong were it not an instance of the PSP. For more on all this, see the discussion of secondary permissibility and secondary wrong below and the criticism of Peter Unger's views in chapter 6.

56. We shall of course have to explain why all this should be important so. Recall as well that it is really the modal form of these claims that is at issue. So it is crucial that it is possible given our act that evil* not be causally upstream from a greater good, or it is possible given our act that evil* and greater good not be causally parallel.

57. In the Loop version of the Trolley Case, the noncausal flip side of the trolley moving away is its being away from the front of the five. The five being free of the trolley from its original direction is not a *further* causal effect of redirecting the trolley away from them.

58. Strictly (as noted above), the five people being free of threats justifies the death of the one only if it is the first stage in the five living significantly longer, which is the greater good (on the continuing assumption that life is a benefit to them). We would only bother to produce the state of affairs where the five are free of threats on the assumption that it is this first stage of the greater good. Furthermore, it would be enough if the flip side of redirecting the trolley, considered independently of further effects of our rescue, were only a structural equivalent of a *part* of the greater good sufficient to justify the death of one person (e.g., two of the five people saved). It could also be a structural equivalent of more than the final greater good, for example, if seven people were saved from a threat that existed independently of our rescue, two of whom would eventually die of the looping trolley. Strictly, it is the structural equivalent of the minimal good that would justify the evil* that should be present when we redirect the trolley. I shall simplify my discussion by bypassing this strict condition and working with a complete structural equivalent of the final greater good. Notice that even in the following case, the structural equivalent (as I have defined it) is the noncausal flip side of redirecting the trolley: We redirect the trolley away from its hit on the five from the right, and this causes a missile that was previously aboard the trolley to detach and head toward them also from the right. (This Missile Case is based on one described by Kasper Lippert-Rasmussen, "Moral Status and the Impermissibility of Minimizing Violations," *Philosophy & Public Affairs* 25 [1996]: 333–51.) Even though there is no time during which the five do not face a threat, the threat to them of the missile arises because of what we do to save them from the trolley. Hence, it does not affect the existence of the structural equivalent, which is what results from what we do to save the five from the initial threat independently of further consequences for them of our doing this. This will be true even if we imagine that the trolley is much slower than the missile, so that if we redirect the trolley, the five would die sooner from the missile than they would die from the trolley, if nothing stopped the missile. Similarly, we would produce the structural equivalent of the greater good, as I have defined it, if we were to redirect a trolley that is headed toward them on a long track away onto a *short* track that loops toward them. The structural equivalent would exist, even though the trolley would then kill them sooner were not the one person on the other track there to stop it. (I owe this last case to Derek Parfit.) Producing a structural equivalent does not mean that, considered independently of the final outcome to which it can lead, it immediately improves the situation of the five. Getting rid of the problem that faces the five to begin with may immediately make things worse for them, as in the Missile Case. (Below, we shall consider different types of cases where the five are worse off as a result of removing the trolley.) It may make no sense to get rid of the problem they initially faced, except for the fact that, if they are to survive, it is necessary to get rid of this problem, *and* the new, worse problem will resolve itself without our having to do anything improper. As I conceive of it, the structural equivalent is present if, when we abstract from new problems created by what we do, the condition of the five is as it would be were the (initial temporal component of) greater good achieved.

59. Recall again that this is actually too strong a requirement in two ways. The final greater good might include the structural equivalent *plus even more good*, but this is not a necessary condition. On the other hand, the greater good might involve only a part of the initial structure but still be large enough to justify the evil*. Strictly speaking, all that is needed is that the *structural equivalent of the minimal good that would justify the evil** be sustained.

60. I first discussed the Miracle Case in *Morality, Mortality*, vol. 2.

61. It is quite all right to do something else in addition that is morally innocent in order to also help stop the trolley from looping, and thus sustain the structural equivalent. But what we do cannot be a mere means to hitting the one (or some other evil*). For example, suppose that we know that the one will be on the sidetrack if we redirect the trolley, but his being hit will only slow down the trolley and we must also pour sand on the tracks farther down the line to

stop the trolley entirely. Pouring sand is permissible. If we did something additional as a mere means to facilitate the hitting of the one, however, the hit would not be the effect of the structural equivalent or means having it as its noncausal flip side. Nor would it be the effect of some other act of ours that is justified in pursuit of a different greater good.

62. Recall that the Double Track Case at least *seemed* to make problems for the DDE(R) and the DTE(R). This was because choosing one track over the other seemed on one interpretation to involve doing something that is not necessary to get the trolley away from the first hit on the five, especially to ensure that the one would be hit. By contrast, if means that have the structural equivalent of the greater good as their noncausal flip side cause (or lead to what causes) the lesser evil*, the theory we are now examining permits redirecting the trolley onto track B, where the one is hit. If we were to go onto track A, where no one would be hit and the trolley would loop, there would be no hope of achieving the greater good even if turning the trolley away produced the structural equivalent of the greater good, and this would rule out acting. Suppose that there were yet another track, C, where the probability of hitting the one (and stopping the trolley) was smaller than if we went onto B. Again, the theory I am presenting raises no objection to redirecting onto B instead of onto C. (I considered different approaches to dealing with the Double Track Case in section IV above.)

63. It might be said, however, that the tractor is not a threat to begin with. That is, the five people would be dead from the trolley and not vulnerable to the tractor threat, unless we redirect the trolley. Because we redirect the trolley away from them, they are alive and thus vulnerable to the tractor threat. So is not the tractor *being a threat* also an effect of our redirecting the trolley? I disagree with this analysis. In the sense that is morally pertinent, I do not think that whether the tractor was a threat to them at the start depends on whether we would redirect the trolley or not. In this same sense, we can say that a person at a given time faces many threats to his life when he faces many opponents, even though he can only be killed once. Furthermore, though we turn the trolley away first, that does not mean it would have killed the five before the tractor; there might be a slow trolley and a fast tractor but there is nothing we can do to stop the tractor except turn the trolley a long time before it would actually hit the five.

64. Again I am assuming that the five free of both threats is the initial stage in their continued survival, which is the greater good.

65. I shall amend this proposal below.

66. If means that produced the greater good only had evil* as a direct side effect, not causally involved in stopping the tractor, that too, would be ruled out by what I have said in C.

67. Here I am responding to Thomas Scanlon, who raised the question: "What is the relation of the DTE to my non-state-of-mind theory?"

68. See chapter 3 for more on why a rational agent need not intend the means to his end.

69. Similarly, in the Prize Party Case described in chapter 4, we act in order to have a fun party and to win a neatness prize and for the second part of this goal the guest's feelings of indebtedness are causally productive.

70. Above, in section IV, and in chapter 4.

71. A nontrolley case like this, called the Secondary Transplant Case was discussed in chapter 4.

72. The DTE does not morally distinguish the Trolley-Organs cases. It would say that what is important is that we act *because* the death of the one will occur rather than *in order* to produce the death in both cases. However, it may still distinguish between turning the trolley, in part, *in order* to save the five from their deadly disease in the first case, but only *because* they will also be saved from the effects of our saving them in the second case. For more on the implications of the DTE for cases in which organs can become available, see chapter 4's discussion of the Secondary Transplant Case.

73. While we shall go on to modify the requirements for permissible harming further below, the Trolley-Organs Case I will not satisfy those requirements either.

74. I say "(at least) a structural equivalent" because the greater good itself would, of course, suffice as a cause of E. E could also be caused by means (or effects of means) noncausally related to the greater good or its structural equivalent. All of this, understood in light of the Model Condition, should be assumed as implicit in what I say.

75. Above I have said repeatedly that strictly speaking in the Trolley Case, it is means that have the first temporal stage of the greater good as their noncausal flip side that lead to a lesser evil*. This first stage is a component of the greater good. So strictly speaking, the cases we have been discussing all along are like the Component Case in one way. They are unlike it, in that in the Component Case we are not just discussing a temporal component of the greater good. We are also discussing a subset of greater good even when we project temporally into the long term survival of the one person.

76. I am here thinking of means that do not overlap with the direct cause of evil*. The indirect effects of means that overlap with the direct cause of evil* are treated like means that have evil* as a direct effect. (as described in part C).

77. I realize that this summary sentence read on its own would be close to incomprehensible. But it should not be too difficult for those who have understood the preceding discussion. As I have said before, I am engaged in a quasi-technical enterprise, where a new vocabulary is necessary to capture a new way of looking at events.

78. I have omitted a step intervening between the consideration of cases and the presentation of the DIJ. It is (what I have elsewhere called) the Principle of Permissible Harm (PPH). (The PPH is one instance of the type, principle of permissible harm. It should not be confused with the type, which includes other instances with different names.) It is a principle summarizing the case judgments in (A)–(E). The DIJ provides the principle underlying the PPH. Possibly, for some readers, considering the PPH first may make understanding the DIJ easier. I introduced a version of the PPH in "Harming Some to Save Others," *Philosophical Studies* 57 (1989): 227–60, and gave a detailed version in my *Morality, Mortality*, vol. 2. A rough version of the PPH is given in chapter 1. Here is a more detailed version, broken into three sections, that differs from the one presented in *Morality, Mortality*. (Step iii is presented in n. 89, as it is formulated after further discussion.)

I. In thinking about the greater good (G) that will justify a particular lesser evil* (E) to innocent, nonthreatening people who are not under comparable threat already, for whom continuing life is a good and who have not consented to evil*, it speaks in favor of permissibility of an act if:

    (i) E can be caused by G or its structural equivalent; or

    (ii) E can be caused by means that have G or its structural equivalent as its non-causal flip side or aspect (or by effects of such means); or

    (iv) E need not be a direct effect of what we must do (or that with which it overlaps) in order to achieve the greater good.

Notice that these conditions (as well as those below) are phrased in terms of necessity and possibility and so involve modal notions.

It speaks against the permissibility of an act if:

    (v) the only possibility provided by that act is that E is a cause of G, unless E is an effect of the structural equivalent of G, or of an event that has this as its noncausal flip side or aspect (or of effects of such events) (as in ii); or

    (vi) the only possibility provided by that act is that a cause of G is an event that has E as a side effect and G as a *mere causal effect*, unless (a) the production of E is mediated by (i) or (ii) for a different G, or (b) E is an indirect effect.

II. It speaks against acts involving or causing E, if there is no G.

III. Possibly, it speaks for the permissibility of agents acting if it is reasonable for them to believe that their acts would satisfy (i), (ii), or (iv), even when they do not. Possibly, it speaks against the permissibility of agents acting, if it is reasonable for them to believe that their acts would satisfy (iv) or (v), even when they do not. (III introduces a state-of-mind component into the theory of permissibility. Those who reject it might still think of III as affecting culpability for objectively impermissible acts or attempts.)

79. In her "Self-Defense."

80. In section VI, I discuss other cases in which the DIJ might permit tactical bombing and I also suggest that bombing may be permitted in cases that the DIJ rules out due to special factors present in war. (Thomson also makes the latter point in her article though she does not say what she thinks the special factors are.) In the Track Trolley Case discussed in chapter 4, something we do (press a button) that is necessary to move the trolley away from the five and to a track where one person sits also moves the track on which that person sits. This second effect is not necessary to move the trolley away from the five. However, the movement of the track overlaps (I believe) with the involvement of the person on it, and this involvement will lead to his being harmed. Hence, our means (in the sense of what we *need* to do to achieve the greater good) would have the direct effect of causing evil*. The DIJ rules this out. There might, however, be variants of the Track Trolley or Tactical Bombing cases in which permissible *indirect* evil* side effects of what we do as a means to the greater good cause the greater good before it is caused in another way. The DIJ could permit this.

81. Notice that evil* could be necessary, given our act, to produce another greater good (G2), but that is not the good that justifies evil*'s coming into existence. Those who focus on intentions could have a modal version of their theory, too, as I noted above (p. 135). That is, to determine permissibility of an act, they might point not to the actual intention of an agent, but rather to whether it is possible for some rational agent to do the act with a good intention. I also argued against going this route.

82. This alteration was suggested by John Martin Fischer.

83. This is on the continuing assumptions that life is a good for these five and that their being saved is the first component in their longer time alive.

84. Notice a difference between the Component Case II and the Tractor Case. In the Tractor Case, when one threat (the trolley) is taken care of, *no one* is yet saved, since another threat to everyone is in the wings. (And there is also no structural equivalent of anyone being saved.) In the Component Case, one person is saved as the flip side of pushing the trolley to the right. Whether this means that there is no component (or structural equivalent of a component) of the greater good present in the Tractor Case once the trolley is redirected is something with which we will deal in the following section.

85. Notice that identifying the good of which something is a component seems to depend on identifying the threat with which we are trying to deal. Proper identification should rule out action in cases such as the following: We can turn the trolley heading toward killing five only a bit so that it is away from hitting one of the five, though it can still hit the other four. Doing this will, as a direct side effect, kill two bystanders. The trolley also hits and paralyzes the leg of another person, and this in turn defuses a bomb that was about to kill six *other* people. Turning the trolley in this case is intuitively not permissible, I think. This is because there is no justification for getting rid of a trolley threat to only one person when this will kill two people as a side effect; it is only if we were concerned with stopping the bomb threat to the other six people that we would do this. But then, relative to the good that could justify the death of two people (i.e., the good of saving the six other people), turning the trolley is a mere means that directly causes the two deaths as a side effect. This is so despite the fact that it has some good as

its noncausal flip-side. If saving the six from the bomb could justify turning the trolley in this case, it could also justify turning the trolley if none of the five facing the trolley threat were saved. That is, turning the trolley does not have a noncausal relation to a *component* of the very good that could ultimately justify the deaths of the two people (or that could at least initially sufficiently justify it).

86. Notice that this case differs from the Missile Case (discussed in n. 58), for the five in this case do not just face a worse (quicker) threat *to come* when we turn the trolley; they are actually in a worse (more painful) state.

87. I was led to construct the Worse-than-Death cases as a result of questioning by Derek Parfit. He was dubious of my original claim that the greater good or its structural equivalent was the flip side of turning the trolley. It was his view that the most I could claim was that the five being free of the trolley threat is the noncausal flip side of turning the trolley (by contrast to its being a causal effect of the turning of the trolley). I tried to defend my original claim (as can be seen by elements of my discussion in earlier sections of the chapter) by (1) emphasizing that I made my claim only about contexts where no other death threat faces the five, (2) emphasizing that strictly it was only the first temporal component of the greater good or the structural equivalent that was achieved when we turned the trolley, and (3) that additional innocent means besides turning the trolley might be necessary to bring about the greater good from the structural equivalent. However, as an aid in trying to take seriously the view that turning the trolley was no more than removing that threat from the five, I created the Worse-than-Dead Case. It convinced me that not even the first temporal component of the structural equivalent of the greater good would have to be a noncausal flip side of moving the trolley in order for turning to be permissible. And this was true precisely because no other death threat was present to the people who were living in a state so bad that death would be good for them. Nevertheless, I will argue that we can say more than that the five being free of the trolley is a noncausal flip side of its removal rather than a causal effect.

88. This point was made by Niko Kolodny.

89. To make the PPH already described (in n. 78) fit the DPP, we could add clause (iii): E is caused by components of G (or their structural equivalents) or by means that have such components (or their structural equivalents) as their noncausal flip side or aspect (or by effects of these), and these components or means could lead to G via (a) good/neutral effects; (b) via evils* smaller than the good of the components, if the evils* produce G; or (c) via evils* that sustain components of G. We would then also have to change (vi)(a) in the PPH to allow that (iii) could also mediate the production of E.

90. For more on this, see chapters 1, 7, and 8.

91. That I first proposed in *Morality, Mortality*, vol. 2.

92. Step 1 is derived from intuitive judgments. If we never come up with morally significant results in this way, we may have to resort to the method of reflective equilibrium which may prune the judgments used as data. We might also try to provide an error theory to account for the intuitive judgments that we exclude as data.

93. What if the trolley is at a crossroads and we must choose to send it toward one person or toward five people? I think that this case falls under the one person being originally selected to be threatened.

94. But he is also wronged when he is the one simply threatened (i.e., not as a result of redirection saving others). This does not justify his sending the trolley from him toward five people. For more on wronging, see chapter 8.

95. An argument like this is to be found in Judith Thomson's "Self Defense."

96. This argument is to be found in my "The Insanity Defense, Innocent Threats, and Limited Alternatives."

97. In chapter 10, I discuss the responsibilities of original and substituting agents further.

98. The discussion that follows is drawn from my "Failures of Just War Theory," and "Terrorism and Several Moral Distinctions," *Legal Theory*, 12 (2006), 19–69.

99. I also believe that it would be permissible to act on the PSP and the EPSP for an alternate reason that does not depend on the factors that actually can justify our acting. So suppose that a great good will be achieved by killing a person as a mere means, in our most recent example. However, we only decide to shoot him because he is short. That is, we would not have taken advantage of the EPSP in order to achieve the greater good if we did not dislike short people. This does not make our act impermissible. For more on this combination of the EPSP and the Principle of Alternate Reason, see my "Failures of Just War Theory."

100. I first considered this question in my "Justifications for Killing Noncombatants in War," *Midwest Studies in Philosophy* 24 (2000): 219–28, on which my discussion here draws. I consider the question again in my "Failures of Just War Theory."

101. Judith Thomson reached this conclusion as well in her "Self-Defense."

102. One could also imagine that the children who will die belong to the country doing the bombing. However, this case would raise questions of whether an extra duty of care is present toward one's own population. It might be this extra duty of care that stands in the way of killing one's own civilians, even if the DDE or the DPP were not a ground for objecting. I discuss this issue in my "Failures of Just War Theory."

103. Suggested first in "Justifications for Killing Noncombatants in War."

104. Notice that another problem may arise, if the greater good consists of *soldiers* not being killed due to the absence of munitions. For the lesser evil* is the deaths of noncombatant children and, typically, just war theory gives preference to avoiding the loss of noncombatants over avoiding the loss of soldiers. Hence, avoiding many soldiers' deaths would not constitute a greater good relative to a few children's deaths. One way to avoid this problem would be to imagine that the munitions would have been used to kill children also. I shall ignore this problem in the rest of this discussion, but it has to be dealt with ultimately.

105. Another problem will arise if the total arms destroyed in a plant do not save enough people to justify direct side effect deaths caused by the destruction, but destroying all the plants would justify these deaths and destroying this plant is necessary to destroying the other plants.

106. For more on this, see my "Failures of Just War Theory."

6

HARMING PEOPLE IN PETER UNGER'S
LIVING HIGH AND LETTING DIE

I. INTRODUCTION

In previous chapters we have made use of intuitive judgments about cases to find moral principles and fundamental factors underlying them. We have especially focused on variations of the Trolley Case. Peter Unger has tried to show that relying on intuitive judgments in cases is a worthless methodology for finding principles, and he has also offered a novel approach to Trolley cases.[1] Given how his views bear on topics with which we have dealt, it is appropriate to consider them in some detail.

Unger, however, deals not only with the questions of when may we harm some to help others and how can we best reason about this issue. He also considers how much we must sacrifice in order to stop strangers from suffering serious losses and whether our distance from them alters our obligations. Substantively, Unger aims to prove the following four claims in the following order: (1) We must, quite generally, suffer great losses of property to prevent suffering and death; (2) we may, quite generally, impose such losses on others for the same goals; (3) we may, quite generally, kill others to prevent more deaths; and (4) we must, quite generally, kill ourselves to prevent more deaths.

Methodologically, Unger aims to show that intuitive judgments about cases that would be presented as evidence against his four substantive claims—a standard technique that nonconsequentialists employ when arguing against consequentialists—

are worthless. He also aims to show that many distinctions presupposed by these intuitive arguments in cases, distinctions to which some nonconsequentialists attribute moral significance, do not matter morally and cannot be used to rebut his (or any) substantive claims. The distinctions whose moral significance he rejects include the distinction between harming someone so that he suffers mortally and not-aiding him when he will suffer mortally, and the distinction between harming someone by re-directing a threat toward him and harming him by using him to stop a threat.

Unger's ground for claiming that intuitive judgments in cases are worthless is that we can construct cases that generate the opposite intuitive judgments. He also thinks the above-mentioned distinctions are useless because we can show that the factors that distinguish the cases where the distinctions seem to matter are not mor-ally significant. He thinks, instead, that we must decide which intuitive judgments are correct and what to do by consulting general moral values, such as the im-portance of reducing suffering and death.

II. UNGER'S ETHICAL METHOD

So far, I have provided only the briefest description of Unger's ethical method. Considered in more detail, we see that Unger actually first proposes that *general* reflection (rather than reflection on cases) reveals our basic primary values, and these values leave no room for the importance of many distinctions between cases relative to the aim of preventing mortal loss. He next tries to show that reflection on particular cases, that supports the importance of nonconsequentialist distinctions, is subject to *negative* distortion. That is, this case-specific reflection is inaccurate because it veers us away (negatively) from the basic values revealed by general reflection. He then supports the claim that our belief in constraints on harming others is often based on such negative distorting tendencies by constructing cases so as to change the intuitive judgments we have concerning the performance of par-ticular acts. Constructing these new cases will make the responses be more in line with basic values that deny the significance of the distinctions at issue. In these re-vised cases, distortion is *positive*, that is, it leads to judgments about cases that agree with, and hence reveal, basic values. (An example of a positive distorting factor, Unger believes, is salience. It is distorting because it is really morally irrelevant how salient an event is; salience should not affect our judgment about a case. However, salience can lead us to have intuitions about cases more in keeping with our basic values, he thinks.)[2]

In sum, we may say that whereas many nonconsequentialists fashion principles to match intuitions, Unger's aim is to show that we can fashion cases and intui-tions about them to match principles.[3] Doing this also, according to Unger, in-volves showing that our intuitions about cases are inconsistent. For Unger, this means that in one case we approve of a constraint on harming; in another case, we disapprove of the very same constraint.[4]

Next, Unger asks us to reflect on the changes he has introduced into cases to alter our intuitions about the permissibility of acts and to see that these changes involve factors that are not in themselves morally significant. Hence, the same acts in cases lacking these factors merit the same response, even if intuitively they do not prompt the same response.[5] The upshot of Unger's procedure is supposed to be that when there is a conflict between the theses supported by general reflection (e.g., reduce suffering) and judgments about particular cases, we should stick with the results of general reflection, for our intuitions about cases are unreliable and manipulable by morally irrelevant factors.

Unger thus presents an *error theory* of nonconsequentialist intuitions in cases and of nonconsequentialist restrictions on both harming others and prerogatives not to make large sacrifices to aid. This error theory is based on the psychological effects of morally insignificant factors. Hence, he thinks, the nonconsequentialist tactic of presenting case judgments that conflict with the principle of minimizing mortal loss cannot be used to defeat the obligation to minimize mortal loss. For example, Unger suggests that one of our primary values is that people's suffering and dying is bad, and more of this suffering is worse than less. Yet, case intuitions sometimes show that we think that we have no obligation to cut off our arm to prevent the loss of another's life. When there is a conflict between intuitions in cases and the primary value, we should stick to our primary value.

Possibly, however, Unger is not consistent in abiding by this recommendation. He considers a case in which, while we are visiting a poor distant country, we meet someone whose leg we can save. He says, "As we intuitively react," it would be "morally outrageous"[6] not to help this person on the grounds that if we save his leg he will reproduce at a greater rate, which will lead to an overall increase in human suffering in that poor land. This intuitive moral outrage conflicts with the general value of reducing overall suffering and death, for future suffering and death is part of overall suffering and death. Does Unger think that it is permissible to side with the intuition that we must help the person in this case rather than with the general value?

I shall assume that Unger would be willing to revise his judgment about this case and side with the general value, and thus leave the man by the road. If he would not, he risks allowing cases to drive the formulation, acceptance, and rejection of normative principles in the way they have for some nonconsequentialists. This would be contrary to his stated view that rather than preserving our original intuitions about cases—a hopeless task anyway, if they are inconsistent—we are (correctly) liberated from them as primary guides to moral truth.

Unger's ultimate thesis is that we should make moral decisions using only primary values. But it must be emphasized that this does not mean that in proving this thesis his method ignores case judgments entirely. In his attempt to prove that we should not rely on intuitive case judgments in deciding what is morally right, Unger himself relies on intuitive judgments about cases (that yield competing intuitions). It is important to his project to show us that our responses to cases will change in the direction of what he thinks are primary values, if he alters cases in certain ways that are morally irrelevant. If our intuitions about cases do not in fact change as he says they will, his arguments against relying on case judgments in deciding what to do will not succeed. Likewise, his arguments against the existence of nonconsequentialist constraints on preventing mortal loss will not succeed and his account of the (supposedly) morally unimportant factors prompting non-consequentialist intuitions will fail. (It is when he asks us to consider whether the alterations he makes in cases that [supposedly] change our intuitions could possibly be morally important in themselves that he relies on reflection rather than on intuitions in cases.)

Of course, it is important that Unger, who believes that intuitions about cases are subject to both positive (i.e., value-tracking) and negative (i.e., value-veering) distortions, have some method besides judgments in cases for identifying correct values. For without knowing what the correct values are, we will not know whether what he thinks are negatively distorted cases really are taking us in the wrong direction. As noted, his method for finding the correct values is that of reflecting directly on general claims, such as the claim that mortal loss should be minimized. This too seems like an intuitive judgment, even if not a case-based one.

I do not believe that Unger is successful in proving either his substantive or his methodological claims as I have described them. In this chapter, I shall critically examine his substantive move from the permissibility of physically harming some people in order to save others in some cases to the claim that, quite generally, we have a duty to physically harm ourselves to save others. His methodological claims will be evaluated as well. Along the way, I will re-present the alternative non-consequentialist account of some of the cases that Unger discusses, which I presented in chapter 5. However, the correctness of this alternative account is not essential to my critical argument. In conclusion, I shall discuss his project of reconciling his views with the ordinary moral judgments with which his views differ.

III. PROPERTY LOSSES AND THE DUTY TO AID

Before proceeding to these issues, however, I will briefly summarize what I have elsewhere said about Unger's claims concerning the duty to suffer losses of property (rather than physical harms) and the permissibility of imposing property losses (rather than physical harms) on others, in order to save people.[7] This is to provide the necessary background for his discussion of physical harming.

Unger is eager to show that we must suffer great losses in property in order to help distant starving people. He contrasts the ordinary intuitive judgment that we should suffer a great deal in order to aid someone who is in an accident near us with our reluctance to condemn someone who does not do much for international famine relief. He thinks that it is salience—the degree to which suffering imposes itself on us to the point where we psychologically cannot ignore it—and a sense that we can take care of a problem entirely in the near case, but not in the distant case that underlie these different judgments. But both of these factors, he thinks, are morally insignificant and cannot justify our different judgments in this set of cases. Hence, in deciding what to do, he thinks that we should rely on the general value that suffering is to be reduced.

To test his analysis, I suggest that we consider a case in which a distant person is the victim of an accident, and the problem can completely be dealt with by our aid. Also imagine that this person's plight is salient because we have long-distance vision. I discuss a distant accident rather than distant starvation, as Unger does, in order to hold constant all factors when comparing a near accident case with helping distant people. This is in addition to holding constant salience and completely dealing with a problem to which Unger points in explaining the different judgments in near and distant cases. I think that our intuitions about some distant aid case can still be different from our intuitions about some case where the victim is near when we hold all these factors constant. This difference may show up, however, only when the cost of aiding is equally high (rather than equally low) in both near and distant cases. We have a duty to aid only the near person at high cost. (For a factor like distance to matter morally, it need only make a difference sometimes, not always.) This suggests that proximity per se plays a role in generating our intuition that we should suffer a large property loss in order to aid. If so, more needs to be said both about the *way* in which proximity affects our intuitions and whether we can *justify* its having a role in generating our intuitions and in morality.

With respect to the first point about the way in which proximity affects our intuitions, I do not think that even if proximity can be morally important, this necessarily means that we *always* have a weaker obligation to aid at high cost a person who is distant from us than to aid one who is near us. Indeed, though it sounds paradoxical, it is *because* nearness matters that we may have a strong duty to help a distant person. For example, suppose that my boat is near a drowning person from whom I am distant. I may be obligated to let my boat be used to help him because *it* is near him though I am not. This case bears on another of Unger's claims: that we may, in general, impose property losses on others in order to help people. Intuitively, he claims, we think that it is morally permissible to take someone's boat to save a drowning person, even if this will cause large, uncompensable damage to the boat, but we also think that it is not permissible to steal money from someone's bank account to help distant people. He does not think that there is any factor of moral significance that explains this difference, and hence we may impose property losses of any sort on others generally in order to provide aid. But I have suggested that if someone's property (such as his boat) is near a victim, she will intuitively be thought to have an obligation to let it be used to save the victim and that she lacks this obligation if her property (e.g., money in a bank account) is not near the victim. This suggests that distance is thought to be of moral importance.

Suppose we can show how proximity is generating our intuitions. The task of showing that we can justify its having this role because proximity is of real moral significance remains. Notice, however, that (contrary to what Unger thinks) if there is a duty to help because of nearness and sometimes no duty to help in the absence of nearness, this does not necessarily mean that we must do our duty to the near person rather than help the distant one. For very often, supererogatory acts—that is, aid we are not duty-bound to give—may be done instead of what is strictly our duty.[8]

IV. THE DUTY TO HARM ONESELF AND OTHERS

A. Unger's Thesis

Unger moves beyond the discussion of imposing losses of property for the sake of saving life and argues for duties to physically harm oneself and others. By using intuitions about cases in which someone is *not* simply giving up his life to save others, Unger arrives by steps at his radical conclusion, that I have a duty to give up my life in order to save the lives of two strangers. That is, Unger does not claim that we have *direct* intuitions about cases to the effect that I have a duty to give up my life to save two strangers. This is so even when their need is salient and my loss is going to completely solve their immediate problem.

The case Unger presents in which our intuitions tell us that we should kill *another* person to save a greater number of people is the Trolley Case, in which a trolley is headed toward killing (in his version) six people, and we may redirect it, though we foresee that it will certainly kill one. Indeed, it would not be wrong to summarize a great deal of what I shall explain in more detail below by saying that Unger attempts to use our intuitions about cases with the *redirection-of-threat structure* to deduce the permissibility of sacrificing people in general in order to diminish overall mortal loss. He does this by arguing that what the redirection-of-threat structure does, and what in large part accounts for our intuition that it is permissible to kill some people in this sort of case, is to *group* people and so over-come our tendency to *separate* people. Hence, whenever we come to group people (even because of a different structure), we will think (correctly, he thinks) that it is permissible to kill some people to save a greater number of others. But when we reflect on how grouping arises, he says, we see that grouping is *not* really morally crucial per se, and so even in cases where there is no obvious grouping, it should be permissible to kill some to save others. Hence, part of Unger's strategy is to rely on our intuition that it is permissible to redirect a threat away from killing six, even though it will then kill someone else, and show that there is no morally signifi-cant difference between this case and others where we would have to kill one to save others, for example, by pushing someone into the threat to stop it. This should leave it open for us to decide to kill based on our reflection on general values.

The traditional Trolley Case is a two-options case: Either we let the trolley kill the six, or we redirect it and it kills one. In being a two-options case, it is like another case where we either let the trolley kill six, or we push someone in front of the trolley to stop it. In discussing the traditional two-options redirection Trolley Case, Unger claims that we think of the one and the six as grouped (he calls this "projective grouping") because they share a connected set of trolley tracks. But in discussing other cases[9]—cases that, I believe, also have a redirective structure, though Unger does not explicitly draw attention to this fact—he points to other factors that produce grouping. These other factors are that the same threat will affect either the one or the six and that the threat going toward the one person is the noncausal flip side of the threat ceasing to go toward the six.[10] Unger thinks that these factors have a role in our thinking because they group the one and six, that is, we think that the one is involved with the six, shares their problems, and hence is "fair game" to be harmed so that the six will survive. This contrasts with our tendency to "projectively separate" someone from the problems that other people are facing, leading us to think it is wrong to involve her in order to save the others.

In addition to grouping versus separating, Unger argues that we respond to what he calls the "protophysical" characteristics of a case, that is, we find it easier to redirect an object already in motion rather than start one up; we find it easier to slow an object down rather than speed it up; and so on.[11] These factors will also affect our willingness to harm someone in order to help others.

If we think of pushing a stationary person in front of the trolley to stop it from hitting the six, we are faced with putting an entity into motion, producing harm to someone who does not share trolley tracks with the six, and producing harm to someone when this is *not* the flip side of the threat to the six ceasing. Some of these factors are important, according to Unger, because they lead us to see the one person as separate and not involved in the six's problem. Unger thinks that projectively separating someone involves treating people unequally,[12] because it gives the one person's claim not to be harmed more weight than is given to the comparable claim of the six not to be harmed by the trolley.

Unger thinks that we can overcome projective separating and so come to find it intuitively permissible to push one person in front of the trolley because we *group* him with the six, by constructing cases that involve *several* options (i.e., more than two).[13] So he constructs the Switches and Skates Case, described as follows:

> By sheer accident, an empty trolley, nobody aboard, is starting to roll down a certain track. Now, if you *do nothing about* the situation, your *first* option, then, in a couple of minutes, it will run over and kill six innocents who, through no fault of their own, are trapped down the line. (So, on your first option, you'll let the six die.) Regarding their plight, you have *three other* options: On your *second option*, if you push a remote control button, you'll change the position of a switch-track, switch A, and, before it gets to the six, the trolley will go onto another line, on the left-hand side of switch A's fork. On that line, three other innocents are trapped and, if you change switch A, the trolley will roll over them. (So, on your second option, you'll save six lives and you'll take three.) On your *third option*, you'll flip a remote control toggle and change the position of another switch, switch B. Then, a very light trolley that's rolling along another track, the Feed Track, will shift onto B's lower fork. As two pretty heavy people are trapped in this light trolley, after going down this lower fork the vehicle won't only collide with the onrushing empty trolley, but, owing to the combined weight of its unwilling passengers, the collision will derail the first trolley and both trolleys will go into an uninhabited area. Still, the two trapped passengers will die in the collision. On the other hand, if you don't change switch B, the lightweight trolley will go along B's upper fork and, then, it will bypass the empty trolley, and its two

passengers won't die soon. (So, on your third option, you'll save six lives and you'll take two.) Finally, you have a *fourth option*: Further up the track, near where the trolley's starting to move, there's a path crossing the main track and, on it, there's a very heavy man on roller skates. If you turn a remote control dial, you'll start up the skates, you'll send him in front of the trolley, and he'll be a trolley-stopper. But the man will be crushed to death by the trolley he then stops. (So, on your fourth option, you'll save six lives and you'll take one.) On reflection, you choose this fourth option and, in consequence, the six are prevented from dying.[14]

In this case, Unger thinks that we will find it permissible to push the one person on roller skates in front of the trolley, even though if it were the only alternative to letting the trolley kill the six, we would find it impermissible. But we should, he thinks, reflect on the psychologically powerful features that differentiate pushing someone in front of the trolley in the Switches and Skates Case from pushing someone in front of the trolley when it is the only option other than letting it kill six people. These features are not really morally important, according to Unger. Hence, we are free to use general moral values to decide what to do and should conclude (by these steps, if not by direct intuition) that it is also permissible to push someone in front of the trolley in the two-options Trolley Case.

Why does Unger think that we *will* intuitively find pushing the one person in front of the trolley permissible in the Switches and Skates Case? Essentially, he thinks that we will have the intuitive judgment because the intervening possible courses of action serve as bridges between what we intuitively find permissible (redirecting the trolley toward the three) and what is initially thought impermissible (pushing the person on skates in front of the trolley). The bridging is supposed to occur in the following way. Redirecting the second trolley (which is already in motion) in the Switches and Skates Case has many of the properties of redirecting the first threatening trolley, so we will think that it is as permissible as redirecting the original trolley threat. And pushing the person on skates in front of the trolley has some of the same characteristics as redirecting the second trolley (where it is the weight of the two people in it that stops the first trolley), so we will think that it, too, is permissible. More specifically, he says, like the six and the three in the first redirection option, the people in the second trolley are on trolley tracks; they are in a trolley that is already moving; and all we must do is redirect the second trolley. And so, he thinks, we will find it permissible to redirect the second trolley with its heavy people into the first trolley threat. The single person on roller skates, like the people on the second trolley, will be in motion once we start him and, like them, he is on wheels (albeit, roller-skate wheels), and it is his presence that causes the trolley to stop. Even though we do have to start the skater up (rather than redirect him) and he is not on any tracks, Unger thinks that the similarities will make us find it permissible to send him in.

Abstractly, the model is that option *A* has properties *abc*, option *B* has properties *bcd*, and option *C* has properties *cde*. Unger thinks that because *B* is in some ways like *A*, and *A* is permissible, we will think that *B* is permissible, and because C is in some ways like B, we will think that C is permissible, too. Hence, C will be permissible, if A is. He thinks that his reasoning holds, even though the resemblance between A and C, when considered directly, is minimal.

Given that, according to Unger, this "bridging resemblance" (my phrase) is all that makes us think that it is permissible to reduce the number of people killed by pushing the one person in front of the trolley, we cannot think that it is only when the bridging resemblance is present that it is permissible to send in the one person. That is, there is nothing intrinsically morally important about this bridging resemblance, except that it helps to overcome inhibitions in a positive direction (given that it leads us to minimize mortal loss, as general reflection [according to Unger] says is correct). For example, there is nothing intrinsically morally important about being on wheels rather than not being on wheels when you are pushed in front of a trolley. Thus, Unger concludes, it is, in general, permissible to push one person into a threat in order to save a greater number.

Unger's theses can be summarized as follows: (1) Our intuitions will be different in the Switches and Skates Case from our intuitions in the traditional two-options Trolley Case with respect to pushing someone in front of the trolley; we think that it is permissible to push the one person in front of the trolley in Switches and Skates; (2) it is projective grouping (via bridging) of the one person with the six that leads us to think that it is permissible to do this to the one in order to help minimize mortal loss to the six; (3) projective separating leads us to believe that we may not involve someone in this way; and (4) if it is permissible to act when people are seen as grouped, it is permissible to act in the same way when they are seen as separate.

B. Criticisms

Let me first summarize briefly my view about each of these four theses of Unger's: (1) My intuitions about the impermissibility of pushing someone in front of the trolley are *not* changed by the introduction of several options, as in the Switches and Skates Case. Intuitively, I do not think that it would be permissible to direct the second trolley so that it stops the first, killing two people on board, if this were the only alternative to redirecting the original threat to three other people.[15] (2)(a) Unger employs a highly contentious notion of grouping, which he is right to think has no intrinsic moral significance, and so it should *not* lead us to change our intuitions about what it is permissible to do. (2)(b) It is not true that people who are grouped, in his sense of grouped, are intuitively thought to be "fair game" to have anything done to them in order to minimize mortal loss. Hence, such grouping is *not sufficient* to account for the permissibility of harming when harming is intuitively permissible. (3)(a) He employs a contentious notion of "separateness," and (3)(b) it is not true that we think that it is impermissible to do harmful things to people who are separate in his sense. Hence, grouping in his sense is *not necessary* to account for the permissibility of harming when it is intuitively permissible. (4) Sometimes, contexts have intrinsic moral significance, and so we cannot draw implications from them about what to do in other contexts. But since the several-options context does not change my intuitions, I think that this point is moot.

(Notice, that I have made reference to "my intuitions" rather than made predictions about what others' intuitions will be. This is because I believe that it is primarily through an individual generating her own intuitive judgments *and then* trying to see what factors account for them and might justify them that we can make progress by a method employing intuitive judgments.)

Let me expand on these points (though not in the same order in which I have presented them). I do not find that my intuition changes about the impermissibility of pushing someone in front of a trolley, whether it is one of two options or one of several options. Indeed (as already noted), I do not even intuitively think that it is permissible to send in the second trolley, when the people on it are ordinary passengers, to crash into the first heavy trolley. Hence, I cannot be accused of inconsistency in thinking that it is wrong to send in a person if it is an option in a two-options case but permissible to send him in when considering a several-options case.[16]

I believe that my intuitions do not change in the Switches and Skates Case because the sort of bridging resemblance that Unger creates between the options in the Switches and Skates Case (and in other several-options cases he discusses) does not ensure that the characteristics that truly account for the permissibility of *redirecting* the trolley threat are present in the other options. This implies that grouping, at least of the sort created by bridging in the several-options case, is *not* the characteristic that accounts for the permissibility of redirecting the trolley threat originally. Further, the fact that option B resembles option A, and option C resembles option B, does not mean that they resemble each other in sharing the property present in A that makes it permissible to redirect the trolley. Suppose that A has properties *abc* and so is similar to B, which has *bcd*, and C is similar to B in having *cde*. This is no indication that C will be permissible, if A is permissible in virtue of *a*. This grouping, if it exists, seems no more explanatory than saying that because all people involved in redirection of the trolley threat are wearing red, we can show that it is permissible to push someone wearing pink in front of the trolley because we can show that it is permissible to redirect the second trolley, whose occupants are wearing half red and half pink. This is part of what I mean when I claim (in my response [2][a]) that Unger employs a contentious notion of how people get grouped.

But there is more to be said about the notion of grouping. If Joe is close to Jim, who is close to Tim, who is close to Tom, then Joe and Tom may be part of a group, in the sense of "not separated by much space," whereas if there were no individuals between them, there would be no group—they would be separated by a significant amount of space. And their being part of a group, in the sense of not being separated by much space, might sometimes have significance for what it is permissible to do to them. This is one way in which we can group people. But this is not Unger's sense of grouping. Rather, as I have said, he thinks we group the person on skates with the six in the Switches and Skates Case in virtue of a *linkage* of similar properties with intervening options. But, if act A is permissible because of some property it does not share with B or C, other similarities between A and B, and B and C do not imply that we may do act C because we may do act A.

Indeed, Unger's understanding of how to make redirecting a trolley and pushing a person in front of a trolley seem equally permissible has something like a sorites structure:[17] Creating a series with (supposedly) slight differences between each member of the series gets us to equate the two extremes of the series, which we know to be distinguishable. Unlike a true sorites, however, a morally significant difference between the first act and the others should stop the illegitimate equivalence in its tracks, as evidenced by the intuitive rejection of the permissibility of sending in the second trolley (as well as the man on roller skates).

I also claim (in response to [3]) that Unger employs a contentious notion of "separation" in projective separating. I think that his concern with grouping and separating is a sort of response to the objection raised to utilitarianism: that it does not take seriously the "separateness of persons."[18] The point of this objection is to emphasize that when one person is harmed to benefit others, the benefits to the others do not compensate the person harmed. This is unlike the case of *intra* personal harm for benefit, where the person harmed is himself compensated by the benefit. The failure of interpersonal compensation is still true of people who are grouped (in any of several senses of "grouped"); the loss to the ones who die is not compensated for by any good to *them*. Hence, we do not eliminate the separateness of persons, in the sense in which this is the basis of objecting to utilitarianism, by grouping them.

There are at least two other senses of "separate persons." First, persons are separate when they are not in a group linked spatially by other persons. Second, persons are separate when they are not grouped together because they do not share the same or similar properties. The latter is the sense of "separate" upon which Unger focuses, corresponding (by denial) to the sense of "grouped" upon which he focuses. (Call these last notions of separate and grouped "Unger-separate" and "Unger-grouped.") Thus, we can put Unger's theses (2) and (3) (summarized above) as the view that when people are Unger-separate, the fact that one person would not be compensated for harm done to him in reducing mortal loss to others *will* be thought morally important enough to make such harming seem impermissible, but when people are Unger-grouped, the fact that the one person will not be compensated for harm done to him in reducing mortal loss to others will not be thought morally important enough to make such harming seem impermissible.

My strategy for showing that Unger-grouping is not what makes harm done to people seem morally permissible (for example, in redirecting the trolley threat) is as follows: Show that when people are Unger-grouped, it is not thought (intuitively) to be permissible to do just anything to one person in order to minimize mortal loss to others; show that when people are Unger-separate, it is still thought (intuitively) to be permissible to do certain things to them in order to minimize mortal loss to others. This suggests that what makes acts that harm permissible or not has nothing to do with Unger-grouping or Unger-separateness. Indeed, rather than permissibility stemming from Unger-grouping versus Unger-separating, grouping or separating in a sense different from Unger's stems (to a large degree) from judgments of permissibility. For whatever factors account for the permissibility of harming, those who may permissibly be harmed *will be* potentially involved with each other (i.e., grouped), and those whom it is impermissible to harm will be uninvolved with each other (i.e., not grouped).[19]

To carry out this strategy, I must first point to intuitions about cases that conflict with the moral significance of Unger-grouping and Unger-separating. Ideally, I should then suggest a principle other than Unger-grouping or Unger-separating that correctly distinguishes between the cases where harming is permissible and where it is not. However, I shall not here spend much time delineating the correct principle.[20] This is because Unger's claim is that by Unger-grouping we can *change* our intuitions about behavior, and only if intuitions change will he be able to support the principle that we may in general harm people in order to minimize mortal losses. So, all we need to do to argue against him is show that Unger-grouping does not affect intuitions as he claims that it does. We need not provide a correct alternative principle.

I have already given my first countercases to the claim that Unger-grouping explains permissibility: My intuitions imply neither that it is permissible to redirect the second trolley in a way that threatens its passengers nor that it is permissible to send in the man on skates in the Switches and Skates Case. Here are further particular examples. As noted, Unger says that in redirection cases, the people on either side of the trolley track are seen as grouped, and grouped people are fair game to be used in order to save others. This is one reason that he thinks that our intuitions tell us that we may redirect the trolley, thereby killing three people rather than six in his case. But if this were so, then we would also think that it is permissible to do many other things to Unger-grouped people. For example, consider a new case in which three people and six people are on either side of a trolley track, and a trolley is headed toward the six. These are grouped people, according to Unger's criteria. But in this new case, redirection of the trolley will only save four of the six people at the cost of *paralyzing the three*, because the trolley will roll back after four have escaped and two people still remain pinned to the first track. However, if we throw the three people who are on the second track in front of the trolley, all six on the first track will be saved, though the three will die (Push-Three Case). Although these latter three people are Unger-grouped with the six, intuitively I do not think that the three are fair game to be caused *greater* harm than they would suffer by redirection of the trolley, in order to save all six.

In a second new case, Push-Three 2, the trolley is headed toward six people. It can be redirected to another track where it will kill three people. However, the hitting of the three on the track will not stop the trolley, and the track loops back to the six. The three and the six are grouped according to Unger's criteria, but, of course, we should not redirect the trolley, as we would then kill nine. May we throw the three from the second track onto the main track, if this will stop the trolley but kill the three?[21] I do not believe that this is permitted. Hence, members of an Unger-group are not necessarily fair game. There are some acts of harming them that still intuitively seem impermissible. This argues against Unger's claim that Unger-grouping is sufficient to account for our intuitions when we judge that it is permissible to minimize mortal loss by harming others.

But what about the factor of protophysics? If we think that it is more permissible to redirect a threat or person already in motion, perhaps this will account
for the judgments of *im*permissibility in both of the Push-Three cases, even when
people are Unger-grouped. For in these cases, we must push people not previously
in motion.[22] Can we find a case where there is Unger-grouping, *no* protophysical
problem, and still there is impermissibility? I have already said that if we redirect
the second trolley in the Switches and Skates Case, there is *no* protophysical
problem and the people are Unger-grouped, yet I think that it is impermissible to
send in the second trolley with people in it.

   Also consider the following case. A trolley is headed toward six people. It can
be directed onto a side track where three people are seated, but this route leads
through the three and back to the six, so it is unacceptable to redirect the trolley.
We can, however, redirect a second trolley, already in motion but threatening
only furniture, toward the first trolley, thereby stopping it. However, the second
trolley will also run into and kill the three people on the side track (Second Trolley
Redirection Case). It is intuitively impermissible to send in the second trolley, even
though the six and the three are grouped in Unger's sense and there is no protophysical problem. Hence, Unger-grouping where there are no protophysical
problems is not sufficient for permissibility.

   Unger also says that when people are *not* Unger-grouped, we think that it is
impermissible to involve them in other people's problems. (So, he has an "if and
only if Unger-grouped will the act be permissible" claim.) In a two-options case, he
argues, a single person who is not on the trolley tracks branching from the tracks
on which the trolley is headed is considered Unger-separate from the six toward
whom the trolley is headed. Yet, my sense is that if we could redirect the trolley
from the six, knowing that it would run *on the grass* killing one person, it would be
permissible to redirect the trolley. Unger also thinks that someone who is sitting in
his yard beneath a mountain far away from the trolley tracks is intuitively thought
to be separate from the six toward whom the trolley is hurtling (Yard Case).[23]
However, my sense is that it is permissible to redirect the trolley away from the six,
even though we foresee that it will tumble down the mountain, killing the one
person sitting in his yard.

   It is interesting to observe that when Unger considers the Yard Case, he does
not consider redirecting the trolley so that as a result of redirection, *it* kills the man
in his yard. Rather, he considers the following sequence of events: We start another
trolley that crashes into the trolley headed toward the six, but the *second* trolley
then tumbles down the mountain, killing the man in his yard.[24] Unger says that we
intuitively find this impermissible. I agree, but this impermissibility is not due to
our killing someone who is Unger-separate from those threatened by the original
trolley, since it is intuitively permissible to redirect the *original* trolley in the Yard
Case. Rather, I believe, it is impermissible because a mere causal means to helping
the six people—the second trolley—will kill another person.[25]

   Furthermore, we can find Unger-separate cases in which there is also what he
would consider a protophysical problem and yet it is permissible to kill one person
to save others. If this is so, the combination of separation and problematic

protophysics will not account for impermissibility. (Hence, Unger-grouping and the lack of protophysical problems will not be necessary for permissibility.) For example, consider the Lazy Susan Case V[26]: A trolley is headed toward killing five people who are seated on a resting Lazy Susan turntable. We cannot redirect the trolley, but we can *start up* the Lazy Susan, turning the five away from the trolley. However, the Lazy Susan will then start a rock slide that will kill an innocent bystander sitting in his yard far away. Here we put into motion a threat and kill someone who is Unger-separate, yet I believe that this action is permissible. It is even permissible to start up the Lazy Susan, I think, if an effect of its turning is to push a stationary bystander who is on the grass into the path of the trolley. So, contrary to what Unger says about protophysics, even in a two-options case, it is not only intuitively permissible to send a threat into someone (as when we redirect the trolley), it is also intuitively permissible to send an Unger-separate person into a threat.

So, I believe that we may harm Unger-separate people in what Unger says is a protophysically problematic way, and we may not harm Unger-grouped people in a protophysically nonproblematic way. Hence, our intuitions concerning the permissibility of harming in a two-options case do not necessarily stem from Unger-groupedness and no protophysical problems, and intuitions concerning the impermissibility of harming in a two-options case do not necessarily stem from Unger-separateness and protophysical problems.

I conclude that neither Unger-grouping nor the absence of problematic protophysical factors, alone or together, is sufficient to determine the permissibility of harming some to save others. Nor is the presence of these factors, alone or together, necessary to determine the permissibility of harming. So, it is not by altering cases to achieve grouping and by manipulating protophysical factors that one can always acquire the intuitions that say it is permissible to push someone into a trolley in order to save others. This further implies that one also cannot reflect upon these as factors that *change* our intuitions—as there is no change wrought by these factors in many cases we have considered—and conclude that because they are per se morally insignificant, we are free to act on general values and harm some people in order to prevent greater mortal loss to others quite generally. The several-options method does not, contrary to what Unger claims, liberate us to act on the values he claims to know are true by reflection on general theses.[27] Rather, it suggests that there is some other principle not identified by Unger that distinguishes permissible from impermissible harms.

C. The Correct Principle of Permissible Harm?

As described in detail in chapter 5, I believe that there is another characterization of factors that are crucial to making it permissible to harm some people in order to prevent greater mortal loss to others. Those who may permissibly be harmed when these factors are present will form a group with those for whose sake they may be harmed. (I would call this "permissibility-grouping.") If Unger's description of when people are grouped did, perchance, partially coincide with this other characterization, it is this other characterization that reveals why they are grouped. Similarly, when protophysical properties are consistent with the characteristics that are crucial to making acts that harm permissible, they will not be problematic; when they are inconsistent, they will be problematic.

Those whom we may not permissibly harm for the sake of others will not form a permissibility-group with those others. But this does not mean (contrary to Unger) that their claim not to be harmed is treated as greater than that of other people. After all, we might harm them for the sake of others if permissible means of doing so were available. The impermissibility of harming them just means that they, like everyone else, including those who need to be helped, should not be treated in a certain way for the sake of others. Suppose that a large number of people are being mistreated, but it is impermissible to stop this because in order to do so we would have to mistreat a smaller group. This does not mean that morality endorses the mistreatment of the larger number. But if it were permissible to do to some people what is now thought to be impermissible in order to save others from comparable mistreatment, morality *would* be endorsing such treatment. This would mean that every person may be treated in these ways that we had thought were prohibited.[28]

What characteristic distinguishes the permissible from the impermissible cases of harming? In other words, what is the correct principle of permissible harm? As I said above, I do not intend to dwell on this question in this chapter, because I do not believe that a detailed answer is necessary for my criticism of Unger to be successful. However, a rough characterization, that summarizes what has been said in chapter 5, is important because it will help us to better understand Unger's method of multiple options. Roughly, the permissible cases involve lesser evil* coming about as an effect, aspect, or noncausal flip side of a greater good, its component, or means that have a greater good or its component as their noncausal flip side. (Recall that the idea of a noncausal flip side can be exemplified in the Trolley Case, where the movement of the trolley away from the six people is the absence of a threat to them, which is their being saved in the context.) The impermissible cases involve lesser evil* either (a) as a means, required given our act, to causally producing a greater good or (b) as the direct effect or aspect of means that produce a greater good as a *causal effect*.

When we turn the Lazy Susan, we move the six people away from the threat— this is the greater good in a context where no other threats are present—and it causes the death of the one person. When we turn the trolley away from the six people, the flip side of this is that they do not have any threat upon them, and this is a greater good. So, the turning of the trolley, which also causes the death of the one, is a means that has a greater good as its noncausal flip side. By contrast, in the Switches and Skates Case, when we send in the second trolley with people on it, this causes the trolley headed toward the six people to stop and also causes the death of the people on the second trolley. Hence, sending in the second trolley is either a means that has the greater good as a causal effect and also directly causes lesser evil*, or a way to have the harmful involvement of two people (whose weight helps stop the first trolley) be a required means that causes a greater good. When we send the man on skates into the path of the trolley, the means itself is bad (as it involves someone in a way that will harm him), and it has a further causal effect of stopping the trolley, and so causally produces the six saved.

Unger finds it odd that we think that it is impermissible to chop off someone's foot in order to save twelve lives while at the same time we think that it is permissible to kill twelve people in order to save a foot.[29] The case he describes in which we do the latter involves redirecting a trolley that will then hit twelve people away from both killing twelve other people and cutting off the foot of a thirteenth.[30] But notice that in this case, it is only because twelve people would be killed anyway if we do not redirect that we redirect the trolley to kill the twelve people who are unaccompanied by a potential thirteenth victim. If chopping off the foot to save twelve violates a principle of permissible harm and redirecting when harm is minimized does not, there is no oddity, contrary to Unger. These cases show that something besides reducing mortal losses is important. I hypothesize that this something is about the high status of persons expressed in our theory of permissible and impermissible harms.

Interestingly, Unger's method of several options can be seen, I believe, as based on a misapplication of the principle that when greater good would be the noncausal flip side of what leads to lesser evil*, action is permissible. Consider that in the Switches and Skates Case, when one agent must decide which of several acts to perform, his performing one act that causes less harm is the alternative to his performing another act that causes more harm. Hence, if an agent sends in the trolley with two people on it instead of redirecting the trolley toward three people, a greater good of three people not being hit is the noncausal flip side of sending in the trolley with two people on it instead. The method of several options can be seen, then, as an attempt to apply the redirection-of-threat model to *the agent considered as a threat*. That is, once the agent decides to redirect the trolley, it may be thought that he can treat himself as a threat who can be redirected from (a) turning a trolley on three people to either (b) sending in a trolley with two people on it or (c) pushing a man in front of the trolley. In general, the idea seems to be that once an agent will be a threat to some, he may redirect himself to minimize the threat that he presents. This idea is what, I believe, underlies the method of several options as Unger uses it, though he does not seem to realize it.[31]

What is wrong with this use of the redirection model and the principle of permissible harm that I suggested underlies it? Why is it still impermissible to send in the second trolley (or the man on skates)? The important general point that must be explained is that *an agent cannot be morally free to do just anything that would otherwise be impermissible simply because it is a less harmful alternative to his doing another act that is permissible.*[32]

Here is a proposed explanation of this general point. Suppose that it is permissible to turn the trolley away from six people and toward three because (roughly) the greater good of the six saved—call this GG1—will be the noncausal flip side of turning the threat toward three people. Sending in the second trolley with two people on it (instead of redirecting the first trolley toward the three) has the three people not hurt—call this GG2—as its noncausal flip side. But GG2 is not the same as GG1. Sending in the second trolley has GG1 as a *causal* effect, and it also results in the deaths of two people. The fact that GG2 (three saved) is the noncausal flip side of sending in the second trolley does not mean that GG1 is the noncausal flip side of sending in the second trolley. Hence, we have a choice between (a) redirecting the first trolley toward three people, which is a permissible way (according to my theory) to achieve GG1 (as it has GG1 as a noncausal flip side), or (b) doing something that harms two different people in a way that (according to my theory) is not permitted in order to achieve GG1. We should not choose the impermissible way when we can choose the permissible way.

Another way of making this point is to characterize the alternatives among which an agent may choose, when he would kill different people on such alternatives, as follows: Once it is permissible for him to do one act that threatens some, he may do only the alternatives that either (1) share the property that made the first act permissible (that is, they have GG1 as their noncausal flip side), or (2) have another property that would make them permissible if they were the only possible way to achieve GG1. For example, if it were an option for an agent to send the first trolley headed to the six toward one person rather than toward three people, GG1 would be the noncausal flip side of this act as well. Hence, this act would be morally different from one where an agent sends in the second trolley instead of redirecting the first trolley toward the three people.

Notice also that there is a moral difference between the case where one sends in the second trolley with two people on it (or pushes in the one person on roller skates), instead of redirecting the first trolley toward three people, and the following two cases: (1) A trolley is headed toward killing three people. I redirect it toward a track where a second trolley sits. The first trolley pushes the second trolley into the path of a third trolley that is headed toward six people. The second trolley stops the third trolley, saving the six people, but two people on the second trolley are killed. (2) Everything is as in case (1), except that the first trolley redirected away from three people pushes a person into the path of the trolley headed toward the six, which stops the trolley but kills the one person. Redirecting the trolley is permissible in these cases.

In these two cases, as in Unger's, doing what would save the three people would involve pushing a trolley, or a person, into the trolley headed toward six people, resulting in fewer deaths. But in these two cases, the threat to the duo or to the single person is the effect of a means (i.e., redirecting the first trolley headed toward the three people) that has saving the three (GG2) as its noncausal flip side. Indeed, Case 2 shows that it can be permissible to do an act, even though it results in evil* being a productive cause of a greater good (saving the six [GG1]) when the evil* is the effect of another good greater than it (GG2) or a means having that good as its noncausal flip side.

But in Unger's case, is it not also true that pushing in the trolley with two people on it (or the person on skates) has the same GG2 as its noncausal flip side? After all, the three people will not be hit because an agent does an alternative act. The crucial difference between my Cases 1 and 2 and Unger's case is that only in Unger's case is it possible to produce GG2 by just *not sending* the trolley toward the three people. They face only a possible act of an agent, rather than a threat already headed toward them. Hence, in his case, it is not necessary to do what sends the trolley with two people on it (or the single person on skates) into the path of the trolley that is headed toward the six, in order to prevent that trolley from being redirected toward killing three people. Doing what redirects the trolley with two people on it is not necessary as a means to saving the three people in Unger's case; the means to saving them in Unger's case is just *not* to send the trolley toward them. By contrast, in my Cases 1 and 2, a trolley is already headed toward the three, and the necessary means to save them is to redirect the trolley, leading to the further consequences described.

Of course, if we simply do not redirect the trolley toward the three people and do nothing else in Unger's case, the six people will be killed. Hence, performing the alternative act of redirecting toward the three is a means necessary *to save the six*, but this is a different issue entirely from what is necessary to save the three. And it has been said that (roughly) a means to saving the six people that also directly causes harm to innocent bystanders should not productively *cause* that greater good but rather have a noncausal relation to that greater good (or be caused by something that has such a relation). Since the alternative acts in Unger's case (i.e., push in the second trolley or push in one person) are not means necessary to achieve GG2 (save the three) but to achieve GG1, these alternative acts should have GG1 as their noncausal flip side. But they do not. Hence, they are impermissible.

D. Harms with an Intervening Agent

In the Switches and Skates Case, I would be the only agent involved in causing harm to others unless I merely let the trolley head toward the six. In another type of case that Unger discusses, I do not alone harm others, but a decision I make to help reduce harm overall can lead to someone else harming others. These are the UNICEF Card and Lesser-Loss-Card cases.[33] In the UNICEF Card Case, if I pick up a UNICEF card, aid will go to many people in Africa, but the villain Strangemind will then send his henchmen to chop off someone's foot in Asia. In the Lesser-Loss-Card Case, if I pick up a UNICEF card, I will save the lives of fifty people in Africa *from Strangemind's henchmen*, but he will then send other henchmen to Asia to chop off someone's foot. Unger thinks that our intuitions are that it is *im*permissible for me to pick up the UNICEF card in the UNICEF Card Case but permissible for me to do so in the Lesser-Loss-Card Case. He distinguishes the cases on the basis of Unger-grouping and Unger-separating.

In the UNICEF Card Case, the suffering people in Africa are not suffering from any problem that Strangemind gave them, so the cause of the threat to the Asian whom Strangemind's henchmen will hurt is different from what threatens the Africans. This makes the Africans and Asians seem separate from each other, according to Unger. By contrast, in the Lesser-Loss-Card Case, the same threat— Strangemind—threatens both the Asians and the Africans, and his henchman's movement to Asia is the flip side of the removal of the henchmen from Africa. This, according to Unger, creates the sense that the one person in Asia and the fifty people in Africa are part of a group. Hence, it seems permissible to help the

Africans by doing something that leads to harming the Asian. Once we see that this is all that grounds our sense of permissibility, we should be free to act on our general values and conclude that it is permissible to pick up the UNICEF card in the UNICEF Card Case as well, he claims.

It should be clear (though he does not make it clear) that Unger has modeled the Lesser-Loss-Card Case on the redirection cases we have been discussing, with the following variation: There are, strictly speaking, two different threats in the Lesser-Loss-Card Case. That is, either one set of henchmen is sent to attack Africans if I do not pick up the card or *another* set of henchmen is sent to Asia if I pick up the card stopping the first set of henchmen. This is by contrast with the villain sending the same henchmen elsewhere. (It might seem that there is another variation introduced into this case. It is my picking up the UNICEF card that is both a means to stop one threat and what starts another. This is by contrast with the stopped threat itself causing another threat. But on reflection it seems that this variation is not really present, for presumably it is Strangemind's recognition of the fact that his henchmen will not go to Africa that is necessary in order for him to send the other henchmen to Asia.)[34]

Despite the variation, I think that, as in the Switches and Skates Case, Unger's aim is to move from the permissibility of redirecting a threat in order to save a greater number to the permissibility of saving a greater number by any means. The first problem with Unger's strategy, I believe, is that picking up the card in the UNICEF Card Case is *not*, intuitively, impermissible. I may save many people despite the fact that (I know that) someone else will, voluntarily and uncoerced by me, make a decision to harm someone else based either on how I act or on what the consequences of my acting are. The same can be said to account for the permissibility of picking up the card in the Lesser-Loss-Card Case.

But suppose we assume, for the sake of argument, that intuitively only action in the Lesser-Loss-Card Case is judged to be permissible. My strategy in dealing with Unger's attempt to assimilate the Lesser-Loss-Card and UNICEF Card cases would be to show that Unger-grouping does not account for permissibility, and Unger-separation does not account for impermissibility.

First, consider those who are Unger-grouped and yet are not fair game to be harmed. In my Lesser-Loss-Card Case 2, if I pick up the UNICEF card (a) Strangemind sends fewer henchmen to kill a group of Africans than he otherwise would have, killing only twenty instead of fifty, but he also sends the rest of his henchmen to chop off the foot of an Asian. So, the one in Asia and the many in Africa are Unger-grouped. But if I pick up the UNICEF card (b) in my Lesser-Loss-Card Case 2, Strangemind will send a henchman to kill the Asian and, because this has such a calming effect on him, he will not send any of the other henchmen he would otherwise send to Africa. I think that it is intuitively impermissible to pick up the UNICEF card (b) in the Lesser-Loss-Card Case 2, even if the only alternative is to pick up the UNICEF card (a) instead. Hence, Unger-grouped people are not fair game. My explanation of the impermissibility of killing the Unger-grouped Asian is as follows: If I pick up UNICEF card (b), my means to saving many lives (the greater good) would be a lesser evil* (having Strangemind be calmed by killing one person). By contrast (and abstracting from the significance of another agent's intervening voluntary act), in the original Lesser-Loss-Card Case and in the Lesser-Loss-Card Case 2 where we pick up UNICEF card (a), the following is true: The lesser evil* seems to be either an effect of means that have a greater good as a noncausal flip side (because threat [1] not facing group [1] is the noncausal flip side of doing what leads to threat [2] facing group [2]) or an effect of the greater good itself (if Strangemind acts to harm the Asian because the Africans will not be threatened).

Now consider those who are Unger-separate. In my Angry Strangemind Case, if I pick up a UNICEF card, money gets sent to save many people in Africa who are suffering independently of any threat of Strangemind's. As a consequence of seeing them so well off, Strangemind gets angry and sends his henchmen to kill an Asian. I believe that it is intuitively permissible to pick up a UNICEF card in this case, even though the Asian and the Africans are Unger-separate. It is permissible (even if we abstract from the significance of another agent's intervening voluntary act) because the *greater good* results in the lesser evil*, even if the lesser evil* is caused by a different threat than that faced by the Africans. (This would contrast with a case in which it is the *means*—our choice—that has a greater good as a mere causal effect and that also triggers, independent of Strangemind's voluntary act, a lesser evil*.) Hence, it is not always impermissible to do what harms those who are Unger-separate.

E. Tolerating and Imposing Nonphysical Harm on Ourselves

Recall that Unger wishes to move from the permissibility of harming others to our having a duty to harm ourselves in order to prevent greater mortal loss. I have examined and criticized a significant part of his attempt to prove the first premise, that it is often permissible to harm others in ways nonconsequentialists would rule out. One route from the first premise, had it been proven, to the conclusion that we have a duty to harm ourselves would involve what Unger calls the Principle of Ethical Integrity (PEI). Roughly, this principle says that what you would permissibly do to others, you cannot fail to do to yourself for the sake of equal or greater reduction in mortal losses.[35] In dealing with cases, as we have seen, Unger's goal is to assimilate our treatment of people in one sort of case (e.g., pushing them in front of a trolley) to other cases (e.g., redirecting a threat toward them). Similarly, his attempt via the PEI is to assimilate our treatment of *ourselves* to our treatment of *others*.

A less direct route to the conclusion is to show, by using cases, that we think we should *tolerate* serious harm to ourselves rather than have others suffer even greater losses. Then we would have to move from showing what we should *tolerate* to showing what we should *impose* on ourselves. I shall first deal with this less direct route, putting off discussion of the PEI. I do this because I have already argued that Unger has not shown that we may always harm others to lessen mortal loss. If we may not harm others, then we cannot show that we must harm ourselves on the ground that we must do to ourselves what we would permissibly do to others.

Perhaps showing that we must tolerate serious harm to ourselves will be a more successful route to the requirement that we seriously harm ourselves. Let us start by examining tolerating less serious nonphysical harm.

In Unger's Bankcard Case, Strangemind will impose a $1,000 loss on your bank account—we start with a property loss—unless you pick up a bankcard, and if you do pick it up, he will send a henchman to chop off a distant stranger's foot. Unger agrees that intuitively we think that it is impermissible to pick up the bankcard. He contrasts this with our intuition, in what he calls the Envelope Case, that it is permissible to refuse to send $1,000 to a charity that would save a distant stranger from losing his life, let alone his foot. Unger thinks that he can account for the intuitive distinction we draw between these two cases on the basis of Unger-grouping and Unger-separating, respectively. Only in the Bankcard Case is the individual who would threaten your bank account the same person who would threaten the distant stranger, and his threatening the stranger is the strict alternative to your not picking up the bankcard. Hence, according to Unger, you think of yourself as grouped with the Asian. This liberates you to what Unger thinks is a true value, that a lesser loss to you is not as important as preventing a bigger loss to another person *quite generally*. Given the actual moral irrelevance (in Unger's view) of Unger-grouping, from this you should deduce that your intuition in the Envelope Case was wrong.

My analysis of the Bankcard Case differs from Unger's, and I do not think the case supports his conclusion. The structure of the Bankcard Case is, once again, like that of a redirection-of-threat case, except that it involves a different agent (Strangemind) voluntarily deciding to do one bad thing if he is prevented from doing another bad thing. (To reflect this, I will call it a "redirection" case.) Picking up the bankcard would involve redirecting Strangemind from causing a small loss to you to his causing a greater loss to others. Hence, it seems wrong to redirect Strangemind. But the impermissibility of doing what leads to harm in the Bankcard Case is not dependent on Unger-grouping or even on the presence of a redirection structure. To see this, suppose that a villain will cause a loss to my bank account and the only means I can use to stop him has as a direct effect that a distant stranger is killed. Here the distant stranger is *separate*, according to Unger's criteria, because what threatens her is my means, and this is different from what threatens me. Yet it is still impermissible to do what helps me and harms her. So Unger-grouping is not necessary to account for why we must tolerate cases of lesser loss to ourselves rather than do what leads to harm to others.

Notice, in addition, that Unger-grouping may make it intuitively morally *easier* (rather than harder) to harm another on our own behalf than does Unger-separation. Suppose that a villain threatens to chop off my legs unless I pick up the bankcard, and if I pick it up, he sends a henchman to chop off a distant stranger's foot. Because this is "redirection" of the villain from greater harm to lesser harm, it may be permissible. (Even if it were strict redirection, it might be permissible.) Such redirection also seems to be endorsed by the values that Unger thinks are correct, that is, it reduces overall severe harm. But if a villain will chop off my legs unless I shoot him, it is not clear that I may shoot him if I know that the bullet will kill the villain but also shoot off the leg of a distant stranger. (This is on the model of its being impermissible to set off a bomb in order to stop a trolley from killing five people when we foresee that it will also kill an innocent bystander. However, it might be permissible for me to shoot, if what we permit in defense of self were broader than what we permit in defense of others. This would, of course, create problems for Unger's PEI.)

More evidence can be given for the view that there is a particular duty to sometimes suffer losses instead of doing what leads to harm (even lesser harm) to other people, rather than any general duty to bear lesser losses in order to prevent greater mortal loss. Such evidence comes from the fact that Unger-grouping is not sufficient to support intuitions that we must suffer losses in order *to aid* those with whom we are Unger-grouped. For example, consider another revision of Unger's case, my Bankcard Plus $1,000 Case: If I pick up a bankcard, I prevent Strangemind from taking $1,000 from my account, but he goes off to chop off a distant person's leg. If I do not pick up a bankcard, he chops off only that same distant person's foot. I could prevent his even chopping off the foot by giving another $1,000 to him. Suppose that I judge intuitively that I should not pick up the bankcard, so as not to be involved in harm to the distant person. I do *not* also intuitively judge that the duty to give the extra $1,000 to aid the person with whom I am Unger-grouped is any stronger (or weaker) than the duty to aid a person from whom I am Unger-separate who would lose a foot in an Envelope Case. Hence, it is not Unger-grouping that is responsible for our different intuitions in the Bankcard and Envelope cases, nor is it grouping that overcomes intuitions that support the Envelope Case.

Suppose that we give a redirection structure to the aid itself. Consider my Keeping Busy Case, in which Strangemind will send a henchman to chop off a distant stranger's foot, but I can prevent this by keeping Strangemind busy removing $1,000 from my bank account. By making Strangemind a threat to me, I redirect him to where he does the least damage. In this case, I and the stranger are Unger-grouped, but intuitively there is no stronger (or weaker) obligation to aid the stranger in this way than in the Envelope Case. Now consider my Generous Strangemind Case, in which Strangemind offers to either give me $1,000 or— the flip side of not doing this—give a distant needy stranger $2,000. Again, there is Unger-grouping of the people, because we are redirecting a benefit, but, intuitively, there is not as strong a duty to refuse the money as there was not to resist Strangemind's taking my money in Unger's original Bankcard Case. Presumably, this is because I would be involved in Strangemind's harming the distant stranger in Unger's Bankcard Case, but only involved in Strangemind's not-aiding the stranger here. Now consider my Joint Venture Case, in which Strangemind offers to give some of his own money to a distant needy stranger, if I allow him to take some of my money. If he cannot take my money, he will not give to the distant stranger. In this case, if I resist his offer, a benefit does not go to the distant stranger with whom I am Unger-grouped. Yet, intuitively, it is no more or less permissible to resist the offer than to refuse aid in the Envelope Case.[36]

In the Keeping Busy Case, my suffering a loss in order to aid another would take the form of my redirecting a threat from a distant stranger to myself. In such cases, I do not merely fail to resist a nonmortal loss that someone else will impose on me; *I impose it on myself.* I concluded that I need no more (or less) impose the loss on myself in that case than in the Envelope Case. But Unger believes that in his Bob's Bugatti Case, our intuitions tell us that we must impose at least a very big financial loss on ourselves. In this case, Bob's Bugatti (in which he has invested his entire retirement fund) is parked on one arm of a branching trolley track. On the other arm is a child and a trolley is headed toward killing her. Unger thinks that we will agree that Bob has a duty to turn the trolley away from the child, even though he foresees that it will certainly cost him his retirement fund. Suppose that we agree. This raises the question: Why is Bob intuitively required to redirect a threat toward his Bugatti, but the person in my Keeping Busy Case is *not* required to redirect Strangemind toward harming his bank account? Four hypotheses suggest themselves.

First, in the Bob's Bugatti Case, someone will lose his life, whereas in the Keeping Busy Case, only a foot is at stake. (But the monetary loss is also lower in the Keeping Busy Case.)

Second, the Bugatti will be destroyed as a *consequence* of turning the trolley away from the child. Hence, the case's destruction is a side effect of means that have a greater good as a noncausal flip side. In the Keeping Busy Case, we intend that Strangemind pay harmful attention to our bank account and, I believe, we conceive of this as a means that has the greater good (of the other person not threatened by Strangemind) as its noncausal flip side. So here our involvement that leads to our financial harm is itself a means to helping another person.[37]

We can make this second point as well by considering another variation on the Bob's Bugatti Case. Suppose that turning the trolley away from killing the child cannot be done quickly enough to prevent its running over the child and partially paralyzing its legs. The Bugatti would also only be partially destroyed by the redirection, leaving Bob with a still-significant retirement fund. However, if instead of redirecting the trolley, Bob sends the Bugatti across the tracks into the trolley, he will completely prevent harm to the child and the Bugatti will be completely destroyed. (Call this Push-the-Bugatti Case.) Do we, intuitively, believe that he must do this for the child with whom he is Unger-grouped? I do not believe so. This means that we get no stronger (or weaker) conclusion from an Unger-grouped case for a duty to aid by imposing losses on ourselves as a mere means to preventing mortal harm (as in Push-the-Bugatti Case) than we would get from a case that involved people who are physically near to us (as they are in Bob's Bugatti) but who are nevertheless Unger-separate.

The third hypothesis to distinguish the Bob's Bugatti Case from the Keeping Busy Case is that physical distance makes a moral difference. The person to be harmed in the Keeping Busy Case is a *distant* stranger, as are those in the Envelope Case. The one in the Bob's Bugatti Case is a *near* stranger. Unger does not believe that physical distance can affect obligations. Perhaps he is wrong about this.[38]

The fourth hypothesis to distinguish the Bob's Bugatti Case from the Keeping Busy Case is that when an intervening agent who acts voluntarily, like Strangemind, is involved, we need not take as much responsibility for preventing harm, because we should not allow ourselves to be manipulated by evil people who are primarily responsible for the harm. On these grounds, it might be argued not only that we should not impose harm on ourselves but that we should not be involved in redirecting more generally. After all, there is a more appropriate way to diminish the threats of evil people: They should control themselves. They are persons, not physical objects like threatening trolleys that have no self-control.

This hypothesis, however, implies that we need not rescue a drowning baby right near us, simply because she was pushed in by an evil person whose aim was to affect our behavior. But this is not true.[39] Note also that in the Envelope Case, as in the Bob's Bugatti Case, evil perpetrators are not the (usual) cause of harm to distant strangers who need the money in the envelope.

In sum, Unger-grouping does not account for our intuitions that we should tolerate losses to ourselves rather than be involved in harming someone, because we also should not harm those from whom we are Unger-separate. Unger-grouping also does not lead us to change our intuitions about how much we should do to minimize loss to others by imposing losses on ourselves in order to aid. The harming/not-aiding distinction and the distinction between suffering losses as a means to aid or as a consequence of aid, rather than the Unger-grouped versus Unger-separate distinction, seem to be doing work in accounting for the intuitions involved in the Bob's Bugatti and Keeping Busy cases. Therefore, we cannot take the next step in Unger's argument, which is to reflect on the per se moral insignificance of Unger-grouping and then deduce the duty to impose losses of property on ourselves in order to prevent greater loss *quite generally*, including to those from whom we are Unger-separate.

In concluding this section, consider Unger's claim that our duty to our dependents (such as our children) might override the duty to impose property losses on ourselves in order to lessen mortal loss to distant strangers. First, I do not understand how, on Unger's view, one has a right to come to have dependents at all, if one foresees that this will prevent one from engaging in projects that minimize mortal loss (as is probably true in our world). For if I have a duty to suffer *mortal* loss in order to minimize mortal loss—a claim of Unger's I will examine in the next section—then it would seem that I have a duty to suffer the loss of having offspring, in the current world as it is, if this would help me to save distant strangers instead.

Suppose, however, that I may permissibly have dependents (perhaps because I am more productive in aiding if I have them than if I do not, due to a limitation of my human psychology). Unger says that I may be justified in not minimizing mortal loss in order to pay for my dependents' education instead. But if Unger wants to take our intuitive judgments about what losses we should undergo in redirection cases, such as the Bob's Bugatti Case, as an indication of what we should be committed to sacrificing for others in general, then his view that we need not give away money that is necessary to provide for our *dependents'* needs would be called into question. This is because if a trolley is headed toward killing a stranger, we should redirect it to a track where it will destroy irreplaceable money needed to educate our dependent (Education Fund Case). If Unger's strategy of assimilating cases were correct, this would further imply that we should give our dependent's education fund away to save a stranger's life, contrary to what he claims.

I, by contrast, suggest that we (or others) may be obligated to redirect the trolley, though it will foreseeably destroy the money, but not to give the money away. On Unger's views, however, to say that I need not give the money to famine relief implies that I need not turn the trolley. Also, Unger's claim (examined earlier) that we should quite generally kill someone else (even as a means) in order to save yet others from mortal loss implies that not saving life is at least as wrong as killing. But this claim, in conjunction with his view that we need *not* sacrifice funds set aside for our dependents in order to save the lives of strangers, implies that we may do what kills others if this is necessary to save the education money for our dependents. Unger's general strategy of equating harming with not-aiding, and not-harming with aiding, combined with the exceptional, nonoverrideable duty to dependents, yields a duty to kill strangers in order to protect funds for one's children's education. This is an unacceptable conclusion.[40]

F. Imposing Mortal Loss on Ourselves

Unger would ultimately like to show that we have a duty quite generally to impose mortal loss on ourselves for the sake of reducing overall mortal losses.[41] So far, when it comes to imposing mortal (rather than property) loss, I have argued that, despite Unger's arguments, direct intuitions or deductions from intuitions show only that it is permissible to redirect threats (or people from threats) in order to minimize mortal loss. Of course, Unger also thinks that reflections on general theses, such as the overriding importance of reducing mortal losses, support imposing mortal loss on ourselves. But his aim was to quell disagreement about the correctness of such general theses by showing that intuitions in selected cases—plus reflection on the moral unimportance of particular factors in those cases (missing in others) that lead to those intuitions—liberate us to follow the general theses. I claim that he has not shown this.

What do we get when we combine what we already believe intuitively about cases with a principle that we should treat ourselves as we treat others, such as his PEI, a general principle that Unger thinks that we accept on reflection? Unger seems to believe that we can, at least, derive the duty to do mortal damage to *ourselves* in redirection cases. And given his assimilation of different types of cases to redirection cases, he believes we can also derive a duty to do mortal damage to ourselves in order to minimize mortal losses quite generally. I emphasize that he *derives* this result. He does not present a case in which one has the direct intuition that one must sacrifice one's life in order to save two strangers, though he thinks that we have case intuitions (as in the Bob's Bugatti Case) that support imposing *property* damage on ourselves. To illustrate what the PEI implies, Unger presents the Trilemma Case: If a trolley is headed toward six people, I should redirect it toward three, but if I can redirect it toward one instead, I should do that. If the one happens to be me, the conclusion still holds.

The only duty that Unger allows may take precedence over the duty to minimize mortal loss is a duty to our closest dependents, for example, our children. But since they, too, have duties to sacrifice themselves to prevent others' losses, what we do for them presumably should be tempered by the thought of what they are duty-bound to suffer for others.[42]

I am not convinced by these arguments. In the Trolley cases, I argued that intuitively it is *permissible* to redirect the trolley and cause mortal loss in order to minimize overall mortal loss, not that it is a duty to do so. But we already know that it is *permissible* for us to suffer mortal loss for the sake of minimizing overall mortal loss; we do not need the PEI to show that we are permitted to sacrifice ourselves for others. If we do not have a *duty* to kill others, the PEI cannot show that we have a duty to kill ourselves.

However, the Trilemma Case does, I believe, provide a scenario in which we have some *duty* to turn a trolley in a certain way, though I do not think that Unger brings this point out. It may be merely permissible, not required, to turn the trolley from six toward three, but if I *am* actually about to do this, and I also have the option to redirect from six toward one other person, then I think, intuitively, I would have a *duty* to redirect the trolley toward the one other person, other things being equal. In other words, I may not have a duty to reduce harm by redirecting the trolley, but if I decide to do so, I have to choose the route that causes the least harm, other things being equal. We have now derived a *conditional duty* to kill one person.

However, other things would not be equal if I would have to suffer a large cost, even downstream, to redirect from three to one other person. Intuitively, I do not think that I would have to suffer a large personal cost to reroute from the three toward the one, any more than to redirect anywhere. (For example, suppose I could easily enough redirect the trolley from six to one except that this would set off a bomb that will kill me. I do not think I then am required to turn the trolley from six to one.)

From these intuitive judgments, in combination with the PEI, we can conclude that I have a conditional duty to turn the trolley toward myself away from the six and the three, if I am the one other person, so long as this causes me no large personal sacrifice. But I *would* have to suffer a large cost if I rerouted the trolley toward myself for I would die. Hence, intuitions in cases, combined with the PEI, do not show that I have a duty to do so.[43]

Could we revise the argument for a duty to harm one versus three, if we redirect from six, so that it implies a duty to harm oneself? Suppose it is permissible for me to redirect a trolley toward three people and I have a duty, given that I would do this, to redirect toward one other person instead. Suppose also that I must abide by the PEI. Then, if I have a duty to impose a loss as large as death on one person rather than kill the three, it is *not* true, it may be said, that I need not redirect from three people toward one other person just because the cost to me of doing so is great. For example, contrary to intuitions, I would have a duty to make a big effort (e.g., break my back) to shift the trolley from three to one. What is odd in this revised argument is that we could find ourselves with a duty to suffer a big loss in order to fulfill a duty to kill one rather than three even if, intuitively, we did not have a duty to suffer such a loss to save the original group of six, as saving them was merely permissible. (For example, I would not have had to break my back to redirect the trolley from the six toward the three if that were my only option.) I conclude that the duty to kill one instead of three to save the six does not give rise to a duty to impose large losses on oneself.

Unger's claim that I morally must redirect the trolley toward myself also conflicts with our ordinary intuitions about what *those others* toward whom we redirect threats may do, whether we think that we are merely permitted or duty-bound to redirect toward them. That is, we do not think that they have a duty *not* to resist the assault on them. If the single other person toward whom I redirect can physically push the trolley away from him, we intuitively think, I believe, that he may do so, even if he foresees that it will kill me, who redirected toward him, or the six toward whom the trolley was originally headed. Intuitively, he may, at least, permissibly *make things as they would have been without redirection* by re-redirecting, even if this does not minimize overall mortal loss. If he may also permissibly harm the agent who redirected toward him, as a side effect of sending the trolley away, he would sometimes be permitted to even make the situation worse than it would have been without the original redirection.[44] Finally, if he has a button that would permit him to turn the trolley away from the six and toward himself, he would not have a duty to use it.

If another person would not have a duty to direct the trolley toward himself, I would not, contrary to Unger, have a duty to do it to myself either even if one accepted the PEI. We impartially universalize the permission not to sacrifice oneself and in this way support the PEI. But in this universalized permission, there is still embedded a rejection of the complete PEI, since all potential victims would be permitted to treat themselves differently from how they treat other people, as they redirect a trolley toward others that they would not redirect to themselves. Our intuitions, at least, support a self-other asymmetry at some level. So, whereas previously I argued, contra Unger, that we cannot move from redirection cases to ones where we directly give up or cause someone to give up something to help reduce mortal losses, here I suggest that one cannot move from what one even has a duty to do to others to what one must do to oneself.

I conclude that Unger's arguments for the conclusion that we have a duty to impose mortal loss on ourselves in order to reduce overall mortal losses fail. More generally, I believe that his inventive attempts to prove his other substantive claims do not succeed. This failure is connected with the fact that his methodological claims are also not sustained; he does not succeed in showing that intuitions in the relevant cases are manipulable by morally insignificant factors nor that intuitive differences in cases are due to the factors that he identifies as, and believes we agree are, morally insignificant.[45]

G. Sensitive Reconciliationism

I have argued that Unger's arguments fail to support his radical conclusions, but of course he believes that he succeeds. So, in addition to presenting substantive normative claims and a theory about how to develop a normative theory, Unger tries to develop what he calls "context-sensitive semantics" in order to make it possible for him to live with the enlightened but speak with the vulgar. That is, he tries to explain how someone who accepts his normative claim that it is wrong not to send a lot of money to Oxfam (the Envelope Case) can still agree with the common folk that not sending the money is not morally so bad. He also tries to explain how someone can believe that it is permissible to steal in order to save distant people from mortal loss and yet still agree with the common folk who morally condemn such theft.

Unger's first explanation relies on distinguishing two contexts. The first context is one in which one's judgment about the correctness of someone's act flows from one's primary normative values (e.g., reduce suffering). The second context is one in which one's judgment about the correctness of someone's act flows from one's secondary values. These values tell us that it is important to know, and be motivated to carry out, the acts that are correct according to one's primary values. If it is hard for someone to know how she should act or to be motivated to act as she should, we may, from the point of view of secondary values, think that she is acting morally well, even if she does not do the morally right act.

However, notice that it is an implication of Unger's context-sensitive semantics that when someone with Unger's normative views speaks with the "commoners," in saying that a person who does not send much money to Oxfam is not doing something morally very bad, he is not really agreeing with the commoners. This is because they are claiming that from the point of view of *primary normative values*, the person is doing okay morally if she does not give money in the Envelope Case, whereas in agreeing, the Ungerite is really just saying that the person is not to be blamed for not doing the right act. If the commoner asks Unger whether the person who does not give to Oxfam is doing something wrong, he is *not* asking whether it is hard for her to know the correct values or to be motivated by the correct values or whether she should be blamed. But that is the question Unger would be answering.

Unger notes that agreement between the Ungerite and the commoners in condemning stealing while the Ungerite believes that stealing is right cannot be explained by Unger's first (supposed) explanation. This is because the thief who acts on Unger's theory, and whom the commoners condemn, is not someone who can be condemned on the basis of secondary values, that is, he cannot be condemned because he does not know a moral truth that it is easy to know or is not motivated to act when it is easy to be motivated by moral truth. Rather, the thief is someone who is imagined to know what Unger believes are true primary values and who *is* motivated to act on them. The commoners just think that his values do not truly justify his conduct.

Unger's suggestion for addressing this second problem is to distinguish a context in which our judgment is based on primary normative values about which act is morally right from a context in which our judgment is based on social norms. However, on this account, Unger is not really agreeing with the commoners, for they do not only claim that stealing is wrong according to social norms (as the Ungerite does), nor do they ask Unger whether stealing is wrong according to the social norms. They are claiming that stealing is wrong according to the true moral values. They are thinking about moral truth, but Unger is thinking about sociological truth when he says that the thief acts wrongly.

What shall we say in a case in which it is easy for someone both to know and to be motivated to do what Unger thinks is correct according to primary values, yet the person rebels and does what Unger thinks is wrong but what the commoners think is right, all according to primary values? For example, suppose that someone grows up in a home of act utilitarians who educate him in accord with act utilitarianism. Nevertheless, the person rebels and represses his tendency to give much of his money away (Rebellious Utilitarian Case). We think that he is doing something permissible, but according to Unger's theory, he does the wrong act, though it was easy for him to do the right act. From the point of view of secondary values, as well as from the point of view of primary values, he seems to be doing very badly on Unger's view. The rebellious utilitarian is unlike the thief who steals for Oxfam and does *well* on both primary and secondary values according to Unger, yet is condemned according to the social norms. From the commoners' point of view, the rebellious utilitarian is acceptable on primary values and does *very well* from the point of view of secondary values, because against all odds, he has found out the truth (as commoners believe it to be). This is a case in which Unger can assent to the common judgment that the rebellious utilitarian's behavior is permissible only by using the social-norm standard, that is, the rebellious utilitarian is doing what is all right according to social norms. But Unger cannot make what he will consider a true moral judgment about the rebellious utilitarian from the point of view of either Unger's primary values or his secondary values and still agree with the commoners.

Furthermore, the introduction of two different standards—secondary values and social norms—for reconciling Unger's theory with common judgment makes for a problem that Unger does not notice. If his reconciliation semantics is correct, he should also be able to agree when the commoners say, "Stealing money to send to Oxfam is *worse* than not giving your own money in the Envelope Case," which is an implication of their views that "stealing to give to Oxfam is wrong," and "not giving money in the Envelope Case is not so bad." But how is Unger to understand that sentence so that he can agree with it? He himself warns us about using two standards (or referring to two standard-determined contexts) simultaneously.[46]

Unger uses two different standards to understand each of the component claims that lie behind the sentence (i.e., he uses the secondary-values standard to understand that not sending money to Oxfam is not so bad and the social-norms standard to understand that stealing is wrong). Will he use both standards in agreeing with the comparative claim? But then is he committed to the claim that it is worse to violate society's norms (using the social-norms standard for the first part of the comparative) than to fail to know or be motivated by the truth when it is hard to do so (using the secondary-values standard for the second part of the comparative)? In excusing someone from doing the wrong act because it is hard to know or be motivated by the truth, Unger gives the impression that he should judge harshly someone who knows the truth and is motivated to act on it, yet instead chooses to abide by society's norm. Why, then, should he condemn so strongly someone who does *not* abide by society's norm and acts on the truth (as Unger sees it)?

There *is* a single standard that Unger could use to translate both components that lie behind the comparative sentence and the comparative judgment of the sentence: the standard of social norms. He could agree with the comparative in the sense that he agrees that society's norms condemn the stealing more than they condemn not giving money in the Envelope Case. But then, when he "agreed" with the commoners, he would never be making a genuine moral judgment—not even one from the point of view of secondary rather than primary values; he would just be engaging in sociological reflection.

The commoners may also make another comparative judgment: They may say that the rebellious utilitarian who does not send his money to Oxfam is in some respects morally superior to the ordinary person in the Envelope Case who does not send his money. He is superior from the point of view of secondary values, for he had to work hard to see the truth that he is permitted to act in this way. By what standard can Unger agree? From the point of view of social norms about primary values, the two agents are equally good. From the point of view of secondary values, as Unger would see it, the rebellious utilitarian is worse.[47] So there seem to be some cases where Unger cannot hold his moral views, and his two translation standards, and also agree with what the commoners say. I conclude that Unger's context-sensitive semantics has significant problems.

There may, it might be suggested, be a different sort of reconciliation possible between Unger's normative views and ordinary nonconsequentialist moral views. In conclusion, let me sketch this possibility and its implication. In ordinary morality, consent by the person to be harmed (when he is competent to give consent) can often justify acts that would otherwise be impermissible. Unger endorses a theory which says one ought to harm people to minimize mortal losses (a limited version of negative utilitarianism). Can such endorsement be taken to be a form of consent to *his* (Unger's) being harmed to minimize mortal losses? At the very least, it implies that he (and others who accept his theory) would not, if they were rational (consistent), raise a moral objection to being harmed to minimize mortal losses. If someone would not, insofar as he is rational, raise a moral objection to our harming him, could ordinary morality permit harming him in ways that would ordinarily be impermissible? For, in many cases, even if people would object to our harming them on grounds of personal preference, if they cannot raise a moral objection to this, we may still harm them.

Of course, Unger may object that others whom his theory says are also eligible to be harmed will not be eligible to be harmed according to ordinary morality, as they do not accept his theory or actually consent to being treated as his theory recommends. This implies that, according to his theory, he and others who believe as he does are unfairly burdened relative to other people, if we treat only them according to his theory. But his own theory, presumably, yields the conclusion that fairness should be sacrificed if it stands in the way of redressing mortal losses. Hence, those who endorse his theory could not rationally raise a moral objection based on unfairness to being harmed to prevent mortal losses to others.

The problem with this attempt at a partial reconciliation between Unger's theory (and also between other theories, such as act utilitarianism) and ordinary morality is that the inability of a rational Ungerite to raise a moral objection does not mean there is no moral objection to be raised. From the point of view of ordinary morality, the absence of consent, even due to a personal preference inconsistent with an incorrect moral theory one holds, will leave in place the moral objection to a harmful act that ordinary morality raises. If Unger's theory is wrong, reconciliation is possible only if the theory's endorsement by its supporters might appropriately be taken as a proxy for their consent to some of the acts it prescribes when done to them. Only then would ordinary morality accept that those who endorse the view that people may be killed in order to reduce mortal losses are likely candidates to be permissibly be killed to reduce mortal losses.[48]

NOTES

This chapter includes parts of "Rescue and Harm: A Discussion of Peter Unger's *Living High and Letting Die, Legal Theory* (March 1999)," my review of Unger's book in *Philosophical Review* (April 1999), and "Grouping and the Imposition of Loss," *Utilitas* (1998). For comments on earlier versions of this chapter, I am grateful to members of the Philamore discussion group. An article on which this chapter is based was dedicated to Mala Kamm, whose persistence, strength, and values inspired it.

    1. Peter Unger, *Living High and Letting Die* (New York: Oxford University Press, 1996).

    2. Unger contrasts his position on intuitions with what he calls "negativism." He describes the latter as the complete denial that intuitions about cases reveal any moral truth. See ibid. p. 13n. Presumably, he says this because positive distortion can lead to intuitions that reveal moral truth. In the same paragraph, however, he also describes negativism not as a methodological stance dismissing intuitions, but as the attempt to bring about consistency between seemingly conflicting intuitions about aiding by denying the duty to aid quite generally, rather than extending the duty to aid quite generally. This makes negativism a substantive position about aiding: We need not suffer any loss to reduce mortal loss. Such substantive negativism also liberates us from what, according to its claim, is negative distorted (i.e., non-value-tracking) intuitions about cases, only it implies that the negative distorted intuitions are the ones that tell us *to aid*. These are the very ones that Unger thinks salience distorts *positively* (i.e., in a value tracking way).

    3. As suggested by Gopal Sreenivasan.

    4. Consequentialists have often accused nonconsequentialists of being inconsistent. For example, they ask, why do nonconsequentialists say that we may redirect a trolley to save five people from being killed by it when we foresee that this action will kill one, if we may not save five people from the trolley by pushing someone in front of it? As we shall see, Unger repeats this criticism, but he also goes beyond it. He tries to show that sometimes we would say that it is permissible to push someone in front of a trolley to save five and sometimes we would say that it is impermissible to do this, and this (he claims) is a clear inconsistency.

    5. Insofar as he tries to change our responses to acts on the basis of altering what he thinks are morally irrelevant features of the context, his technique is like the framing technique used by cognitive psychologists Daniel Kahneman and Amos Tversky. See chapter 14 for a discussion of Kahneman and Tversky.

    6. Unger, *Living High and Letting Die*, p. 37, n. 7.

    7. For more on the issues discussed in this brief summary, see chapters 11 and 12.

8. I discussed this in chapter 1, and I discuss it in connection with whom to aid in chapter 12.

9. See Unger, *Living High and Letting Die*, chap. 5.

10. Unger here follows, I believe, my focus on this flip-side aspect of the Trolley Case, as presented first in my "Harming Some to Save Others," *Philosophical Studies* 57 (November 1989): 227–60, and then in my *Morality, Mortality*, vol. 2. I continue to focus on it in chapter 5 in this volume.

11. Unger, *Living High and Letting Die*, pp. 101–8.

12. Ibid., p. 100.

13. The method of aptly combining cases, which Unger also describes, is just a way, I believe, of creating cases with several options. See Unger, *Living High and Letting Die*, pp. 106–14.

14. Unger, *Living High and Letting Die*, p. 90.

15. It is possible that this intuition can (and should) change when we conceive of the second trolley as a device meant to be used to stop other trolleys on which the people have inappropriately been placed. A person on skates, however, is not someone using a device meant to be sent in to stop trolleys, and so there would be no shift in the intuitive judgment that we may not send that person in front of the trolley.

16. However, I have also said in my response to Unger's (4) that there is, in general, no inconsistency in thinking that an act of a certain type is impermissible in one context and that an act of the same type is permissible in another context. For example, I believe that pushing a person in front of the trolley is impermissible even if it would merely paralyze him in a two-options case. But suppose that it is permissible for me to redirect a trolley from five people toward one, thereby killing a person on the other track. Suppose that I am about to do this, when I find out that if I push that one person on the track in front of the trolley instead, it will only paralyze him. Since it is better *for him* if I push him in front of the trolley than if I redirect the trolley toward him, it is permissible in this context to do what it would not have been permissible to do in another context, where I had no option of redirecting a trolley that would kill him. This is an example of the Principle of Secondary Permissibility (PSP) that I discussed in chapters 1 and 5. Unlike what is true in the Switches and Skates Case, here there is a *morally important* difference between doing the act in one context rather than in another because, only in one context will someone suffer less harm than he would otherwise have suffered.

17. This is a form of argument that Unger is famous for using in his early skeptical work in epistemology.

18. This is one of John Rawls's objections. See Rawls, *A Theory of Justice* (Cambridge, MA: Harvard University Press, 1971), pp. 29ff.

19. In chapters 4 and 5, I considered a possible exception to this. In the Tree Trolley cases, it seems that the determination of who is uninvolved, in the sense of *physically* nonsusceptible to a threat, or involved, in the sense of *physically* susceptible to a threat, precedes and determines permissibility.

20. Having tried to do this in chapter 5.

21. I owe this case to Michael Otsuka.

22. I should point out that my intuitions do not agree with Unger's in some of the cases he uses to support his theory about protophysical distinctions. For example, he says that if there is a resting bomb that will explode and kill five people, we intuitively think that it is *not* permissible to *start* it rolling away from them when it will foreseeably kill an innocent bystander. By contrast, he says, we think that it is permissible to redirect a bomb that is already in motion away from five it will kill, though we foresee that it will kill an innocent bystander. But I think that it *is* permissible to start the first bomb moving; it is a threat to the five and may be moved away though it harms the one. It is possible, however, that if a threat (e.g., germs) were already

incorporated *into* a person, then ejecting it from him when this results in its being directed toward others is wrong. For example, should a doctor tell five patients to cough, when he knows this will cure them but fatally infect a bystander? This is a Threat Incorporated type of case that I briefly discussed in chapter 5.

23. See Unger, *Living High and Letting Die*, p. 98.

24. Ibid.

25. As argued in chapter 5., mere means that have a causal relation to the greater good should not directly cause the lesser evil*.

26. Lazy Susan cases I—IV were discussed in chapters 1 and 5.

27. In his review of Unger's book, David Lewis accepted that varying grouping and protophysics accounts for our intuitions, about what seems to be morally correct. However, contrary to Unger, he denied that these factors are not really morally relevant. See David Lewis, *Eureka Street* 6 (1996). I have denied that these factors account for our intuitions and also denied that they are really morally relevant.

28. For more on this, see chapters 1 and 8 in this volume.

29. See Unger, *Living High and Letting Die*, pp. 121–23.

30. Unger notes that intuitively we might *not* redirect when on balance we only maximize utility by a smaller amount than a foot. I discussed the question of what is an "irrelevant utility" in such cases (and in others as well) in detail first in F. M. Kamm, "The Choice between People, 'Common Sense' Morality, and Doctors," *Bioethics* 1 (1987): 255–71; and then in F. M. Kamm, *Morality, Mortality*, vol. 1 (New York: Oxford University Press, 1993), chaps. 5–10. See also chapters 1 and 2 in this volume.

31. Suppose one had a case with several options but with different agents in control of each option. For example, A could redirect the trolley toward the three; B could send in the trolley with two in it; C could send in the man on skates. C knows that if he does not send in the man on skates, A will turn the trolley toward the three, unless B sends in the trolley with two. Will those who think (mistakenly, I would say) that a single agent with several options may send in the man on skates, also think that C may do so in order to prevent A and B doing worse? I doubt it, for in this case no agent is redirecting himself to do less harm.

32. This is consistent with the Principle of Secondary Permissibility (PSP), as I argued in chapter 5. The PSP allows that sometimes it is permissible to do something to someone in the second instance that it is not permissible to do in the first instance to the very same person. But Unger is concerned with harming other people, not the same person who would otherwise have been harmed.

33. Unger, *Living High and Letting Die*, pp. 126–28.

34. Hence the Lesser-Loss-Card Case is not like the following two versions of the Trolley Case: (1) I press a button that causes the trolley headed toward five people to be diverted onto a track with no one on it. Pressing the button also sends out a death ray that kills a bystander. (2) I press a button that sends out an electric current that redirects the trolley headed toward five people to a track with no one on it. The electric current also moves down another track and electrocutes the person on the track. In these cases (discussed in chapter 5), pressing the button itself causes two different things and they are cases in which a mere means to greater good causes lesser evil*.

35. Unger, *Living High and Letting Die*, pp. 139–40.

36. If I see my refusal as a way of stopping a plan that Strangemind already had to give aid to the stranger—and I see this as a form of making the stranger worse off than he would have been without my refusal—would I, intuitively, think that I should allow Strangemind to take my money? I do not think so. Someone's making his continuing aid contingent on my aid cannot, by itself, obligate me. If Strangemind puts the offer as a case in which he will follow my lead (i.e., if I

am willing to lose money, he will lose money too), I also do not think that our intuitions suggest a stronger obligation to aid than we think exists in the Envelope Case. However, it is true that I can do more good when I help in these other cases, than when I aid in the Envelope Case. This is because I have the power to make someone else also aid, and so more is at stake in my refusal. This can create psychological pressure to help. (This mechanism is at work in a small way when one is told that one's employer will match one's charitable donations.)

37. In addition, our helping has a causal relation to providing someone else with a benefit in the Envelope Case; the benefit is not a noncausal flip side of our involvement. However, I doubt that the latter difference has any moral significance, for, I argue, I have no greater obligation to keep Strangemind busy (where the benefit is a noncausal flip side of his involvement with me) than to send money in the envelope.

38. For more discussion of this issue, see chapters 11 and 12.

39. I discuss this issue further in "Harming Some to Save Others from the Nazis" in its revised (unpublished) version. The published version is in *Moral Philosophy and the Holocaust* ed. E. Garrard and G. Scarre, pp. 155–168 (Hants, UK: Ashgate, 2003).

40. In this connection, it is interesting for me to remember an early discussion in which Unger argued for the position that one might harm others to benefit one's family. At that time, his ground for this claim was that one had no duties to anyone but one's family. His more recent views try to combine the claim that we have very strenuous duties to others trumped only by duties to one's family.

41. He does not expect people to do what they are morally required to, but this does not show that they do not have the duty.

42. Unger, *Living High and Letting Die*, p. 155.

43. Suppose that I realize that if I were the one to be killed, I would decide not to redirect *at all*, but if someone else were the one to be killed, I would decide to redirect. Have I then violated the PEI because I respond differently to a situation as a function of whether I am in it or not? It seems so. But then I might as well violate the PEI *and* also reduce the total number harmed by turning only from six toward three, and not toward myself.

44. We noted this in chapter 5. We also noted, possibly, that the one may not use *means* that will stop the trolley that is redirected toward him, if as a side effect it harms the original six, unless this is a substitute for his capacity to permissibly turn back the trolley that would have done the same or more damage to the six. (This makes it secondarily permissible.) Nor may he turn the trolley away in a direction where it harms six people who were *not* originally threatened by the trolley. He would also not be permitted to redirect a trolley that was originally coming at him, foreseeing that it will then kill six people. Furthermore, suppose that Strangemind had redirected a threat from killing people in Africa to imposing a loss on someone's bank account—a property damage. I do not believe that this person is permitted to redirect back Strangemind to killing people in Africa. Property loss versus mortal loss makes a difference here. This is consistent with the Bankcard Case.

45. In discussing Unger's substantive and methodological views, I have tried to examine the details of his cases and arguments. This approach differs from, and yields somewhat different results from, discussions by others. For example, in her review of *Living High and Letting Die*, Martha Nussbaum ("Philanthropic Twaddle," *London Review of Books*, September 4, 1997) concedes that Unger shows that there are irrationalities in our ordinary thoughts about aiding. (Philip Kitcher seems to agree. See his "Global Health and the Scientific Research Agenda," *Philosophy & Public Affairs* [32] Winter 2004, pp. 36–65.) I have argued that Unger does not show this. In his review of *Living High and Letting Die*, Colin McGinn ("Saint Elsewhere," *New Republic*, October 14, 1996) presents Unger as drawing his conclusion about a strong duty to aid distant people from a general commitment to producing the best state of affairs. But, in

fact, Unger attempts to derive his conclusions about aiding independent of that particular general commitment.

46. Unger, *Living High and Letting Die*, p. 166.

47. Possibly Unger could commend someone for taking the difficult step of thinking for himself, even if he gets the wrong answer when he could easily have had the right answer.

48. This connects with Kant's view that a murderer wills his own death, for example, by capital punishment. For if murder is wrong, how can the fact that a murderer wills the principle that permits it, make it right to treat him according to an incorrect principle? But if consent of the victim can make an act that would otherwise be impermissible, permissible, and if willing a principle is a form of consent to acts implied by it, the consent can justify what the incorrect principle cannot justify. In Kant's case, however, willing implies acting on rather than merely endorsing.

SECTION II

Rights

7

MORAL STATUS

In one sense, moral status can be defined as what it is morally permissible or impermissible to do to some entity. In this sense, rocks may have the moral status of entities to which, just considering them, it is morally permissible to do anything. This is what we can call the "broad sense" of moral status. An important point in talking about status in the broad sense is to distinguish it from what actually happens to an entity. For example, if one's moral status makes it impermissible for someone to kill you, you do not lose that moral status merely because you are impermissibly killed. One way to reduce the number of morally bad things that happen in the world is merely to populate it with entities whose status is such that it is permissible to do anything whatsoever to them. Yet most would not think that such a world—for example, one with only rocks in it—would be a morally ideal world, better than one in which there are entities such that some ways of treating them would be morally impermissible, even if it happens that they are sometimes actually treated impermissibly. Presumably, this is because the more important an entity is, the more it matters how one treats it, and it is better to have a world populated by more important entities.[1]

There is a different sense of moral status where the contrast is not between what it is permissible to do to an entity and what happens to an entity. It might be suggested that the contrast is between entities that in some important sense "count" morally in their own right, and so are said to have moral status, and other entities that do not count morally in their own right. "Counting morally in their own right" is a narrower sense of moral status. This implies that in the broad sense of moral status described above, some entities have no narrower moral status. For example, ordinary rocks do not count morally in their own right. But there are also different ways to count morally and, perhaps, different degrees to which one may count in any given way.

When we say that something counts morally in its own right, we are often said to be thinking of its intrinsic worth or value rather than its instrumental value. If it were morally right to treat animals well only because this would promote kindness between persons, animals would count morally only instrumentally. That is, they should be treated well not because they count in their own right, but only because of the effects on others of treating them well. But Christine Korsgaard has argued that the true contrast to mere instrumental value is having value as an end, not having intrinsic value.[2] For example, if an animal counts morally in its own right, there is no further end that need be served by our treating the animal well in order for us to have a reason to treat it well. If something is an end (in this limited sense), it need not mean that it has value that can never be trumped nor that it should never be treated as a mere means.[3] At minimum, it means only that its condition can provide a reason (even if an overrideable one) for attitudes or actions independent of other considerations.

Korsgaard argues that some things may be ends in virtue of their intrinsic properties that give them their intrinsic value, but others may be ends in virtue of their extrinsic properties. The intrinsic properties are all of an entity's nonrelational properties.[4] Its extrinsic properties are properties that it has in virtue of its standing in relation to other things. For example, Ronald Dworkin claims to have a theory of the intrinsic value of even nonsentient, nonconscious life, such as is found in an early embryo. But he also says that this value comes from the history of the embryo, in particular the investment that nature or God has made in it. This is not a theory of the intrinsic value of a life but of its extrinsic value since it derives the value of the embryo from its particular history and its relating to God or nature rather than from properties it has independent of history and relations.[5] An entity's ability to produce an effect (i.e., be an instrument) is a relational property holding between it and the effect. It is possible, given what Korsgaard has said, that something could be worth treating as an end because it is capable of causing an effect, even if it never does. Hence, I take it that the narrower sense of moral status involves, at least, something having value as an end rather than as an instrument whether because of its intrinsic or extrinsic properties.

A work of art or a tree may count in its own right in the sense that it gives us reason to constrain our behavior toward it (for example, not destroy it) just because that would preserve this entity. That is, independent of valuing and seeking the pleasure or enlightenment it can cause in people, a thing of aesthetic value gives us (I think) reason not to destroy it. In that sense, it counts morally. But this is still to be distinguished from constraining ourselves *for the sake of* the work of art or the tree. I do not act for its sake when I save a work of art, because I do not think of its good and how continuing existence would be good for it when I save it. (Nor do I think of its exercising its capacities or performing its duties. Acting for the sake of these might also involve acting for an entity's sake, though it need not involve seeking what is good for it.) Rather, I think of the good *of* the work of art, its worth as an art object, when I save it for no other reason than that it will continue to exist.

By contrast, when I save a bird, I can do it for its sake, because it will get something out of continuing to exist, and it could be a harm to it not to continue. It seems that something must already have or have had the capacity for sentience or consciousness in order for it to be harmed by not continuing on in existence.[6] This is because an entity having such characteristics seems to be necessary for it to be a beneficiary or victim. It must be able to get something out of its continuing existence, and capacity for sentience or consciousness seems to be necessary for this. (I do not think that either capacity is a necessary condition for us to be able to act for the sake of the entity, since each without the other is sufficient.) Having the capacity is not the same as actually being, for example, sentient. It is also not the same as merely having the potential to be sentient, where the latter implies that an entity has the potential to have the capacity that then gets exercised.

So, we see that within the class of entities that count in their own right, there are those entities that *in their own right and for their own sake* could give us reason to act. I think that it is this that people have in mind when they ordinarily attribute moral status to an entity. So, henceforth, I shall distinguish between an entity's counting morally in its own right and its having moral status. I shall say that *an entity has moral status when, in its own right and for its own sake, it can give us reason to do things such as not destroy it or help it.*

On this account, a nonsentient, nonconscious embryo lacks moral status but could count morally in itself (e.g., give us reason in its own right not to destroy it) because of its intrinsic and extrinsic properties, such as what its potential is. This is different from its merely having instrumental value because it will in fact give rise to a person who has moral status. For even if the embryo is not instrumental to there being a person, because it is deprived of an environment in which to develop, its having the potential could still give it greater value than an embryo that lacks the potential, I think. (Similarly, a Chippendale dining table may have value in itself and more value as a work of decorative art if it can also turn into a magnificent writing desk, though it will not.) Notice that an embryo can have greater value in its own right if it has the potential to become an extraordinary person (e.g., Beethoven) rather than an ordinary person, even if these persons would, were they to exist, have the same moral status, and even if the embryo will not, in fact, generate anyone. (The instrumental value of an embryo will also be greater if it will generate Beethoven rather than an ordinary person, even if these two persons' moral status does not differ.)

If an embryo can matter in its own right, this does not mean that its continued existence is good for it, or that it is harmed by not continuing on, or that we can act for its sake in saving its life. Similarly, an ordinary table might, by magic, be turned into a table that has the capacity to develop into a person and it may be good to be a person, but can a table be the sort of thing that is harmed by not getting the good of the fulfillment of this capacity? It does not seem so.[7] The person who would come from the embryo also cannot be harmed by never coming to exist. But we can act for the sake of a person who will develop from the embryo by doing things to the embryo not for its sake, but for the sake of the person who will exist. (I shall return to this issue below.) The fact that an embryo may have intrinsic value in virtue of its extrinsic properties could account for why it might be wrong to use it for frivolous purposes. If so, the ground for objecting to such acts would be like the ground for objecting to making lampshades of the flesh of deceased human persons (who had died of natural causes). The flesh has no moral status, but it has an extrinsic relation to once-living human persons who had moral status, and so it may give us reason in its own right not to use it in certain ways. (The embryo's particular intrinsic and extrinsic properties, of course, differ from those of the dead flesh.)

Those things for whose sake we can act when we save their lives may or may not give us as much reason to save them as entities whose existence cannot be extended for their own sake. For example, if we had to choose whether to destroy the Grand Canyon or a bird (holding constant the number of people who would get pleasure or be enlightened by each), it could be morally wrong to choose to destroy the Grand Canyon. This illustrates how something can count morally because it can get something out of life, and so have moral status, without it giving us more reason to act in its favor than other things whose going on in existence, in their own right, is more significant. Sometimes, the remarkableness of something or its uniqueness calls for more protection than does something else's having moral status.

We can have duties to behave in certain ways toward entities that count in their own right and, as a subset, to entities that have moral status. But this still does not imply that all of these are entities *to which we owe* it to behave in certain ways. There is a difference between one's having a duty to do something and having a duty *to* a specific entity to do it. The latter is known as a "directed duty," and typically it has a correlative, that is, a right or claim had by the entity to which the duty is owed against the person who owes it.[8] Correspondingly, there is a difference between doing the wrong thing (for example, in not fulfilling a *non*directed duty, such as a duty to promote the good) and *wronging* some entity in failing to perform the duty owed to her. The entity to whom a duty is owed is not necessarily the entity who is benefited or affected by the object of the duty. For example, if you owe it to me to take care of my mother, I am the rightholder, not my mother, even though the object of the duty is to benefit her. You wrong me, not my mother, if you fail to help her. Arguably, the ideas of respect for persons and the dignity of the person are connected to the idea that one *owes it to a* person to behave in certain ways, and also that what the person wills and that to which she has claims, rather than what is good for her, can give us a duty to her. This is in contrast to it being simply wrong to treat someone in certain ways because, for example, one owes it to God not to or because it would not maximize utility to do so, and one has a general duty as a rational being—but not owed to anyone—to maximize utility. So just as only some entities that count in their own right are entities which have moral status (as I defined it), so it may be that only some entities that have moral status are owed things and have rights against us.

It is tempting to think that these entities have a *higher* moral status than other entities which also have moral status (as I defined it). At the very least, there are reasons to do things with regard to them that do not apply to other entities, for example, we owe it to them. (The distinction is analogous to the one that applies in cases where A is in need of assistance, but B is not only in equal need but has been promised assistance while A has not been.)

The possibility of wronging some entities opens up the further possibility that moral status in the broad sense with which we began may not be completely defined by how it is permissible to treat an entity. This would be so, if it were sometimes permissible to do something to an entity and yet one still wronged it in the course of acting permissibly. Those entities which would be wronged in the course of a permissible act would have a different moral status from those which, while capable of being wronged in other situations, would not be wronged in the course of the same permissible act. It is tempting to think that those we could wrong in the course of a permissible act would also have a higher moral status than those not so wronged. Hence, there would be yet another indication of moral status expressed by when one would be wronged.

For example, as described in chapter 5, those nonconsequentialists who think that constraints on harming persons have thresholds beyond which they may be overridden are called "threshold deontologists." A way of understanding their views is as follows: Suppose a constraint expressed respect for persons and revealed something about their high moral status. We wrong the person if we violate the constraint, as we owe it to him not to do it. If it is wrong (i.e., impermissible) to do the act that wrongs the person, even as the costs of not doing so go up, then the wrong we would do to him must be very serious. The fact that it would be impermissible to treat him in the prohibited way, as the cost of not doing so goes up, is a further mark of his high status.

Suppose the costs go above a threshold and it becomes permissible, that is, *not wrong*, to override the prohibition. Still, we could be wronging him in doing the overall right act. What would be the evidence for this? That we had to compensate him or apologize to him? But these acts might be required even if we overrode a constraint *without* wronging someone in doing so. For example, when we infringe a right, it is said that we *permissibly* override it (by contrast to violating it, which involves impermissibly overriding it). An example of this might be: I take someone's car without his permission to rush someone to the hospital in a grave emergency. In this case, we may still owe an apology or even compensation to the owner. (That there is this negative residue to be made up might, of course, also be an indication of someone's moral status.) Yet, perhaps, we have not wronged the owner in permissibly overriding his right. A mark of this might be that it would be morally wrong of him to resist our taking his car simply on the grounds of his property right.[9]

By contrast, recall the Trolley Case: A runaway trolley is headed toward killing five people. We can redirect it onto another track, but then someone immovably seated there will be hit and killed by the trolley. It is commonly thought to be permissible to do this.[10] However, I argued in chapter 5, it would not be impermissible for the one person toward whom the trolley is redirected to resist our doing this. For example, if he could press a button and send the trolley away, back where it came from, even if we or the five originally threatened would be killed,

I think this would be permissible. This is true even though he may not, in general, do what leads to harm others to save himself. The permissibility of someone's resisting our permissible act is, I think, evidence for the fact that we still wrong him in acting permissibly and in (permissibly) infringing his right.[11]

The fact that someone could still be wronged, even though we act permissibly, and the fact that a great cost would be needed to make it not wrong to do what wrongs him are both marks of his high moral status. This status, however, no longer gives rise to the impermissibility of treating him in certain ways. That too is a mark of his status, as it would be even higher if an even greater cost (or any cost) would have to be sustained rather than override the prohibition.

To what sorts of entities is it possible to owe things or behaviors? Thomas Scanlon has argued that only entities capable of judgment-sensitive attitudes are entities to whom we can owe certain treatment. (Scanlon does not speak of rights as the correlatives of directed duties, but I believe the addition of rights talk in his system would be appropriate.) Entities capable of judgment-sensitive attitudes form attitudes or decide on actions on the basis of evaluating certain factors as reasons, that is, as, normatively speaking, considerations in favor of an attitude or action. For example, they do not just respond to aspects of their environment (as a cat would); they see these aspects as considerations in favor of or against action. Scanlon's view seems to be that if some entity can evaluate our conduct toward her so that she can see a reason for us to act or not act in that way, then we may potentially owe it to her to act or not act in that way. He also seems to think that a creature capable of judgment-sensitive attitudes governs herself in the light of reasons, and so it is only to such self-governing creatures that we can owe things. (It is possible, however, to imagine that the capacity for judgment-sensitive attitudes does not go so far as to involve self-governance in the light of reasons. For example, a creature might take certain factors in the environment as true reasons to pursue food but not be self-conscious and so not self-governing. I am not sure what Scanlon would say about owing things to a creature if these two conditions were pulled apart.)

Scanlon thinks that animals count morally in their own right and give us reasons to act for their sake. Hence, our conduct toward them can be right or wrong, independent of further considerations, but it cannot be owed to them, and they cannot be wronged when we behave wrongly. This is because (he assumes) they are not capable of judgment-sensitive attitudes. Furthermore, he thinks that while we have a reason to help an animal in need, we can have the same reason to help a rational being in need plus an additional reason absent in the case of the animal, that is, we can owe it to the rational being to help him. On this account (as noted above) the "greater" moral importance or value of rational beings (persons) could get fleshed out (in part) as the additional factor present in our relations with them, that is, we owe things to them or, as I would also say, they have rights against us. But, in addition, the fact that they have reasons for willing one thing rather than another could imply that what we owe them relates to what they will rather than to what is merely good for them. This gives them greater authority over what is owed to them.

If only rational beings can, strictly, be the subjects of directed duties or have rights, what shall we say of infants or the severely retarded? Scanlon's view seems to be that in virtue of their relation to rational beings—that is, they are early or failed members of a type whose norm it is to be rational—they too have some rights.[12] Here their extrinsic properties are giving them these rights. Why does this not apply to embryos, too, we might ask? Scanlon does not say. Perhaps it is because, at least when what is at issue is being destroyed or being kept alive, an entity must be at the stage where it would either have the capacity to get something out of going on living or have the capacity to set itself to achieve a goal by going on. Then we could act for its sake in saving it. Infants and the severely retarded can get something out of going on, as well as having rights in virtue of merely extrinsic properties. As I argued above, even if an embryo would lose out on what would turn out to be a good life, given what it is now, it is hard to see how it is harmed by this loss or why it is morally important whether it loses further life.[13]

This leaves it open that we should still react differently to entities at given stages of development depending on such extrinsic properties as whether they could, or will in fact, develop into entities for whose sake we could act or to whom we might owe certain things. If the entities could, but will not in fact develop into such other entities, they may still be more remarkable entities than those entities that could not. If they will in fact develop into such other entities, then to some degree they should be treated so that the latter do not suffer and do not fail to get what they are owed.

I say to "some degree" only. Some hold that if we have duties pertaining to an embryo, it is because of the person to whom it will give rise. They think it follows from this that duties that exist while there is only an embryo should be as strong, and of the same type, as duties we have to the person once he has developed, if we are certain that the embryo will give rise to a person. I would argue that this is not true, with respect both to doing what causes a future person to be worse off than he might have been and with respect to helping a future person to avoid being worse off.

Here is an example in which, I believe, it is permissible to affect a future person by doing something to the embryo from which he develops, though it is not permissible to affect the person in the same way by doing something to the person once he exists. Suppose that a woman has given a fetus genes that will result in a future person with an IQ of 160. She decides this IQ is too high, not for the good of the person who has the high IQ, but for the good of the family. As a result, she takes a drug during early pregnancy in order to reduce the future person's IQ to 140. I call this the 160 IQ Case. It is a case of causing a person to be worse off than he would otherwise have been. I believe that this is permissible (for reasons to be given below). But it would not be permissible, I believe, for the woman to give her child, once it exists, a pill that reduces his IQ from 160 to 140. What is the difference between affecting the future person by affecting the embryo and directly affecting the person himself? An embryo, not yet being a person, is not the sort of being who has a claim over, or is entitled (i.e., has a right, is owed) to keep a characteristic it has, such as a makeup that will generate a 160 IQ. In addition, the person who will develop from the fetus will not fall below an acceptable level of life if he has only a 140 IQ, so he is not owed a 160 IQ. (A 140 IQ is already far above the minimal standard owed by parents to the people they create.) These two facts are crucial to the permissibility of taking back IQ points from the embryo, IQ points that the parent gave it. If the embryo is not yet a person—and even though it will give rise to one—taking away characteristics it has (which will have an impact on the person to be) is no different from not giving him those character-istics to begin with. And presumably, one would have a right not to give a future person that one created genes sufficient for a 160 IQ. But since a child is already a person (I assume), he is entitled to keep the beneficial characteristic he has, even if doing so raises the child far beyond the standard he is owed. Hence, I believe that it is impermissible to give the pill to the child, even if doing so would not cause his IQ to fall below the minimum owed to one's child.

By contrast, suppose that we owe a good chance of an IQ of at least 100 to people we create. In this case, doing something in pregnancy to an embryo that results in a person having an IQ below 100 may well be as impermissible as doing to the later child something that lowers its IQ to below 100.[14]

Once a creature is of the sort that can have rights and be owed things, not all of its rights relate to what bears on its interests (i.e., some aspect of its well-being). I am interested in pursuing this point because I hope that it helps show that some rights are directly concerned with expressing the fact that one has the moral status of a rightholder rather than with the interests of the rightholder. I hope that it will also bring us back to the first sense in which we can be concerned with moral status, namely, as it contrasts with what actually happens to entities and whether they are actually treated as they should be. (These are topics that will concern us in chapter 8.)

NOTES

This chapter is based on parts of my "Moral Status and Rights beyond Interests" (unpublished), which was presented at the Conference on Moral Status at Santa Clara University, April 2002, and on my "Moral Status and Personal Identity: Clones, Embryos, and Future generations," *Social Philosophy & Policy*, 22, 2, Summer 2005, pp. 283–307.

1. Seana Shiffrin seems to have a different view. She is concerned to avoid unconsented to harm to entities who are or will be capable of consent, because she thinks greater benefits to them cannot by themselves compensate for lesser harms to them. (Only avoiding greater harms can justify unconsented-to lesser harm.) Suppose we treat coming into existence to a very good human life like a benefit. Shiffrin thinks that even a good life has inescapable harms. Among these, she thinks, are the burdens of moral choice, pain, rights violations, and having to cope with death. Hence, she concludes, even an average parent, in creating a life overall well worth living, is involved in tortious conduct and may owe compensation to his child.

I disagree with Shiffrin's analysis of ordinary creation as tortious and calling for com-pensation. First, it seems odd to me to treat as problems or as being in a harmed state some of the very things that give value to human life, such as moral choice. It is possible that some of the things that give value and meaningfulness to human life are not best thought of as benefits to the person (namely, as improving his well-being). Hence, deciding whether creating a human person is right or wrong requires more than weighing what are goods and evils to the person created.

Second, I believe that Shiffrin's argument implies that we should reduce the benefits to, and the importance of, entities in order to avoid harming them. I believe her view implies that creating creatures incapable of moral choice, never in pain, and unaware of truths, such as the prospect of death, for example, extremely happy, long-lived rabbits who have no other problems, would be preferable to creating human persons as they are now. But I think this is the wrong conclusion. It would be wrong, and would have been wrong at the beginning of creation, to substitute such creatures for continuing humanity. Arguably, if it would be wrong to eliminate difficulty at the cost of either reducing the overriding benefits to the entity we create or reducing the importance of the entity we create, one should not be liable for compensation for certain unavoidable problems if one produces the benefits and values that outweigh those problems on balance. See S. Shiffrin, "Wrongful Life, Procreative Responsibility, and the Significance of Harm," *Legal Theory* 5, no. 2 (1999): 117–48. I consider her views further in my "Baselines and Compensation," *San Diego Law Review* 40 (2004): 1367–86.

2. See her "Two Distinctions in Goodness," *Philosophical Review* 2, no. 481 (April 1983): 169–95.

3. So this is not the stronger sense of end-in-itself mentioned in chapter 1.

4. Except, perhaps, relations between its parts.

5. See his *Life's Dominion: An Argument about Abortion, Euthanasia, and Individual Freedom* (New York: Knopf, 1993).

6. I say "have had" in order to deal with the following sort of case: Suppose someone with the capacity for consciousness goes into a coma and also loses the capacity for future consciousness. Suppose further that somehow we could bring back this capacity in such a way that the *same person* would be conscious in the future. It would then be for the sake of the person who originally had the capacity for consciousness that we would bring back the capacity and its exercise. By contrast, if an entity had always lacked the capacity for consciousness, there would be no one for whose sake we would bring about the capacity for consciousness.

7. Perhaps this fact is overdetermined. First, the table is not the sort of entity that can be benefited by continuing to exist. Second, it is not benefited by becoming something radically different from what it is now (for an entity is only benefited by future existence if *it* is what will exist). These two factors may also be true of embryos. But there could be entities of whom the first factor is not true, while the second factor is true. Some hold that an embryo can be harmed in not developing into a person, and it could get something out of continuing on though it lacks sentience and consciousness. But the harm to it has no moral significance because it is harm to an entity that lacks moral status. That is, its characteristics give us no reason, in its own right and for its own sake, to prevent harm to it. But suppose that an embryo will develop into a mildly retarded person. Will it be harmed in being prevented from developing into such a life that is worth living, in the way that a person would be harmed if he were killed rather than allowed to live on with mild retardation?

8. An exception may exist if there are duties one has to oneself, for one cannot have rights against oneself. In giving his theory of moral wrongness, Thomas Scanlon emphasizes what we owe to others. See his *What We Owe to Each Other* (Cambridge, MA: Harvard University Press, 1999). I have criticized Scanlon's use of his account of "owing to others" as the basis of an account of what it is for something to be wrong. I suggest that it may better be understood as what makes it possible to wrong someone. I also believe that his theory, therefore, could appropriately make use of the notion of a right. See my discussion of his book in chapter 16.

9. However, it could be that the wronging is not very great and this is why he should not resist given what is at stake.

10. We examined this view in chapter 5.

11. Similarly, if torture of an innocent person were ever justifiable, then this would not mean that the victim would not be within his rights to resist the torture. Permissible resistance is not always a mark of our wronging someone, however. For example, in a boxing match, it is permissible for me to try to knock out my opponent and it is permissible for him to try to stop me. But I would not wrong him if I knocked him out, because it is the authorized (and, let us assume, morally permitted) point of the activity for each of us to try to do this to the other and to try to resist its being done.

12. Notice that basing rights on this relation to a *type* is not the same as basing rights on a relation to particular individuals, such as parents who love the retarded child.

13. As noted above (n. 7), this could be both because it is not now the sort of being that can be harmed by non-existence and because what it would become in future life is so radically different from what it is now. It was also noted that others say that the embryo *is* harmed by this loss, but given what it is now, harm to it has no moral significance.

14. I first presented this argument in *Creation and Abortion* (New York: Oxford University Press, 1992), and the present discussion of it also appears in "Genes, Justice, and Obligations to Future People," *Social Philosophy and Policy* 19, no. 2 (2002): 360–88. Note that it is not strictly the absence of personhood that is critical to my argument, but rather the absence of an entitlement to keep what one has been given. For we can imagine a case that involves a person all along, and yet has the same general characteristics as the 160 IQ Case. In the Million Dollar Case, I put one million dollars into a box for a person to take out tomorrow. Before tomorrow comes, I change my mind and take the money back. This could be permissible, though my second act makes the person worse off than she would have been had I only performed the first act.

8

RIGHTS BEYOND INTERESTS

I. INTRODUCTION: MORAL RIGHTS, HUMAN RIGHTS, LEGAL RIGHTS

Rights are most often thought of either as claims to something or as protected options to act, though these categories are not exhaustive. (By "claim," I do not mean that anyone does [or even is permitted to] engage in the act of claiming, but only that someone is entitled to something.) That someone has a right can provide a unique reason for action on the part of others or, less likely, the rightholder himself. For example, that someone has a right to something can be a reason for according it to him independent of other reasons, such as that it would produce some good or satisfy a preference. Furthermore, this reason seems to function as an exclusionary reason. That is, it excludes our considering certain other factors that would ordinarily be reasons. For example, if someone has a right to something that someone else wants, the other person's desire is not merely outweighed, it is irrelevant in deciding who should have it. It is because rights exclude consideration of many other prima facie reasons that they come close to putting an end to an argument about what to do. However, if not all considerations are excluded by rights, then rights need not provide the final say.[1]

In addition, a right provides a distinctive reason for an agent who, in virtue of someone's right, has a correlative duty. (By contrast, if someone will suffer if I do not help him, this too is a distinctive reason to help, but it may not give rise to a duty to help.) Importantly, this correlative duty is *owed to* the rightholder in particular. Not all duties we have are owed to particular people. For example, we might have a duty to promote the good but not because we owe it to anyone to do so. We might have a duty not to execute murderers but not because they have a right not to be executed. Individual persons who are conscious agents are typical bearers of rights. However, infants are not agents, and yet they are commonly thought to have rights. Possibly, groups also have rights.[2]

Moral rights are said to exist independent of any legal system and of their recognition by people; one shows that they exist by moral arguments. A certain subclass of these, human rights, tells us what is owed to each human person just in virtue of her/his being a human person. So they are said to be universal human rights independent of their recognition by everyone or their enunciation in human rights law. There are at least two ways in which the claim that there are such human rights can be understood: (1) All that is needed in order to come to have certain rights is that one be a human person; (2) All that is needed in order to come to have and continue to have certain rights is that one be a human person. While there may be some rights that satisfy (2), most rights that are now considered human rights do not satisfy it. They only satisfy (1). For example, the right to free movement, the right not to be killed, and the right to free speech may all be forfeited in virtue of one's conduct. Hence, if there are human rights in sense (1), then this does not mean that every human person always has such rights just in virtue of being a human person.

Consider some practical implications of this. Some argue against capital punishment on the ground that it violates a human right not to be killed. They favor incarceration instead. But in the same sense (1) in which there is a right not to be killed, there is a right not to be deprived of liberty. If one can forfeit a right to liberty by bad acts, and so can be permissibly incarcerated as punishment, then it is not clear why one could not forfeit the right not to be killed (even when one is not presently a threat). Some argue that there is a human right not to be tortured. Others argue that it would take the need to stop a ticking bomb that threatens an enormous number of people to justify torturing even those who set the bomb. But suppose that a villain is about to set a bomb that will shortly kill one child. Presumably, the villain has no right that we not kill him, if only this would stop his setting the bomb. Furthermore, torturing someone for a short period seems less bad for him than death. Then why does the villain also have no right not to be tortured, if torturing him rather than killing him, would also stop his setting the bomb? And if we are unable to kill him, but only able to torture him in order to stop his setting the bomb, might he not also have no right not to be tortured?

Legal rights depend on the legal system, but they may sometimes reflect and be justified by moral rights. Suppose that a law grants person A a claim to have something, but person B has a moral right that person A not have that thing, and these are the only relevant facts. Some might suggest that in this context "it's the law" provides no reason for the permissibility of A's possessing the thing at issue. However, if there were not such a conflict between moral and legal rights, then "it's the law" could provide a reason for A's possessing the thing, even if morality does not require his possessing it.[3] On this view, whether any reason is given by "it's the law" is conditional on the law's relation to moral rights. This view could be denied on the ground that a legitimate process of creating legal rights does provide a reason to obey even immoral laws.

In this chapter, I shall first consider certain conceptual aspects of rights (both moral and legal) and then move on to more substantive issues about the ground of rights, conflicts between rights and promoting goods, and conflicts between different rights. In these discussions, I shall draw on key elements of nonconsequentialist theory—especially inviolability, the harming/not-aiding distinction, and distinctions among ways of harming people—already developed in previous chapters.

II. CONCEPTUAL BASICS

The most famous conceptual scheme of rights is due to W. N. Hohfeld.[4] His typology includes four types of rights. The first is a claim-right held by person A against another person B. It is (on Hohfeld's view) equivalent to (i.e., it exists if and only if) B has a duty to A in respect of the content of the claim, for example, that he be off A's property. The claim-right can be negative (to noninterference) or positive (to some contribution). The right is directional, that is, directed toward someone (possibly everyone), and is spoken of as a right against someone. It entails that the latter person has (or people have) a correlative and directional duty to the rightholder. Hence, if B owes something to A and B fails in his duty, he not merely acts wrongly, he wrongs A. A's right against B need give no one else any duty to A, for example, to see to it that B perform his duty to A, or even not to interfere with what A has a claim to have from B. In virtue of this, a claim-right that A has against B need not involve what is known as a restriction (or constraint) on interference by (all) others with that to which A has a claim. Only if A has a claim *against all others* is there a duty in them to A.

As Joel Feinberg notes,[5] in a world without rights held by people, there could still be duties; not all duties to do something for A are duties (owed) to A that are correlative to rights held by A. Instead, I might have a duty, for example, correlative to God's right that I do something for A. If I fail in this duty, I may have done something wrong to A. I may even have treated A incorrectly in the light of his properties, perhaps affecting him badly. But I could do all of this without wronging A (even if he is the object of the duty), because it is not to him that I owed performance of the duty. The right in A adds the idea of owing something to A (though it may add more than this); A holds the debt of B in some way.[6] This, I shall say, makes A the subject of the duty.[7] Arguably, being such a subject of a duty (not merely an object of it) is crucial to the idea of the dignity of the person.

As Judith Thomson emphasizes,[8] it is possible that B ought not carry out his duty x to A (correlative to A's right), in virtue, for example, of his having more important duties to others.[9] Further, the truth of this need not be a reason to believe that B has no duty x to A in the circumstances and A has no correlative right. That is, we need not think of A's "right to x from B" as a specified "right to x from B, except when m, n, o, . . ." Instead, A's general (nonspecified) right to x from B may be nonabsolute, not a bottom line, and so infringeable, but it is because he still has this right in circumstances m, n, o, etc., that he may be owed compensation if the right is infringed.[10] Hence, it is not that one has a right only if someone ought to grant it.[11]

Thomson takes the view that if we may permissibly infringe someone's right, when we do so we have not wronged her. It is only in violating a right (i.e., not granting it when we ought to) that we have wronged someone. But is it not possible to wrong someone in the course of doing what we ought to do? For example, suppose that A has a right that I not cause him great pain, but I ought to do this to A in order to save thousands of people though he did not cause their plight. It seems to me that I have wronged A, although I merely infringe and do not violate his right. One mark of this may be that it is permissible (not merely excusable) for him to resist my action, even if not all permissible infringements may be permissibly resisted.[12] This suggests that it may be possible to permissibly wrong someone.

Thomson suggests that it is conceptually part of the idea of a right, partly in virtue of its infringeability, that it implies subsidiary duties besides the duty strictly correlative to it: Either one carries out the correlative duty, or one has a subsidiary duty to seek release from the rightholder and/or a subsidiary duty to provide compensation to him. These three alternatives are not equally good, however, as the performance of the duty that is strictly correlative has pride of place.[13] It is also possible (given, for example, conflicts with other overriding rights or duties) that one also ought not carry out any of the subsidiary duties. In sum, there is no necessary conceptual connection between there being a right and its being true that, as a bottom line, something ought to be done about it.

Rights might be nonabsolute and still be so-called trumps over utility, if they are overridden by factors other than utility or even if they override all but very great utility (or disutility) considerations.[14] But I doubt that all rights—rather than just the most important human rights—cannot be overridden by moderate utility considerations. If so, many rights will not be trumps over utility, as well as being nonabsolute for other reasons. And even the most important human rights may have utility or disutility thresholds that are just extremely high.

Hohfeld's second type of right is the privilege. A has a privilege relative to B with respect to x, if he has no duty to B, for example, to refrain from actions with respect to x. So he is at liberty relative to B with respect to x; this liberty is usually understood as involving a bilateral option, a choice to do or not do something with respect to x. However, A might have a duty to B or C to do something with respect to x; even if he then had no option whether to act, he could still have a right to do so and in this sense be at liberty to do so. (While Hohfeld did not speak of "liberty to do," it is common to extend the notion of not being under a duty to refrain so that it applies to actions per se.) But A's liberty does not entail a duty on the part of anyone not to interfere with his actions with respect to x. (Hence, liberties may be the Hobbesian conception of rights, in so far as Hobbes thought that there was no constraint on others interfering with what we are at liberty to do.) A liberty to do something in the sense that involves a bilateral choice and some claim against others to noninterference with either choice would be what Thomson refers to as a "cluster right," that is, one that contains more than one sort of right. H. L. A. Hart notes that the claims often associated with liberties to do something do not entail duties strictly correlative to the object of the liberty.[15] I may be at liberty to look at you, but you have no duty to let me look at you if you may permissibly put up a screen in front of you. The duty you have in relation to my liberty (if there is a cluster right) is one you may also have apart from my liberty, that is, not to poke out my eyes (as a way of interfering with my liberty to look at you).

Is the idea of a liberty right also the idea behind what moral philosophers refer to as "prerogatives"? For example, Samuel Scheffler speaks of having a prerogative not to promote the good, which is not, however, accompanied by a constraint on anyone from forcing one to promote the good.[16] I do not think that a liberty right is quite like a prerogative, for such a prerogative implies that it is morally permissible (i.e., it is not morally wrong) to not promote the good. By contrast, the idea of having a liberty right (or a claim-right) is not so strong, as there may be moral (or legal) rights to do what is morally wrong. For example, while I have a liberty right because I have no duty to you to refrain from doing something, it could still be morally wrong of me not to refrain.[17]

Finally, in Hohfeld's scheme, the third and fourth types of rights are powers to alter the rights of oneself and others, and the rights that are immunities from the powers of others to alter one's rights. These last two are metarights, because they are about the first two types of rights.

III. THEORIES OF RIGHTS AND CORRELATIVE DUTIES

Are rights prior in any sense to their correlative duties so that they are the ground of these duties? Hohfeld's view is that a claim-right is equivalent to a directed duty. This "if and only if" relation is still compatible with rights giving rise to duties. On Thomson's view, however, a claim-right just is a directed duty, and this involves the denial of a priority relation. Suppose that either of these views were true. Then, if one had duties to oneself, one would have a right against oneself. But this is implausible. Does not the fact that duties to oneself are at least possible, but rights against oneself are not, argue against equating duties owed to A with A's rights? One possible way to respond to this challenge is to analyze duties to oneself as duties that are proper responses to the characteristics one has, for example, rational humanity. Only in this sense are they "owed" to oneself. By contrast, my owing to another person is owing to him (not merely owing a response to his characteristics, even if it is in virtue of these that I owe something to him). Hence, he can hold a debt against me in a way in which I cannot hold a debt against myself when I have a duty to myself. If duties to oneself are not "owed to" in the way that duties to others are, there is no question of a right being present.

However, even if duties to oneself could be owed to the person in the right way, this would not show that rights are prior to and give rise to such directed duties, as there are no rights of the person against himself that are prior to the directed duties either.

Perhaps the following thought experiment will help with this issue. Imagine a one-person world with A in it. It would make sense, I think, to say that A has rights, in the sense that the characteristics he has make it the case that if person B existed, B would have a duty *to* A not to treat him in certain ways. Though we conceptualize the right as involving a potential directed duty, its source in characteristics of A leads us to think of A's right as prior to any duty. Certainly, in a one-person world with A as a rightbearer, it would not make sense to say that anyone actually has duties to A. Further, in the one-person world, A might have a right to be helped even in the absence of any helper with a duty to help him. The evidence for this might be that we think that there should be brought into existence others who will have a duty to help him. Suppose, by contrast, that duties owed to C were based not on characteristics of C, but rather on characteristics of the dutyholder D. For example, suppose that D is a criminal and his punishment is to obey the next stranger who appears. Hence, if C were the next person to appear, he would have a right that D obey him. This right stems from D's characteristics, which give D a directed duty. In this case, I think that it makes sense to think of the directed duty as giving rise to the right, because it is properties of the duty-holder that give rise to the duty/right pair.[18]

In the world without C, does D have a duty? I do not think so. So there is a sense in which rights can sometimes exist without anyone actually having the directed duties to which they give rise, and though directed duties can give rise to rights, such directed duties will not exist if an actual rightbearer does not.[19]

If one thinks that rights involve (at least potentially, even if they are not reducible to) duties owed to someone, then there is essential reference in the duty to someone other than the agent of the duty. This other person is the rightholder. Some theories of rights focus on some characteristic of the rightholder (e.g., his interests) that gives rise to (or are the content of) the specific duty/right pair. Other theories of rights focus on a power—either to choose or to make claims—that the rightholder is said to have in addition to his being the subject of a directed duty. Let us briefly consider some of these theories.

A. Beneficiary and Choice Theories

According to Bentham, to have a right is to be the intended beneficiary of a duty. Hart famously raised the Third-Party Beneficiary cases as an objection to this view. For example, I can have a right that you take care of my mother. My mother is the intended beneficiary, but I have the right against you, and you owe the duty (whose object is my mother) to me. I am thus the subject of the duty.[20] The mark of my having the right, Hart says, is that my choice is a valid ground for determining whether you should give the aid to my mother; for example, I can waive the right and release you from the duty. If I decide to release you from your duty, my mother has no power to stand in the way of your being released. The mark of my having the right is not that I will be benefited by it being carried out. Herein lies the origin of Hart's Choice Theory of Rights.

It is worth noting several things about the third-party beneficiary case:

(1) We can agree that my mother can set the condition on being aided. That is, if she does not wish to be aided, the person who owes it to me to aid her may not do so. This, however, is consistent with her not having the right; setting a condition is not the same as having the power to call for the right to be carried out or to cancel the right. When my mother refuses to be aided, the person who owes it to me to aid her still has the duty, for if she changes her mind, he should perform the duty to me that he has had all along. Making it impossible for someone to carry out a duty is not the same as canceling it. Hence, her setting the condition on aid is not enough to show that my mother, not I, has the right to her being cared for.

(2) It might be said that I, too, am an intended beneficiary—not just an unintended beneficiary—of the right. This is because my interest (in the sense of what is in my interest) in being able to make contracts so that I get what I want is in question. (This interest can be at stake and satisfied, even if this means that other interests of mine are thereby set back.) Still, since my mother's interests are also aimed at in the satisfaction of this duty, how can an intended beneficiary theory decide whether I or my mother is the rightholder? At the very least, being an intended beneficiary is not sufficient for saying who has a right, unless we both have rights. But if we both have rights, we should again consider why my waiver alone, even if my mother is opposed, is sufficient to release the agent from his duty and her refusal to be aided does not cancel his duty.

(3) If (as [2] claims) I am also an intended beneficiary, this might be used to help show that it is my right, not my mother's. Suppose that my desire for my mother's welfare is weak; I do not want it very much. Then it is only weakly in my interest that a contract backing a weak desire be fulfilled. Suppose that my mother's interest in her welfare, by contrast, is strong, as her life is at stake in getting the aid. Suppose that the right that she be aided comes in conflict with a quite strong unrelated right or with a quite significant good. Intuitively, I believe, given the facts of the case, the right that my mother be aided could be easily overridden. This is likely to be true only if the stringency of the right reflects my weak interest rather than her strong interest. Hence, I am the rightholder.

Independent of deciding who is the intended beneficiary, Hart's Choice Theory of Rights raises several issues: (a) He believes that inalienable rights present a problem for his theory and that they will have to be dealt with as immunities from the power of others or oneself to change one's status, not as protected choices of the rightholder to cancel or demand fulfillment of his right. But it is possible to waive even an inalienable right.[21] For example, I may waive, on a given occasion, my right to speak even if I cannot alienate my right to speak. (b) A third party such as a judge, not I, may have the power to relieve someone of his duty to me. But this does not show that the duty is not owed to me, but rather, is owed to the third party who can release him.[22] (c) Perhaps it is the power to "claim" in the sense of "insist on" the right, rather than the power to waive or cancel it, that is crucial. Feinberg emphasizes such an activity of claiming.[23] But claiming (like waiving or canceling) is a separate act; it is possible that I might have a right and correlatively someone owes me something, and yet I have no right to insist on (or right to waive or cancel) getting the thing that is owed.

B. Interest Theory

Joseph Raz offers an Interest Theory of Rights. In one account of it, he says that some entity has a right if and only if some interest (i.e., aspect of the well-being) of the entity (which is capable of being a rightholder) is sufficient to ground a duty.[24] Raz contends that a right based on an aspect of someone's well-being need not contribute to his overall well-being. Also, he says, it is possible that the interest that gives rise to the right is not represented in that to which someone specifically has a right. So, for example, I may have a right to my shirt because it is in my interest to have personal property, even if my interest in having my shirt specifically is not strong enough to generate a right to it. The right to the shirt is then a derivative right from a more general right to property grounded in the interest in having personal property.

Raz also offers a second, slightly different account of his Interest Theory of Rights: There is a right if and only if some interest (i.e., aspect of well-being) of some entity capable of being a rightholder is sufficient to ground a duty to care for and promote the interest in a significant way.[25]

The first and second accounts of Raz's theory have different implications. For example, suppose that you have a very high level of well-being. This may be sufficient to ground a duty in me to see that your well-being does not increase further (for reasons of equality with others, or because you do not deserve so much well-being). On the first (but not the second) account of rights, you would have a right that I carry out this duty, but this hardly seems true. This case helps us to see that Raz's first account differs from Bentham's in that Bentham requires that the rightholder be a "beneficiary" of the duty. Only Raz's second account incorporates this element.

The second account, however, implies that if you are very sick, and this is sufficient to give me a duty to help you in some significant way, you have a right that I help you. But it is possible that I have a duty to help you—I morally must help you—and this merely because it would be greatly in your interest to be helped, without you having a right that I do so. For to claim that you have a right to be helped by me is to claim more than this: It is to claim that I have a directed duty *to you* (as subject), so that if I do not act I would not only be acting wrongly, I would also *wrong* you.[26] In the absence of such a correlative right, if you are not helped, you lose out because I did not do my duty, but you have no more (or less) ground for complaint, nor were you any more wronged by my failure to respond, than anyone else. A right would give you in particular a moral entitlement to the aid being given. But the fact that I have a duty stemming from your interest does not give you, any more than anyone else, a moral entitlement to my fulfilling the duty.

These problems arise, I believe, because in both accounts of rights that Raz offers, the duty is not described as a directed duty owed to the person who has the right. (Even the second account does not say that we owe the promotion of someone's interest to him.) When Raz claims that a right is more than a correlative duty, he does not have in mind a *directed* duty, that is, a duty owed *to* someone.[27]

I have suggested that there might be duties that your interest is sufficient to give rise to in me without your thereby having a right. It is also possible, I think, for someone to have rights where there is no interest (i.e., aspect of well-being, according to Raz) of his sufficient to give rise to a duty (even derivatively). If I simply endow you with the right to some of my money, your interest in having the money or property in general played no role, let alone a sufficient role, in my now having a duty to give you my money. This leaves it open that it may be in my interest to have the power to endow you with a right, but it is not an interest of yours (that the right with which I endow you serves) that gives rise to the right, even indirectly. Your having a right that does not stem from your interests is consistent with it being in your interest to have the right (though your interest in having a right also played no role in grounding your right). Your having such a right is even consistent with the possibility that you could have no right that was not in some way in your interest. Yet, in fact, I do not believe that it is true that you could have no right that was not in some way in your interest. I might endow you with a right to do something (a privilege relative to me, plus a claim against me to noninterference), though it serves no interest (and even defeats all interests) of yours to have it. For example, I give you a nontransferable right to set off a nuclear weapon when you are angry. Other examples of rights that do not arise from the interests of the rightholder (even if, as a side effect, they serve his interests) include a parent having a right to obedience from his child, or a priest having a right to respect from his followers.

Raz himself says that the stringency of a right can outstrip the importance of the interest that it most directly protects. In some cases, he thinks that this is because the interests which give rise to a right or which determine the stringency of the right are not necessarily the interests of the person which the right specifically protects. He says: "The main reason for the mismatch between the importance of the right and its contribution to the rightholder's well-being is the fact that part of the justifying reason for the right is its contribution to the common good."[28] An example is the importance of a journalist's right to free speech, which is mostly, he thinks, a function of the interests of the journalist's audience.

It is not clear that his account of the importance of a right outstripping the interest it directly protects in the case of the journalist is consistent with his two accounts of the relation between rights and interests. On these two accounts, a right is present when an interest of the rightholder is sufficient to ground a duty. But if the satisfaction of the interests of others is the reason that the journalist gets a right to have his interest protected, his interest is not sufficient to ground the duty of noninterference with his speech. Perhaps, the journalist's interest in writing is sufficient to ground a weak right, but the great stringency of the right is a function of interests that do not ground the right? Yet Raz speaks of the interests of others (in a case like the journalist) as "part of the justifying reason" for the right (not just for its stringency). A Razian might, however, argue that what grounds someone's right is this person's interest, and some other factor accounts for the stringency of the right.[29] I shall not explore this possibility, though, since I am concerned to argue that rights and their stringency could reflect something other than interests.

In the case of many rights, someone having a right may come about entirely because this serves the interests of others rather than her own interests. For example, it is theoretically possible for a police officer to have a legal right to use a gun in defense of everyone except herself. An intelligent being may have the (legal and moral) right to protect animals simply out of concern for the animals' interests and not his own.

Could some rights be justified completely independently of serving any being's interests, let alone the interests of the rightholder? The example of the priest who has a right to respect might be one. Persons might have a right to treatment as equals—which is an essentially comparative right—without our duty to them being based on their interests. Rather, I would say, this right is based on their nature as persons and not necessarily related to any aspect of their well-being. Even if it turns out to be in their interest to have this nature, the right derives from their nature and not from their interest in having it. A person's right to treatment as an equal may even lead to leveling down (i.e., taking away from some without giving to others), thus serving no one's well-being. If there were an independent "dignitary interest" in being treated as an equal (i.e., because it promotes some aspect of psychological well-being), it need not be because this treatment serves that interest that a person has a right to it. It may simply be fitting to treat a person no differently from anyone else. Suppose that each individual were on a separate planet and knew nothing of his treatment or well-being in comparison with others. We might still think that equality was required, possibly by leveling down. Another example is the right to punish which, on a retributive theory, is justified independently of concern for anyone's interest. It may be a burden to punish others; it is a burden to them to be punished; and it may not be expected to do society good. Yet, we may have a right to see to it that someone receives what he deserves, as a way of taking human agency seriously.[30]

Finally, in this vein, consider another example Raz gives that involves an ordinary citizen's right to free speech. He claims that her right to free speech is more important than her interest in speaking freely that it protects. His account of this is that she has a strong interest in benefiting from the free speech of others. Indeed, Raz claims that his own interests would be better served by living in a society where others have a right to free speech and he lacks it than in a society where he has the right and others lack it. In this case, it is not as a producer of speech but as a beneficiary of it that one's interests are most important. An implication of this view is that a given person has the strong right to speak only because it would not be possible to deny it to him without denying it to others as well. Raz's Interest Theory of Rights requires the nonseparable allocation of a strong right of free speech in order to account for its strength in any given person. For if allocation were separable, the really strong right would be the right that others be free to speak.[31]

However, if we do not remain wedded to the Interest Theory of Rights, we can recognize that any given person's interest in speaking freely is not great, and yet still argue that he has a strong right to free speech, even when its strength is independent of serving (directly or indirectly) any other interest of his or anyone else's. The right to speak freely may simply be the only appropriate way to treat people with minds of their own and the capacity to use means to express it. Even if their interests would be set back only slightly by interfering with their free speech, the permissibility of doing so (including their having no right that such interference not occur) would imply that they were beings of a quite different sort.[32] Not recognizing a person's option of speaking is to fail to respect him. Someone may waive (or perhaps even alienate) this right in order to promote his greater interests. But to say that any given person is not entitled to the strong right to free speech is implicitly to say that no person is so entitled noninstrumentally. That is, it is a way of saying that certain crucial features of human nature are not sufficient to generate the right in anyone. And this seems to be a mistake.

On the alternative account I am offering of why the importance of a right can outstrip any interest it directly protects, we might say that some rights are a response to, or an expression of, the good (worth, importance, distinctive capacities) of the person, his authority over himself, and his limited authority over others, rather than a response to what is good for the person (that is, what is in his interests).[33] If it is in a person's interest to be a being of this sort, the right is still not a response to this interest, but simply to his worth as a person. (The interest gets protected as a side effect, not as the point, of the right.) The strength of the right is not a mark of the strength of the interest it directly or indirectly protects, but a mark of the fact that the right is a response to basic, morally crucial characteristics of persons. Hence, it is a response to a characteristic of persons that may itself be a necessary presupposition of the importance of protecting their interests.[34]

We could try to take account of the two concerns upon which I have focused so far in criticizing the Interest Theory of Rights by revising Raz's formulation as follows: Some entity has a right if and only if some interest *or other aspect of the entity (including properties that make it capable of being a rightholder)* is sufficient to give rise to a duty owed *to the entity*. This revision manages, I think, to deal even with cases in which someone (in virtue of her properties) is owed noninterference with her promotion of the interests of others (e.g., animals). However, it is not clear that it deals with cases in which someone endows you with a right for reasons quite unrelated to your interests or properties (as in the case where I give you a nontransferable right to blow up a bomb when you are angry). It is this class of cases, I think, that pressures us to eliminate the first part of the formulation having to do with the ground of rights when formulating what it is for an entity to have a right.

Raz's version of the Interest Theory of Rights treats interests as what give rise to rights. Another type of an interest theory of rights might remain mute about what gives rise to a right. It might only claim that what a right is about (regardless of how it originates) is the protection of some interest (still defined as some aspect of someone's well-being). I interpret "about" to mean not just that a right always has an effect on someone's interest, but that it is the point of the right to do so. I think that many of the examples discussed above also could be used to argue against this view. For example, a person's right to free speech does not, according to my account, have as its point an aspect of her (or others') well-being (e.g., that she [or they] not be psychologically frustrated).

Some general thought experiments may also be helpful with respect to all versions of the Interest Theory of Rights: Can we imagine a person who has no interests and yet could have rights? Or could we imagine a person whose well-being will remain constant no matter what he does, what others do to him, and what permissions everyone has, yet he has rights? Presumably, these people could have reasons for action besides expected effects on their well-being. Hence, if they, for example, had a duty to worship God, they might have a right to freedom of worship. Or, as the acquisition of knowledge can be a worthwhile activity even if it does not increase anyone's well-being, such persons might have a right to acquire knowledge.[35]

IV. RIGHTS AND CONFLICTS

Even the Interest Theory of Rights does not imply that a right that protects an interest thereby promotes interests overall within the life of one person or overall among people. Hence, there may be conflicts between respecting rights and promoting interests. (I shall refer for the time being to maximally promoting interests as producing the greater good.) This should be no surprise, since to say that someone has a right to something is ordinarily a way of excluding the calculation of overall goods and evils in deciding how to treat him. (Hence, as noted above, the right is sometimes referred to as one type of "exclusionary reason.") Suppose the balance of good over evil recommends that A get x. In an act-consequentialist system that maximizes the good produced, this will mean that someone has a duty to provide A with x. If the balance of good shifts even a little bit in another direction, A should not have x. The idea that A has a right to his life in this system would be redundant for "produces the most good for A to have his life" or "it is right that A has his life." But the idea of a right is meant to *contrast* with such ideas, not be synonymous with them.[36] On the act-consequentialist view we are considering, if we could save two lives by taking another person's life, the one would have no right to his life. That his right appears and disappears in this way makes the idea of special sovereignty over his life (which is the usual notion of a right to life) misplaced. Despite the fact that his interests are given equal weight with those of others in the calculation of what is good overall, he is ultimately treated as a resource for promoting the good. However, a notion of a right that is not redundant in this way could be given by a rule-consequentialist system: Overall, according rights and not balancing goods and evils on each occasion will maximize the good brought about. This is a theory of rights (in the ordinary sense) but only as instruments for maximally promoting interests of everyone overall.

Nonconsequentialists, by contrast, try to justify a system of rights that has noninstrumental value and that may conflict with bringing about the greatest good overall (even eventually or indirectly). Furthermore, even if this greatest good is sensitive to the distribution of goods among people, so that, for example, priority is given to the interests of the worst off, nonconsequentialists will insist that a right might stand in the way of producing this fair distribution. For example, the worth of each individual may imply that each has rights to bodily integrity, and these can interfere (overall and in the long run) with the distribution of body organs so that the number of years lived by all people are maximal and fairly distributed.

However, the concept of a right need not imply that respecting a right will always take precedence over the greater good (either at the act or the rule level). Rights need not be absolute, but rather, may have thresholds beyond which the calculation of goods and evils is reintroduced.[37] I may have a right that you give me something, but if a great good is possible only by transgressing my right, this may be permitted. In such a case, the right will have been infringed rather than violated. The more good we must sacrifice rather than transgress the right, the more stringent is the right by at least one measure. It has been claimed that some fundamental human rights are stringent enough to stand in the way of even great goods, whose achievement they prevent. This may be because the rights represent the worth of the person, which is the presupposition of the importance of promoting interests. But rights can also conflict with the personal interests of agents who have to act in accord with them. For example, someone's right to be saved by his bodyguard may give the bodyguard a duty to give up even his life for his employer. There are then at least two measures of the stringency of a right: (1) how much good overall that could otherwise be produced is needed to override it, and (2) how much personal good an agent must sacrifice to fulfill the duty associated with the right. As we shall see, these two measures need not always coincide. This will be true, for example, if a right that an agent must do a great deal to accord does not require much good, alternatively produced, to override it. Indeed, less alternative good may be necessary to override it than to override another right that an agent need not do a great deal to accord, as we shall see.[38]

Rights may also conflict with other rights. The two measures of stringency may not coincide here either. For example, a right that an agent must do a great deal to accord (and so is very stringent in that sense) might be overridden by another right (which is more stringent in the sense of "capacity to override") that an agent need not do as much to accord. Rights that protect interests may even conflict with maximizing, *ex ante*, the protection of the very interest the right directly protects of the very person whose right it is. We shall now consider each of these types of conflicts and ways of measuring the stringency of rights.

A. Conflicts between Rights and the Greater Good

1. Consider first the conflict between rights (both positive and negative) and great goods not protected by rights.[39] Can the good override the right if it is produced by aggregating small goods distributed over many people who are all better off than the rightholder, or must someone among those who will lose out on a good face being worse off than the rightholder would be if his right is overridden? The latter view (which involves pairwise comparison of individuals one at a time) seems

more plausible than the former.[40] So, one reason that rights can trump goods is that the total good is not distributed over persons in the right way.[41] But it is still possible that the aggregate loss to many people, each of whom will lose out on as much (but no more) good than the rightholder would lose, and who would be as badly off without the good, provides a reason to override the right, for example, if five will die unless one is killed. (We will consider below whether achieving goods distributed in this way may still not override rights. It is also possible that the aggregate loss to those who would each lose out on less than the rightholder but who would each still be worse off than the rightholder provides a reason to override the right.)

2. Ronald Dworkin tried to explain why some rights trump great goods, in the sense that they must not be transgressed for the sake of producing the great goods, even if we take utilitarianism as a background theory. He argued that the satisfaction of the external preferences of some people whose object involves denying the equal weight of the preferences of others should not be counted in a utilitarian calculation to determine how much good is at stake if we do not act. He thought that this was true even if individual people will suffer more (through lack of satisfaction of their external preferences) if we do not act than the people whose interests we would act against would suffer. Rights that trump aggregated utility may be, in his view, heuristic devices that represent the elimination of such external preferences from a social calculus without our actually having to do this elimination on each occasion.[42]

This explanation of why rights trump goods, however, does not explain why anyone should have a right that trumps aggregated preferences that are not inappropriately external. For example, why does one person have a trump right not to be killed when we could save the lives of five people by killing him, and each person prefers to survive? Dworkin's explanation of rights as trumps in terms of eliminating external preferences also does not specifically call for pairwise comparison to see how badly off each individual would be and how much he would lose out on getting; it would allow us to use a large aggregate of nonexternal preferences, each of which is a preference for a small good for oneself when one is already quite well off, in order to override someone's right to be protected from a severe loss.

3. Judith Thomson offers an account of why some rights must never be transgressed, even to achieve great goods not involving inappropriate external preferences and even when a great number of people would each suffer as great a loss and be as badly off if the great good is forgone as the rightholder would be if his right is transgressed. Her view is, in a sense, that there is not enough morally relevant good in the world to override some maximally stringent rights. This is because, she argues, in deciding whether to transgress a right, we must do pairwise comparison to see how badly off each individual whose good helps to compose the aggregate good would be if we do not transgress the right. Further only if someone will suffer a fate sufficiently worse if a right is not transgressed than the rightholder would suffer if his right is transgressed can the transgression be justified. But sometimes it will not be possible for any one person to suffer such a fate. For example, on her view, we must not violate the right not to be killed of one person (even if we kill him painlessly) in order to save 1,000 people from drowning

through natural causes very painfully. This is because no one of 1,000 will suffer a fate *sufficiently* worse than the rightholder would. Thomson's account allows, however, that there are rights such that someone could suffer a sufficiently worse fate than the rightholder, and then the right might be permissibly infringed.

One problem here is that her view also seems to ignore the possibility that there are rights whose stringency is not a function of the interest at stake but of the worth of the person and the capacities that make it possible for him to be a rightholder. Hence, even if someone will suffer a much worse fate than the rightholder would, the right might not be infringeable. For example, someone's fate may be much worse if another person's freedom to read pornography is not limited than the reader's fate would be if it is limited, and yet it could be wrong to limit that other person's freedom to read pornography. A second concern is that her view seems to imply that an increasing number of people who will suffer a sufficiently worse fate does not add to the justification for infringing the right beyond what we had with one person. After all, why should the sufficiently worse fate aggregate in a morally relevant way when equally bad fates do not, in her view?[43]

4. Yet another proposal as to why a right should take precedence over a great good is that the transgression of a right always produces a worse outcome than does the absence of the great good (perhaps, for example, because it is worse to die by way of a rights violation than to die of natural causes). This proposal seems extremely implausible, in part, because it would imply that we never have a reason based on considerations of the greater good to override a right. The implausibility can be brought home by considering the following hypothetical case: Suppose that someone is about to kill one person in order to save five people from a naturally occurring disease, but though he will kill the one, he does not have a very good chance of actually saving the five. We can either (1) stop him from killing the one, or (b) provide the five people with some medicine that we have developed in order to save them. We cannot do both (a) and (b). We might reasonably choose to save the five people because their dying is a worse state of affairs than is the one in which the one person is killed. Yet, if the rights violation resulted in the worse outcome, we would have strong reason to prevent it instead. The deep error in the proposal is to think that the right that someone has that others not treat him in a certain way is a reflection of how bad a state of affairs would exist if he were treated in that way. If that were true, furthermore, five people's being treated in that way would be an even worse state of affairs, and it would then be quite generally permissible to kill one person in order to save five from being killed. But this is wrong.[44]

Thomas Nagel thinks that this deep error results from trying to explain an agent-relative requirement (that gives to each agent a duty that *she* not do something to *her* victim) in terms of what has agent-neutral negative value, that is, a bad state of affairs involving a rights violation that anyone has a duty to prevent.[45] Those who treat rights violations as new types of negative values (in addition to, or as taking precedence over, such things as pain or setbacks to interests) that are used to evaluate how bad an outcome will be, and who say that we have a duty to produce the best outcome so understood, are called *rights-consequentialists*. An alternative view is that rights are "side constraints";[46] they can tell us not to do something to a person, even if its being done would stop a worse state of affairs from occurring as, for example, when the same sort of setback to interests or transgressions of rights will be done to a greater number of other people.

5. But now consider a variation on the agent-relative view that claims to provide yet another justification for rights taking precedence over the greater good. Some have interpreted the view that there are agent-relative duties in such a way that the focus is on the agent rather than on the right-bearing potential victim and in such a way that a form of consequentialism results. For example, some say it is *my* transgressing the right in order to produce a great good that produces the worse state of affairs (at least from my perspective) relative to the absence of the great good. On this view, any agent must not do something when doing that thing will bring about the worse state of affairs from the agent's perspective. Here an agent-relative evaluation of the outcome is combined with a consequentialist perspective, and it is in order to avoid the worse outcome so construed that an agent should not transgress the right.[47]

The agent's concern with *his* not doing something might also be put in a non-consequentialist framework. It might be said that one's responsibility to not transgress a right is greater than any duty one has to produce the best outcome, because one must not be the sort of agent who does certain types of acts (even if doing them does not produce the worse outcome from my perspective). The emphasis in this sort of nonconsequentialist account shifts from the significance of the right of the potential victim as a side constraint (which implies that I have a duty to her not to do something to her) to the importance for a particular agent of his not being a certain sort of agent.

Both the consequentialist and nonconsequentialist versions of this focus on the agent suggests that if another agent were to transgress the right of the victim for the sake of the greater good, one would not have, on balance, a good enough moral reason to stop him. But suppose, for example, that B will violate A's right not to have his arm removed in order to save five lives. Do I have a good enough moral reason (even if not a duty) to put aside my activities to stop the transgression, rather than let it be the cause of the greater good? I think I do.[48] On the other hand, if it were most important that *I* not be involved in acts of a certain type, should I not reduce the number of such acts in which I am involved? May I kill one person now as a means to stop a threat I started yesterday that will soon kill five other people? (This question can be raised in connection with both the consequentialist and nonconsequentialist versions of agent-relativity that we are considering. For the outcome in which I kill five people is worse from my perspective than the one in which I kill one person.) I think I may not kill one person as a means to stop my being the killer of five.[49] What if another agent were about to kill someone as a means to stop the lethal threat I *started* yesterday to kill five other people today. Do I still have sufficient reason to stop him from transgressing the one person's right? What if the one person he is about to kill seeks minor assistance from me to escape. Do I have sufficient reason to help him, even though it means that *I* will wind up the killer of five others? I think that the answer is yes to both these questions.

These cases suggest that it is a mistake to interpret agent-relativity as based on an agent's concern with her own agency that ordinarily leads her not to transgress a right, and a mistake to think that agent relativity so interpreted explains why respecting rights can take precedence over certain greater goods. Rather, it is because the right I would come up against should not be transgressed in order to achieve the greater good that I must not transgress it, even though its being transgressed by me is not the worst state of affairs either from my perspective or anyone else's.

Indeed, the existence of rights has the following implication in cases of conflict with producing greater goods. Suppose that B is intending to violate A's right not to be killed in order to save many other lives in an accident. However, there is only a small chance that A's being killed will succeed in saving the others. It is certain, however, that I can save the others. I believe that it is correct for me to save them, though this will not stop B from violating A's right. (I have a reason to stop B, but I have even more reason to save many lives.) Now, suppose that my route to saving the others becomes blocked. It is consistent for me, as someone who would have tried to save the lives of many, now to act on the reason I have to stop B from violating A's right, even if this means that the many will not be saved.

6. My approach to understanding how respect for some rights can take precedence over producing the greater good can be illustrated by considering the right not to be harmed, and the fact that the impermissibility of overriding it expresses a degree of inviolability of the person.[50] High inviolability can serve one's interest in life, but that is not all it is about, I think. (One might sometimes have a nonoverrideable right not to be harmed by A, even if one will otherwise be similarly harmed by B. In this case, one's interest in life will not be protected by the right against A; nevertheless, the right may exist.) Further, there may be other ways to treat a person that serve the same interests that are served by inviolability, and yet there is no right to these other forms of treatment.[51] Inviolability is a status—a description of what it is not permissible to do to a person—and it does not depend on what happens to a person. Even if one is violated impermissibly, one does not lose one's inviolability. (Hence, it involves the broad sense of moral status discussed in chapter 7. But in addition it describes a particular form of moral status in the narrower sense described in chapter 7 because it says that certain things may not be done to the person.)

The permissibility of my leaving A, who will have his right transgressed by someone else, so that I can go and save others, does not imply that it is permissible for anyone to harm A. However, if it were permissible to harm him in order to save others, or if it were morally wrong to stop him from being harmed in order to save others, this would involve morality endorsing his being harmed in order to save others and hence endorsing a less inviolable status for the person. So, insofar as respecting a right not to be harmed involves respecting a status of inviolability, whether one has succeeded in respecting the right does not depend on whether the person is in fact violated or his interests set back.

Carrying this account of rights further, we can see that in the conflict between rights and the greater good, it is possible to offer an account of why an agent should not transgress a right that is, in a certain way, good-based. To do this, however, we need to expand the idea of the good to include more than promoting interests. We also need to move beyond the consequentialist idea of producing the good. That is, there may be a type of good that already exists but that would not exist if it were permissible to transgress the right of one person in order to save many lives. This is the good of being someone whose worth is such that it makes him highly inviolable and also makes him someone to whom one owes nonviolation.[52] This good does imply that certain of one's interests should not be sacrificed, but inviolability matters not merely because it instrumentally serves those interests.[53] Overall and *ex ante*, it might not even serve those interests, as the impermissibility of killing someone in order to save many others in an accident can actually reduce *ex ante* every individual person's chances of survival. Inviolability is a reflection of the worth of the person. On this account, it is impermissible for me to harm the person in order to save many in the accident, because doing so is inconsistent with his having this status. If I harmed him, it would, of course, be my act that did so, but that it would be my act is not what gives me the reason to avoid it. I should avoid it because it is inconsistent with his status.

Furthermore, inviolability is a status that every person has only if it is impermissible to transgress any given person's rights. This is a function of the universalizability of moral status that one has qua person. Every person who dies in an accident because it is impermissible to harm another person in order to save her also has high inviolability, but only because it is indeed impermissible to harm that other person. If the properties that a person has qua person were not sufficient to give rise to high inviolability in one person, they would not do so in all others. This means that if it were permissible to harm the one to save the others, no one would embody the sort of good that is expressed by high inviolability.[54]

It is important to distinguish the good (in the sense of worth) of the person, which may give rise to his inviolability, from its being good for the person to be a person of such worth and, hence, inviolable. Even if it is in his interest, this is not the source of the rights associated with his being inviolable. He must have a certain nature, rather than an interest, in order to be worthy of inviolability. Furthermore, any interest he has in being the sort of entity who is inviolable would also be distinct from any interest he has in being recognized as this sort of a being. (The latter is what is sometimes called a "dignitary interest.") His interest in this recognition could not be the fundamental reason that he has the right that is to be recognized. Indeed, it may only be his having the status that marks him as the sort of entity whose interests and desires (e.g., to have his rights recognized) should be given serious consideration.

Note that I have not here explained why the worth of persons expresses itself in high inviolability rather than a status of high "saveability." The latter might require us to sacrifice one to save many from natural death. But, in this connection, I believe that the following point is important. The status of persons qua persons is a function of what is true of any one person. If you should be saved simply because you are in a group with more people, this does not indicate that you or the others as individuals have higher saveability, but only that the numbers of people could affect what we should do. Strictly speaking, a status of high saveability would have to show up as a duty to do a great deal to save any one person. But it would be paradoxical to say that it showed up in the permissibility of killing one person to save someone else (other things being equal) from death or less than death; in the latter case, the one who would be killed is the one who should most be saved.[55]

As noted above, the inviolability of persons need not be absolute. First, someone may be inviolable with respect to one thing (his life) but not another (his hair). Second, the degree (or magnitude) of inviolability with respect to these things could vary. The degree of inviolability could be measured by how bad the fates of others must be before we may override the right or possibly by how many people will suffer bad fates. Unlike Thomson's view (which I described above), the position I am describing now is not committed to not aggregating the losses of individuals who will suffer as much if not aided as the rightholder would suffer if his right were transgressed. That is, it does not seem committed to the view that increasing the number of people whose fates would be comparable to the right-holder's is irrelevant to whether we may transgress the right. It is just that one of the goods that counts against the rights transgression is the good of each person being someone whose status involves inviolability.

Would it be permissible to destroy one great art work—an entity that counts in its own right—to prevent several other comparable artworks from being de-stroyed in a natural disaster? I believe it would be permissible. Would it be per-missible to destroy one non-rights-bearing animal in order to minimize the deaths of others in a natural disaster? Arguably, yes. Would it be permissible to destroy one developing embryo to save others from being destroyed in a natural disaster and so allow them to develop? I believe so. This sacrificeability of one entity of these types for the sake of others of their type is in sharp contrast with the way it is permissible to treat a person.

It is tempting to hypothesize that this indicates that there is a relation between the two different contrasts to having moral status (described in chapter 7), that is, (1) what happens to one, and (2) lacking moral status. The first contrast is to the broad sense of moral status, which refers (roughly) to what it is permissible to do to an entity. The second contrast is to a narrow sense of moral status in which it refers to a particular way of mattering. The hypothesis is that only if an entity has a subtype of narrow moral status (i.e., being a rightholder to whom things can be owed) can respect for an individual's moral status take precedence over what happens to other members of the subtype. If one lacks this particular moral status, all that matters is what actually happens to entities of a type in aggregate within the constraints of fair distribution (such as priority to the worst off).[56] (The latter would apply both to those who have no sake for which one can act and those who have a sake for which one can act.)

To understand the hypothesis, we should distinguish an intraentity and an interentity claim. In an intraentity case, it might insult an animal, for example, to train it to act in ways atypical for its species even if this increased its well-being. It is possible that respect for the animal's particular moral status should take precedence over its own well-being. In this case, what *happens* is that it loses well-being if respect is shown to its moral status. The intraentity case is different from the interentity case (with which we began) that involves sacrificing the entity or even treating it in insulting ways (ordinarily incompatible with its moral status) to eliminate problems for other members of its type. Arguably, this is permissible with animals and objects. In this case, what *happens* is that a certain moral status itself is not respected in one individual in order to prevent harm to other individuals. This implies that none of the individuals of the same type, including those helped, have a moral status that provides high inviolability. In the case of persons—as I said above—if it were permissible to kill one person to save others, no person would have a certain particular status (a certain sort of inviolability) qua person. So respect for the status of every person, including those many who will be treated badly, is taking precedence over preventing bad outcomes for them. If all this were true, it would show that the nonsubstitutability of the individual is less strong in the morality of nonpersons than in the morality of persons.

However, the hypothesis—that only if one has the narrow moral status to which things can be owed, can respect for an individual's moral status take precedence over what happens to other members of the type—does not seem to be true. Entities whose value is purely symbolic, like flags or holy entities, should not be destroyed for the sake of saving others of their type. Yet these entities are not rightholders. (If this is true of purely symbolic entities, but not of embryos, this suggests that the value of the embryo does *not* always reside merely in its role as a symbol of human life. An embryo may serve merely as a symbol when we are *not* interested in the future development of embryos. Hence, we may think it makes sense to destroy one embryo for the sake of the future development of other embryos but not for the sake of their survival as mere embryos in a freezer where their only role is to serve as symbols of life.[57])

7. I have pointed out that some views on why a right may override the greater good nevertheless allow that as the number of people who would suffer losses increases, there can be more reason to transgress the right. On other views, the numbers do not count. Let us consider the issue further for it will help us evaluate the view just presented (in section IVA(6)). Consider what I call the $5 Case: Each of twenty people will lose his $5 bill as a result of a gust of wind blowing it away. The only thing that will get the money back to each is taking away A's $5 bill, which alone survives the storm, and investing it to recoup the lost $100. Unfortunately, A will soon be gone and will not be able to benefit from the investment.[58] It is indeed wrong, I think, to take A's $5 in order to prevent a permanent loss to each of the others that is no greater than the loss that he will suffer. It is true that if it were permissible to take his $5 for this purpose, the claim of any person, including those who benefit, to his $5 would be a weaker claim. It is only if it is impermissible to take A's $5 that each of the others would have a stronger right to keep his $5 (if he had it). (This is all analogous to what was said above (in section IVA(6)) about the inviolability of one person and all persons.) However, even if all this is true, no one thinks that the right to keep one's $5 is a very strong right nor that people are financially inviolable. The test of the right's low stringency is the fact that if one other person were to lose a really important good unless we permanently deprived A of $5 without his consent, it might well be permissible to do so.

The $5 Case shows that we can generate the same type of argument for the impermissibility of taking A's $5 in order to save twenty other people's $5 bills as we can generate for the impermissibility of taking A's life in order to save twenty other lives. That is, if it were permissible to do so, it would be true of every person that he is less inviolable and that his right is not as stringent. I do not deny that this is true, but what, I ask, is implied by it being true in *both* types of cases? Perhaps what is implied is that the ability of a right to "stand up" to the aggregation of similar losses to many people is not an adequate measure of the strength of the right nor of the degree of inviolability of the person. Perhaps, it is rather an indication (as Thomson's view suggests) that it is an error in the logic of rights to consider the number of people who would benefit when deciding whether to infringe a right. In the $5 Case, it seems that the impermissibility of taking A's $5 in order to stop equal and aggregated losses to others does not reflect a high degree of inviolability of anyone's possession of $5; it is more the case that we think that it is in some way illogical to count the equal losses of many other people.[59] This view, however, conflicts with both the judgment of some that once the number of people who will lose their lives becomes great enough, we may infringe the one person's right to life in order to save them, and with the judgment that if her right gave way before the needs of a smaller number of people, this would be an indication that it is a less stringent right.

These judgments suggest that an alternative conclusion should be drawn from the $5 Case: A right's ability to stand up to an aggregation of similar losses in many others (call this the Horizontal Test of Stringency) on its own is not sufficient as an indication of the stringency of the right. Rather, there must be some connection between (a) the seriousness of infringing the right as measured by how it stands up to preventing various losses in a single other person (call this the Vertical Test of Stringency) and (b) the right's ability to stand up to aggregated losses, in order for the latter Horizontal Test to also be a measure of the right's stringency.

Let us summarize a bit. In section IIIB, I questioned the Interest Theory of Rights on the basis of Raz's claim that the strength of a right often seems greater than the weight of the interest it protects. I suggested that this might be because it reflects the nature and worth of the person rather than his interests. More recently, I have discussed why sometimes the most important interests of a person (e.g., to not die) seem to be given greater weight than the comparable interests (e.g., to not die) of many others. One answer I have considered to why this is so is that the worth of each person is implicated in the impermissibility of violating one of them (and, by implication, in the strength of his claim to his life). I suggest that the strength of the right can outstrip even the interest it protects because it expresses something true of all people (that they have strong claims not to be interfered with) that surpasses the interests of any of them. Without denying this view, I have also raised a question about whether the failure of aggregated losses to count against a right is sufficient to show the stringency of the right (and the degree of inviolability of the person) or is rather a reflection of the fact that counting aggregated losses would evince a deep logical error in understanding the stringency of rights.

8. Now let us consider another aspect of the conflict between rights and goods not protected by rights: that the quantitative degree of inviolability (its magnitude) is not all that matters. As emphasized throughout Part 1 of this book and especially

in chapter 5, the manner in which it is permissible and impermissible to interfere with a person is also of significance. By "manner of interference," I mean to refer (throughout) to the required causal relations that hold between what we do, the harmful involvement of the person, and the good we hope to achieve, as discussed in chapter 5. Someone might have the same quantitative degree of inviolability if it were permissible to interfere with him only in way x and not in way y as if it were permissible to interfere only in way y and not in way x. Yet, the former might be the correct and the latter the incorrect way to treat a person.

This topic bears on another approach to arguing against an Interest Theory of Rights and to defending the claim (in section IVA[6]) that inviolability is not merely about protecting someone's interest in life and bodily well-being. Raz observes that interests may not give rise to all of the rights that might protect them. I believe that he does not adequately explain why this is so, and that any such explanation will be inconsistent with an interest theory (whether it is about the origins of rights or about the content of rights). I believe that the fact that the same interest can go unprotected in one way and yet be protected in another way indicates that it is at least more than the presence of an interest in a creature capable of having rights that grounds or explains the content of the right; it is also the manner of treatment of the person that would be involved in affecting his interests that is crucial to whether a right exists and what is its point. In this sense, the interest (i.e., some aspect of well-being) is not sufficient to ground a duty when there is a right.

In discussing conflicts between rights and goods, we have so far seen one example of this: Even if we may not harm (e.g., kill), it could be permissible to allow harm (e.g., let die). Here it is not a question of different ways of interfering with the same interest, but of interfering versus not promoting. The most obvious interest at stake (living) is the same in both cases. However, typically, when we kill we deprive someone of the life he would have independently of us; when we let die, someone loses life that he would have had only by making use of our services. His sovereignty over his life is only at stake when we kill. (The aider's sovereignty over her efforts is at stake when the question arises for her of whether or not to let die.) This, rather than interests alone, helps account for the presence or absence of rights.

Might we say that it is in one's interest per se to be sovereign over one's life, as distinct from it being in one's interest to be alive? But we have also seen that one could permissibly leave someone who is being deprived of the exercise of his sovereignty (when someone else is killing him) to do something else, such as save twenty people from drowning. Hence, sovereignty's being in one's interest would give rise to a right not to be killed, but not to a right to be helped to avoid an attack on one's sovereignty. Why is this so, when the interests affected are the same? (Notice that the sacrifices that we as agents would have to make rather than kill someone or rather than let someone die could be the same, and yet there could be a right not to be killed but no right not to be left to be killed. Hence the difference in the cost to agents need not account for the presence or absence of the rights.) No doubt, if it were permissible to kill, morality would endorse the transgression of a person's sovereignty over herself, but it need not do so if it is merely permissible to allow a transgression (that itself is still impermissible). But we still need an explanation of why letting the transgression occur can be permissible when its effects on everyone's interests (victim, agent, and others) are the same as the impermissible killing.

The importance for the generation of rights of the different ways in which interests can be protected is shown in the interpretation of the claim that rights trump goods. Those who support this claim may want to insist that the deliberate transgression of a right is not permitted in order to bring about certain goods, but the cases we have considered above show that this does not commit them to the claim that we should always sacrifice the same goods in order to prevent the deliberate transgression of the same right. In this sense, rights do not trump goods. (Recall that it was permissible to save many people from a natural disaster rather than rescue one person from being killed by someone [in his misguided attempt to save the many].)

Even talk of the impermissibility of the deliberate transgression of a right is not sufficiently precise. And here we come to the heart of the idea that the manner in which we interfere with a person matters: Hold constant the interests of the rightholder in, for example, life and personal sovereignty, as well as the interests involved in promoting the greater good. It is still true that there are some ways in which a person has a right not to be deliberately interfered with to achieve goods and other ways in which a person has no right not to be deliberately interfered with to achieve these same goods. The Trolley cases (discussed in earlier chapters) illustrate this. It is permissible to save five people by redirecting the trolley onto a side track, though we foresee that it will thereby hit and kill one person. We would not impermissibly transgress the one's right not to be killed, if we were to redirect the trolley. However, it would not be permissible to push an innocent bystander into the trolley as a way of stopping the trolley—his right not to be killed would be impermissibly transgressed if we did this. One way of putting the point might be that the *strength* of a right not to be killed is not solely a function of the interest it most obviously protects (i.e., life for everybody in all of these cases), but also of the way in which the interest is affected. Another better way of putting the point, is that the Trolley cases imply that there is no right not to be killed in a certain manner (e.g., as a consequence of redirecting a threat so as to bring about a greater good). These cases will then show that the manner in which someone's interests will be affected is relevant to generating a right and/or is part of what the right is about.

Of course, in order to support these judgments about cases we need a general account of when and why it is permissible to kill in one way but not in another. As I have said in earlier chapters, I believe that the correct account will say something about how greater goods should be causally related to such lesser evils* as harm to people, and this will not represent a concern merely for the interests of potential victims.[60] Nor will it, I believe, reflect a concern for the interests of agents. For example, the permissibility of redirecting the trolley and the impermissibility of pushing someone into the trolley is not a function of the difficulty for the agent of doing each. For we could imagine that pushing the one person into the trolley is also accomplished by redirecting a trolley, this time a second trolley (on its way to harming no one) so that it gently pushes the one person into the first trolley. In any case, if difficulty to the agent were a crucial factor, this would give an agent only an option not to throw someone into a trolley, not a duty not to do so. The correct account of when and why someone's right not to be killed is not infringeable, or when and why the right exists, may be a further reflection of our concern with the worth of the person rather than merely with interests that are important to him. This would mean that a concern with how the greater good should be causally related to lesser evils* has something to do with concern for the worth of the person. Since I believe that a principle concerning causal relations reveals part of the point of nonconsequentialism, I also believe that a principle that reveals part of the point of nonconsequentialism will help account for the strength or existence of different rights.

In previous sections, I questioned the Interest Theory of Rights by arguing (1) that the strength of some rights is greater than the weight of the interest it protects, because the right implicates the worth of the person, not only his interests, and (2) that the right protecting one person's interests could have greater weight than the same interests in many others, because the right implicates the worth of each of the people. In this section, I have questioned the Interest Theory of Rights (both as a theory of the origin and the content of a right) by arguing (3) that it is the manner in which we would affect interests, and not interests alone, that is crucial both for generating rights and for the stringency of rights.

B. The Conflict between Rights and Personal Interests

So far, I have considered how rights might interfere with the achievement of, or be overridden by, greater goods. But if a right may be overridden by a greater good, this does not settle the question of what we must do. Suppose, for example, that A has a right that B meet him for lunch, but on his way to lunch, B sees C in need of a kidney transplant that B could provide. It would do such a great deal of good to help C that it is permissible for B to fail in his duty to A in order to help C. But, presumably, we think that B is still not required to give his kidney in order to bring this great good about. Hence, it is supererogatory for him to do so; he has no duty to do it. However, if he wishes to do so, he may;[61] he would be mistaken to think that A's right could only be overridden if he, B, had a duty to save C at the cost of a kidney. Supererogatory acts may, therefore, come into conflict with rights and override them.[62]

In this case, A will lose so little if his right is overridden that we might think he should waive it. But suppose that D has a right against his bodyguard, E, to have his life saved, even at great personal expense to E. E now faces a choice between saving D or saving 10,000 strangers. I do not think that D is obligated to waive his right to E's services. Yet, I believe, it is permissible for E to abandon D in order to save the 10,000 Strangers. (This does not imply that he may kill D in order to save the 10,000, for a positive right to have one's life saved may be overridden because it is a weaker right than the right not to be killed even though both rights protect the interest in life.) E may abandon D, even if E would not be willing to sacrifice as much personally to save the 10,000 as D will lose if he is not helped, or as E *would* have been willing conscientiously to lose for D's sake, had it been necessary to carry out his duty to D. Still, if the effort that E must make in order to save the 10,000 is considerable, and so his aiding is supererogatory, then it is still not true that his duty to D must take precedence over supererogatorily aiding.

If the cost to E of saving the 10,000 is small (and, hence, saving them is not supererogatory), then he faces a conflict of a *duty* to save 10,000 (though it may not be a duty with a correlative right) and a duty to save D (where there is a correlative right). Arguably, E ought to save the 10,000 and ought not honor D's right to have E save his life. Suppose that the 10,000 even have a right that he save them at small cost to himself. Then it may be true that E should fulfill the right that is less stringent by the measure of how much he personally must suffer to meet it rather than fulfill D's right, which is very stringent by the measure of how much he must do to meet it.

So far, we have seen that the greater good may take precedence over a right just insofar as we compare these two factors, but whether we are required to do what brings about the greater good can depend on how bringing it about would affect us. This is because considering the two factors of an agent's personal good and the greater good, it is often supererogatory for him to produce the greater good. But now we can ask, if someone is not obligated to make great efforts to bring about the greater good that can trump a right, why is he obligated to make such great efforts in order to accord someone that right?[63] There are some things one can be required to make a great effort to do, even if one cannot be required to make a great effort to maximize the good. These might be considered minimal, crucial aspects of morality, or else agreements that one has undertaken voluntarily, with advance warning and with reliance by others. Yet, if one wishes, one may sometimes maximize the good rather than do what one can be required to make a great effort to do. So, even if E is not obligated to give up his life to save the 10,000, and he may save the 10,000 instead of D, he may also be obligated to give up his life to save D when doing this does not interfere with his saving the 10,000. D's right can be stringent relative to E's efforts (while the greater good is not stringent relative to E's efforts), but D's right is not stringent relative to the greater good. This, of course, does not imply that every right could require maximal efforts from the person who is duty-bound. If there is no specific contract to the contrary, for example, your obligation to meet someone for lunch, when his reliance would not be costly to him, could be overridden by the fact that the cost to *you* of doing so is losing your job.

Suppose that, in the circumstances, E knows that if he were to accord D his right, he would actually suffer the loss of his life, which he is obligated to suffer in order to fulfill his duty to D. Suppose further that this same loss is physically required in order to save the 10,000, if E does that alternative act. Does the loss of E's life, ordinarily supererogatory for purposes of saving the 10,000, now become obligatory for that purpose because the loss is no greater than what E will wind up actually suffering in any case if he does his duty? I do not think so; someone might raise a moral objection to being obligated to do for the sake of one end (greater good) something he will merely conscientiously do for another end. Someone may refuse to suffer the large loss for the sake of the greater good per se, though he will bring about the greater good instead of according a right.

However, this does not mean that E is never obligated to give his life as a means of saving the 10,000. Suppose that E can save the 10,000 at a small cost to himself if he abandons D. Alternatively, if he takes a more dangerous route that will cost him his life, he can save both the 10,000 and D. Suppose he really owes as much as his life to satisfying D's right. Then if he wishes to save the 10,000, he must choose the more dangerous route, I believe. The fact that he would produce a great good that could override D's right will not excuse him from fulfilling the duty to D at the maximal obligatory cost. In this case, E gives his life only indirectly for saving the 10,000; given his choice to save them, he must do so in a way that fulfills his duty to D, given that this is possible. (Of course, if E sees that the actual cost to him of saving D will have to rise above what it would otherwise have been had he not also chosen to save the 10,000, he may decide not to save the 10,000.)

C. Conflicts of Rights

1. TYPES OF CONFLICTS

If rights can conflict among themselves, this suggests that even when a right cannot be granted, it is nevertheless a real right, not just a factor that has to be considered in determining what rights there are.[64,65] It has been claimed that rights conflict only because the duties to which they give rise conflict.[66] However, suppose that two people have rights to medicine when there is only one indivisible portion available, but no third party has a duty to provide either with the medicine. It seems here that the rights conflict, but no one need have a duty that conflicts with any other duty. The conflict arises because each rightholder is at liberty to use the medicine in virtue of his right to it, and yet each has a duty to abstain from its use (correlative to the right each has to exclude the other). These duties to abstain are not in conflict (since both can abstain simultaneously); rather, the liberty and the duty that each has are in conflict.

When rights conflict because duties that are correlative to them conflict, the duties can be in one agent who cannot fulfill them both. We can call this our "agent-relative conflict." There can be such conflicts because there is a conflict of negative rights with negative rights when one agent who is, for example, in charge of a runaway trolley headed to five must decide how to direct it—toward killing A or toward killing B.[67] There can be conflicts of negative rights with positive rights, as when an agent must decide whether to harm someone in order to fulfill an obligation to aid someone else. There can be conflicts of positive rights with positive rights, as when an agent owes aid to ten different people and can help only one.

We can also understand rights as in conflict when different agents are responsible for fulfilling correlative duties. We can call it an "agent-neutral conflict" when the following is true: If one agent will meet the requirement of the rightholder to whom he is obligated (by way of negative or positive rights), another agent will not meet the requirement of the rightholder to whom he is obligated.

A particular type of agent-neutral conflict arises when an agent must transgress a negative right to prevent another agent from violating negative rights. In this case, the second agent will fail to do his part in satisfying rights no matter what happens, but the rightholders he fails will not suffer the violation of their rights if the first agent intervenes. Notice that, in this case, from the agent-relative perspective, the first agent faces a conflict between fulfilling a negative duty and helping someone else avoid the violation of his negative right. If such help is covered by a positive right for assistance, from the agent-relative point of view there is a conflict between a negative right and a positive right, even while it is a conflict between a negative right and a negative right from the agent-neutral point of view. All of these types of conflicts can occur between rights involving the same interests or involving different interests, for example, less and more important interests.[68]

2. CONFLICTS AND STRINGENCY

a. How should we resolve the conflicts? It might be claimed that we should decide on the basis, first, of the stringency of the rights involved (that is, whichever right is stronger takes precedence) and then, given that their stringency is the same, on the number of rights that will or will not be fulfilled. Again (as in earlier sections of this chapter), we are asked to measure the stringency of rights. Thomson suggests that the stringency of rights is a function of the importance of the interests they protect.[69] She further suggests that, when we face a conflict of rights, at least in an agent-relative conflict, we should accord the one that would involve the more important interest, and where interests are the same we should accord the greater number of rights.

But it has already been argued above that one should accept that the stringency of a right may be out of proportion to the importance of the interest it protects. So, for example, suppose that a negative right not to have his arm cut off protects person A against everyone, and a positive right to assistance from her bodyguard protects the life of B. If interests were the only measure of the stringency of rights (even if not a full account of the ground of rights), it would be permissible for the bodyguard to take off A's arm if doing this were the only way to fulfill his duty to save B's life. But this is impermissible. Indeed, Thomson makes use of the impermissibility of doing this to argue that there are no positive rights to assistance. But it is clear that there can at least be contractual positive rights to assistance between a bodyguard and his client.[70] So, I think one must conclude from this case that the stringency of rights is not only a function of the interests at stake, but also of the type of right and the way in which its nonfulfillment would treat the person. The bodyguard may, however, fulfill the positive duty to save his client's life, even if this means that he leaves another client to lose her arm, failing in his positive duty to that other client. (Still, it would be an oversimplification to say that negative rights are more stringent than positive rights, especially when the importance of interests is held constant. For example, a bodyguard might have a positive duty, correlative to his clients' positive rights to have their lives saved, to redirect an out-of-control trolley from killing five of his clients toward killing one other person instead.)[71]

Similarly, in a case that seems to involve a conflict of negative rights, the stringency of rights is not merely a function of the interest they protect. Suppose that we could stop a runaway trolley from killing five people either (a) by redirecting it onto a track where it will kill one person, or (b) by pushing another person in the way of the trolley when we know that this will (only) paralyze him. Even though the interest at stake in the latter case is less than that in the former, it may be permissible to do the former and not the latter, thereby infringing at least a general right to life rather than a right not to be caused paralysis.[72]

Finally, it seems possible that right A could come with explicit assurances that it will not be overridden, even if the agent faces a conflict between according it and according right B, which protects a weightier interest than does right A. It seems possible for such an assurance to sometimes generate a valid commitment to accord the right involving the lesser interest.[73]

I conclude that, at least in agent-relative conflicts, even if we should choose to accord the most stringent right, this will not necessarily be the one protecting the most important interest. In agent-neutral conflicts, it seems clearly incorrect that we should resolve conflicts by according the most stringent right. For this would imply that A should take off someone's arm in order to stop B from killing someone else. Here, the relative stringency of the rights may not be in dispute—the right not to be killed may be stronger than the right not to have one's arm removed—and yet we should not decide what to do on the basis of this fact.

b. Without telling us what gives rise to the stringency of a right, Waldron suggests a method for measuring rights' stringency that involves agent-neutral conflicts. He takes it that we might measure the strength of the right not to be tortured relative to the right to free speech by noting that we would not torture someone no matter how much free speech would be lost through the acts of others if we did not. This is evidence that the right not to be tortured is much stronger than the right to free speech, he thinks.

There are, I believe, significant problems with this procedure for measuring the strength of rights. We should not compare the strength of two rights, R_1 and R_2, per se, by comparing (a) the strength of the prohibition on causing the transgression of R_1 as a means with (b) the letting happen of the transgression of R_2 as a side effect (if we do not infringe R_1). The variation in the contextual features that are associated with R_1 and R_2 (means versus side effect, causing versus letting happen) may account for the impermissibility of transgressing R_1 to stop transgressions of R_2.[74] (We noted above that the permissibility of torturing would involve morality endorsing a less inviolable status for persons; by contrast, the permissibility of letting free speech be violated rather than torturing does not endorse the permissibility of violating free speech.) So with these different contextual factors, we would not be measuring the weight of R_1 versus R_2 per se. Yet this is how the procedure Waldron uses works.

Using Waldron's procedure, one could even prove that R_1 is stronger than R_1, for it may be impermissible to transgress one person's right not to be tortured as a means to stop any number of other people from being tortured. Yet, it is clear that R_1 cannot be stronger than itself. The procedure could also "show" that R_1 is stronger than R_2 and R_2 is stronger than R_1. For one may have a right not to be tortured to death (R_1) to save people from having their right not to be killed without being tortured (R_2) violated, and one may also have a right not to be killed without torture (R_2) to save people from having their right not to be tortured to death (R_1) violated. But it would entail a contradiction to say that R_1 is stronger than R_2 and R_2 is stronger than R_1.

c. The correct way, I think, to test for the relative stringency of R_1 and R_2 is to test them in cases that equalize all factors in the contexts of the two rights. Here are some tests—all in agent-relative conflict contexts—that at least satisfy this principle of equalization:[75]

(1) *The Choice Test.* If the only way to achieve a certain goal is to transgress R_1 or to transgress R_2, as means to the goal, which right would one sooner transgress, given that one has to transgress one of them? (This test leaves it open that we do something wrong whatever we do.) The suggestion is that one should transgress the weaker right, when all other things are equal.[76]

(2) *The Goal Test.* How important a goal must one have for it to be permissible to transgress R_1 as a means to the goal? to transgress R_2? The suggestion is that transgressing the stronger right requires a more important goal, when all other things are equal.[77] (This test corresponds to the test discussed in section IVA: How great a good is necessary to override a right, at least if overriding the right is a means to the great good?)

(3) *The Effort Test.* How much effort would one be morally required to make (or how great a loss would one be morally required to suffer) (a) to avoid transgressing the right as a side effect, (b) to accord the right, or (c) to compensate or undo the effects of the transgression? (In this test, [a] and [b] correspond to the test discussed in section IVB: How much must someone do to fulfill the duty correlated with the right?) The suggestion is that the stronger right will require more effort.

The Choice Test is in one way more revealing than the other two, because two rights may differ in strength and yet the weaker one be so strong that maximal efforts are needed to avoid transgressing it and maximally important goals are needed to justify transgressing it. Remember, however, that at least in agent-neutral contexts, the measure of the strengths of the rights per se does not determine what to do.

There are at least three problems with these tests, however. First, the Effort Test and the Choice Test may give conflicting answers (as was emphasized in section IVB). For example, a bodyguard may be required by contract to make a much greater sacrifice to prevent the paralysis of one of his clients than he would be required to make to save the life of another client who has a right against him to be helped. Yet, it might be correct for him to choose to abandon the client who will be paralyzed in order to save the one who will die. So, the Choice Test says that the second is the stronger right and the Effort Test says that the first is the stronger right.

Second, the Effort Test and the Goal Test may give conflicting answers (as we saw above). A bodyguard may be required to make a much greater effort to save one client's life than he would be required to make to fulfill the right of a second client, service to whom will save 10,000 lives of group B. Yet, the goal of saving 5,000 lives of group A could override the first client's right but not override the second client's right, service to whom will save 10,000 lives.[78] So, by the Goal Test, the second is the stronger right, and by the Effort Test, the first is the stronger right.

The third problem with the tests is that the use of these tests to measure the stringency of rights depends on an assumption of transitivity: For example, if R_1 is not overridden by avoiding loss x and R_2 is, then R_1 will override R_2. Yet it is always possible, due to a particular interaction between R_1 and R_2, that this is not so. Hence, these tests are at most prima facie indications of the stringency of a right in comparison to another right. For example, suppose that person A has a right to assistance even if it costs us a great deal, but person B has a right to assistance only if it costs us a bit. Even if we can say that the claim of A to aid is more stringent than the claim of B, when each is considered in isolation, it is possible that when the two are in conflict, we should grant B his right at low cost to us. This might be because B is the parent of A, and childrens rights should never be served before their parents rights.[79]

In using these tests (or others like them), it is important to realize that just because R_1 and R_2 sometimes give the same result when we apply the stringency tests to them, this does not mean that they are per se as stringent. We cannot prove a universal truth that R_1 is as strong as R_2 by, for example, showing that in some equalized contexts we must spend the same amount to avoid transgressing each. For as the cost of not transgressing goes up, R_1 may require it and R_2 not. But if R_1 yields a different result from R_2 in even one test case, and R_2 offers no comparable different result from R_1, then we have evidence that R_1 differs in strength from R_2 per se. (Only one counterexample is needed to deny a universal truth.)[80]

d. Waldron offers yet another way to determine the relative strength of rights. He says that if we take a right seriously, we must take it to generate associated duties, in addition to the primary duty not to violate it. For example, in the case of the duty not to torture, there are associated duties to punish torturers, to educate against torturing, and so on. But surely, he says, all of the duties associated with the right not to be tortured are not stronger than any duties associated with free speech. For example, duties to punish violations of free speech might be stronger than the duties to educate against torture (as measured, let us say, by how many resources we should devote to each). But if some duties associated with the stronger right can be outweighed by some duties associated with the weaker right, then, he suggests, the stronger right is not so strong after all and might, after all, be outweighed by sufficiently important considerations stemming from the weaker right. (Here he moves backward from the weakness of some duties associated with the original right to the weakness of the original right. This argument has a reductio form. That is, if we assume that a right has great strength, we can show that it does not have such great strength.)

I do not think that Waldron's argument, whose ultimate goal is to determine the strength of a right, is correct, though one of its points seems correct. Does taking rights seriously imply taking associated duties—aside from the primary one of not deliberately transgressing the right—as seriously? When Ronald Dworkin said that some rights are trumps over utility, could he have meant to imply that we must suffer the same loss of utility in order to prevent someone from violating those rights (or to facilitate the exercise of the right) as we must suffer rather than deliberately violate those rights?[81] If he did, the claim that rights are trumps would be implausible.[82] It is a merit in Waldron's discussion that he denies that all duties associated with a right are equally strong.[83] Many of these duties are correlative to positive rights associated with some of the negative rights that are trumps, for example, the right to police protection to prevent killings. These are real positive rights even if they are not trumps over utility in the same way as the negative right from which they derive.[84]

As I noted above, I think that this point gives us reason to deny that when a right is present it is because an interest in a creature capable of having rights is sufficient to give rise to a duty. For example, if the interest in not being tortured were sufficient to give rise to a duty not to torture, then one would have a right that any behavior that has a high probability of resulting in torture be equally prohibited (given the same cost of doing so), including not helping to prevent torture. But if the right not to be tortured is also about morality ruling out the treatment of persons in a certain particular manner leading to torture, then we could account for why there would be both a very strong right not to be tortured that trumps the foreseen loss of utility if we do not torture and not as strong a right that torture be prevented. One may even have a right against an act of torture that is known to have a low probability of success and not have as strong a right to aid that has a high probability of preventing certain-to-occur torture. Hence, not forgoing as much good to prevent tortures as we forgo rather than torture is not inconsistent. This is just the thesis of non-consequentialism—that the state of affairs resulting (e.g., interests that are affected) can be the same, and one way of the state of affairs coming about is prohibited and another (i.e., not aiding) is not prohibited—as applied to the violation of rights.[85]

However, it is a mistake in Waldron's argument to conclude from the fact that duties associated with a supposedly strong right can be weak, and also outweighed by some duties associated with a supposedly weaker right, that the strong right is not so strong after all. Strong subsidiary rights may be a mark of a strong right, but their presence is not necessary for the right to be strong. It is also a mistake to conclude that preventing some violation of the weaker right could, after all, outweigh deliberately transgressing the stronger one. If the manner in which the interest is affected is important, the deliberate transgression might not be outweighed, either in agent-relative or agent-neutral conflicts, even if other ways of affecting the same interest can be outweighed by concern for the weaker right.

For example, A's right not to be pushed in harm's way when this will cost him his leg may be weaker than B's right not to be pushed in harm's way when he will be killed. But in discussing the Trolley Case, we have seen that the former right is stronger than B's right not to be killed as a consequence of redirecting the trolley in order to save a greater number of people. Though the interest in being alive is stronger than the interest in not losing a leg, the different manners of treatment help to determine the strength (or even existence) of the respective rights. But this does not show that we may push B in harm's way when he will be killed in order to prevent A from being deliberately put in harm's way when this will cost him his leg.[86] I conclude that this argument of Waldron's, which involves considering subsidiary duties, is not the way to show that a right cannot be strong enough to trump the protection of different rights.

3. MINIMIZING RIGHTS VIOLATIONS BY VIOLATING RIGHTS?

Let us consider in some detail how the considerations that I have highlighted in discussing conflicts of rights might play out in a much-discussed type of case involving conflicts from the agent-neutral perspective between negative rights. We can imagine that unless agent 1 kills Joe, agent 2 will kill Jim and Susan.[87] Waldron once claimed that if we have an interest-based theory of rights and we are concerned about rights, then this sort of conflict of negative rights should lead agent 1 to kill Joe.[88] This is so, even if concern for rights would not imply that someone should kill Joe in order to save Susan and Jim from a fatal natural disaster. (It was the latter sorts of cases that we considered when discussing conflicts between rights and the greater good in section IV.) Hence a distinction is being drawn between transgressing a right to promote the greater good and transgressing a right to minimize violation of comparable rights. Some have even claimed that it is paradoxical or irrational not to kill Joe, if one is concerned with rights. Waldron said that if agent 1 must not kill Joe regardless of what the other agent will do, this will be because we accept a duty-based rather than a rights-based theory. The theory will be duty-based, he said, because we focus on the significance for an agent of killing and see it as something he must not do; we do not focus on the interests of the potential victims who are protected by rights.

This is like the model that I discussed in section IV A(5) above, which attempts to derive a constraint on the agent from "inside (the agent) out (to the victim)" rather than from "outside (in the victim's right) in (to the agent)."[89] I think that this model is wrong, for reasons similar to those I have given in sections IVA(5) and (6), as well as elsewhere.[90] I will allow myself to briefly recapitulate these reasons in order to show the relevance in this context. First, note that it is not clear that a duty-based account that focuses on what it means for an agent to kill would always tell agent 1 not to kill when (intuitively) he should not. For if agent 1 has (or will) set a bomb that will kill Jim and Susan unless he now kills Joe, an agent's concern for his not killing might imply that he prevent more of his killings by killing Joe. Yet it seems impermissible for agent 1 to do so.

Second, consider the Art Works Case: If someone loves art, he will be disposed to preserve and not destroy art works. What should this person do if he must destroy one art work in order to prevent someone else from destroying five equally good ones? Presumably, it is permissible for him to destroy one to save the five. This suggests that the constraint on harming persons is not derived from inside the agent out, but from outside her in, since the constraint reflects the kind of entity upon which she would act—a person, not a work of art.

Third, there are, I believe, duty-based views that focus on the quality of an agent's act or state of mind rather than on a victim's right, but these views do not take note of the "agent's mark" on the act, victim, or outcome. For example, the quality of the act or state of mind in which an agent must engage if he kills the one person is repellent. The act would be the agent's if he did it, but it is not essentially it being his rather than someone else's, but what it is in itself, that is repellent. Advocates of this view might claim that the repellant quality of the act can explain why an agent should not kill one person now to save a greater number of people even from the agent's past or future bad acts. However, notice that the explanatory structure of this duty-based constraint would be essentially the same as a rights-based constraint. According to both constraints, one instance of either a duty-type or right-type stands in the way of minimizing misconduct involving many instances of the same duty-type or right-type. If the logic of concern for the duty does not require that we minimize its transgression but simply not transgress it, why should the logic of the concern for the right require that we minimize its transgression?

I believe that a rights-based theory that focuses on the rightholders who are potential victims of rights transgression could require agent 1 not to kill Joe. It is, at least, not irrational or paradoxical to be concerned about rights and yet not minimize rights violations by transgressing rights. The argument for this involves a variation on what was said above (in section IVA[6]) in discussing conflicts of rights and goods (and hence some repetition is called for). If it were permissible for agent 1 to kill Joe in order to prevent the violation of comparable rights in Jim and Susan, this would have to mean that Joe has a weaker negative right not to be killed than if it were impermissible to kill him. (This will be true even if it were permissible to kill him because we would be infringing his right, rather than because he merely had no right not to be killed. A right that could not permissibly be infringed would be stronger.) Since what is true of him is true of everyone else—as we must universalize moral properties had qua being a person—Jim and Susan also would have weaker negative rights. To be protected by weaker negative rights indicates that one is less inviolable and, I think, this indicates that one is a being of less worth. The stronger one's negative right, the more inviolable one is. This inviolability is a status, that is, it tells us what it is impermissible to do to a person; it has nothing necessarily to do with what happens to a person. If Jim and Susan are left to be killed because Joe is not killed, they are violated but they are no less inviolable than is Joe. This is because morality did not endorse the permissibility of killing them; they are wrongfully killed. By contrast, if it had been permissible to kill Joe in order to save Jim and Susan, morality would permit a form of killing and hence endorse reduced inviolability for everyone, expressing the view that each individual is a less important type of being.

Concern for a right can rationally be expressed not by acting as though the right everyone has is weaker, so that it is permissible to minimize the violation of this weaker right, but by acting in accord with the strength of the right. It is important to emphasize that it is a difference in the permissibility of killing, and not any actual killings, that would signal a change in the status of the person. Furthermore, both what it is impermissible to do and the associated degree of inviolability are not legislated by our choosing any given morality; we do not make people inviolable. They either are or are not inviolable. If they are, we should act in accord with this.

If there is a strong negative right, agent 1 could be required not to kill Joe, but not for an essentially agent-focused reason, such as that he should be more concerned with his agency than with the agency of others (or more concerned with his agency now than with his earlier or future agency). Rather, he will be required not to kill Joe for an agent-neutral reason (i.e., a reason that has force for every agent); the high inviolability of any person he comes up against is expressed by a strong negative right protecting persons. Agent 1 should be stopped by the right of any person he would kill, but not because there is anything special about that person (e.g., his being this agent's victim) or because there is anything special for the agent in it being his act that kills. (This is not to deny that it is special for him to be a killer.) The justification I have offered for not minimizing rights violations focuses on the distinction between a person's status (i.e., what it is permissible to do to him, expressing what sort of being he really is) and what happens to a person, and also on the distinction between having a higher and lower status, rather than on the distinction between what I do and what another agent does.

When no interests at all are at stake if rights are protected, it becomes especially clear that a concern for rights alone does not necessarily lead to the minimization of rights violations. Consider the Priest Case. Each priest has a right that I bow to him, simply as a mark of respect. One priest is coming down the road, so I should bow. But behind him are coming five priests. They will have passed beyond the point where I can bow to them, if I bow to the first one. In addition, someone else will fail to bow to all of them, and I could prevent this by not bowing to the first priest. It seems clear that I should fulfill the right of the first priest whom I come across. This case suggests that it might make more sense (even if it would not be right) to transgress a right to protect interests per se (i.e., for the sake of the greater good) rather than out of concern for minimizing violations of the right.[91]

The analysis I have provided of why it is not irrational to refuse to transgress a right in order to minimize such transgressions in others implies that, at a higher level, the agent-neutral conflict between Joe's right not to be killed and the same rights of Jim and Susan disappears to some extent. Suppose that it were significant for each one of them (whether they thought so or not) that he or she is a being worthy of high inviolability. Then, Jim and Susan are the "beneficiaries" of the impermissibility of killing Jim. Of course, they will not benefit in the sense of remaining alive (or in having their right enforced and recognized by people), as he does. And "remaining alive" (and secondarily, the interest in the enforcement and recognition of rights) is presumably the interest that the Interest Theory of Rights sees the negative right as protecting. The conflict in rights disappears to some extent at a higher level, consistent with an Interest Theory of Rights, only if it is in a person's interest to be someone who is worthy of inviolability, to be the sort of entity who truly merits this status. (This involves modifying the notion of interest as an "aspect of well-being.")

But we may reject even this attenuated form of an interest theory. An alternative account of the right (and other fundamental human rights) is that the status to which it gives rise expresses a good that is not so much in a person's interests as it is a good in him (in the sense of worth he has) that makes his interests worth protecting. It might make the world a better place to have in it entities who deserve this status; it might be an honor to those who have the status to have it. But the status is not important primarily because it is in the interest of the person to have it or because it serves (if it does serve) the other interests of the person. On this account, fundamental human rights, at least, are not concerned with protecting a person's interests, but with expressing his nature as a being of a certain sort, one whose interests are worth protecting. They express the worth of the person rather than the worth of what is in the interests of that person, and it is not unimaginable that it will be harder to protect some interests of a person just because of the worth of him as a person.[92] It is still true that at a higher level, the conflict between the rights, so conceived, of Joe and the tandem of Jim and Susan disappears to some extent—the latter two could not have this right, this status, if Joe did not, and this is separate from their having the right enforced.

Another way of putting this point is in terms of what rights exclude as reasons for overriding them. If people have high inviolability in certain respects, then the rights expressing that inviolability will specifically exclude certain factors as reasons for infringing the rights. For example, a right expressing high inviolability of life could hold (or imply) that "the person's right not to be killed will not be over-ridden even for the sake of saving many more people from being killed." This is what Raz would call a right functioning as an "exclusionary reason." Suppose that Jim, Joe, and Susan each has this right, but Jim and Susan will have their right violated. The permissibility of violating Joe for the sake of the right they all share would be self-defeating. That is, it would be self-defeating for it to be permissible to maximize protection of the right by violating Joe for the sake of Jim and Susan, because the right specifically says not to do this. The right could not be protected by it being permissible to do what in essence denies that anyone has this right. This would be a "futilitarianism" of rights.[93]

The analysis I have provided here of negative rights in agent-neutral conflicts can be applied to other rights, such as the right to free speech, when transgressing the right in one person would prevent its transgression in others. Indeed, we can see a contrast between the outcome this analysis yields and the outcome yielded by Waldron's analysis of conflicts among free speech rights.[94] Waldron considers the case of a conflict in the rights of free speech of the Nazis and the Communists. The Nazis want to speak freely and if this has a predictable effect, the Communists will lose their right to speak freely. (Waldron must mean that the Communists will lose their legal right to free speech, for nothing the Nazis could do would make the Communists lose their moral right to free speech.[95] Hence, I will assume that, in Waldron's case, the Communists' legal right to free speech will be violated.) May we interfere with Nazi free speech for the sake of the right of free speech itself, that is, to prevent the legal right to free speech of the Communists from being violated? Waldron gives three reasons for saying yes: (1) The speeches they claim the right to make would bring an end to the form of life (i.e., all exercising the right to free speech) in which the idea of free speech is conceived; (2) the content and tendency of the speech is incompatible with the very right asserted; and (3) to count as a genuine instance of free speech, a person's contribution must be related to his opponent in a way that makes room for both to exercise free speech.[96]

Waldron's views, it seems to me, yield a weaker form of the right to free speech. Perhaps such a weaker right is required if we are to achieve a goal of maintaining the exercise of some right to free speech for people overall. But if each person has a stronger right to free speech, this right could (on the model I presented above) exclude as a reason to limit it protection of the exercise of free speech. That is, the strong right can represent a status that each has as a free-speaker, even if respect for this status results in some other people (who still have the very same status) not speaking freely because their rights are improperly violated. While it might be wrong to exercise this strong right to stop others' free speech—there is a well-worn distinction between exercising a right and doing the right thing—and while we might infringe (i.e., permissibly transgress) the right for the sake of a particular good, namely, more people actually exercising some sort of right to speak, this is not the same as justifying transgressions of the right out of concern for the stronger right to free speech itself. If it is permissible to infringe the right for the good of people speaking freely, all I am claiming is that we are not thereby acting out of concern for, or protecting, the stronger right.[97]

4. *EX ANTE* PERSPECTIVES

Cases that involve conflicts of rights (or conflicts between rights and interests) among individuals can, from a sufficiently *ex ante* perspective, be made to seem like cases in which individuals would, in a *hypothetical* agreement, have alienated their strong rights in order to promote their own interests. To see this, consider again the case of killing one person (in a way that is ordinarily considered a violation of a right) for the sake of saving five from being killed. There are (at least) two types of *ex ante* perspectives we can take on this. From either one, any person considers that he might be either the person who will be sacrificed or one of the five who will be saved by the sacrifice. In *ex ante* 1, each is thought to have a small probability of being a person who in his *actual* life never has any chance of being one of those to be saved but will certainly be the one sacrificed, and a large probability of being a person who in his actual life never has any chance of being the one sacrificed but will certainly be one of the saved. In *ex ante* 2, each is a person who in his *actual* life will have both a small probability of being the one sacrificed and a large probability of being one of the five saved. I think that the *ex ante* 2 perspective offers a stronger ground for arguing that it is rational *ex ante* to alienate rights not to be sacrificed in such a situation. For it is more difficult to impose a loss on a person who in his *actual* life never himself had a chance of benefiting from an arrangement that now costs him something, even if he is conceived of as having had, *ex ante*, a chance of being a person who actually certainly stands to benefit (which is true in *ex ante* 1).

From each of the *ex ante* perspectives, there are two attitudes to take toward the two different positions—the sacrificed or the saved—that might be occupied. In taking the first attitude, each person conceives of the position of the sacrificed as one that *he* himself has a small probability of falling into. (This can be true either through his being someone who in his actual life has the small probability of being sacrificed or through being someone who has the small probability of being a person who in his actual life will certainly be sacrificed.) This way of thinking allows each to imagine that no one may actually fall into the position of being sacrificed. However, in fact, we know that someone will definitely fall into that position. So, each should rather take the second attitude, which involves each thinking of the position of the sacrificed person as one in which he himself not only runs a risk of being, but as a position that some person will actually occupy. Indeed, perhaps he should consider only that it is a position that some person will actually occupy.[98]

How should each of us conceive of that actually unlucky person, if there were an *ex ante* agreement to kill him in order to save five people, at a time when he will refuse to be killed? We should conceive of him as someone who (in *ex ante* 2) was willing to have an actual life in which he will run a risk of being killed (at a time when he would be unwilling to be killed) in order to maximize his own chances of not being killed. (This is because he has a higher chance of being killed as me of the five, if he is not willing to run this risk.) People take risks of death all the time so as to increase their probability of survival, as well as for other lesser goods. For example, some people take a risk of dying from a drug's side effect by taking a drug that has a much higher probability of saving their lives. But in our case, unlike this case, the death would be imposed deliberately at a time when we know that it can no longer be in the interest of the person to risk it. It was just in her interest *ex ante* to run the risk of being put in this position later.[99]

Could we defend retention of rights against the rationality of such *ex ante* alienation by hypothetical agreement. One approach is to invalidate the relevance of *ex ante* reasoning for moral conclusions as a whole. On this view, we must decide how to treat a person simply by considering what we would do to her and how this compares with what we would otherwise do to others. The fact that each person has the same probability of being a person who will be treated in a certain way and that each maximizes her chance of satisfying her interests in living on by the permission to treat a person in that way has no bearing on deciding whether that form of treatment is morally permissible.[100] (The fact that we each ran a small risk of being a slave in order to maximize the good in our lives by having slaves does not justify slavery.)

Another (related) approach is to argue that the right not to be treated in certain ways is not alienable *ex ante*, whether for the sake of maximizing the chances of satisfying one's own interests or for fundamentally altruistic reasons (e.g., because one is afraid that one will lack the courage to sacrifice oneself for others at a later time though one, in principle, wants to act in that way). This is because, it is claimed, the right against such treatment at a time when one does not will it expresses the worth of the person, which is the ground of the importance of promoting people's interests to begin with. This leaves it open that it is permissible, at the time the loss is to be imposed (or the nearest conscious time to it), to willingly allow oneself to be sacrificed for the sake of others. (The latter is an act that is more appropriately described as waiving a right to not be sacrificed rather than alienating it.) Such a willing act of self-sacrifice contrasts with an unwilling sacrifice, which is the final step in a strategy to maximize one's own (or others', if one is an *ex ante* altruist) interests *ex ante*.[101]

There is at least one problem with this approach that designates the right not to be sacrificed for others as inalienable. For one can show that this very same right which is not alienable *ex ante* in one context may be alienable *ex ante* in another. And it seems that whether it is alienable or not is a function not of how many people would suffer a loss comparable to the loss suffered by the person sacrificed, but rather, of how much worse would be the fate of any person who stands to benefit from that sacrifice.[102]

Consider, for example, that it might be wrong to agree *ex ante* (or act as though one had agreed) to cut off someone's arm at a time when he is not willing to give it in order to save the arm of each of five people (from a natural disaster or from being cut off by a villain), even though such an agreement would maximize everyone's chances of keeping an arm. Does this mean that the right not to have one's arm cut off against one's will in order to help others is inalienable *ex ante*? To help answer this question, consider the Two Diseases Case,[103] in which there are two diseases in a community. One, the Arm Disease, causes one and only one arm per person to fall off and is very prevalent among a part of the population whose members we can identify beforehand. The second, the Death Disease, is very rare in a different part of the population that we can identify as susceptible to it. The only thing that cures the Arm Disease is a serum made by taking the finger of a person who was susceptible to the Death Disease but did not get it, and the only cure for the Death Disease is a serum made by taking the arm of a person who was susceptible to the Arm Disease but did not get it.

I believe that it would be in the interest, *ex ante*, of all involved to make an agreement to provide the resources necessary to make the serums at the time they are needed and that enforcement of this agreement would not be morally wrong. This is so, even though this is (in part) an *ex ante* I type of agreement, because actual people will know the disease to which they are susceptible. There is a high incidence of the Arm Disease, so there is a high probability that the people who were once susceptible to the Death Disease will lose a finger in exchange for having avoided the small risk of a big loss to them, that is, death. There is a low incidence of the Death Disease, so there is a low probability that a person who was once susceptible to the Arm Disease will lose an arm (ultimately) in exchange for having avoided a large risk of losing an arm.

This is a case in which an Arm Disease person would have to pay with the very item he had attempted to increase his probability of keeping (i.e., his arm) at a time when it is known that it is no longer in his interest to do so (for he no longer faces the threat of the Arm Disease), having received only the benefits of the increased probability of protection from the Arm Disease. In this case, the arm would be sacrificed to prevent an even greater loss (death) to another person. That is, what the person who is sacrificed loses is significantly less than what the person who is saved would lose if he were not saved. There is also another factor that may be crucial to making the agreement permissible: There is actual reciprocity between the two groups, even if not between any person who is sacrificed and her beneficiary.

Finally, note that the way in which a transgression of a negative right would come about seems crucial to whether or not a mere greater number being saved from the *same* loss can justify an *ex ante* agreement leading to a transgression. In this regard, consider the Ambulance Cases. In Ambulance Case I,[104] a community has to decide whether to have an ambulance. If it has one, it will save many lives that would otherwise be lost, but a small number of people who otherwise would not have died prematurely will be hit by the ambulance as it races to the hospital. Indeed, we may imagine that (for some reason) it is known to be only people who would not need the ambulance to save their lives who will be hit by it. At the time of the agreement, however, no one knows whether she is such a person. This is an *ex ante* 1 type of case. Is it permissible for the community to have the ambulance? Perhaps so, and even more certainly, it would be permissible in *ex ante* 2 type of cases, where each person knows that she has a chance of being hit or of being saved. In this case, preventing a greater number of equally great losses (deaths) seems sufficient reason to introduce the ambulance.

Now consider Ambulance Case 2. The same community is deciding the rules for the performance of the ambulance. More lives overall will be saved if it is agreed that when the ambulance is on its way to the hospital with many people whose lives are to be saved, and delay would be fatal to them, it will not stop—even though it could—to keep from running over someone in its way. Should the community agree to this? Another possibility, in Ambulance Case 3, is for the community to agree to install new brakes that (somehow) make it impossible for the ambulance to stop before hitting someone whenever more people are in the ambulance who could be saved than would be hit in the road, and delay would be fatal to the former. These agreements seem impermissible.

People's right not to be killed could be presented as a reason for not introducing vehicles that might kill them, if no benefit would come from having such vehicles. But in Ambulance Case 1, the benefit, coupled with the fact that no one does anything to cause harm aside from running vehicles justified for the sake of benefit even when there is a risk of unavoidable harm, seems to defeat an objection based on a right not to be killed. In Ambulance Case 2, by contrast, the community would sanction doing what will (as a side effect) kill someone when it could easily be avoided (albeit, at the opportunity cost of saving more lives). This way in which the death would come about makes the objection from the right not to be killed appropriate, and the greater number of those who will die is insufficient to override it. In Ambulance Case 3, making it impossible to easily avoid killing someone because this will save more lives seems similarly ruled out by the right not to be killed.[105]

NOTES

This chapter is based on my "Rights" in *The Oxford Handbook of Jurisprudence & Philosophy of Law*, ed. J. Coleman and S. Shapiro, 476–513 (New York: Oxford University Press, 2002). Part of its point is to see if nonconsequentialist distinctions drawn independently of rights also bear on the theory of rights.

1. For the idea of exclusionary reasons, see Joseph Raz, *The Morality of Freedom* (Oxford: Oxford University Press, 1986).

2. Consider the following case as possible intuitive support for the existence of group rights: Suppose that members of a group (who identified with the group) have been killed

unjustly because they were members of the group. They have no direct family descendants. Had they or their descendants lived on, they would have had a right to compensation for persecution. Would it be unreasonable to argue that the group to which they belonged has a right to receive the compensation (just as familial descendants would have) and a duty to use it for other group members? This is a case in which the compensation is owed to the group; it is not merely a matter of it being just that they get a fair share of money. For the group might be very well off, having more than its share of goods. Indeed, if the members of the group did not have a right to the money, it would be morally wrong to give it to the group, because the money would be better spent on others.

3. That a factor can be a reason in one context but not a reason in another, I call the Principle of Contextual Interaction. I discussed it in chapter 1. For more on this, see my *Morality, Mortality*, vol. 2: *Rights, Duties, and Status* (New York: Oxford University Press, 1996).

4. W. N. Hohfeld, *Fundamental Legal Conceptions* (New Haven, CT: Yale University Press, 1923).

5. Joel Feinberg, "The Nature and Value of Rights," *Journal of Value Inquiry* 4 (1970): 263–267.

6. Doctors were very willing to think of themselves as having duties (for example, in virtue of the Hippocratic Oath or stemming from their professional role) and to think of their patients as being the object of these duties. However, they resisted the idea of patients having claim-rights against them, and this implies that they resisted the idea of having a duty (owed) to the patient.

7. Thomas Scanlon, in his *What We Owe to Each Other* (Cambridge, MA: Harvard University Press, 1998), emphasizes both owing things to others and the distinction between acting wrongly and wronging someone. Yet he does not connect these notions to a theory of rights, as I believe he should. I also believe that the account he provides for "wrong" is better understood as an account of wronging. However, suppose it is possible to wrong someone even if we do not act wrongly. (This was suggested in chapters 5 and 7.) If we did not act wrongly, could we still be failing to give someone what is owed to him? If so, then acting wrongly is not the only one way of wronging. It would be a sufficient but not a necessary condition of wronging. For discussion of these issues, see chapter 16.

8. Judith Jarvis Thomson, *The Realm of Rights* (Cambridge, MA: Harvard University Press, 1990).

9. Duties correlative to rights might also be overridden by supererogatory acts. On this, see chapter 1, my *Morality, Mortality*, vol. 2; and below.

10. It might be said that the existence of a right to compensation does not show that one had a right that was infringed (or violated). Rather it shows that one has a right that is composed of disjuncts. For example, one has a right either to have one's car or to be compensated if it is taken in an emergency. If either condition is met, there is no right that has been infringed (or violated). But is it not because someone still has the right to his car that his interests may take precedence in a conflict. For example, if we may take A's car to rush B to the hospital, this does not mean that A does not have rights over the car in the circumstance. For if A were in equal need of getting to the hospital and we could only take one person, he should have priority as it is still his car. By contrast, if A loses his rights in the car when B is in great need, we should only toss a coin to decide between them with A getting componsation if not the car. Thomson distinguished between infringing a right (permissible) and violating a right (impermissible). I shall also distinguish between permissibly transgressing a right (infringing) and impermissibly transgressing a right (violating). So "transgressing" is ncutral as between being permissible and being impermissible. Also note that violating a right is different from violating a person. The latter is some sort of physical intrusion, regardless of whether it is permissible or impermissible.

For Thomson's distinction, see her "Ruminations on Rights," reprinted in her *Rights, Restitution, and Risk: Essays in Moral Theory*, ed. W. A. Parent (Cambridge, MA: Harvard University Press, 1986); and her *The Realm of Rights*.

11. In the law, it is more common to use "has a right" as equivalent to "must accord a right." See also n. 65.

12. See my discussion in chapter 7.

13. Given that this is Thomson's view (see her *The Realm of Rights*, p. 94, n. 7), it is odd that she claims (ibid., p. 96) that if one pays compensation, it is inappropriate to feel guilt at not having carried out the duty strictly correlative to the right. Might not guilt be appropriate because one has not carried out that part of the right whose fulfillment has pride of place?

14. I owe this point to David Enoch.

15. H. L. A. Hart, "Bentham on Legal Rights," in *Oxford Essays in Jurisprudence*, 2d series, ed. A. W. B. Simpson (Oxford: Oxford University Press, 1973), pp. 171–201.

16. Samuel Scheffler, *The Rejection of Consequentialism* (New York: Oxford University Press, 1982). We discussed prerogatives in chapter 1.

17. David Enoch also argues that even if I have a moral duty to you to refrain from some act, I can still have a moral right (at least against everyone but you) not to do the duty. On his view, I may even have a right against you to decide whether I will carry out my duty to you and, hence, a moral right not to do my duty to you (though the duty is correlative to your right that I do something). See David Enoch, "A Right to Violate One's Duty," *Law and Philosophy* 21 (2002): 355–84.

18. Joseph Raz says that rights give rise to duties; duties do not give rise to rights (see *The Morality of Freedom*). But in this case, a duty does seem to give rise to a right.

19. In addition, if a general right is connected with several directed duties (each of which involves a particular correlative right), then at least the general right seems prior to the duties. That general rights can give rise to new duties, Raz sees as the dynamic character of rights, and he points to this as grounds for thinking that rights are prior to duties. See Raz, *The Morality of Freedom*, p. 171. He says that rights can give rise to new duties that do not now exist though we know that the right exists. For example, if someone has a right to an education, this may give rise, he thinks, to many duties (not just one) correlative to it; which ones it does give rise to may vary with time and place. Rights can be dynamic in this way when the object of the right is more general than the specific duties it generates. (This is also connected to Raz's point that not all ways in which an interest, such as having an education, can be promoted give rise to duties.) But notice that when the general right gives rise to these duties, it seems that it will simultaneously give rise to subsidiary rights that are strictly correlative to (and, for all that the dynamic character of rights implies, may be no more than) the directed duties.

20. Hart, "Bentham on Legal Rights."

21. See Joel Feinberg, "Voluntary Euthanasia and the Inalienable Right to Life," *Philosophy & Public Affairs* 7 (1978): 113.

22. This point was raised by Peter Graham.

23. Feinberg, "The Nature and Value of Rights."

24. Raz, *The Morality of Freedom*, p. 166. Raz affiliates himself with a broadly Benthamite theory of rights. However, note that Bentham's theory does not require that an interest in the (intended) beneficiary be sufficient for a duty in order that there be a right, even if the right is lodged in the beneficiary. Bentham's theory leaves it open that A's directive that B promote C's interest is necessary—in addition to C's interest—to give rise to C's right (on the assumption that the theory is not wrong to locate the right in C). So Raz's theory (which points to someone's interest as sufficient to ground a duty) seems to ignore the possibility that an agent can, in virtue

of having a certain power, endow someone with a right, assuming that the recipient has the properties that make him capable of being a rightholder at all. Another contrast with Bentham will be noted in the text below.

25. Raz, *The Morality of Freedom*, p. 183.

26. But recall from my discussion above that I also believe that it is possible to wrong someone without acting wrongly.

27. The same is true of Feinberg. Indeed, when Feinberg contrasts a right with a duty, he contrasts a duty that is owed to someone with other duties. His defense of the view that rights are prior to correlative duties is thus weak. See Feinberg, "The Nature and Value of Rights."

28. Joseph Raz, "Rights and Individual Well-Being," in his collection *Ethics in the Public Domain* (New York: Oxford University Press, 1994), p. 55.

29. David Enoch's suggestion.

30. This example, modified, is owed to Larry Temkin.

31. Presumably, one does not have a right to others actually speaking—though this is what is really in any given person's strongest interest, on Raz's analysis—since others would then have a duty to speak.

32. Thomas Nagel presents a similar argument in his "Personal Rights and Public Space," *Philosophy & Public Affairs* 24 (1995), 83–107.

33. The rights that are due to the worth of the person and his authority over himself (and resultant authority to limit others' behavior toward him) are presumably rights that all persons come to have just in virtue of being persons and are (at least) fundamental rights of human persons. (Though recall that this does not necessarily mean that all human persons have these rights regardless of what they do.) I shall not in this chapter broach the question in detail of what these human rights are, but it may be useful to raise a warning flag in connection with how to determine what they are. When some point to a person's capacity for agency in the light of reasons, they derive a fundamental human right to free agency, including perhaps rights to conditions for the maintenance of that agency. Perhaps this is a correct move, but we must be careful how we interpret it. I have already suggested that a fundamental right to free agency need not derive from such agency being a good for the person. Now notice that if we remove someone's kidney against his will or interfere with his actions on several occasions, we do not yet interfere with his being a free agent nor with the conditions for his being a free agent. (James Griffin has pointed this out in unpublished material.) But it is a mistake to think that it is permissible to do whatever leaves someone still able to be a free agent even when this interferes with particular decisions he makes as a free agent. Respect for someone as a free agent requires respect for at least some particular expressions of his agency. However, his decisions as an agent to exert control over things need only be respected when they concern what he has a right to control (or at least to try without interference to control). So if he makes a decision to give up his own kidney, his decision should be respected. When he decides to donate your kidney, his decision need not be respected. This suggests that in addition to any fundamental right to free agency, there will be fundamental rights to those things that make one a separate person (e.g., one's body parts), whether or not those things are necessary conditions for being a free agent. This is what I mean by referring to a person's authority over himself.

34. I shall have more to say (in section IVB) about how a right and its stringency may not be a function of the interest it protects. The points I have made about the possible independence of rights from interests also bear on the theses of Louis Kaplow and Steven Shavell in their *Fairness versus Human Welfare* (Cambridge, MA: Harvard University Press, 2002). Kaplow and Shavell assume that satisfaction of preferences, rather than satisfaction of interests, is of fundamental importance. But they do not see rights as ways to satisfy preferences; rather, they criticize rights for interfering with the satisfaction of preferences. When a right would interfere

with the satisfaction of every person's preference, it would be irrational to act on it, they claim. I suggest, though, that the view that one has a right and a duty to seek retributive punishment out of respect for human agency should not be reduced to a preference. And even if pursuing it interferes with the satisfaction of everyone's preference, it need not be irrational to act on it. Furthermore, how can we assume that the satisfaction of preferences is of fundamental importance? The objects of some preferences are worthless, as when they do not represent true interests or correct values. Even when this is not a problem, we may wonder whether the satisfaction of the preferences (or interests) of some creatures matters unless the creatures themselves matter. (David Velleman emphasizes this in "A Right of Self-Termination?," *Ethics* 109 [April 1999]: 606–628.) And perhaps certain rights reflect the worth of certain creatures (e.g., persons versus penguins), and such worth is a necessary presupposition of the importance of satisfying their preferences and interests. (It may also be an argument against satisfying some preferences that doing so would conflict with respect for what gives the creatures the worth that grounds the importance of satisfying their preferences.)

35. Suppose creatures without interests, or where interests could be satisfied without rights, could have rights nevertheless. Does this mean that a common reason for denying that human embryos have a right to life could be wrong? Embryos are nonconscious, nonsentient forms of human life. Because this is so, it seems possible to deny that they are harmed by the loss of future life or that it is in their interest to be kept alive, even if that future consists of becoming a sentient and conscious person. On account of this, it is tempting to conclude that human embryos have no right to go on living. But, I have just argued, creatures without interests could have rights. Hence, if human embryos lack rights, this is not only because they lack interests, but also because they are not subjects at all, unlike the persons without interests or whose interests are not affected by rights whom I have considered and who might have rights.

36. So if Bentham's theory of rights said that having a right makes one the intended beneficiary of an *act-consequentialist duty*, this could only be a necessary, not a sufficient, condition for having a right in the sense that contrasts with the vagaries of act-consequentialist duties.

37. We said the same about principles of permissible harm, that they might be overridden. But notice that it might be the case that a principle of permissible harm itself overrides a right. Then we may wrong someone in doing what is permissible.

38. This is applying to the discussion of rights points I made in discussing supererogation and obligation in chapter 1, based on discussions in *Morality, Mortality*, vol. 2, chap. 12.

39. Under "goods," I include both strict benefits and the avoidance of harm.

40. For more discussion of pairwise comparison, see chapter 2. We are here trying to apply some of what was said there to contexts involving rights.

41. However, note that, according to some consequentialists, the goodness of outcomes depends in part on how well principles of distributive justice are fulfilled.

42. Ronald Dworkin, "Rights as Trumps," in *Theories of Rights*, ed. Jeremy Waldron, pp. 153–167 (Oxford: Oxford University Press, 1984).

43. Thomson is careful to distinguish her view about what to do when a right conflicts with achieving goods from what should be done when providing goods to one person conflicts with providing goods to many, independent of rights. In the latter case, it is permissible, on her view, to aggregate (at least) goods to many who would suffer equally bad fates if not aided and who can be aided equally. So, in the absence of rights, one should save ten people rather than save one person. (This is an issue we discussed in chapter 2.)

44. A more moderate view—that every rights violation is a worse outcome than *many* other bad events, even if not all bad events—is also subject to this last objection. Additionally, it is subject to the following counterexample: It seems at least permissible to save one person from drowning instead of saving another from being murdered. But why is this so, if the rights

violation is so much worse an outcome? (This is an example originally offered by Thomas Scanlon. But see chapter 9, pp. 296.)

45. See Nagel, "Personal Rights and Public Space."

46. The term is Robert Nozick's. See Robert Nozick, *Anarchy, State, and Utopia* (New York: Basic Books, 1974).

47. See, for example, Amartya Sen, "Rights and Agency," *Philosophy & Public Affairs* 11 (1982): 3–39.

48. And this is not because I would otherwise be intending the act by another's hand, for I need not be intending it. For example, I may be a very busy person, and making some effort so that transgressions do not occur is an imposition I would like to avoid, yet I have a good reason, given how the person will be treated (even taking into account the greater good this transgression will produce), to make the effort.

49. I am imagining in all of these cases that the killing would be done in a way that violates the correct principle of permissible harm.

50. I first discussed this approach in my "Harming Some to Save Others," *Philosophical Studies* 57 (1989): 227–60; also in "The Structure of Nonconsequentialism, the Person as an End-in-Itself, and the Significance of Status," *Philosophy & Public Affairs* 21 (1992): 354–89; *Morality, Mortality*, vol. 2, and chapter 1 in this volume. I repeat some of what was said in chapter 1 to see how the ideas play out in the specific context of rights. What I say about the inviolability of persons is meant to apply only to innocent, nonthreatening persons, who do not consent to violation. Nothing I say denies that it is permissible to violate aggressors, threats, etc.

51. I shall expand on this point in section IVA(8) below.

52. The latter point is necessary to distinguish an inviolable person from an inviolable object (for example, a religious artifact) that, let us assume, should not be violated even to prevent damage to other such objects. We do not owe it *to* that object not to violate it. It was Michael Thompson who emphasized to me that inviolability as a status must be combined with the directedness of the duty not to violate, to which inviolability gives rise in the case of persons.

53. In this connection, as noted above, it is useful to consider the case in which someone will die soon anyway, so that killing him to save others does not really interfere with his interest in well-being. It can still be wrong to kill him, if he does not give his consent. (This is compatible with it being easier to justify killing him than killing someone else who would not soon die anyway.) We might also show that inviolability is not merely for the sake of interests it protects by showing that other ways of treating the person besides violating him can set back the same interests to the same degree; yet these other ways of setting back interests are permissible while violation is not. I consider this point in detail in section IVA(8).

54. It might be argued that the best state of affairs is one in which it is true that people have high inviolability (and so it is often impermissible to violate them) *and* someone acts *impermissibly* in violating one person in order to save more from being violated. But this only shows that our aim should not be to *produce* the best state of affairs but rather to act in accord with the values (such as the inviolability of persons) that exist.

55. This point—that status is determined person by person and is not affected by numbers— may be related to Thomson's position that numbers do not count in deciding whether to transgress a right for a great good (even if they count when transgressing a right is not at issue).

56. Robert Nozick raised and rejected the view that deontology is for persons and utilitarianism is for animals (in *Anarchy, State, and Utopia*, p. 42 (New York: Basic Books, 1974)). Utilitarianism is wrong for animals, I think, if it means that one animal can be made to suffer a great loss in order to prevent small losses to a great many animals already better off than it.

57. For more on these issues see my "Moral Status and Personal Identity: Clones, Embryos, and Future generations," in *Social Philosophy & Policy* 22 (2005): 283–307.

58. I first presented this sort of case in my *Morality, Mortality*, vol. 2, chap. 11.

59. I shall return to this issue once more in the text below.

60. For specifics on this, see chapter 5.

61. Nor does his wishing to do it make it his duty to do it. On this point, see my "Moral Improvisation and New Obligations," forthcoming in *NOMOS*. XLIX, Moral Universalism and Pluralism eds. Mi Willcams and H. Richardson, Nyu Press, 2007.

62. This case, those that follow, and the discussion of them apply what I first said in my "Supererogation and Obligation" (and in chapter 1 in this volume) to the subject of rights, in particular.

63. For a more elaborate version of the argument that leads to this question, as well as the argument that answers it, see chapter 1 in this volume and *Morality, Mortality*, vol. 2.

64. For more detailed discussion of conflicts of rights in general, see my "Conflicts of Rights: Typology, Methodology, and Nonconsequentialism," *Legal Theory* 7 (2001): 239–54; and chapter 9 in this volume.

65. Terminology in the law sometimes suggests the opposite, namely, that a court decides who has a right in a conflict situation, rather than whose right is more stringent. (I do not mean to imply that it is *only* if conflicts of rights exist that we can conclude that a right exists even if it should not be granted.) It would be especially troubling if courts behaved as if there were only interests, rather than even prima facie rights. For suppose one person has a life threatening illness and another has a less serious illness that causes paraplegia. If only interests determine who has a dispositive right to a scarce drug, the fact that the person who faces paraplegia owns the drug should make no difference, as a type of consideration distinct from interests, to who gets to have the drug.

66. See Jeremy Waldron, "Rights in Conflict," in his collection *Liberal Rights* (Cambridge: Cambridge University Press, 1993).

67. Waldron (ibid.) suggests that in an agent-relative system of only negative rights (where a duty tells an agent that he must not do something) there cannot be conflicts of duties, but this trolley case shows that this suggestion is wrong. A slightly different case involves an agent who has a choice between (a) not defusing a threat he started in the past to one person that is about to come to fruition and (b) starting a threat now to someone else in order to defuse the first threat. In this case, the agent will become the violator of negative rights whichever act he does, but at the present time he faces a conflict between according a negative right and fulfilling a positive duty to aid his potential victim of a negative rights violation. Such a conflict can arise, because systems that have only agent-relative negative rights in their foundation should, I believe, entail positive rights to aid from a perpetrator when a negative right has been or threatens to be violated.

68. For a more detailed typology of conflicts of rights, see chapter 9.

69. Thomson, *The Realm of Rights*. Above, in section IVA, I described another sense of stringency as a function of how much good is needed to permissibly override a right. Connecting these two ideas says that the amount of good that is needed to permissibly override a right is a function of the importance of the interest protected by the right.

70. Might it be said, however, that the contractual right that B has is not "to be saved by his bodyguard," but rather to be saved only by certain means? It is always possible, though, that one can be saved by *those* certain means only if one takes off A's arm, yet this is impermissible. (For more on this issue, see chapter 9, n. 22.) Thomson herself argues (in "Physician-Assisted Suicide: Two Moral Arguments," *Ethics* 109 [April 1999]: 497–518), that there are some "natural" rights to be provided with help, for example, a child has a right to be helped by her parents. In addition, she claims—though I do not agree—that terminating such help (and even not providing it) when it is necessary for life can involve killing the child, rather than letting

the child die. These additional claims, combined with her claims that the stringency of a right is a function of the interest it protects and that numbers of rights matter, imply (the incorrect view, I believe) that a parent may kill a bystander in order to save the lives of his two children. For, on Thomson's account, whatever the parent does, he will kill someone: Either he will kill his two children in not helping them or he will kill one bystander to help the children.

71. Aggregating rights is not always correct, of course, when it disregards the interests involved. Suppose that A on island A has a contractual right against us to have his life saved, and so does B on island B, but we can only go in one direction. On island B is also to be found C, who has a contractual right against us to have her sore throat cured, which we could do as well if we went to help B. I think that it would be wrong to let the far less significant right of C decide whether A or B gets his important right satisfied. C's right is a morally irrelevant right in this context. This is an implication of our discussion of similar issues in relation to morally irrelevant goods independent of rights. See chapters 1 and 2; and *Morality, Mortality*, vol. 1.

72. Admittedly, however, I do not think there is a specific right not to have the trolley redirected.

73. A particular case in which this is true might be modeled on a different one constructed by Judith Thomson (in "Killing, Letting Die, and the Trolley Problem," *Monist* 59 (April 1976): 204–17). Suppose that city authorities have invited a person to visit the trolley tracks and this person comes only on the condition that his safety from trolleys (that would even merely paralyze [rather than kill] him) is guaranteed. If a trolley is at a crossroads and we must head it either toward paralyzing this person or toward killing someone else, we may not direct it toward the visitor.

74. This also implies that interests at stake in each right are not all that is relevant to stringency. Even if we reject the moral significance for permissibility of an act of the intending/ foreseeing distinction, characterization of the differences between these cases, on grounds I offer in chapter 5, may be morally significant.

75. These tests are based on ones I developed to compare killing and letting die. On this, see *Morality, Mortality*, vol. 2.

76. One could have an analogous Choice Test (and also the following Goal Test) involving the rights being transgressed as mere side effects.

77. Alon Harel argues that free speech could be infringed for the sake of preventing insult but not to win a war, though the latter is a more important goal. But here all things are not equal; free speech during war plays an important role in seeing to it that the war is justified and pursued correctly, whereas free speech for insult has no comparable virtue.

78. In an extended sense, an Effort Test and a Choice Test could also diverge when the conflict is between a supererogatory act and a positive right. In some cases, one might voluntarily (not as morally required) do more to accomplish a supererogatory act than one was required to do to meet the positive right, and yet one should not choose against satisfying the right in order to accomplish the supererogatory act instead. (In section IVB, above, I described different conflicts between the Choice Test and the Effort Test: One might be required to make a great effort to do a duty but not to do a supererogatory act, and yet the supererogatory act could permissibly be chosen instead of the duty.)

79. For discussion of these sorts of (apparent) intransitivities, see *Morality, Mortality*, vol. 2, chap. 12.

80. The issues here are similar to those in the discussion of whether the duty not to kill is more stringent than the duty not to let die. See my discussion of that issue in chapter 1 and in *Morality, Mortality*, vol. 2.

81. We also raised the issue in section IVA(8). Notice also that Dworkin's formulation does not speak to whether a right can trump an aggregation of equally strong rights. And indeed,

Dworkin may believe that we may transgress one person's right in order to minimize the transgression of rights of other people. See Dworkin, "Rights as Trumps."

82. It may be possible, therefore, that some arguments in public policy that call for action to prevent violations of rights use the rights-as-trumps argument incorrectly.

83. Note also that while Waldron is quite right to recognize that a fourth-ranked duty associated with torture may be outweighed by a second-ranked duty associated with free speech, this still does not show that the n-ranked duty associated with the stronger right R_1 would not always outrank the n-ranked duty associated with R_2. However, evidence for even this additional claim might be provided by the following example: While the right not to be tortured to death is, arguably, stronger than the right not to be deliberately killed without torture, this alone does not imply that rescuing victims from attempts at death by torture is more important than rescuing victims of ordinary attempted killings. Here is an account (that I do not necessarily endorse) of why this could be so. Torturing mistreats someone in a way that is even more inconsistent with his nature as a person than killing him is. But when we have to decide whom to leave to his sad fate, we would not be endorsing either form of inappropriate treatment. Therefore, only the largest part of loss that each person would suffer might be relevant in deciding whom to help, and the additional pain and insult from torture might not be a great enough difference, relative to the evil (of death) that both face, to deny each an equal chance to be saved.

84. For the relation between such positive rights that back up negative rights and positive rights more generally, see chapter 9.

85. Dworkin himself makes use of the intention/foresight distinction, thought by some to underlie parts of nonconsequentialism, in his defense of a right to have a willing physician assist suicide. He considers the objection that such a right (and an associated right of a doctor to act on it) may lead to many violations of the right not to be killed against one's will through mistaken exercise of the right. While he grants that a sufficient number of such foreseen mistakes might weigh against the right to assisted suicide, he insists that the government's intending to deny (and thus violate) someone's right to assisted suicide must be contrasted with its foreseeing (but not intending) other violations of rights. See his introduction to "The Philosophers' Brief to the U.S. Supreme Court," *New York Review of Books*, March 27, 1997, pp. 41–47.

86. This issue is related to my discussion of Peter Unger's views in chapter 6. Of course, nothing I have said implies that if we face a conflict between (a) A being killed as a consequence of redirecting a trolley to save a greater number or (b) A having his leg deliberately taken off to save a greater number, we must choose (a). We may sometimes do what it would be impermissible to do (take his leg off) if it were the only thing we could do, as a substitute for what it is permissible to do, if this is in A's interests. I have called the principle that permits this the Principle of Secondary Permissibility (PSP). See chapters 1 and 5 for more on this.

87. In this case, the greater number of rights that will be transgressed is distributed interpersonally. Different issues would be raised if all the transgressions would occur in one person.

88. Jeremy Waldron, "Introduction," in Waldron, ed., *Theories of Rights.*

89. As in Stephen Darwall, "Agent-Centered Restrictions from the Inside Out," *Philosophical Studies* 50 (1986): 291–319; and Elizabeth Anderson, *Ethics and Economics* (Cambridge: Cambridge University Press, 1993).

90. See, for example, chapter 1 in this volume, and *Morality, Mortality*, vol. 2.

91. This position contrasts with the one taken by Amartya Sen, I believe. See his "Rights and Agency," *Philosophy & Public Affairs* 11 (Winter 1982): 3–39. For more on this, see my *Morality, Mortality*, vol. 2.

92. Here we might recollect Mill's view that it is better to be Socrates dissatisfied than a pig satisfied.

93. This analysis brings together (1) the view that minimizing the transgression of rights would wind up defending only a weaker right, with (2) the view that there is something logically incoherent with counting the number of people whose rights will be violated when deciding whether to transgress the right. (Earlier we discussed the view that it is illogical to count the number of people whose interests, unprotected by rights, will be affected, when deciding whether to transgress a right.)

94. Waldron, "Rights in Conflict."

95. I owe this point to Peter Graham.

96. I do not really understand (3). How could it be necessary to know the content of someone's speech in order to know if his speech was genuinely free speech?

97. This is on the continuing assumption that the right to free speech is to be the same for all persons, that is, we are not imagining that some people have a weaker right so that others have the stronger right to speak (i.e., even if their speaking has a chilling effect on others actually being able to speak freely).

98. Thomas Scanlon emphasized the distinction between these two attitudes in his "Contractualism and Utilitarianism" in *Utilitarianism and Beyond*, ed. Amartya Sen and Bernard Williams, pp. 103–128 (Cambridge: Cambridge University Press, 1982).

99. As I noted in chapter 4, Judith Thomson is willing to make use of *ex ante* alienation of one's right not to be killed in order to justify killing some to save a greater number of others in a suitably described Trolley Case: (Roughly) this is when *ex ante* alienation decreases each person's *ex ante* probability of losing what is important to him. See Thomson, *The Realm of Rights* (Cambridge, MA: Harvard University Press, 1990). As I noted in chapter 4, one problem is that the same considerations would also justify an agreement to press a switch that will cause a trolley worker who is standing on a bridge to fall into the trolley to stop it. Yet, the latter way of killing the person seems impermissible. For further discussion of this see my *Morality, Mortality*, vol. 2.

100. I believe that Thomas Scanlon holds such a position. See Scanlon, *What We Owe to Each Other*.

101. This approach to arguing against *ex ante* alienation of a right would have to be modified somewhat, if it were permissible to allow oneself *ex ante* to be harmed at a time when it is still for the sake of one's own interests that this happen. This is so even though one will at that very time refuse consent. (For example, I might agree *ex ante* that I will be given a drug that *might* kill me, for the sake of its expected great benefits to me, though I will refuse permission through weakness of will at the time the drug is given.) This is a form of alienation of a right not to be interfered with, I think, but for the sake of a good that one still seeks at the time of the sacrifice.

102. I take this as support for the view described in section IVA(7) above, that aggregation's role in the permissibility of infringing rights (by contrast to its role in distributing scarce resources) can depend on factors aside from sheer numbers of people suffering equal or similar fates. Such factors as preventing a sufficiently *worse* fate in each of many people or a sufficiently *serious* similar fate in each of many can be crucial.

103. I first discussed this case, as well as the Ambulance cases that follow, in my *Morality, Mortality*, vol. 2.

104. Suggested by Ronald Dworkin.

105. I think that there is some similarity between my use of the Ambulance cases and Scanlon's discussion of the (ir)relevance of the probability of harm to deciding on principles governing conduct in his *What We Owe to Each Other*, pp. 206–9. I believe that *how* (i.e., the way or manner in which) we would harm someone plays a large role in Scanlon's judgment of cases, though he may not in his book recognize this sufficiently. For my discussion of "how" factors in Scanlon, see chapter 16.

9

CONFLICTS OF RIGHTS

A Typology

I. INTRODUCTION

In previous chapters I have considered what ought to be done (and which theory explains what ought to be done) when there is a conflict for an agent between his respecting the negative right of one person and his respecting the same negative right of others. He faces this problem when, for example, he must decide whether to direct a runaway trolley away from five and either toward one person or toward two people. In this situation, it was argued, an agent may minimize transgression of rights. We have also considered what ought to be done when there is a conflict between an agent respecting a negative right and his preventing the violation of the same negative right in many others by other agents. I considered cases of this type in which the agent may permissibly redirect a threat sent by a villain to five away from them and toward one person instead.

In this chapter, I shall examine the ways in which rights may conflict (or at least seem to conflict) in greater detail. This will still be a sketchy survey,[1] but I believe that it may be helpful. Among the questions I shall consider is whether we may minimize transgression of positive or negative rights by transgressing fewer positive rights of other people. I shall also again (as in chapter 8) consider how the resolution of the conflicts is not solely a function of the weight of the interests involved and what this suggests about the correct theory of rights.

II. TYPES OF CONFLICTS

When an attacker who threatens to cut off someone's leg is killed by his potential victim in self-defense, it is sometimes said that there is a conflict between the right of the attacker not to be killed and the right of a person not to be harmed. However, this is a pseudo-conflict of rights, since the attacker's right not to be killed is in some way weakened by his being a threat, at least for the purpose of eliminating the threat he presents. Considered alone and not weakened, how would we rank the rights involved in this case? How does the right not to have one's leg be cut off compare with the right not to be killed? If I heard of two people, one of whom was threatened with violation of the first right and one of whom was threatened with violation of the second, I would think it right to help the second person first, other things being equal. This is some indication that I believe that the second right is stronger. But this need not determine how we resolve all problems involving such rights, since in some cases the right may be weakened. For example, we may help the person who is attacked rather than the attacker. Henceforth, I shall consider conflicts among unweakened rights.

I shall now supply a typology of cases in which rights conflict because duties correlated with them conflict. That is, I have a duty as correlative to two rights, and these duties conflict.[2] I do not claim that this typology is exhaustive. We can divide rights into negative and positive rights.[3] Insofar as this is possible, negative and positive rights may protect the same interests. The negative rights have correlative duties of noninterference and the positive rights have duties of provision. For example, a negative and a positive right can both protect life, as in a negative right not to be killed and a positive right of a drowning person to be saved by a lifeguard. Negative and positive rights may protect different interests, though, as when a negative right protects the interest in not having one's leg broken and a positive right exists against a lifeguard to protect one's life. A positive right may derive from a violation of a negative or a positive right, as when we must give help to someone we have harmed, or give much help to someone whose minor positive right we failed to accord. I shall call rights of the latter sort "derived positive rights."[4] Alternatively, a positive right may be a "pure" positive right, for example, a right to aid that stems from a promise to aid.

What about positive rights that help to *prevent* the violation of negative or positive rights? If the positive rights involve person P having a duty to prevent herself from violating a negative right by doing something other than just refraining from violating the right (for example, tying herself up so that she does not violate the right), then these positive rights are like the derived positive rights already described. If they involve person P preventing person R from violating negative rights, they come closer, I think, to pure positive rights, but only if we take a so-called agent-relative perspective that can result in treating the rights violations of other agents differently from our own.[5] Even if we take this perspective, we may think that positive rights that give someone a duty to prevent a violation of another's *right* by a different agent might fall into a different category from a simple right to be provided with assistance. So I shall call this category of positive rights "mixed." (Notice that the right whose violation we prevent may be either negative or positive, so there might be a mixed positive right held by Q against P to prevent the failure of R to fulfill a pure [or derived] positive right of Q's.)

We can put these distinctions together in the following way to represent possible conflicts of rights:

(1) Negative versus negative
  (a) same interests
  (b) different interests
(2) Negative versus positive
  (a) same interests
    (i) positive derived
    (ii) positive pure
    (iii) positive mixed
  (b) different interests
    (i) positive derived
    (ii) positive pure
    (iii) positive mixed
(3) Positive versus positive
  (a) same interests
    (i) positive derived versus positive derived
    (ii) positive derived versus positive pure
    (iii) positive derived versus positive mixed
    (iv) positive pure versus positive pure
    (v) positive pure versus positive mixed
    (vi) positive mixed versus positive mixed
  (b) different interests
    (i) positive derived versus positive derived
    (ii) positive derived versus positive pure
    (iii) positive derived versus positive mixed
    (iv) positive pure versus positive pure
    (v) positive pure versus positive mixed
    (vi) positive mixed versus positive mixed[6]

But now there are also two different senses of conflict stemming from two different perspectives: the agent-relative perspective and the agent-neutral perspective (as these terms were employed in chapter 8, section IVC). The agent-relative perspective on conflicts states that the conflicts are between rights that give conflicting duties to one agent or otherwise create internal conflict in one agent. The agent-neutral perspective on conflicts states that the conflicts are between rights that give *different agents* different duties. For example, when there is a conflict of rights from an agent-neutral perspective, it can be that either rightholder S will have his right transgressed (permissibly or impermissibly) by agent R or rightholder Q will have her right transgressed (permissibly or impermissibly) by agent P, but they will *not* both have their rights respected. If agent R carries out her duty to S, agent P will *not* carry out his duty to Q, and so rightholder Q will suffer a transgression. If agent R does not carry out her duty to rightholder S, agent P will at least not transgress a right against rightholder Q. (Agent P may fail in his duty to respect the right insofar as it is up to him but be prevented from succeeding in transgressing Q's right by R's intervention.) In virtue of this sort of conflict, agent R may believe that she is under a duty (not correlated to that right of Q that would be transgressed by P) to prevent P's failure to abide by a duty strictly correlative to Q's right. If there is this sort of conflict of rights from the agent-neutral perspective, it will then follow that agent R will herself (i.e., from an agent-relative perspective) face a conflict of duties, between the duty she originally had to rightholder S and a mixed positive duty to rightholder Q. Hence, when exploring the categories listed above, we could consider each in its agent-relative (A) and agent-neutral (B) forms.

III. SPECIFIC CONFLICTS

A. Negative versus Negative

I shall now consider selected types of conflicts that are generated by combining our categories. Can negative rights conflict with negative rights covering the same interest, giving a particular agent conflicting duties? (This is [A][1][a], where A stands for the agent-relative perspective.) As noted in chapter 8, Jeremy Waldron says that making all rights both negative and agent-relative rules out conflicts of rights.[7] But suppose that an agent in Trolley Scenario 1 is permitted to send a deadly trolley either down track A or down track B, because otherwise it will go to track C, killing five people. (This could be permissible even if the five people had no positive right against the agent to be saved.) Joe is on track A, and Jim is on track B. It seems that each has a negative right not to be killed, and the agent who wishes to save the five has to decide whether to do what will certainly kill Joe or certainly kill Jim. Hence, contrary to what Waldron claims, even a system that has only agent-relative negative rights seems able to give rise to conflicts of rights. I believe that Joe and Jim each has a right that the agent use a random decision procedure to select which one of them will be killed.

This case shows that even when conflicts of rights reflect conflicts between fulfilling two different duties, the conflict itself may arise for reasons other than that doing our duty leads to it. For it is, arguably, not our duty to redirect the trolley away from the five. Further, the fact that a conflict of negative rights will ensue if we do redirect the trolley is not a sufficient reason to make it impermissible to redirect the trolley.

What if, in Trolley Scenario 2, Jim and Susan are on track B, while only Joe is on track A, and the trolley would kill those it hits? How should this conflict be resolved? We may, I think, send the trolley toward Joe. In resolving this sort of case, each person has a right only to be balanced against his equal and opposite number, and the remaining person on one side helps to determine the outcome.[8]

Within category (A)(1)(a), there is a slightly different case worth considering, since it bears on the balancing explanation just given. Consider Trolley Scenario 3, which is just like our previous case, except that while Joe and Jim would be killed by the trolley, we know that Susan would only be slightly bruised. She has a negative right not to be bruised, but should this play any role in deciding how to redirect the trolley? In conflict cases, if Joe has a right to be balanced against Jim, and the remainder provided by Susan helps to determine the outcome, then the agent should choose to send the trolley toward Joe. But my sense is that Susan's right is a morally irrelevant right in this context. (Hence, there seems to be a Principle of Irrelevant Rights.)[9] This is because if the right she has is transgressed, what she would suffer is much less than what Jim would suffer if his right is transgressed; their rights would be transgressed in the same way, and from Jim's and Joe's personal points of view, it is not irrelevant whether Jim or Joe is the one to survive. To deprive Joe of an equal chance, which he would have in a random decision procedure, in order to prevent the additional rights infringement to Susan is a moral mistake, I believe. My point here is to show that an agent who is faced with a conflict of negative rights, where an equal number of rights protecting the same interest lies on either side, should not necessarily always minimize violations of negative rights, in particular when other rights at stake protect lesser interests.

What if Susan stood to lose a leg? Here, her negative right protects something much more important to her than avoiding a bruise, and it may, I think, at least weigh in favor of sending the trolley toward Joe.[10]

We can now consider category (B)(1)(a) (where B stands for the agent-neutral perspective). That is, the same negative rights are in conflict but we consider the conflict from an agent-neutral perspective. A case that exemplifies this is one where unless agent R kills Joe, agent P will kill Jim and Susan. If one takes an agent-neutral perspective on the conflict of negative rights, it might be that a new conflict of rights arises for P in the special case where Jim and Susan have a mixed positive right against him. This new conflict is the conflict between his duty to respect a negative right and his mixed positive duty (corresponding to their mixed positive right) to stop negative-rights violations. I have argued[11] that it is not irrational for a rights theory to prohibit one agent from transgressing one person's negative right for the purpose of minimizing the transgression of other people's negative rights by other agents in cases where there is no specific right these other people have to be aided. The point I wish to make now is that it is an implication of that argument that even when the potential victims of the other agents have mixed positive rights to assistance against an agent, the agent can be prohibited from transgressing the one person's negative right. (But I do not want to claim that the correct rights theory would always prohibit such action.)

Is it possible that negative rights in conflict could protect the same interest and yet one right be stronger than the other because the strength of a right may not be a function solely of the interest it protects?[12] Suppose that different manners of interfering with a right that protects an interest were differentially permissible. By "different manners of interfering," I mean to refer (throughout) to the causal relations that hold between what we do, the harmful involvement of the person, and the good we hope to achieve.[13] Then, in a conflict, we should not necessarily be indifferent as to which negative right we transgress. For example, suppose that a villain heads a trolley toward killing five people. To stop it from killing them, we could either (i) push John in front of the trolley to stop it, thereby killing John, (ii) redirect the trolley away from the five to a track where it will kill Rachel, or (iii) redirect the trolley to a track where it will kill Peggy and Rita. (Call this the Multiple Option Case.)[14] In this conflict, we should choose to kill Rachel because it is permissible, I believe, to kill by redirecting the trolley but not by pushing a person in front of the trolley. If we could not follow course (ii), we should do (iii) rather than (i). Hence, in this conflict, we should kill more people—transgress more negative rights—in one way rather than transgress someone else's negative right in another way.

Now, we come to category (A)(1)(b), cases where an individual agent faces a conflict between negative rights that involve different interests. For example, suppose that an agent must direct a trolley so that it either kills Joe or breaks Jim's leg. Other things being equal, the agent should avoid violating the right that protects the more important interest, at least when the differential strength of each right is a function solely of the interests it protects. But some differences in interests are too small to be morally relevant. For example, suppose that directing the trolley toward Paul breaks his leg and directing it toward Simon breaks his leg a bit more severely (or breaks his leg and bruises his finger), so that the conflict is between negative rights protecting different interests. Given that each person is capable of avoiding the larger part of the loss—the part it is reasonable to care most about avoiding—and each wants to be the one not to sustain that loss, the additional loss to Simon seems irrelevant, even if avoiding it is covered by a negative right. This is an application of the Principle of Irrelevant Rights (and Irrelevant Goods) to the question of which right or set of rights is more stringent.

Suppose that next to Jim are five other people, each of whom would also suffer a broken leg if hit by the trolley. If we send the trolley toward Joe, however, he will die. Because on Jim's side each of the six as an individual would suffer a far smaller loss if his negative right is transgressed than Joe would, it would be wrong to avoid transgressing the large aggregate of all of their rights. The principle that would justify this is giving preference to the person who will be worst off if his right is transgressed. Suppose that each of Jim and the five people would be totally paralyzed and assume that this paralyzed condition is not as bad as death but much worse than a broken leg. If Jim alone were to face that prospect, we would still turn the trolley toward him rather than Joe. I believe that even when each of many would suffer their terrible loss, it is still correct to turn the threat toward them rather than kill Joe. (This conclusion is consistent with there being some greater number of people, each of whom would suffer such a significant loss, for whose sake it is permissible to cause Joe the greater loss.) This contrasts, as we shall see, with the permissibility of according positive rights to help that Jim and his companions have rather than according Joe his positive right for help, even when he will die and they will not.

Decisions about cases in which negative rights that protect different interests conflict is again complicated by the fact that the strength of a right may not be a function solely of the interest it protects, and so the differential strength of the rights may not be a function solely of the differential interests they protect. For example, suppose that we modify the Multiple Option Case slightly so that options (ii) and (iii) are the same, but in option (i) we would push John in front of the trolley, thereby paralyzing his legs (but not killing him). In this conflict, I believe that it is impermissible to choose (i) rather than (ii), and if one cannot do (ii), one should do (iii) rather than (i). Hence, it is not always the case that when there is a conflict among fulfilling negative rights, we should transgress the one that protects the weaker interest.

B. Negative versus Positive

Moving on to conflicts between negative and positive rights, consider an instance in category (A)(2)(a) (i.e., agent-relative, negative/positive conflicts where interests are the same). The conclusions for which I shall argue here are general and apply to any negative rights and positive rights related in the same way. I shall use the negative right not to be killed and the positive right to have one's life saved for purposes of illustration.

Suppose that I must kill Joe in connection with saving Jim and Susan from a fatal threat that I presented to them in the past and that is about to come to fruition. Assume further that the manner in which I threatened Jim and Susan is the same as the manner in which I would kill Joe. I have a positive duty *derived* from a (potential) negative-rights violation that is in conflict with negative rights of the same sort. Hence it is a case of A(2)(a)(i). It is illuminating to consider various ways in which the death of Joe could come about and how what we may do varies with them. The general claims for which I shall argue, based on what these cases reveal, are (1) the interests involved will stay constant in all variations on the way of killing Joe to save Jim and Susan, and yet sometimes the killing will be permissible and sometimes not (so this will reinforce the similar claim made above in discussing conflicts of negative rights); and (2) the fact that it is sometimes impermissible to kill Joe shows that a negative right not to be killed can be stronger than (even an aggregate of) positive rights derived from the negative right protecting the same interest. That is, the positive right to aid even one's own potential victims can be weaker than someone else's negative right. Both (1) and (2) suggest that the strength of a right is not solely a function of the interest it protects (i.e., life for everybody in all these cases), but also of the manner in which the interest is affected (to the same degree). This assumes that there is no other reason that it is impermissible to kill besides the rights involved. This may be a further reflection of our concern with the worth of the person rather than with what is in his interest.[15]

Consider five ways in which Joe might be killed in connection with saving Susan's and Jim's lives in (A)(2)(a)(i) to fulfill their derived positive right (against me, who started the threat to them): (a) I have to kill Joe for his organs and provide them for Jim and Susan; (b) in order to divert a trolley on its way toward killing

Jim and Susan, I must set a bomb that, as a foreseen side effect, will kill bystander Joe; (c) I have to push Joe in front of the trolley that is headed toward Susan and Jim in order to stop it, as only his being hit will stop the trolley, and doing so will kill him; (d) I have to turn a trolley that is headed toward Jim and Susan onto a track where Joe will be killed; or (e) if I save Jim and Susan from the trolley that is headed toward them, they will breathe (by contrast to their not breathing at all if dead), and this will change air currents in a way that moves deadly germs in the air in Joe's direction.

I believe that killing Jim in (a), (b), and (c) is impermissible and killing him in (d) and (e) is permissible, and this is due to the rights that Joe has and lacks in each case. The interest in life in all of the cases is the same among all of the people. Hence, we cannot attribute the fact that Joe's right not to be killed in two cases is strong enough to stand in the way of the derived positive rights of Jim and Susan to the fact that the right protects a stronger interest. There is, I suggest, a difference in the strength (or perhaps even existence) of rights not to be killed that is not a function solely of the interest it protects, but of how we kill.

As we have seen in Part 1 of this book, many theories have been offered to account for the differences in the permissibility of killing in order to aid in cases (a) through (e). I shall not again discuss all these theories here. A possible non-consequentialist principle that could account for the differences put in terms of rights is (roughly put) as follows: (1) We may permissibly transgress someone's negative right as an effect of a greater good (or component thereof), or of means having the greater good as its noncausal flip side, even when the person's right being infringed plays a causally useful role in sustaining the greater good by dealing with new threats that arise from our efforts to produce the greater good; and (2) it is impermissible to transgress someone's negative right as a direct effect of, or as part of, what we do to produce the greater good—though this does not mean that the right against doing this is absolute.[16] Although the principle tells agents what they may and may not do, I do not think that it is essentially concerned with the agent's point of view. That is, I think that its strictures reflect something about the person whose rights we might transgress and how his nature makes it the case that we owe it to him not to treat him in certain ways. This is my reason for thinking that the objection to certain ways of treating people is victim- and rights-based.

The principle described implies that the right not to be killed that Joe has and that conflicts with the rights to be saved of Jim and Susan may be permissibly transgressed in (d), in particular, but not in (a). Recall, however, that this does not mean that Joe is not at liberty to try to stop the trolley from hitting him by turning it either back toward the one who turns it toward him or toward those who would have been hit if it had not been turned. (He is at liberty to do this, but others may try to interfere with his doing it.)[17]

It is also possible to show that a negative right is stronger than a positive right in a case of type (A)(2)(a)(i) by employing a version of what I have called the Choice Test for stringency. In this test, we must choose which of two acts to do on the assumption that we will choose the act that transgresses the least stringent right.[18] So, for example, suppose (in a new case) that Jim has a derived positive right that I give him $500 to save his life, but it will cost me $500 to see to it that I do not kill Joe. I cannot do both. It seems to me that Joe has the stronger right.

Finally, it would be permissible for me to not fulfill a derived positive right against me that Joe has to have his life saved in order to instead fulfill a derived positive right against me of Jim's and Susan's to be saved. But (as I have argued) it is sometimes impermissible to kill Joe in order to fulfill these rights of Jim's and Susan's. This shows that a negative right (of Joe's) is stronger than a derived positive right (of Joe's). This way of measuring the strength of the rights in question employs what I call the Goal Test.[19] That is, the less stringent right (the derived positive right) may be transgressed so that we can pursue a goal (helping Jim and Susan), but the more stringent negative right may not be transgressed so that we can pursue the same goal. However, the Goal Test does not involve a direct conflict between the derived positive right and the negative right whose strength is to be measured. Hence, it only gives indirect evidence for how a conflict between them should be resolved.[20] (We must be careful in using all tests for stringency to test *certain manners* of transgressing a negative right, as some ways of transgressing a negative right may be permissible in order to satisfy the derived positive rights of Jim and Susan, as I have already said.)[21]

The results for (A)(2)(a)(i) that we have considered apply as well, I think, to (A)(2)(a)(ii) and (iii) and to (B)(2)(a)(i), (ii), and (iii). Each of the specific scenarios (a) through (e) in the case above instantiates general manners in which someone might be harmed. Let us henceforth take (a) through (e) to refer to these manners. Then, for example, in an agent-neutral conflict ([B] case), if P has a pure positive duty correlative to others' rights to have their lives saved, R should not facilitate performance of the duty by killing Joe in manners (a) through (c). However, if P has such a duty to save two lives, it is permissible for R to facilitate performance of the duty by redirecting a threat away from killing the two even if it kills Joe.

Under the category of negative rights conflicting with positive rights that protect the same interests is the following sort of case: A side (or all sides) in conflict, in addition to having rights at stake protecting the same interest, has rights protecting lesser interests. For example, Joe's negative right not to be killed conflicts with Jim's contractual right to have his life saved and Susan's contractual right to be saved from a broken leg. Or, the right of Jim not to be killed and the right of Susan not to be bruised conflicts with Joe's contractual right to have his life saved. The first issue that these cases raise is whether, when an equal number of *equal* interests protected by rights is present on either side, there is something to be said for giving equal chances to each side, even if this means killing *n* people to save *n* people. (Recall that it was said that when we had a choice between killing Jim or killing Joe, each had a right to the use of a random selection procedure.) Suppose that we should not be willing to kill to save merely to provide an equal chance of living to those on conflicting sides.

The second issue is whether anything but the major interest (i.e., life) should determine whether we cause death in manners (d) and (e), when we should refuse to cause death just to save lives. Above we saw that a smaller interest (or set of such smaller interests) could sometimes be relevant to deciding what to do when negative rights conflict with negative rights (protecting the same large interest). This was when the smaller interests were still large by comparison to the major interests. Could lesser interests also be relevant when negative rights conflict with positive rights (protecting the same large interest). Consider such a case. I suggest that it would be permissible to redirect a trolley away from Jim and Susan to fulfill positive rights to save him from death and her from being completely paralyzed, even though we foresee that Joe will be killed. Hence, the significant lesser loss (paralysis) covered by a right makes killing Joe permissible, even though Jim on his own would not have had a right to an equal chance that he be saved or that Joe be killed. Smaller additional losses covered by rights may be irrelevant goods, however (as explained above).

Now we must consider cases where the negative and positive rights protect different interests, that is, cases (2)(b)(i)–(iii). There are two possibilities: The negative right protects the stronger interest or the positive right does. Consider cases of the former type first. For example, suppose that I must kill someone in order to fulfill a contractual obligation to save each of five people from being completely paralyzed, assuming that total paralysis is not as bad as death. This case might raise at least two issues we have already discussed, that is, how large the smaller losses have to be for aggregation of such losses to make a moral difference and whether the manner of causing death makes a difference. Only manners (d) and (e) described above are eligible. I suggest that it would not be permissible to redirect a threat that will paralyze the five, thus fulfilling the right of five people to avoid total paralysis but transgressing another's right not to be killed. (This does not necessarily imply that as the number of people who will be paralyzed increases, the conclusion will remain the same.)

What if the negative right protects a weaker interest than the positive one does? For example, may one do what will break Joe's leg in order to save Jim from death? If we break Joe's leg in manner (d) or (e), it seems clear that doing so is permissible. Permissible infringements of the negative right are intuitively plausible, even in manners (a) through (c), though my sense is that, unlike what is true if we use manners (d) or (e), compensation is owed for this harmful interference.

C. Positive versus Positive

Finally, we must consider the conflicts of positive rights versus positive rights. I shall only consider some of the many possible cases that raise interesting issues here. One question arises: Are positive rights, like negative rights, sensitive to the manner in which they would be transgressed? Is there something analogous to the principle of permissible harm described in section B for not-aiding when rights are involved? To answer this question, we can consider cases of not-aiding some in order to aid others that differ in ways analogous to manners (a) through (e). In all of these cases, all parties have positive rights to be aided. Consider first cases in which the interests of each person are the same.

Here is a case involving not-aiding analogous to (a): Jim and Susan have a positive right against a doctor to an organ transplant. However, a shortage of organs develops. The doctor omits to give another patient, Joe, his medicine, in order that he will die, for then his organs can be used to fulfill the positive rights of Jim and Susan. Not fulfilling Joe's positive right to the medicine is impermissible. Hence, we should not always decide whom to aid merely on the basis of the number of rights protecting the same interests that we can fulfill.[22]

Here is a case involving not aiding analogous to (b): We are busy setting a bomb that will move away the trolley heading to kill Jim and Susan, who have a positive right to our aid. As a result, we cannot simultaneously use means to fulfill Joe's positive right against us to be saved from another trolley headed toward him. In this case, it is our using certain necessary means to help Jim and Susan that results in Joe's death, but it is permissible not to save Joe. (This is by contrast with the impermissibility of using means whose direct effect is causing Joe's death in [b].)

Here is a case involving not aiding analogous to (c): A strong wind is about to push Joe over a bridge and in front of the trolley headed toward Jim and Susan. The trolley would kill him. Suppose Joe has a right against us to save him from falling, which we can easily do. However, Joe being hit by the trolley is necessary to stop the trolley, and Jim and Susan have a right against us to be saved from the trolley, a right which we cannot fulfill in any other way but by allowing Joe to fall. It is impermissible not to fulfill Joe's positive right.[23]

Here is a case involving not aiding analogous to (d): A life-saving raft that Joe has a positive right to have from us is on its way to him. Then we see that Jim and Susan are drowning. We redirect the raft away from Joe toward Jim and Susan, thereby fulfilling their positive right against us to send a raft to save them. In this case, it is permissible not to fulfill Joe's positive right.[24]

Here is a case involving not aiding analogous to (e): If I fulfill Jim's and Susan's positive right against me to be saved, their being alive rather than dead means that they will consume resources (that any person needs) that are the only resources I could (and would) otherwise have used in order to fulfill Joe's positive right that I save him. It is permissible to fulfill the positive right of Jim and Susan, though it leads to my not being able to fulfill Joe's positive right.

These cases show that though the interest that the right protects is constant, the permissibility of not fulfilling Joe's positive right is sensitive to the *manner* in which it would come to be unfulfilled. This is a step in showing that there is a principle dealing with not-aiding that is in some ways similar to (though in some ways different from) the particular principle of permissible harm described earlier.

Another interesting issue, raised by conflicts of positive rights when the interest protected by each right is the same, is whether one should fulfill the positive right that derives from one's violation of a negative right rather than satisfy a pure positive right that one owes. This is a case of (A)(3)(a)(ii). For example, should Joe's bodyguard forgo saving Joe from paralysis in order to stop or (somehow) undo his (the bodyguard's) impermissibly paralyzing Jim? I believe that he should. Preventing oneself from taking away from someone what he has quite independently of us (his ability to move) takes precedence, I think, over a promise to someone else to provide him with that sort of thing (e.g., by preventing Joe's paralysis that would occur independently of our act). I think that this is interesting because if the bodyguard faced a conflict of positive duties (correlative to rights) between (a) saving Jim from *someone else's* failure to abide by Jim's negative right and (b) saving Joe from paralysis due to a natural disaster, (a) would not necessarily take precedence over (b).[25] In the latter conflict, I am imagining that Jim has a contractual right to the bodyguard's help when he is a victim of *someone else's* violations of his negative rights (mixed right), and Joe has a pure positive right to aid against the bodyguard. Here, the fact that there is a rights violation that causes one person's need for help is not a factor that helps determine whom to help if the interests in both cases are the same. This contrast between the role of rights violations in A (agent-relative) and B (agent-neutral) cases is interesting because some[26] seem to have concluded on the basis of the second (agent-neutral) case that a rights violation makes no difference to whom we should choose to aid when interests are the same. The case where the bodyguard would himself have violated the right of one of the people he must now aid defeats this conclusion.[27]

Suppose that the conclusions of the preceding paragraph were taken to a social level, where the government is thought of as the agent who acts to fulfill positive rights. (Again, by "positive," I mean rights to be provided with something, not rights that are legislated [by contrast with moral rights].) These conclusions would imply that if individuals have positive rights to both medical care and to police protection (against the violation of negative rights by other individuals), according rights to the latter (given the protection of equal interests) would not necessarily take precedence over the former. This is so even though the latter involve aid to prevent or undo violation of negative rights. Deriving this conclusion involves taking seriously the fact that the government that must help is not the agent who will have violated the negative right.[28]

However, suppose that social institutions such as government exist, in part, to help citizens to share the burdens of each one's duty to prevent his violation of negative rights and to fulfill positive rights that derive from prevention (or repair) of violations of negative rights. If these duties are more stringent than the duty to fulfill pure positive rights or other derived positive rights (given that equal interests are at stake), then perhaps we could justify according a right to police protection before a right to medical care. This is because we would have, by the idea of interpersonal sharing, reduced all mixed positive rights in question to derived positive rights. That is, the sharing of burdens changes the cases from agent-neutral (where we undo or prevent the effects of others' transgressions, in response to mixed rights) to agent-relative (where we undo or prevent the effects of our own transgressions. Furthermore, suppose that no one had any noncontractual pure positive (welfare) rights or even mixed positive rights. We might still justify some positive rights, such as the mixed positive right to police protection of one's negative rights, at the social level by reducing what would have been mixed positive rights (had they existed) to derived positive rights. We can do this by invoking individuals sharing their individual obligations to fulfill derived positive rights to prevent or undo the violation of negative rights.[29]

When conflicts between pure positive rights involve the same interests, the issues of balancing and aggregation that we discussed above return. In addition, there is a question of whether it matters what sort of pure positive right is at issue: a contractual right or a human (person) right to aid (assuming that there are such rights). A slightly different issue is raised by the following case: Suppose that Joe and Jim each contracted and paid for a portion of a life-saving drug to which no one has an equal right simply in virtue of being a person. Joe is on one island and Jim on another, and we only get to one in time to save him. I believe that each has a right to an equal chance to the drug. However, what if Susan is near Jim, also needs the drug to save her life, and could successfully use the part of it that Jim does not need, but she did not contract for it. Should her need count in determining to which island we should go? It seems to me that it should *not*, though if Jim wins in a random choice between him and Joe, he *and* Susan should be helped. (Perhaps she even has a right that something to which she per se has no right not be wasted.) Joe should not be deprived of his right to an equal chance to have what he has as much of a contractual right to as Jim, given its importance to him, on account of Susan's need in the absence of her contractual right, when need is not a ground for a right.

Positive rights that protect lesser interests may be combined with rights that protect greater interests, on one side, or positive rights (aggregated or not) that protect lesser interests may be alone against positive rights that protect weightier interests, on the other side. In some of these cases, the issues of whether to honor the right involving the weightier interest or whether to allow an aggregation of rights that protect lesser interests to override arises again. However, because we will not have to transgress a negative right of the person who has the weightier interest, I suggest that fulfilling the aggregation of rights that involve significant but lesser losses may often override fulfilling the positive right of the person with the weightier interest.[30] Whether this is true will depend, in part, on the manner in which the failure to fulfill the positive right that protects the strongest interest comes about. For example, it is impermissible to leave unfulfilled Joe's right to have his life saved in order that his death make available his organs, a serum from which will enable us to fulfill the positive rights of 100 people that we help them to avoid paralysis. However, this does not mean it is always impermissible to do what fulfills the rights of many people to each avoid a significant lesser loss rather than fulfill the right of Joe to avoid a more serious loss *because* Joe's organs will be available once he dies. For example, we might decide to spend our time distributing medicine to the many to stop their total paralyses rather than save Joe's life, even though we know that our medicine will have a potentially fatal side effect on each. We do this because we also know that Joe's death will make available his organs from which a life-saving serum for the many can be made.[31]

The manner in which the positive right would not be fulfilled will also be important to the permissibility of, sometimes, *not* fulfilling many positive rights that protect strong interests in order not to fail to fulfill a positive right that protects a lesser interest. So, we should not fail to fulfill Joe's positive right to medicine that prevents him from being a paraplegic in order to gain scientific knowledge from his illness, which is necessary and sufficient in order for us to fulfill a positive right of Jim and Susan against us to save their lives.

If it is sometimes permissible to accord many positive rights that protect lesser interests rather than accord a positive right that protects a weightier interest (as I have suggested), we must take seriously the following implication. Where x, y, and z are decreasing losses, n and m represent the number of such losses, and m>n: If $n(y) > x$, and $m(z) > n(y)$, transitivity implies that $m(z) > x$. It should be obvious that using this argument repeatedly would, if transitivity holds, lead to the conclusion that sometimes we should not fulfill Joe's right to be saved from death in order to help a billion (or more) people, each of whom would suffer a headache that each has a right we help to alleviate. This is, I believe, obviously the wrong conclusion. One way to hold that $n(y) > x$, but not $m(z) > x$, is to insist on comparing the size of x with the size of z to make sure that they are not too far apart. If they are too far apart, the aggregate of $m(z)$ cannot outweigh x, even if it can outweigh $n(y)$, which outweighs x. This implies that whether we should help $n(y)$ will be a function of the choices we have. If we have only the choice between $m(z)$ and $n(y)$, we should choose $m(z)$. If x is also an option along with the other two, however, we should choose $n(y)$. This means that the presence of an option upon which we would not act in any case (x) should result in a change in our choice from $m(z)$ to $n(y)$. This is not irrational.[32] Let us consider a particular case in more detail, assuming that everyone has a right to be aided.

Joe will die if we do not treat him, but only if we do not treat him could we save 1,000 people from quadriplegia. Assuming that quadriplegia is not as bad as death (so that we would save one person from death rather than one person from quadriplegia), it still seems permissible to save the greater number. Suppose Joe was never on the scene, and we just had a choice between helping 1,000 quadriplegics or helping 10,000 paraplegics. It seems permissible to help the greater number. Now suppose we face a choice involving all three types of people. We can save 10,000 people from paraplegia only if we save neither Joe nor the quadriplegics. I believe that it is disrespectful of Joe to attend to paraplegics who will lose much less than he, rather than save his life, but not disrespectful to him to save many who would suffer the much worse condition of quadriplegia. Hence, when Joe is present, one may go so far as save the quadriplegics but no further. ("Disrespectful to consider" is not transitive.)

Consider further variants on this case. Suppose that as a result of our decision to help the quadriplegics, Joe is now dead, but we have not yet given our resources to the quadriplegics. Should we treat the paraplegics instead, as we should have had Joe's life never been at stake? This would be wrong, I think, because the only legitimate reason for Joe now being dead (and so not available for help) is that we had a superior reason to help the quadriplegics rather than him. We should act only on the reason (i.e., help the quadriplegics) that would have justified our letting Joe die, given that he is dead because we decided to act on that reason. We must not forget the *history* of how we came to be at the point of helping the quadriplegics when we decide between them and the paraplegics.[33]

In sum, the aggregation of rights that protect lesser individual interests may matter, even if protecting them involves the failure to accord other positive rights protecting greater individual interests; however, qualitative considerations constrain the quantitative ones. That is, the size of the interest at stake (and compared pairwise) in each person matters.[34]

NOTES

This chapter is derived from my "Conflicts of Rights: Typology, Methodology, and Non-consequentialism," *Legal Theory* 7 (2001): 239–54. It adds new material but also omits sections of that article (at 243–46 and 250–54) that are already present in chapter 8. It should be thought of as a continuation of section IVC in chapter 8.

1. Though still more detailed than that presented in chapter 8, section IVC. I will make use of the theory of rights developed in chapter 8 and also theories about how conflicts over scarce resources should be resolved and when it is permissible to harm some people in order to save others, developed in chapters 2 and 5. The point is to see how these discussions can be applied to conflicts of rights. Other discussions can be found in my *Morality, Mortality*, vols. 1 and 2 (New York: Oxford University Press, 1993 and 1996).

2. See chapter 8, section IVC, for an argument that these are not the only kinds of conflicts of rights.

3. This contrast makes use of a sense of "positive" that is different from the one it has when we contrast moral rights and positive rights. The latter sense usually means "rights that are the result of governmental actions."

4. Negative rights might be derived from the violation of positive or negative rights as well. (Peter Graham reminded me of this.) For example, if I fail to give you something that I owed to you, you might get a right that I not take away something else from you. Such derived negative rights are less common than are the derived positive rights, I believe. I shall not discuss them here.

5. For a description of "agent-relative" and its contrasting idea, "agent-neutral," as employed to describe conflicts of rights, see chapter 8 and also below.

6. In keeping with what was said in n. 4, I will not consider conflicts between negative rights derived from either positive rights or (pure) negative rights. It would be interesting if these negative rights had a different significance from nonderived negative rights.

7. Jeremy Waldron, "Rights in Conflict," in his *Liberal Rights* (Cambridge: Cambridge University Press, 1993).

8. Of course, this is a conclusion that requires more argument, possibly of the sort I provided in chapter 2.

9. This principle corresponds to the Principle of Irrelevant Goods that I discussed in chapters 1 and 2, and in my *Morality, Morality*, vol. 1 (where it was called the Principle of Irrelevant Utilities).

10. Why this is so requires much explanation that I shall not provide now. See chapter 2 for more discussion independent of rights, that could be applied to rights.

11. See chapter 8.

12. I argued in chapter 8 that the strength of a right need not be a function solely of the interest it protects. In section IIIB, below, I consider another argument for this claim.

13. As described in chapter 5.

14. This case is based on the Switches and Skates Case presented by Peter Unger in his *Living High and Letting Die* (New York: Oxford University Press, 1996). Criticism of Unger's conclusion about this case and further support for my conclusion here is provided in chapters 6 and 8. I also say something more in defense of my conclusion in section IIIB below. I am here assuming that there is some sort of negative right that will at least be infringed if we redirect a trolley toward someone, rather than simply that there is no right not to be harmed by having the trolley redirected.

15. Again, I take this to be a consideration weighing against a theory of rights that focuses solely on interests. For more on this, see chapter 8.

16. I discuss this principle in detail in chapter 5, where I call it the Doctrine of Productive Purity (DPP). However, it is there laid out without employing the notion of rights.

17. See chapter 5 for more on this.

18. I discussed this test in chapter 8.

19. Described in chapter 8.

20. And it may be subject to intransitivities due to interaction effects. See chapter 8 for more on this.

21. In chapter 8, I also discussed another test for measuring stringency, the Effort Test.

22. Some might say that Jim and Susan have no positive right against their doctor to be saved, only to be saved by certain means but not others. This can then be given as a reason for there being no conflict of positive rights between saving them and saving Joe with medicine to which he has a positive right, even though his being saved means that his organs will not be available for Jim and Susan. But if we say that Jim and Susan have a positive right to be saved by a particular means, such as medicine, it is always possible that getting the medicine will only be possible if (for some reason) we first get Joe's organs. Then we shall either have to say that there is a conflict between Jim's and Susan's positive right to be saved by medicine and Joe's positive right to have his life saved by medicine, or else we shall have to say that Jim and Susan have no positive right to be saved by medicine. (In general, for any way in which we try to limit Jim's and Susan's right, we can imagine that not aiding or harming Joe is necessary for fulfilling that limited right.) Suppose that one just says that Jim and Susan have a positive right to be saved only if it does not involve transgressing Joe's rights in a certain manner. This description of their positive right seems just to incorporate all of the reasoning we would have gone through in deciding how to resolve a conflict between positive rights, if we assumed that Jim and Susan had a positive right and then showed that it could not be permissibly fulfilled due to Joe's positive right. Furthermore, it seems to stem from a view that there is no positive right unless it must be granted. But if we think that rights can exist even if, because of a conflict, they cannot be fulfilled, we need not accept this view of positive rights.

23. But notice that it is permissible to *not* fulfill Joe's positive right in the following case: A strong wind is about to push Joe off a bridge, as a consequence of which he will die. We can either fulfill Joe's positive right to our help or else fulfill Jim's and Susan's positive right to our help to stop a trolley that is headed toward killing them. We may help Jim and Susan. What if the only way to save Jim and Susan will cause them organ failure, from which they would shortly die, were it not that organs could be collected from Joe once he dies that could be transplanted into Jim and Susan? It is still permissible to stop the trolley rather than help Joe, even though the only reason it is permissible is that Joe's organs will counteract a bad effect of our saving Jim and Susan. This case is like cases discussed in chapters 4 and 5 in which we act because an evil* will sustain a greater good.

24. It might be thought that the following is a not-aiding case analogous to (d): A trolley is headed away from Jim and Susan and toward Joe. Joe has a positive right that we help him to avoid trolley threats, but helping him means that we do what makes the trolley go back toward Jim and Susan. But this case involves a conflict between not-aiding Joe and *causing harm to* Jim and Susan. Hence, it is not an example of a conflict of positive rights.

25. This case (with my addition of contractual rights to aid) is based on an example of Thomas Scanlon's. Samuel Scheffler referred to Scanlon's example in his *The Rejection of Consequentialism* (Oxford: Oxford University Press, 1982), p. 109.

26. For example, Scheffler and Scanlon, as cited in the previous note.

27. There could also be a conflict for one agent between fulfilling a pure positive right and fulfilling derived positive rights to prevent or undo his violations of positive rights. In such cases, since positive rights will be transgressed whatever he does, fulfilling one has no priority over fulfilling the other (given the same interests), I think.

28. If the government itself has a negative duty not to interfere in some respects with its citizens, its merely doing so would not involve its fulfilling a positive right. However, if it had violated or might violate the negative right that some of its citizens have against it, it could have a derived positive duty to expend resources to remedy or prevent its violation. Nevertheless, as noted in section IIIB, if such a derived positive duty were in conflict with the government respecting the negative right in other citizens, it might not be permissible to transgress the negative rights of these others. (The manner in which interference would occur may be crucial, of course.)

29. Stephen Holmes and Cass Sunstein, in *The Cost of Rights: Why Liberty Depends on Taxes* (New York: Norton, 2000), argue that justifying (what I call) pure positive welfare rights at the social level is no more (or less) difficult than justifying positive rights to police protection to prevent violations of one's negative rights. However, I have suggested that, while it is true that both are positive rights in the sense of providing resources, arguments for derived positive rights based on negative rights can be separated from arguments for pure positive rights. Alan Gewirth, in "Are All Rights Positive?" *Philosophy & Public Affairs* 30 (2001): 321–33, points out that Holmes and Sunstein want to argue that all rights are positive in two senses that I have distinguished. First, they claim that to have any "teeth," moral rights must be positive in the sense of "legislated," or otherwise be the creation of government (call this positive G). Second, they claim that creating the legal rights is already a positive act in the other sense of "positive," as the government is providing us with something. This is true even if it legislates a negative right. But we can object to Holmes' and Sunstein's argument, for the government's legislating rights would fulfill a *positive* right in the sense of a right to be provided with something—call this positive P—only if we had a positive right (P) to such governmental legislative action. Assume that we do have such a right. (It cannot be a legal right; it must be a moral right.) This does not mean that the negative right which we have a positive right that the government legislate is itself a right to some positive assistance. And it remains open for someone to say that we have positive P rights to the government putting into law (as positive G rights) negative rights, but we do not have positive P rights to the government putting into law rights with positive P content. Further, for reasons given in the text, we might have a moral right to have the government fulfill derived positive rights even if not pure positive rights.

30. For more on this sort of distinction between negative and positive rights in a context where the aggregated interests do not involve any rights, see chapters 1 and 16 in this volume and my *Morality, Mortality*, vol. 1.

31. A similar point was made in n. 23, and is discussed in more detail in cases not necessarily involving rights in chapter 4.

32. All of this will also be true when we must choose whom to aid where no rights are involved.

33. The analysis of these cases is reminiscent of the argumentative structure in the discussion of supererogation and obligation in chapter 1. In the argument's slots, doing one's duty is the substitute for helping Joe; doing the supererogatory is the substitute for helping the quadriplegics; and pursuing personal goals is the substitute for helping the paraplegics. Considered on their own, personal goals may take precedence over supererogatory conduct. Personal goals may not, however, take precedence over the duty. In the context where we permissibly abandon our duty in order to do the supererogatory act, it is no longer true that we may refuse to do the supererogatory act and pursue personal goals instead. We should either be doing our duty or doing the supererogatory act. And this remains true even though at the time we would do the supererogatory act, it is no longer possible for us to do our dutiful act instead.

34. I also consider this approach to stopping the downward movement to aggregating smaller losses in chapter 16.

SECTION III

Responsibilities

10

RESPONSIBILITY AND COLLABORATION

I. INTRODUCTION

In previous chapters, I have discussed the form of the constraint on harming other people and how this relates to rights that individuals have. In doing so, I have emphasized what I called a victim-focused account of constraints. I have also considered the difference between killing and letting die (including letting be killed). Now I shall consider agent-focused concerns that may also have a role in constraining agents from transgressing negative rights and in deciding to let die rather than kill.[1]

The doctrine of negative responsibility holds that individuals are *just as* responsible for things they allow to happen or fail to prevent as they are for things they bring about.[2] In an attempt to criticize this doctrine, which he believes is an important component of consequentialism, Bernard Williams uses a case commonly referred to as Jim and the Indians. Here is his description of it:

> Jim finds himself in the central square of a small South American town. Tied up against the wall are a row of twenty Indians, most terrified, a few defiant, in front of them several armed men in uniform. A heavy man in a sweat-stained khaki shirt turns out to be the Captain in charge and, after a good deal of questioning of Jim which establishes that he got there by accident while on a botanical expedition, explains that the Indians are a *random*

group of inhabitants who, after recent acts of protest against the government, are just about to be killed to remind other possible protesters of the advantages of not protesting. However, since Jim is an honored visitor from another land, the Captain is happy to offer him a guest's privilege of killing one of the Indians himself. If Jim accepts, then as a special mark of the occasion, the other Indians will be let off. Of course, if Jim refuses, then there is no special occasion, and Pedro [the Captain's assistant] here will do what he was about to do when Jim arrived and kill them all. Jim, with some desperate recollection of schoolboy fiction, wonders whether if he got hold of a gun, he could hold the Captain, Pedro, and the rest of the soldiers to threat, but it is quite clear from the set-up that nothing of that kind is going to work: any attempt at that sort of thing will mean that all the Indians will be killed, and himself. The men against the wall, and the other villagers, understand the situation and are obviously begging him to accept. What should he do?[3]

Here are some arguments for and against Jim killing one of the Indians:

(i)(a) The *act-consequentialist* will argue that Jim clearly should kill the one Indian because it maximizes the good. It is better that one dies than that twenty die.[4]

(i)(b) Further, the act-consequentialist will argue that if Jim does not kill the one, he will be responsible for the deaths of all of the Indians. If he could have prevented the Captain from killing them and did not, he has *negative* responsibility for the deaths and for the Captain causing the deaths. This is so even when one of the causal links to the deaths of the twenty is the intervening act of another agent, the Captain.[5]

A *nonconsequentialist* might argue for the permissibility of Jim killing the one Indian and do so in the following ways:

(ii)(a) The one would die anyway, so he is no worse off than he would otherwise have been, while the other Indians will be better off if Jim kills the one than they would otherwise have been. Killing the one is thus a Pareto optimal move for those the Captain threatens.[6] It is at least not against the one Indian's interest to be killed by Jim and in the interests of the other Indians. (Call this factor "Pareto.")

In this respect, the case is different from one in which Jim would have to kill a bystander who would not have died anyway as a result of what the Captain will do, in order to save the Indians (Bystander Case). In the Bystander Case, a nonconsequentialist would think that Jim may *not* kill the one. This is because the bystander has a right not to be killed in the particular way Jim would kill him when he would be made significantly worse off, even if his death minimizes the number of people who get killed.[7] The bystander's right acts as a constraint on Jim's autonomy, even if Jim were willing to kill the bystander. Further, neither the Bystander Case nor Williams's Jim and the Indians Case is like one in which we redirect a threat, or redirect persons away from a threat, thereby killing someone who would not have soon died (as in the Trolley Case). In cases where we would have to redirect a mechanical threat, nonconsequentialists typically think that the way in which we kill one bystander, who would not otherwise die, makes killing permissible in order to save a greater number.[8] Would they also agree that if we could, we might redirect an agent like the Captain, so that he harms one person who would not otherwise have been harmed instead of harming a greater number of other people? I believe this would be permissible too.[9]

(ii)(b)(1) It would be in the *ex ante* self-interest of *each* of the Indians for Jim to select one to be killed, since they will then *each* have a reduced probability of being killed. (Call this factor "Better Off.") There is reason to doubt that (ii)(b)(1) is necessary. For we could change the case so that the Captain says that if Jim kills one particular Indian, say, Gonzalez, the Captain will not kill the others (Gonzalez Case). Now it will not be *ex ante* to Jim's killing in the interest of each that Jim kill someone. Does this change the permissibility of Jim acting when the Captain makes his offer? I do not believe so, even though it is morally significant that Jim's killing Gonzalez is now just a way of saving the others (without making Gonzalez worse than he would otherwise have been), and so is not the upshot of any scheme that was *ex ante* in Gonzalez's own interest.[10]

(ii)(b)(2) If each knows that Better Off is true, we may imagine the case (as Williams does) in which each asks that Jim shoot one Indian. Then we would have another reason for Jim to agree, that is, the actual *consent* of each person to Jim doing so. Perhaps they consent on the ground that before they know who will be shot, it is in each one's interest to have Jim shoot someone. (Call this factor "Consent.")

This argument for the permissibility of Jim killing one Indian is consistent, on the nonconsequentialist view, with the rejection of the claim that Jim would be responsible for all of the deaths if he does *not* kill.

Suppose a nonconsequentialist could endorse even Jim killing Gonzalez on the basis of Pareto (independently of [ii][b][1] and [2]). Why could he not then also endorse killing anyone who will soon die in order to save others? For example, why could he not endorse killing a patient who will soon die anyway in order to retrieve the patient's organs in optimal conditions so that he may save five lives with those organs (Organs Case)? But in the Gonzalez Case, Jim does to one Indian what would otherwise have been done to him (i.e., he kills him instead of the Captain killing him) or does something better for him, and to stop a threat he shares with others. By contrast, if we were to kill the patient for his organs, the patient would be killed rather than otherwise die a natural death, he would have his organs used rather than otherwise simply die, and to stop a different threat than he faces. These differences from what would otherwise happen may affect permissibility.

Suppose it is important that Jim does to the Indian he kills only what the Captain would have done to him or something better. This implies that the nonconsequentialist argument for the permissibility of Jim killing the Indian that we have considered (which does not specifically include consent of all parties) should not necessarily imply the permissibility of Jim killing the Indian in the following case: Regardless of what Jim does, the Captain will inject the nineteen Indians chosen at random with a slow-acting fatal toxin. But only if Jim, rather than the Captain, kills the one remaining Indian, the Captain will allow Jim to also use that Indian's organs in order to make an antitoxin that will save the nineteen.[11]

On the basis of this discussion, we can add that if (ii)(b)(2) (Consent) were not part of the nonconsequentialist argument, we should substitute (ii)(c): Jim does to the one Indian only what would otherwise have been done to him or something better for him, and the one Indian has happen to him only what would otherwise have happened to him or something better for him. (Call this "Identity or Better.")[12]

(iii) Williams argues that while it may be permissible to kill the one Indian, it is not clearly so. That is, the decision is not merely a matter of weighing the lives saved versus the life lost and the unhappiness of Jim at doing the killing. In particular, he argues that in refusing to shoot, Jim would not affect the world through the Captain nor make the Captain shoot. But if Jim were morally obligated to shoot because the Captain would otherwise shoot more people, this would mean that the Captain's aims and intentions affect Jim's actions so that these actions are no longer the expression of Jim's own aims and projects. This constitutes an attack on Jim's integrity as an agent. (Williams must think that this is so, even though the Captain also does not strictly *make* Jim shoot; Jim has a choice and is not personally under a threat.) These are the criticisms that Williams raises against the doctrine of negative responsibility. They have come to be known as the Integrity Objection.

If the Integrity Objection is to be successful,[13] it must not merely reflect concern that one's acts not be manipulated by someone else. For suppose an evil person pushes an infant into a pond where he will drown if I do not save him. The evil person does this merely in order to "control" my behavior because he knows that I would stop my other activities in order to save the infant, and he wanted to disrupt my day. If I know all of this, does it give me strong reason not to save the infant? I do not think so. This suggests that it is crucial to the Integrity Objection that one will have to do an act otherwise objectionable (e.g., killing rather than saving).

Among the arguments a *nonconsequentialist* (including Williams) might offer for Jim *not* killing are:

(iv)(a) Jim has a commitment to his own values, and his personal values may commit him to nonviolence against innocents. The Integrity Objection may be about such interference with one's values.

(iv)(b) In killing, Jim collaborates with evil, given that the Captain has arranged for the killings, and by jointly intended coordination he will use Jim to carry out part of his aims. This complaint could not exist if the Indians were under a threat from a completely natural disaster.

(iv)(c) As suggested in the discussion leading to the Identity or Better factor, it might not always be permissible to do what is in the *ex ante* interests of all of the victims. Here is another example: Suppose that a stranger who is coming to live in a town gives a local citizen the option of having the stranger either (1) murder one person or (2) work at a chemical plant (when no one else would), when he foresees that the activities there will result in the deaths of twenty townspeople. It is in the citizen's interest, *ex ante*, that the stranger commit the one murder rather than work at the plant, since it lowers the citizen's chances of dying. Yet it is impermissible to commit murder and far less wrong to work at a plant where ordinary procedures foreseeably cause more harm.[14] This objection really amounts to saying that the Pareto factor is not sufficient reason for killing.

My primary aim in this chapter is to consider the possibility that a nonconsequentialist should take the collaboration argument (iv)(b) as sometimes a consideration *for* Jim killing one Indian rather than against it. Hence, I wish to consider the possibility that, at least in some special circumstances, there is something to be said in favor of collaboration with evil. I shall try to show this by comparing two sorts of cases—those in which agents like Jim are put in positions that give them the opportunity to harm others at the request of a villain and those in which agents like Jim are put in positions that give them the opportunity to harm others *not* at the request of another person—and arguing that we are often more willing to recommend an agent harming others in the first case than in the second. The factors of Pareto, Better Off, and Identity or Better, which a non-consequentialist might give in favor of an agent killing someone, as well as the Integrity Objection against killing, can be present equally in both types of cases, yet sometimes it is the presence of collaboration that may make killing permissible or at least morally less problematic.

I also aim to defend two broader claims. First, it is a neglected aspect of Williams's case that, instead of it being true that if Jim does not act, he has negative responsibility for the deaths of the Captain's victims, it is true that the Captain has *positive responsibility* for killing one Indian if Jim does act. More specifically, my first claim here is that in some cases the positive moral responsibility for Jim's act, which would otherwise have been Jim's, is the Captain's. The second claim is that it is morally more acceptable for someone in Jim's position to act when the positive moral responsibility for the act will be the Captain's than when it will not. A corollary of these two claims is that in circumstances where we deal with illegitimate authority, a certain sort of responsiveness is preferable to taking the initiative just because it makes possible the switch in positive moral responsibility. I shall also consider how these claims relate to Williams's criticisms of consequentialism. In this connection, I consider the possibility that, contrary to what Williams thinks, the Integrity Objection to consequentialism is not raised by his case of Jim and the Indians, since it is only raised by cases in which positive moral responsibility remains with an agent. In conclusion, I shall examine the implications of my discussion for two further questions: (1) Do my claims help to distinguish the behavior of Jim from that of George, a character in another case that Williams presents? (2) What do my claims imply about physician-assisted suicide and euthanasia?[15]

II. THE CAPTAIN CASES

In this section, let us consider variations on Williams's Jim and the Indians Case (henceforth W). I shall refer to these variations as the Captain cases (henceforth C).[16]

Consider C(Scan): Everything is as in W, except that there is only the Captain who would shoot (without Pedro); the Captain does *not* make his offer to Jim; and the Indians themselves are not in a position to ask Jim to shoot or not to shoot. Rather, Jim has an infallible brain-scanning device that tells him that the Captain will kill all of the Indians unless Jim kills one, in which case the Captain will release the other Indians. The Captain is inaccessible, and if Jim acts, he will do so without telling the Captain or the Indians anything.

I claim that it would be a much more serious moral matter for Jim to kill the one Indian in C(Scan) than for him to do so in W. Indeed, it might be impermissible to do so in C(Scan), even if it were permissible to do so in W. Furthermore, C(Scan), not W, is closer to a generic sort of case for consequentialist reasoning, since consequentialist issues arise when we can maximize the good; it is not necessary that someone offer us the opportunity to do so. So in focusing on W rather than C(Scan), Williams might not be making the strongest case against consequentialism, if acting in W is easier to justify than acting in C(Scan).[17]

Since I removed two factors (in addition to Pedro) from W to create C(Scan), it is also possible to imagine two other cases: C(Request), in which the Captain makes no offer but the Indians know of the result of the brain scan and ask Jim to shoot, and C(Offer), in which the Captain makes his offer but the Indians are not in a position to ask Jim to shoot or not to shoot. In C(Request) there is *ex ante* consent of the potential victim (and Pareto is true if Jim shoots) but no offer; in C(Offer) there is no victim consent or refusal but there is an offer by the Captain. I would make an additional claim about these cases, that Jim has a weaker moral reason not to shoot in C(Request) and C(Offer) than in C(Scan). If the claim about C(Offer) is true, then it supports the conclusion that "collaboration with evil" can be a consideration that overrides other objections to killing.

Now consider C(Jim's Offer): Everything is as in C(Scan) (where the Indians are not in a position to ask Jim to shoot or not to shoot and the Captain makes no offer to Jim), except that *Jim offers* to the Captain to kill one of the Indians if the Captain will then not kill the rest. (Jim might do this rather than just kill the one Indian, because he is unsure about the scan that predicts how the Captain will react after Jim kills an Indian, and Jim wishes to elicit a promise. But even if Jim had no brain scan of the Captain, he might make the offer.) In this case, there is also collaboration with evil, that is, some sort of jointly intended coordination of behavior between the evil Captain and Jim. However, I would claim, it is morally more problematic for Jim to make the offer to kill than for him to act on the Captain's offer, and even possibly that he should not do the former while he may permissibly do the latter. If this is so, then we should say that "collaboration with evil at the instigation of the evil party," not simply collaboration, may sometimes be a factor that overrides other objections to killing.

Now consider C(Complete): The Captain has set a bomb, which is now completely out of his control, so that it will kill all of the Indians *unless* Jim kills one, in which case the bomb will not go off. The Indians are not in a position to ask Jim to shoot or not to shoot. In this case, the Captain's action would not intervene between Jim's inaction and the death of the Indians, because the Captain's part is complete once he sets up the bomb in a certain way.

Is the fact that the Captain's act would not come after Jim's decision morally relevant in deciding whether Jim has negative responsibility for any killings he does not prevent? I believe that if one thinks that he would have no negative responsibility in the other cases, one should also think that he has none in C(Complete). In C(Complete), however, I claim, it may not make a difference to the moral difficulty or the moral permissibility of Jim killing an Indian whether the Captain offers to let

Jim shoot or whether Jim simply takes advantage of the known effect of shooting. Either way, it is permissible for him to shoot.[18]

III. POSITIVE MORAL RESPONSIBILITY

I claim that the Captain cases so far can be divided into two types: T1 and T2. Tentatively, we can describe T1 as involving Jim's collaboration in a scheme in which the Captain has responsibility for creating the contingency of the better outcome—in which he does not kill—on Jim's killing, and for making an offer based on this. It may be more permissible for Jim to kill in T1 cases than to kill in T2 cases. We can tentatively describe the T2 cases as ones in which Jim simply acts to prevent the worse outcome or where Jim's collaboration is in a scheme in which he has responsibility for initiating the contingency of the better outcome, in which the Captain does not kill, on Jim's killing.

I claim that there is a moral difference between T1 and T2, even when it is true of both that good is maximized; the factors of Pareto, Better Off, and Identity or Better apply to both; the Captain is a malicious, morally responsible agent; and Jim is against being a killer. What I believe accounts for the difference in permissibility between the two types of cases is that, in T1 cases, the Captain has *positive moral responsibility* for the consequences of Jim's act. I take this to mean that he is to be held completely morally responsible in the sense of being to blame for, being at fault for, the negative consequences of Jim's act. He is also completely responsible, in the sense of being accountable, for the negative consequences (i.e., liable for criticism, punishment, or compensation for the death).[19] This is true even though Jim kills someone and the Captain winds up killing no one. That is, I take it that Jim is causally responsible for the death of the Indian. Furthermore, his choice to shoot was what I shall call a responsible one, because it was voluntary and he was in a sound state of mind. I do not deny that insofar as causing death is an intrinsic negative, Jim has done something intrinsically negative.[20]

The moral responsibility for killing that the Captain has is *in addition* to the other things for which the Captain is responsible and accountable as a result of his own acts, for example, threatening and endangering people. If Jim shoots an Indian to stop the Captain from killing all of the Indians, the Captain is responsible for the killing in T1 cases, in the sense that he is completely blameworthy for the murder; he is a perpetrator, not just an instigator.[21] We lay the negative consequences of the act at the Captain's doorstep and not just "negatively," that is, because he allowed Jim to kill, but positively, as something he brought about *because he made the offer*. The Captain asks Jim to do something if Jim wishes to stop the Captain from doing worse. This offer is an act,[22] an act soliciting Jim to become involved in the Captain's lethal plan, an act that aims to incorporate Jim's actions into the Captain's plans and actions. The offer is designed to encourage Jim to kill, where killing is something he does for the Captain so that the Captain (or his underlings) do not kill, and it involves claiming to make a commitment to Jim if he does kill. The fact that the offer is such an act, however, is not sufficient to account for the Captain's complete

positive moral responsibility for the negative consequences. For recall C(Jim's Offer), in which Jim makes the offer to the Captain. When the Captain agrees, this is an
act as well (that encourages and claims to commit), yet in that case I do not think that
positive moral responsibility for the negative consequences (e.g., death) of Jim's act is
placed *completely* at the Captain's doorstep, though he may share in them and be the
only one properly punished for murder. The Captain's act in T1 cases, but not in
C(Jim's Offer), is the *initiation* of a lethal plot.[23]

However, Jim can be completely morally responsible and accountable for the
good consequences both of his own act of killing the one and of the Captain's *not*
killing nineteen, if the Captain chooses not to shoot because Jim does. The Captain
gets no credit for the reduction in the number killed by his making an offer to, or his
accepting an offer from, Jim. This is, in part, because he could have saved all twenty
by simply deciding not to kill, independently of what Jim does. (It may also be
because he did not reduce the number to be killed for the purpose of reducing the
number killed, but rather in order to honor or involve Jim.)[24]

Characterizing Jim as a *substitute actor* who acts on behalf of someone else comes
closest to capturing the way in which responsibility gets shifted from the agent, Jim,
to the Captain in T1 cases, I believe. I shall call such a substitute actor someone's
Agent (capitalized to distinguish this sense of agent from the idea of a moral agent). A
lawyer who carries out an eviction of a poor tenant is the Agent of his client who owns
the building. When it is permissible for the lawyer to be an Agent in this capacity, he
is not morally responsible for the bad effects of his act; it is his client who is morally
responsible and accountable. Responsibility gets shifted. Indeed, it can sometimes be
morally permissible to be an Agent and do an act as an Agent, without its being
morally correct for anyone (including the client) to do the act if one is not an Agent.
So insofar as a client has a right to do what is wrong, he may sometimes do something
any person morally ought not do through an Agent who acts permissibly qua Agent.

However, in traditional Agent roles, the client is also morally responsible for
the *good* consequences of the Agent's behavior. This is because the professional
Agent does not usually decide to do the client's bidding because he can thereby
bring about a greater good that the client does not *simply* intend. (Evidence that a
client does not simply intend a greater good is that he could bring it about without
involving an Agent at all, but does not.) Jim, by contrast, does the Captain's
bidding so that he can bring about a greater good that the Captain does not simply
intend. Hence, the good consequences are at Jim's doorstep.

When someone chooses to become an Agent, she is morally responsible for
that choice, but this is not the same as moral responsibility for the consequences of
the acts one performs as an Agent. Choosing to be an Agent will involve evaluating
how bad what one is asked to do is and what good will be achieved by being an
Agent. Suppose, for example, that someone is paralyzed and needs an Agent to
carry out his wish to break a beautiful vase he owns. Someone might believe that
increasing the autonomy of paralyzed people is a good and decide to help the
person to do something intrinsically wrong that the paralyzed person would have a
right to do. But if a paralyzed Vermeer asked to have a picture he had painted
destroyed, one might think it wrong to become the Agent who destroyed it, even if

Vermeer would have a right to do the wrong thing and destroy his own paintings. If it is wrong to become an Agent, one might well retain moral responsibility for the bad consequences of the acts one performs as an Agent. (Notice that consistent with thinking it wrong to be the Agent of destruction, one might think it permissible to be an Agent who provides a tool of destruction to a paralyzed Vermeer who is unable to reach it but capable of using it. Here it is one's act of destroying a sublime art work per se that one should find unoverrideably objectionable.)

I suggest that the fact that one can maximize the good and that the factors of Pareto, Better Off, and Identity or Better are reasons in favor of killing can help justify someone in becoming the Captain's Agent, and the fact that the Captain will have positive moral responsibility and accountability for the negative consequences understandably helps one to make the decision to be an Agent. The permissibility of being the Captain's Agent, of course, cannot depend on the Captain having a right to do the wrong act (as the paralyzed person discussed above has). So, if I am correct, it must sometimes be permissible for one to be an Agent for someone who is doing what he has no right to do, even when one is not under duress.

Why does the fact that the Captain will have complete positive moral responsibility and accountability understandably help someone to make the decision to kill? Here is one suggestion. Some have discussed Williams's case as raising the question of Jim's preserving or losing his "moral purity" (or "dirtying his hands").[25] One way to deal with the question of moral purity is just to note that one cannot lose one's moral purity by doing the right act, and so deciding what is the right act must be done independently, and precede determination, of moral purity. But it is possible that the distinction between T1 and T2 cases tracks another sense of moral purity, namely a concern not to be responsible for bad aspects of even a right act. Perhaps someone who acts as an Agent for another can retain such purity, because moral responsibility for negative aspects (e.g., deaths) will then belong to another. We might call this hyper-purity. By contrast, even if Jim killing in C(Scan) were right, he would, I suggest, have some moral responsibility and accountability for negative aspects or consequences of his act. This responsibility for the negative aspects of one's act that an Agent lacks may give rise to the sense that one has lost one's moral purity, *even when one does the overall right act*, thus understandably giving one more reason not to act. (The accountability may also increase the burden on one.)[26] This sort of reason for not acting can help account for the wish of someone in C(Scan) that he had never come on his botanical expedition and had stayed home instead, though then all twenty would have died. (Of course, Jim in C[Offer] may have the same wish simply because he will kill someone. By contrast, a consequentialist should not regret having landed on an opportunity to save nineteen lives.)

On the Agent analysis of W and C(Offer), Jim's position can be compared to the position occupied by those citizens who, according to Michael Walzer,[27] want to vote and work for politicians who will bear the responsibility for the nasty acts the citizens want done for the greater good, but not done by themselves. They want the opportunity to assist (by voting for or working for) those who will do, and bear the responsibility for, the nasty acts. Jim, by contrast, will do the nasty act but in a context where he too will assist someone who will bear the responsibility for it.

In sum, positive responsibility thus has at least three components: (1) There is the component of who responsibly (i.e., voluntarily and of sound mind) does the act of killing. I do not deny that Jim has this responsibility as he chooses to be causally responsible for killing. The second and third components of positive responsibility are who is (2) morally responsible and (3) accountable for the consequences of Jim's act, in virtue of other acts (such as the Captain's offer) responsibly undertaken. There is a division of the second and third components: who is morally responsible and accountable for the good aspects of the consequences and who is morally responsible and accountable for the bad aspects of the consequences. In T1 cases, Jim is completely morally responsible and accountable for the good aspects, but the Captain is completely morally responsible and accountable for the bad aspects. This helps to preserve Jim's moral hyper-purity described above.[28]

IV. RESPONSIBILITY AND NEGATIVE CONSEQUENCES

On the basis of cases W, C(Scan), and C(Offer), it might be suggested that the following four conditions together are *sufficient* to make the Captain completely morally responsible and accountable for the negative consequences of the killing Jim brings about: (I) The Captain is fully able to desist from killing the Indians if he chooses to. (II) The Captain responsibly chooses (i.e., voluntarily and in sound mind) to make it the case that his not killing is contingent on Jim's killing. (The capacity to do this is dependent on the truth of [I].) (III) He informs Jim, by way of his offer, of his (i.e., the Captain) making his behavior contingent on Jim's behavior, making it reasonable for Jim to believe that the Captain's not killing is contingent on Jim's behavior. (IV) The fact that one can maximize the good and that the factors of Pareto, Better Off, and Identity or Better apply *contribute* to making it morally permissible for Jim to kill the one Indian.[29]

Are any of these four conditions (I, II, III, IV) *necessary* for *any* responsibility for the negative consequences to be with the Captain? There is reason to doubt that (II), (III), and (IV) are necessary for this. That is, the Captain can have some responsibility without them. This also gives us reason, as we shall see, to doubt our tentative characterization of T1. Let us first consider (IV). We know from the Gonzalez Case, in which it is known from the start that the Captain asks Jim to kill one particular Indian, that the factor of Better Off is not necessary. That is, it need not be in the victim's *ex ante* interest that Jim kill him. Further, suppose that the Pareto factor weighing on the side of permissibility were not present because, for example, the person Jim would have to kill is an innocent bystander who would not die soon anyway. If, in the Bystander Case, the Captain offers Jim the opportunity to kill the innocent bystander, and Jim does so in order to save the Indians, he will do the morally wrong act, I believe. Will the absence of this factor mean that the Captain is *not* at all morally responsible and accountable for the killing? I believe not.

Jim is reasonably expected to avoid doing the wrong act in the circumstances, especially given that neither his judgment nor his integrity are undermined by any threat to his own well-being. Yet, this need not make the Captain have no moral responsibility and accountability for murder in the Bystander Case. It is possible that in the Bystander Case *both* Jim and the Captain would bear responsibility for the negative effects of shooting the innocent bystander. If so, this would imply that the Pareto factor is not necessary in order for some responsibility to lie with the Captain. (For my purposes, I need not prove this, since everything I want to say would hold if Jim alone were morally responsible and accountable for wrongful killing in the Bystander Case.) Still, (IV), or at least maximizing the good, and the factors of Pareto and Identity or Better might be necessary in order for *complete* responsibility for the negative consequences of Jim's shooting to lie with the Captain.

Does the contrast between C(Offer) and the Bystander Case imply that if Jim does what it is at least not wrong for him to do in the circumstances, the Captain alone will be fully morally responsible and accountable for a wrong, and if Jim does what it is wrong for him to do, the Captain will not alone be fully morally responsible and accountable for the wrong? Perhaps, but it is misleading to say this, because part of my claim is that when the good would be maximized and the factors of Pareto, Better Off, and Identity or Better apply, it could still be true that Jim should *not* kill the Indian, unless the Captain makes the offer. This is because sometimes Jim's act could be right only *because* the offer makes *complete* positive moral responsibility and accountability for its negative consequences lie with the Captain. That the Captain will alone be morally responsible and accountable for the negative consequences is part of what makes it permissible for Jim to kill the Indian. (It is, of course, possible that the immediately preceding claim is false. If so, it could still be claimed that the fulfillment of [I] through [III] above in conjunction with Jim doing an act that is *permissible* in virtue of maximizing the good and the factors of Pareto, Better Off, and Identity or Better [IV] makes the Captain completely morally responsible and accountable for murder, and his responsibility and accountability makes what is already a permissible act justifiably less problematic and more attractive to Jim.)

Why does an act become either permissible or more attractive if complete positive responsibility for negative consequences lies with the Captain? I have already indicated (in section III) that it may have something to do with a refined conception of moral purity—hyper-purity—but there is more to be said that must be postponed (until section VI below). We must first deal with other aspects of the location of positive responsibility.

Notice that what I have said implies that if Jim's act will be permissible in C(Offer), this does not mean that there is no wrong for the Captain to be guilty of. Suppose that the Captain was worried about murdering people, but wanted to have them killed anyway. Could he arrange to threaten the twenty, so that Jim could reasonably be induced to accept an offer to kill one instead, and then *no one* would commit murder (understood as unjustified killing)? But this scheme of indirection does not work. Jim's act would not be wrong, in part, because it was reasonable for him to believe that the Captain would otherwise have killed everyone, and *that* act would have been wrong. To use some legal language, in some cases it is the solicitor's proposed wrong act that helps make the solicited act (Jim's) *not* wrong and makes the solicitor morally responsible and accountable for the negative consequences of the solicited act. In such cases, *the wrongness of the solicitor's proposed act attaches to the solicited act (even if in diminished form)*, and the solicited act attaches to the solicitor. That is, it is a wrong killing of one person instead of a wrong killing of twenty that attaches to the Captain. In sum, the Captain, instead of Jim, not only gets moral responsibility for negative consequences, he also gets treated as though he had done a wrong act of killing, when no wrong act of killing actually occurred.

That Jim does not do the wrong act in killing the one Indian in W or C(Offer) means that the Captain, if he should be so inclined, could not justifiably have Jim punished for his action. But the location in the Captain of all positive moral responsibility and accountability for negative consequences, and the attribution of unjustified killing to him, should mean that the Captain may permissibly be punished for murder. This liability for punishment cannot be defeated, I believe, by the claim that if Jim acts, we can now never know for sure that the Captain would have killed or ordered anyone to be killed. Indeed, I think that the liability cannot be defeated even if we find out that the Captain would not, in fact, have killed anyone (or ordered anyone to be killed). This is because the Captain made it *reasonable* for Jim, at the time he had to make his decision, to think only that the Captain would do the killing if he, Jim, did not kill one Indian. This is part of what (III) states.

If the Captain would not have killed anyone, then Jim does not kill someone who would have died anyway, nor does he maximize the good. Furthermore, (II) is not true. For if the Captain would never have killed, he cannot have made his *not* killing contingent on Jim's behavior. On one view of this scenario, Jim has still not committed a wrongful act in killing, in part because it was only reasonable for him to have believed that the Indian would have died anyway, that he would maximize the good, and that the Captain's not killing was contingent on his act. Then the Captain is still completely morally responsible and accountable for one murder. On another view, Jim did a wrongful act, as he killed someone who actually would not otherwise have died, he did not lower anyone's probability of dying, and did no good at all. But the reasonableness of his beliefs about the act imply that he is not at fault in doing it. This leaves it open that the person who led him to believe that his act would have the factors that make for permissibility is the one who bears responsibility for the occurrence of the impermissible act.[30] Hence, on both views, the Captain need not be responsible for fewer deaths than he would otherwise have been responsible for in order to still be completely responsible for one murder as much as if he himself had pulled the trigger. Although it is reasonable to think that Jim will do the Captain a favor if he kills one Indian, thereby making the Captain responsible for fewer deaths, this need not be how things turn out in order for the Captain to be morally responsible for one death. This is one reason that the Captain might consider not making the offer and avoid putting his fate into Jim's hands. (In what follows, I will adopt the first view on permissibility. But I do not think that the results with respect to moral responsibility for negative and positive consequences would change, if we adopted the second view.)

If (II) is not necessary for locating (some or all) moral responsibility for negative consequences in the Captain, then the tentative version I gave of T1 above is incomplete, because it does not capture all of the cases in which Jim can rely on the Captain having complete positive moral responsibility for negative consequences. After all, the tentative version requires that the Captain makes the better outcome—in which he does not kill—contingent on Jim's act. Hence, T1 should now be revised so that it applies to cases where Jim's collaboration is in a scheme in which the Captain has responsibility, by way of his offer, for making it only reasonable for Jim to believe that the Captain creates the possibility of a better outcome contingent on Jim's killing.

In this section, I have argued that not only does the Captain have moral responsibility and accountability for negative consequences, but he is to be treated as morally responsible for a wrong act of killing even though no one commits such an act and no one would have committed it.[31] I have also argued that (II), part of (III), and (IV) are unnecessary for responsibility to be shifted to the Captain, though it being only reasonable for Jim to believe that the conditions they enumerate hold may be necessary.

Throughout this discussion, I have thought of Jim as collaborating with a villain. We could also speak of Jim's "complicity" with a villain. This suggests that Jim is the accomplice to the Captain's crime. But someone who actually kills, as Jim, does is typically thought of as "the principal," while the person who solicits a principal is thought of as the accomplice. It certainly seems odd, however, to think of the Captain, who is in control of creating threats to people and making offers to Jim concerning his killing, as a mere accomplice to Jim's act. (In the same sense, it would be odd to refer to a Mafia boss as an accomplice to those he solicits to (wrongly) kill victims.) But those who believe that the Captain is the accomplice in this scenario, should conclude that it can be much worse morally to be an accomplice than to be a perpetrator (like Jim) who actually kills, and that an accomplice can bear all the responsibility for negative consequences of the principal's act.

V. DURESS, AUTHORITY, AND MORAL RESPONSIBILITY

May moral responsibility and accountability for the negative consequences of Jim's act lie with people other than the Captain? For example, what if the potential victims are asking Jim to accede to the Captain's offer (as in W and C[Request])? The fact that Jim responds to their wishes is consistent with the Captain still being the only one morally responsible for the death of the one Indian, insofar as it is a negative effect. This is because the request by the Indians is a morally permissible response to the Captain's threat to them. If it were wrong of them to ask Jim to act, and Jim would not have done the killing but for their request, then the Captain would not be *completely* morally responsible for the murder of the one Indian. So the fact that the potential victims' request is made under duress must not merely excuse a wrong request by them; the request must be *justified* in order for the Captain to have full moral responsibility.

Suppose that we are in C(Request). The Captain never makes an offer, but all the Indians ask Joe to kill one of them. Suppose Jim acts permissibly in killing, in part because he is reasonable in believing that he will maximize the good and that the Pareto factor holds, and in addition there is the Indians' request. Then, I believe, full responsibility for the negative effects of the act shifts first to the Indians but does not remain with them. If they had all asked Jim to kill one of them in response to a natural threat to them, the moral responsibility and accountability for the negative effects would remain with them. But if they make the request because they are under a threat from the Captain, then while Jim most directly loses responsibility for the negative effects of his act *to them*, they lose this responsibility to the Captain. Again, this means that all negative consequences are placed at the doorstep of the Captain, but the good consequences may now be placed at the doorstep of the Indians (and perhaps Jim, since he does take on causal responsibility for a death for their sake). Furthermore, the killing should be treated as a murder that the Captain performed. So in C(Request), where the Captain makes no offer, the location of complete positive moral responsibility in the Captain rather than in Jim comes about indirectly.

Furthermore, the Captain need not make any offers to the Indians (e.g., "If you ask Jim to kill one of you, then I will not kill all of you") in order for the killing to be his moral responsibility. This is because he places them under a great, unjust personal threat and this seems to be enough to shift full moral responsibility to the Captain for the negative consequences of acts that diminish his threat to them, so long as these acts have other properties in favor of their permissibility. In C (Request), we can say something like "the Captain made the Indians do it," though he did not specifically tell them what to do and they could have chosen to do nothing. By contrast, putting someone in Jim's situation in W or C(Scan), with the possibility of doing something to help others, is not for the Captain to put Jim under duress. Jim cannot say "the Captain made me do it" in the way the Indians can.

In this way, I believe, the Argument from Duress works differently from the Argument from Necessity with respect to the location of positive moral responsibility for negative consequences. That is, placing some under a threat that justifies their request that someone be killed works differently from placing someone who is not under a threat in a situation where he finds it necessary to choose the lesser evil. An offer is necessary for the location of complete positive moral responsibility in the villain rather than in the agent who acts from necessity. No offer is necessary for the location of complete moral responsibility in the villain rather than in the people he places under duress. At least this is so, if I am right that in situations like C(Scan), where the Captain makes no offer and the Indians make no request, then the Captain cannot be held morally responsible for a killing that Jim commits.

These cases highlight the effect that legitimate and illegitimate authority have on the moral value of an act. The Indians have rightful authority over their own lives, and their offer to Jim in a case of natural disaster threatening them would give them positive moral responsibility for (the negative and positive aspects of) Jim's act. Since killing one of them is an act that it would have been permissible for them all to agree to perform, it has an overall positive value (as a permissible killing) when it is conceived of as an act carried out by their Agent, Jim, at their request. By contrast, the Captain *usurps* authority from the Indians over their lives. Hence, from his offer he gets positive moral responsibility for the negative aspects of Jim's act, and relative to the Captain the act has overall *negative* value (i.e., it is a wrongful killing). As argued above, this negative value comes from the overall negative value of the Captain's proposed act of killing the twenty, which was impermissible, in part, because it involved usurping authority over the Indians' lives.

VI. INITIATION VERSUS RESPONSIVENESS

Consider again cases where Jim retains some positive moral responsibility for negative consequences, there being no *complete* location of responsibility elsewhere. Two important cases of this sort, I believe, are C(Scan) and C(Jim's Offer).[32] In the former, no one makes an offer or requests that Jim kill one Indian, and I think that the Captain does *not* get positive moral responsibility or accountability for the killing as if it were his own act. In C(Jim's Offer), Jim makes the offer to the Captain that the latter's conduct be contingent on Jim's, and positive moral responsibility and accountability get shared, albeit for different things, *only* the Captain gets positive moral responsibility for murder.

To repeat, C(Scan) is important because it is closer to the sort of case that is generic for act-consequentialist reasoning, that is, doing something to prevent a bad outcome when that act produces a less bad outcome. (However, it is atypical in that the less bad outcome is part of what would (or would only reasonably be thought to) have occurred anyway.) What prevents the Captain from having positive moral responsibility for Jim's killing in C(Scan) as if it were his own act? What makes Jim's killing more problematic in C(Scan) than in W or C(Offer)? The answer to both of these questions is, in part, that Jim *initiates* steps to save the Indians from the threat. That is, he is not merely *responsive* to the offer or request of other people. He thrusts himself into the situation rather than being implicated by the offer. Likewise in C(Jim's Offer), Jim takes the initiative and (reasonably believes that he) creates the contingency between the Captain's behavior and his own.

Is mere responsiveness to be favored over initiation in general, though? Hardly. After all, in C(Request), the potential victims take the initiative in making an offer to Jim, and yet complete positive moral responsibility for the negative consequences is located in the Captain. But, to repeat what was said above, here they act under the threat that the Captain has imposed, and this seems to be enough to shift full moral responsibility to the Captain for the negative consequences of what legitimately diminishes his threat. In C(Request), we can say something like "the Captain made the Indians do it," though he did not specifically tell them what to do, and they could have chosen to do nothing. But putting someone in Jim's situation in W or C(Scan), with the possibility of doing something to help others, is not the Captain putting Jim under duress. Jim cannot say "the Captain made me do it" in the way the Indians can.

To some, this will signify that self-interested concern (duress) is more pressing for initiating action than is other-directed concern. But I do not think that this—that is, whether one's act relieves oneself of a threat or another of a threat—is the heart of the matter. For Jim might be willing to *initiate sacrificing himself*. He might, for example, offer his life to the Captain rather than shoot one of the Indians in C(Scan), if this would stop the Captain from killing twenty. Responsiveness is not morally preferred to his doing this, because being responsible for one's own death is morally different from being responsible for another's death, given that one has authority over one's own life but not over those of others. What is problematic for Jim is initiating the contingency that leads to the Indian's death. It is not so problematic for all the Indians to initiate this same contingency, since it is one of their lives they sacrifice. So it is not the pressure of self-interested concerns, thought of as a mere excuse, that is at work in justifying an initiative. It is authority over oneself as part of a justification for action that helps to make initiation acceptable.

This is all consistent with the above division of cases, into T1 and T2, tracking different locations of moral responsibility that can affect the moral appropriateness or attractiveness of Jim killing. I argued earlier that when there is an initiative on Jim's part for taking the life of the Indian in T2, moral responsibility for negative consequences is not completely elsewhere; when Jim is responsive, it is completely elsewhere (T1).[33]

However, suppose, in a new case called C(Offer to Indians), that Jim initiates an offer *to the Indians* whose content is either that (with their permission) he will initiate a contingency between his behavior and the Captain's (by making an offer to the Captain) or simply that he will kill one of them in order to stop the Captain. Here he initiates an offer with the proper authorities over the Indians' lives (namely, all the Indians), not with the Captain. His taking this initiative and the Indians' consenting are consistent, I believe, with the Captain having complete moral responsibility and accountability for the negative aspects of Jim's act. Hence, the line that separates T1 from T2 (i.e., the line between responsiveness and the initiation of action that takes others' lives) does *not* quite coincide with different locations of complete moral responsibility for negative consequences. C(Offer to Indians) suggests that it is initiation independent of consent of the proper authorities—the absence of mere responsiveness to the improper authorities in C(Jim's Offer) being an instance of this—that coincides with the more morally problematic act of killing by Jim.

Now suppose that the Captain has already done all he could do to bring about deaths, as in C(Complete), where he has set a bomb that is now beyond his control, and this will cause the deaths unless Jim kills one Indian. (His killing one Indian, we may imagine, alone can defuse the bomb.) Without any offer from anyone or consent of the proper authorities (though not against their wishes), Jim kills one Indian. Still, the positive moral responsibility and accountability will lie completely with the Captain, I think. Again, T1 does not coincide with the location of responsibility away from Jim, if we take this as a case that involves Jim's initiation. However, if complete responsibility is to lie with the Captain in the absence of the Captain's offer and the Indians' consent, it waits upon the villain's doing everything necessary that will cause harm to occur and Jim's responsiveness to this. In C(Complete), Jim is not so much doing what (it was only reasonable to believe) another person would have done as producing a consequence of what someone has done before what someone has done produces that consequence, and his doing this saves the other Indians.

But what of a case (like W) in which the Captain has ordered Pedro to kill the twenty? Is it not like C(Complete), in that the Captain has done everything necessary to get people killed? Is Pedro not like the Captain's bomb? Recall that I redescribed all of the cases (excluding W) so that there was only the Captain, not Pedro. But if Pedro were like the Captain's bomb, then that would explain why, even if someone should not shoot in C(Scan) without an offer, it would be permissible for someone to shoot one Indian in a case that is like C(Scan) in all respects except that Pedro will carry out the Captain's orders.

However, I do not think that Pedro is like the Captain's bomb. The Captain will be responsible if Pedro kills, and Pedro, unlike the bomb, will also be responsible if he kills. The Captain and Pedro will only be responsible for a death if Pedro (whom the Captain has ordered) does everything *he* must do that will ensure the killing. But Pedro has not yet done this unless he has fired *his* bullet. And so if Jim, who is in the bushes, kills an Indian without Pedro or the Captain or the Indians making him an offer, complete responsibility for the death will not shift to (Pedro and) the Captain for the reason it shifts in C(Complete).

In connection with such two-villainous-agent cases, it is worth considering a variation on C(Scan) that involves two virtuous agents. In this case, Joe is in the bushes and sees that Jim is about to act on a less generous offer that the Captain has made him: If Jim kills *two* people simultaneously (with two guns), the Captain will not kill the twenty. Joe has (nontransmittable) brain scan information that Jim lacks to the effect that if only one Indian is killed, the Captain will also desist. If Joe kills one Indian, a life will be saved, but where will moral responsibility for the death lie? One possible approach takes it that once Jim has accepted the offer to shoot, all other good agents are *implicitly* licensed by him (as if he made an offer to them) to achieve at a lower permissible cost the good results he seeks. Hence, they become his Agents, and as Jim would not have moral responsibility and accountability for the negative aspects of two deaths, so Joe would not have such moral responsibility and accountability for the one death. Hence, there are reasons for Joe to shoot without an offer that are not present for Jim in C(Scan).[34]

Let me end this section with a better description of the T1 and T2 cases:

T2: Jim initiates the scheme to harm someone independently of getting consent from the proper authorities when the villain has not done everything that he must do that will cause harm to occur.

In these T2 cases, Jim killing the one is problematic because positive moral responsibility and accountability for the negative consequences do not lie completely elsewhere than in Jim. Further, T1 should not be restricted to no-initiation cases, or else it will fail to capture all of the morally less problematic killings by Jim, such as C(Complete) and C(Offer to Indians). Hence T1 should be:

T1: Jim does not initiate the scheme to harm someone unless it is with the proper authorities or it is in a context where the villain has completed what has to be done to cause harm.

VII. KEEPING MORAL RESPONSIBILITY
WHERE IT DESERVES TO BE

Let us now reexamine the claim that responsiveness is morally preferable to initiating a killing in some cases *because* there is a bias in favor of Jim killing when
positive moral responsibility and accountability for negative consequences are located with someone else rather than with Jim. There is a problem with this claim. In
order to see what the problem is, let us examine the following case.

Suppose that some rocks will fall, killing all of the Indians as the result of a
natural disaster. The Indians are not in a position to approve or disapprove of Jim's
killing one of them in order to save the others. In such a case, I believe, there is also
no bias against Jim's killing one Indian if this will save the rest, even if moral
responsibility is not located away from Jim. This suggests that there is a bias in
favor of responsiveness because there is a bias in favor of locating moral responsibility for negative consequences in another person, *if that person is morally responsible for the threatening condition.* That is, *if* a person would be fully responsible
for a bad outcome if we did not intervene (or it is only reasonable to think he
would be), then there is a bias in favor of his remaining fully morally responsible
and accountable for whatever harm occurs. If no person is responsible for a threatening condition, then it does not matter in the same way whether responsibility is
located away from Jim. So Jim's responsiveness allows moral responsibility for the
negative consequences of a negatively valued act to remain with the villain.[35]

Here we may also have another part of the explanation of *why* there is a bias
in favor of acting when moral responsibility and accountability for negative consequences are located elsewhere. If the only concern were that Jim not be morally
responsible for the negative consequences of the act and retain moral hyper-purity
(in the sense discussed above), then there would be as much bias against his acting
to stop the natural disaster as to stop the Captain in C(Scan). That there is
not suggests, I believe, that it is keeping moral responsibility where it deserves to
be that is crucial. Because moral hyper-purity is also lost when one does the
lesser evil for the sake of the greater good in a natural disaster case, keeping moral
hyper-purity is not determinative. We might say that keeping moral responsibility where it deserves to be is a *condition of respectful agency* in a world of different
agents.

In W and C(Offer), the malicious mastermind of the entire problematic situation has the initiative in bringing about Jim's act and will, I have argued, alone
be morally responsible and accountable for a crime that is more commensurate
with his behavior than is the mere crime of threatening people but not actually
harming them. That this should be attractive is connected, I believe, to the outlook
of a retributive theory of punishment. According to retributivism, it is simply
morally better that someone who deserves evil gets it. Here it is not pain and
suffering, but sufficient discredit to his moral record that he deserves and gets.
Because the Captain gets the discredit of moral responsibility for the negative
consequences of Jim's act of killing, he also deserves punishment for murder.
Another way of putting this point is that, in virtue of threatening the Indians and

making it necessary for Jim to kill one, if twenty are not to die, the Captain *deserves to deserve* punishment for a murder. (This is true even in C[Scan].) But only if he becomes morally responsible for the negative consequences of Jim's act does the Captain actually deserve this punishment. He can become responsible by making the offer. (Deserving to deserve punishment is not the same as actually deserving punishment. Another example of this is as follows: A attempts to kill B, but fails to do so through a freak of nature. He may deserve to deserve punishment for murder, but he does not actually deserve such punishment because he did not kill B. This is true, even though he may have deserved to have the responsibility of having killed someone and did not deserve the fortuitous act of nature that interfered with such responsibility.)

Collaboration has negative aspects, for example, dealing with evil people.[36] Yet, I wish to argue, it sometimes not only reduces harm but also keeps moral responsibility and discredit where it belongs, and preserves moral hyper-purity in an agent. When we realize this, we see that it sometimes releases us morally to do what we should otherwise not do quite so easily. The strongest claim would be that sometimes it is permissible to do the killing *only because* the Captain will be completely morally responsible for its negative consequences; one should not do it *unless* the Captain will be totally morally responsible for these. This does not mean that the fact that Jim can make moral responsibility be located in the Captain (while saving lives) provides a *primary* reason for his action in the sense that Jim should kill *in order to* make the Captain responsible. If one either acts or omits to act *in order to* bring about something, one does not merely act or omit to act *depending on whether* that thing happens. By contrast, the latter is all that need be true when one acts *because* the location of complete moral responsibility is in the Captain. That responsibility will be located with him can be a condition of action, without being a purpose in acting, and then it is (what I call) a secondary reason for action.[37,38]

This, however, does not mean that Jim should always prefer to be in the situation where the Captain has complete moral responsibility for the negative consequences of Jim killing. For imagine C(Scan Secondary), in which Jim is in the bushes, as in C(Scan), and he knows the following: (1) If he kills one Indian without any offer from the Captain (or request from the Indians), the Captain will desist from killing the twenty. (2) If he does not kill as in (1), the Captain will bring him out of the bushes and make him an offer that involves his killing two people. In this situation, given that Jim will do something to save the Indians, he knows that he will either kill two (with the Captain having moral responsibility for it) or he will kill one. Since he will kill people no matter what he does, it is understandable that it would be more important to him that he kill fewer people and save more people than that the Captain bear complete moral responsibility for the killings. (I have already said that being causally responsible for a death is a negative that cannot be transferred from Jim.) However, this is only true if his killing the one Indian from the bushes has all of the characteristics favoring its permissibility except the offer. (This last caveat is crucial; Jim should not choose to kill one innocent bystander, as in the Bystander Case, instead of two Indians.) By contrast with C(Scan Secondary), in each of the other cases we have been considering, Jim faces the choice of killing someone or killing no one. (This case bears its name because, I think, it is an instance of what I have called the Principle of Secondary Permissibility [PSP], which says that sometimes it is permissible for an agent to do something that might otherwise be impermissible for him, when it is the alternative to his doing something with worse consequences that it would be permissible for him to do if it were his only choice.)[39]

Why not just *declare* that the Captain will be completely morally responsible for murder in C(Scan)? (Or even that he will share moral responsibility for killing with Jim?) Why not declare that whenever an evil person threatens others, she must take into account that she will be morally responsible for the negative consequences of at least certain acts that someone else does to diminish the bad consequences of the evil person's threat? My sense is that who has moral responsibility for what (unlike legal responsibility) cannot be determined by declaration. In C(Scan), the Captain had no idea that Jim knew what the Captain was going to do; the Captain did not direct or ask Jim to act. The Captain did not offer to reduce his threat if Jim acts or in order that Jim act. The Captain cannot become completely morally responsible for the negative consequences of Jim's act just because it was reasonable to believe that the Captain would have done what Jim does and worse, and Jim acts as he does specifically in order to minimize the harm that the Captain does. Something else is necessary. If the Captain has not yet done what needs to be done to ensure harm, he can become morally responsible for the negative consequences of Jim's act only through another one of the Captain's acts, such as his offer.[40]

If the Captain were not in this way completely morally responsible for the murder of one Indian, we might still, *as a punishment* for actions for which the Captain is uncontroversially responsible (such as setting up a threatening situation), treat him *as though* he were completely morally responsible for a murder. But this is different from saying that we punish him because he *is* completely morally responsible for a murder. It is the latter that I am arguing is true in some cases. The following thought experiment may further support the view that the Captain's additional act is crucial to making him morally responsible for the negative consequences of Jim's act. Suppose that we have a legal system that punishes the Captain as if he were completely morally responsible for murder when Jim kills one Indian in C(Scan). Suppose further that the Captain reforms and regrets the situation he set up, which led to Jim's act in C(Scan). Would not such a reformed criminal, if he were just thinking of his own life, be glad that Jim had acted but also that he had not made the offer to Jim?[41] And is this not because without it, he is not morally responsible for the killing, though he is morally responsible for the conditions which made it more reasonable for Jim to kill? (This thought experiment, admittedly, does not show that he alone would have moral responsibility for the negative consequences if he had made an offer. But this is not the point at issue here.)

The key point to be drawn from this section is that, when harming others is in question, an agent's (note the lowercase *a*) responsiveness is morally favored because, when dealing with an illegitimate authority who has not yet done what must be done to ensure a harm, it permits the location of complete positive moral responsibility and accountability in the villain. And this is favored because it *preserves* the villain's sole moral responsibility for causing unjustified harm. Even if acting without the offer is not necessarily impermissible, in such a case moral responsibility for the negative consequences of killing (even in the course of an overall permissible act) stays with the agent.[42]

VIII. THE ROLE OF AGENT REGRET

A. I have argued that Jim does no wrong in killing the one Indian when complete moral responsibility for the negative consequences lies with the Captain. I have also argued that he does not bear moral responsibility for the negative consequences caused in doing this overall permissible act. But ought Jim, nevertheless, have what Williams calls "agent regret"?[43] *Agent regret*, as Williams describes it, involves identification with and regret for one's involvement with some harm that one causes, even if one does nothing wrong that makes one the cause of the harm.[44] His example of this is someone who backs out of his garage nonnegligently and with reasonable care and yet he unluckily hits and kills a child (who was also not at fault). He is causally responsible but morally innocent in every way. Williams thinks that it is only appropriate that his attitude toward the child's death be different from the attitude that is appropriate for a bystander to have, even though he did no wrong. Furthermore, it might be expected that he would feel responsible for going to some expense to comfort the family of the child.

Let us first consider the components of a situation in which agent regret is said to be appropriate:

(1) The act that is faultless does not fit under the description "*harmful* act." The harm is an untoward side effect of the faultless act, and so it is not the production of harm per se that would be faultless (as it is in W, C[Request], and C[Offer]).

(2) Though the act is faultless, if one knew what the bad side effect of it would be, one should have chosen to do some other act (or omission). One should also have been willing to undergo costs (greater than that required of a mere bystander) prior to the act in order to change it, or to see that it did not have these effects.

Presumably, one should have paid such a cost to stop the bad effect of one's act if one had known it was coming, even if, up to the point of knowing, one was faultless in doing the act. This may help explain the fact, which Williams notes about his case, that even if one did not have pre-act knowledge of the coming bad effects, one should undergo post-act costs to ameliorate the harm to the victim's family. For suppose that the faultless act has been done and an unforeseen bad side effect—the hitting of the child—has occurred, but his death can be avoided if the driver makes a sacrifice after she acts. Presumably, she has special responsibility—more than does any bystander—to do something in this situation, too, even though she did nothing wrong in doing the act that put the child in danger. Why is not the reason for this responsibility the same as the reason to do something after one acts, but before the act causes the hitting of the child, to prevent the hit one foresees only after one acts, after all one is faultless in acting in both circumstances? And is not the view that supports this conclusion the same one that can account for why the agent should recompense the family in some way, if her faultless act immediately kills the child? (Of course, in the latter situation she may be required to do less than if she could save the child, because the good to be achieved is less.)

This reasoning relies on the idea that one has a duty to see to it that there is no harm that one causes, either by not harming or by undoing or ameliorating the harm that one causes. (Call this View 1.) This contrasts with View 2, that one has a duty not to be a *cause* of harm, but once one is such a cause, one cannot decide what one should do henceforth independently of considering whether one was able to avoid being such a cause. According to the latter view, if you should and could have taken measures prior to causing harm to prevent it but did not, you must pay afterward. This could be because, arguably, you have an option of paying prior to causing harm or after causing harm (if payment completely remedies the harm) when the option of paying prior to the harm was available. But if the option of paying prior to the harm to prevent it was *not* available, you have no duty, according to View 2, to pay post-causing harm. The problem with View 2 is that the reasoning that supports your responsibility for paying pre-harm when your behavior was faultless also seems to support your responsibility for paying post-harm, independently of considering what options you had pre-harm. This may have implausible implications, but it is hard to see why the reasoning is wrong. I believe that deciding between these two views is a deep problem.[45]

(3) In Williams's driving case involving agent regret, the faultless act was an act that one had an option to do. That is, duty did not require one to go for a drive, though one could see no reason not to do it. I shall call it an "option act," rather than a dutiful act. We could imagine, by contrast with Williams's case, that one had a moral duty to back the car out of the garage at that time, perhaps because doing exactly that was necessary to save someone's life. (This is not to say that one would have had a duty to do it to save someone's life if one had known that the child would be killed.)[46]

My sense is that (3) is a crucial factor in whether an agent ought to feel and act on agent regret. If in doing a nonfaulty act, an agent was doing only what she had to do as a matter of duty, then if there is an unforeseen harm, she need not feel agent regret. There was no other way she was permitted to act at the time. This is so, even if (1) and (2) are also true (e.g., if she had known that the harm would happen, she should have not done what would otherwise have been her duty). This means that when the act was her duty, the fact that she would have had to pay costs to avoid the harm had she foreseen it does not imply that she has to pay costs to remedy the unforeseen harm once it occurs.[47] Hence, it is not merely being an agent that matters for agent regret, but whether one was an agent who did an option act. If one need not have done what one did—though one had no reason at the time not to do it—agent regret seems to become appropriate. The person in Williams's case who drove out of her driveway had no duty to do so; she was acting on her preferences. It is open to her to wish that she had not acted as she did; it is not open to someone who did her duty when harm was unforeseeable to wish that she had not acted as she did. (Can she say, "I wish I had been lax and lazy about doing my duty, then this would not have happened?")[48]

In some cases, one should continue with the act that is one's duty, even if one knows that the harm will occur (i.e., [2] does not hold) but producing the harm is not itself one's duty (i.e., [1] holds). For example, a doctor has a duty to continue the only operation that can save a life, even if he comes to foresee that it will cause the patient some harm. Here, too, it is not incumbent on a decent agent to feel agent regret for the bad effects of his act. In this case, however, this is because the doctor can truthfully say, "I had to do this act because a life is at stake and preventing a greater evil outweighs the bad to the patient."

Suppose that an act is optional, but even if one had foreseen the harm that would be its side effect, one need not have changed course nor paid to avoid causing the harm. (This may be because the harm is small, unlike the death of a child, or because others should bear the harm in order to support one's being able to do optional acts.) Here, too, agent regret seems inappropriate. Hence, while an option act or an act chosen contrary to duty that causes harm may be a necessary condition for agent regret, it is not a sufficient condition. So it seems that only an option act (or an act chosen contrary to duty) that one either should have avoided once one knew of a harm it would cause (or paid a price to make harm-free) is the sort of act that can appropriately give rise to agent regret.[49]

B. How does all of this bear on the Captain cases? It was said that even if the Captain has moral responsibility for the death, Jim is causally responsible. Further, I have not argued that it is Jim's duty to save the greater number and shoot the one Indian in W, C(Request), or C(Offer). So he is causally responsible for a harm resulting from an act he had no duty to do, though he would not make someone worse off than that person would otherwise have been (unlike Williams's driver).[50] Presumably, we ordinarily have a duty not to kill someone even if he will soon be improperly killed by someone else, and we also have a duty to save lives. These duties conflict in this case. However, if we decide that it is only permissible and not obligatory to kill the Indian (even when Better Off applies), then we will not clearly have resolved the conflict by concluding that one of the duties—to save lives—is stronger. However, the reason that Jim's killing the Indian is not his duty may be different from the reason that driving one's car in Williams's case is not one's duty and also different from a reason provided by what is owed to the Indian. That is, if it were not a great deal to ask of someone that he kill another person (even when that person will be killed anyway), perhaps saving the Indians would be Jim's overriding duty. We would not be morally indifferent about Jim saving the Indians the way we are indifferent about whether someone takes a drive. But we may think that his killing is only permissible because it is beyond the call of duty—that is, supererogatory—on account of its cost to him. The cost to him that makes the act supererogatory is the burden of doing something he should reasonably want to avoid doing (killing, at least when death is bad for someone), whether he bears responsibility for the harm or not. The cost represents an agent's *self-concern* rather than his concern (and responsibility) for those who suffer because of what he does.

Suppose that Jim's act in C(Offer) is not a duty only for this reason. Then, when he chooses to act, he should not, I think, be deprived of any relief from agent regret that would come to someone who was performing his duty.

The second point about the way the discussion of agent regret bears on the Captain cases is that (1) does not apply. That is, the act Jim does is supposedly nonfaulty, even when the act is described as deliberately harming or involving the Indian in a harmful way. That the act is harmful in this case is taken into account when we decide that Jim's act was *not faulty*. In the Captain cases, involving someone in a harmful way is not the side effect of a faultless or even dutiful act; either the death is sought or the involvement that one foresees will cause death is sought, and yet the act is supposed to be faultless because it can be completely justified. However, many cases in which the agent justifiably but deliberately harms or wrongs someone are often described by nonconsequentialists as involving a negative "residue." In these cases, unlike ones where the harm is a side effect of a dutiful act, the fact that one is justified in, for example, telling a lie or causing pain to someone in order to fulfill a duty is not thought to relieve one of the responsibility to make up for the affront to that person. This is so even if one does the overall right act. In earlier writings, Williams discussed such cases in which obligations conflict,[51] arguing that even when we know which obligation we should carry out, we have failed to do something else we ought to have done—our act is in this way faulty, and it leaves a negative residue that calls for some action (such as making amends). But suppose that we ought not to kill and we ought to save lives, and these obligations are in conflict when we can only save lives by killing. If we had to kill a person who would not soon die anyway, then it would usually be the wrong decision to kill. But when we decide not to kill in such a case, then there is no residue at all left by not fulfilling the duty to save lives. Suppose that in some case the number of lives that would be lost is so great that it is right to kill someone who would not otherwise soon die in order to save the people. I suggest that we need not say that we have done anything wrong, if we are justified in acting. But we might say that we have (permissibly) wronged the person we kill in doing the right act. He is wronged in the sense that (a) nothing about him or what he has done called for this sort of treatment, and (b) he might even permissibly resist our killing him, though it interfered with our saving the great number of people.

The Captain cases, however, differ from this case in that the person killed would have soon been killed by someone else and Better Off holds (so it is ex ante in the interest of the one Jim kills for Jim to shoot). Would the person to be killed in C (Offer) have a right to resist being killed by interfering with Jim's act at the expense of the other nineteen people, when the twenty will all be killed anyway by the Captain? It is hard to believe that this would be permissible. Nevertheless, Jim will be killing someone who neither deserves nor is liable to being killed, and so is wronged.[52]

Now suppose that Jim's act in C(Offer) did wrong someone in the course of doing a right act, and not only as a side effect. The additional factor that should relieve Jim of dealing with a negative residue is that he can pass on responsibility to the Captain. This is so if Jim is justified in being an Agent for the Captain, and the role of Agent allows him to escape the sort of identification with the act and its consequences that gives responsibility for residues. By contrast, in C(Scan) where Jim is in the bushes and he shoots, his act may be justified, but whatever negative residue there is lies at his doorstep. I take this to mean that a form of agent regret and responsibility in Jim could be appropriate in C(Scan) if wronging occurred.

Now consider the Agent for the paralyzed Vermeer (in the case I discussed above). He might have refused to be an Agent, so as to avoid his doing the overall wrong act of destroying a beautiful vase. But if there were justification for becoming Vermeer's Agent to do this act and even nobility in the role, Vermeer must be identified with the wrong act, not his Agent.

IX. RECONSIDERING WILLIAMS'S INTEGRITY OBJECTION

Suppose that the moral difference for which I have argued between C(Scan) and C(Offer) exists. Let us consider what implications this has for some of Williams's criticisms of consequentialism. As we have seen, he says that consequentialism attacks people's integrity, for their actions would be determined as much or more by other people's projects and values as by their own. He also says that it involves a sort of moral Gresham's Law with bad acts driving out good acts.[53] This is because the good acts that some people would have performed are replaced with acts that would otherwise be bad, which they find are necessary to stop even worse ones.[54] A morally significant distinction between C(Scan) and C(Offer) would not help to support either the Integrity Objection or Gresham's Law criticism, because the distinction points to an argument *in favor of* Jim killing the one Indian in C(Offer). (However, the distinction is not one that a consequentialist can use either, because it supports an argument *against* the equal moral acceptability of killing in C[Scan], and an act-consequentialist should *not* morally distinguish that from C[Offer].)

Further, the distinction between C(Scan) and C(Offer) raises a new problem for Williams's Integrity Objection, because it seems that the Integrity Objection may not even arise in W (or in C[Offer]), if these are cases where complete positive moral responsibility is located in the Captain.[55] That is, when complete positive moral responsibility for the negative consequences of one's act is located in someone else, one is truly in the position of being someone's Agent (i.e., acting from his values and projects), but *in a way that does not disrupt or reflect on one's commitment to one's own values and projects.* It is true that Jim may *choose* to be the Captain's Agent, and he has positive moral responsibility for that, but this is different from having positive moral responsibility for the negative consequences of his act. It is also true that sometimes one should refuse to be someone's Agent because the act required is too inconsistent with one's values (as I noted in discussing Vermeer's Agent destroying a Vermeer painting). Given that Jim cannot avoid being causally responsible for a death if he kills, if he were a pacifist, this would be a reason for not becoming the Captain's Agent. And yet this does not show that one may not sometimes do what one would otherwise think it wrong to do without this giving rise to the Integrity Objection, simply because one is doing it as an Agent. By contrast, if Jim kills an Indian in C(Scan), it is because he accepts that he must adopt *as his own* the project of making the world go as well as possible even when he has moral responsibility for all of the consequences. This may be a significant alteration in his own projects or of the reasons he gives for pursuing his own projects.

Could it be argued that Williams's Integrity Objection just is the concern that consequentialism requires that people turn themselves into Agents of others' projects rather than acting on their own projects?[56] I would respond that if this is Williams's conception of the Integrity Objection, he is not really describing an attack on one's integrity. For if we think about the lawyer who evicts his client's tenants, he does not necessarily lose his integrity (in the sense of being true to his own values and projects), whether or not his client does the overall wrong thing in ordering the eviction. This is because it is not always wrong to be someone's Agent, even when one's client's values are opposed to one's own, and when one is an Agent one's act does not necessarily reflect badly on one's commitment to one's own values.

What if one is *always* an Agent, though? Is Williams saying that if one always must be an Agent, one loses one's integrity by never being fully morally responsible for the consequences of any act? Perhaps. But my own sense is that there is a better conception of the Integrity Objection, and it applies when a person is thought to be under an obligation to act as a utilitarian agent and supplant or adjust his subordinate values and projects in order to pursue the greater good. Consequentialism is threatening because it requires this in requiring one to seek the greater good and (if one takes a *non*consequentialist perspective on doing this) because one then bears the moral responsibility for the lesser evils one causes in seeking the greater good. This contrasts with what is true when one is an Agent for another person. Perhaps my point can be put in the following way: There is a difference between being a utilitarian agent and being an Agent (even) of a utilitarian.

If Jim, in W or C(Offer), would be acting like the Captain's Agent and get no positive moral responsibility for the negative consequences of his act, does he then have a *duty* to be the Captain's Agent, given the good he can do? If he does, then if he fails to perform this duty, will he not have negative responsibility for the deaths of the twenty? But, as I suggested above, Jim has *no* duty to be the Captain's Agent, because he can reasonably wish to avoid causing the death of an innocent person, given that nothing can make this part of positive responsibility transfer away from him. If Jim is sufficiently opposed to doing this, he is no more required to become an Agent than a lawyer is required to become the Agent of an evictor or someone is required to become the Agent of a paralyzed Vermeer intent on destruction (even of vases).

Williams is also concerned that the consequentialist thesis of negative responsibility by Jim for the deaths of twenty ignores the fact that the causal chain to harm would run through another agent's (the Captain's) act.[57] My proposal for the location of positive moral responsibility in the Captain also does not help Williams with this point. For how can we claim that Jim does *not* have negative responsibility because the Captain intervenes to bring about a consequence and Jim did not make him do it, if we also claim—as I have argued we should—that the Captain *does* have positive responsibility when Jim intervenes to bring about a consequence and the

Captain did not make him do it? The crucial difference between the cases is that the Captain, not Jim, originates the threat to the Indians and makes the offer; Jim's threat is reactive to the Captain's offer and diminishing of his threat. So it is background acts of the Captain's, rather than his subsequent intervening act, that are most important for determining moral responsibility in these cases.

X. RESPONSIBILITY IN SCIENTIFIC RESEARCH AND MEDICAL ETHICS

Finally, our analysis may help us to say something about other cases. First, it may play a part in explaining a moral difference that Williams thinks exists between W and an additional case he presents bearing on negative responsibility. Second, it may help us to understand responsibility in physician-assisted suicide and euthanasia.[58]

A. George's Case

Here is Williams's description of George's Case:

> George, who has just taken his Ph.D. in chemistry, finds it extremely diffi-
> cult to get a job. He is not very robust in health, which cuts down the
> number of jobs he might be able to do satisfactorily. His wife has to go out to
> work to keep them, which itself causes a great deal of strain, since they
> have small children and there are severe problems about looking after them.
> The results of all this, especially on the children, are damaging. An older
> chemist, who knows about this situation, says that he can get George a de-
> cently paid job in a certain laboratory, which pursues research into chemi-
> cal and biological warfare. George says that he cannot accept this, since he is
> opposed to chemical and biological warfare (CBW). The older man replies
> that he is not too keen on it himself, come to that, but after all, George's
> refusal is not going to make the job or the laboratory go away; what is more,
> he happens to know that if George refuses the job, it will certainly go to
> a contemporary of George's who is not inhibited by any such scruples and is
> likely if appointed to push along the research with greater zeal than George
> would. Indeed, it was not merely concern for George and his family, but
> (to speak frankly and in confidence) some alarm about this other man's excess
> of zeal, which had led the older man to offer to use his influence to get George
> the job.... George's wife, to whom he is deeply attached, has views (the
> details of which need not concern us) from which it follows that at least there
> is nothing particularly wrong with research into CBW. What should he do?[59]

Williams believes both that George clearly should not participate in the re-
search and that Jim may well be right to shoot the one Indian in W. He suggests two possible explanations for the difference in the cases: (1) the immediacy (and certainty) of the good effect that Jim will have (versus the mere possibility of

George's saving lives) and (2) the identifiability of the persons who will be saved by Jim (versus the unknown [and possibly future] people who will be saved in George's case). Another point along these lines that Williams does not mention is that if George will harm people, then it is not clear that these will be only a small subset of the very same people who would have been harmed anyway (e.g., by the other chemist). This is clear in Jim's case. It may also be worth noting that how long one will be involved in a project that one despises differs in the two cases—a few minutes in Jim's case versus possibly years in George's.

Could another moral difference between the cases have to do with the difference between substituting for a villain and substituting for a wrongful collaborator with a villain? In the W and C cases, we know that someone who is set on doing evil will be able to kill many people even if no one helps him. In George's Case, the situation is more like one in which someone set on doing evil needs people, such as scientists to help him do so. Without them, he cannot fulfill his evil aims at all.[60]

In cases where someone set on evil can only accomplish this with others' help, the correct thing is for no others to collaborate. If one of them breaks this rule and wrongly collaborates without sharing the evil goals, he may do so for various reasons. Among these may be his mistaken belief that someone else will wrongly collaborate anyway, and he may as well get the benefits of collaboration. Are there reasons not to substitute for this wrongful collaborator, in order to minimize harm, reasons in addition to any not to collaborate with a villain who could accomplish his own aims?

In both types of cases, whether one substitutes for a villain or for a wrongful collaborator, someone (the villain or the wrongful collaborator) would definitely bring about great harm that need not have occurred and do so for bad reasons. If each had acted as he should have (not being a villain, not wrongly collaborating), then no harm would occur. In the case where a villain could act alone, he is noncompliant with ideal moral conduct. In the wrongful collaborator case, there is also noncompliance with an ideal solution (of noncollaboration) to deal with evil. In both types of cases, those who try to remedy the wrongful conduct would have to abandon the same rule as the villain or wrongful collaborator abandoned.

And yet, in the wrongful collaborator case where the initial collaborator does not share evil goals, the necessity of evil occurring (by contrast with the certainty of its occurring) seems absent. That is, there was a noncollaboration solution to the problem of evil that no one lacking an evil goal could have rejected. Nothing bad had to happen, though, of course, it will. Furthermore, it is only because the rule not to collaborate is broken that the villain has the power to succeed. Hence, in collaborating to diminish the effects of wrongful collaboration, one would do the same type of act—breaking the noncollaboration rule—that empowered the villain to begin with. This seems especially hard to do, I think.

By contrast, in the case where the villain has the power without collaboration to do evil, evil's occurrence seems necessary in the sense that it is the agent's goal. Furthermore, the collaborating act one would do in order to diminish the harm of the villain is not the type of act that empowered the villain to begin with.

Are these factors grounds for thinking that George should not collaborate in order to correct for incorrect collaboration of another scientist, grounds that leave it open as to whether Jim should collaborate to stop the evil a villain can do without collaborators who do not share his goals? But these factors are not relevant if the initial collaborator shares the evil goals, and the other scientist in George's case is described so as to make us think he does share the goals.

We should note a factor on the other side that favors collaboration: It is not certain that George will harm anyone as a result of his research. It is certain that Jim will harm someone. But it is also not certain that the other scientist will harm someone, and that diminishes the reasons for substituting for him.

What does our analysis of the role of an offer in Jim's case imply about George's Case? In George's case, his competitor for the job is not the one who makes it only reasonable to believe, by way of an offer, that *his* not producing more deadly chemicals is contingent on George producing less. Someone else—the older man—makes an offer to get George the job. So it is not quite true that it would be at George's initiative that the reduction of a greater evil takes place by the doing of some lesser evil. But the person who makes the offer and can arrange for the reduction in evil is neither the person whom it is only reasonable to believe would otherwise have done the chemical research nor its victim. Hence, I believe, there would be no relocation of positive moral responsibility (for an act with negative value) either in the older man *or* in the competitor, if George did the research. Would our response to George taking the job be different if he did so because the more productive candidate offered to back off from what he truthfully portrayed as his certain success and the certain use of the chemicals only if George took the job? My suggestion is that our reaction would differ, at least if we thought George's work would kill no one but a subset of the other candidate's victims, in part because it is now the case that the other candidate will have moral responsibility for any deaths that George's research causes.

B. Physician-Assisted Suicide and Euthanasia

Finally, consider the relevance of our discussion to the issue of voluntary active euthanasia (where a patient requests that a doctor kill him) and active physician-assisted suicide (where a doctor prescribes a lethal drug that a patient takes).[61] There are at least two ways in which these issues are typically presented in a context that assumes patient competence. The first takes the view that doctors have a duty of medical mercy.[62] That is, one of the projects to which they commit themselves is the relief of the misery of their patients. On some people's view, this implies that doctors can be obligated to kill a patient in order to relieve his suffering, if this does not sacrifice a greater good that the patient might have in staying alive and it is consistent (or at least not inconsistent) with the patient's wishes. The second way in which these issues are typically discussed emphasizes the patient's autonomy. In certain contexts, it is said, patients may decide that it is best for them to die. It is then either (a) a doctor's duty to serve the patient's will, at least when it is not obviously against the patient's interests to do so, or (b) it is permissible for a doctor to serve the patient's will, at least when it is not obviously against the patient's interests to do so. Hence, on the second view, it is at least sometimes permissible for a doctor to prescribe lethal drugs and even kill a patient (when the patient is unable to carry out the act), because the doctor may act as a patient's Agent in carrying out her wishes when doing so is not obviously against her interests.[63]

On the second view, the doctor commits himself to the project of being the patient's Agent, at least so long as this is not obviously against the patient's interests, rather than to the project of doing what is best for the patient, so long as this is not against the patient's wishes. There is a reversal of emphasis in these two accounts. Only the second view *need not imply* either that the doctor agrees with the patient's decision to die or that the doctor is fulfilling his own project to do what is best for the patient in seeking the patient's death. It can even be argued that in prescribing the lethal drug, the doctor's intention is to give the patient a choice about ending her life; his intention need *not* be to end the patient's life. Hence, objections to physician-assisted suicide on the ground that the doctor acts because he intends the death may be misplaced.[64]

But notice that intending that the patient have a choice can also lead a doctor to actively kill a patient when the patient decides that he wants to die but he is unable to kill himself. Yet if the doctor does not in this case kill for the patient's good, but only to carry out the patient's wishes when it is not obviously against the patient's interests, then this active killing is *not* appropriately called euthanasia. This is because euthanasia involves killing the patient for his own good. (It can also be argued that even if it is one's aim to produce this good, it is euthanasia only if one does produce the good.) Hence, there is a form of active killing of the patient to which the patient consents that may be permissible even though it is not euthanasia. In this form of killing, unlike assisted suicide by provision of lethal drugs to be used by the patient, the doctor causes the patient's death and does the patient's bidding, when it is not obviously against the patient's interests to do so (though it may be).

My central claim is that only on the Agent model of the doctor does positive moral responsibility and accountability for all of the negative consequences of killing the patient or the provision of lethal drugs (in physician-assisted suicide) lie at the patient's doorstep. What is true on the beneficence model of the doctor who either performs voluntary active euthanasia or assisted suicide? On the beneficence model, seeking the death because it is good for the patient is at least a project of the doctor's. Let us assume the patient also seeks his own good (though he could seek his death, when it is good for him, for some other reason). Both decide the patient's death best fulfills their individual projects. But the doctor cannot fulfill her project without the patient's consent. Even though this is true, it seems to me that the doctor is more than the patient's Agent once she gets the consent. Doctor and patient are like two people who set up a project on the land of one of them. For this reason, doctor and patient may share positive moral responsibility and accountability for any negative consequences.

I suggest that if complete positive moral responsibility for negative consequences would be at the patient's doorstep in the Agent model, this might be a reason for the doctor to act as an Agent when she otherwise would be reluctant to act from beneficence. This includes cases where she thinks that the patient is doing the overall right thing from the point of view of his interests in choosing death, but she does not act because of this belief.

Does the doctor on the Agent model get positive moral responsibility for the *positive* consequences of her act? Not if she only acts as the patient's Agent, and the good consequences of death are sought by the patient. In this respect, this case differs from W. In W, it is Jim and not the Captain who aims at better consequences for the Indians simply because they are better consequences for the Indians. That is his reason for becoming an Agent. On the Agent model of the doctor, in a killing that the patient requests which is not obviously against the patient's interests (as well as in active physician-assisted suicide), positive moral responsibility for the negative consequences would also pass to the person who has legitimate authority over the patient's life, namely, the patient.

Does this mean that it would be permissible for a doctor to initiate the offer of help, given that she makes the offer to the legitimate authority? The model of Jim's relation to the Indians suggests that it is permissible, but special conditions may be present in the doctor-patient relationship that suggest it is not. For example, inequality of power in the relationship might lead a doctor's offer to be taken up by a patient who does not really want to die. The offer may transmit more than the information that an Agent is available to do the patient's bidding; it may transmit the idea that death is the right thing to seek.

The distinction I have drawn between two ways of conceiving the doctor's behavior is sometimes not recognized in discussions of these topics. For example, Dan Brock (in discussing stopping treatment) says: "Both physician and family members can instead be helped to understand that it is the patient's decision and consent to stopping treatment that limits their responsibility for the patient's death and that shifts responsibility to the patient."[65] Brock, however, also says in discussing active physician assisted suicide: "Seeking a physician's assistance, or what can almost seem a physician's blessing, may be a way of trying to remove that stigma and show others that... the decision for suicide was... justified under the circumstances. The physician's involvement provides a kind of social approval."[66] But, I believe, what makes the first claim true may make the second claim false. For it is only when the doctor is merely an Agent that moral responsibility for the negative consequences of the killing lies completely with the patient, and then helping the patient or killing him does not imply that the doctor has blessed the patient's decision or shown that it is justified under the circumstances.[67] Could it also be that what makes the second claim true makes the first claim false? For if a doctor acts because she approves of the patient's choices, then she may also be acting for the sake of her own goal to do good for the patient, as the patient acts for his goal, and this could give the doctor a share in moral responsibility for both the negative and the positive aspects of the death. But it is also possible that Brock's particular scenario allows one to imagine that the doctor is still only an Agent. She is an Agent whose views about what is best are fortuitously achieved and free her to act as Agent, without having to commit to a goal of beneficence.

NOTES

This chapter is based on my "Responsibility and Collaboration," *Philosophy & Public Affairs* 28 (1999): 169–204. For comments on earlier versions of this chapter, I am grateful to the audiences at the Law School of the University of California, Berkeley; the Johns Hopkins University and Union College Departments of Philosophy; the members of the New York University Colloquium on Law, Philosophy, and Social Theory (especially Professors Richard Arneson, Ronald Dworkin, Gertrude Ezorsky, Liam Murphy, Thomas Nagel, and Sigrun Svavarsdottir); the members of the Law and Philosophy Group at the University of California, Los Angeles; the editors of *Philosophy & Public Affairs*; and Leo Katz, Kristi Olson, and Michael Otsuka. I also thank Graham Hughes and David Richards for advice on the law.

    1. In chapters 11 and 12, I shall consider a factor that may also have an agent-focused explanation that determines whom we aid.

    2. Bernard Williams, "A Critique of Utilitarianism," in *Utilitarianism: For and Against*, ed. J. J. C. Smart and Bernard Williams, p. 94 (Cambridge: Cambridge University Press, 1973).

    3. Ibid., p. 98.

    4. A rule-consequentialist may answer differently. Even an act-consequentialist may answer differently if he believes that the consequences of killing in this case would be to encourage other evil people to make innocent bystanders into killers by threatening to kill a greater number (when they would not otherwise threaten to do so). I shall assume that the case can be imagined so that it will not have any further negative consequences and is an isolated and soon-forgotten episode.

    5. There are really two other agents in this case: the Captain and Pedro. For most of this chapter, I shall treat them as one, imagining that the person who makes the offer to Jim and the person who would actually kill the Indians are the same, namely, the Captain. I shall reintroduce Pedro in section VI. Under the Nuremberg Doctrine, a soldier like Pedro has a duty not to carry out the orders of someone like the Captain. Williams does not say that, in order to avoid having to carry out orders himself, Pedro urges Jim to shoot. Does this raise a problem for the Captain's responsibility for murder if Pedro shoots? That is, can the Captain say that he cannot be held to account for a deed that would not have occurred had the subordinate been doing *his* duty under the Nuremberg rule? It seems clear that the wrong act of ordering a killing can indeed make someone responsible for a killing, though Pedro's prohibited shooting is necessary for the killing to occur. However, since Pedro killing the twenty could also have been prevented if *he* had not shot them, Pedro also has positive responsibility for their deaths. Who has the heaviest burden of responsibility, according to consequentialism? Is it the *last* person whose omission of killing would have prevented the deaths or the person who failed to interfere with that last person who, it was known, would not omit to kill? Presumably, a consequentialist would decide this question by considering the consequences of each assignation of responsibility. For example, if we hold most responsible the last person who could have altered the outcome (for example, by omitting to kill), this may encourage people to leave to the last moment the prevention of bad consequences. If we hold most responsible someone further up the line, we encourage nipping disasters in the bud.

    6. Notice that (ii)(a) requires that some of the *Indians* will be better off. Without this condition, Pareto optimality would permit killing in the following case: The Captain asks Jim to kill all twenty Indians, or else the Captain will do it. Only if Jim kills all twenty will this save an innocent bystander from being killed by someone else. This is a case in which Jim killing people improves a situation and makes no one worse off (which is what makes it Pareto optimal). (I owe this case to Michael Otsuka.) But we may doubt that Jim shooting the twenty

is permissible in this case. (Possibly, this is because it does not rescue any of those who face one threat, but instead uses them to save someone else from a different threat.)

7. I have allowed myself to use the same name as was used for a case in earlier chapters, in which we would use a bystander to stop the trolley. This is because the use made of the person here has the same moral significance as the use of the bystander in the trolley case.

8. For my analysis of the case in which the bystander would have to be killed and of the Trolley Case, see chapter 5. Also see earlier discussions in *Morality, Mortality*, vol. 2 (New York: Oxford University Press, 1996), chaps. 9 and 10. I am aware that if participants imagine themselves sufficiently *ex ante* to the situation they are in, it may have been in the interest of *everyone*, even the person who turns out to be the bystander in the Bystander Case, to agree to the bystander being shot. This is because there was a time when no one knew who the bystander would be, and at that time each would have a greater chance to live if the bystander would be shot later. I will not discuss this issue here, but do so in chapters 5 and 8 and in my *Morality, Mortality*, vol. 2, chap. 11. The necessity doctrine in the law, which allows someone to produce a lesser evil in order to avoid a greater evil, unfortunately does not carefully distinguish among these various cases. See Glanville Williams, *Criminal Law: The General Part* (London: Stevens, 1961).

9. For a discussion of such cases see my "Harming Some to Save Others from the Nazis," in *Analytic Philosophy and the Holocaust* (Ashgate, 2003), and an unpublished modified version of that article.

10. The Gonzalez Case is based on one that Julia Driver presented in her lecture "Negative Responsibility," given at City University Graduate Center, May 3, 1996; it was reflection on that case that led me to write the article on which this chapter is based. In Driver's case, Mary is the mother of five children. Joe wants to kill her, but if he does so, he will also kill her five children. We can stop Joe from killing the five children by ourselves killing Mary. There is, however, an important difference between Mary and anyone Jim would kill (whether it is Gonzalez or any one of the Indians). We might assume that a mother would want to sacrifice her life to save her children, especially when she would die anyway. This could rightly play a role in our deciding whether to kill her. But the desire to sacrifice one's life to save others is not the same as the desire to take a chance of being the one who will be shot to save others *in order to* reduce one's own chance of dying. This difference in the victim's motivation might reasonably play a role in determining whether to kill someone. This is because, in Mary's case, at the time we kill, we kill someone who wants to die to save others, but in the cases involving Jim, at the time we kill, we do not kill someone who wants to die to save others.

11. However, if the Captain would have taken the single Indian's organs, then it may be permissible for Jim to do the same in order to save the nineteen.

12. I am grateful to Kristi Olson for the addition of "better" here.

13. I do not believe it is.

14. I owe this example to Leo Katz.

15. In the published article on which this chapter is based, I also considered whether my claims help us to distinguish morally among the behavior of various types of collaborators with Nazi persecution. This section has been omitted as it was expanded into a separate article; see my "Harming Some to Save Others from the Nazis."

16. I refer to them as the Captain cases, not as the Jim and the Indians cases, since I wish to focus on the role of the Captain's offer.

17. Those who think that collaborating with evil makes acting in W worse than acting in C(Scan) will think that Williams picks an unfairly hard case, which is not typical of consequentialism, due to a property that C(Scan) lacks. Of course, C(Scan) is not a typical consequentialist case either since the less bad outcome (one death) is part of what (it is supposed) would have occurred anyway (the death of twenty).

18. To put in relief the cases I have presented, now consider cases in which life and death are not at issue, but the distinction between C(Scan) and C(Offer) to which I have pointed is also in play. Suppose that Albert is about to deliberately tell a story that will embarrass twenty people. However, he makes Jim an offer: If Jim will tell a story that embarrasses only one of the people, Albert will desist (Case A[Offer]). In an alternative scenario (Case A[Scan]), Jim knows with certainty (through a brain scan) that he can only stop Albert if he tells a story that will embarrass one of the people, though he must act alone without an offer from Albert. My sense is that in A(Offer), Albert will have positive moral responsibility for Jim's telling the story and that acting in A(Offer) is morally favored over acting in A(Scan). (Ned Block suggested that the use of non-life-and-death cases might better highlight the factors that I believe are at work in the life-and-death cases, because some might think that the factors of life and death would swamp these other factors. Richard Arneson, Liam Murphy, and Sigrun Svavarsdottir helped me to construct the A cases.)

19. By "completely," I mean that he has *all* of the moral responsibility and accountability; he alone has it. I also mean to include in this that he has *full* moral responsibility and accountability; he has it to the highest degree. Two people could share full responsibility, but then neither would have complete moral responsibility. The assignment of all positive moral responsibility and accountability for negative consequences to the Captain assumes that Jim chooses a way to kill the one Indian that has no unnecessary negative effects. What if the Captain's specific offer is to desist if Jim shoots *three* of the twenty, but Jim is aware (through his brain scanner) that the captain will also desist if he kills two of the twenty. Given that it would be permissible for Jim to kill the three if the other alternative were not available, Jim may now carry out the best possible act whose other conditions favor permissibility, knowing that positive responsibility for *it* will also be the Captain's. This is so, even if responsibility for this act would not have been the Captain's without his offer, and his offer did not specify killing two people.

20. In distinguishing between causal responsibility, being to blame, and being liable for further responses to the act, I am relying on distinctions drawn by Joel Feinberg in his "Action and Responsibility" and "Sua Culpa," both in his *Doing and Deserving* (Princeton, NJ: Princeton University Press, 1970). He also says of the person who is to blame that the act can be charged to him or placed as an entry to his record (reputation) ("Action and Responsibility," p. 128). I say that the negative consequences of Jim's act can be placed at the Captain's doorstep.

21. One type of analysis of collaboration might distinguish between accomplices and perpetrators, distinguishing them by the fact that the perpetrator is the one causally responsible, and identifying the perpetrator as the principal. I am disagreeing with such an analysis: I am suggesting, instead, that the principal is not always the one who is causally responsible. I shall return to this point below.

22. And so understandably crucial in giving rise to positive responsibility, as Jerome Schneewind emphasized to me.

23. Cannot the Captain also become completely and fully responsible for the negative consequences of Jim's act by deliberately putting much information in Jim's way about the connection between his act and the Captain's possible behavior? What if Jim is even *told* about the contingency point blank by the Captain without the latter making an offer? Perhaps positive responsibility for Jim's act is located in part in the Captain in these cases, relative to ones where the Captain does not do anything in particular to bring about Jim's act. But, I think, it does not shift completely, as when Jim accepts an offer. When Jim acts without the Captain's claim to be committed—a claim to commitment that cannot be made by mere inducements to Jim to act—he is not like the Captain's Agent (a concept to be explained in the text below) and, as we shall see, this is important. Of course, the Captain may not really be committed—he might shoot the rest of the Indians anyway—though he claims to be. This is irrelevant to his responsibility for the negative consequences of Jim's act.

24. As Christopher Grau pointed out to me, someone who does harm that he could have avoided entirely, but does less rather than more simply in order to do less, may deserve credit for the good consequences of fewer being harmed. If we take Williams's description of the Captain nonironically, the Captain's motivation is best described, I think, as follows: He seems to be the sort of person who thinks that Indians can be treated as toys. Hence, letting a guest shoot an Indian is really a way of honoring the guest. The guest's involvement in the sport is such a wonderful occasion that some of the toys can be given a gift (here, the gift of life). If we take the account ironically, the Captain's motivation is only to toy with Jim as well.

25. For example, Thomas E. Hill, Jr., in "Moral Purity and the Lesser Evil," in his *Autonomy and Self-Respect* (Cambridge: Cambridge University Press, 1991).

26. If Jim would do the *right* act if he killed the Indian in C(Scan), there is no fault in the act. So how could it be *his fault* (the first sense of moral responsibility for a bad effect) that the death occurred? (By contrast, the Captain's behavior is full of fault, in virtue of which a death occurs.) But the fact that Jim's act is right does not exclude it having bad consequences for which he might be morally responsible and accountable. It also does not exclude it from being faulty (even unavoidably so) in one aspect, if he wrongs someone in the course of doing the overall right thing. The latter might be especially true in the Gonzalez Case.

27. In his "Political Action: The Problem of Dirty Hands," *Philosophy & Public Affairs* 73 (1973): 160–80.

28. It is important to reemphasize that this apportioning of responsibility for the consequences does *not* depend on the view that there is a fixed amount of responsibility for any act and that a fixed amount can either be had by one person or had in diminished amounts by different parties. Many people can each have full responsibility for the negative consequences of an act (or for the occurrences of an event) when this means they are all responsible to the highest degree. For example, this is so if many villains participate in killing someone. Each one's responsibility will, however, not be complete, for completeness also implies having *all* of the responsibility, that one is the only one with full responsibility.

29. Claire Finkelstein suggested that whether the Captain has sole positive responsibility for the negative consequences also depends on Jim's reasons for shooting. If these reasons have nothing to do with saving the greater number from the Captain's threat, she suggests, positive responsibility does not lie totally with the Captain. For example, suppose that Jim would not have killed because of the Captain's offer if he had not also always had a desire to kill an Indian. (Because the Captain's offer provides the opportunity for Jim to act, responsibility will still be the Captain's in part on Finkelstein's view.) I am doubtful about this. For if someone chooses to make himself an Agent only when this dovetails with his personal interests, can he still not be just an Agent?

30. These two views represent different views about whether even an ideal agent's perspective on an act should be incorporated into permissibility judgments. Thomas Scanlon argues that whether it was reasonable for an agent to believe something was true of his act is relevant to judgments of permissibility of the act. See his "Permissibility and Intention," *Proceedings of the Aristotelian Society* Suppl. 74 (2000): 301–17. Judith Thomson argues that what is in fact true of the act, independent of what it was reasonable for an agent to believe, determines the permissibility of his act. But she also thinks that whether an agent is at fault or to blame can be a function of his reasonable beliefs. See her *The Realm of Rights* (Cambridge, MA: Harvard University Press, 1990).

31. In this way the case is unlike one in which a gangster is someone's Agent; when his boss gets partially blamed for a wrong act, it is because a wrong act (on either view of permissibility) was done by the gangster Agent.

32. We already discussed another such case above, where Jim kills an innocent bystander (Bystander Case). Another one, arising from a natural disaster and with no offer from potential victims, will be discussed in section VII below.

33. I use the contrast between initiation and responsiveness, rather than between activity and passivity, since Jim acts (kills) whether he initiates a scheme or responds to one in order to save Indians.

34. What if the Captain's offer to Jim specifically excludes allowing anyone but Jim to minimize harm to the Indians? Does this imply that Jim would not be free to license others to act for him with the assurance that the Captain and not Jim will have moral responsibility for the killing? I do not think so. A villain who makes Jim an offer has implicated himself in Jim's act of killing and in any act that permissibly reduces the harm that comes from his offer being taken up.

35. This analysis dovetails with a reason for Jim not to kill at all when a villain (or even a well meaning but mistaken person) rather than a natural event creates a threat. This reason is that there is another way for the disaster to be avoided, namely by the villain fulfilling his responsibility not to do a wrong act. Jim has fulfilled his responsibility not to do wrong acts and, it might be said, it is not his further responsibility to make up for other people's failures, as if those other people were natural disasters that could not have avoided creating threats. If the villain bears the negative moral consequences of the killing, then that comes closer to his bearing full responsibility for not threatening people.

36. Christopher Kutz argued (in conversation) that collaborating with evil people is wrong in part because it requires us to treat them during our interactions as though they had a normal normative status when, in fact, they are people who deserve to be shunned or punished.

37. For further discussion of the distinction between doing something *in order* that *x* come about and doing something *because x* will come about, see chapter 4. Samuel Scheffler emphasized to me that Jim does not kill in order to make the Captain responsible.

38. Similarly, we should not do something in order that a freak of nature *not* interfere with the Captain shooting the twenty, in order that he then deserve punishment for murder. This is so, even though he deserves to deserve it. I introduced the distinction between primary and secondary reasons for action in chapter 4.

39. For more on the PSP, see chapter 5.

40. Recall that in C(Complete), when Jim interferes with the consequences of the deadly act that the Captain has already done, there is no offer necessary in order for the Captain to have complete moral responsibility. It is only when it is only reasonable for us to believe that the Captain *will do* something, and we act to forestall it, that the offer is necessary.

41. Of course, a reformed criminal would also prefer that the twenty had not been killed. This is why he prefers that Jim have acted in C(Scan) without his offer and have moral responsibility for the negative consequences of the act. For even if Jim acted wrongly in killing in C(Scan), his wrong would not be as great as the one the Captain would have at his doorstep if he were morally responsible for killing twenty Indians or even one Indian, when it was in his power that no one be killed. It is understandable for even a reformed Captain to think in this way. But it is not appropriate *for Jim* to prefer his acting in C(Scan) to his acting on an offer from the Captain just because any wrong he did in C(Scan) would be less than the wrong for which the Captain would be responsible if he made an offer. After all, only one Indian would get killed in either case, and the Captain deserves to have moral responsibility for the bad consequences if anyone does, and furthermore, responsibility for them as a murderer.

42. At this point, it is useful to consider a possible relation between American law and the analysis I have provided. In their discussion of the Model Penal Code on duress (2.09), Sanford Kadish and Stephen Schulhofer (in their *The Criminal Law and Its Processes*, 6th ed.

[Boston: Little, Brown, 1995], pp. 903–7) note (but do not approve of the fact) that the code permits the necessity defense to both natural and manmade threats, but permits duress as an excuse only when there is a "do-it-or-else" threat, not a nonperson-caused threat. They quote (ibid., p. 906) the Model Penal Code's final commentary (Model Penal Code and Commentaries, Comment to 2.09 [1988], pp. 378–79):

[T]here is a significant difference between the situations in which an actor makes the choice of an equal or greater evil under the threat of unlawful human force and when he does so because of a natural event. In the former situation, the basic interests of the law may be satisfied by prosecution of the agent of unlawful force; in the latter circumstance, if the actor is excused, no one is subject to the law's application.

I have suggested that it is the desirability of a villain having responsibility for murder that lies behind giving weight to the Captain's offer. There is a bias against acting when this will not happen. The Model Penal Code commentary may seem to be expressing a similar view. However, as we have seen, I also wish to claim that the prosecution of the originally threatening person for a murder is not always appropriate when another agent kills to reduce evil. Furthermore, the interest in having a villain be responsible for murder need not imply that when there is a natural disaster and no villain, there is also a bias against acting. I have also distinguished between those "do-it-or-else" situations that involve a threat to the agent (duress) and those that do not.

43. Williams discusses this and its connections with the phenomenon of moral luck in "Moral Luck," in his *Moral Luck* (Cambridge: Cambridge University Press, 1981), pp. 20–39.

44. In other cases of moral luck, one has done something wrong, but it is no worse than what others do who are not unlucky enough to harm someone because of their wrong act.

45. I first discuss these issues in my "The Insanity Defense, Innocent Threats, and Limited Alternatives," *Criminal Justice Ethics* 6 (1987): 61–76, and again in *Creation and Abortion* (New York: Oxford University Press, 1992). Here is one seemingly implausible implication of View 1: Suppose that there is a relation between costs that should be undertaken in order to avoid an act that one foresees will have a bad effect and costs morally required to respond to unforeseeable harmful effects once they have occurred. Then people who do not act at all, but are innocent threats to others (e.g., someone shot out of a cannon), would have responsibilities via what I shall call *cause regret* (if not agent-regret) to respond to unforeseeable harm once it occurs. This is because if someone is a human missile and he finds on himself a button by which he can redirect himself even at some cost to himself, then it is not implausible to think that he should press it in order to avoid causing harm. He has this responsibility, though he is not at fault for being a missile. I suggested (in chapter 5) that this implies that if he had no button—not just if he fails to press one he has—that we may impose a comparable cost on him to divert him in order to prevent harm. Does his responsibility to press the button also imply that, even when he has no button to press, after he causes the harm, and it can be remedied, he should be responsible to bear some cost to remedy it? Admittedly, he is not at fault, but he was also not at fault in the case where he had to press the button on himself that would impose a cost on him. If he would have been at fault not to press the button, why is he not at fault if he does not pay the same cost postharm to remedy harm?

46. Similarly, for cases where someone does something negligent and unluckily causes harm, we could imagine a comparison case where his doing an act that involves negligence is required by duty. For example, suppose that a driver is part of an experiment that is necessary to improve road safety, and his duty is to drive negligently (for example, while mildly intoxicated). He does this and, unlike other test drivers who do the same, unluckily harms a child.

47. This differs from the conclusion I reached when discussing the problem of agent regret and moral luck in my *Morality, Mortality*, vol. 2. There I concluded that if one should and could either omit the otherwise dutiful act once one knows it leads to harm or, prior to acting, pay to

avoid the harm, then one should pay after the harm occurs when harm was unforeseeable and the act was one's duty. The reasoning to support this is similar to that described in the discussion of View 1 above. Here I am suggesting that dutiful acts be treated differently. Again, this raises the question of whether View 1 or View 2 is correct.

48. The view that doing one's duty can relieve one of agent regret in the way an optional act does not fits with Kant's view that one should not lie to a murderer about the location of his intended victim (see Immanuel Kant, *On the Old Saw: That May Be Right in Theory, but It Won't Work in Practice*, tr. E. B. Ashton [Philadelphia: University of Pennsylvania Press, 1974]). If one really had a duty not to lie in this case, not interfering with the death of an innocent person because one was doing one's duty is not something about which one should feel agent-regret. If one chooses to lie in order to save a life when one need not (and even should not) do this, how things turn out becomes very important. For if the innocent person is actually killed as a result of one's choice to lie (because without one's knowing it, Kant says, he has gone in the direction that one gives in one's lie), one is open to agent-regret. (One chooses to lie, but, of course, if one had a duty not to, this is not really a morally permitted option. So perhaps, my view should rather be that if one does an optional act *or* makes a choice contrary to duty, then one is open to agent regret.) This does not mean that Kant was right that one really has a duty not to lie to the murderer (or even that one has a duty not to lie to an innocent bystander, who asks us in which direction the innocent victim has gone while the murderer is within earshot). But *if* one has no duty not to lie in these cases, then it is only if one has a duty *to lie* that one can be relieved of agent regret if the victim dies only because one lied. (There is, of course, also the issue of agent regret for the lie itself, at least when told to a bystander who has not forfeited his right to the truth. As will be seen in later discussion, regret for the lie itself, even if lying is dutiful, should be treated differently, I think, from regret for its bad side effects.)

Williams also discusses, in "Moral Luck," the case of Gauguin, who disregarded his duty to his family in order to paint. He says that whether Gauguin did the right thing will depend on the outcome, i.e., on whether he was a success at painting. On any account of permissible acts that is purely objective (i.e., that disregards what agents could reasonably know at the time of acting in determining permissibility), Williams's conclusion is quite understandable. For suppose that a duty is nonabsolute and could permissibly be overridden by good enough consequences or fulfillment of a conflicting duty, if we knew that these would come about. Then on the objective account, regardless of what we knew or reasonably believed, if the good consequences or fulfillment of the conflicting duty do come about, then the act was permissible. Williams is disagreeing with Kant in thinking that consequences can determine whether an act contrary to duty is right. But given what I have said about the lie-to-save-a-life case, Kant also seems to have thought that where one does not do one's duty (and acts contrary to duty), one is a hostage to consequences in a way that one is not hostage to consequences when one does one's duty. However, Kant did not, thereby, think that not doing one's duty could be right in virtue of positive consequences; just that negative consequences will lie at our doorstep.

49. Kristi Olson has suggested that a different distinction is what is really important to whether agent regret is appropriate. If you would regret not doing the act as well as doing it, no agent regret is appropriate. If you would not regret *not* doing the act (even if it was your duty) once you know of its consequences, but regret doing the act, then agent regret is appropriate.

50. Jim as an Agent is unlike the lawyer who, as an Agent, evicts a tenant. The lawyer actually has a duty to act as he does, though he has a choice as to whether to be a lawyer for the building owner. In his case, he may wish that he had not done his duty, in the sense either

that he wishes he had not become someone with that duty or that he should have realized that the harm that would occur overrode his doing his duty.

51. In his "Ethical Consistency," reprinted in his *Problems of the Self* (Cambridge: Cambridge University Press, 1973), pp. 166–86.

52. Suppose that the one Indian that Jim would kill became capable of escaping the Captain and Jim. I think that the Indian could permissibly resist Jim's act, even by killing Jim, even though this means the other nineteen people will be killed by the Captain. But this is because the single Indian would not now be killed soon anyway by the Captain.

53. Gresham's Law in economics involves bad money driving out good money.

54. He says: "A Gresham's Law operates by which the bad acts of bad men elicit from better men acts which, in better circumstances, would also be bad." Bernard Williams, *Morality: An Introduction to Ethics* (New York: Harper and Row, 1972), p. 104.

55. In a case like C(Request), where consent of the victims to Jim's act is present, the victims' responsibility may also defuse the Integrity Objection. Hence in W, where there is also victims' consent, defusing the Integrity Objection might be overdetermined.

56. Samuel Scheffler suggested this.

57. I believe that Williams means another agent's *subsequent* act. If so, would this imply that he thinks that Jim *does* have negative responsibility for the deaths of twenty if he does not kill one Indian in C(Complete), for there the Captain's act would not follow Jim's omission? But presumably he should not think this. On some of these issues, as well as the difference that natural disasters make, see Ann Davis, "The Priority of Avoiding Harm," in *Killing and Letting Die*, ed. B. Steinbock (Englewood Cliffs, NJ: Prentice-Hall, 1980), pp. 173–214.

58. It also suggests a possible moral distinction in the behavior of those who collaborated with the Nazis. For this, see my "Harming Some to Save Others from the Nazis."

59. From Williams, "A Critique of Utilitarianism," pp. 97–98. I will put to one side two interesting questions raised by this case: (1) Why is there a strain on the children if George's wife goes to work when George could take care of them? (2) Is it morally wrong (and under what circumstances) to go after a job *because* one knows that one will do it less well than someone else, even, perhaps, with the intention of, at least in part, sabotaging the goals of one's firm?

60. The distinction between these two types of cases was emphasized to me by Sebastian Martens.

61. Here I focus only on problems raised by collaboration. I have discussed other aspects of this issue elsewhere. See my "A Right to Choose Death?" *Boston Review* 22 (1997): 20–23; "Physician-Assisted Suicide, the Doctrine of Double Effect, and the Ground of Value," *Ethics* 109 (1999): 586–605; "Physician-Assisted Suicide, Euthanasia, and Intending Death," in *Physician-Assisted Suicide: Expanding the Debate*, ed. M. Battin, R. Rhodes, and A. Silvers, pp. 28–62 (New York: Routledge, 1998); and "Ronald Dworkin on Abortion and Physician-Assisted Suicide," in J. Burley, ed., *Dworkin and His Critics* (Oxford: Blackwell, 2004), pp. 218–240.

62. On this, see Margaret Battin, "Euthanasia: The Fundamental Issues," in her *The Least Worst Death*, pp. 101–129 (New York: Oxford University Press, 1993).

63. Even when it is against a patient's interests to die, a doctor can be required to remove life support if the patient wishes it.

64. Judith Thomson makes the latter point in her "Physician-Assisted Suicide: Two Moral Arguments," *Ethics* 109 (1999). I am here leaving aside other types of objections to focusing on an agent's intention in deciding whether an act is impermissible. We considered these objections in chapters 3 and 5. See Thomson, ibid., for her arguments about the irrelevance of intentions for determining the permissibility of action in the context of assisted suicide.

65. Brock, "Voluntary Active Euthanasia," in his *Life and Death* (New York: Cambridge University Press, 1993), p. 211.

66. Ibid., p. 230.

67. Though it may show that it is not a form of conduct that is completely beyond the moral pale or obviously against the patient's interests, because then the doctor would not even be permitted to be an Agent.

11

DOES DISTANCE MATTER MORALLY
TO THE DUTY TO RESCUE?

I. INTRODUCTION

In chapters 1 and 2, I discussed how we should distribute aid, if we have a duty to aid or if we just decide to aid. In chapter 9, we considered these questions when there were positive rights to aid. Now I will consider whether and how our duty to aid might be affected by physical distance.

What is the problem of distance in morality (PDM)?[1] The Standard View holds that this is the problem of whether we have a stronger duty to aid strangers who are physically near to us just because they are physically near than we have to aid strangers who are not physically near (that is, who are far), all other things being equal. A Standard Claim concerning this problem is that to say distance is morally relevant implies that our duty to aid a near stranger would be stronger than our duty to aid a far one, given their equal need.[2]

Notice that the Standard View about the PDM concerns only aiding strangers whom we have not promised or contracted with to aid. It is not thought to be a problem of whether we have stronger duties, in general, to those who are physically near. So, for example, the negative duty not to harm strangers or the duty to keep promises and contracts to aid strangers are not thought to be stronger to those who are near than to those who are far. Those who think distance does matter morally do not, of course, think that it is the only factor that matters. For example, if I can help more strangers at a distance or fewer who are near, the difference in numbers might be a reason to help the group of distant people. If the distant people are members of my own community and the near people are not, I may have a stronger duty to aid the distant. Furthermore, to say that distance matters is not to say that we need do *nothing* to help distant strangers, nor is it to say that we must do *everything* to help strangers who are near. There may be an upper limit on how much we must do to aid strangers. To say that distance matters could be just to say that, other things being equal, we will have to do more for the near than for the distant because they are near (but not do more *for the far* because they are far).

I maintain that the Standard View is not an accurate description of the PDM and that the Standard Claim—if distance matters morally, we have a stronger duty to aid a near stranger than a far stranger, given their equal need—is also not correct. These are the primary issues with which I shall be concerned both in this and the next chapter. (Chapter 12 may be read independently of this chapter.)[3] There are eight major points I wish to make: (1) If we are to use hypothetical cases to help to answer the question of whether distance matters morally, we must use properly equalized cases and not deduce negative results from just one negative case. One of the methodological issues discussed in chapter 1 of this volume—how to determine whether a set of contrasting factors is a morally relevant distinction—will be revisited here. (2) We must distinguish the possible moral importance of absolute proximity (nearness) from relative proximity and from just any difference in distance. We must also give an operational definition of *proximity*. (3) Before considering whether we can justify any intuitions about proximity, we must see whether these are indeed intuitions about proximity or rather about salience. (4) We should distinguish the role of proximity in relation to aid owed in accidents from aid for basic justice. (5) All previous discussions of this proximity issue have misconceived the PDM. (6) The Standard Claim is wrong. As odd as it sounds, it is easy to show that if there were a strong duty to aid based on proximity, this would itself imply that we can have as strong a duty to aid far strangers as to aid near strangers. (7) I accept that intuitive support is not enough to justify a principle of morality. We must find morally significant ideas underlying intuitions for the principle to be justified. When we consider how we might *justify* intuitions that proximity matters morally, we may find it helpful to contrast negative rights (which are not affected by proximity) with positive aid (which might be affected by proximity) and to consider the possibility that duties related to proximity are concomitants of agents' having an option to act from an agent-centered perspective. (8) A duty to take care of what is near but no duty to take care of what is far does not necessarily imply that we have a duty to take care of what is near rather than what is far.

I shall deal with points (1)–(4) in this chapter and (5)–(8) in the next. I consider (6)—if there were a strong duty based on proximity, this could be a reason that we have a strong duty to aid distant strangers—to be the most striking result. I believe that it overturns past conceptions of the PDM and reconceives it into what I call the New Problem of Distance in Morality.

II. METHODOLOGICAL ISSUES I

A. Intuitive Judgments and Equalized Cases

Peter Singer has famously been concerned with famine relief. In connection with this concern, he has denied the moral significance of distance.[4] He says: "I do not think I need to say much in defense of the refusal to take proximity and distance into account. The fact that a person is physically near to us . . . does not show that we ought to help him rather than another who happens to be far away."[5] Yet, a classic set of cases that has been used to illustrate the fact that our intuitions support a stronger obligation to help the physically near, and thus give rise to the PDM, was presented by Singer.[6] Here are his two examples:

Pond Case: I am walking past a shallow pond and see a child drowning in it. If I wade in and pull the child out, my $500 suit will be ruined. Intuitively, I ought to wade in to save him.
Overseas Case: I know that there is a child starving to death overseas. To save him, I must send $500. Intuitively, I am not obligated to do so.[7]

There is a problem with these cases, however. If we are using cases to see whether distance per se matters, all other factors in the cases should be held constant. If we are going to use intuitive judgments about cases to test the thesis that distance is morally relevant, we can learn from the use of this method when it is applied to deciding whether the difference between harming and not-aiding (or killing and letting die) is morally relevant.[8] In discussing that issue, the methodological point we learned was that we must construct perfectly *equalized* cases. That is, in order to see whether one variable (near/far, kill/let die) makes a moral difference, we must compare two cases that differ only with respect to this variable, holding the contextual factors constant. But Singer's set of cases does not satisfy the equalization condition. For example, in the Pond Case, the child who is near is assumed to have had an accident, but the need of the child who is far in the Overseas Case is not due to an accident, but perhaps due to the absence of basic economic justice or to a natural disaster. The Overseas Case child is not a fellow citizen nor a member of the community of those who would be called on to aid; the Pond Case child probably is. In the Pond Case, the ruined suit occurs as a side effect of someone doing something minor to aid; in the Overseas Case, the monetary loss is the means to aid. In the Pond Case, the potential helper may be the only one who can help. This condition is likely not present in the Overseas Case. Further, the far child in need is probably one of many such children; the near child is thought of as unique.[9] Hence, we can take care of the whole nearby problem in the Pond Case, but only part of the far problem in the Overseas Case. In the Pond Case, we may be assured that our efforts will be efficacious; in the Overseas Case, perhaps we cannot be sure that our efforts will pay off.

As an example of how to remedy at least some of the contextual inequalities in Singer's set of cases, we could construct the following two sets of cases:

Near Alone Case: I am walking past a pond in a foreign country that I am visiting. I *alone* see many children drowning in it, and I alone can save one of them. To save the one, I must put the $500 I have in my pocket into a machine that then triggers (via electric current) rescue machinery that will certainly scoop him out.
Far Alone Case: I *alone* know that in a distant part of a foreign country that I am visiting, many children are drowning, and I alone can save one of them. To save the one, all I must do is put the $500 I carry in my pocket into a machine that then triggers (via electric current) rescue machinery that will certainly scoop him out.
Near Many Case: I am walking past a pond in a foreign country that I am visiting, and I and many others see many children in it drowning; any of us can save one of the children, but the others will not. To save one, I must put $500 I have in my pocket into a machine that will certainly scoop him out.
Far Many Case: I and many others know that in a distant part of a foreign country that we are visiting, many children are drowning; any of us could save one of the children, but the others will not. To save one, all I must do is put the $500 I have in my pocket into a machine that will certainly scoop him out.

My sense is that I have a stronger duty to the near child than to the far child in both sets of these cases, and this could be due to distance. If these cases were equalized for all factors aside from distance, then it is only the difference between near and far that could account for the different judgments about duties. Of course, the different judgments may not be due to distance, as there may still be important differences between these cases besides distance.

What conclusion could we draw if we found *one* set of equalized cases in which our intuitive judgment is that a difference in distance from two strangers makes *no* moral difference? The following might be such a set of cases:[10]

Near Costless Case: Everything is the same as in the Near Alone Case, except that all I must do is flip a switch right next to me to save the child.
Far Costless Case: Everything is the same as in the Far Alone Case, except that all I must do is flip a switch right next to me to save the child.

We cannot conclude that distance is *never* morally relevant simply by showing that one time or even sometimes it makes no difference to the strength of a duty in equalized cases. This is because a property that makes no moral difference in some equalized contexts may make a difference in other equalized contexts. (This is what I call the Principle of Contextual Interaction. We also learned about it in discussion of the killing/letting die distinction.)[11] For example, in a context where the cost of aid to the agent is low and the effects of not-aiding are great to a stranger, the duty to aid a stranger who is near and the duty to aid a stranger who is far may be equally strong. (This would, of course, imply that if there were a conflict between the two, it is at least permitted to toss a coin to decide whom to help.) Indeed, it is the point of some contexts to make distance a morally *ir*relevant feature. So if we are government officials who must aid citizens, the fact that one citizen is near and another is far is irrelevant. The role of government officials and the status of citizen are intended to make some other sorts of considerations (e.g., distance) morally irrelevant.

By contrast, we can show that distance *is* morally relevant (at least judged intuitively) by showing that we think it matters morally sometimes—even one time—in equal contexts, even if it does not always make a moral difference.[12] Hence, when someone argues that distance could make a moral difference, he is not committed to saying that it often or always does. For example, if famine relief implicates issues of basic justice, and distance is not relevant to the duty to promote basic justice, distance could still matter morally when aid to prevent accidents is at stake (as in the Pond Cases). Similarly, we may see the difference that distance can make only as we vary the size of the cost required to provide equal aid in a near and a far case, or as we vary the seriousness to an individual of not being aided. It may be that high costs must be borne in near cases but not in far cases. (The difference between the Far Costless Case and Far Alone Case tests this hypothesis.) It may be that even less serious problems must be taken care of in near cases but not in far ones.

The methodological point is that we must not only create equalized cases, we must also *alter* certain contextual factors equally in the near and the far cases to see if we find some cases where distance intuitively matters. It is not just equal contexts that are important, but different equal contexts. We could also vary the probability of success of the aid equally in both cases to see, for example, whether we intuitively believe that we are obligated to aid in the near case but not in the far case when the probability of success is low in both. We could see whether we think we must do as much to *make us able* to help those who are far as we must do to make us able to help those who are near. (For if we have a duty to help those who are far, that need not only mean that we should help if we can, but that we should also make ourselves be able to help.)[13]

When people say that distance is less morally relevant in the modern world than in past ages, they may have in mind that in a context where it is quite costless (in time and effort) to reach others with aid and to help others, distance is not relevant per se. They may also have in mind that in a context where people are interdependent with others who are far (via economic and communicative relations), distance is not relevant per se with respect to whom we should aid. (Notice that when they put these points of ease of access or interdependence by saying "no one is far from anyone any more," they thereby unwittingly give credence to the view that farness per se does indeed matter.)[14] However, all of this could be true, and distance can still be morally relevant. For when costs to reach or to aid people are high and people with whom one is not interdependent ("strangers") are involved (even when all other factors are equal), we may have a duty to pay the costs only for those who are near.

B. Distance versus Relative Distance

What if there were no equalized pair of cases in which intuitive judgments suggested that nearness in some way made the duty to aid stronger? Even this result might be consistent with distance having moral relevance sometimes. This can be shown by considering single cases in which the features of near and far are combined. For example:

Near/Far Case: I learn that in a distant part of a foreign country that I am visiting, a child is drowning. Someone else, just like me in all respects, is near him and also knows of his plight. Either one of us could successfully help by depositing $500 in a device, one of which is near each of us, that will trigger a machine that will scoop the child out.

Who has a stronger obligation to help in the Near/Far Case? In the Far Alone Case, the only person who can help is far. Suppose, contrary to what I have suggested, that it were true that in the Far Alone Case, one judges that one has as strong a duty to help, even at great cost, as one would have in the Near Alone Case. This would be consistent with the person who is near in the Near/Far Case having a stronger duty to aid than the person who is far in that very case does. (This would be comparable to a brother having as strong an obligation to take care of his deceased sister's child as he has to take care of his own child, but having a much weaker obligation to take care of her child if his sister is still alive to take care of it.)

However, the Near/Far Case may only measure the intuitive importance of *relative* distance.[15] That is, when one person who can aid is nearer than another, other things being equal, the duty to aid of the nearer may be greater, at least sometimes. This leaves it open that the physically nearer person could be far away in (more) absolute terms and yet still have as strong a duty to aid as someone who was physically near*er* and near in (more) absolute terms. It would be an interesting result in itself to show that *relative nearness* matters morally, at least sometimes, but this is still not the same as showing that (more) absolute nearness matters.[16]

If we are still concerned to determine whether nearness itself (and not relative nearness) matters morally, we could try the following methodology: (1) Show that a far person (in absolute terms), when no one is near, would have a weaker duty than a near one would have when no one was far. (One could use the Near Alone and Far Alone cases to test for this.) It would then be shown that *distance per se* rather than *relative distance* has (at least at the intuitive level) moral significance. (2) If, contrary to my suggestion, showing (1) is not possible, we could use (a) a Near/Far Case in which the distances of agents from a victim were all far in an absolute sense, but differed relatively, and (b) a Near/Far Case in which the distances of agents from a victim were all near in an absolute sense, but differed relatively. If the difference in the individual distances (especially in [a]) makes no difference to duties, then we would have evidence that relative distance is not a relevant factor.[17] (3) The evidence in (2) would suggest that in a Near/Far Case where one agent is near in absolute terms and the other far in absolute terms, it would be nearness, not relative nearness, that causes a difference in duty. Such a difference in duty would indicate that nearness per se matters, even if the duties of those who are near and far were the same (contrary to my suggestion) when no agent is near. It turns out, then, that it could be very important to run the test in (2) and that even uniformly negative results in Near Alone and Far Alone types of cases would not settle the question about the moral relevance of distance per se (at least at the intuitive level).[18]

C. A Succession of Cases

Another methodological question is whether we can imagine each case separately from the likelihood of its being only one of a number of cases. In the Near Alone Case and the Far Alone Case, we are asked to imagine them as isolated cases. But suppose that we could expect many identical Far Alone cases arising in succession. Then, if we aided in one case, what reasons could we give for not-aiding in the next case, and then the one after? But the aggregation of all of the aid would consume much of our life. We are not required to give up so much in order to aid, it might be said. So perhaps, it might be said, we are not required to aid in any of the cases.[19] (In real-life cases, aid to those who are far [at least from affluent countries] may involve issues of basic economic justice that should be societal and institutional concerns. This is an additional factor, besides aggregation of aid, that may be held to account for our refusal to aid in even one case.)

I disagree that this aggregation problem implies not aiding in one case. It is incorrect, I believe, to judge what we should do in one case on the basis of what we need not do if many cases were to arise. Even if there is no distinction between the cases taken individually, the cumulative effort or cost is different in aiding once versus many times. Even if there is no magic cutoff point such that the difference between aiding ten times and aiding eleven times, for example, will involve making more of a total effort than is required, we can set an arbitrary cutoff so as to aid sometimes but not to go on aiding when the aggregate total effort will clearly be more than required.

Furthermore, it is not true that this problem of aggregation only arises where there are potentially many cases needing aid. We can imagine one near accident case that would require many small bits of aid over time, so that we would start off giving a certain amount but, as time went on, more and more would be required to make the rescue a success. We could in this case also set an arbitrary cutoff point so that we do not wind up doing more than we are required to do through the inability to say why, at any point, one small additional bit of aid should make any difference. If we can stop the aggregation in this way in one near case, we could stop it where the potential for providing more aid than is required arises through many cases. Hence, the threat of future obligation need not be a reason for deciding how we act in the first case at the beginning of the potential series. (It might, however, explain not giving minor aid in one case if the case fell in the middle of the series. Hence, in our methodology for deciding whether the near/far distinction ever counts morally, we should assume that our cases do not fall in the middle of such a series.)

In concluding this section, I suggest that, intuitively, there is a difference between the Far Alone Case and the Near Alone Case (or there will be a difference for some degree of cost or effort). I also suggest that there would be an intuitive difference in the Near/Far Case, even if helping were costless, though in the absence of the test suggested in (2) in section B, this might be due to the factor of relative nearness. If there is an intuitive difference between the Near Alone Case and the Far Alone Case, this implies that if the near person in the Near/Far Case failed to help, the far person should (intuitively) still *not* be obligated to aid at the cost of $500. (But it is possible that there is some lesser cost or effort such that the intuitive judgment is that the near person would be obligated to sustain it first, and if she did not, the far person would be obligated to sustain it.) Yet, if all factors besides distance have been equalized in the Near Alone Case and the Far Alone Case, and at some level of effort or cost there was thought to be a difference in obligation, these cases would show that, at least intuitively, distance per se matters to what obligations we have.

I also suggest that absolute nearness could be shown to matter even if it merely gives priority to one person having an obligation as well as if it eliminates another person having an obligation, at least sometimes. Whether relative nearness matters rather than absolute nearness, or as well as absolute nearness, is a different and interesting question that it is, nevertheless, crucial to discuss in connection with whether absolute nearness gives priority to one person's obligation, even if its absence does not eliminate another (far) person's obligation.

III. MEASURING DISTANCE

Would the result that absolute distance matters per se show that, intuitively, any difference in distance can have moral significance, or rather that a certain type of difference in distance may sometimes have moral significance? There is a difference in distance when one child is near me and another child is in a distant part of the country. But a third child could fail to be near me, yet be much closer to me than the one who is in a distant part of the country. Would there be any case in which our intuitive responses would tell us that our obligations to this third child were weaker than to the near one but stronger than to the more distant one? The claim that (1) all intervals of distance could matter intuitively, at least sometimes, is different from the claim that (2) the distinction between the near and the far (where the non-near is the far) could matter. The latter claim is compatible with there never being any intuitive differences in our obligation to the second and third children. I suspect that it is really claim (2) with which the PDM is concerned. Hence, we really want to know whether absolute proximity (nearness) matters intuitively.[20]

What is the intuitive measure of proximity? Let us first try to answer this question for the standard type of case that has been considered in the literature, namely, the distance from an agent to a needy stranger. First, is the distance measured by finding where the agent stands and where the needy stranger stands? Suppose that I stand in a part of India, but I have *very* long arms that reach all the way to the other end of India,[21] allowing me to reach a child who is drowning in a pond at a great distance (Reach Case). Intuitively, I think that this case is treated as one where the child is near. Suppose that the child is so far away in India that I cannot reach there even with my long arms, but the child can reach toward me with *her* long arms so that she is within my reach. Again, I think that this case is treated as one of a victim who is near. These cases might suggest that one intuitively relevant measurement of distance between strangers (whom I shall henceforth call the agent and the victim) is from the *extended* parts of the agent's body to

a 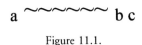 b c

Figure 11.1.

the extended parts of the victim's body.[22] The question then is: Are these extended parts near or far from each other? In the Reach Case, they are near.

Notice that this does not necessarily mean that someone with long-distance reach is near everyone who is *within* the territory from his central location to the outer rim of his extended reach. For it is possible that his reach is not continuous, as illustrated in figure 11.1.

Suppose that an agent is at *c*. He may reach to *a* and all the way back from *a* to his centered location, but his arm may fail to *extend and stop* within area *a* to *b*, so he has no reach there. It extends and stops again between points *b* and *c*. Intuitively, there can be a point somewhere between *a* and *b* from which he is distant, even while he is near a physically farther point at *a*. (I shall ignore such unusual cases in the following discussion.)

Suppose that within a short period of time, we can bring people near each other's extended parts by a vehicle. Then they are *near by that vehicle*, it might be said. The measurement of near-by-vehicles is at least in part temporal. It seems to combine a nontemporal notion (extended parts are nontemporally near) with a temporal notion (how long it takes to get near as measured nontemporally). If it takes a long time to get extended parts physically close, people are far-by-vehicles. But perhaps nearness is then mostly a function of the length of time it takes to traverse a physical distance. That is, for any given period of time, different vehicles may cover different distances; someone may be far-by-car but near-by-plane. Once we relativize near and far to a vehicle, I believe, we are dealing with a set *length of time* (not distance) that it takes to bring people to a certain distance from each other's extended parts. If within a certain length of time (yet to be determined), we can by vehicle bring people to a certain distance from each other's extended parts, they are *near-by-vehicle*.

For example, suppose that A's extended parts are several feet away from B's, but A suffers from a disease that makes him move very slowly unaided, say, an inch an hour. If he is in his wheelchair, he covers the distance quickly. Should we say that he is near-by-wheelchair and far unaided? It seems we must, if we allow that someone can be near-by-vehicle when he is far-on-foot. Or, suppose that a fast vehicle can get us to a point many miles away almost instantaneously, but cannot traverse a route to a half-mile away. We will be nearer the first point than the second, by the temporal measure.

By contrast, if our notion of what is near is nontemporal or is a function of the time it takes for an unaided normal human being to traverse a distance, someone who moves very slowly can still be near and someone who has a very fast vehicle can still be far. Having a fast vehicle can make it very easy to help those who are far, and this may be why our duties to these far people are as great as to those who are near (as in the Far Costless Case, where it was easy to aid for a different reason). A test of this hypothesis

is to raise the efforts required to get the fast vehicle going. If we are already near because we are near-by-vehicle, the efforts or money we are obligated to expend to get the
vehicle going should be as great as those we are obligated to expend for someone we
are near-without-vehicle. I suspect that the efforts required differ, at least intuitively.

For example, suppose that A is near-by-car to C, whereas B is near to C
without any alteration in his current location. If B would have to expend $500 to
save C, would A (in a separate case not involving B) have to expend $500 on
getting a car to go to C, if there were then no further cost to speak of in saving
him? In other words, does near-by-car give one the same obligation to engage in a
more costly rescue as is had by someone who is near *tout court*? I do not think so.
(Other cases to consider in this connection include: (a) Would A have to transmit
the $500 to help C just because he is near-by-car, instead of using it to go by car so
as to have his extended parts be near C's? It seems very odd to think that even
though we do not have to go anywhere by vehicle in order to be able to help C,
because of start-up costs, whether we are near-by-vehicle could determine whether
we have an obligation to transmit aid at this same cost. (b) Would A have a duty
to go by car costlessly in order to then pay the $500 to save C, if he had to pay this
if C were near? This is more likely to be so, I think because it is initially like Far
Costless.

I conclude that the non-relativized-to-vehicle sense of near is primary for our
intuitive sense of when we must do more to aid. Hence, I shall accept a notion of
near that is *not* only temporal (or is only temporal in the sense of a distance it takes
a normal, unaided human a short time to traverse).

As I have already suggested, when people speak of a "shrinking world," one
thing they seem to have in mind is that an increasing number of people are near in
the sense of "easy (costly neither in time nor in money) to become near in the
ordinary sense" (where the latter may be a distance [between extended parts] that it
takes a short time for unaided, normal humans to traverse). Again the ordinary
sense of near is needed to boot up the new idea, which we might call "neasy," and
so the ordinary sense cannot be eliminated or completely substituted. If people
were neasy, would we have as strong an obligation to expend as much to aid them
as we do for people who are near (in the ordinary sense)? If absolute distance
matters morally, the answer should be "not always," as exhibited in case (a) above
in which A is neasy but need not therefore, spend the $500 on C.

I have used the cost test to see whether near-by-vehicle is the same as near. But,
of course, the costs we are required to expend to aid could be the same, and yet
near-by-vehicle not be the same idea as near. This would be because distance does
not matter morally. The crucial point seems to be that near-by-vehicle is parasitic
on a more fundamental idea of nearness, as shown by the fact that the vehicle is
used to bring people close, as measured by the nearness (independent of vehicle) of
their extended parts.

Now suppose that in the Reach Case, no part of me that reaches the child is
efficacious in helping her. Is the intuitively relevant measurement of the distance
between an agent and a victim from the *efficacious extended* part of the agent's body
to the extended part of the victim's body? Possibly not. When a nonefficacious

extended part of me is near an extended part of the victim, could I be strongly obligated to help by the use of an efficarious device that is mine, even though it is far from both me and my victim? If the answer is yes, then it need not be an efficacious part that is near the victim in order for me to be near. In this regard, there are several different types of hypothetical cases it is worth distinguishing.

In one case, I am extremely large, so that an extended part of me that is near a victim is far from the part of me that would be efficacious in helping. For example, my right hand is near the victim but it is my left hand, now miles away, that could be moved to help. Intuitively, I am obligated to move the left hand. Here, I am efficacious in aiding, both in that I can do something to bring a far means close and in that the means is a part of me and I am close.

In a second case, my mechanical means that could be helpful in rescuing the victim is at a distance, but I could trigger it by pressing a remote control button. Here, what is near the victim is not completely efficacious, but also not totally inefficacious, since I who am near the victim can trigger the remaining means of aid. The question in this case is whether, intuitively, if I am not totally efficacious with what is near, I have an obligation, in virtue of being near the victim, to do what I can to activate the tools of rescue that are still far. If I am near the victim with my precious Stradivarius violin, which is also near to me,[23] and its destruction would save someone's life, intuitively I have to destroy it. But if I am near the victim, do I have to press the remote control button and transport my far Stradivarius for destruction if this is necessary? Intuitively, I do not think so. This leaves it open that there are some means I do have to transport by remote control just because I am near the victim.[24] If I know that I could be called upon to sacrifice my Stradivarius if it were near, this, of course, could give me a reason to never have it near in situations where I might be obligated to sacrifice it. It does not seem to me that this is inconsistent with having a duty to sacrifice it if it is near.

This is in some respects like the following case:[25] A nervous person is coming to live near my apartment. If I am near when he becomes needy for support, I will have a moral duty to help him. If I know this is true, this could give me a reason to be out of town when he comes, if the efforts I would be obligated to make for him are burdensome. But it would be ex ante in the self-interest of each of us (given that a trip will be disruptive to me and will leave him all alone) to agree that I should stay and when he needs help just be obligated to do something minor for him that has at least some chance of helping him. I do not believe such an agreement can override the duties I would have in virtue of being near to a person in need. Hence (unless other factors are present in the case), the non-Pareto optimal choice (e.g., do not be near) may be the only morally acceptable one. Similarly, in the Stradivarius Case, the morally acceptable choices could be to leave the violin at a distance or be obligated to use it when you are near the victim and the violin is near you.[26]

In a third case, I am near a victim but I am totally inefficacious, unable even to activate a far device that would be efficacious. Because I am near, should someone else who is far but who has authority to act for me and knows that I am near the victim, activate my means of rescue that are far? Only if I who am near would be obligated to do so if I could, I think.

IV. SALIENCE, RECOGNITION, AND PERSONAL ENCOUNTER

Now let us turn to an issue—salience—that bears on whether the Near Alone Case and the Far Alone Case were equalized for all factors besides distance. In the Far Alone Case as described, I do not directly *see* the person drowning, but in the Near Alone Case, I do. Hence, these cases are not correctly equalized. It might be that this difference makes the need salient in the Near Alone Case but not in the Far Alone Case, and salience rather than distance accounts for intuitive differences between the two cases. Furthermore, it may be that in the Near Alone Case, the victim sees me (and I know this), but this is not so in the Far Alone Case. Call this the factor of recognition. If these factors are present, the agent certainly has a personal encounter with the victim in the Near Alone Case, but not in the Far Alone Case. These are additional failures to equalize cases, and these factors might affect intuitive moral judgments.

The salience of need refers not only to the obviousness and inescapability of noticing need, but also to the continuing imposition of this knowledge on us. Peter Unger,[27] for example, says that salience is not always present when something is clearly visible close up, since we may well be able to pass over what we notice. The salient event, according to him, is the one that attracts and holds our attention so that we cannot stop thinking about it; it presses itself upon us. So need that is near and obvious may not be salient, if I can simply put the need out of my mind. This understanding of salience suggests that it is "subjective salience" (S_s) with which Unger is concerned: Whatever a person cannot get out of his mind is salient to him. But there is also a notion of "objective salience" (S_o), which suggests that something should attract and hold one's attention or is such that it would attract and hold the attention of a normal (or ideal) observer. Need that is at a distance could be salient. Suppose that I have very long-distance vision and can see great need directly at a distance; the need is then obvious but still not near. The need may also be salient (S_s) in that I cannot get the scene out of my mind. The need may be salient (S_o) in that I should not be able to get it out of my mind, and a normal or ideal observer could not do so. Hence, we could equalize salience in the Near Alone and the Far Alone cases by assuming that direct observation in both cases gives rise to salience (in both senses, S_s and S_o).

Could we equalize for the absence of salience by making direct observation absent in the Near Alone Case, as it was in the Far Alone Case originally? Not necessarily. Some need that is near (or far) may be salient, even though it is not obvious or directly observed. For example, suppose that I am informed by a detecting device that someone just outside my door is drowning and I could help. Even though I cannot see or hear him (and he cannot see or hear me), his need can be salient to me in the sense that I cannot stop thinking about it, and a normal or ideal individual would not stop thinking about it (Door Case). The absence of direct sensory awareness of and/or active engagement with the victim, I believe, implies that there is also no *personal* encounter with the victim in the Door Case. (By contrast, if I am speaking with a distant person on the phone [or even communicating via e-mail with him as he reads and responds to my message], there is a personal encounter.)[28] Further, in the Door Case, since the person cannot see or hear me, the recognition factor is also absent.

We should equalize the Near Alone and Far Alone cases for the presence or absence of salience, personal encounter and recognition. So, let us imagine that there is no recognition and no personal encounter in these cases, but salience due to a continual message sent by a detecting device (as in the Door Case) is present in both cases. My claim is that when the Near Alone and Far Alone cases also both have salient need, it is nearness and not salience that gives rise to our intuition that we have a strong obligation to help in the Near Alone Case. If the Near Alone Case were salient and the Far Alone Case were not, I claim that it would be nearness and not salience that gave rise to our intuition that we have a strong obligation to help in the Near Alone Case. That is, when we think we have a strong obligation to aid in the Near Alone Case and not in the Far Alone Case, it is the difference in distance represented by the cases rather than the difference in salience that is determinative of the sense of obligation. This is contrary to what Unger argues for.[29] He thinks that it is salience—I suspect S_s—and not nearness that our responses to cases track, even though he does not think salience can be theoretically justified as a true morally relevant difference determining obligations.

Here is the key point in showing that it is not S_s of need that our intuitions about obligation track: The mere fact that we cannot take our mind off of someone's need does not mean that we would think it impermissible to do what *would* take our mind off of it, if we could, even though this would interfere with our aiding. If we do not think that there is some other reason besides S_s for why we have a duty to aid, we should believe intuitively that we may eliminate S_s, even if this interferes with our aiding. This indicates that S_s alone is not generating the intuition that we have an obligation to aid, for if we believed that S_s gave rise to an obligation, we would think it wrong to alter the salience if this reduced our tendency to help. For example, suppose I think that it is permissible to turn off my detecting device if this will help me stop thinking about the long-distance need and make it less likely that I will aid in the Far Alone Case. It is probably because I believe that I am not strongly responsible for helping that distant person that I think it is permissible for me to eliminate the S_s of this need. Hence, the S_s of the need does not imply that I will think I have a duty.

Furthermore, suppose that a person I see through my long-distance vision is truly striking, dressed in vibrant colors, and dramatically exhibiting his need. He stands out from a few other equally needy people. Further, his need *should* be salient and would be salient to a normal or ideal observer. It is so. I do not intuitively believe that I have a greater obligation to this person than to the others at a distance, even if I feel under more psychological pressure to aid.[30] This is a case where S_o is not a function of moral factors but purely visual ones.

By contrast, suppose that the person outside my door in the Door Case is in great need, and as I said before, his need is salient (S_s and S_o) even though I cannot see or hear him. (In this case, his need would be S_o on account of moral, not visual, factors.) May I take a pill to eliminate its salience or turn off the machine that gives me knowledge of his condition in order to reduce salience, if this reduces the chance that I will aid? (It is possible to eliminate S_s, and if one makes oneself into a non-normal, non-ideal observer, it is possible to eliminate S_o in oneself. However, one cannot eliminate the truth that something deserves [for moral or nonmoral reasons] to be salient to a normal observer.) If I think that I am obligated to help someone who is near, I should not eliminate salience if it is necessary to help me fulfill my obligation. A sign that I intuitively believe that it is nearness that obligates me to help is that once I am near someone who needs help, I do not think I am permitted to move myself from him to a greater distance merely in order to avoid being near in order to avoid an obligation. Contrast this with my sense that I am permitted to change the salience (S_s or S_o due to nonmoral factors) of need, if no other factor obligates me to provide aid. If I intuitively thought that such salience obligated, I would think that I am not permitted to change it to avoid being obligated, as I believe that I am not permitted to change nearness, once it is in place, to farness merely in order to avoid being obligated.[31]

While the Permissibility of Elimination Test that I have been using cannot (conceptually) apply to S_o when S_o is due to moral factors, we can also show that such S_o is not the source of obligation. For it is not because a need ought not to be forgotten that we should aid; we should aid because such need has another property (e.g., pain and suffering of a near victim) in virtue of which it ought not to be forgotten (i.e., in virtue of which it has S_o).

I have argued that we may not alter the characteristic (our nearness), if we correctly believe that it gives us an obligation, once we have the characteristic, in order to avoid the obligation. This does not, however, mean that we *have to acquire* the characteristic; that we may not avoid having it. For example, if I want to have a quiet vacation, intuitively I may permissibly avoid going to places where I am likely to have an obligation to aid those near me. By contrast, if I have an obligation to aid that is independent of distance, I may well have a duty to go to a place where I can be useful.[32]

But here is a problem. Recall our earlier discussion of the Stradivarius Case and the Nervous Visitor Case. If it is permissible to avoid acquiring the characteristic that gives one a duty, it may well be to the mutual advantage of an agent and the person who could be aided by her to compromise on the demands made of the agent in virtue of her nearness in order to induce her to be near. For example, if I want to avoid being imposed on and so stay in my own backyard, I may deprive myself of enjoyment I can have if I go to a hotel in a place where accidents happen. I also deprive someone who needs my help of even such minimal assistance as calling for an ambulance when he is truly desperate. Could we imagine a hypothetical agreement that yields a Pareto optimal outcome? I get to be near someone and only have to do a small fraction of what would be required of me just in virtue of being near an accident. As I said above, I believe, intuitively, that it is not morally acceptable to limit the duty in this way. If one is near, one cannot in this way be relieved of the full responsibilities incumbent on someone who is near. This is true, I believe, even if it implies that fewer people will allow themselves to be near needy people.

In sum, I suggest that when we equalize the Near Alone and Far Alone cases for salience, absence of personal encounter, and recognition, the duty to aid is stronger in the Near Alone Case, and distance is driving our intuitions.[33] Not only are salience and distance different concepts, but far things can have all varieties of salience and near things can lack all varieties of salience. Salience alone does not intuitively ground an obligation (let alone truly ground an obligation in being theoretically justified). Some evidence for this is that we think it is permissible to eliminate salience when there are no other grounds for the obligation to aid even though this reduces our chances of aiding. Obligations do, at least intuitively, seem to vary with the near and non-near in some cases; near things should be salient if this aids us in meeting the obligation that nearness generates. The obligation can be avoided by staying far rather than being near, but it cannot be limited merely by reasoning based on the mutual self-interest of the agent and the needy stranger. At least, I claim, this is the report of our intuitive judgments.

V. METHODOLOGICAL ISSUES II

Two different sorts of objections may still be raised to the conclusion that, at least intuitively, we care about distance. The first objection does not deny that we respond intuitively to distance per se.[34] However, it claims that the genesis of our tendency to respond in such a way undermines the idea that we care about distance per se. For example, because nearness and effectiveness of aid have usually been connected, we become "hardwired" to respond to nearness itself. We then do so even when effectiveness is stipulated as equal in near and far cases of aid. But really it is effectiveness that (causally) explains the role of distance in our intuitions. One answer to this objection, I believe, is to find an alternative explanation for why distance should have its intuitive role. Another response is to deny that we are so "hardwired" that we cannot respond to factors in a hypothetical case as they are described. This response bears on a second objection.

The second objection claims that because distance is usually associated with other factors, for example, effectiveness, we cannot really imagine the equalized cases we are asked to imagine;[35] for example, though we are told to imagine a case where nearness makes no difference to effectiveness, we will continue to imagine the Near Alone Case as involving greater effectiveness. Hence, we are not judging distance per se to matter. I believe that this objection has a too-depressing view of our ability to imagine and respond to unrealistic cases, a view not typically held about other subject matters. For example, newborn babies cannot speak English. But suppose that I ask you to imagine that one baby has an innate capacity to do so and then to consider how you would treat it differently from ordinary newborns. Do people find this impossible to do, and would they continue to report the responses they have to infants who could not speak English? I doubt it.

VI. UNGER'S VIEWS AND THE TWO-SUBJECT QUESTION

In concluding this chapter, let us consider how Peter Unger argues against the intuitive significance of distance in the course of his discussion of variations on two cases: the Sedan Case and the Envelope Case.[36] In the first version of the Sedan Case, we are driving by some stranger who is near us. He needs to be taken in our car to the hospital, but he will bleed over the seats and this will result in costly damage to our car. In the first version of the Envelope Case, we are asked to send money to needy strangers who are far away. (Their plight is not the result of an accident and thus implicates basic justice. The Sedan Case and the Envelope Case, like the Pond Case and the Overseas Case, are not equalized.) Intuitively, we think that we have a stronger duty to aid in the Sedan Case than in the Envelope Case. The question is: What difference between the cases accounts for our intuitive responses (even if it does not justify them)? Unger's strategy in answering this question is to consider various candidate differences by, for example, (a) removing the difference from the Sedan Case to see whether our intuitions change from the original Sedan Case, and (b) adding the difference to the Envelope Case to see whether this changes our intuitions from the original Envelope Case.[37]

Unger removes nearness from the Sedan Case and claims that when we hear on our car radio that someone at a distance needs aid, our sense of obligation to drive him to the hospital is not reduced. If nearness were purely a temporal notion, near-by-car in the Second Sedan Case would be as near as near-by-foot in the original Sedan Case. This would explain why our sense of duty would not change. But I have suggested that this purely temporal notion of distance is not right.[38] An alternative explanation is available, however. If having a vehicle makes aid easy, aid at a distance may be as obligatory as near aid (as in the Far Costless Case, for a different reason). But aid will eventually be costly in the revised Sedan Case (as it is in the original Sedan Case), because the damage will be done to our car. So how can costlessness be an explanation of an equally strong obligation? (Recall that in section III, I too presented a case (b) where one had to easily go a long distance to then expend a lot to help.)

Unger's Sedan cases might point out the importance of *how* the cost comes about in generating our intuitive sense of what we owe. What I have in mind is that, in these cases, what we are called upon to do per se (even when we get to the person) is easy and costless. The significant cost is a further effect of what we do; that is, the car gets bloody, needs to be repaired, and that will cost. This is in contrast to a case where the cost is what must be directly invested upfront, as in the Near Alone and Far Alone cases, where we put the $500 in the machine, or where we must pay the cost to get the car set in motion. (It is also, to some degree, in contrast to case (b) described in section III where someone is neasy but must pay $500 to help when he gets to his victim. I have already noted that in the Pond Case, the cost is a further effect; in the Overseas Case, the cost is upfront.) In general, it may be that, at least intuitively, costs that (roughly) are upfront to helping someone can defeat obligations, even when the same costs as further effects cannot. If this were true, then we would expect only upfront costs to defeat an obligation to the distant more easily than they would defeat an obligation to the near. Why, it may be asked, is the upfront/downstream distinction morally significant, if the outcome in terms of harm to the agent and the victim would be the same? It represents the difference between what an agent must do and what he will suffer as a result of what he will do. If the distinction matters, presumably it has something to do with how people should be treated, both victim and agent, in bringing about an outcome. One sort of treatment (not paying up-front) is not disrespectful of the victim; another sort of treatment (not doing what is easily done because of downstream payment to come) is disrespectful of the victim. Why is this? Perhaps because its flip side is that requiring that an agent do something costly up-front to aid is disrespectful of the agent, but requiring that he ultimately pay downstream is not. But why is this? More will have to be said and it may relate to what imposition on a person is a means and what is a side effect.[39]

Next, Unger considers a version of the Envelope Case to which nearness is added: On vacation, someone visits a poor country. Near his vacation house are sick children. He receives an envelope in the mail from a local charity asking for money for the children next door. Unger thinks that, at least intuitively, we believe that the visitor does no wrong in not giving the money. From this, he concludes that nearness is not relevant to an obligation to aid. One alternative analysis of this case explains why the visitor does no wrong in not-aiding, by distinguishing issues of basic *justice* from *accidents*. If the children are sick because of a failure of social justice, as a nonmember of the society, the visitor is no more (or less) obligated if he is near than if he is far. But if the children are sick due to an accident, the visitor should save even one of many if that is all he can save, and presumably he does this without the intermediary of an envelope to charity. I have only claimed that intuitions in cases involving accidents and individuals who can aid—Singer's Pond Case was of this type but not the Overseas (famine) Case he compares it with, as I have already noted—track the presence or absence of proximity. I have not claimed that responding to issues that are the responsibility of states or organizations tracks proximity.

However, the class of events to be distinguished from those involving issues of social justice includes more than accidents. I am not sure how to describe this larger category. For example, if someone is deliberately shot, this is not an accident, and yet a visitor should help in this case also.[40] It is tempting to think that the distinction is between those events that mark a change in the normal course of events ("emergencies") and those that are par for the course. However, if a new economic crisis occurs just as one visits a foreign country, this does not turn an issue of economic justice into one for which nearness generates a duty to aid. Having gestured in the direction of the distinction I have in mind, for purposes of this chapter, I shall simply distinguish between basic justice and accidents.

It is worth pointing out that in drawing this distinction, I may be taking a stand on the so-called two-subject question: Should issues of basic social justice be distinguished from issues implicating the individual's duty of beneficence or rescue,[41] or do the latter underlie and also reflect the former? The view that there are two subjects (justice is separate from beneficence) is Rawlsian.[42] By contrast, some (e.g., Liam Murphy)[43] claim to see only one subject: The duty of beneficence underlies the concern for basic justice, and the same principles that govern institutional action to achieve basic justice should govern individual morality.

Suppose that there is a duty for an individual to directly aid in the Near Alone Case and no duty when social justice is at stake nearby as he visits in a foreign country. This supports the two-subject view. Murphy argues that our duties to aid in general (including to support just institutions) are based on having a duty to do our fair share to promote the good. When others fail to do their fair share, we are not required to do more than our fair share to pick up the slack. However, he himself notes that this principle does not seem to cover many rescue cases. For example, suppose that one person has an accident near several of us, and all of the others fail to do their part in a rescue. I am then obligated to do *more* than my fair share, I think. This would also support my claim that principles governing rescue in accidents are different from aid to achieve basic justice (or beneficence in general).

The view that certain issues are "political, not ethical" is also confirmed by the possibility that individual action to correct for certain political failures always misses its mark. For example, suppose there were a government duty, as part of basic justice, to tax so that wealth is distributed in accord with the Difference Principle. If the government fails in its duty, and citizens voluntarily give up their money to create a distribution in accord with the Difference Principle, this does nothing for political justice per se, because the state is still unjust. Furthermore, if even the worst off in the society are very well off in absolute terms, the government might still have the same duty of distributive justice. But citizens would have no ethical duty as individuals to voluntarily redistribute their wealth.

Individuals have an ethical duty to support (including by taxes) institutions and organizations providing basic justice or compensating for its absence. The strength of the duty may vary with social membership—stronger to one's own society, weaker to other societies (other things being equal)—even if it does not vary with distance, as the individual's duty of rescue sometimes seems to. Individuals may also have duties to support institutions that deal with emergencies and accidents. If one is in a foreign country, is there a stronger duty to organizations concerned with such events that occur near where one is rather than with far events, other things being equal? Is there a greater obligation to organizations concerned with such events far from one in one's own society, but an even stronger obligation to organizations dealing with such events near to one within one's own society? These are questions I raise but leave unanswered.

Finally, if we intuitively think that obligations can vary as a function of proximity, we can account for our responses to two puzzles that Unger raises.[44] In the first one, someone who has already given a lot to Oxfam feels morally free to refuse to respond to another request for life-saving aid. The same person, however, does not feel that simply because she has already given a lot to Oxfam, she may refuse services to a person she meets on the road who needs life-saving aid. Since Unger denies the significance of distance, he concludes that one cannot refuse the additional Oxfam request for aid to distant lands any more than one can refuse to aid the person on the road.

But suppose that we think we have a duty to help those who are near and not as strong a duty to help those who are far. Then, by our intuitive lights, giving a great deal to Oxfam either will not have been a duty or will have satisfied whatever duty of direct aid we have to the distant. By contrast, performing supererogatory or dutiful acts of a certain type at one time does not necessarily relieve one from doing a different type of duty at a later time, for example, to help the stranger one meets on the road.[45] But doing a supererogatory act at one time or fulfilling one type of duty *can* relieve one from doing more of it at a later time, hence the sense that one may permissibly decline the additional Oxfam request in good conscience.

What if one has already performed a duty—for example, saved someone whom one came across on the highway—and then one receives a request from Oxfam? Having performed a strenuous stringent duty can make it permissible to refuse to do a strenuous supererogatory act or a less stringent duty, if what was involved in the stringent duty depleted the resources also needed for those other acts. If one's money is not depleted by hard work, the duty to send money to Oxfam can remain after working hard on the highway. Can having performed one strenuous duty of one type relieve one from performing another of the same type, for example, saving the next person on the highway? Yes, if there is a limit to the costs one must incur to perform such duties. Hence, it is not merely that one has aided in the past that is relevant to future action. Whether one's aid was supererogatory, whether it was a different type of dutiful act, and how costly it was can affect what one must do in the future.

Unger's second puzzle arises in connection with his views on what he calls "futility thinking." This is the tendency to not help anyone if one cannot help a significant proportion of those who need help. (He claims that salience, as a matter of psychological fact, helps to overcome futility thinking.) The puzzle is: When do I *not* have a case in which I can only help a nonsignificant proportion of those who need help? Unger says that the case in which I can definitely save the only person near me who is drowning in the pond is *not* a case in which I can take care of "the whole problem," any more than I do when I save a few of those doomed by starvation in distant Africa.[46] This is because the one person who is drowning is just one of many people in the world who are drowning. But suppose that we intuitively distinguish morally between cases of near and distant aid. Then it is understandable that when I take care of the only person near me who is drowning, I think that I have completely dealt with a problem. (It remains true, however, that futility thinking will not excuse someone from saving one of many near people who are drowning.)

NOTES

I thank Liam Murphy for suggesting that I examine the topic of whether there is moral significance to physical distance. I am indebted to the students and faculty of my graduate classes in ethical theory at UCLA and NYU for their discussion of the ideas in chapters 11 and 12. I am grateful for comments from Alexander Friedman, Sigrun Svavarsdottir, Derek Parfit, and audiences at the Philosophy Department Colloquia at the Graduate Center, City University of New York, the University of Calgary, the Conference on Nationalism and Borders at the University of Utah, and the Pacific Philosophical Association 1999 panel on Aiding Distant Strangers. I am also grateful for the discussion at the Conference on Moral Theory, Le Lavandou, France, June 1999, where my commentator was Marina Oshana, and for discussion at the Conference on the Moral and Legal Limits of Samaritan Duties at Georgia State University, where my commentator was Violetta Igneski.

1. I originally referred to this as the Problem of Moral Distance, but I became convinced that this term suggested something different (e.g., the difference in people's moral systems or moral relations).

2. Throughout, I use "obligation" and "duty" interchangeably and without the implication that someone has a correlative right. I do not think this is crucial to my argument.

3. My discussion in this and the next chapter combines material from my articles "Faminine Ethics: The Problem of Distance in Morality and Singer's Ethical Theory," in *Singer and His Critics*, ed. D. Jamieson, pp. 162–208 (Oxford: Blackwell, 1999); "Rescue and Harm: A Discussion of Peter Unger's *Living High and Letting Die*," *Legal Theory* 5 (1999): 1–44; "Does Distance Matter Morally to the Duty to Rescue?" *Law and Philosophy* 19 (2000): 665–81; and "The New Problem of Distance," in *Duties to Distant Needy*, ed. D. Chatterjee, pp. 59–74 (Cambridge: Cambridge University Press, 2004).

4. I discuss other aspects of his views on famine relief in chapter 13, "Peter Singer's Ethical Theory."

5. Peter Singer, "Famine, Affluence, and Morality," in *World Hunger and Moral Obligation*, ed. William Aiken and Hugh LaFollette, pp. 22–36 (Englewood Cliffs, NJ: Prentice-Hall, 1977).

6. In ibid. and in Peter Singer, *Practical Ethics*, 2d ed. (Cambridge: Cambridge University Press, 1993).

7. In picking the dollar amount, we must be sensitive to whether the demand is on an average person or a billionaire. I am assuming an average person in my examples. Below, I shall deal with the importance of testing the different amounts required of any given person.

8. For details, see my *Morality, Mortality*, vol. 2 (New York: Oxford University Press, 1996). For a shorter description, see chapter 1 in this volume.

9. This last factor may give rise to the question: Why select one far person over another to help? Nearness in the Pond Case, by contrast, can select (distinguish) whom I should help. However, suppose that the reverse were true in another set of cases: Many people are drowning near me of whom I can save only one, and only one is in need *anywhere in the world* at a distance. Intuitively, I still believe that I have a stronger obligation to help one of the near at a cost of $500 than the far one. That is, even when nearness is not a characteristic that distinguishes someone from others, it can intuitively seem to be a reason to act. However, suppose that nearness had only a distinguishing role. Then if all the needy were far and nothing else distinguished them, we might just toss a coin to find out who will be the beneficiary of our duty to give far-aid (if the duty were equal in strength to our duty to give near-aid).

10. Suggested by Connie Rosati.

11. On these phenomena, see my "Killing, Letting Die: Methodological and Substantive Issues," *Pacific Philosophical Quarterly* 64 (1983): 297–312; Shelly Kagan, "The Additive Fallacy," *Ethics* 99 (1988): 5–31; and my *Morality, Mortality*, vol. 2.

12. I believe that the times it makes a difference must be ones that do not just appeal to intensional contexts. For example, the fact that saving someone who is near rather than far is the object of an agent's special desire is not relevant to showing there is a moral difference.

13. These tests are modeled on ones suggested for killing and letting die (in my *Morality, Mortality*, vol. 2, chap. 4) and for testing the relative stringency of rights (in chapter 8, this volume). It might also be suggested that we could run a Choice Test, i.e., if we could only save someone near or someone far, but not both, which should we choose? However, I think that this test may have its limits, because we are often free to choose to do what we have no duty to do rather than do our duty (as discussed in chapter 1). I will explain this point in chapter 12.

14. They also introduce a debatable notion of what it is to be far. For example, if it takes a short time to get to a place, that place is not far. But that may not be true. For more on this issue, see below.

15. I owe this point to Matthew Coleman Niece.

16. There is even a further complexity, for is it possible that relative nearness matters at some absolute distances and not at others?

17. I say "especially in (a)," because if relative distance mattered only within absolute nearness, it would still be true that absolute, not relative, nearness stands in contrast to being far.

18. There is, of course, a way different from the Near/Far Case of combining near and far in the same case. Rather than have one victim with a near agent and a far agent, we could have one victim far from, and one victim near to, one agent. We then ask, for example, whom he has a duty to help if he cannot help both. This is a form of the Choice Test. The problem with this test, however, is that we are not always obligated to do our duty before doing a nonduty or a weaker duty (as discussed in chapter 1). Hence, if we did not have a duty to help the-near-victim-rather-than-the far-one, this would not show that there was no duty to the near victim that was stronger than any duty to the far one. I shall discuss this issue further in the following chapter.

19. As suggested in David Schmidtz's "Islands in a Sea of Obligation: The Nature and Limits of the Duty of Rescue," *Law and Philosophy* 19 (2000): 683–705.

20. I owe this point to Julia Driver and Jerrold Katz. It overlaps somewhat with the issue in section IIB.

21. I owe this case to Tyler Burge.

22. We shall re-examine the hypothesis below.

23. Note that if I am *very* large, my violin could be near to me but not near to the victim to whom I am near. It is its nearness to me that seems important, when I am near the victim. Notice that nearness seems relevant here both because the agent is near the victim and because the means are near the agent.

24. Suppose that our nearness to a victim implies, as I have said, that we at least should sometimes activate some distant means to help the victim. Aware of this source of obligation to use some means, it might still be permissible to see to it that these far means *cannot* be activated by remote control. Is it possible that only those distant means which the agent can make efficacious *while still retaining his initial nearness* to the victim are the ones he is obligated to use? But we often have to leave a near victim, making ourselves far, in order to get means that help him. What if the movement away in order to get means puts us near another victim? Are we then obligated to help the new victim rather than the original one assuming that his need is equal and we cannot aid both? I think not, since we already have an obligation to help the first one.

25. I discussed it in *Morality, Mortality*, vol. 2.

26. This is my response to Alexander Friedman's suggestion that if it were permissible to leave the violin at home so as not to have it available for destruction, it cannot be true that I have a duty to destroy it if it is with me.

27. In Peter Unger, *Living High and Letting Die* (New York: Oxford University Press, 1996), p. 28.

28. The distinction between a personal encounter and nearness was emphasized to me by Franklin Bruno and Richard Miller.

29. In Unger, *Living High and Letting Die.*

30. One way in which salience works is to help me really understand someone's need. But when I understand what her need is really like, I now also understand what every other person who is not as salient, but who is as needy, is going through. So, insofar as salience is revealing of need, one would expect that salience would lead me to help everyone—salient or not—who is so needy. It would not bias me in favor of helping just the person who is, in fact, salient.

31. It might be thought that I may eliminate my salient knowledge of the far need because it came to me via an *unusual* sense; long-distance vision is unusual for our species. By contrast, my knowledge of the person near me comes via my ordinary senses, and perhaps this is why I may not eliminate it if this interferes with my aiding. But in the Door Case, I get the knowledge of the near person via an unusual machine. Similarly, we can imagine that I could not know of the person outside my door if I did not have a detecting machine. I do not believe that the fact that I am unusual in this respect means that I have a right to ignore his plight once I find out about it nor to move so that I am far with the aim of avoiding or eliminating an obligation.

32. Similarly, Peter Singer believes (and should believe, given his other views) not only that I have an obligation to give away money once I have it, but that I must go and earn money in order to have it to give away. (Here "having the money" functions like "near," and if near versus far does not matter, then "having money" does not matter relative to "could have money.")

33. Of course, if part of S_0 is what should not be forgotten due to properties that give rise to a duty, we cannot equalize for S_0. If distance were not driving our intuitions, but personal encounter were a morally relevant factor, this would also be a significant conclusion. Suppose that long-distance vision *made for* a personal encounter (though it would not involve recognition unless I not only saw the victim but he also saw me). Suppose also that it would be permissible to turn off my long-distance vision and so stop a personal encounter with a distant person (in the absence of recognition, at least), though this interfered with aid, but it would not be permissible to do this with a near person in an otherwise comparable case. This would be evidence that a personal encounter did not give rise to an obligation, but nearness did.

34. The objection is based on one raised by Wlodek Rabinowicz.

35. This objection was raised by Thomas Nagel. It is also raised by Richard Hare in arguing against using empirically unlikely hypothetical cases as counterexamples to utilitarianism.

36. Unger, *Living High and Letting Die,* pp. 24–36.

37. The first step in Unger's strategy, I believe, is a sounder way than the second of seeing whether a factor had an effect in the original Sedan Case. This is because if a factor is exported into the Envelope Case, as in the second step, it may have no effect in its new context, but this will not show that it had no effect on its original context. (This is due to the Principle of Contextual Interaction.) For discussion of these points, see my *Morality, Mortality,* vol. 2, and chapter 1 in this volume.

38. Of course, it is possible that degrees of nonnearness matter (which is a hypothesis we put aside above).

39. I do not deny that we need an explanation of why up-front costs would matter more than downstream costs. On the same issue, see chapter 16. It seems that "up-front" involves costs that are a means to saving by contrast to side effects of saving and then, it might be thought, things claimed in chapter 5 would be relevant. But throughout chapter 5, we considered evil* to include involvement of the person in a way that will presently lead to his harm, and this is true of someone who helps initially at low cost in the Sedan Cases. The principles we were investigating in chapter 5, however, dealt with harm done to others, not with what agents

must do to themselves. It remains open, therefore, that not distinguishing involvement that is a means and harm that is not a means is correct in one context but incorrect in another.

40. I owe this point to Marina Oshana.

41. Thomas Scanlon, Violetta Igneski, and others distinguish rescue, helpfulness, and beneficence. See chapter 16 for discussion of Scanlon's views and chapter 12, "The New Problem of Distance in Morality," for discussion of Igneski's views.

42. See John Rawls, *A Theory of Justice* (Cambridge, MA: Harvard University Press, 1971).

43. Liam Murphy, "Institutions and the Demands of Justice," *Philosophy & Public Affairs* 27 (1998): 251–91.

44. Unger, *Living High and Letting Die*, pp. 60–61.

45. Exceptions can arise if doing the supererogatory act has the further effect of *raising* the costs of performing one's duty. For example, suppose that Albert Schweitzer has been serving the poor his whole life supererogatorily, and this results in his only having a few days left in his life to play the organ. The cost of giving up his *last chance* to play the organ might relieve him of certain duties to others.

46. Unger, *Living High and Letting Die*, p. 41.

12

THE NEW PROBLEM OF DISTANCE
IN MORALITY

I. INTRODUCTION

Suppose that our intuitions were correct in suggesting that proximity can alter our obligation to aid.[1] Is this *translatable into* (i.e., is it just another way of understanding) or does it imply (what I have called) the Standard Claim, that we have a stronger duty to aid strangers who are physically near us than to aid strangers who are far from us given their equal need? All discussants of the problem of distance in morality (PDM) of whom I know think that the Standard Claim follows. Indeed (as we said in chapter 11), the Standard View of the PDM holds that the PDM just is the problem of whether we have a stronger duty to aid strangers who are physically near to us just because they are physically near than we have to aid strangers who are not physically near (that is, who are far), all other things being equal. If I do have a stronger duty to help a near person than a far one, does this imply that it would be wrong of me to help the far person rather than the near one? (Call this the Standard Implication.) I shall argue that the Standard Claim is false and that it is not a translation nor an implication of the view that proximity can matter morally. I shall also argue that the Standard View misconceives the PDM and that the Standard Implication is at least questionable. In the course of making these arguments, I shall also consider how we might *justify* intuitions that proximity matters morally.

II. WHAT IS NEAR TO WHAT?

I shall rebut the Standard Claim by considering certain selected cases. First, how-ever, it will be useful to show how the strategy I shall use to defeat the Standard Claim relates to my discussion of how to measure distance (in the previous chapter, section III). There, I considered how we measure the intuitively relevant distance between agent and victim. We saw that in the standard near cases, victim and agent are near, as measured from where their centers are located. Yet, we get intuitions that are like those for the standard near cases when only the agent's and the victim's extended parts are near. But in trying to answer the question of how we measure distance between strangers, we had to broach the problem of distance *between things other than the agent and the victim*, namely, the distance between the agent and the agent's means (of aid), and between the victim and the agent's means. This is because the part of the agent that is near may not be efficacious, and so the agent's means may not be where part of the agent is. In the standard cases, not only the victim but also the means are near the agent. Furthermore, the means also belong to the agent. (For example, he has his money with him or can use his body, and they are efficacious.) But in one nonstandard case we examined, the potential means (a Stradivarius) was distant from the agent (and also from the victim).

But this is just the tip of the iceberg. The separability of the agent and his means leads us to think about the separability of other factors that are usually present together in the standard cases. There are four separable factors on which I shall focus: agent, victim, threat, and means. Under means, I shall consider (for the most part) two categories: agent's means and victim's means. Cases I consider that involve one category of means will not (unless specifically noted) involve the other category of means. Distance (in the sense of near or far) can vary between each factor and the other three. The general point of all of the selected cases that I shall present in this section is that the intuition that in a particular case nearness matters morally does not, contrary to what is commonly thought, conflict with the intuition in the very same case that we have a strong obligation to help distant strangers.[2]

In the first case, suppose that I alone am *near to a threat* that will shortly travel and kill someone who is far from me (and I know this). (Call this the Agent Near Threat Case.) Do I have a duty to help that far-away person by defusing the threat? My sense is that, intuitively, my duty to stop the threat to him is strong, just as I have a strong duty to help in a case where I alone am near someone who needs help. Furthermore, my obligation is stronger than if the threat to a far person were itself far from me.[3] So, without leaving the level of intuitive responses, we see that when the threat is near to the agent but the stranger is far, the agent still has a strong duty to help. Hence, if nearness is intuitively important, this very fact may imply that we have strong obligations to aid distant strangers. I consider this result to be very important. It shows that the PDM should be understood differently from the Standard View. The standard description of the PDM—that the distance between ourselves and needy strangers matters morally—is too narrow, since it is also the distance between ourselves and threats that seems to matter. Furthermore, contrary to the Standard Claim, our intuitions do not tell us that we always have weaker obligations to aid strangers who are far than those who are near, holding need constant, and they also tell us that this is consistent with proximity making a moral difference. This is because it may be our *nearness to a threat* to distant people that is morally relevant. Hence, the Standard View and the Standard Claim are wrong. Neither is a translation of the view that distance can be morally relevant, and the Standard Claim is not an implication of it.

Another reason the result in the Agent Near Threat Case is important is that it reduces the plausibility of the claim that the reason I am strongly obligated to help when I am near is that a member of my community or fellow citizen is at risk. For a threat that is near to me is not a fellow citizen or community member. (We have also, of course, eliminated these variables when dealing with near people by imagining cases where agents are in foreign countries.) Those who think that proximity is of no significance will also be committed to our having as strong an obligation (e.g., one that is not defeated by significant costs) to stop a threat to far people that is far from us (call this a far threat) as we have to stop a threat to far people that is near us (call this a near threat).

Note also that when the victim is near to the agent but the threat to him is still far from both him and the agent (call this the To-Be-Victim Case), the agent's intuitively felt obligation can still be as strong as in the case where the threat is near both to the victim and the agent, and the victim and the agent are near one another. This is so, at least when the threat, which is now far, will eventually affect the victim while he is still near to the agent. (What if a stranger near the agent needs help now to intercept a threat that is still far and that would intersect with the stranger once he is away from the agent? I doubt that the strength of obligation is less here.) So, our obligations, intuitively, are not limited to people we are near *who are already facing a threat.* (I will, though, still use the term *victim* to describe people who will face a threat later if not helped now.)

We can conclude that, intuitively, we think that we have greater obligations to take care of *what is in the area near us*, whether this is a threat that will cause harm at a distance, or a person who is or will be a victim. The fact that an agent can be obligated to aid because she is near a threat is an important consideration in conceptualizing the issue of distance as involving the agent's special relation to the area near her. An alternative would be to say that a victim acquires certain rights over the things near *him*, including persons. But a threat cannot acquire rights over agents near it. This suggests that we should focus on the agent's relation to the area near her rather than the victim's claims on what is in the area near him.[4]

With what means are we obligated to help? If the agent herself is near the victim or the threat, intuitively, while there may be some far means that she can be obligated to use, we have noted (in chapter 11) that she need not transport her distant valuable Stradivarius. However, she may have to forfeit her valuables that are near her. (Call this latter the Valuable Means Near Agent Case.)

Now, consider a third case in which the agent is far both from the victim and from the threat to the victim (and the threat is either close to or far from the victim), but the agent's means are near to the victim. (Call this the Means Near

Victim Case.) I suggest that, intuitively, we think that the agent has a strong obligation to let his means be used (or to activate them if he can by remote control) because something efficacious that he owns is near to the stranger, even if he himself is not.[5] By contrast, intuitively, the agent is not obligated to let his (distant) means be used simply because any nonefficacious item of his (e.g., his T.V.) is near the stranger.[6] Furthermore, if the agent is far from both the stranger, the threat, and the agent's means, the agent is only obligated to allow his means near the stranger to be used.

Does the significance of the Means Near Victim Case open a truly vast potential obligation? Consider that one's money now seems to be locatable almost anywhere as a result of cash machines.[7] Suppose that there is a cash machine in a distant part of India, and with it I could access my money if I were there. If my money is there whenever I need it (or whenever anyone who has my code needs it), why is it not simply *there*? I believe that there is still a difference that may have moral significance between (1) things of mine being transmitted to distant India rapidly, or things that are not mine *becoming* mine rapidly (in virtue of exchanges in bank balances), and (2) what is mine being there, in distant India, already. Certainly, my money cannot now actually be wherever there is a cash machine that would give me money if I were there, for that would mean my assets were enormous, when actually they are very small. Some may think, "My money is relevantly present in any cash machine, if all that it takes is an electronic message for some of the cash in this machine to be mine."[8] However, the fact that a message is necessary in order for the cash "to be" mine is important, I think. Consider an analogy involving a boat. There is a boat near people in need of it. Using it to help them will cause very expensive damage to the boat. Just by transmitting an electronic message, I (or anyone with the code) can make the boat be mine in virtue of a "boat-credit" I have. This does not show, I believe, that the boat is already mine. Suppose that if it were mine, I should let it be used to help the people and if it is not mine, it is not usable at all. This does not imply, I think, that I must make it mine so that it can be used. The same can be said for money.[9]

Now, suppose that the agent is far from both the victim and the threat (which is far from the victim), but the agent's means are close to the *threat* to the victim, though far from the victim. (Call this the Means Near Threat Case.) Again, I suggest that, intuitively, we think that the agent has a strong obligation to let these means be used to defuse the threat because something efficacious she owns is near to a threat that will eventually harm the victim. If the agent is far from the victim and the threat, and her means are also far from the victim and the threat, intuitively, the agent would not be strongly obligated to aid, barring some other relevant consideration.

The Means Near Victim and Means Near Threat cases suggest that means— which are by definition *efficacious* for helping—that belong to the agent function like the presence of his extended part in obligating him to provide aid. But recall that in chapter 11 we said that the agent's presence *need not be* efficacious in order for him to be obligated, for example, to use at least some of his distant things to help. By contrast, intuitively, what he owns must be efficacious in order for him, at a distance, to be obligated to help by triggering the means by remote control. It bears reemphasizing that if something I own is near a victim or a threat but it is not an efficacious device, intuitively, I am not obligated to trigger something else that I own that would be efficacious but is at a distance from both the victim and the threat. (I shall return to this point below.)

Once again, intuitions support the claim that I can be obligated to help those who are not near me, even while also confirming that, at an intuitive level, nearness seems to matter morally. This is contrary to the Standard View of the PDM and the Standard Claim (according to which the significance of nearness is taken to make the obligation to distant victims weaker than the obligation to near ones when needs are equal). In our most recent cases, it is distance between the agent's efficacious device and either the threat or the victim that is morally relevant. These cases also show that describing the PDM so that it only involves reference to the distance between *ourselves* and victims or threats is misleading, since it may also pertain to the distance between our *means* and victims or threats.

It is now possible to see an important relation between the case in which my means are close to the victim (or to the threat to the victim) but I am distant and the cases in which an agent who is near a victim (or near a threat to a victim) makes use of means that belong to neither him nor the victim, but to someone else who is distant (Distant Owner Case).[10] For example, suppose that a rich foreigner is in Chicago, but his boat is at Cape Cod, where a stranger is drowning. I am at Cape Cod, observing the victim, and the boat is near to me and him. One possible justification for my taking the boat to help the victim is that if the owner of the boat were near, he would have a duty to use his boat (if this were not physically dangerous for him) to help the victim. He is not near, but his means are, and so, according to what I argued above, he is intuitively thought to be obligated to let his means be used. In taking his boat, I help him to fulfill the duty he has even while he is in Chicago, in virtue of his means being near the drowning stranger, to let those means be used. (It is possible, however, that someone might permissibly do something that imposes a greater loss on another person than he would have to impose on himself. We saw this in considering whether a person toward whom a trolley is permissibly redirected might permissibly send it back.)

Peter Unger discusses a case like the Distant Owner Case, which he calls the Yacht Case. In his Yacht Case, an agent takes a boat that belongs to another person to help someone near him. The rescue will result in a million dollars' worth of damage to the boat for which he cannot compensate. Unger compares this with the Account Case in which a delivery boy to the office of a rich person can do a computer transfer of funds from the rich person's account to UNICEF's. Unger claims that our intuitions are approving of providing assistance in the Yacht Case and disapproving in the Account Case. He further claims that there is no morally significant difference between the cases.

One difference between these cases, is that one involves an accident and the other may implicate basic justice issues. A further difference, which might be suggested on the basis of my analysis, is that the owner's yacht in the Yacht Case is near the victim, whether or not the owner of it is, but in the Account Case, *both the owner and his means* are far from the needy victims or the threat to them, at least so long as his money is not located near to the people whom UNICEF helps. In the Yacht Case, when I take the yacht to help someone, I could, in part be acting on someone else's duty, based on the nearness of his property. In the Account Case, I cannot say that I am enforcing an owner's obligation to the victim, if nearness is a ground for obligation. It is also true in the Account Case, but not in the Yacht Case, that the *agent* (in the Yacht Case, this is the person near the drowning victim) is not near the stranger. (I shall return to this issue below.)

If the nearness of the yacht but not the account were explanatory of different intuitions, what about the following Revised Account Case? On his way to make his delivery, the delivery boy sees someone in danger nearby. (As in the Yacht Case, the danger was caused by an accident rather than an omission of basic justice.) Only if he transfers funds out of the rich person's account will he activate a machine that will help the endangered person. Here we have made the account and the agent near the victim. Further, suppose that the money that would be transferred in the Revised Account Case comes from the personal yacht-repair account of the owner; that is, it is money that was set aside for a luxury rather than for a business item. Also, the money must go into the machine only for a short period of time in order to save the stranger; however, it is foreseen that as a side effect some of the money (a million dollars) will get eaten up in transaction costs.[11] I suggest that these changes, which equalize the cases, in combination with nearness, make the delivery boy's transfer intuitively as acceptable as the yacht agent's transfer.

Of course, the agent who is near the victim, intuitively, has an obligation to do something to aid because *she* is near. If the boat were unowned property, she would, intuitively, have the same obligation to use it. But if the boat is owned, I suggest, she is also acting in the light of whatever obligation the owner has to let his boat be used. Suppose that the owner had no obligation, perhaps because his boat remaining where it is located is necessary to the owner's survival. Then, even if two people would drown without it, it would be wrong for the near agent to take the boat. By contrast, suppose that the boat were unowned, but the rich foreigner's life also depended on its remaining where it is. If two other people would die if the near agent did not use it, I think that she may use it.

What if the agent is far away but knows of the victim on Cape Cod? Is he strongly obligated to move (by remote control) the means at Cape Cod that is owned by the foreigner who is in Chicago? If it is easy to activate the means—just flip a switch with no further costs—I believe he could be strongly obligated. The claim is just that the obligation to help is not as strong as if the agent were near, as measured, for example, by up-front costs to the agent that he must sustain.

Now, suppose that the boat of the foreigner in Chicago is close to him but *at a distance* from the victim (it is on Lake Michigan). I am near the victim (or threat) on Cape Cod. Is it the case that I have a strong obligation to move the Lake Michigan boat to help the victim? Is it even thought to be permissible for me to do so? These are, of course, two different questions. The first question also suggests two separate issues: What do we think my obligation is, and what do we think the obligation is of the owner of the boat? When the owner is distant from the victim or the threat,[12] and his means are as well, intuitively, he has no strong obligation to aid. (This can imply that he need not suffer significant up-front costs in order to aid or even significant downstream costs.) So, in this case, I may not be able to justify bringing his distant means to use at Cape Cod by saying that I am partially the agent of his obligation. Could my obligation to do something in virtue of my nearness give rise to an obligation on my part to use the means that another is thought to have no obligation to use and that belong to him? This is what Unger seems to be considering when he imagines the following case: I am near a drowning stranger, and I must forge a check on a billionaire's account in order to buy a yacht to save the stranger. The yacht will be destroyed in the course of the rescue and no compensation can be provided. I doubt it. More likely, I am thought to have a strong excuse rather than a justification for taking the billionaire's means.

But notice that this is still different from the case in which I am *not* near a victim or a threat, and I am tempted to use means that are costly (up-front or downstream) that are not near the victim or threat and whose owner is not near the victim or threat. (Arguably, this is what is true in Unger's Account Case.)[13] If the means that are distant from me are *unowned*, and I have a strong obligation to do something arising from my nearness to the victim, I do, intuitively, have a strong obligation to employ these distant means by remote control. If they are owned by me, the answer seems to vary depending on the cost (e.g., I need not move my distant Stradivarius for its destruction in order to aid someone).

Classifying all of these Distant Owner cases as one type of case, let us consider another type of case. It is a version of the Near Alone Case in which I see a life-saving machine that belongs to a victim (who is far) floating in the pond near me. Unless I throw my $500 jacket in the pond (thereby ruining it), the victim's machine will sink in the pond, and the stranger will die. The point here is to construct a case in which *the means belong to the victim, the agent knows this, and these means are near the agent when the victim and threat are far from him.* (Call this the Near to Victim's Means Case.) In this case, intuitively, I think that the agent has a strong obligation to save the machine that will help the distant victim. If the victim's machine were distant from the agent (and the victim and threat were also distant), there would not, intuitively, be such a strong obligation.[14] Once again, an intuitive judgment tells us that the strong obligation to help a distant victim is consistent with nearness having moral significance and, contrary to the Standard View of the PDM, it is our nearness to the victim's means, not to the victim, that is relevant.[15]

One hypothesis for why being near a victim's means is significant is that what is owned by a stranger stands in for him, and we react as though he were near. This is on the model of the agent's means being close to the victim (discussed above).[16] But this is not quite right, and indeed it is not an accurate extension of the model. For it is not enough that *just anything* belonging to the victim be near the agent; for example, if his T.V. set is floating in the pond, this does not obligate the agent to give money to help the distant victim. It is only if the victim's efficacious means that can help him are near that the agent has a stronger obligation to rescue these means. By contrast, a nonefficacious victim (i.e., someone who can not help himself) being near an agent does trigger the obligation to aid. And, as noted above, in the case of an agent's means being near a victim from whom the agent is distant, the *efficaciousness of the agent's item, not mere ownership of it* (as with a TV), is necessary for obligation.

Does this mean that what triggers an obligation to use some (if not all) distant means when one *person* is near another, though neither person is efficacious, is fundamentally different from what triggers an obligation when something that belongs to one person is near another? But, it may be said, an agent even when he is not able to help directly can be partially efficacious by triggering his efficacious distant device. In this sense, even if he is not directly efficacious, he can *relate usefully* to a victim. A device, it may be said, must be able to do this to be analogous to the presence of an agent. Efficacious means are clearly like this, and the agent's T.V. is not.[17] However, (in chapter II, section III) we considered a case in which the agent can do nothing, but his employee sees him near the victim. This too, it was said, should trigger the employee to help the agent fulfill duties he cannot carry out personally. By comparison, a completely inefficacious device of the agent's near the victim triggers no similar duties.

What about the victim's nonefficacious property that is close to the agent when the stranger is distant? It is more puzzling that for a duty to arise, what belongs to the victim has to be efficacious or be able to relate usefully to his need than that what belongs to an agent must be so. For the victim himself *is not efficacious, nor need he relate usefully to his own need* in order for someone to have a duty in virtue of being near him. However, the victim, unlike his device, can be benefited. The characteristic shared by cases in which the agent's means are near the victim or the victim's means are near the agent seems to be that *only what is pertinent to satisfying the need of the victim* (whether it is a person who can be benefited or a machine that can help) is relevant to establishing an obligation. The victim is certainly pertinent to satisfying his need, even if he is not efficacious, and so is his efficacious means, unlike just anything he owns—such as a T.V.

Let us move on to yet another type of case. An agent's efficacious machine, which is distant from the agent, the threat, and the victim, *is near the victim's means*, which is distant from the agent, the threat, and the victim. (Call this the Means Near to Means Case, because it is a case in which the means of both the agent and the victim are present.) My means can rescue the victim's means that can then help him. My sense, in this case, is that, intuitively, I have a stronger obligation to aid in virtue of some form of nearness than if there were no nearness at all. Once again, I intuitively seem to have a duty to help someone who is far from me, and yet this is because nearness is intuitively a matter of moral significance. This time, it is nearness of my means and the victim's means that is morally relevant.

Notice that what I have concluded implies that the intuitions about the sources of an agent's obligation may be overdetermined. For example, an agent's sense that he is obligated may arise because he is near the victim, while the same agent may also believe that he is obligated because his means are near to what will threaten the victim. An interesting question (that I shall not here answer) is: Does overdetermination increase the strength of the obligation? For example, is the duty to help someone who is near me to avoid a threat to which I am near when my nonvaluable means are near to both of us greater than the duty to help someone who is near me to avoid a threat that is distant from me when my nonvaluable means are distant from me, the victim, and the threat?

My *tentative* conclusion in this section is that the *New* PDM should be understood as whether we can justify our intuition that we have a greater responsibility to take care of what is going on in the area near us or near our (efficacious) means, whether this involves needy strangers, threats, or means belonging to strangers. The complete PDM is not just about whether we have greater responsibility toward strangers who are near us.[18]

III. PRIORITY AMONG FACTORS

Given that all of these factors are relevant to the New PDM, is there still some greater weight given intuitively to some of these factors relative to others? For example, if different factors were considered as separate cases and the same degree of effort were required, what would a Choice Test indicate? If we have "threat near agent" (T_N), "victim near agent" (V_N), "victim's means near to agent but far from victim" (VM_N), "agent's means near to victim but far from agent" (AM_N), there are six possible combinations of these factors to consider in determining the weight of each factor relative to the others. (I have not included all factors for consideration, such as victim's means near agent's means.) Let us consider them on the supposition that I am a noncitizen of France visiting France and all of the strangers are somewhere in France. Further equalize for the near and far victims being detected but unseen and unseeing of the agent.

1. *T_N versus V_N.* In one near pond, there is a fast-moving threat to a faraway victim and, in another near pond, there is a different victim. To which pond should the agent go if one life is at stake in either choice and times of death would be the same?[19] Perhaps to the pond with the victim. If so, $V_N > T_N$. But what if T_N will kill two distant strangers? Then, T_N may dominate V_N. If so, the dominance of $V_N > T_N$ is not very great.

2. *T_N versus VM_N.* In one near pond, there is a threat to one far victim, and in the other near pond is a different far victim's means. Intuitively, there may be some sense that one should go to the pond with the threat. This may be because one wants to avoid being associated with the *cause* of death more than to be associated with a rescue from death. (This may be piggybacking on the loss/no-gain distinction.)[20]

3. *T_N versus AM_N.* In a near pond, there is a threat to one distant victim and, at a distance, the agent's means are near another stranger. Is there a sense that the agent should deal with the threat rather than trigger the means? If so, this may be because it is the *agent* rather than his means that is near. On the other hand, the agent's means are near the victim *himself* rather than the threat. So, the duty to trigger one's means may be stronger.

4. V_N *versus* VM_N. One victim is near an agent and also a distant victim's means are near the agent. Intuitively, there is a sense that one should go to the near victim in need, but this may be overridden if a greater number of distant victims would be helped by the means.

5. V_N *versus* AM_N. One victim is near an agent, and the agent's means are near one distant victim. V_N intuitively takes precedence over activating the distant means, but if a greater number of distant victims could be helped by AM_N, this may override the weight of V_N.

6. AM_N *versus* VM_N. One distant victim's means are in a near pond, but the agent's means are near a different distant victim. The duty to help each victim seems to be equal in strength.

My tentative conclusion from the previous section was that, intuitively, there is a greater felt responsibility for a threat, victim, or victim's means when they are in the area near an agent or an agent's means than when they are far from these. Now we can add to this that, intuitively, the responsibility to aid the near victim is stronger than the duty to stop near threats, and both obligations are stronger than the duty to rescue a victim's near means or activate an agent's distant means near a victim, other things being equal. Furthermore, nearness to an agent has greater significance than nearness to an agent's means. In some sense, then, $V_N > T_N > VM_N$, and $A_N > AM_N$, when other things are equal.

Does this result undermine the rejection of the Standard Claim, because that claim implies that the duty to aid victims who are near is stronger than the duty to aid victims who are far even when threats to them are near? Not necessarily, because the Standard Claim also applies to these situations when we do not have to choose whether to deal with the near victim or a near threat (to a far victim). Priority in conflicts is consistent with as much being required of us to deal with a near person as a near threat to a far person in separate situations. Further, even if the Standard Claim were strictly correct, we could argue that, through failure to consider all of the factors pointed to by the New PDM, we risk underestimating how much we might have to do in order to help a far victim *in virtue of the importance of proximity*, even if this is less than what needs to be done in order to help a near victim. Hence, the Standard Claim would at least be seriously misleading.

IV. TEMPORALLY VARIOUS CASES

Our tentative formulation of the New PDM was based on consideration of near cases in which aid is to be rendered at the time the agent or his means are near the victim, the victim's means, or the threat. But what if, for example, when the agent is near to the victim (or to-be-victim) he does not know of her plight? Consider the following case, which I call a temporally various case:

Near-then-Far: I am passing near a child drowning in a pond, a child whom I am able to help. But, through no fault of mine, all of the following are true: I do not know that I am near the person, I do not know that he is in danger, and I do not know that I can help. After I am far away, I learn that I was near him when he was in danger, and I could have helped. I can still save him from that danger, in the way I could have when near, by putting $500 in a device that will activate a machine to scoop him out.

I believe that, intuitively, the obligation to help is stronger than it would be if I had never been near. Hence, I can be obligated when I am far because I once was near the person when he was in danger and I was capable of helping him by means I should have used. The strong obligations I have to take care of the problems that are going on in an area near me are not limited to problems in the area near me at t_n, the time when I have the obligation.

We can imagine variations on this case. What if, when I was near (a) the person was not in danger but only became endangered once I was far; (b) the person was a to-be-victim, the threat to whom existed at the time and I could have stopped it; (c) I would have been unable to help when I was near, but am now able to do so; (d) I knew that the person was in danger but not that I was near; (e) I knew that I was near the person, but not that he was in danger; or (f) I knew that the person was in danger and near, but not that I could help. Intuitively, I think that in (a) our obligation is *not* stronger than in ordinary far cases. So, the fact that I was near someone does not mean that I have a stronger obligation to help, if it is only when I am far that he is in danger. If we had an obligation when (c) is true, this would show that obligations in temporally various cases do not depend on a failure to have done what one could have done when near. If there is no obligation in (c), then this suggests that obligations in temporally various cases depend on failures. I shall leave this case undecided.

Now we should consider different temporally various cases. In these temporally various cases, I was near a *threat* to a distant person or near a far victim's means when it could have been useful for rescue, but I did not know it. I am now far from the threat and the means (as well as the victim), but am able to stop the threat or get the victim's means (that are still needed for the same purpose) to the victim. My sense is that, in these cases, it is also true that now that I am far, I have a greater obligation to help because I once was near.

What if, in these temporally various cases, it is not I but my efficacious means that were near to the victim or the victim's means? My means were then not known to be near or useful. Now they are far but can still be useful. My sense is that, intuitively, the obligation to aid is greater than in other far cases. A possible difference between *my* having been close and *my means* having been close is that it is only the means that were close and unused that one may now be obligated to use when far. But if *I* was near in the past, it is not only what I could have used at the time to help that I may be required to use now that I am far.[21]

In another form of temporally various case, a problem is now going on in an area from which I and my means are now, and have always been, far, but the problem will still be present when I or my means are near in the future. It is only now, however, that I or my means can deal effectively with the victim, the threat, or the victim's means. Intuitively, I do not think that I am more obligated to deal with a problem that will be near (to some relevant variable) but is far than with ordinary far problems, though I am sometimes more obligated to deal with what has been near but is far. A past tie based on nearness seems to linger once it exists, but a future tie does not obligate before it exists.[22]

So, we can further revise our tentative conclusion: The New PDM should be understood as the problem of whether we can justify our intuition that we have a greater responsibility to take care of victims, threats, or means belonging to the victim that are or were in the areas near us or our (efficacious) means. The fact that if distance mattered, it could matter in all of these ways implies that those who reject the moral importance of distance will be committed to rejecting much more than just the claim that our duty to aid strangers could depend on the distance between them and us (unless the rejecters can explain why distance could matter in all types of cases except the latter).

V. WHY DISTANCE COULD MATTER

I have dealt with whether and how—"let me count the ways"—we *intuitively* think that distance matters. Now, we should consider whether we can justify these intuitions, for I accept that intuitive support is not enough to justify a principle of morality that refers to distance in deriving obligations. We cannot, I think, truly justify the moral relevance of distance in some contexts without a theory explaining why this factor should have relevance. Such a justification could involve deriving the importance of distance from some notions that clearly have moral significance. This helps to justify the intuitions and any moral principle relying on them. In the absence of a clear justification linking distance with notions having clear moral significance, intuitive judgments that support the moral relevance of distance in some cases might be subject to debunking explanations. Debunking explanations are meant to explain away rather than justify our intuitive judgments. If we could not only provide a positive theory of why distance matters sometimes, but also show that debunking explanations are incorrect, we would further support the principle that distance can be morally relevant in some cases. Let us consider some of the debunking explanations first.

It may be suggested that proximity matters as a heuristic device that correlates with morally significant factors, though it itself is not morally significant.[23] One of these factors might be the need to set limits to our duty to aid strangers to avoid being overburdened; being responsible in accord with proximity is a way to set these limits. Another factor might be the need to help those with whom we potentially have cooperative relations, and given our nature, these have typically been near rather than distant people. But I doubt that these factors explain the apparent moral significance of distance. And, indeed, the revised description of the nature of the intuitive bias in favor of the near that I have suggested can be used to show that these hypotheses are not adequate.

First, being responsible only for those who are near, or, as I have alternatively described our intuitions, being responsible for what goes on in the area near us or our (efficacious) means will not by itself necessarily limit the burdensomeness of our obligations, for we may be near many needy people. (Indeed, if Asian Indians were responsible for helping those far away in East Hampton, New York, rather than those who are near, they would have less burdensome obligations because the needy population of East Hampton is far less than that of India.) Furthermore, if one had long-distance reach, one's responsibility could be very great if responsibility were a function of proximity. But this would be, admittedly, a different world from the present one, and the limits theory we are considering might say that if we had such long-distance reach, proximity would *not* be our method for drawing limits. Nevertheless, I doubt that we can just legislate proximity in and out of relevance in this way. Indeed, I believe that the considerations favoring limits on duties to aid are not reflected in the grounds for favoring responsibility in accord with distance. Rather, these limits would be needed to *override* the proximity-based reasons that favor responsibility in order to limit that responsibility. (So, those who are near many needy people may limit their responsibilities by referring to upper limits on costs they must incur even to those who are nearby.)

In addition, there could be other *geographic* delimitations on aid, if the purpose of geographic zones were to limit the requirement to aid. New Yorkers could (now that it is physically possible) be responsible for helping only those in Santiago, Chile. If setting limits on aid were all that justified giving us greater obligations for what goes on in the area near us, there would be no more reason to choose that form of limitation than any other (efficacious) geographic way of limiting responsibility. But it seems more than an arbitrary choice whether we do it one way or another.

Notice also that if alternative geographic delimitations are to function the way delimitation by near versus far functions, they must share the other characteristics of the delimitation by near versus far. It must be true, for example, that if New Yorkers are responsible for dealing with *threats* arising in Santiago that will hurt people in Paris, then they will also be responsible for rescuing Parisian's means of rescuing the Parisians when those means are in Santiago. When we discover that nearness affects our relation not only to people but also to threats and to victim's means, it may be harder to suggest that some other geographic delimitation is substitutable for proximity.

What of the second hypothesis, that distance tracks potential cooperative relations?[24] If I visit Switzerland, I have no reason to believe that there will be further relations between me and the Swiss victim, and yet I am, intuitively, more strongly obligated to help him if he is near than if he is at a distance, subject to a threat distant from me, and distant from my means while I and my means are distant from his means. Furthermore, if he is distant from me, but I am near to his means or to the threat to him, or, alternatively, he, his means, or the threat is near my means, then I do have the stronger duty to aid. Yet, in these cases, there has neither been nor is there potential for future cooperative relations. Finally, the near/far distinction may apply to creatures with whom we could not have cooperative relations. For example, if I come to know about (without interacting with) a dog that is suffering near me, my obligation to aid is intuitively greater than my obligation if I am the only one who can help a distant dog.[25]

Consider a third hypothesis for why distance seems to matter morally. It might be said that, traditionally, people to whom we are strongly connected and to whom we, therefore, have greater responsibilities tend to live physically close to us. We then mistakenly invert these factors of connectedness (or responsibility) and nearness and think that when people are physically close to us, we have greater responsibilities to them. One problem with this debunking theory is that it implies that we do not really have a duty to aid those with whom we are unconnected (that is, strangers), even if they are near.

Further, can this debunking theory explain the cases in which we intuitively think that we have a duty to deal with a *threat* that is near us and will affect a distant person, but not to deal with a threat that is far from us and will affect a distant person? Is there an independent account of threats with which we must deal, such that, so described, these threats also tend to be close? Do we then mistakenly invert these factors, saying that the close threats are the ones with which we must deal? Perhaps, it may be said, people are typically threatened by things that are close to, rather than far from, them. Since we must take care of threats to people to whom we are connected, and since these tend to be people who are near, the threats we come to be responsible for taking care of are typically close threats. In other words, the debunking theory would say that we invert "threats to people with whom we are connected" with "near threats."

An implication of this debunking theory is that if threats to people with whom we are connected had been distant (or if people to whom we were connected had been distant), we would have mistakenly thought that we were more responsible for distant threats (or people) *because they were distant* than for close threats (or people). If we doubt that we would have been subject to *that* inversion, we should doubt that our concern with nearness is the product of an analogous inversion.

The final alternative explanation I shall consider of some of the cases I have described, one which denies that distance per se is of moral significance at least sometimes, is offered by Violetta Igneski.[26] She argues that in those situations where distance seems to matter, it is not really distance that is driving our intuitions. Rather, what she calls the "moral determinateness" of the situation in which we find ourselves accounts for our intuitions. She says that a situation has moral determinateness when the following is true of it: (1) a specific agent (2) must do a specific act (3) for a specific person (4) in order to immediately bring peril to an end. She further claims that when these characteristics obtain, an agent cannot choose among various options as to how to help, when to help, or whom to help. When the four characteristics are present, we are in a "rescue situation," according to Igneski. Nearness will seem to matter, she claims, only when it coincides with a morally determinate (i.e., rescue) situation.

By contrast, a situation is morally indeterminate when we have the option of how to satisfy the duty to help people. In such situations, we can choose how, when, and whom to help; in such situations, it could also be true that *which* agent must act to help a specific victim is not determinate.

Let us now try to get clearer about the distinction between morally determinate and indeterminate situations by examining the Joe Case. Suppose that I find myself in a situation where only I can save only Joe, and I can only do so by throwing him a raft precisely at t_r. If I have no other duties, I *must* throw Joe the raft. Notice that there are two different sorts of "must" involved here. One sense is purely instrumental: *If* I am to save Joe, I must throw the raft at t_r, as nothing else will cause him to be saved. This makes the means determinate, and we can say that it makes the situation "instrumentally determinate," because a specific agent has no choice about how or when to act if she is to save a specific victim. But this is not the same as saying that I must save him in a second, normative sense of "must," according to which I have a duty to throw Joe the raft because I have a duty to save him. I believe that Igneski is employing the normative "must" when she says that a situation is morally determinate, that is, that there is a very particular thing that an agent is morally obligated to do.

In the Joe Case, I have deliberately asked us to imagine a morally determinate situation where there are no other duties I could have besides throwing the raft. This is because I believe that the best way to get clear about the distinction between morally determinate and indeterminate situations is, at least to begin with, to think of the duty to throw the raft as a *pro tanto* duty. That is, barring the presence of other duties I have, there is something very specific that I am morally obligated to do. (We should try, in distinguishing morally determinate from morally indeterminate situations, to avoid assuming what should be done if there are other duties (determinate or indeterminate) with which a conflict might arise.)

By contrast, consider a morally indeterminate situation. In the absence of other duties, the duty of helping people gives me a duty *that still includes options*. I may help now, or at any one of many later times, any one of a number of different people in any one of a number of ways. Furthermore, the people I can help can also be helped by other people; each of the many situations calls on no specific agent. So *instrumentally*, there are many ways to pursue the duty of helping people, and morally I am not obligated to pursue any one way in particular; though morally I must do something to fulfill my duty of helping.

I shall now pose some questions about the distinction between determinate and indeterminate situations and duties as I have described them:

(1) Is it urgency that determines whether the duty of rescue is present rather than a duty of ordinary aid, because urgency tracks determinateness? Igneski says that in a rescue situation, "an agent is bound to some specific act to immediately end peril."[27] This, however, is not the same as "something we (in the instrumental sense) must *immediately* do can end peril." Determinateness, as she describes it, seems compatible with, for example, only I being able to rescue only Joe using only a raft at a *specific time immediately after I encounter him a month from now*. Here too, there is no choice as to when to save, but it would not be described as urgent because it is not something I must immediately do. Hence determinateness does not imply urgency. Nevertheless, there will eventually be a duty to rescue. In indeterminate situations, while it is true that different agents have a choice among many different people and among many different times and among many different means, it is also true that for some person who needs help, it may be only immediately, and only in one way, that he can be helped. If he is not helped now in that way, then *he* will be

lost. Hence, it is urgent for him to be aided. Yet there is no duty of rescue, because there will still be others to be helped by any agent. I conclude that urgency need not be present in determinate situations and can be present in indeterminate ones.

(2) Is it true that rescue situations must involve determinate duties, as Igneski claims? Consider the Indeterminate Rescue Case: Three people are near a pond where A, B, and C are drowning. A raft, a boat, and a life preserver are available to save them, and there is an hour in which to save all of the people. Given where they are in the water, not everyone can be saved at once. Hence, each agent must choose *a* person, *a* device, and *a* time at which to save, but not any particular person, device, or time. This situation does not meet Igneski's criteria for a determinate situation, but it seems to be a rescue situation with a strong duty to aid someone nonetheless. Perhaps this is because nearness is involved. But then this would mean that nearness might matter even when the situation is *not* determinate, contrary to what Igneski claims.[28]

Suppose that we have a far case that is indeterminate in the same way as the Indeterminate Rescue Case. My claim is not that the duty to aid someone could not be as strong in the Far Indeterminate Rescue Case as in the Near Indeterminate Rescue Case. For example, if the cost of aid were low, there could be a strong duty in the Far Indeterminate Rescue Case to do one of the acts. Hence, even in far cases, indeterminateness does not correlate with the absence of a strong duty to rescue. As the cost goes up, however, the duty in the Far Indeterminate Rescue Case might be defeated, I claim, unlike the duty in the Near Indeterminate Rescue Case.

In some types of near and far indeterminate cases, we may know in advance that the options will extend over long periods of time. (This is what Jesus meant when he said that the poor will always be with you.) Given that one need not always be aiding someone, may one decline the first *near* opportunity to aid and give aid later, if one would not have been obligated to also aid later had one aided at an earlier time? Perhaps, but this seems more clearly true when we are involved in a far indeterminate case.

(3) Would an instrumentally determinate far case be morally determinate, as it should be if it is determinateness that is crucial? I agree that it could be, as in the Far Costless Case presented in chapter 11 where the cost to aid is very low. In a case of a distant person in need, when there is some particular agent whose act would be instrumentally determinate to ending peril, my claim is not that the agent has no (*pro tanto*) duty to act. One of my claims is just that as the costs involved in acting go up, a duty to aid a distant person may be defeated, whereas a duty to aid a near person would not be. But even in a near case with instrumental determinateness, there may not be *pro tanto* moral determinateness. For example, if giving up one's life is physically necessary in order to save a particular victim at a particular time, there may be no duty to perform such an action.

(4) Is it true that the cases I have used in discussing the New PDM imply that determinacy matters? Igneski says (in commenting on my earlier work), "Kamm redefines what it means to be close" because "all the cases that Kamm counts as near are also cases where the solution is specific enough to ground a duty to do some particular act of rescue and the cases that she counts as far are cases where the situation

is not specific enough to ground a duty of rescue."[29] I think that this is wrong. I do not believe that I have changed our notion of being close. I specifically gave the Far Alone Case, where there is also a specific determinate act (in Igneski's sense) that the agent instrumentally must do though he is far rather than near. Furthermore, in all of the cases I presented involving rescue, nearness to a victim or nearness to a threat could be altered so that the cases involve a choice of types of acts to do, choices among victims to rescue (already presented in the Near Alone Case), and choices among threats from which to save victims. I do not think that the intuitive judgments will change, just because the cases lack what Igneski calls determinateness.

(5) Suppose it is true that there is only one kind of act I *instrumentally* must do in the determinate situation and not only one kind of act I *instrumentally* must do in the indeterminate situation to help someone. Suppose also that there is one kind of act I *morally* must do in the morally determinate situation *when there are no other duties I have*. It is a mistake to think that this proves that, in the determinate situation, "the agent is morally bound to fulfill her obligation in a very specific way,"[30] when this is taken to mean that I morally must perform the determinate *pro tanto* duty rather than one of the options I have as part of my indeterminate *pro tanto* duty. After all, the world could be such that I have both determinate and indeterminate *pro tanto* duties at a given time, and much more good could be accomplished by my doing the indeterminate duty.[31] And those I have an option of helping under a *pro tanto* indeterminate duty may only be relieved from peril if I aid now instead of performing the *pro tanto* determinate duty. (Recall that the fact that a victim must be helped now or die does not make the duty determinate, if there are many others in the same situation.)

Igneski believes that the morally determinate duty is a perfect duty and the morally indeterminate duty is an imperfect duty. Kantians commonly hold that when there is a conflict between perfect and imperfect duties, the perfect duties take precedence. This may be why she thinks that, what I have described as the *pro tanto* determinate duty takes precedence over the *pro tanto* indeterminate duty. Suppose it were true that perfect duties take precedence over imperfect duties. If the *pro tanto* determinate duty does not always win out in conflicts with the *pro tanto* indeterminate duty, this will be evidence that it is wrong to think that a *pro tanto* determinate duty is equivalent to a perfect duty. It seems clear that I have a perfect duty not to kill someone by throwing him in the water to make him a human life preserver, or by doing something that as a direct side effect kills him. But suppose that the only way to fulfill my *pro tanto* morally determinate duty to save two people is to kill someone else by throwing him into the water to make him a human life preserver, or to throw a raft to the two that I know will hit and kill someone swimming near by. It is clear that I must let the two drown rather than do what is necessary to save them. Is this a conflict between *two* perfect duties, one of which is *more* perfect than the other? Rather, it may be that the duty that dominates is the perfect duty, and even a *pro tanto* morally determinate duty to aid the two is an imperfect duty. In any case, the fact that a *pro tanto* morally determinate duty can be dominated by a perfect duty suggests that it may not have the immediate dominance over imperfect duties that a perfect duty is said to have.

But suppose that the *pro tanto* determinate duty to aid *is* morally overriding with respect to one of the options of the *pro tanto* indeterminate duty to aid. It is still not clear that this is implied just by the ideas of these two types of situations/duties. Such an implication must be argued for, and Igneski does not do this. That a situation is *pro tanto* morally determinate does not show that it is *overridingly* morally determinate when there is an indeterminate duty with which it conflicts. Could it have precedence because if we do not do it when it must be done, someone will perish, but we can act on an option of how to fulfill an indeterminate duty at any time? The problem with this, though, is that at least one of the options in the indeterminate duty may also not be available at another time (e.g., some particular people will perish far away because we did not aid at a particular time). So why may we not select one of those options instead of the *pro tanto* determinate rescue?

Hence, once we are in a world where there is a *pro tanto* indeterminate duty as well as a *pro tanto* determinate one, the overall situation may become morally indeterminate, for all that Igneski has said.[32] It seems, though, that if one bypassed the *pro tanto* morally determinate duty in order to perform one of the options in the *pro tanto* indeterminate duty, one could no longer treat the latter as a mere option. That is, one *has* to be saving someone at a given time if one is not performing the *pro tanto* determinate rescue at that time. By contrast, if one is not performing one option of an indeterminate duty at a certain time, one need not be fulfilling another duty.

I have argued thus far that a situation need not be determinate in order to involve the duty of rescue (as opposed to an ordinary duty to aid); both determinacy and indeterminacy may be true of situations involving near and far, but the duty to aid when the victim (or threat or victim's means) is far may be defeated by certain factors that do not defeat the duty to aid when the victim (etc.) is near. I have also argued that the duty in a determinate situation is not necessarily a perfect duty.

(6) Recall that I claimed (in section IIB, chapter 11) that the thesis that nearness matters morally could be defended, even if (i) an agent who is near and (ii) an agent who is far (*when no one is near in an absolute sense*) always have the same duties. Suppose that when someone is far, there is also someone who is near, and the near person has priority to perform rescues, other things being equal. This would be enough to show that nearness mattered in some way. This bears on the issue of determinate versus indeterminate cases in the following way. Suppose that in state 1, the world is such that only those who are near are able to provide aid. Many of these aiding situations may be determinate, and then, according to Igneski, there are strict duties to aid. In state 2, the world has changed, so that for each of those previously determinate situations, many other agents who are far away are able to aid the victims in many different ways. All of the determinate aiding opportunities then become indeterminate from the point of view of both those who are near the victims and those who are far from them. This opens up the possibility that some people who would have been helped previously will not be helped, because helping them is now one option among many for everyone. If the near person had a stronger duty because he was near, this "problem" would be less

likely to arise. (It would still arise to some degree, though, if a strong duty did not always take precedence over a weaker duty or nonduty that did more good.)

VI. PROXIMITY, THE DUTY NOT TO HARM, AND AGENT-CENTEREDNESS

Now let us consider a nondebunking explanation of the moral significance of distance. Perhaps it will help to understand why proximity may affect the duty to aid by considering why it does *not* affect the duty not to harm. That is, negative duties and rights can behave very differently in response to proximity than some positive duties. We have at least as strong a duty not to harm someone who is far as not to harm someone who is near. I suggest that this is because in standard cases in which we would harm someone, we would deprive her of what she would have had independently of our aid. These things that people have independently of our aid are protected by the negative right relative to us. This "protective coating" goes with the person wherever *she* is located—near or far. Hence, the strength of her negative right is something that has its source in her, not us, and is based on properties located where she is. Efforts we make not to harm someone involve doing things in order not to impose first on that to which she has a right.[33]

This contrasts with someone who needs our help: If we do not aid, he will lose something that he would not have without our aid, that is, something he would not have independently of our aid. If we do help him, in a sense, he imposes first on us. The focus would then seem to be about what comes *from us* and adds to what the person would have independently of us. This may seem to help explain why the focus is on *us* in aiding, and hence on where *we* are.

But this is much too quick for at least two reasons: (1) Even when someone is near us and he needs aid, he still stands to lose out on only what he would not have without our aid. If this factor explains why the focus is on the agent rather than the victim, it can seem to justify the absence of *any* duty to aid, even to aid those who are near. (2) Suppose that someone has a positive right to aid based on considerations *other* than his being near to us, for example, promises. In this case, a person's right to this aid and our duty to aid do not disappear just because he is not near.

All of this suggests that (a) we have to show that we have a special responsibility to do something about what goes on in the area near us or our means (hence, nearness is a sufficient condition for some duties), and (b) we have to show that there are some duties to aid whose *origin* lies in nearness, so that when nearness is not present, the duty is not present (hence nearness is a necessary condition for some duties). That is, if we have a duty to aid a stranger—even though the fact that he needs our aid means that he stands to lose out on only what he could not have without us—the strength of our duty is connected with the following facts: The focus in aiding is on the agent from whom aid comes and who is imposed on first, and the agent has a responsibility for the area around him or his means.[34]

Now, why might he actually have such responsibility for the area around him or his means? Here is one suggestion. It is commonly thought that one has a moral prerogative to give greater weight to one's own interests and projects rather than giving equal weight to oneself and to others.[35] This *agent-centered* prerogative allows us to give weight to things out of proportion to the weight they have from an impartial perspective. This prerogative, while agent-centered, is not fundamentally egoistic. That is, it also protects our choice to engage in projects that are not concerned with promoting our own well-being. We may use it to devote our lives to others. The prerogative gives us a permissible option, not a duty, to act from a partial perspective. But possibly, if one takes advantage of the option to give weight to things out of proportion to the weight they have from an impartial perspective, there is also a *duty* generated from the perspective on life from which one then acts, to take care of what is associated *with the agent*, for example, the area near her means. After all, we are locatable beings, positioned at the center of our world in virtue of our taking an agent-centered perspective. We also identify with our means that are locatable. This suggests that the person who does not act on the partial perspective option, but treats herself impartially relative to others quite generally, would not have a greater duty to take care of the area near herself or her means than the area that is far.

I do not mean to imply that the prerogative itself gives rise to duties; its point is to give agents options, not obligations. (Of course, if one exercises one's options, for example, to enter into a contract, one may generate obligations for oneself.) It is the mindset of one alternative covered by the prerogative—focusing on what looms larger for an agent than for the impartial perspective—that is supposed to help explain the duty to aid related to the agent's location or the location of his means.

But, it may be asked, would not this mindset rather imply that an agent should have a duty to take care of what is near the things or people he cares about rather than near himself? After all, the partial perspective is not necessarily egoistic. Here is a possible answer. Some (e.g., Samuel Scheffler) have argued that it is not possible to derive duties not to harm from the concern for the agent's perspective that underlies the prerogative.[36] That concern may generate options for an agent, but not duties for him. Others (e.g., Thomas Nagel, at least in some of his work) have tried to derive such a duty not to harm from what looms larger to an agent. That is, Nagel (at one point) thought that an agent must be more concerned with the victim he would harm than with others' victims whom he might save by harming someone.[37] While I do not think that this account of the duty not to harm is correct,[38] it might suggest that concern for the agent's perspective can give rise to some other duties. Most important, Nagel's account claims that the agent can have a duty not to harm a perfect *stranger*, not merely someone about whom he cares from his agent-centered perspective. The person comes to have greater significance to the agent only because he would be the object of the agent's act. The analogue in the area of aiding, I suggest, is that an agent might be obligated not to leave a perfect stranger who comes to have extra significance only because of his location near the agent or his means, even if he is not related to projects about which the agent antecedently cares. (So caring about the area near one need not be a mark of an egoistic perspective.) Further, if the duty to aid those who are near may sometimes permissibly be supplanted by a desire to do more good for those who are far (as I shall argue below), the duty to the near generated by agent-centered considerations would not need to be strong enough to withstand consideration of the greater good in the way that the duty not to harm a stranger should often be.

Notice that this explanation (like the discussion in chapter 10 of responsibility and collaboration), finds a place for agent-focused reasons within a nonconsequentialist theory that emphasizes a victim-focused account of negative rights (as discussed in chapters 1 and 8) and of some positive rights (for example, covered by promises and contracts). In chapter 10, the emphasis was on agent-focused reasons for harming or not-harming. Here, it is on agent-focused reasons for aiding or not-aiding.

VII. WHAT MUST WE DO?

Suppose that I do have a duty sometimes to help a near person and not a far one (or a stronger duty to help a near person than a far one). Does this imply that in such cases it would be wrong of me to help the far one rather than the near one (as the Standard Implication says)?

Peter Unger believes that this Standard Implication holds, for he argues that to say we have a duty to aid the person near us but not a duty to aid distant people implies that we have a duty to save one person close to us rather than do what will save many who are at a distance.[39] In discussing whether distance per se affects our intuitions about the obligation to aid, I have tried to keep constant the number of people and the losses they will suffer in the near and far cases. Theoretically, therefore, everything I have said is consistent with our having a duty to save two in the far case rather than one in the near case. But I now wish to assume that the intuitive bias in favor of the near is strong enough so that there is *no* strong duty (e.g., one for which one would have to sacrifice a significant amount) to rescue several in the far case, but there is a strong duty to rescue one in the near case. The question is whether this implies that we have a duty to save one person close to us rather than do what will save many who are at a distance.

One ground for the Standard Implication would be the claim that in a choice between a duty and a supererogatory act, one always has to do the duty. But this claim is not true, even within a nonconsequentialist ethical theory.[40] If I have a duty to meet someone for lunch because I promised to do so, but on my way I see that I alone can save someone who is dying of kidney failure by giving him my kidney, I may save him rather than go to lunch. Though giving the kidney is a supererogatory act that goes beyond the duty to aid, it may take precedence over the duty to keep my lunch engagement. Furthermore, a supererogatory act may take precedence over a duty, even in a case where the person to whom I am obligated would lose much if I do not fulfill my duty toward him. For example, suppose that I have promised to save one person from paralysis that threatens him, but as I am about to help him, I see 1,000 people drowning nearby. Aiding them, but not the one, would cost me my leg, so it is supererogatory of me to save them, but doing so can override my duty to help the one, I believe. Some philosophers (e.g., Scheffler) have argued that we may have responsibilities based on relationships and that dealing with these responsibilities is a legitimate reason for not adopting a purely impartial perspective.[41] The cases I have now been examining show that if we have particular responsibilities, and there are legitimate reasons not to take an impartial perspective, this does not yet prove that it is *impermissible* to respond to a more impartial perspective if we choose to do so.

All of this suggests that even if it is sometimes wrong not to save a near person when there is nothing else to do and not wrong to fail to save a greater number who are far, if one had a choice between saving the near or a greater number of the far, one might permissibly do the latter. That is, it may not matter morally which act one does, and this is compatible with its being a duty to help the near but not the far. This case follows the model that in doing the supererogatory, one does more good than in doing one's duty, and this could be a reason for substituting one act for the other.[42]

Unger himself would, presumably, wish to make use of the permissibility of doing a supererogatory rather than an obligatory act. This is because he argues that we have a duty to give our money to help the poor (i.e., it would be wrong not to),[43] but he also argues that it is permissible and morally worthwhile to steal from others to help the poor, though it may not be wrong not to.[44] This means that it is supererogatory to steal. Put to one side whether we agree with these claims of Unger's. Just note that if he believed that the duty took precedence over the supererogatory act, he would be committed to thinking that a person who had few resources (but more than the poor) would have a duty to give these to the poor rather than steal a lot of money from a rich person in order to give it to the poor, even when he was willing to steal. But, presumably, Unger would think that it is permissible to do the supererogatory act instead of the dutiful one, when one cannot do both. This suggests that he too should deny the Standard Implication that if we have a duty to help the near but not the far, we should help the near instead of the far.

But I also wish to argue for the further claim that when the amount of good that is done by taking care of the near and taking care of the far is the *same*, we may have a choice of what to do, even if taking care of the near is our duty and taking care of the far is not.[45] This requires an extension of what I have previously argued about the relation between supererogation and obligation. If I have promised to meet someone for lunch, it would usually be wrong for me to choose instead to meet someone else for lunch whom I had not promised to meet when no more good is, thereby, done. Or again, if I have a duty to take care of my child, while I might sometimes instead choose to make even a supererogatory sacrifice to help many children who are not mine instead, it seems wrong to substitute fulfilling a duty to my child with doing only as much good supererogatorily for someone else's child.

However, there are other cases where substitution of an equal good that we are not required to bring about—at equal cost—is permissible. For example, we may have a right to require that you come into work on any day Monday through Friday (giving you a duty to do so), but not to require work on Sunday because that might interfere with your religious observance. Still, it would be just as good if you came in on Sunday instead of Monday, and it would be permissible to do that. We may have no right to require that you keep your own desk clean because to do so would be paternalistic, but we might permissibly require you to clean up others' desks. Still, given that all we care about is that there be clean desks, you could as well clean your own if you would prefer. Likewise, it may be that given you live from the permitted agent-centered perspective, it is permissible to require you to take care of what is close to where you (or your means) are located, but not permissible to require as much of you to take care of what is far. Yet you may permissibly substitute helping those who are far. Hence, the Standard Implication may be wrong even in cases where we can produce equal amounts of good.

It may seem odd that if one act is required and another not, we may sometimes nevertheless do the latter rather than the former. I have tried to explain why this is so. On the other hand, it seems natural to think that if two acts are equally required, it makes no difference which we do. So, for example, suppose that it is equally easy to flip a switch and save someone who is far or flip a switch and save someone who is near. Arguably, we are equally required to do each, and we may choose to do either one if we cannot do both. But I also wish to argue that it is not, in general, true that we may substitute one required act for another. Suppose that it costs very little to save a life and also costs very little to avoid killing someone. It might well be argued that I am equally required to do both. Yet, if I can only do one, I must avoid killing rather than save the life. The greater stringency of the negative than the positive duty shows up in this way.[46] This will be true even if there is a positive right correlative to the positive duty, for example, if I have promised to help someone. By contrast, in the choice of aiding a near or aiding a far person costlessly, we are dealing with positive assistance in both cases, and this may account for the possibility of choosing either act.

In permitting a supererogatory act as a replacement for a dutiful one, we must be aware of the possibility of motivational oddities and errors. Under the category of oddities, consider someone who only develops an interest in doing, at considerable effort, the supererogatory act that does more good once he realizes that he has a duty to do something very onerous. Under the category of error, note that I am not claiming that if one is going to do a duty at a certain cost, the only rational thing to do instead is a supererogatory act that does more good at the same cost. For example, someone who has never thought of saving distant children might think that given that she now has a duty to spend $500 on the near child, she might as well spend it in achieving the better consequence of saving several distant children. There is no requirement to always produce the best outcome, I believe. These cases differ from the one in which someone who is independently motivated to save distant children wishes not to give up that act in order to do less good for someone who is near. In this case, at least these motivational oddities, or errors about what is a rational requirement, do not arise.

It is now time in our discussion of supererogation to notice that there may be a moral difference between different types of supererogatory acts that bears on whether the Standard Implication is true. Consider the case in which I must choose between my obligation to one person and saving at supererogatory cost to me 1,000 near people. Here, saving the 1,000 people would be at least one of my duties (even if there were no correlative right) were it not for the great cost to me of doing it. If it were costless to me, then this duty would, I think, conflict with my duty to keep my promise to save one person (even though there may only be a correlative right in the case of the promise). Because we are (often) free to absorb a cost if we want to, an account (such as I have provided) of why one kind of supererogatory act may compete with a duty is available. But it is not necessarily the great cost to me that makes aiding those who are far away not be a duty. We intuitively think that it has something to do with distance per se; a high cost that would be required in the Near Alone Case would not be required in the Far Alone Case.

On the basis of this difference, it might be suggested that we are not free to make the plight of those who are at a distance as important to us as those who are near in order that the supererogatory act compete with a duty. (Similarly, it might be argued that what great costs we will absorb is up to us, but it is not in our power to make helping members of other societies a competitor with helping fellow citizens in our own society, holding constant their need and number.) If it were not permitted to put this particular type of supererogatory act in competition with the duty, this would be a ground for the truth of the Standard Implication that is independent of the claim that duties always take precedence over nonrequired acts. It would support the view that we *must* aid a smaller number of near people (even foreigners) rather than aid a greater or equal number of those (foreigners) who are far away. I shall not pursue this issue further here. Suffice it to say that if we are to fill in the outlines of a conception of duty that varies with distance, we need to deal with this issue.

NOTES

1. In chapter 11, I tried to show that there is an intuitive judgment that distance matters morally.

2. Again, as in the previous chapter, I am focusing on accident, not basic justice, cases.

3. I use "duty" and "obligation" interchangeably here.

4. However, note that the latter conceptualization may offer a better account of why (intuitively) an agent may not be required to make available the same resources (e.g., his Stradivarius) to aid when they are far from the victim (and the agent) as when they are near the victim though far from the agent. I discuss such cases below.

5. If the means is the agent's employee, he does not, of course, own the employee. Nevertheless, I shall understand him to have a relation to his employee similar to ownership, for our purposes.

6. Notice that I treat a nonefficacious item differently from the way I treated a nonefficacious part of the agent himself (in the previous chapter). More on this below.

7. I owe this point to Sigrun Svavarsdottir.

8. I owe this point to Derek Parfit.

9. Liam Murphy suggests an alternative response: Money is too abstract to be dealt with like concrete means. (However, if my money were in a sack next to a child in distress, this might not be so, I suggest.)

10. As a matter of biography, it was through trying to explain what goes on in such a case that I stumbled upon the possibility of separating the locations of the agent and his means in relation to the victim.

11. I add this change because of the possible moral difference (discussed in chapter 11) between upfront and downstream costs. In the Distant Owner and Yacht cases, we use the boat and as a side effect damage it. We do not destroy the boat as a means (e.g., for wood to make a raft to save someone). But in Unger's Account Case, giving away the person's money is not a side effect of using the money, it is our means to saving people.

12. And the stranger's means, as we shall see below.

13. In that case, the agent is distant from the victim and threat; the means he would use are distant from the victim and threat; and the owner of the means is distant from the victim and threat.

14. Possibly, when a victim has the means to alleviate his condition but is far from them, there is still an impetus for those who are also distant from these means (and from the victim and threat) to help the victim get his means, greater than if his rescue depends totally on means belonging to others. This is not because there is reduced cost in saving him if we use his means (since there may be no such reduction), but because there is a sense in which he is *more self-sufficient.* This issue deserves further examination.

15. This case is different from an agent being near his own (not the stranger's) means, which I have *not* said by itself gives an agent an obligation to a far victim. Though I have said that if his being near gives the agent an obligation, whether his means are near him or not, then the distance of his means from him can affect whether he has an obligation to use them. Recall the case of the near versus distant Stradivarius.

16. This extension of the model was suggested by Franklin Bruno.

17. What about the agent's computer that is near the victim or threat, and cannot help directly but can monitor the scene and trigger the use of the agent's means that are distant from the victim? Is the agent intuitively thought to be obligated to let the computer trigger the same sort of distant device that the agent, were he near, would be obligated to trigger? I suggest that he is.

18. The selected cases we have examined in some detail can be generated, along with many others, from mechanically combining the four different factors (agent, victim, threat, means) and the four categories of means (agent's means, victim's means, third parties' means, unowned means). It is also possible to consider who "owns" the threat. (I owe this point to Franklin Bruno.) In what follows, I shall ignore threat ownership and also the possibility that means belong to third parties or are unowned. The problem is simply to consider what intuitions one has about one's obligation to suffer a loss to save an innocent stranger from death in cases involving all possible combinations of the factors. Figure N.1 illustrates the cases and the route for generating them. V stands for "victim," A stands for "agent," AM stands for agent's means, VM stands for "victim's means," T stands for threat, r means "in relation to," N stands for "near," and F stands for "far."

Let us consider the cases in this figure. Are some of the possibilities inconsistent with each other because the relevant properties are not instantiatable? For example, if the agent is near the victim, and the agent's means are near the agent (1), is it impossible for the means to be far from the victim (4)? Theoretically, it is possible for the agent to be far enough from a still-near victim while the means near him are far enough from him that the means are far from the victim. Still, as I imagine the cases, if the agent is near the victim, and the threat or means are near the agent, they are also near the victim. This means, for example, that (1) and (4) do not coexist, and also that cases in III mimic cases in I. When agent and victim are near and the threat is near each, we can know whether the means are near the threat just by knowing if the

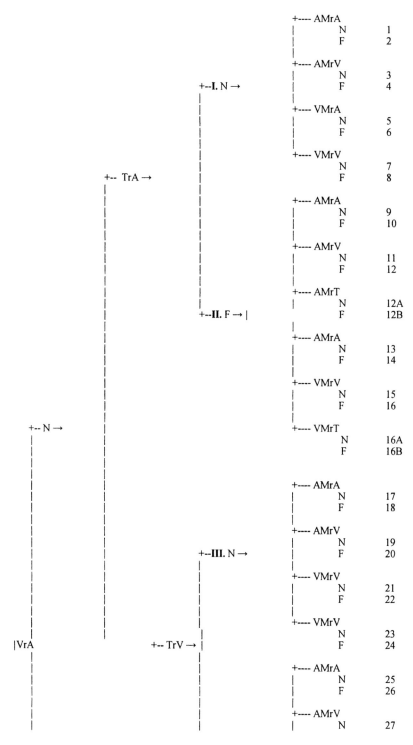

Figure N.1.

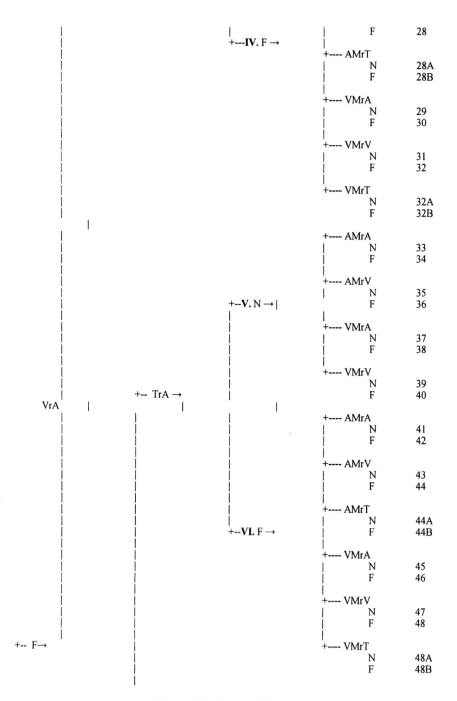

Figure N.1. (*continued*)

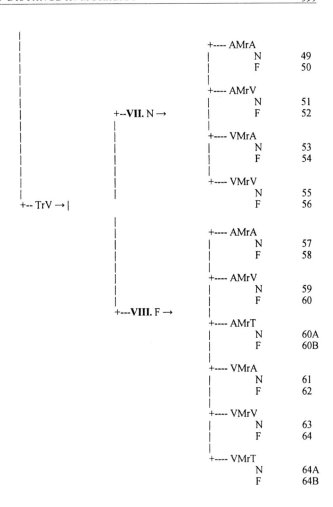

means are near or far from the agent. But when the threat is far from the agent (II), we need to consider *separately* whether the means are near or far from the threat (hence, cases 12A and 12B and 16A and 16B). Cases in IV also mimic cases in II. Nevertheless, focusing on cases in IV, where the threat is far from the victim, highlights the fact that an agent can be obligated to aid a near victim, who is not yet subject to the threat. Also, this is a case where the need of the victim is likely not to be salient. (I owe the first point to Franklin Bruno.)

In V, if agent and victim are far and the threat is near to the agent, it is far from the victim. We can also assume that this implies that if the means are close to the agent, they are close to the threat, and if they are near the victim, they are far from the threat. When the threat is near the agent, if the agent's means are near the victim (in 35), they should be used to help the victim, either by being brought by remote control to deal with the threat near the agent or to protect the victim they are near who is not yet affected by the threat. (I am assuming the cost incurred is the same either way.)

In VI, when the threat is far from the agent and the victim is also far from the agent, this does not mean that the threat is near the victim. There are many different ways to be far from the agent. Here we must also consider separately whether the means are close to the threat, hence 44A and 44B and 48A and 48B. In VII, when the threat is near the victim and the victim is far from the agent, I assume that the threat is far from the agent, and when the means are close to the victim, they are also close to the threat. In VIII, when the threat is far from both victim and agent, we must also consider whether the means are close to the threat, hence, 64A and 64B.

Once again, our conclusion is that if the agent or agent's means are close to the threat or to the victim or victim's means, then intuitively, the obligation to aid will be strong. This includes cases where the victim is distant and yet the intuitive obligations to aid are strong.

19. Alexander Friedman reminded me to equalize the latter factor.

20. For discussion of this distinction, see chapter 14.

21. If my device was not useful at the time it was near but it is useful now that it is far, then it was not a means at the time, and I do not think that its past presence obligates me now. This conclusion has to be, in some way, consistent with what we say about (c). That is, if I was near a person in danger in the past but could not then have helped, then could I have a greater than ordinary obligation when I am now far and can help? Is it possible that a person should be obligated to use new means to aid with troubles he has been near, and yet not become obligated to do this because of improvements in devices of his that were once near troubles, although he was far?

22. Possibly, if the temporal gap between nearness and then farness is very great, the past tie is wiped out. I shall not here investigate this degree-of-temporal-gap question.

23. That it might correlate or have been correlated with effectiveness was mentioned in chapter 11.

24. Suggested by Tyler Burge.

25. This case was suggested by Jerrold Katz. We must remember to hold constant factors such as amount of effort required and also vary the amounts of effort to test for higher efforts being required near than far.

26. In Violetta Igneski, "Distance, Determinacy, and the Duty to Aid: A Reply to Kamm," *Law and Philosophy* 20 (2001): 605–16. My discussion of her work in this section is based on what I say in "The New Problem of Distance," in *Duties to the Distant Needy*, ed. D. Chatterjee, pp. 59–74 (Cambridge: Cambridge University Press, 2004).

27. Igneski, "Distance, Determinacy, and the Duty to Aid: A Reply to Kamm," p. 611.

28. When several potential agents are near a victim and only one of the agents is needed to aid (another indeterminate situation), it is still the duty of each to be sure someone else will aid before she walks away. Is the same true in a comparable case where one is far from the person needing aid? In both situations, if one could not walk away if one were the only person, one would have to be sure someone else had picked up the slack, I think.

29. Igneski, "Distance, Determinacy, and the Duty to Aid," pp. 613, 614, commenting on my "Does Distance Matter Morally to the Duty to Rescue?"

30. Igneski, "Distance, Determinacy, and the Duty to Aid," p. 612.

31. I try to argue for this in more detail in section VII. Even a supererogatory act, rather than an option under an indeterminate duty to help, could override the *pro tanto* morally and instrumentally determinate act. I discussed this in chapter 1.

32. This dovetails with my view (discussed below in section VII) that the duty to those who are near may not necessarily take precedence over helping, even supererogatorily, those who are far.

33. For more on this, see chapter 1 in this volume and my *Morality, Mortality*, vol. 2 (New York: Oxford University Press, 1996).

34. This special responsibility is not to be identified with any property-like stake in the area around him, as this would imply that he not only had special responsibilities for, but also special privileges or rights in, the area near him. But this need not be true.

35. See Samuel Scheffler, *The Rejection of Consequentialism* (Oxford: Oxford University Press, 1982) and chapter 1.

36. In Scheffler, *The Rejection of Consequentialism*.

37. See Thomas Nagel, *The View from Nowhere* (New York: Oxford University Press, 1986).

38. See my *Morality, Mortality*, vol. 2 and chapters 1 and 8 in this volume for criticism.

39. Unger, *Living High and Letting Die*, p. 55.

40. I first tried to show this in my "Supererogation and Obligation," *Journal of Philosophy* 82 (1985): 118–38. For an expanded version of the article, see *Morality, Mortality*, vol. 2, chap. 12; for a short discussion, see chapters 1 and 8 in this volume.

41. See Samuel Scheffler, "Individual Responsibility in a Global Age," *Social Theory and Practice* 21 (1995): 219–36.

42. Notice, however, that in the specific context in which one fails to do one's duty in order to do what is supererogatory, one does not, in general, retain the option not to do what is supererogatory. But still, one may not have to do everything in order to do the supererogatory act that one would have had to do in order to accomplish one's duty. For more on this, see my *Morality, Mortality*, vol. 2, and chapters 1 and 8 in this volume.

43. Unger, *Living High and Letting Die*, chap. 3.

44. Ibid.

45. This is a different view from one (at least, at one time) held by Richard Miller, which says that there is nothing to the distinction between near and far except that, when all else is equal, "near" can pinpoint a direction for us to move in a way that "far" cannot. The view I am now arguing for says that, when all else is equal, we may choose the far despite a duty to the near. Miller's view was expressed at the American Philosophical Association panel on Aid to Distant Strangers, Pacific Division Meeting, Berkeley, CA, April 1999.

46. I call this the Choice Test for stringency of a duty. On this Choice Test, see section III above, *Morality, Mortality*, vol. 2, and chapter 8 in this volume.

SECTION IV

Others' Ethics

13

PETER SINGER'S ETHICAL THEORY

I. INTRODUCTION

In previous chapters, I have, to a large extent, investigated aspects of nonconsequentialist ethical theory as I see it.[1] In this last section of the book, I will exclusively examine the views of consequentialists as well as of nonconsequentialists whose perspectives differ from my own. In this chapter, I shall consider both the kind of consequentialism to which Peter Singer subscribes and his conception of the role of moral reasons. Based on what he claims in various places in published works, I shall first reconstruct and critically examine his general normative theory. I shall often contrast his views with alternative possible conceptions. I shall then give particular attention to his arguments for the claim that the distinction between killing and letting die has no moral relevance. The examination of his ethical theory will also help us to evaluate his views on such practical issues as famine relief, treatment of the disabled, and animal liberation, with some surprising results.[2]

II. SINGER'S GENERAL THEORY

In *Practical Ethics*, Singer commits himself to a general two-level theory about the content of morality, a theory of the sort that Richard Hare advocates.[3] The higher level which is basic is strictly impartial consequentialism. The lower level (which is implied by the higher level in conjunction with empirical facts) consists of rules or types of character traits that we ought to develop. Apparently, on Singer's view, the rules need not to be merely rules of thumb that we may break on occasion, because he says that it could be better from the point of view of maximizing good consequences overall that we not be able to think of breaking the rules, even if doing so would maximize good consequences on certain occasions. This is why I think that he is committed to the possibility that we should develop certain *character traits* or *patterns of thinking* that make it impossible to think of breaking rules that maximize good consequences overall, even if following the rules does not lead to maximizing the good on a particular occasion.[4]

There is a second two-level theory to which Singer commits himself, but it does not provide us with the content of a normative theory. Rather, he claims, it describes the *motivation to be moral*.[5] He does not think that the higher-order motivation is derivable from a commitment to rationality per se. Instead, he posits self-interest as the higher-order rationale for an individual's being moral.[6] Being moral is in one's self-interest because it is the best route to a meaningful life, he thinks. A *meaningful life* is good independently of happiness (understood as preference satisfaction). According to Singer, happiness may be achieved by a sociopath as well as, or better than, a moral person, but the sociopath cannot have a meaningful life. Hence, Singer seems to believe that it is more in someone's interest to have a meaningful life than to have one in which his preferences are satisfied.[7]

At the lower level in the motivational structure is *moral conscientiousness*. That is, while self-interest can reasonably motivate us to be moral by the route described above, being moral involves acting for the sake of morality, not for the sake of self-interest.

Is Singer's account of the motivation to be moral plausible, given his view about the content of morality? As already described, he understands the content of morality at the higher level to involve strict consequentialist impartiality, and (as we shall see below) its content at the lower level is also very much concerned with producing the best state of affairs from an impartial point of view. Singer thinks that pursuing the impartial good is a secure basis for a meaningful life, and he contrasts the impartial good that he believes is the point of morality with purely personal aims to which, he thinks, one is not likely to remain committed.[8] But, in fact, many people find meaningful lives through work and personal relations, and they are capable of stable attachment to these. (Indeed, when Singer describes an environmentally sound lifestyle, he seems to describe just such a life based on engaging work and personal relations, without its meaningfulness being related to maximizing the good from an impartial view.) If meaningful lives are frequently possible outside of a commitment to impartial morality, Singer's motivational argument for being moral will have difficulty dovetailing with his view about morality's content. (If enjoying work and personal relations did not require morality in any form, whether strictly impartial or not, a meaningful life would not necessarily require any morality.)

Furthermore, there may be an inconsistency generated by the employment of *two* two-level models. For if the search for a meaningful life involves a commitment to an impartial perspective, such a commitment suggests that one becomes conscientiously committed (at the lower level in the motivational model) to the strictly impartial theory. But the strict impartial theory is at the higher level in Singer's normative model, and the morality of day-to-day life at the lower level, does not necessarily involve a strictly impartial perspective on each occasion. Indeed, one may be asked to forget about the primacy of strict impartiality if one is to act in accordance with morality's dictates. If this is so, then the meaningfulness of one's life could not derive from a conscious attachment to impartiality, even if impartial good were the ultimate justification of one's daily morality.

A general problem with the two-level model of normative theory is that it is most workable (even if not correct) when only a few know the truth about the impartial consequentialist foundations of morality, and the rest just know about the commitment to rules or the maintenance of traits of character. But if we imagine one person knowing the real impartial consequentialist foundations of his morality, it is hard to see how *he* can treat the rules or traits as unbreakable and right in themselves, even though this may be necessary in order to maximize good consequences. It is possible that at a prior time he should have known the true foundations of his morality and then induced amnesia so that he now has forgotten it. If inducing amnesia is the only route to maximizing the good, he should follow it, according to consequentialism. One's life might then be meaningful because of its objective connection with impartiality, but one would know this only for a short period of time. Is a meaningful life the source of whose meaningfulness one does not know about what Singer has in mind?

An alternative possibility is that someone can put out of his mind the true impartial moral theory in daily life and only be aware of it in reflective moments. But here there is probably more danger of a spillover that will reduce one's commitment to rules. Still, if awareness of the true impartial moral theory were occasional, one might be able to have a *sense* of the meaningfulness of one's life, if its meaningfulness did depend on involvement with an impartial morality, in addition to just having an objectively meaningful life.

III. THE MORAL POINT OF VIEW AND NORMATIVE THEORY

Let us try to reconstruct in more detail both the idea of the moral point of view and the content of the two-level normative theory to which Singer subscribes. Singer believes that the strict impartiality of the higher level of normative theory is suggested by, but not a necessary implication of, the very idea of the moral point of view. He thinks of the latter as a justification of conduct in terms of the good of all. Impartiality involves (a) equal consideration of the relevant interests, where interests are now to be understood as what each would *rationally* prefer for herself, and (b) maximizing the satisfaction of these interests, though, perhaps, not in accord with the importance of the interests. Let us elaborate first on Singer's idea of the moral point of view.

A. The Nature of the Moral Point of View and the Weightiness of Moral Considerations

Singer's conception of the moral point of view militates against the idea that, *at its basic level*, the moral point of view permits agents to weigh things partially, that is, out of proportion to their weight from an impartial point of view. This understanding of the moral point of view contrasts with the ones offered by Samuel Scheffler[9] and Thomas Nagel.[10] They think that morality at its most basic level itself endorses a prerogative to care and sometimes to act from the personal point of view rather than the impartial point of view. (In Scheffler's view, in particular, at a basic level in morality, the fact that doing what is approved of from the impartial point of view would interfere, both in content and in motivational source, with someone's acting from the personal point of view can rule out the dominance of the impartial view in morality.) In their views, morality's demand for impartiality is sometimes satisfied by merely granting the prerogative to act from a personal point of view to *everyone* equally. Singer's conception permits acting on a partial point of view only at the lower level of normative theory, if it is a means to producing the best outcome impartially understood. Singer can only allow that, at a basic level, someone's personal perspective is one factor, to be combined with other factors and other person's perspectives to yield an impartial point of view which is dominant.

There is a related issue that offers a challenge to the weight that Singer gives to the moral point of view, rather than to its nature. That is, is the moral point of view, whether it requires impartiality or not, dominant over other points of view? Some, such as Susan Wolf, have argued that it is not.[11]

In considering this view that moral considerations may be overridden, note that there are at least two senses of "overriding the moral." One is that an explicitly moral type of consideration (such as fair treatment or overall human welfare) can be overridden by, for example, an aesthetic consideration in a way that does *not* imply that acting in accord with the aesthetic consideration is immoral. That is, the conduct is still consistent with the moral point of view. For example, if the presentation of a great work of performance art requires the telling of a small lie, then while a moral wrong occurs to the person who is lied to in the process of the aesthetic achievement, it may not be morally wrong to pursue the aesthetic achievement. (This is similar to "overriding the impartial" by personal considerations that Scheffler's view allows, for such overriding is supposed to be consistent with, though not demanded by, the moral point of view.)

Even if we believe that moral considerations can be overridden in this way by nonmoral ones (i.e., consistent with our still doing the morally right thing overall), we can believe that a consideration's being moral gives it extra weight relative to its being an economic or aesthetic consideration. That is, a very serious aesthetic consideration can override a very slight moral consideration (e.g., great art versus a minor impoliteness). But a very serious moral consideration may always weigh more than what is an equally serious consideration from the aesthetic perspective. We might think of this in the following way: First, we weigh the seriousness of some behavior from each of various points of view—for example, moral, aesthetic, economic—and then we attach multiplicative factors for the categories. If the multiplicative factor for morality versus aesthetics is three, then if an act ranks at the highest level of seriousness in the moral category, it may get an overall score three times greater than an act that also ranks at the highest level of seriousness in the aesthetic category. The most serious offense from an aesthetic point of view can thus never override the most serious moral offense.[12]

A second sense of "overriding the moral" is that a prohibition, all things considered from the moral point of view, can be overridden by what is demanded from some other (e.g., the aesthetic) point of view. An example of this would occur if, though it is morally wrong to kill someone in order to produce a great picture, we should nevertheless kill him because producing the picture has great aesthetic merit. Singer would clearly reject the latter sense of overriding the moral, and even those who support a big role for the personal point of view in determining what morality requires can agree with him on this.[13]

Hence, those who disagree with Singer over the role of partiality *within* the moral point of view can still claim that the moral point of view is not overrideable. They can also agree that even though minor moral considerations can be overridden by more important nonmoral considerations, to lead to an act that is morally permissible, the moral considerations must have a greater weight in virtue of their category than considerations coming from other categories.

B. Equal Consideration of Interests

One component of impartiality (in the higher level of Singer's normative theory) is equal consideration of interests. What types of interests does Singer think should get equal consideration? The relevant interests include more than the interest in pleasure and avoidance of pain, for Singer thinks we have an interest in having a meaningful life, even if we do not know that we do or are too irrational to have a preference for it. (One complication with claiming that only interests [i.e., rational preferences for self] count in Singer's view is that he sometimes allows us to count not only people's rational preferences but the *effects* of their *irrational* ones. For example, in discussing immigration,[14] he recognizes that people's irrational prejudice against newcomers may lead to social disruption, and then the true interests of newcomers [and perhaps even those who are prejudiced and who would be involved in the disruption] are not served by immigration.)

The relevant interests include those of any sentient being, and these interests are to be treated in a strictly nonspeciesist way. While higher animals may have different interests than lower ones (for example, in achieving friendship or knowledge), pain per se is equally bad in whichever species it occurs, and each species can have the same interest in not having pain. Presumably, he believes that this is true of pleasure per se as well. Further, suppose that there were no additional morally significant reverberations (e.g., reflection on pain or pleasure) that gave rise to new interests (for example, in having pleasant prospective thoughts) in any one species. Then, according to Singer, one would have as much reason to produce pleasure in a mouse as in a person (whether the person is a human or a member of another species, such as a self-conscious, rational Martian). This point helps us to distinguish two different strands in Singer's thought: nonspeciesism and (what could be called) non-locationism. Those who believe that pain occurring in a person matters more than pain occurring in a nonperson, such as a mouse, believe that the location of pain matters. Singer denies this. But those who think that location matters can also be nonspeciesists, for they would not necessarily distinguish morally in important respects between a Martian person and a human person.

Singer does, however, distinguish between beings in whose interest it is to go on living and those who have no such interest,[15] based on the presence or absence, respectively, of self-consciousness. The latter are replaceable beings (i.e., so long as one replaces the goods their lives would have provided, there is no loss in painlessly killing them). This is because they have no sense of themselves as continuing entities (i.e., no self-consciousness), and so cannot form the desire whose object is their continued existence. Hence, though Singer is famous as an animal liberationist, he is not opposed to killing non-self-conscious animals painlessly. Given his non-speciesism, humans who are not self-conscious also, on his view, lack an interest in their own continuing survival and are replaceable.

Let us consider some of these views. First, might there be an asymmetry between pleasure and pain? Even if it were as bad a state of affairs for there to be pain in a mouse as in a person (considering pain independent of its reverberations), perhaps it is morally more important that a good thing, such as pleasure (independent of reverberations), happen to a more important being (a person) than to a less important one. If we just focus on pain, is there as much reason to prevent as well as not cause pain in an animal as in a person? If so, Singer's view implies that we should be engaged in a great rescue effort to deal with the pain that exists, but that we do not cause, in animals. An alternative view is that what we have reason to do is not only a function of how bad a state of affairs will occur if we do not act but also of whether we owe it *to* someone to deal with the bad state of affairs. Thomas Scanlon, for example, holds that only those who can act for reasons are creatures to whom we can owe things, hence "owing to" is not an additional reason to eliminate the pain of nonrational beings.[16] Scanlon admits that on his account, we would need further grounds to justify helping nonrational beings who are human (such as the severely retarded), if we do not care for similar problems of nonhuman animals of equivalent intellectual status.

What might such a ground be? Just as some moral theories allow an individual to give his own interests greater weight sometimes, it may be that a species (or type) may give preference to its members (or to individuals related to those in a type). Such a ground, however, will only yield an *option* to care for the retarded humans, not a duty. (It will also imply that any rational species has no reason to care more for nonrational members of a different rational species than for any nonrational being of a nonrational species.) There is the additional possible moral significance of a state being abnormal and tragic when it occurs in one species but normal in another species that grounds a special duty of care. So, for example, suppose we have a scarce drug that can raise IQs in any species to a normal human one, and this would be a benefit to any individual regardless of species. Should we give it to a retarded member of a rational species or to a cat?

What of Singer's view that nothing wrong is done if we eliminate non-self-conscious beings so long as good produced in the world does not diminish? Something can continue over time even if it does not know that it does, and the absence of self-consciousness need not mean that there is no psychological self in the sense of a single mind that is a locus of thought and experience, and that continues through time. If such a being's future time were to be filled with good experiences, these good experiences would be *its* good experiences. Is it not in its interest to have these? Death would deprive it of this, and so it seems that there is a reason not to kill it, even if it is not a very strong reason. On the other hand, even self-conscious beings who think of themselves as going on in time may not have desires to continue. As well, if they are not psychologically closely connected to their "future selves," they may not lose much that is currently strongly in their interest to have, if they do not live on.[17] So self-consciousness and a desire to go on living seem to be neither necessary for death to be against one's interests nor sufficient for death to be strongly against one's interests. Self-consciousness, however, might be thought to bear on how important it is that one's interests be satisfied. But on Singer's view, for example, pain or pleasure per se has no greater disvalue if it located in a self-conscious than in a non-self-conscious being.

Objections may also be raised to Singer's placing *interests* at the foundation of morality. First, Singer himself considers the objection that nonsentient entities with no interests might have intrinsic moral significance, for example, trees, the planet, or works of art. (He rejects this view but wishes to argue that such entities should sometimes be protected against the current economic interests of sentient beings, because their loss would affect the interests of future sentient beings.)

A second, more general objection to focusing only on the interests of sentient beings is that many of the things that make individual lives have worth are not concerned with interests but rather, for example, with the capacity for rational agency, responsibility, and respect for what someone wills rather than for his interests. These characteristics should play a part in moral theory independently of their effect on the interests of sentient beings, it might be said. These characteristics may serve the interests of sentient beings, but they are not important merely because they serve these interests. For example, it may be right to punish people because they deserve it, even if it is in no one's interest that this be done, as an expression of taking agency and responsibility seriously. Finally, for contractarians (such as Scanlon) the foundation of morality lies not in a concern with promoting interests but in a concern to be able to justify one's behavior to others who are affected by it. How interests are affected will play a role in the justification of behavior, but it is not the only thing that plays such a role nor is the promotion of interests rather than establishing justifiable relations the ultimate point of morality.

C. Maximizing the Satisfaction of Interests

A second component of impartiality in Singer's view, is maximizing the satisfaction of interests in accordance with their importance. (Given his non-locationism, in whom an interest would be satisfied does not, per se, affect its importance.) In

"Famine, Affluence, and Morality," Singer does not commit himself to more than negative utilitarianism, that is, minimizing suffering has significance even if maximizing happiness does not. But in *Practical Ethics*, he moves beyond mere negative utilitarianism to maximizing positive values as well as minimizing negative ones.[18] Some things Singer says also suggest that he is not a straightforward aggregationist. That is, they suggest that he believes that it is more important that the most important interests be satisfied first, even if satisfying the aggregate of many more less-important interests would produce greater overall satisfaction. (The aggregation of the satisfaction of *equally* important interests is clearly part of this view.) One could support this interpretation by pointing to such quotes as the following: "True scales favour the side where the interest is stronger or where several interests combine to outweigh a smaller number of similar interests"; and "Slavery prevents the slaves from satisfying their interests . . . and the benefits it confers on the slaveowners are hardly comparable in importance to the harm it does the slaves."[19]

However, Singer has stated that he *is* a straightforward aggregationist.[20] This implies that he would aggregate small benefits to billions of slaveowners (if there were such), and they could outweigh lives of great deprivation to a few slaves. It also implies that if he had a choice between saving a few thousand people dying of starvation or else curing the headaches of each of an enormous number of people, he would do the latter. Hence, despite his fame as an advocate of famine relief, Singer's theoretical position does not offer as strong a defense of such aid as does a position that emphasizes giving priority to satisfying the needs of the worst off even if this interferes with maximal aggregate benefits.

If Singer changed his position to endorse giving priority to satisfying the most significant interests, this would not mean that he endorsed maximin (i.e., always benefiting the worst-off before benefiting those who are already better off). He explicitly rejects maximin on the basis of cases suggested by Derek Parfit,[21] in which we can do much less to help the person who would be the worst off than we can do for someone else. (For example, if we can either help a blind man not lose a finger or help a fingerless person not go deaf, we should do the latter, even if it is worse to be blind and fingerless than to be deaf and fingerless.) I believe that this is correct.[22]

Another aspect of Singer's maximizing consequentialism is that he should accept that even small differences in expected outcome can *always* give us a reason to choose the better outcome. This would account, in part, for his view that if we must ration a scarce life-saving resource, we should give it to an able-bodied candidate rather than to a disabled candidate, since, other things being equal, we produce a better outcome if we save the former. Singer also employs a certain sort of reasoning from behind a veil of ignorance to reach this conclusion.[23] Singer is known for his view that abortion and infanticide of the disabled are permissible, but he is thought to believe that once the disabled are persons (i.e., they attain self-consciousness), their lives should not be ended against their will any more than anyone else's. As his views on the distribution of scarce life-saving resources show, however, this does not mean that he believes that we have as much reason to save the life of a disabled person as a nondisabled one, other things being equal. This conclusion, of course, also depends on his view that it is better for the person himself to be able-bodied than to be disabled, for that is why the outcome in which the nondisabled person lives is better than the one in which the disabled person lives. His evidence for this claim is that it is an uncontroversial assumption behind our ordinary medical policies of trying to prevent or cure disabilities.

I believe that Singer is wrong to think that it is inconsistent with believing that a disability is bad to sometimes ignore disability in a life- and death-rationing choice between a disabled and a nondisabled person. This is because a difference in outcome could be morally relevant *in one context* (for example, giving us a reason to prevent or cure disabilities) but morally irrelevant in another context. I call this the Principle of Irrelevant Goods.[24] Consider the following scenario: One person is on island A, and another person is on island B. They share all of the same properties, except that one just recently lost a hand, and the other did not. We can save the life of either one, but not both. Each will be as badly off as the other if we do not help him (dead). But if we help the person without the hand, we do not produce as good an outcome because it will involve a life without use of two hands and this is not as good as a life with two hands, other things equal. (Call this the Hand Case.) I think it is morally wrong to decide whom to aid on the basis of who will have the additional hand.

The Principle of Irrelevant Goods can account for the right decision. The explanation of the applicability of the principle in the Hand Case is that what both people are capable of achieving (a long, good life) is the part of the outcome about which each reasonably cares most or, put differently, what is reasonably held to be most important for each person can be had by either—a long, good-quality life. Furthermore, we should take seriously from an impartial point of view the fact that each person, from his personal perspective, wants to be the one to survive. Fairness may require, therefore, that we not deprive either of his equal chance for the great good of extended survival just for the sake of doing what results in the better outcome. The benefit of an additional hand is irrelevant in this context, though not in another where we must decide whether to prevent someone losing a hand. This is especially true because the one person in the Hand Case who would have the additional benefit is someone who would already be getting the other great benefit of additional life. That is, it is a case of a greater good being concentrated in one of the two people rather than a case in which the greater good is dispersed over a third person. Here is an example of the latter: We can either (1) save the life of A, who lacks a hand, or (2) save the life of B, who lacks a hand, and also save C (who is under no threat of death) from losing one of his hands. In this case, the fact that we can save one person and also save a hand in another person might give us a reason not to save A. The distinction between these cases is not captured by a theory like Singer's, which is concerned with a total in the outcome rather than with its distribution per se. (Nor is it captured by his view that behind a veil of ignorance each person should think of himself as having an equal chance of being disabled or able-bodied, and then maximize his ex ante expected utility by agreeing to a policy that always helps the able-bodied. An alternative view of the veil of ignorance is that it is a device that forces us to identify with the fates of the actual people who will wind up in different positions in life, rather than a device for imagining that I have a chance of falling into any position, though, of course, I will occupy only one of them. If we are forced to take seriously the fate of each [by, for example, even keeping ourselves ignorant of probabilities of being in any position], then we are more likely to consider that though one can "care more to have" the property of being able-bodied, one may "care about" the life one has as a disabled person just as much as an able-bodied person cares about his life.)

On the basis of the Hand Case, we can see that it is compatible with recognizing that not having a hand makes a life worse (other things being equal) and makes an outcome worse (other things being equal) to think that, relative to the question of whose life we should save, it could be a morally irrelevant consideration. Hence, targeting funds to replace a missing hand because life without it is worse than life with it is not inconsistent with giving equal weight to saving the lives of the disabled and the nondisabled. This is contrary to what Singer's maximizing consequentialism and his use of the veil of ignorance imply.[25]

Notice also that the fact that we ordinarily seek to cure disabilities if we can must be taken by Singer to imply both of the following: (1) the disability per se is a bad thing; and (2) the disability does not bring with it anything else good that outweighs its badness, making the life with it as good or better than the life without the disability, other things being equal. But (2) could be false even if (1) were true, and the question is whether our trying to prevent or cure disabilities is *necessarily* evidence that (2) is true. (Of course [2] might be true even if seeking to prevent or cure disability were not evidence for its truth.) Here is a reason to think it is not necessarily evidence for (2). It is compatible with thinking that life A is better than life B to try to prevent someone from *having* to live A. This is because a better life in the sense of a more meaningful or worthwhile life might be a much harder one to live (e.g., as a mendicant saint). Living such a life might be supererogatory for a person. Hence, unless they consent to it, we should, out of concern for them, try to prevent them having no choice but to live the harder life. If it were for this sort of reason that we tried to prevent or cure disabilities, doing so would be compatible with the life of the disabled being as good as or better than the life of the nondisabled.[26]

Like many other consequentialists, Singer insists on the moral irrelevance at the highest level of moral theory of the distinction between harming and not-aiding per se, and so maximizing may proceed without a side constraint on harming some in order to help others. He also seems to accept the moral equivalence of harming and not aiding per se at the lower level of his normative theory, and so I shall discuss it in the next subsection.

D. The Lower Level of the Normative Theory

The lower level of Singer's two-level normative theory is concerned with the rules or traits of character that will further the impartial goals of morality, even if they do not themselves embody impartiality. The only point I wish to make about Singer's subscription to rules that on occasion do not maximize good consequences is the role that slippery slopes play in their construction. Singer recommends a very general rule against eating non-self-conscious animals, though he believes that it is strictly permissible to raise, kill, and eat them if this does not cause them pain. His recommendation that we not have a more fine-grained rule that permits eating some animals is based on a concern that we may slip into eating nonhuman self-conscious animals, or cause the non-self-conscious but sentient ones pain in raising or killing them. But in the case of euthanasia of persons, he recommends a very fine-grained rule, which allows us to kill some people, rather than a general rule that excludes killing in cases even where it is strictly permissible. He apparently does not fear a slippery slope to other killings in this latter context. What might account for the difference in his willingness to tolerate a fine-grained rule and possible untoward effects in these two contexts? While Singer does not say as much, it is possible that what accounts for the asymmetry is how bad the effects will be if we have a more general rule: Having an overly general rule in the case of not eating animals deprives people mostly of gustatory pleasure, while in the case of euthanasia, a more general rule against killing would prevent people who are in great pain or misery from ending their lives. The cost of each of the general rules is very different.

I. KILLING AND LETTING DIE

Some of the rules and policies that Singer recommends at the lower level seem straightforwardly impartialist, with minimal alteration from what they would be at the higher level. He denies the moral significance of the harming/not-aiding distinction, and consistent with this, he accepts a strong doctrine of negative responsibility whereby we are as responsible for harm we could have prevented as for harm we cause, holding constant all other factors extrinsic to the harming/not-aiding distinction (e.g., motive or the effort required to aid or not harm). When he discusses this issue in detail,[27] he considers the particular distinction between killing and letting die. He claims that we mistakenly think that killing is worse than letting die in itself because of factors extrinsic to killing and letting die, not intrinsic to them. That is, extrinsic factors that commonly accompany killing are different and morally worse than extrinsic factors that commonly accompany letting die. In order to show that it is factors extrinsic to killing and letting die that cause us to think that killing and letting die differ morally in themselves, he first adopts the strategy of taking the factors that are common in killing cases—for example, bad motive—and putting them in letting die cases. This is a way of equalizing killing and letting die cases for all factors aside from killing and letting die. Indeed, that we can take the factors present in killing cases and put them in letting die cases, he seems to think, *shows* that these factors are extrinsic to killing per se.

But this last conclusion is not true, because it is possible to export into a case of letting die a property that is intrinsic to (i.e., essentially true of) killing but not to letting die, and so *necessarily* common to killing cases. It is also possible to export a property that is intrinsic to letting die (but not to killing) into a case of killing. An example of the first is "causing death"; this is essentially true of killing, I believe, but can be true of *some* letting die cases. For example, suppose that A unplugs B from a life support machine that belongs to A and to which B has no right. If B dies of lack of life support, I think that A lets B die, though he (in part) causes his death. An example of the second is "someone losing out on only life he would have had with my help"; this is essentially true of the person whom I let die, but it can be true of the person I kill in *some* killing cases. For example, this will be true if I fatally stab someone to whom I am providing life support and who would not have lived without the support.[28]

Suppose that we export a property intrinsic to killing into a letting die case and it makes the letting die case morally worse, but no property intrinsic to letting die makes a killing case worse when it is exported into a killing case. Then this would be evidence that killing but not letting die has an intrinsic property that can make behavior worse. This, in turn, would be evidence for a moral difference between killing and letting die per se. If letting die has an intrinsic property that, when exported into a killing case, makes the case less bad, but killing has no property that has the same effect when exported into a letting die case, this would also be evidence for an intrinsic moral difference between killing and letting die. (Notice that this is true even though some particular cases of killing and letting die do not differ morally, perhaps because they have had properties intrinsic to the other behavior exported to them.)

In the cases I have described, it seems that the "causing" property of killing, when exported to a letting die case, does not really make the case of letting die morally worse (e.g., when I unplug a life support system). However, the intrinsic property of letting die I have described—namely, "losing out on only life someone would have had with my help"—does sometimes make a killing easier to justify. (For example, fatally stabbing someone to whom I am already providing life support at great cost seems more acceptable than killing someone who is independent of me or even someone who imposes on me to the same degree but does not receive from me life-sustaining aid.) If so, this is evidence for an intrinsic moral difference between killing and letting die.

"Evidence" does not mean conclusive evidence, however, for the fact that an intrinsic property has a significant moral effect when exported does not necessarily mean that it has the significant moral effect on its home ground, that is, the behavior from which it is exported. This is another example of the Principle of Contextual Interaction, which holds that properties may interact differently within different contexts. It is only if the property has the same effect on its home ground as it does when exported to a different behavior that we have secure evidence for an intrinsic moral difference between killing and letting die. I see no reason to believe that the property I have described does not have the same effect on its home ground as when exported. Singer does not consider that some factor intrinsic to letting die can be shown to make it less bad per se than killing per se, in the manner I have described above.

And he believes that he has shown that it is only factors extrinsic to killing that make killing cases worse than letting die cases, because he thinks that equalizing the killing and letting die cases only for these extrinsic factors leads us to make the same judgments about letting die cases as we make about killing cases. I have argued that mere exportability does not show that a property is extrinsic. But I also disagree that we make the same judgments about killing and letting die cases whenever extrinsic factors are equalized. (I will shortly discuss cases bearing on this issue.)

Given all this, the second step in his strategy[29] is to consider whether factors that are typical in letting die cases but extrinsic to letting die—these factors are just the reverse of the extrinsic factors typical of killing cases—not only *explain* our differing reactions to typical killing and letting die cases, but also *justify* them. Singer's claim is that these extrinsic factors do not justify our differing reactions.

To show this, he takes extrinsic factors commonly found in letting die cases and adds them to killing cases. He claims that his aim is to show that such factors do *not* make the killing morally acceptable. But, he concludes, if there is no intrinsic difference between killing and letting die, they should not make letting die acceptable either. For example, that we are ignorant of who the victim of our not-aiding will be—typical of many but not necessarily all letting die cases—should not help make letting die permissible if our *not* knowing whom we will kill does not make killing permissible. But notice that we could invert this strategy, that is, we may show that there *is* an intrinsic moral difference between killing and letting die by showing that extrinsic factors that make letting die permissible do *not* make killing permissible. (This would show that equalizing killing and letting die cases for extrinsic factors does not necessarily lead us to make the same moral judgments about the cases.)[30]

Singer himself gives us an example of this inversion. He discusses the extrinsic factor of great effort and how burdensome it typically would be to aid many people. We would, given his line of reasoning thus far, expect him to argue for the *im*permissibility of letting die, by seeing whether the argument from burdensomeness would affect permissibility when killing is in question. For presumably, that we had to make a great effort to avoid killing someone would *not* defeat the duty not to kill. For example, suppose that if I drive down road A, I will run over someone stuck in the road. I have a duty to take road B, even if it is dangerous and will cause damage to my car. This would imply, if killing were not intrinsically morally different from letting die, that comparable burdensomeness should *not* defeat a duty to save life. It is striking that Singer does not inquire into whether the argument from burdensomeness defeats a duty not to kill. Instead, he merely accepts that we cannot require "moral heroism" from people when it comes to aiding.[31] But if we can require someone to suffer a lot rather than kill an innocent bystander (i.e., it is not moral heroism to do so), and not require this of him to aid an innocent bystander (whom he has not already harmed), this suggests that there *is* a moral difference between killing and letting die per se.

An additional example that is commonly used to support the thesis that there is a per se difference between killing and letting die holds all extrinsic factors equal:

(a) I must rush five dying people to the hospital to save them. To get there on time, I must speed over a road where I know one person is stuck, thereby killing him. This is impermissible.

(b) I must rush five dying people to the hospital to save them. To get there on time, I must speed past someone drowning in a pond, thereby allowing him to die. This is permissible.[32]

In this set of cases, the extrinsic factor is our goal on a particular occasion, and a goal that makes letting die permissible does not make killing permissible.

Of course, that the distinction between killing and letting die sometimes makes a moral difference does not mean that it always does. But to rebut the general thesis that there is no intrinsic difference between killing and letting die per se, we need present only *one* case where the moral difference between the two shows up. By contrast, to support the thesis, it is not sufficient to present one case where the difference does not matter morally. Singer typically presents one striking case where some distinction that nonconsequentialists emphasize does not seem to make a moral difference, and then he concludes, without considering many other cases, that the distinction is not morally significant per se.[33]

Suppose that cases exist in which our intuitive judgments support a moral distinction between killing and letting die. What could explain such a moral distinction? *Why* do some essential properties of letting die have different moral significance than those of killing? One possibility is that persons are entitled to certain things that are both related to their identity as separate persons and that they have independently of our help, for example, their bodies (when they are not dependent on our providing them with life support). They are entitled to these things even if they do not, in any deep sense, deserve to have the body they have. If this were so, then if we harm them and thereby cause them to lose these things that they have independently of our help, this would be an encroachment on their entitlements. However, if we do not aid someone, she loses out on only what she would have had with our help (rather than what she would have had independently of us). Further, our help may be something to which she is not entitled because such an entitlement would conflict with our entitlement to personal resources that are connected to what makes us a separate person.[34]

I conclude that Singer's arguments to show that there is no intrinsic moral difference between killing and letting die do not succeed.

2. PRINCIPLES GOVERNING AID

Independent of whether there is a per se moral difference between harming and not-aiding, Singer suggests two principles that might govern providing aid:[35] (1) unless something of *comparable* moral significance is at stake, we should help to relieve suffering; or (2) unless something of moral significance is at stake, we should help to relieve suffering. Both of these principles focus on reducing suffering rather than promoting the good. The first principle is more stringent in favor of aiding than is the second, and it is the one Singer favors.

Sometimes Singer fails to distinguish the first principle from the second. For example, while defending the first principle, he argues that it does not require one to give up family relations, because most people find such relations necessary for a flourishing life, and to give them up would be to sacrifice something of great moral significance: "Hence, no such sacrifice is required by the principle for which I am here arguing."[36] But the principle for which he is arguing says that we need not sacrifice anything of "*comparable* moral significance," and something that is very significant in the life of a person is not necessarily of *comparable* significance to the loss of many lives, which his sacrifice might prevent.

Let us examine the two principles in greater depth. First, consider how they overlap. They both are supposed to yield strict duties to aid, that is, something that it is wrong not to do and is not merely a matter of supererogatory generosity. They apply independently of whether those who aid and those to be aided belong to different societies, regardless of the distance between them, and regardless of whether there are other people who should also be aiding but do not. They also both imply that what one has a duty to do is not merely what would be fair for one to be required to do if others also fulfilled their duty to aid. Presumably, Singer believes that even if we are treated unfairly by other potential aiders who renege on their duties, thereby requiring us to do more than our fair share, the unfairness to us is less important than the bad consequences to others if we do not aid.

Notice, however, that even if we agreed with these claims, it would still be possible to argue that before we do more than our fair share, we have a right to *force* those who would renege on their duties to aid to provide aid as well. Furthermore, if we are treated unfairly *by those who need our help*, perhaps their unfairness to us does override their need for aid. This may be one argument—though not the one Singer gives—to support his suggestion that we should deny aid to those who do not use birth control or appropriate farming techniques and thereby bring on their problems of overpopulation and famine. However, this unfairness argument could not be used to deny aid to the children of those who have acted unfairly. Given the importance of saving the children's lives and also the importance of our not-aiding those who treat us unfairly, it would seem that we should *force* the unfair parents to change their behavior as we provide aid to the children. Oddly, given his dismissal of the harming/not-aiding distinction, even at the lower level of the normative theory, Singer is at pains to argue (independently of considering consequences) that he would not *coerce* those needy people who are responsible for causing their own plight into improving it.[37] (Perhaps, he means that he would neither harm nor not aid them in order to coerce a positive change in their behavior.) However, if they do not change their bad behavior, we are at liberty, he says, not to aid them because (and only because) our aid would do no good. This means that he thinks we may let them die, even if our coercion would have a better outcome (cause them to live). It is hard to see how this is justifiable from a consequentialist perspective that is concerned with satisfying interests.

Now consider in greater detail how Singer's two principles of providing aid differ. What the less stringent principle implies depends on what is of moral significance. It seems to imply that if a promise is of moral significance, then we need not break a minor promise in order to relieve much suffering. But this is not true. Further, suppose that consumerism is necessary in order to create the wealth needed to save people from starvation, but consumerism itself has negative moral significance (as Singer suggests when he says that "consumer society has had a distorting effect on the goals and purposes of its members").[38] Then the second principle implies that we ought not create the great wealth needed to save people from starvation if the only way to create it is to foster consumerism. This seems to be at least a debatable issue.

Singer thinks that the more stringent principle implies that one must bring oneself and one's family down to a level such that if one did any more in order to aid, one would be worse off than those whom one is trying to help.[39] But this does not seem to be the correct limit, for it calls for something like a pairwise comparison of myself and any given individual I might help, to see if anyone I might help is worse off than I would be if I helped him. But Singer supports aggregation, not pairwise comparison, and it is possible that making oneself and the few people in one's family *worse off* as individuals than those whom one is trying to help might still prevent great suffering in each of many individuals and might prevent more suffering in *aggregate* when we total even minor losses in the many people whom our sacrifice helps. (This is especially likely to be true, given the relative costs to feed people in different countries; the money that comes from my depriving myself of food even if I let myself starve can be used to buy meals for hundreds of people in Africa.) For example, I think that, considered impartially, the death of me and my family at a young age is not of comparable moral significance to the avoidable deaths of thousands of others at even a slightly greater age. Further, remember that Singer believes that there is no per se moral difference between killing and letting die (or between intending death as a means and foreseeing death as a side effect). Then I should be required to do what will foreseeably kill me and a few others in order to save many lives and also to intentionally kill myself and a few others in order to save many lives. Hence, Singer's stringent principle, especially when combined with a commitment to aggregation of equal and even lesser losses, demands more than he says it does. Singer does not explicitly draw these conclusions, but Peter Unger, who considers himself a follower of Singer, draws some of them.[40]

If the more stringent principle requires such great sacrifice, it would certainly require that someone sacrifice his arm in order to save lives, because the loss of an arm is not of comparable moral significance to the loss of lives. If I believe that I am not morally required to sacrifice my arm in order to save lives, it is not because I believe that someone's arm not being lost is of comparable moral importance to eliminating much suffering or to the continued survival of many people.[41] The evidence for this is that I agree that if a third party has to choose between saving my arm or saving other people's lives, it is perfectly understandable that he should save their lives rather than my arm. If I do not believe that loss of my arm is of comparable moral significance to the loss of lives, yet I believe that I am not required to sacrifice my arm to save lives, must I reject Singer's more stringent principle?

One way to avoid an affirmative answer to this question is to argue that people's having the negative right to lead their own lives, so that they are not mere devices for reducing overall suffering and death (unless they choose to be), is of greater moral significance than saving a greater number of lives.[42] If it were morally required of people to make large sacrifices in order to prevent all sorts of suffering and death, or permissible for them to be sacrificed by others to that end, their status as beings with a certain type of personal independence and inviolability would be lost. It is the loss of this status, rather than the loss of an arm, that may have greater moral significance than the saving of many lives. Importantly, this status is not lost if it is permissible to save many from dying of starvation rather than prevent the violation of someone else's negative right for the purpose of reducing suffering. Neither is the status lost if it is impermissible for me to sacrifice your arm to prevent many other people's arms from being taken from them in order to promote the greater good. This is because even if many people lose their arms and are thus treated impermissibly, their status as people who have a right not to have their arms taken is not lost unless it is *permissible* to take their arms. Morality does not endorse the permissibility of taking people's arms if it allows them to be abused in this way rather than endorse the abuse of someone else to save them. Hence, the greater moral significance of having the status of a being with a right to lead its own life does not imply that we should prevent actions that are disrespectful of this status rather than save many lives or that it is a worse state of affairs when someone is improperly killed to save others than when many more die of starvation. But morality would endorse abuse if it were permissible to take the arm of one person in order to save the arms of others. (The status of independence is also lost if it is required of you to give your arm in order to save lives, though no one may take it from you.) Some may find this view about the importance of a certain sort of status of the person attractive, though Singer would not.[43] It offers a way of retaining even Singer's more stringent principle, in the face of possible counter examples, by identifying a status the retention of which is of greater moral significance than the saving of lives.

A methodological note is necessary. I have argued against Singer's stronger principle by considering its implications for particular cases, such as whether I have a duty to give my arm in order to save people in Africa from famine. Our intuitive response to this case may be that I do not have such a duty. Singer seems to believe that even if we have this negative intuitive response, and a positive response to the case is implied by principle (1), this does not defeat the principle. He says, "[T]he way people do in fact judge has nothing to do with the validity of my conclusion [that we must give away a great deal to famine relief]. My conclusion follows from the principle . . . and unless that principle is rejected, or the arguments shown to be unsound, I think the conclusion must stand, however strange it appears."[44] This suggests, at least, that Singer does not think that a moral principle that seems plausible on its face (or follows from plausible higher-order principles) could be defeated by our intuitive judgments about cases. Hence, a conflict between intuitions and principles may just remain, and the intuitions will remain unjustified. Perhaps he thinks that an error theory can be provided to account for such intuitions.

I disagree with Singer on methodology. First, he also relies on some intuitive judgments—those about the plausibility of general principles, such as "maximize the good." I think that our intuitions about general principles must be tested against our intuitions about the implications of general principles for cases. Second, we have seen that Singer himself relies on intuitions in cases in his attempt to defeat the principle that there is a moral difference between killing and letting die, so his methodological position does not seem consistent. Third, I do not think that our intuitions about cases are less reliable than those about principles. This is, in part, because we do not have a reliable grasp of a principle itself without considering its implications.[45] In particular, I think that one argument that Singer has given for not relying on intuitions in cases can be shown to be wrong.[46]

He believes that our judgments about when we may not kill are a function of our evolutionary history. In earlier times relevant to our evolution, we could only kill people by attacking them personally, not at long distances with mechanical means. Psychological studies of our intuitions show,[47] he thinks, that we intuitively think it wrong to kill in the first way but permissible to kill in the second way. This is how he explains the intuitive judgments that we may not push someone in front of a trolley headed toward killing five people in order to stop it but we may push a button that will redirect the trolley away from the five even though the trolley will then kill one other person.[48] If our intuitive judgments just reflect our early evolutionary history, they do not reveal anything about moral truth and should not be used to test or develop theories.

I do not think that Singer's evolutionary explanation of these different Trolley Case intuitions is correct. For it implies that we would also intuitively think it permissible to push a button that directs a piece of machinery toward one person, in order to push him in front of a trolley headed toward killing five people, thereby stopping it. But, intuitively, I think it is just as impermissible to do this (at long distance and by mechanical means) as it is to push someone into the trolley. As Singer describes it, the evolutionary explanation could not account for this intuition of impermissibility because the case involves the use of machinery. In addition, one can imagine a case in which it is intuitively permissible to push someone into a trolley without mechanical means in order to stop the trolley from hitting the five. The five people are attached to one of my arms and the trolley is coming at them. To my other arm is attached another person. If I rotate myself, I get the five out of the way of the trolley, but the other person is thereby placed in the way of the trolley. Doing this seems as intuitively permissible as redirecting the trolley away from the five. Hence cases where I personally push someone in are not always thought to be impermissible.

I believe that intuitive judgments can serve to build a theory and reveal new principles that underlie them. That is, these intuitions about cases should not float freely in a purely negative role if they are to justify our rejection of a certain principle. Rather, they are the basis for uncovering other, correct principles which are to be further justified by consideration of the principles themselves and the morally significant ideas that underlie them.[49] In the next chapter, we shall consider in more detail the reliability of intuitive judgments.

NOTES

1. Not exclusively so, however. For example, I have examined some alternative views on deontological constraints in chapter 3, on instrumental rationality in chapter 4, and on rights in

chapter 8. In addition, I have examined Peter Unger's consequentialist position (which, I think, is implied by Singer's) in chapter 6, and in chapters 11 and 12, I considered Singer's and Unger's view that distance should not make a moral difference to our duty to aid.

2. My discussion of his theory and views on practical issues is largely based on Peter Singer, "Famine, Affluence, and Morality" (henceforth FAM), reprinted in *World Hunger and Moral Obligation*, ed. W. Aiken and H. LaFollette, pp. 22–36 (Englewood Cliffs, NJ: Prentice-Hall, 1977); and Peter Singer, *Practical Ethics*, 2d ed. (henceforth *PE*) (New York: Cambridge University Press, 1993). This chapter is a revised version of part of my "Faminine Ethics: Peter Singer's Ethical Theory," in *Singer and His Critics*, ed. D. Jamieson, 162–208 (Oxford: Blackwell, 1999). Other parts of that article formed the basis for discussion of Singer in chapters 11 and 12.

3. See R. M. Hare, *Moral Thinking* (New York: Oxford University Press, 1981).

4. We might consider this to be a form of what Derek Parfit describes as "rational irrationality" when he endorses similar character traits. See Derek Parfit, *Reasons and Persons* (New York: Oxford University Press, 1984), part 1.

5. Discussed in the final chapter of Singer, *PE*.

6. He does not discuss the claim that morality is a system that it is rational for each agent to want all agents to follow. He merely focuses on the question "Why should *I* be moral?"—the question that a free-rider on the moral behavior of others might ask.

7. Singer, *PE*, p. 328. It is possible that his view is that *rational* preferences include the preference for a meaningful life.

8. Singer, *PE*, p. 334.

9. See Samuel Scheffler, *The Rejection of Consequentialism* (New York: Oxford University Press, 1982).

10. See Thomas Nagel, *The View from Nowhere* (New York: Oxford University Press, 1986).

11. See her "Moral Saints," *Journal of Philosophy* 79 (1982): 419–39.

12. To illustrate this, consider the following hypothetical case: Suppose that different committees have been established to consider a policy, with each committee representing a different point of view, such as economic, aesthetic, etc. Now suppose that we have time to listen to the report of only one committee. Which committee should we choose? One suggestion is that we should choose the committee that is such that if we run afoul of its advice, we will have gone wrong in the most serious way. This is a maximin policy: Avoid the worst possible outcome by adopting the policy with the best worst-case scenario. While an error in the aesthetic area could be more serious than an error in the moral area, the worst possible error can *only* occur in the moral area. That is, the worst possible aesthetic error cannot be as serious as the worst possible moral error. So maximin tells us to consider the moral committee's advice. (But is trying to avoid the worst state of affairs a policy that is biased in favor of morality? It is possible that the best state of affairs requires aesthetic greatness, though it also involves avoiding great moral wrongs. Is it rational to risk the worst [great moral wrong] for the sake of ensuring the *possibility* of the best?) That the moral category bears this relation to other categories can be seen after we make a choice about what to do, even if we are not conscious of weighing categories when we ordinarily decide what to do (as Joseph Raz claims in "The Central Conflict: Morality and Self-Interest," presented at the Colloquium in Law, Philosophy, and Social Theory, New York University Law School, October 17, 1996, p. 9). That is, on reflection, we can consider how we judge the weightiness of factors from different categories in various cases. For example, we notice that a consideration that is slightly important from the aesthetic point of view is trumped by a factor that is even less important from the moral point of view. In this way, we learn that being a *moral* factor counts for more. Therefore, while Raz may be correct to say that, in deciding on conduct, we consider factors as reasons independently of their categories, it

would be incorrect to conclude from this either that there are no categories of reasons that vary in weightiness or that reasons do not have extra weight simply because of the category to which they belong (that is, because of a property they share with other reasons in their category).

13. For example, Thomas Nagel, given his view in *The View from Nowhere*, would agree. Scheffler, however, does not commit himself to the dominance of the moral point of view even when it incorporates the personal perspective at a basic level. See Samuel Scheffler, *Human Morality* (New York: Oxford University Press, 1993), and my discussion of that book in "Rationality and Morality: A Discussion of Samuel Scheffler's *Human Morality*," *NOUS* 29 (1995): 544–55.

14. In chapter 9 of Singer, *PE*, "Insiders and Outsiders," pp. 261–62.

15. Obviously, the lack of interest does not merely mean that they are not interested in living on, it means it is not bad for them not to live on.

16. See his *What We Owe to Each Other* (Cambridge, MA: Harvard University Press, 1998), and chapter 7 in this volume, where I discuss his view on this issue.

17. See Parfit, *Reasons and Persons*.

18. See, especially, Singer, *PE*, pp. 14 and 37.

19. Singer, *PE*, pp. 22 and 23. The way he interprets his principles governing aid also suggest that he is concerned with satisfying the most important interests first. See section D (2) below for discussion of this.

20. In his response to an earlier version of this chapter in D. Jamieson, ed., *Singer and His Critics*.

21. See Derek Parfit, "Innumerate Ethics," *Philosophy & Public Affairs* 7 (1978): 285–301.

22. For my discussion of this issue, see my *Morality, Mortality*, vol. 1 (New York: Oxford University Press, 1993).

23. See his "Shopping at the Genetic Supermarket," available on-line at http://utilitarian .net/singer/by/2002....02.htm and his "Double Jeopardy and the Use of QALYs in Health Care Allocation," reprinted in *Unsanctifying Human Life* ed. H. Kuhse (Oxford: Blackwell, 2002).

24. I discussed this principle in detail as part of a nonconsequentialist theory of distribution in *Morality, Mortality*, vol. 1. See also chapters 1 and 2, this volume.

25. For more on the disabled and the Principle of Irrelevant Goods, see my "Deciding Whom to Help, Health-Adjusted Life Years, and Disabilities" in *Public Health, Ethics, and Equity*, eds. S. Anand, F. Peter, A. Sen, pp. 225–242 (Oxford: Oxford University Press, 2004). There I further argue that *how* a difference in outcome comes about in a given context can also make a difference as to whether the difference is morally relevant. This also conflicts with Singer's views, I believe.

26. I discuss this further in "Disability, Discrimination and Irrelevant goods" (unpublished).

27. His detailed discussion of this issue is in *PE*, pp. 224 ff. My detailed discussion of this issue is in my *Morality, Mortality*, vol. 2 (New York: Oxford University Press, 1996), chaps. 1–4. Some of the points I make there and will make here are also made in chapter 1, this volume. My discussion of Singer's methodology in using contrasting cases to show that distance does not matter morally to aiding is in chapter 11.

28. Singer himself presents a case that involves exporting into a letting-die case a property which is a cousin of one that is essentially true of a killing: "Finally, it may well be that the doctor is personally responsible for the death of the infant she decides not to operate upon, since she may know that if she had not taken this case, other doctors in the hospital would have operated" (*PE*, p. 225). Here, a doctor, in taking a case, makes it impossible for another to

provide life-saving aid that he would otherwise have provided. Killing essentially involves making it impossible for another to provide life-saving aid.

29. Starting in Singer, *PE*, p. 215.

30. I discuss this strategy in detail in *Morality, Mortality*, vol. 2, chap. 4, and briefly in chapter 1, this volume.

31. Singer, *PE*, p. 228.

32. For possible problems with this example, see chapter 5.

33. This is true of James Rachels as well. See his "Passive and Active Euthanasia," *New England Journal of Medicine* 292 (1975): 78–80, and contrast its use of cases with the use of cases by Philippa Foot in her "Euthanasia," *Philosophy & Public Affairs* 6 (1977): 85–112.

34. Another possible rationale for the harming/not-aiding difference does not assert that people are entitled to certain things they have which are intimately related to their identities as separate persons. It only claims that other people are *not* entitled to these things.

35. Singer, FAM, p. 24. In *PE*, pp. 230–31, he only presents the first principle.

36. Singer, *PE*, p. 245.

37. Singer, FAM, p. 35.

38. Ibid., p. 32.

39. Singer, *PE*, p. 26.

40. See Peter Unger, *Living High and Letting Die* (New York: Oxford University Press, 1996). Unger does not seem willing to aggregate small losses to many to override great losses to a few, however. I discussed Unger's views on these matters in detail in chapter 6. Because I think Singer should also draw at least these conclusions from his more stringent principle, chapter 6 should be considered a criticism of some implications of Singer's theory.

41. However, I may believe that someone's arm not being lost is of comparable importance to the creation of many *new* lives.

42. It might be said that if they choose to be devices for reducing overall suffering and death, they still cannot turn themselves into mere devices, for their having the authority to choose whether to be devices implies they are not mere devices. While I sympathize with the thought behind this view, I think it is possible to distinguish what one is at the time one makes the choice from what one turns oneself into by the choice, and the latter could be a mere device.

43. I argue for such a view of the status of inviolability in my *Morality, Mortality*, vol. 2, chap. 10; and in chapters 1 and 8, this volume.

44. Singer, FAM, p. 28.

45. I have argued in chapter 6 against Peter Unger's attempt to show that intuitions about cases are inconsistent and undependable. I will examine Daniel Kahneman's work in so far as it bears on dependability of intuitive judgments in the next chapter.

46. In his "Intuitions and Ethical Theory," presented at the James Rachels Memorial Conference, University of Alabama, Birmingham, September 26, 2004.

47. In the work of Joshua Greenberg.

48. As discussed in chapter 5.

49. This is the route I followed in chapter 5.

14

MORAL INTUITIONS, COGNITIVE PSYCHOLOGY, AND THE HARMING/ NOT-AIDING DISTINCTION

I. INTRODUCTION

In previous chapters, I have made liberal use of intuitive judgments about cases and principles. I have also discussed the difference of opinion between some non-consequentialists and some consequentialists (such as Peter Unger and Peter Singer) about the use of such judgments. Are the methods and results of cognitive psychology relevant to the questions these philosophers ask about the form and validity of a moral theory and the methods used in doing moral philosophy? In this chapter, I shall examine aspects of this very large question by considering some of the methods and results of psychologists Daniel Kahneman and Amos Tversky, especially in connection with their development of Prospect Theory.

This chapter has four main sections. In section II, I shall present certain claims made by Kahneman based on his and Tversky's work.[1] His claims concern moral theory, the use of intuitions, and the identification of the bearers of utility. I shall discuss how a philosopher might respond to some of these claims (saving responses to the remaining claims until other sections below). I shall also explain how I conceive of the critique of moral theory that can be derived from Kahneman and Tversky's views. In section III, I shall deal in more detail with the theory of gains and losses in Kahneman and Tversky's work and its relation to the supposed moral contrast between harming and not-aiding that has been discussed in earlier chapters. In section IV, I shall consider what a moral theory based on the loss/no-gain distinction of Prospect Theory might look like. I shall conclude in section V by considering some attempts to preserve the reasonableness of intuitions collected in experimental tests.

II. KAHNEMAN AND TVERSKY'S VIEW AND SOME RESPONSES TO IT

Kahneman claims that most contemporary moral theory (with the notable exception of work by Robert Nozick) aims to describe *end states* (ideal or not); for example, it aims to describe what is a good distribution of burdens and benefits, without considering the changes—that is, losses to some or gains to others—that would bring about this end state. In contrast, it is an essential claim of Prospect Theory that people do not behave as if utility were a function of end states per se but of changes, that is, of new states relative to prior states. Experimental data suggest that people behave as if the utility of a state is higher if it represents a gain and lower if the same state represents a loss. These data also show that people are more averse to a loss than they are pleased by a gain, so a *no-gain* that leaves them in a certain end state is considered less bad than a loss that leaves them in the same end state. Let me expand on this a bit.

Prospect Theory is a behavioral decision theory, that is, it tries to explain how people actually make decisions. It asserts that (1) people tend to be risk averse with respect to achieving gains from what they identify as the status quo, (2) people tend to be risk preferring with respect to preventing threatened losses from what they identify as the status quo, and (3) people are more averse to prospective losses than they are positively attracted by prospective gains (which explains [1] and [2]). In connection with these three points, Kahneman claims that philosophers' use of their intuitions, independent of examining experimental data that show (1)–(3), would lead them to continue to represent consequences in terms of end states rather than considering the changes that lead to the end states.

How could philosophers respond to these points? Deontologists or non-consequentialists have always been concerned with *how* end states come about, for example, one such concern is whether the acts (or omissions) necessary to achieve even a fair end state are right. They argue that we may not be permitted to do certain acts (e.g., harming people), even though these acts lead to the best end state. Such theorists point to a moral distinction between harming and not-aiding, whereby it can sometimes be permissible, for example, to refuse to aid with the consequence that a person dies, but impermissible in a comparable case to actively harm with the consequence that someone dies. Furthermore, moral theorists who emphasize the harming/not-aiding distinction in how end states come about came to make such a distinction not by experimental data, but by relying on their own intuitions. For example, Philippa Foot, relying on her own intuitions, argues for the moral importance of a harming/not-aiding distinction.[2] Philosophers may not, however, have developed this distinction, as Kahneman does, by conceiving of the *consequences* so that they include how an end state comes about (i.e., assigning utility to changes up or down). They may be correct in not doing so, as we shall see.

The role of these nonconsequentialist philosophers can be obscured by having in mind—as Kahneman does—the work of John Rawls, whose views on just economic distribution might rightly be said to ignore such distinctions as whether a fair economic distribution comes about by causing a loss or not producing a gain.[3] Even Rawls, however, says that each person has an inviolability recognized by justice, so that we may not sacrifice one person in order to improve the condition of another. What weakens this statement as a response to Kahneman's concern for the difference between end states that come about by losses or no-gains is Rawls's view that one way to sacrifice someone for the sake of another is to fail to improve his condition when he is worse off, even though helping him causes the condition of someone better off to decline. Rawls's view that we should not allow A to become worse off than B just so that B may be made even better off than he already is does not exclude making B worse off so that A, who is worse off than B, is improved.

Does Kahneman's concern, as so far described, involve anything more than an apparent criticism of traditional consequentialist or other end-state theories?[4] I think that it does. A theory that describes people's intuitions as employing the loss/no-gain distinction could be presented as an alternative to, or an explanation of, a theory that describes people's intuitions as expressing the distinction between *harming* and *not-aiding*.[5] Focusing on the loss/no-gain distinction might be thought to replace the harming/not-aiding distinction as a fundamental account of people's intuitions. Furthermore, since the theory that uses the harming/not-aiding distinction can be connected with a theory that says people ascribe greater stringency to negative rights (not to be harmed) than to positive rights (to be aided), people's view on rights may be thought to be ultimately explicable as the response to a distinction between losses and no-gains. Negative rights will be thought to be more stringent because people are more averse to losses.

If this transformation were possible, then we might take the next step and try to undermine the normative correctness of theories that emphasize the distinction between negative and positive rights by undermining the worth of the intuitive judgments that support the loss/no-gain distinction. If these intuitions are unreliable, they cannot support the correctness of a nonconsequentialist normative theory. And indeed, it is an important element of Prospect Theory to argue that by framing a case in one way rather than another—that is, by manipulating factors that should be irrelevant—we can induce people to see the same facts as either a no-gain or a loss. In particular, the frame does this by leading people to alter the baseline in the case, so that what would have been a no-gain relative to one baseline will be a loss relative to another. Arbitrary framing affects what people identify as the status quo baseline for the purpose of determining what counts as a loss and what counts as a no-gain. Because of their susceptibility to framing effects, people will choose inconsistently in the sense of making different and opposed choices in decision problems that are essentially identical and differ only in trivial variations in their characterization that are not morally relevant.

For example, experimental subjects give different responses about the necessity of a health-care policy to deal with a coming Asian flu, depending on whether we say either that (a) without the policy, 400 of 600 people will lose their lives, or

(b) without the policy, we can only save 200 of 600 people. In description (a), the baseline suggested by the phrasing is a state in which people are now well but face getting worse; the baseline suggested by the phrasing in description (b) is the near-death state people will be in if there is no intervention, but from which there can be improvement. Subjects think that it is worse if people lose their lives than if they do not gain them, and they are more averse to a policy in which people lose their lives than one in which the same number are not saved.[6] Hence they would prefer the policy in (a) to having it in (b), though it is the same situation described differently.

If judgments of fairness/unfairness, permissibility/impermissibility, or lesser/greater worth depend on the perception of no-gains or losses, and if framing affects these perceptions, then the judgments cannot really be of great moral significance. This can suggest—surprisingly, given where we began—that moral theories that ignore change and focus on end states are really the most sensible ones. This means a return to traditional consequentialism and other end-state theories. And indeed, while Kahneman at first seems like a critic of a normative end-state theory (like traditional consequentialism), the sense one ultimately gets of his view is that actual people's intuitions about losses and no-gains lead them astray and are thus not a sensible basis on which to construct a moral theory.

The points I have been making can be used to support claims that might be made on the basis of Kahneman and Tversky's work. The claims can be summarized as follows:

1. In moral theory, the significance of the harming/not-aiding distinction is supported largely by appeal to people's intuitive responses to cases.
2. Prospect Theory indicates that people's intuitions about cases may be better explained as resting on a loss/no-gain distinction than on a harming/not-aiding distinction.
3. To the extent that people's intuitions about cases are explained as Prospect Theory suggests, the intuitive support for the normative significance of the harming/not-aiding distinction per se is reduced.
4. The loss/no-gain distinction that is claimed to explain people's responses to cases is normatively confused and does not make normatively good sense, as people actually deploy it.
5. So, nonconsequentialist moral theory is undermined in two ways: Its core harming/not-aiding distinction is an idle wheel that does not explain people's actual moral judgments about cases, and the distinction to which people actually appeal in reaching nonconsequentialist conclusions about what is fair or morally right is confused.
6. By helping to raise doubts about the nonconsequentialist enterprise without raising any comparable doubts about consequentialism, Kahneman and Tversky's work indirectly supports normative consequentialism.

The problem raised by framing is part of Prospect Theory's more general critique of the use of intuitive judgments of cases. Many moral theorists have relied on intuitions in both building up and challenging theories. Kahneman directs certain warnings to those who do this. He notes that intuitions (which he says assign "weights") may not accord with rules that we find morally plausible.[7] For example, Kahneman presents a set of cases, each of which was presented to a separate group of subjects. In one case, a person gets robbed at a grocery store that he has frequented many times before, while in the other case, a person gets robbed at a grocery store he goes to for the first time because his regular store is closed (Grocery Store Case). Subjects who hear the second story award higher compensation to the victim than do those who hear the first story. However, when subjects are allowed to consider the two cases together, they reject the principle of differential treatment. The assumption is that when subjects consider several cases, they consider whether a general guide to conduct (i.e., a rule) that gives weight to certain differentiating characteristics could be right. Kahneman distinguishes between gathering intuitions about different cases *inter*personally versus *intra*personally: Intuitions that do not accord with plausible principles arise interpersonally when we get intuitions from different subjects on one case at a time and when no individual subject (intrapersonally) reflects on the two cases together. Furthermore, he warns us that when intuitions do accord with morally plausible principles, it need not be any representation of these principles that gives rise to the intuitions.

What might philosophers say about these methodological points? With respect to Kahneman's first concern—intuitions being inconsistent with plausible principles—some philosophers claim to use the method of *reflective equilibrium*, which allows them to reject certain intuitions about cases on the ground that these intuitions are not in equilibrium with principles that are supported by other intuitions or arguments. Indeed, it may be inappropriate to call a judgment about a case a moral intuition if it has not first been reflected upon. For example, run *inter*personally, a case with a black victim may yield lower compensation than a case with a white victim. This does not mean that some subjects had a moral intuition that being black affects how much money one deserves and then, when presented with both cases, realized that the intuition does not accord with a moral principle. Rather, the subjects did not have a moral intuition at all; they had a prejudice. We should also consider the possibility that when subjects are presented with one case, they are (appropriately) doing something different from what they do when presented with two cases together. If this is so, the intuitions had in a single case would not necessarily be in conflict with a rule that governs the treatment of both cases.[8]

Furthermore, philosophers use *intra*personal, not *inter*personal, testing of cases, so the errors resulting from the latter need not threaten their results. That is, a philosopher relies on her own intuitions. This is primarily because she is not only data collecting but data analyzing. It can be much more valuable to have one person's intuitions in combination with an analysis of what moral concepts underlie them than to collect the intuitive judgments of many people. When the philosopher begins this process, she typically begins with one case and then automatically considers whether she would have the same response in another case in which certain factors are modified from the original. The basic requirement of moral rationality, namely, that we universalize the maxims of our conduct, itself embodies the requirement that one person consider many cases in which an act would be performed and not just one. (However, the fact that philosophers often do not respond to one case without thinking of another, and especially the possibility that their considering several cases together might yield different intuitive judgments than considering each case in isolation, may threaten an assumption about the purity of a philosopher's intuitions. While the intuitions would not necessarily be generated by a prior conscious commitment to a theory, they may be impure because they are the result of a coherentist frame of mind [i.e., one that tries to make intuitions hold up as a sensible whole]. This is a problem worth thinking about.) On the other hand, one person, considering intuitions in multiple cases, can be led not to alter or discard any intuition but rather to alter or discard a principle he had thought underlay an intuition.

Kahneman's second concern—that intuitions could accord with but not be caused by consideration of principles—seems to focus on the psychological unreality of the correct principles as generative of moral intuitions. Some philosophers may be attracted to the idea of the psychological reality of deep moral principles that generate intuitions, principles of which we are not ordinarily aware and which can be unearthed and brought to consciousness. But philosophers need not insist that the correct principles are psychologically real. Heuristic shorthands may be part of human psychology without normative theory being adversely affected. The bigger problem is whether the intuitions are inconsistent with a plausible moral theory.

III. THE THEORY OF GAINS AND LOSSES IN RELATION TO THE HARMING/NOT-AIDING DISTINCTION

1. Having pointed to several issues that arise in the relation between Prospect Theory and moral theory, I now wish to focus on the relation between a theory that holds that the loss/no-gain distinction is important to people and a theory that holds that the harming/not-aiding distinction is both normatively important and important to people. I will begin by reconsidering the methodology used by philosophers who have discussed the harming/not-aiding distinction. Given the merits of at least one aspect of this methodology, namely the technique of *equalizing cases*, I shall consider whether the data that supposedly support Prospect Theory are derived from such equalized cases. I will suggest that the cases presented by Kahneman and Tversky to experimental subjects are not always well crafted, so the data do not accurately show what the subjects think. I shall then contrast the loss/no-gain and harming/not-aiding distinctions and suggest some responses to the six claims described above as possible implications of Kahneman and Tversky's work. I will argue that the harming/not-aiding distinction should not be collapsed into the loss/no-gain distinction. The importance of the harming/not-aiding, rather than the loss/no-gain, distinction may actually be supported by Kahneman and Tversky's own data. In addition, the harming/not-aiding distinction is not subject to the same framing effects as the loss/no-gain distinction is, and so susceptibility to these framing effects cannot be held against it as a basis for a nonconsequentialist theory. However, there are reasons to think that in order to arrive at morally satisfactory judgments about

a wide range of cases, we must engage in subtle refinements of the basic harming/ not-aiding distinction.

As we have seen in earlier chapters, what some philosophers who argue for a moral distinction between harming and not-aiding have done is construct cases that are alike in all respects other than that one is a case of harming and the other a case of not-aiding. It is only if all other factors are equal that we can be sure that people's responses to cases speak to the question of whether harming and not-aiding per se make a moral difference. It can be very difficult to construct equalized cases, and often philosophers think that they succeed when they do not.[9] Here is a sample set of cases: (1) Jim wants to get Jane's inheritance, so he pushes her down in the bathtub, holding her head under the water until she drowns. (2) Bill wants to get June's inheritance. He sees her drowning in the bathtub, and while he could easily help her, he refrains, intending that she drown.[10] In these two cases, motive, intention, effort (involved in not killing and in aiding), etc., are the same. Only one case is a case of harming and the other a case of not-aiding.

The concern to equalize all factors besides the ones whose significance one is testing should also be of concern to psychologists who do experimental testing of intuitions. It is often not clear that Kahneman and Tversky's test cases fulfill this equalization requirement. For example, Kahneman claims to be measuring the significance to people of the difference between losses and no-gains, where the end state to which they lead is otherwise the same. Notice that the distinction between loss and no-gain is different from the distinction between an *imposed loss* (which I take to be an instance of harming) and a *denied gain* (which is an instance of not-aiding), for someone could lose something or not gain it as a result of natural events rather than deliberate human behavior. If we are really testing for the loss/ no-gain distinction, we should not test for this other distinction, and we certainly should not compare a case in which a loss is imposed by a deliberate human act with a case in which someone fails to gain through something other than the deliberate refraining from helpful intervention. If we were to compare such cases, we would introduce a factor—human decision-making—in only one case, and this might be responsible for a differential response to cases, leading us to conclude that one case is worse than the other. Similarly, if one considers a case in which there is an imposed loss of something to which one has a right, we must compare it to a case in which there is a denied gain of that to which one also has a right.

Now consider whether some of Kahneman and Tversky's best-known cases are equalized properly. The Snow Shovel cases were used by them to determine whether loss versus no-gain per se makes a difference in people's judgment of fairness:

Snow Shovel Loss Case: A spring blizzard leads a store to raise the price on its snow shovels.
Snow Shovel No-Gain Case: A store does not reduce the price of its snow shovels when it gets them cheaper from its dealer.

In both cases, the final price is the same. The first case is considered unfair, while the second is considered fair. Kahneman claims that people tend to normativize the status quo as something to which they have a right and are entitled, unless there are specific barriers to doing this (e.g., if the baseline is a sale, people would not think that they had a right to sale prices). Hence a movement down from the status quo (raised prices) is not only a loss, but a deprivation of that to which people think they are entitled. A failure to get an improved price is a no-gain, and people do not think that they are entitled to the additional benefits.

These Snow Shovel cases involve not only loss and no-gain, but also imposed loss (harm) and imposed no-gain (a deliberate refraining from benefit), but this additional factor is equalized.[11] In addition, the Snow Shovel Loss Case involves a store taking advantage of people's increased need for snow shovels due to a blizzard. (The term *blizzard* even suggests that there is the possibility of danger from the weather.) This may be economically rational, but morally it might be thought to be wrong. The Snow Shovel No-Gain Case is not equalized for this factor, as no blizzard is mentioned. If we *remove* this factor from the Snow Shovel Loss Case, in order to equalize for everything except the difference we are testing, we get a case in which (where there is no spring blizzard and no increased need) the store just increases its price on snow shovels. Does this seem unfair? I do not think so.

The lack of unfairness of raising prices when there is no blizzard and no increased need for snow shovels also seems to conflict with the claims that the status quo is normativized and that customers would lose that to which they believe they are entitled. In any case, the sense in which consumers are entitled to a price in the market seems markedly weaker than nonmarket entitlement, since Kahneman says that his data also show that it is not considered unfair to impose a loss on a consumer from the status quo if this is necessary for the seller to keep himself from falling below his status quo. But it is not ordinarily permissible to take from someone that to which he is entitled in order to prevent a loss to oneself of that to which one is entitled. (For example, I cannot take someone's property in order to compensate for a theft of my property.) If imposing a loss to keep oneself from falling below one's status quo is not seen as unfair (even in a spring blizzard), and not giving a price break when one would fall below one's status quo if one gave it is not seen as unfair, this suggests that it is not only whether one imposes a loss on or denies a benefit to others that is crucial. What is also important is whether the seller provides himself with a benefit relative to his status quo or instead prevents a loss to himself by raising the price, and whether he avoids imposing a loss on himself when he does not lower the price.

An additional question related to entitlement that the Snow Shovel cases raise is whether Kahneman and Tversky's subjects ever yield responses that exhibit the belief that there are no-gains of that to which one is also entitled. In such a case, the status quo is not normativized, and people fail to get that to which they believe they are entitled, but no loss is involved. Considering such a no-gain case would equalize for the (supposed) belief in entitlement in both loss and no-gain cases, unlike the Snow Shovel cases. (Certainly, normative theory allows for situations in which people stand to gain an improvement to which they are entitled and to which they believe they are entitled.)

Suppose that we *add* the blizzard to the Snow Shovel No-Gain Case rather than remove it in the loss case (as we have discussed so far), thereby equalizing the cases in the other direction. Then is it as bad to refuse to pass along one's savings to consumers in a time of blizzard and consumers' great need as to raise prices? If not, *this* would suggest a difference between harming and not-aiding others, that is, between imposed loss and deliberate not-benefiting of others in at least one context.[12]

Next, consider just the degree of equalization in Kahneman and Tversky's Knee Damage cases, in which subjects' responses show that someone would demand more money *ex ante* in exchange for losing the use of a knee than she would demand *ex post* (as compensation) in return for not regaining the use of a knee. This set of cases especially associates the loss/no-gain cases with what is known as the Endowment Effect: Our having something seems to endow it with a value that objects we do not have, or even no longer have, lack. (This is obviously related to what Kahneman and Tversky think is the tendency to normativize the status quo.) It is worth emphasizing that in the *ex post* case, we consider someone who would get compensation for the loss of a function she *once had*. Hence, this case also involves something that was lost as well as not gotten. This is to be contrasted with a case in which someone is asked how much he wants as compensation for never having had, or simply not gaining, knee function. Because the *ex post* no-gain case in the Knee Damage cases is equalized with the loss case for something one has already had, it is a very extreme test of the difference made by loss and no-gain.[13]

2. (i) So far we have considered whether some crucial test cases are equalized, how they could be equalized, and what our responses would then be to them. Now we come to the central question: Is Prospect Theory's loss/no-gain distinction the same as the nonconsequentialist's harming/not-aiding distinction? I believe that the two are not the same and that the loss/no-gain distinction does not explain the harming/not-aiding distinction. I have already noted that imposed loss is different from loss per se and that imposed no-gain is different from no-gain per se. But, in addition, there are two other major points here. First, the harming/not-aiding distinction is about what the agent does or does not do (as well as what the victim undergoes), while the loss/no-gain distinction is only about what the victim undergoes. Second, and most important, given the way that Prospect Theory describes a loss, it is possible for one to suffer a loss as a result of someone's not-aiding. For example, according to Prospect Theory, if one frames facts in a case so that the baseline state of someone is his being alive and well, then *if we do not take action* to save him from an upcoming threat (as in one of the Asian Flu cases), there will be a loss of life.

Further, if Prospect Theory emphasizes that the crucial distinction is between suffering losses (even as a result of not being aided) and not receiving gains, it should predict that people would be as disturbed at our deciding not to prevent a healthy person from losing life as at our *causing* him to lose life (by killing him, for example). But this is just what the thesis of the moral distinction between harming and not-aiding denies. The harming/not-aiding thesis claims that losses caused by an agent's act will often violate negative rights and that this is morally of a different quality than failing to help someone avoid even what is identified as a loss from a normativized status quo.

The harming/not-aiding distinction is often present in cases in which there is a distinction between someone's losing what she would have continued to have independently of our involvement (when we harm), and her *losing* what she would have continued to have only with our involvement (when we do not aid). The harming/not-aiding distinction is also often present in cases in which there is a distinction between someone's losing what she would have continued to have without our involvement (when we harm) and someone's *not gaining* what she would have only with our involvement. This further implies that according to a theory that emphasizes the harming/not-aiding distinction, as the frame in the not-aiding cases switches from a loss-producing baseline to a no-gain-producing baseline, the moral judgment about the permissibility of not-aiding does *not* change. It can be permissible to not-aid in both cases (where there is a loss and where there is no-gain), and both cases are to be contrasted with harming. The correct application of the concepts of loss and no-gain may vary with baseline changes that are facilitated by different frames. The correct application of the concepts of harming and not-aiding does not vary in relation to the same baseline changes. This suggests that the harming/not-aiding distinction as it is employed in moral theory is not subject to the same framing effect as the loss/no-gain distinction as it figures in the psychological experiments run by Kahneman and Tversky.[14]

As pointed out above, the loss/no-gain distinction focuses on what happens to a victim. The harming/not-aiding distinction focuses on what an agent does to a victim. Even if a victim will be harmed (e.g., by B), A's relation to him can still be that of not-aiding him rather than harming him. Suppose one thinks that the reason an agent should not harm someone is fundamentally that his victim has a claim against him not to be harmed rather than that the agent has concerns about how his own life will go if he acts in certain ways.[15] This still does not mean that the focus in harming is on the victim in the sense that his condition as *being harmed* (rather than suffering a loss without human intervention) determines that we should aid him (i.e., to stop his being harmed by someone else) as well as not harm him.

The distinction between the harming/not-aiding distinction and the loss/ no-gain distinction can be further reinforced by noticing the following: It is also possible that in addition to harmings that involve losses, and not-aidings that involve either losses or no-gains, there are harmings that involve no-gains (but do not involve not-aiding). Suppose that B is to make a delivery of a life-sustaining drug to A, who is now dying. I interfere with the commencement of B's delivery by removing the engine of his car (Delivery Case I). This seems like a case in which I harm A (not merely do not aid him), but perhaps people would also think that A is not receiving a gain. (If I interfere with the car that is already on its way [Delivery Case II], they may think that I have caused a loss, because they think of the baseline as one in which A will get the drug and live.) Is harming that involves a no-gain judged as less bad than harming that involves a loss? If it is, then to the extent that what is a loss and what is a no-gain is subject to framing effects, certain judgments of whether a harm is wrong will also be subject to such effects. Nevertheless, if we find a harming to be less bad because it is framed as involving a no-gain, one may still think that it is worse than the not-aiding that involves either a no-gain or a loss. Then the effects of framing will not affect the moral significance of harming relative to not-aiding. Indeed, I suggest that the significance of harming overrides any differential response to gains and losses in the Delivery cases, and we intuitively think that both harms are equally wrong.

If the harming/not-aiding distinction is not subject to the same framing effect as the loss/no-gain distinction, this does not deny the possibility that moral theory might use a loss/no-gain distinction if it is careful to identify losses versus no-gains with a normatively appropriate status quo baseline. The fact that lay experimental subjects are tricked by framing effects into identifying the baseline from which to judge losses and no-gains does not gainsay the possibility that moral theory could use the distinction in an unconfused way. Further, the fact that one can describe the use by moral theory of a harming/not-aiding distinction that is not vitiated by arbitrary framing effects does not show that experimental subjects would not behave inconsistently in deploying such a distinction.[16]

(ii) Joel Feinberg is a philosopher who thinks that not helping someone to avoid losing what she already has (by contrast with not helping her to gain something she has never had) is morally equivalent to harming.[17] But the implications he draws from this are not in accord with Prospect Theory. For Feinberg (apparently) also thinks that all cases in which we prevent someone from losing what she already has count as preventing losses. By contrast, Prospect Theory claims that we can frame some of these cases as no-gains. (An example is the Asian Flu Case in which we say that some people will not keep on living because they are not saved from the coming Asian flu rather than say that some will not go on living because they will *lose* their lives to the Asian Flu.) Feinberg also thinks that failing to help someone to regain what he has already lost can be as wrong as causing the loss or not preventing the loss. But Kahneman's data (exhibited in the Knee Damage cases, for example) suggest that when we fail to do something to help someone regain what she no longer has, we are dealing with a no-gain case, and its disutility is less than that of a loss. (This is the implication of the fact that people demand less money for not regaining the use of a knee than they demand in exchange for losing it.)

I believe that in Kahneman and Tversky's system, "no-gains" refers to (a) uncorrected losses that have already occurred either by being (agent/non-agent)-caused or not prevented, (b) no new improvements, and (c) some cases of not maintaining what someone has already (e.g., the framed no-gain Asian Flu Case). "Losses" refers to (a) (agent/non-agent)-caused losses, and (b) unprevented losses (e.g., the framed loss Asian Flu Case).

Some may suggest that people will always set the baseline from which they judge losses and no-gains at what would have happened without intervention, rather than where things actually are. If they do this, then not-aidings will overlap with no-gains; there will be no not-aidings that involve losses. But notice that if such a projection gave the baseline, this would be inconsistent with the responses to the Asian Flu cases. There, given the prediction that 600 people will die if we do nothing, subjects did not always set the baseline at a state in which all 600 died, and they sometimes judged that unless a certain policy were enacted, people would *lose* their lives (i.e., fall from where they are now, that is, alive).

However, suppose the baseline were always set by what would happen without intervention. Prospect Theory might then predict that not preventing death should usually be seen less negatively than causing a death (assuming that death is bad for a person). This is because staying at the baseline is a no-gain and, according to Prospect Theory, this is better than moving down from a baseline. By contrast, causing death usually moves someone down from a baseline that is set by projecting continued life if no intervention ensues.[18] Setting baselines in this way would support the view that the harming/not-aiding distinction overlaps at least with the imposed-loss/denied-gain distinction.[19]

Suppose that this were so. Would it mean that the harming/not-aiding distinction and the imposed-loss/denied-gain distinction are subject to framing effects? If an imposed loss is defined as an *intervention* that alters for the worse an interventionless projection, it is not clear how problematic framing can occur any more. For problematic framings arise when different standards are used to determine the baseline—sometimes things are framed so that the baseline is the point at which the person is presently (e.g., alive) so that he can then suffer a loss relative to this, and sometimes things are framed so that the baseline is the point at which someone would wind up without intervention (e.g., dead), so that he fails to be saved from it. If the baseline is set in one way only, it will not be subject to confusion.

The question would still remain, though, as to whether the imposed-loss/denied-gain distinction is morally significant. If we think that the separateness of persons is morally significant because people are entitled to have special authority over themselves, then someone's imposing the loss of what someone else would have had independently of him will not be morally inconsequential; the imposition feature is conceptually true of imposing loss and not of denying gain, and the removal of what someone else would have had independently of oneself only occurs in imposing loss.[20] In addition, making use of another's efforts for an aiding project will also have moral significance. On these grounds, someone might object to imposed loss but not to deliberate no-gain.[21]

(iii) Let us return to the assumption that the way people set baselines implies that there can be cases of not-aiding that involve losses (as in one of the original set of Asian Flu cases) and that once these cases are under a frame, they are not describable as no-gains. We can then further illustrate the differences between the harming/not-aiding distinction and the loss/no-gain distinction by considering cases like ones introduced by Foot.[22]

Car Case 1: We are about to start rushing to the hospital in a car with five dying people in the back. Beside the road, someone, whom only we can help, is dying, but if we help her, we will not save the five. It is permissible to let the one die.

Car Case 2: We are about to start rushing to the hospital in a car with five dying people in the back. In the middle of the road is a healthy person who cannot be moved. If we go on to the hospital, we will, as a foreseen side effect, run over and kill her. We should not run over the one.

The justifications for the difference in the moral judgments are supposed to be connected to the greater stringency of the duty not to harm (the one) over the duty to aid (the one or the five) and also the permissibility of producing the greater good when we do not harm. But it has been suggested by Tamara Horowitz that we can explain (if not justify) the difference between the judgments by the loss/no-gain distinction.[23] In Car Case 1, she says, we conceive of the one and the five as being on the brink of death from which we must save them (a gain). So we face a choice of no gains in each case. In Car Case 2, we think that the one on the road is all right, but she will lose her life if we drive on. By contrast, the five who are dying in the back of the car will (merely) not gain life if we do not rush to the hospital. So we face a choice of a loss versus a no-gain.

I believe that Horowitz's proposed explanation of our judgments of permissibility and impermissibility does not succeed. Suppose that we frame things so that the one person beside the road in Car Case 1 is in good shape but will be fatally attacked by a wild animal unless we stay with her. The case then involves a choice between preventing *loss* of life to the one—if the model of the Asian Flu cases is correct—and providing a gain to the dying five. Yet, we still should save the five. Avoiding loss to one does not trump avoiding no-gain to five here, although Horowitz thinks that in Car Case 2, avoiding a loss can trump saving five lives. Suppose that it were a choice between saving the one person beside the road who will suffer a loss if we do not aid and saving *only one* person in the back of the car who will not gain if we do not go to the hospital. There should be no preference for the one who will lose his life; we might toss a coin. (Similarly, Timothy Hall points out that if the one person on the side of the road is well but needs a shot now to avoid *soon* getting and dying from a fatal infection, and another person on the other side of the road is at the point of death and will equally soon die unless he gets a shot now, it would seem odd to favor the first person.[24] Just because our failure to give him the shot will allow him to suffer a loss, but the other person will have a no-gain if we do not aid, is no reason for preference.) Here, when we allow a loss rather than cause it, no distinction between losses and no-gains surfaces. This suggests that it is the harming/not-aiding distinction rather than the loss/no-gain distinction that is morally significant.

Suppose that we re-frame Car Case 2 so that the five people are in excellent shape; they just need a shot of a flu vaccine, the last supply of which is available only now at the hospital, in order to prevent their soon dying from the flu that is coming into town in a few hours. Then not saving them would be framed as preventing losses rather than no-gains. We still should not prevent these five losses of life by driving over one person who is on the road, causing a foreseen loss to him. So even when there is no contrast between a loss and a no-gain in a case, we are not permitted to do what harms (by causing a foreseen loss) in order to aid (by preventing a foreseen loss).

3. Now let us consider further whether Kahneman and Tversky's own data should be interpreted as supporting the view that people's intuitions conform to a

harming/not-aiding rather than a loss/no-gain distinction. Let us add a third variant to the two Snow Shovel cases discussed above: The price of the snow shovels to the consumer and the store owner is going up during a spring blizzard because of action by the manufacturer, who is solely aiming to increase his profits. However, the store owner is, independently, being provided with a huge reduction on another type of item, which only those who do not buy snow shovels purchase (Snow Shovel Case 3). Is it perceived as unfair for the store owner not to share her increased profit with the consumers in order to offset their loss—a loss she does not cause—when she can do so without lowering her profit from the status quo? If the loss/no-gain distinction, rather than the harming/not-aiding distinction, is determinative, the intuitive judgment should be that the store owner should prevent the price of snow shovels from rising by aiding because she then prevents a loss. (Unlike the original Snow Shovel No-Gain Case, which, of course, involved a no-gain to the consumer, this case involves preventing an imposed loss on him.) But I doubt that the response of Kahneman and Tversky's subjects will be that the store owner is wrong not to prevent the loss. This would support the crucial role in intuitive moral judgments of whether the agent harms or does not aid rather than merely whether the victim undergoes even an imposed loss rather than a deliberate no-gain.

Here is another set of Kahneman and Tversky's cases (which they present *inter*personally) that support this point: (a) An employer cuts wages by 7 percent in a period of high unemployment and no inflation, and (b) an employer raises wages by 5 percent in a period of high unemployment and 12 percent inflation. The first case is judged to be unfair, the second to be fair by respondents. Kahneman suspects that this response is irrational for it involves thinking that workers who wind up in the same end state are treated unfairly when their employer lowers their salary but fairly when the salary raise she gives them only compensates partially for losses due to inflation. However, while in both of these cases there are losses to the workers overall, in the first case the employer causes a loss, in the second the employer only fails to prevent a loss that is not caused by her but by an outside force, namely, inflation. It is not surprising to a theorist who supports the significance of whether an agent harms or does not aid that only the employer in the first case is charged with unfairness (even if it is not ultimately correct for him to be so charged). Beyond this, the important point to emphasize, as nonconsequentialism does, is that it is consistent with a victim being indifferent between two end states, with regard to their effect on her own welfare, that she evaluate differently the conduct of the agents who could put her in each of the states. One person may treat her fairly, the other unfairly. Furthermore, from their own points of view, victims may prefer being treated fairly, for considerations other than their own welfare may count, even from the victims' point of view.

I conclude that Kahneman and Tversky's experimental data do not help to undermine the possible moral importance of a harming/not-aiding distinction. First, this is because their data do not support its substitution with a loss/no-gain distinction in the account of people's intuitions. Indeed, the data may support the presence in people's intuitions of a harming/not-aiding distinction, because arguably loss versus no-gain by itself would not explain many intuitive responses that could be explained by harming versus not-aiding. Second, the data do not support the susceptibility of the harming/not-aiding distinction to framing effects of the sort associated with the loss/no-gain distinction. Of course, as noted above, use by subjects of the harming/not-aiding distinction might be susceptible to certain other distinctive fallacies, and the loss/no-gain distinction might be used by moral theorists in such a way as to avoid framing effects.

IV. THE LOSS/NO-GAIN DISTINCTION AND MORAL THEORY

Given that the loss/no-gain distinction is different from the harming/not-aiding distinction, it may be worthwhile considering what sort of moral theory could be built on the former distinction. (It should be noted that Kahneman and Tversky are not themselves concerned with constructing a normative theory, even if they are concerned with providing a description of how people decide what has normative significance.) Nonconsequentialists who give weight to the harming/not-aiding distinction are sometimes thought to preach an ideology rather than defend a true morality because of the conservative tendency of a system that puts constraints on harming individuals in the way of maximizing the overall good. But this is conservatism relative to consequentialism only if the idea of each individual person's having a status of significant inviolability is a conservative idea; I do not believe that it is. A moral system built on a gain/no-loss distinction might be conservative in a different way. Recall the Knee Damage cases. Suppose that we know that while someone takes a very dim view of losing the use of her knee, she will not care as much about regaining it once she has lost it. Then, while someone should avoid improperly removing a capacity, he may be thought to not be under much moral pressure to reinstate it even if he can. By contrast, a nonconsequentialist theory should (I think) treat the failure to return something that one has improperly taken as seriously as it should treat the original taking (barring conflict with a duty not to engage in another improper taking),[25] and one's responsibility in this regard may be independent of the strength of the preferences of the victim. On this view, the no-gain of that which was previously rightly possessed and improperly taken away should count for a great deal, at least relative to the culpable agent.

At a more general level, Kahneman and Tversky's most basic claim is that people's responses indicate that they take changes rather than end states to be the "bearers of utility." Suppose losses are counted for more than no-gains. This implies that there will be some level of wealth, A, such that even though it is higher than level B, taxing someone at A so that he loses x but is still above B, in order to provide a gain of $x + n$ to someone at B, who will not then be higher than $A - x$, will not be favored. The bigger gain to B will not be worth the lesser loss to A. This is not, therefore, a maximin theory. It does not always favor helping the worst off, because a negative value is introduced just in introducing a loss to some, regardless of the size of the loss. (It is not clear whether the negative value of the loss per se also increases as the size of the loss increases.)

Maximin theories, which emphasize fairness in order to justify taxing the better off to benefit the worst off, may also emphasize diminishing marginal utility (DMU), because DMU emphasizes the reduced value to the better off of what is taken from them.[26] I do not know what Kahneman and Tversky think about the interplay between DMU and the loss/no-gain theory, but DMU may reduce the conservative tendency of the loss/no-gain thesis if what the person loses is less important to him because of DMU. It is also important to note, in relation to the conservatism issue, that even if there is an asymmetry of responses to losses and no-gains, this need not hold when end states are *not* held equal, that is, it could be judged to be worse to stay at a very low wealth level through a no-gain than to fall to a moderate wealth level.[27]

I am trying to derive some normative implications from the supposition that aversion is greater to losses than to no-gains, but it is important to reemphasize that traditional nonconsequentialist theory may be right when it says that degrees of aversion are not necessarily relevant to deciding what is right and wrong. For suppose there were more aversion to a no-gain that leaves one at a lower absolute level than to a loss that leaves one at a higher absolute level. This would have no direct implication for the permissibility of bringing about in one person that loss to which there is less aversion for the sake of preventing a no-gain in another person to which there is more aversion. For example, it is not necessarily permissible to reduce one person's health to level B in order to improve someone who is at health level B − n, even when the reduction is less averse to the first person than the no-gain is to the other person.

Nor should assigning utility to changes rather than end states be thought to imply that our normative results improve if we now set about, for example, *minimizing* the new source of negative utility, namely, losses. That is, merely changing the items that are bearers of utility does not change the theory of what is right from having a consequentialist structure, wherein we seek to bring about (typically maximize) the good or avoid (typically minimize) the bad. It does not change this theory into a nonconsequentialist one; it only tells us to maximize (or minimize) different things. So if the consequentialist structure is wrong, it will be wrong to decide what to do by merely balancing losses and gains, even holding constant the welfare involved in these. This is another reason that the loss/no-gain distinction is not a replacement for the harming/not-aiding distinction in a normative system. For, in saying that harming is worse than not-aiding per se, a nonconsequentialist system does not tell us to minimize occurrences of harmings rather than not-aidings, nor to balance harmings against not-aidings, even holding constant the welfare involved in these. Furthermore, it does not necessarily permit us to harm one person in order to minimize harm to others. For example, if five people will suffer a loss because of the acts of another person, this does not mean that I may cause a sixth person to suffer a comparable loss in order to prevent the loss to the five. (I am assuming that we can frame the case so that harming the one is seen as preventing a loss to the five not just as not providing a gain, as Prospect Theory employs these terms.) This is true even if there is more aversion to five losses than to one loss, and more negative utility to five losses than to one.[28]

Another problem with trying to construct a normative theory based on a simple loss/no-gain distinction (as much as trying to construct it on a simple harming/not-aiding distinction) is that it fails to account for all of the cases where it is permissible to harm or tolerate loss for the sake of gain. For example, in the Trolley Case, it is thought permissible to redirect a trolley that is headed toward killing five people onto another track where, we foresee, it will kill one. If we interpreted the Trolley Case as involving a loss to the one and only a no-gain to the five who are about to be hit by the trolley, and this were the dominant factor in deciding how to act (as Horowitz's analysis suggests), one would be unable to explain why it is permissible to redirect the trolley threat.

Finally, emphasizing the loss/no-gain distinction overlooks the indignation that many feel about the condition of people who have never received the goods they deserve by right. Kahneman might avoid this problem by claiming that if we are owed by right something good, then its absence is always a loss, since the baseline accords with the claim of a right. But if one has never had that to which one has a right, it seems clear that no-gains, not losses, are involved. It is best, I believe, if we denormativize the status quo, neither assigning to it what we are owed nor saying that it is what we are owed. The status quo will certainly not be endowed with normative significance if we understand that the current status of some people can itself be the product of injustice. Mere possession does not yield entitlement. It can be acceptable for some to lose what they were never entitled to have and for people to be provided with gains consisting of that to which they have a right.[29]

V. THE REASONABLENESS OF INTUITIONS IN EXPERIMENTAL TESTING

If people's intuitions in certain contexts are unreliable or shown, on reflection, to be irrational, we should be hesitant to rely on them in those contexts. So far I have argued against the view that intuitions about cases involving a harming/not-aiding distinction are unreliable because they shift with framing in the way that intuitions in cases involving a loss/no-gain distinction might. Furthermore, I believe, the harming/not-aiding distinction is connected with a reasonable thesis about persons' special authority over themselves.[30]

At this point, I would like to consider whether in certain cases in which Kahneman and Tversky claim that people's intuitions lead them astray, they really do and, if so, why. My previous strategy in dealing with the attacks on non-consequentialism that (I said) could be derived from Kahneman and Tversky's work was to show that problematic shifts in judgment about cases (dependent on framing) did not touch the harming/not-aiding distinction. Now the point is to see whether certain shifts in judgment are problematic. The general point I shall be interested in making here is that a framing effect is arbitrary only if the different descriptions that frame are equivalent in all morally relevant respects, that is, they are merely alternative ways of saying what has exactly the same moral content. Whether two characterizations are morally equivalent—that is, whether they include the same morally relevant factors—is a judgment that depends on moral theory, which picks out some factors as relevant and other factors as irrelevant. Kahneman and Tversky may ignore the possibility that two descriptions of a puzzle case to which subjects respond differently, but which researchers regard as essentially equivalent, really involve significantly different moral factors and are nonequivalent in crucial respects.

I shall consider several puzzle cases in order to explore the possible arbitrariness of framing effects: (1) Schelling's Tax Case; (2) the preference for more pain rather than less; (3) the Knee Damage cases (again); and (4) the Grocery Store cases (again). In beginning this reinterpretation of some of the cases that Kahneman presents, let us first consider again the idea of framing. Kahneman claims that framing effects occur when we give different descriptions that are extensionally the same, and yet our responses to them differ.[31] But this is not a complete account of framing, for the same event can be described as my writing a check or as a very particular interaction of certain molecules, and it is quite reasonable that my response to it under each of these extensionally equivalent descriptions should differ. But framing effects are supposed to lead to different responses that cannot be reasonably justified on account of the frame, that is, the frame must introduce what is seen, at least on reflection, to be a difference that should be irrelevant to different responses. What we should *not* do is look for extensionally equivalent descriptions, one of which eliminates from our awareness factors that are morally relevant differences, and then condemn the different response induced by the description that has morally relevant features. For example, we might describe an event as "maximizing utility" or as "killing one to save five." The former description, of the two that could be extensionally equivalent, eliminates a morally relevant characteristic that is only observed in the latter description.

(1) The first puzzle case I shall consider is one that Kahneman attributes to Thomas Schelling. Kahneman writes:

> Schelling reports asking his students to evaluate a tax policy that would allow a larger child exemption to the rich than to the poor. Many readers will immediately respond, as Schelling's students do, that this proposal is outrageous. Schelling now points out to his students that the child exemption assumes that the default case in the tax table is a childless family and that special adjustments are required for families with children. Of course, the existing tax schedule could be rewritten in which a family with two children would be the default case. A tax surcharge for childless families would presumably be imposed. Should this surcharge be as large for the poor as for the rich? Of course not. In this example and in other framing effects, a strong preference can be overturned by altering a superficial feature of presentation. The intuitions that are evoked by formulating the problem in terms of exemptions and surcharges are incoherent, and neither intuition survives when the inconsistency is pointed out. The only formulation of the tax problem that avoids this arbitrariness is a complete table that determines the after-tax income of

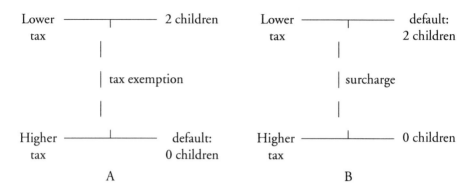

Figure 14.1.

families for every level of pre-tax income and number of children. In this situation, a description in terms of final states is superior, precisely because it avoids powerful intuitions that can be manipulated.[32]

This problem is represented in figure 14.1.

If the tax surcharge for not having children were larger for the rich than for the poor when the default line is two children, this would just mean that the tax exemption for the rich having children would be larger than the tax exemption for the poor when the baseline is at zero children. If the increase in taxes is greater for not doing x, the decrease (or non-increase) in taxes must be greater for doing x.

Although this explanation of incoherence in subjects' responses is understandable, let us also try to make sense of subjects' responses against a greater exemption for the rich and for a greater surcharge on them. The term *exemption* suggests that we first determine what the government may by right take from a citizen's income for various purposes and then consider exempting people from that. Call this amount to which the government has a right t. If the government wants to encourage childbirth, it may give some of what is its by right, t, back to a citizen.

The term *surcharge* suggests a penalty, that is, it suggests that the government has first taken all it has a right to from citizens, and then, if they do not have children, more is taken from them. But this is to take from citizens what is theirs by right. This could be an injustice if promoting childbirth is not a sufficiently important goal. If you do have a child in order to avoid the penalty, the government in this scenario could be interpreted to have the authority to let you keep that to which you already have a right. This could be seen as an abuse of governmental authority, since the government had no right to threaten such a penalty to begin with.

Therefore, it might be permissible to give exemptions (in the sense of returns on legitimate taxes) for a good cause, but not to impose surcharges (in the sense of taking legitimate personal property). This could be true even if the system of exemptions and the system of surcharges each left one at the same absolute level (which could happen if what one strictly owed in taxes was higher in the exemption case and lower in the surcharge case). But if a surcharge (as I have defined it) is to be imposed on anyone, it should be imposed on the rich, who can afford it. On the other hand, if the government will give back a portion of that to which it has a right, it should give to the poor, who need it. In figure 14.1, if the taxes to which the government has a right, t, come from the default position in A, then the "surcharge" in B is not a real penalty: It represents merely not getting a return from what is the government's by right. In a sense, on the no-return versus penalty analysis just provided, the two-children level cannot be a default position, if default tax represents what the government has a right to from you for contributions to such things as defense, education, and so forth, and if promoting childbirth is a goal for which the government may not permissibly increase your taxes. (On the no-return versus penalty analysis, the case would be analogous to it being permissible for the government to draft anyone for war but also to exempt people who decide to have children, even though it would be wrong to draft people when there was no war just because they did not have children.)[33]

(2) Now we come to the paradoxical cases in which more pain is preferred to less, in the sense that people, on the basis of memories, choose a future episode that will have more pain rather than less.[34] All subjects must go through three trials in which one of their hands is placed in painful icy water. In the first trial, the hand is kept in for x minutes, then immediately taken out. In the second trial, the hand is kept in for x minutes, then for $x-n$ minutes in somewhat less icy water, and then taken out. Subjects are asked which trial they prefer to repeat, and most say the second. Kahneman claims that their behavior follows the Peak-and-End Rule, according to which people evaluate a past experience according to how bad its worst point was and how it ended, rather than according to how much total pain occurred, which depends both on the pain's intensity and its duration. An intense pain experience that ends abruptly is evaluated as being worse (and its repetition is avoided) than an intense pain experience that peters out into a less intense pain experience, though overall the latter experience lasts longer and has more total pain than the former.

This case distinguishes *experienced* disutility from *decision* disutility, since people will decide to repeat the more painful experience in the future. Kahneman further suggests that since we spend more time with memories of experiences than having the experiences, perhaps we should choose which experience to have based on the memory we are likely to have of it. (He claims that we *are* our memories.) This also implies sometimes choosing to have the more painful experience.

Let us consider the last normative recommendation first. I do not think that we are our memories. It is possible that a person does not remember the most worthwhile things she has done in her life. Yet she and her life are constituted, in good part, by what she has done and the character that led her to do these things. If memory were all that counted, should a person who knows she will not remember anything (e.g., she will soon die) not do something worthwhile? (Sometimes people think, if I will die soon, I should go to see Venice. And someone else incorrectly says: "What is the point, as you won't be around to remember it?") If memory were all that counted, it could be the case that only "apparent memories" count. Then we would have to do what will result in our having the most pleasant illusions of our past, even if these result from bad experiences and worse acts. Then memory would disconnect from character and the ability to assign moral responsibility properly. I conclude that we should not choose only on the basis of what our memories will be like, though we should perhaps try to make our memories reflect the true nature of what has happened.

How can we justify the seemingly irrational focus on the peak and end of an experience, which can lead to the preference for more overall pain? Intuitively, inclines (representing increasing goods or decreasing bads) are preferable to declines (representing increasing bads or decreasing goods); it is preferable for events to conform to an incline rather than a decline, even when total utility is held constant.[35] One would rather start as a clerk and move up to be president than the reverse, even with total utility held constant. This does not seem irrational to me. If it is not irrational, it is because the narrative structure of one's life matters, in addition to the utility it contains. I believe that what Kahneman's results may suggest is that narrative structure can apply to what I would call *parsed events* rather than to life as a whole. Let me explain.

If a painful experience ends abruptly, this is a movement on an incline to a better state of affairs (no pain) sooner and more steeply than if the pain is followed by diminishing pain before stopping. So overall, one's life is on a steeper incline if the pain stops abruptly earlier than if it stops later after petering out. But suppose a parsed event, such as a medical examination, is conceived as being over when all pain ends. Then *that event* within one's life would end on an incline (less bad, more good) only if the pain peters out rather than if it ends abruptly. The state of absence of pain would be conceived as a new event or situation, and if pain ceases abruptly, the previous event does not end in an incline; rather, the previous event is seen as merely intense pain. If one could incorporate the absence of pain, so that it is seen as part of the medical exam itself, by, for example, keeping the patient in the exam room for a comforting massage after the abrupt removal of the pain, the medical exam event would also end on an incline. Then people would not need to choose additional but less intense pain in order to achieve an inclining event. Two alternatives to this are to get people to focus on what will really happen to them, where this involves making them strongly aware of how much time is being spent in pain, or to get people to see that it is an incline over the course of one's life, rather than within parsed events, that is important. However, I do not think that parsing events so that they have narrative structures is necessarily irrational.

(3) In the above discussion of the Knee Damage cases, we argued that *re*gaining what was once rightfully ours should have great importance. This impugns intuitions that subjects have in the Knee Damage cases. Furthermore, if one is owed something by right that one has never had, not gaining it should be a more serious matter than both not gaining that to which one has no right and losing what one has but to which one has no right (other things being equal, and assuming that the status quo is not, by definition, that to which one has a right).

However, something can also be said to make the Endowment Effect (endowing what one actually has with extra value) seem not so unreasonable. In the *ex ante* Knee Damage case, where loss of function is yet to come, there is vulnerability to some sort of intrusion and decline (and when these occur, there is a declining narrative structure).[36] These factors of intrusion, vulnerability, and decline are not present if one fails to regain the lost item. Attending to these additional negative factors does not strike me as irrational. But, in addition, once the events that are characterized by these negative factors are in the past, these negatives may be rated differently. This asymmetrical rating of future negative factors and past negative factors can help account for the reasonableness of at least a prima facie tendency in the direction of the subjects' intuitions in the Knee Damage cases. That is, they do not ask as much for having suffered bad things (even the additional negative factors, such as decline) as for suffering them in the future.

The asymmetry in attitudes toward future and past is part of a general phenomenon. Derek Parfit pointed out this asymmetry in connection with future pain and past pain.[37] We would prefer to have it be true that we have had a great deal of pain in the past rather than have it be true that we will have a small amount of pain in the future. This means that after the great deal of pain is over (and there is no memory of it), we do not care about it. Hence, the compensation for it we demand *ex post* might be less than what we would demand *ex ante* in exchange for undergoing it. In the Knee Damage case, of course, the disability is *not* in the past, it remains with someone. So how is it like pain that is over? An answer is that the particular negatives identified above as being associated with a loss—intrusion, vulnerability, and decline—will be behind us when the question of compensation *ex post* arises. Hence, we do not care about them as much. (Notice that these additional negatives of loss are not "behind us" when the question is how much we would take in exchange for remaining without some capacity that we have never had.)[38]

(4) Finally, let us return to the Grocery Store cases. The award of higher compensation for the person who is attacked in a grocery store he goes to for the first time is not irrational, if awarding compensation on the basis of how unfair an event is, rather than merely on how much one unjustly suffers, is not irrational. If someone has on many occasions reaped the benefits of a risky enterprise (e.g., going to the store), there is less unfairness to her if she "pays the (admittedly unjust) price" eventually. If someone pays the price without having gotten the benefit, this seems more unfair. (The positive version of this case may be the gambler who wins without ever having gambled before, as opposed to the gambler who wins after a long round of losses.) A possible problem with this analysis is that the visitor to the new grocery store did get benefits from going regularly to another grocery store in the past, presumably. Why should this factor not count?

Another possibility is that what people measure in the intra- and interpersonal presentation of the two cases is different and that their responses are sensible relative to this difference. When presented with one of the cases, the subjects merely register by their award amount how terrible is the event that has happened to someone (perhaps including the unfairness discussed above). But in the *intra*personal presentation (i.e., when both cases are presented to one person), the issue of equality between the victims arises, and the question of their suffering (versus the cosmic badness of the event in which they are involved) may appropriately come to the fore. This could lead to awarding equal compensation.

Something comparable may occur when we consider what to do in the following two cases: (a) A is thrown into a lake by a villain, and (b) B falls into a lake by accident. The former may be, all told, a worse event. But if we have to decide whom to save from drowning, we ignore this difference and just decide on the basis of who is more likely to die or whom we are more likely to save. (If the likelihood of the death and the rescue of each is equal, we might just toss a coin to give them an equal chance.)[39] Even if we thought that preventing an injustice was an additional good to be achieved only in saving A, this can become (what I call) an irrelevant good by comparison to the good that we can achieve whomever we save and the fact that A and B each wants to be the one saved. Hence, a difference that matters when we evaluate badness of outcomes (i.e., a villain caused the plunge) becomes irrelevant when we have to decide how to treat the two people considered together.[40]

In the Knee Damage cases too it may be appropriate, when considering the *ex ante* and *ex post* cases separately, to use awards as a measure of how it is reasonable to respond to future loss versus past loss (thus exhibiting the asymmetry between attitudes toward past and future, as discussed above). But when we consider *ex ante* and *ex post* circumstances together, we should focus on the mere absence of function in the knee as the preeminent evil.

If the context where cases are considered together can reasonably make certain factors irrelevant that are relevant when a case is considered by itself, this could be a very important factor of which to take account in the design of experiments and in the interpretation of experimental data. (It is, however, also possible that changing judgments when cases are presented intrapersonally represents a failure to understand the factor that accounted for one's intuitive judgment to a case in isolation, leading to the imposition of "false rationality" that treats the cases as equivalent.)

A general point about these attempts to construe the experimental results as reasonable is that they point to factors that prima facie favor the subject's responses, that is, factors that—were there no opposing considerations—could reasonably determine a response. Sometimes it seems that these factors should be swamped by other factors. For example, perhaps it would not be irrational to pay with some extra pain in order to live on an incline rather than a decline over the course of one's whole life, but this is not true if the incline just consists in an extra bit of lower future pain (as in Kahneman's case). If there is irrationality, it may lie not in attending to certain factors, but in giving them too much weight or giving them weight too generally.

A final note should be made about a possible problem in making predictions of *overall* irrationality in judgments based on the sorts of data provided by Kahneman and Tversky: Some of the judgments they describe seem to move in opposite directions, and this suggests that the judgments might possibly cancel out each other's effects. For example, if people think that losses are worse than no-gains, they also (it is said)[41] tend to underestimate the likelihood of events leading to losses occurring. Hence, in an expected utility calculation, the increased negative value of a loss may be balanced by assigning a reduced probability to its occurrence. Another example can be seen in the Knee Damage cases, which Kahneman and Tversky take to imply that people demand less compensation after a loss than they would demand prior to the loss to undergo it because they assign higher value to something they have (the Endowment Effect). Above, I suggested that another way to interpret these cases is that people place greater value on avoiding certain negative factors involved in losing per se, which are not present in merely being without something. However, once these negative factors are in the past, the asymmetrical attitudes toward past and future negatives takes over. Hence, greater compensation for losses gets cancelled by the fact that the losses are in the past rather than to come.

NOTES

    1. This chapter is based on my article of the same title published in *Ethics* 108 (1998): 463–88. That article was an outgrowth of my comments on Daniel Kahneman, "The Cognitive Psychology of Consequences and Moral Intuition" (the Tanner Lecture in Human Values, University of Michigan, Ann Arbor, November 1994). As such, most references are to that lecture. For another account of Prospect Theory, see Daniel Kahneman and Amos Tversky, "Prospect Theory: An Analysis of Decisions under Risk," *Econometrics* 47 (1974): 263–91. I am grateful to the Department of Philosophy at the University of Michigan for giving me the opportunity to comment on Kahneman's paper, and to the audience and Kahneman for responses on that occasion. I am also indebted for comments to the participants in the Philosophy and Decision Theory Seminar run by Michael Bratman and John Ferejohn at Stanford University in the spring of 1995; to the audiences at the Conference on Morality and Ideology, Lady Margaret Hall, Oxford University, June 1996, and the Philosophy Department, Rutgers University, October 1996; and to Timothy Hall. I thank Professors Jonathan Baron and Richard Arneson for their detailed written comments. I am especially grateful to Daniel Kahneman for his very worthwhile discussion of the relation between notions employed in moral theory and results in empirical psychology, and for discussing his views with moral philosophers.
    2. See Philippa Foot, "The Problem of Abortion and the Doctrine of Double Effect," in her *Virtues and Vices and Other Essays* (Berkeley: University of California Press, 1978), pp. 19–32.
    3. In John Rawls, *A Theory of Justice* (Cambridge, MA: Harvard University Press, 1971).
    4. And is it even a criticism of these normative theories that people's actual judgments in experiments do not accord with the theories? Recall (from chapter 13) that Singer says that actual judgments that do not accord with a theory's implications do not defeat his theory. Let us put to one side this very general question in order to see some possible further implications of Kahneman's view.
    5. Robert Nozick, in his *The Nature of Rationality* (Princeton, NJ: Princeton University Press, 1993), p. 60, writes: "Doesn't the relation of the bringing about/allowing to happen distinction to a baseline seem suspiciously like that of the gain/loss distinction to its baseline? This last, of course, is a favored example for framing effects." If bringing about a death is considered harming and allowing it to happen is considered not-aiding, then this might be like the loss-versus-no-gain distinction. However, Nozick draws a parallel between bringing about/allowing to happen and gain/loss, in that order. Does he mean that the distinction between bringing about saving someone's life and allowing the life to pass away are like the gain/loss distinction? If so, then he is trying to make a different point from the one I am making.
    6. I draw my conclusions about this case by implication from a similar case discussed by Tamara Horowitz in her "Philosophical Intuitions and Psychological Theory" (paper presented at the Rethinking Intuition Conference, Notre Dame University, South Bend, Indiana, April 1996). I am grateful to her for sharing her paper with me. (Her paper was eventually published in *Ethics* 108 [1998]: 367–85.) She says:

Kahneman and Tversky presented one group of subjects with this decision problem: Imagine that the United States is preparing for an outbreak of an unusual Asian disease which is expected to kill 600 people. Two alternative programs to fight the disease, A and B, have been proposed. Assume that the exact scientific estimates of the consequences of the programs are as follows: If program A is adopted, 200 people will be saved. If program B is adopted, there is a one-third probability that 600 people will be saved, and a two-thirds probability that no people will be saved. Which program would you choose? The subjects in a second group were given the same cover story with the following description of two different alternative programs, C and D: If program C is adopted, 400 people will die. If program D is adopted, there is a one-third probability that nobody will die and a two-thirds probability that 600 will die. Once again, the subjects were asked which program they would choose. Programs A and C are equivalent from the point of view of expected survival as are programs B and D. Nevertheless, a majority of the first group of subjects chose program A over program B while a majority of the second group of subjects chose program D over program C. So when the outcomes were stated in positive terms, "lives saved," subjects tended to be risk averse whereas when the outcomes were stated in negative terms, "lives lost," subjects tended to be risk seeking. . . . In the framing process, the agent chooses one possible outcome of her actions as the "neutral" outcome. And she classifies the other possible outcomes as either "gains" or "losses" relative to this neutral outcome; that is, she classifies outcomes as either "positive" or "negative" deviations from the neutral outcome. . . . in this case it is assumed that subjects shift reference points because of the overall phrasing of the decision problem. . . . In the first part of the experiment, for example, the results of disease-fighting programs are formulated in terms of "people saved." So one can hypothesize that subjects choose the outcome in which 600 people are dead as the neutral outcome. But in the second part of the experiment, programs are described in terms of "people dying." So it is reasonable to assume that subjects choose the outcome in which 600 people live as the neutral reference point. . . . this shift in neutral reference point presumably forces the subjects to evaluate disease-fighting programs as leading to positive deviations in one case but negative deviations in the other. (pp. 370–75)
(I would revise this last sentence in Horowitz to "preventing negative deviations in the other.")

She also says: "People tend to be risk averse when it comes to gains, risk seeking when it comes to losses, and their response to losses tends to be more extreme than their response to gains." (p. 372) In the case Horowitz discusses, subjects risk losing 600 people to avoid definitely losing 400 of them. They do not see a reason to risk losing 600 people in order to save more than 200 people. This is not the same as saying that they would not do as much to save 400 as to prevent 400 from dying. But if the conclusion we should draw from the former cases is that they care more about losses than about no-gains, we should be able to conclude that they would pay more to avoid one than the other. (However, for a contrary intuition about a similar case, see section III of the text below.)

7. This should remind us of Unger's contrast between intuition in cases and basic values (see chapter 6).

8. I shall consider this possibility in reanalyzing the Grocery Store Case data below.

9. See my *Morality, Mortality*, vol. 2 (New York: Oxford University Press, 1996), part 1, on this issue.

10. These are modeled on cases presented by James Rachels in his "Active and Passive Euthanasia," *New England Journal of Medicine* 292 (1975): 78–80.

11. By "deliberate" I mean only that someone decides to not aid, not that they aim at a person's not having a benefit. They may decide not to aid merely because they decide the expense is too great.

12. In his comments on a draft of this chapter, Timothy Hall suggested that people may think that in the time of a blizzard, they are entitled to a certain price, whether they have it already or not. Then a harming-versus-not-aiding distinction would be overridden by the entitlement to a price.

13. In these cases, we are also dealing with something closer to a pure contrast between loss of what was had versus no-gain of what was had. This is because no agent (deliberately) harms or refrains from aid. That is, the loss case is due to illness or accident and repair of the knee is not possible.

14. It also suggests that Nozick was wrong if he thought that the loss/no-gain distinction was like the harm/not-aid distinction (see n. 5). Further, if cases of not-aiding in which someone already has something (and will not retain it without our aid) always involved a loss rather than a no-gain (even if, for example, people were framed as already at the point of losing the item, from which point we must raise them up), then all cases in which we do not prevent the loss of what someone already has will involve losses as much as will cases of harming. Yet some non-consequentialists claim that not-aiding in these cases may be permissible when harming in comparable cases is not. For more on this, see the discussion of Feinberg below.

15. This is the victim-focused view I defend in *Morality, Mortality*, vol. 2, and in this volume in chapters 1 and 8.

16. I owe these points to Richard Arneson.

17. See Joel Feinberg, *Harm to Others* (New York: Oxford University Press, 1984).

18. Exceptions are cases where C will be killed by A even if B does not kill him. In this type of case, we would think that B causes C's death and harms him even if the baseline is set at C's death already, and so there would be causing a death without loss relative to a projected baseline. We may, by contrast, set the baseline at C alive now regardless of A's expected act, so there is loss and harm when B kills C.

19. Still, there is no *perfect* overlap. For example, our refusal to join in giving aid may lead others to abandon a life-saving project that they were going to undertake before we intervened. Here a person moves down from the baseline of projected rescue, even though we simply did not aid. This is not a harming, even though it would (on the view we are considering) be a movement down from the baseline. We can also harm someone who would have suffered the same loss anyway, and yet he would not lose anything relative to his baseline, understood as projected fate without our interference.

20. Though it does not occur in all cases where we impose loss. For more on the properties conceptually true of harming and not-aiding and so of imposed loss/denied gain, see chapter 1 in this volume and my *Morality, Mortality*, vol. 2. For more on the significance of special authority over oneself and it's relation to nonconsequentialist distinctions see chapter 3.

21. Of course, when A will kill C even if B does not, we can only object to B interfering with what C *has now independently of B*, though C would not retain it even independently of B's interference.

22. In Philippa Foot, "Killing and Letting Die," in *Abortion: Moral and Legal Perspectives*, ed. J. Garfield and P. Hennessey, pp. 177–85 (Amherst: University of Massachusetts Press, 1984); and subsequently discussed by Warren Quinn, "Actions, Intentions, and Consequences: The Doctrine of Doing and Allowing," in his *Morality and Action*, pp. 149–74 (New York: Cambridge University Press, 1993). I have modified the cases so that we have not yet started to rescue the five.

23. See Horowitz, "Philosophical Intuitions and Psychological Theory."

24. In conversation.

25. On this, see chapter 9.

26. For example, the value of ten more dollars to a man who has $1 million is far less than the value of ten more dollars to that same man when he only had $1 to his name. The utility of additional wealth thus falls as one's wealth increases.

27. Some suggest that if one were either (a) to fall to moderate wealth from truly enormous riches, so that one suffers a great loss, or (b) to remain at moderate wealth through not gaining a potentially large sum, then one might be worse off than someone who is at a lower wealth level through failing to gain a slight improvement (and perhaps also through suffering a slight loss?). (I believe that Thomas Nagel claims this. See his *Equality and Partiality* [New York: Oxford University Press, 1991].) This is supposed to be true, even though the second person remains at a much lower level of wealth in absolute terms than the first person. I do not believe that Kahneman is committed to either (a) or (b) just by claiming that a loss counts for more than a no-gain. Nagel uses comparative judgments—where might I have been as well as where am I—in order to judge how badly off someone is. Like Kahneman and Tversky, he rejects merely relying on end states. But, unlike them, he seems not to give greater weight to losses than failures to gains. (Thomas Scanlon's judgment of who has the biggest complaint seems to incorporate a similar view. See his *What We Owe to Each Other* [Cambridge, MA: Harvard University Press, 1998].)

28. For more on this and its relation to inviolability, see chapters 1 and 8.

29. Kahneman predicts that people will oppose affirmative action if it requires that we fire people from jobs they already have (a loss), but not if it fails to give all people an equal chance to get (gain) the same job. He also claims that people will agree that we may build new toilets that are handicapped accessible, even if, because of the increased expense of such facilities, there will not be as many toilets overall for the population. But there will be an additional negative reaction to dismantling regular toilets already in existence, when the expense of doing so is what leads to fewer toilets overall for the population. However, suppose that many jobs are now held by people because of past unjust discrimination against others, or that toilets that are not handicapped accessible should never have been built. Then these considerations may lead us to not distinguish policies in accord with the loss/no-gain distinction.

30. As described above, in section III. For more on this, see chapters 1 and 3.

31. Kahneman, "The Cognitive Psychology of Consequences and Moral Intuition," pp. 10–11.

32. Ibid., pp. 7–8.

33. Timothy Hall suggests an alternative justification of people's responses to Schelling's cases: An exemption is an amount of earned income that is exempt from taxation. A surcharge is the amount of tax paid. Whether someone who is poor or someone who is rich has a child, arguably the same amount of money is needed to raise the child. Hence, the amount of the exemption from taxes should be the same. If a person does not have a child, she will not get the exemption, so more of her earned income is subject to taxes. But this does not settle the question of the tax rate, i.e., of how much taxes (surcharge) the rich and the poor should pay. Arguably, the tax rate should be higher on nonexempted income for the rich than for the poor. Hence, the use of terms such as "exemption" and "surcharge" can explain why people think that the exemption should not be greater for the rich than for the poor, but the surcharge should be greater for the rich than the poor.

34. Kahneman, "The Cognitive Psychology of Consequences and Moral Intuition," pp. 17–18.

35. For more on this, see Michael Slote, *Goods and Virtues* (Oxford: Clarendon, 1983); my "Why Is Death Bad and Worse than Pre-Natal Nonexistence," *Pacific Philosophical Quarterly* 60 (1988): 161–64; David Velleman, "Well-Being and Time," *Pacific Philosophical Quarterly* 72 (1991): 48–77; my *Morality, Mortality*, vol. 1 (New York: Oxford University Press, 1993),

pp. 67–71; and my "Rescuing Ivan Ilych: How We Live and How We Die," *Ethics* (January 2003): 202–33.

36. See n. 35.

37. In Derek Parfit, *Reasons and Persons* (Oxford: Oxford University Press, 1984).

38. The asymmetrical attitudes toward past and future can also be made use of to explain our asymmetrical attitude toward death and prenatal nonexistence: Both involve non-existence, and so involve the absence of goods we could otherwise have had, yet most people are concerned about death but not about prenatal nonexistence. Parfit suggests that this is (at least in part) because the absence of a good through prenatal nonexistence is always behind us, and we therefore care less about it, but the absence of a good through death is yet to come. I have also suggested that the particular negative factors associated with decline (discussed above in the text) occur with death and not with prenatal nonexistence; hence, these negatives also are only in our future, never behind us. For detailed discussion of this, as well as of Parfit's view, see my *Morality, Mortality*, vol. 1, part 1; for a brief discussion see my "Why Is Death Bad and Worse than Pre-natal Nonexistence?"

39. These cases were presented by Thomas Scanlon, as quoted in Samuel Scheffler, *The Rejection of Consequentialism* (New York: Oxford University Press, 1982). I also discussed a different aspect of them in chapter 9.

40. For more on the Principle of Irrelevant Goods, see my *Morality, Mortality*, vol. 1, and in this volume chapters 1 and 2.

41. See Cass Sunstein, "Probability Neglect: Emotions, Worst Cases, and Law," *Yale Law Journal* 112 (2002): 61–107.

15

HARMS, LOSSES, AND EVILS IN GERT'S MORAL THEORY

I. INTRODUCTION

In chapter 14, I considered psychological evidence concerning intuitive judgments. I was especially concerned to see if people's judgments about the difference between harming and not-aiding amounted to their judgments about a difference between losses and no-gains as these notions are understood by some psychologists. I concluded that these were different sets of judgments. This conclusion can, I believe, help us to better understand the moral theory offered by Bernard Gert.

Gert claims that "the goal of morality is the lessening of evil."[1] He thinks well of Hobbes's view that "the utility of moral and civil philosophy is to be estimated, not so much by the commodities we have by knowing these sciences, as by the calamities we receive by not knowing them."[2] In addition, Gert thinks that this view represents common morality, and he aims to provide a justification of that common morality.[3]

I shall consider whether morality on Gert's understanding really is concerned with avoiding or lessening evils in the Hobbesian sense. First, I shall briefly describe Gert's views on evils and goods and conduct related to them. Then I shall provide my own characterization of the various ways in which the evil/good and harming/aiding distinctions may interact in this view. Having done this, I shall consider how concerned Gert really is with lessening evils. I shall argue that Gert, as a nonconsequentialist, is actually committed to an understanding of the harming/not-aiding distinction consistent with the one I describe in chapters 1 and 3.

II. GERT'S VIEWS

According to Gert, the point of morality is to lessen evils, not to promote goods. Evils are things that it is irrational for an agent to seek or not avoid. This category includes loss of goods. Gert also thinks that it is an evil to be in a deprived state, that is, to have insufficient goods relative to a social standard of sufficiency. Among the primary rules of morality are five telling us *not to cause evil*: Do not cause death, pain, loss of ability, loss of freedom to act or be acted upon, or loss of pleasure (or opportunities for pleasure). To cause losses of goods such as freedom or pleasure (or the opportunity for the latter) is to cause evil. A moral ideal—not a moral rule—tells us to also *prevent* evils (that we do not cause). Sometimes we can break rules that require us not to cause evil in order to prevent greater evils. It is only a utilitarian ideal, not a moral ideal, that tells us to promote goods, according to Gert.

III. THE NEGATIVE AND THE POSITIVE

I believe that there are two senses of the contrast between the negative and the positive in Gert's system. The first is that between evils and goods. The second is that between harming and aiding. It will help us in thinking about the relation between Gert and Hobbes to consider these two sets of factors in relation to each other. The following figure presents some relationships among these four factors, though it does not necessarily represent in all cases Gert's thinking about these factors (N stands for "negative" and P for "positive"). The following paragraphs explain figure 15.1.

The column labeled "Evils (N)" is intended to represent *only* the evils that are *not* the loss of goods, for example, pain or disability with which one began life. I shall refer to evils that involve the loss of goods as N*. Arguably, death is an evil primarily because (and when) it involves the loss of the goods of life or because life itself is a good. Loss of ability, freedom, and pleasure are also evils that involve losses of goods. N and P represent both negative and positive objects and negative and positive behaviors:

(1) represents causing evils that are not the loss of goods.

(2) represents interfering with the goods that someone has (and would have continued to have). Hence, it involves causing N* (the loss of goods had).

(3) represents interfering with someone getting new goods. When Gert speaks of causing the loss of opportunities for pleasure, I think that he has this in mind. Hence, it involves causing N* (no potential goods).

(4) represents preventing (or undoing) evil that is not just loss of a good and that is not caused by human interference.

(5) represents preventing (or undoing) evil that is not just loss of a good and is caused by human interference. The distinction attended to between

	Evils (N)	Goods (P)
Harming (N)	(1) NN	(2) N*P$_1$ (3) N*P$_2$
Aiding (P)	(4) PN (5) P(NN)	(6) PP$_1$ (7) PP$_2$ (8) P(N*P)$_1$ (9) P(N*P)$_2$

Figure 15.1.

(4) and (5) is not, I believe, given importance in Gert's system. Some, however, may think that the factor of preventing an evil caused by human interference is important in deciding whether to aid or not.

(6) represents preventing (or undoing) the loss not caused by human interference with a good someone has (or had). As such, it prevents an evil N*.

(7) represents providing someone with a new good. It may involve preventing (or undoing) an evil N* if the person is already deprived. Otherwise, it does not prevent an evil, but just provides a good.

(8) represents preventing (or undoing) the loss, caused by human interference, of a good someone has (or had). Hence, it prevents an evil N*.

(9) represents preventing (or undoing) the loss, caused by human interference, of an opportunity for a good. Hence, it prevents an evil N*.[4]

Gert claims that there can be a fine line between preventing the loss of a good like pleasure when someone is not deprived (part of the moral ideal of preventing evil) and simply providing someone with pleasure (a utilitarian ideal). (This would be especially true if there were no human interference involved in the loss, I think.) Strictly, however, preventing losses takes precedence over providing goods, even when one of the following conditions obtains: (i) the loss would leave someone no worse off than someone else will be if he does not receive a good; (ii) the loss would leave someone *better off* than someone else will be if not given a good; or (iii) the loss would reduce someone's condition slightly, and our aid could produce a greater benefit to someone else.[5]

IV. GERT, HOBBES, AND COMMON MORALITY

I shall now raise three points in support of the claim that both Gert and common morality are more concerned with the harm/aid distinction than with the evil/good distinction as Hobbes might be taken to have understood it.

First, in Gert's system, suffering a loss (through natural or human intervention) is an evil. Often, however, even a large loss (and hence, not a trivial one) will leave one still quite well off. Yet Gert thinks that there is a moral rule not to cause such losses. Could these be the sorts of evils that Hobbes thought we should flee the state of nature to avoid? As they leave us still well off, it seems unlikely. If all people ever did to each other was cause the loss of pleasure or cause occasional broken legs, it seems unlikely that life would be short, nasty, and brutish *without morality*. I am not denying that there are many losses that do result in very bad conditions, and so we might flee a state of nature to avoid them. I am only pointing out that Gert's system does not make a point of *only* ruling out such flee-the-state-of-nature losses.

Gert seems to be more concerned with the harming/not-aiding distinction, when this is understood as the distinction between (a) causing someone a setback of his condition (regardless of how badly off this would leave him) and (b) not helping to improve his condition.[6] This distinction is different from the loss/no-gain distinction that Gert also accepts, but to which he gives less weight. Emphasizing the latter distinction but not the former would give as much importance to helping to prevent a loss as to not causing it.[7] But Gert gives less weight to helping to prevent a loss than to not causing it, though he thinks that preventing a loss has more weight than providing a gain, even when persons would wind up in the same position through loss and no-gain.

Concern for the harming/not-aiding distinction (and even the loss/no-gain distinction) contrasts with concern for the distinction between people not being in bad conditions and their being in good conditions. It is the latter distinction that is more likely suggested by the ordinary contrast between evils and goods. Insofar as Gert is concerned with the harming/not-aiding distinction, even when caused losses do not lower someone to a bad condition, I believe that he is really concerned with a morality that gives emphasis to the *separateness of persons*, rather than a morality that seeks to diminish evils. Such a morality says that we have a strong duty to avoid interfering with what others have independently of us and we have a weaker duty to aid, because to have a duty to aid requires interference with what we have independently of someone else for the sake of their having what they would not have independently of us.[8] This sort of morality coheres with Gert's frequent assertions that we could abide by the five moral rules with respect to everyone without doing anything, but we would have to do something (and, hence, probably not do something for everyone) if we had to aid people.

Second, if Gert really believes that common morality is concerned with reducing evils, he should, for example, think that it permits the killing of one person in order to save two from death (or from being killed) or the maiming of one in order to save another from death. Such minimization would also apply to those evils of loss that would leave us not very badly off. Yet he does not endorse minimizing evils in general. Rather, he thinks that the amount of evil we would prevent has to be very much larger than the amount of harm we would cause in order for the rule against causing evil to be overridden by the moral ideal of preventing evil.[9] In other words, there are probably rules that would reduce evils more than Gert's rules do, yet they are not the rules of common morality.

Third, if the loss to you of obeying the moral rule not to harm someone is even greater than the loss you would cause her, common morality still insists that you may be required to suffer the loss. For example, if a villain (or natural disaster) threatens to break your leg and your arm unless you break someone else's arm, it is not permissible to break the other person's arm. If common morality were concerned with reducing evils (understood either as bad conditions or losses), such an action would be permissible.

I conclude that Gert and the common morality he seeks to describe and justify are more concerned with the distinction between harming and not-aiding and respect for the separateness of persons than with either the avoidance of evils or the avoidance of losses.

NOTES

This discussion of Gert began life as a comment on "Accentuate the Negative: Negative Values, Moral Theory, and Common Sense," by Douglas MacLean. Both MacLean's paper and my comment were presented at a conference on Gert's Moral Philosophy at Dartmouth College, 1999, and appear in *Rationality, Rules, and Ideals: Critical Essays on Bernard Gert's Moral Theory*, ed. Walter Sinnott-Armstrong and Robert Audi (Lanham, MD: Rowman and Littlefield, 2002). I am grateful for the stimulus to thought provided by MacLean's paper and for the comments by one of the editors of the Gert volume, Walter Sinnott-Armstrong.

1. Bernard Gert, *Morality: Its Nature and Justification* (New York: Oxford University Press, 1998), p. 253. All citations to this volume are hereafter referred to as *Morality*.

2. Ibid., p. 2.

3. Ibid., p. 13.

4. Some distinctions were added to this figure thanks to discussion with Shelly Kagan.

5. In emphasizing avoiding losses rather than promoting goods, Gert emphasizes some of the factors that Daniel Kahneman and Amos Tversky emphasize in their Prospect Theory. For more on Prospect Theory, see chapter 14.

6. I shall here ignore the point I made in chapter 1, that some terminations of aid seem to involve causing a loss even though they are not harmings but not-aidings.

7. For more on the difference between the loss/no-gain and harming/not-aiding distinction see chapter 14.

8. This is only a shorthand description of an account of the harming/not-aiding distinction that I have given in my *Morality, Mortality*, vol. 2 (New York: Oxford University Press, 1996), and in chapters 1 and 3, this volume.

9. Gert, *Morality*, p. 125.

16

OWING, JUSTIFYING, AND REJECTING

I. INTRODUCTION

In this final chapter, I shall discuss contractualism and its attempt to generate moral principles by taking seriously the perspectives of individuals rather than by maximizing the goodness of outcomes. I shall do this by examining Thomas Scanlon's contractualist theory of morality, focusing on those parts of it that bear on the issues we have discussed in previous chapters in this book.[1]

By now, Scanlon's original formulation of what wrongness is has become famous: "For an act to be wrong is for it to be contrary to a principle which no one could reasonably reject who was searching for informed, unforced agreement on principles for mutual regulation with others similarly motivated."[2] His more recent formulation is somewhat different: "An act is wrong if and only if any principle that permitted it would be one that could reasonably be rejected by people moved to find principles for the general regulation of behavior that others, similarly motivated, could not reasonably reject."[3] In section II, I focus primarily on Scanlon's views on wrongness, value, and the theory of contractualism. A major conclusion I reach in this section is that while Scanlon believes that he is giving an account of wrongness, he actually gives what is better described as an account of wronging. Section III focuses on reasoning that may be employed in deriving moral principles in a contractualist framework. Two major conclusions that I reach in this section are (1) that Scanlon assumes nonconsequentialist distinctions that one would have thought his system should attempt to justify, and (2) that there are significant problems with his views on aggregation.

II. WRONGNESS, VALUE, AND CONTRACTUALISM

A. The Formulation of Wrongness and the Scope of Morality

Let me begin by making clearer certain aspects of Scanlon's account of wrongness. It gives one the impression that he believes that contractualism is concerned with determining which acts are wrong or right. His more refined view seems to be that contractualism is also concerned with *what reasons and forms of reasoning could be licensed* by contractors as adequate for acting in certain ways, since acts are wrong when no adequate form of reasoning could justify them.[4] For example, a reasonable principle would rule out breaking a promise for the reason that it is inconvenient to keep it, but not rule out breaking promises for other selected reasons (pp. 157, 199–201). However, there is another way to put this that places more emphasis on the properties of an act rather than on possible reasons of an agent: The fact that keeping a promise has the property of being inconvenient is not grounds for not keeping the promise.

Scanlon emphasizes that his account of wrongness is not meant to be a definition. The definition of wrongness that contractualists and noncontractualists alike could accept is something like "violates important standards of conduct and is therefore open to serious criticism" (p. 10). My understanding is that Scanlon's account of wrongness fills in the "standards" placeholder in this definition with a particular account of the standards, that is, they are principles that people could not *reasonably reject* (henceforth abbreviated RR). Nor is his account a description of what makes an act be wrong. Scanlon distinguishes between the property of wrongness and the properties that make acts wrong. The latter properties (for example, brutal killing, causing pain for its own sake, etc.), in making acts wrong, make them have the additional property of wrongness of which Scanlon's contractualist formulation is an account.[5] Nor is his account merely a higher-order summary of all of the particular properties that make acts be wrong. The account of wrongness is intended to help us understand both the content and reason-giving force of "wrong." But, Scanlon thinks, it only does this for the part of morality that deals with what we owe to each other (what I shall call M1). Scanlon believes that there is another, noncontractualist form of wrongness that is not reducible to our failing to render what we owe to others, though it may be related to this idea (p. 173). (I shall call this part of morality M2. M2 includes being inhumane in failing to give certain things that we do not owe [p. 238].) Hence there is a *fragmentation of morality in his view into M1 and M2*.

The contractualist account of wrongness speaks of principles that people could not RR. The flip side of the idea of reasonable rejection in Scanlon's system is justification to others. If we do an act that is permitted only by a principle that someone could RR, we will not, Scanlon thinks, be able to justify our act to others on grounds that they could not RR (p. 5). In Scanlon's system, being able to justify to others is just as important as not violating principles that no one could RR (or more weakly, not doing what would be ruled out by every principle that no one could RR).

Is there not a problem, though, with the idea that the possibility of justification to others includes reference to, and is a flip side of a concern with, their reasonable rejection? One concern is that ordinarily it seems that someone could reasonably reject at least our doing something, and yet we could justify our doing it to him. For example, suppose that a bodyguard owes it to his client to save his life, but the bodyguard faces a conflict between doing this and saving the lives of a thousand people. Given the size of the loss to the client and the existence of a contractual obligation, I think that the client could reasonably reject his being left by his bodyguard; he need not release the bodyguard from his obligation to him. (This is consistent with his not being able to reasonably reject being abandoned for the thousand, if he had no contract for assistance.) Yet, it also seems that the bodyguard could justify his conduct to his client, if he leaves his client in order to save so many people. However, in this case, either neither party is appealing to a principle that *no one* could RR, or else each is appealing to unrejectable principles that are relativized to the situation of each. (That is, it is unrejectable that the client need not release his bodyguard and unrejectable that the bodyguard may decide to abandon the client.)

A second concern about the relation of "justification to" and "reasonable rejection by" relates to the scope of morality. In his discussion of the scope of the morality of right and wrong (pp. 177–87), Scanlon argues that MI applies to any creature with judgment-sensitive attitudes (p. 179), that is, attitudes that are adopted or withdrawn in accord with appreciation of reasons. He notes that not all such creatures need be capable of morality or be able to form the idea of morality as a set of principles that people could not RR. A problem may arise, therefore, because the ability to have some attitude responsive to a consideration weighing in favor of the attitude, combined with an appreciation that the consideration is a reason, does not ensure that one can decide whether one reason is stronger than another, an ability that seems necessary to be able to RR. It does not even imply that one is self-conscious or capable of judgment-sensitive attitudes concerning oneself or what is done to one. In other words, the ability to appreciate and to act on reasons need not mean that one is self-governing, for one might have judgment-sensitive attitudes only concerning other things or other people. Would we owe a creature with such a limited capacity for judgment-sensitive attitudes, and hence such a limited capacity for RR, justification of acts toward him? Scanlon might assume that all creatures capable of judgment-sensitive attitudes have "capacities for reasoning and rational self-direction" (p. 100) and so really think that it is these latter characteristics that are crucial to being in the scope of MI. Alternatively, he might believe that once creatures are responsive to reasons at all, the appropriate way to value them is to treat them according to the best system of reasons, whether they would recognize all of these reasons, and engage in RR, or not.

Suppose that MI applies to creatures we can think of as being owed a justification, and any creature capable of having any judgment-sensitive attitudes can be thought of as being owed a justification. M1 will then not necessarily involve justification to creatures who are capable of reasonable rejection of principles or grounds of action. So it seems that Scanlon's account of wrongness, in order to dovetail with his account of the scope of M1, should be put in terms of "cannot be justified to" rather than in terms of "can be reasonably rejected by." He himself says about those capable of judgment-sensitive attitudes but not of moral reasoning:

> [T]he idea of justifiability to such beings nonetheless makes sense, and . . . we have reason to care about it. Claims about what it would be reasonable for them to accept if they were moved to find principles that others also could not reasonably reject involve a minimal counterfactual element. Moreover, their capacities for reasoning and rational self-direction call for the kind of respect that entails treating them only in ways that they could (in this minimally counterfactual sense) not reasonably object to. (p. 180)

One of the concerns I have expressed is that some creatures capable of judgment-sensitive attitudes and recognition of a reason might not *weigh* reasons and/ or might not have what we would ordinarily call the capacity for rational self-direction. Furthermore, given that the thought of reasonable rejection is sometimes counterfactual, even if only minimally, it seems that the requirement to justify oneself to someone is what is still more basic to M1.

In addition, the foundational reason that Scanlon gives (p. 106) for focusing on reasonable rejection is that it is a proper way of valuing beings who can assess reasons and govern themselves according to this assessment. If this is so, then if a being lacks these capacities, as someone with a judgment-sensitive attitude might, why does appropriately valuing him entail thinking about what he could RR? On the other hand, it might be said, if justification to creatures with judgment-sensitive attitudes involves considering what they could counterfactually RR, then focusing on reasonable rejection should have a foundation other than that it is a way of valuing reason-assessing, self-governing creatures who *are* capable of reasonable rejection.

In sum, one concern I have is that Scanlon's account of wrongness and his foundation for it that focuses on RR is not perfectly consistent with his account of the scope of M1 put in terms of the possibility of "justification to."[6]

B. Foundation of the Account of Wrongness

As noted above, the foundation for Scanlon's contractualist account of wrongness is to be found in his theory of value and valuing. Indeed, in some ways, I think that the chapter on value is the key to the whole book. In general, he is there trying to show that different things that are of value require different ways of valuing; bringing about a maximal amount of a valuable thing is often not the appropriate way to value it.[7]

When he discusses respecting the value of human life (pp. 105–7), he offers two interpretations of it. The first concerns the value of a life *to* the person who lives it, and this amounts to the reasons it gives him for going on living. So respecting the value of human life in the first sense amounts to respecting the reasons someone has to go on living (at least insofar as his life itself provides the reasons). If there are no reasons a person has to go on living and he does not want to go on living, then it may be permissible to end his life.[8]

The second interpretation of how to value human life (pp. 105–7) is, in my view, what is crucial as a foundation to his moral theory. It is not concerned with the value of a life *to* the person but rather with the value *of* a person (understood as a being capable of responding to reasons.) According to Scanlon (pp. 105–6, 169), appreciating the value of the person must involve recognizing and respecting her capacities to assess and act on reasons. Now comes the crucial point: The way to value the rational and self-governing capacity in a person is to treat her in accord with principles that she could not RR, and this is to treat her according to principles of right and wrong on Scanlon's account of wrongness ("[T]he idea of justifiability to others and the idea of their value cease to be distinct" [p. 171]). So Scanlon hopes to connect a theory of value and how to value with a theory of right and wrong.

This is Scanlon at his most Kantian, relying on the second formulation of the Categorical Imperative to "treat humanity in oneself or others always as an end and never as a mere means," where this is interpreted as treating persons according to principles they could not RR.[9] A non-Kantian feature, however, is that Scanlon thinks of the morality of right and wrong as "what we owe to each other." He does not attempt to derive any obligations to oneself as Kant did.

Does Scanlon's view that respecting the value of a person involves acting according to principles he could not RR imply that we can reject a principle on the ground that it does not respect the value of persons only if we mean that the principle tells us to ignore people's reasonable rejection of principles? No, for he specifically says (p. 106): "I do not claim that this is the only possible response to the problem of understanding the requirements of valuing human life," and (p. 169) "[r]ecognizing the value of human life is also . . . a matter of seeing that it is a bad thing . . . when their lives go badly." Hence, there could be further information being given about a principle in saying that it does not respect the value of a person that could serve as a reason for reasonably rejecting it. If so, there must be some other way one can respect the value of a person besides treating her according to principles she could not RR.

However, Scanlon distinguishes between a person's life going badly and a person's valid claim being denied (p. 169). Respecting people's valid claims is a way of valuing persons. He says (p. 169) that some may think that the content and reason-giving force of the valid claims can *lead* people to RR certain principles. He denies this, however, because on his view valid claims only come about *as a consequence* of the reasonable rejection of principles, leaving behind principles no one could RR that give rise to valid claims. (One then has a claim not to be treated in a way that could only be licensed by a rejectable principle and not to be treated in a way that violates a [or all] non-rejectable principle[s].) Yet, I think that it makes sense to reject a principle *because* properties people have give them a valid claim to certain sorts of treatment. Scanlon denies that we can in this way reject a principle because it does not respect the value of a person.

Let us suppose, as Scanlon thinks, that the primary way to respect the distinctive value of people is to heed principles that no one could RR (p. 169). Why ought we to value people appropriately? It cannot be because they could RR a principle that permits our not valuing them, because it is only if we must first value them appropriately that we must heed their reasonable rejection. If we want to say that it is *wrong* not to value people appropriately (i.e., it is wrong not to heed principles that no one could RR), this will have to involve a sense of wrongness that is not given by Scanlon's contractualist formulation of wrongness, because it is needed as the foundation of the normative significance of the contractualist formulation. So a noncontractualist sense of "wrong" seems to be needed in order to get the entire contractualist system (not only M2, as Scanlon thinks) off the ground. Furthermore, we cannot say that the value of persons is only a conception of themselves whose nonacceptance they could RR, for we should care about what they could RR because they have value independently of what they believe about themselves, a value to which we respond appropriately by attending to what they could and could not RR.

So at the foundation of Scanlon's theory there must be an objective theory of value. We might say that the answer to why we ought to appropriately value what is objectively valuable—it is wrong not to—is simply that this is the only rational response to it (using "rational" in a broad sense to include reasonableness as well as mere consistency). So the requirement to be rational gives rise to the "wrong" at the base of contractualism. But Scanlon thinks that the failure to avoid other behavior that is not rational (e.g., making mistakes in math) is not always as serious as the failure to value persons (pp. 149–57). So the significance of failing to recognize and respond appropriately to the reasons there are must vary, depending on the reason in question.

Scanlon says at one point that his account of why we should avoid acting on principles that people could RR is avowedly heteronomous. We should do so in order to be able to live in a desirable way with other people; being able to justify ourselves to others brings us "in unity with our fellow creatures" (p. 163). This proposal seems to contrast with the simple idea that the value of persons is objectively great, that is, the reasons we have for treating them in a way that reflects their rational powers is very strong (as compared with other reasons we have for doing other things). It seems to me that it would be better if Scanlon just followed the latter route to account for why we should care about reasonable rejection by others, rather than introducing what he calls heteronomous reasons.[10]

Notice that Scanlon's view leaves it open that what accounts for the value of the person (namely, his rational capacities) can be different from what provides a person with a reason to go on living (that is, his rational capacities need not make his life of value to *him*). So merely retaining and even exercising one's rational capacities, while one is suffering greatly, may not provide a person with a reason stemming from his life to go on living. Further, on Scanlon's account, respect for rational beings is about heeding their reasonable views, not necessarily about promoting and protecting their rationality. Hence, it is consistent with the fact that someone's life is not worth living and that this gives him sufficient reason to end his life, that he himself has great worth because he is still a rational being.[11]

C. Wrongness, What Makes Something Be Wrong, and Transparency

When individuals decide whether a principle is one they could RR, they must consider reasons for rejecting it. These reasons must be provided (in part) by properties of the acts that the principle would allow, properties other than that the acts are allowed by a principle that someone could RR. In other words, for the persons who RR a principle, it is not their reasonable rejection that can be a *reason* for rejecting a principle. To use language that Scanlon uses in another context, their own reasonable rejection is *transparent* from the first-person point of view; one sees through it to the reasons for it. It is the transparency of well-being from the first-person point of view—that is, while well-being may result from the pursuit of goods and projects, it is not aimed at by an agent—that leads Scanlon to downplay its role for the person himself. Further, it is the transparency of desire satisfaction from the first-person point of view when someone makes a judgment about the goodness of something that leads Scanlon to reject the Desire Satisfaction Theory of Goodness (p. 388, n. 29). That is, that something satisfies his desire cannot be taken *by an agent* himself as a reason that something is good; rather, the thing's other properties give him reason to think it good and hence to desire it. Yet Scanlon takes a property—namely, that a principle could be RR—that is also transparent from the first-person point of view of moral reasoners to be a centerpiece of his moral theory. This means that he would reject any account of "wrong" for M1 that makes it equally non-transparent from all points of view.

Why does this property that is transparent to those who reason about principles become a centerpiece? It is because, whereas Scanlon accepts what he calls the "buck-passing" view of goodness, according to which all of the importance of goodness is captured by the properties that give rise to it, he believes that "the fact that an act is wrong seems to provide us with a reason not to do it" (p. 11) and that "[i]t is the particular reason-giving force of this idea of moral wrongness that we need to account for" (p. 152). His solution is, of course, "to explain more clearly how the idea that an act is wrong flows from the idea that there is an objection of a certain kind to people's being allowed to perform such actions and ... an act's being wrong in *the* sense described can provide a reason not to do it" (p. 153). (The "sense described" is M1.)

Suppose that we, as agents deciding to act, would reject acting in a certain way for only the very same nontransparent reasons for which others must reject principles that would allow us to act in that way. Does this imply, in Scanlon's view, that we will not have sufficiently shown respect for the value of persons, because we will not have rejected acting in this way on account of a further property the act has—a property transparent from the first-person point of view of those who consider and reject principles—that is, it is not in accord with principles that no one could RR? No, for while Scanlon thinks that wrongness per se has considerable reason-giving force, he also thinks that a morally good person "more often will be moved directly by these more concrete considerations without the need to think that 'it would be wrong.'...The latter thought is more likely to come to the fore... [when] we have failed to do what we ought or are feeling tempted to." This seems to reduce the importance of the reason-giving force of wrongness as a property had by an act, the property that his theory is concerned to understand. However, he also thinks that the reason we consider concrete considerations that make an act wrong (rather than the wrongness of it)[12] is that "the source of motivation[,]...the ideal of justifiability to others...provides a higher-order reason to shape our...practical thinking in ways that...others could reasonably be asked to license us to use" (p. 156). Also, we avoid taking into account "considerations...that others could reasonably refuse to license us to count as reasons" (p. 157). So for any given set of concrete considerations that make something be wrong, attending to them (rather than wrongness per se) is important, according to Scanlon, because others could RR our not doing so.[13] But this (their own reasonable rejection) cannot be the reason that these *others* think it is important for us to attend to concrete considerations. *They* will have other reasons for thinking it is important that people consider these matters. Are we fully respectful of others if we just consider *those* reasons for considering the concrete considerations? If so, what gap in how to value persons is left to be filled by attending to their reasonable rejection?[14] I shall call this the Gap Question.

Similar things could be said about being concerned with justifiability to others. In ordinary speech, if I were to say, "I cannot justify this particular act," I think that this would be merely a signal for me to focus on the properties of the act that make it wrong as a reason for not doing it. The point of saying, "I cannot justify (to others) the act," is to get me to focus on those properties or effects it has and not do the act because of them. It is not a signal for me to focus on the property of not being able to justify the act to others or not being able to stand in the relation of justifiability to others. (Similarly, if we say that we *can* justify an act, this is a cue to take our mind off the properties of the act.)

Now consider further the relation between a property, such as "being a brutal killing," that makes an act wrong and the property of wrongness. The property of wrongness is present in many acts that have relatively little impact on people's lives as much as it is present in a brutal killing. Presumably, as a potential victim, I would care much more about your brutally killing me than about your failing to take seriously the fact that I could RR the principle permitting your act. It is hard to believe that I would think it more a sign of your not valuing me as a person that you do not take my reasonable rejection seriously than that you do not take seriously the property that makes the act wrong (that is, it takes my life brutally), especially when many acts that have relatively little impact on people's lives could be reasonably rejected as well. This would show that compared with the reason provided by the act's wrongness, on the contractualist account of wrongness, stronger reasons not to do an act are often provided by the properties that make the act in question wrong.

There may also be similarities between the structure of the contractualist account of wrongness and the Rational Desire Theory of the Good that Scanlon criticizes. This latter theory is intended to remedy the Desire Satisfaction Theory by limiting the objects of desire to those it is rational to desire. However, rather than just accepting an Objective List Theory of the Good, which identifies what is good with the items on the list, it insists on making reference to the fact that the objects could be rationally desired in its account of their goodness. Scanlon, among others, criticizes the Rational Desire Theory, noting that the satisfaction of desire is really playing no role in the theory of the good. All of the work is being done for the theory of the good by having entities whose properties give one reason to desire them. But it seems that the structure of his contractualist account of wrongness has a similar problem, insofar as it does not focus either just on simple rejection (comparable to simple desire) nor on what properties would serve as reasons for rejection (comparable to properties of good objects that give a reason for desire). It insists on making reference to the fact that there is rejection by someone based on those properties. The same holds for the "justification to" prong of the theory: It is not enough that a certain reason cannot justify an act; the theory insists on reminding us that there are no reasons that can justify the act *to* someone. *Someone* could reject those *reasons* as support for that *act*; we could not justify to *someone* that *act* for that *reason*. The theory insists on three-place relations among reason, act, and others, rather than the two-place relation between reason and act. But, in fact, the presence or absence of reasons for the act, independent of someone's attitude toward those reasons, may do all the work.

In Scanlon's theory, the power of certain entities to rationally judge behavior toward them is supposed to make *them* quite generally a presence in our M1 thinking. This is independent of any other properties they have that rightly make them a presence in our moral thinking and make our acts affecting them right or wrong. I think for this reason that the theory gives others a role in the wrong place, an unnecessary role, even an oppressive role, at least if the theory is about explaining the property of wrongness. It seems that once there are beings who understand the reasons why something is wrong in people's behavior toward them, it is *that* they would evaluate the behavior (or reasons for the behavior) that gets attended to in order to understand the wrongness of the act. That we would fail in their eyes becomes constitutive of wrongness. At some level, it will be incomplete just to attend to the reasons they attend to in judging our failure. This seems implausible to me, at least as an account of wrongness.[15]

D. "Owing to" and the Model of Rights

In his discussion of the scope of M1, Scanlon says that in a broader sense of morally wrong (M2), we can morally mistreat creatures that have no judgment-sensitive attitudes. So, for example, causing pain to such an entity will provide us with a moral reason not to act that we also have with respect to creatures who have judgment-sensitive attitudes. But in the latter case, we have an additional reason not to act, namely, we *owe it to them* not to cause them pain; not causing them pain is then part of M1. The thought here seems to be that if a creature has reasons for its conduct or attitudes, then offering justification to it is appropriate, and this connects with the idea of owing the creature not only a justification but also particular acts or particular forms of practical reasoning. We cannot owe anything to the creatures who are not capable of the judgment-sensitive attitudes.

Furthermore, we can do a morally (M2) wrong act if we cause pain to a creature that has no judgment-sensitive attitudes but, Scanlon says, we *wrong* only the creature to whom we also fail to give what we owe. On Scanlon's view, those who can understand that something is a consideration in favor of or against doing something have a type of claim on our attention that those who can only *be affected* by what is a consideration in favor of or against doing something lack.

Many philosophers who make use of the idea of *rights* have similarly emphasized the idea of "owing to someone" and "wronging someone" as distinct from merely being obligated to do something or doing the morally wrong thing.[16] They associate A's having a right with B's owing something *to* A in particular. This also involves a three-place relation among, for example, agent, act, and one to whom the act is owed, and it typically goes along with B's consciousness of A's being entitled to something from him.[17] Importantly, it is possible to owe something to someone who is not the person affected by our doing the act. This is true if I owe it to you to take care of your mother. It is hard to see how one could owe it to one animal to do what affects the well-being of another animal when this does not bear on the first animal's well being. We could try to transmit the idea of the additional reason that owing gives us by the following case involving rights: A and B need something equally, but I have promised it to A. I now have an additional reason for giving it to A. In this case, I owe it to A because A has a right against me. Arguably, the idea of respect for persons involves not only the idea that persons ought not to be treated in certain ways, but also that we owe it to a person in particular not to treat him in that way. This line of reasoning contrasts with the ideas that we owe it to God not to treat the person like this or that not treating him like this is implied by a duty (not owed to anyone in particular) to maximize the good.

Yet Scanlon never says that M1, which is all about what we owe to each other, has anything to do with rights. This may be because he thinks that we should not equate "something's being owed to someone" with her having a right to it. Even if this is so, I think that the emphasis that Scanlon places on "owing to" makes it illuminating to consider whether his construction of M1 has been inspired by the theory of rights and whether the connection of M1 with rights can help us to answer the Gap Question raised in section IIC above. Before considering this in more detail in section IIE below, we should note some differences between certain elements of rights theory and Scanlon's theory of M1.

In rights theory, once it is decided that we owe something to others, they could often RR our not giving it to them. This is not the same as deriving what we owe them from the possibility of their reasonably rejecting principles that do not imply our debt. In rights theory, if we do not give what we owe, we might owe a justification of our failure. This is different from deriving what we owe to others by considering what we could not justify to them. One reason that a rights theorist might think it wrong to derive what we owe to others from what others could RR or what we could not justify to them is that there are many things we do *not* owe to people whose failure to provide we nevertheless could not justify to them or that they might RR. For example, failure to provide an animal with pain relief is something we perhaps could not justify to persons, but we still might not owe it *to* a person to provide this pain relief to the animal.[18] In rights theory, we think of having to relate to others once we know that we owe them something. In Scanlon's system, we are to start with the thought that others are owed the possibility of justifications for how we treat them and from this derive what else we owe to them. So we see that Scanlon uses certain notions common in theories of rights, but uses them in somewhat different ways.

As noted above, it is possible that not all of what we owe to others in Scanlon's system would be identified by him as correlative to their rights. Rather, he may think of what we ordinarily think of as rights as correlative to a subset of what we owe. (He would then also reject the view that rights are nothing but directed duties.) Figure 16.1 is one way of representing how the components of Scanlon's theory might dovetail with rights.

Rights are typically thought of as nonabsolute; they are (permissibly) in-fringeable for the sake of valuable things that are within the scope of M2 (and hence *not* owed in senses (A) or (B)), let alone for the sake of things covered by (A) or (B). Scanlon claims that what we owe to others (M1) should not be overridden by acts covered by M2 (pp. 187, 220–21), though we may owe it to people to modify what they owe to us in order that they be permitted to act on the reasons they have for being responsive to values in M2 (p. 221). This position seems to commit him, for example, to its being wrong to breach the noninterference we owe to someone in order to stop him from killing dogs merely for the fun of it, as concern for animals fall under M2, even if it is right not to make it the case that people owe it to us to kill dogs in this way. However, suppose that what we owe to each other in Scanlon's system had properties like those we associate with rights. Rights can be permissibly infringed for the sake of valuable things not owed in senses [A] or [B], and when they are infringed it is often for the sake of the valuable thing itself, rather than merely out of concern that a person might have reason to act in a way that is responsive to valuable things, and so he should not owe it to us to not act in that way. Then M1 might also be infringeable for the sake of things outside it, that is, for

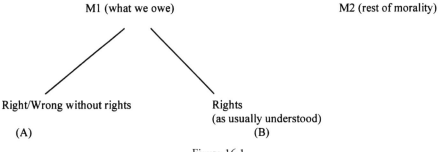

Figure 16.1.

things covered by M2, even independently of our owing it to someone to allow him to be responsive to the reasons provided by things covered by M2.

What I would call the "redundancy effect" in the theory of rights may also bear on Scanlon's claim that an additional reason is provided by our owing something to someone. If everyone had a strong human right not to be killed, then my giving someone, in addition, a personal promise not to kill him adds nothing to his right against me. Reasons, as Scanlon would be the first to note, are not simply additive. Is it possible that, similarly, there are some wrong acts (falling into M2) that are of a type such that we would not have any additional reason to avoid doing them to a person just because we owed it to her not to do them?

E. Wrongness and Wronging: Against the Fragmentation of Moral Wrongness

In section IIC, I discussed whether we owe it to people to consider, in particular, that they could RR any principle that permits our act or whether it is enough to consider the reasons they consider in rejecting the principle (for the reasons they consider them). I asked whether we are fully respectful of others, if we just consider such reasons, and if so, what gap in how to value persons is left to be filled by attending to their reasonable rejections. I called this the Gap Question. In section IID, I discussed further the ideas of owing to someone and wronging someone (by contrast with just having a duty to do something and doing the wrong act). Now I shall try to bring together these discussions to show that what Scanlon thinks is an account of wrongness is better understood as an account of wronging and that a possible answer to the Gap Question is that focusing on the fact that others could RR something emphasizes that, in our relation to persons, wronging and not just doing the wrong act is crucial. (This answer depends on its being true that one can wrong people only if they could RR.) Furthermore, I shall argue, if Scanlon's account of wrongness is better thought of as an account of wronging, this leaves the way open for a unified idea of wrongness.

In Scanlon's system, having judgment-sensitive attitudes leads both to being owed the possibility of a justification and to being owed acts. If we fail in giving what is owed, we wrong someone. If we need the idea of a capacity to reasonably reject principles, it is only because of its connection with a property (that is, a capacity for judgment-sensitive attitudes) that relates to *owing* and *wronging*. It is not needed to account for the *wrongness* of acts.

This is true even if, when we wrong someone, that will be by doing a wrong act,[19] and even if, when we do a wrong act but do not wrong someone, two further implications (not needed for the judgment of wrongness) follow: We cannot justify our behavior to other persons, and they could RR our behavior (or principles licensing it). That is, when we do a wrong act but do not wrong, it is because the act is wrong that we cannot justify it to persons and they could RR it; it is not because we cannot justify it that it is wrong. When reasonable rejection or inability to justify is no more than an implication of wrongness—as when we cannot justify the wrong treatment of animals—it does not imply that we owe it either to the animals or to persons not to mistreat animals. It also does not imply that we owe to anyone the possibility of justifying our conduct to animals; after all, we could be unable to give a justification (for a wrong act such as mistreating animals) that we do not owe.

Suppose that the *wrongness* of the act that wrongs someone need not essentially make reference to "inability to justify to" or to "rejectability by," even if *wronging* should make reference to these things. Then the wrongness of acts that are done to creatures with judgment-sensitive attitudes and the wrongness of acts that are done to other entities would not involve two different senses of wrongness; there would be no fragmentation of moral wrongness into M1 and M2. M1 would just involve *wronging* (the failure to do what we owe to someone), in addition to wrongness. (Though we might say that wronging is itself a property that can make an act wrong, this would not account for the wrongness of the act that made it possible for it to be an instance of wronging in the first place [assuming we can only wrong by way of wrong acts].)

How does this all imply that wronging can be identified with "acting contrary to principles that no one could RR or acting in a way we could not justify to them"? The possibility of owing to x and, therefore, of wronging x is said to depend on the capacity by x for judgment-sensitive attitudes and reasonable rejection of principles. Suppose that wronging consists in not refraining from a wrong act with respect to someone who is owed acts that are not wrong. Someone who is owed that is only someone (usually) capable of reasonably rejecting (via the exercise of judgment-sensitive attitudes) the principle leading to that act. So *wronging* would be doing an act to someone (who is also the person in virtue of which the act is wrong) that is contrary to a principle that he could RR (or acting in a way that could not be justified to him).[20] On Scanlon's account, we owe to people not only certain acts; we also owe it to people to be able to justify our acts to them. But being unable to justify to someone how we act to him is not itself doing a wrong act in addition to the wrong act we do. Doing an act to someone that is unjustifiable to him, I suggest, is best seen (in Scanlon's system) as another way of characterizing the act as one that (in addition to being wrong) *also* wrongs him because we owe it to him not to do it. The Gap Question asked why we have to be aware of the rejectability of a principle. The answer seems to be that this is related to knowing that a violation of it is a wronging in addition to being wrong. The Gap Question also asked why in deducing the wrongness of an act we have to be aware of any factor beyond the factors that those who would RR principles rely on to reject principles. This question presupposes that a principle is not determined to be wrong by those who RR on the basis of the fact that they can RR it. However, suppose that they decide not only that a principle is wrong (thereby ruling out acts permitted only by it), but also that they are owed nonperformance of acts that are permitted only by the principle. Then they, as well as we, might have in mind the factor that distinguishes them from creatures who cannot be owed nonperformance of wrong acts. This factor (according to Scanlon) is that they are capable of judgment-sensitive attitudes and of reasonable rejection. If all this were true, then we, in deciding that we owe others not to do what they could RR, still need not, thereby, be aware of any factor beyond what those who reject principles must be aware of.

I have argued that Scanlon's account of wrongness is really an account of wronging on the assumption that wronging occurs by a wrong act being done. But what if it is possible to wrong someone in the course of doing an act that is *not* wrong? For example, suppose that in order to save someone's life I must break a promise to someone else not to use his valuable property. The property is important enough to the promisee that he would not be morally wrong in not releasing me from the promise just so that I may save a life. Nevertheless, what he will lose if I do not keep the promise is much less than the life at stake for the other person, and this plays a part in its being right for me to save the life even by breaking the promise. Is the promisee wronged? Scanlon might say that we can justify our seemingly abusive conduct to this person and while he need not have granted us our liberty to act against him, he could not reasonably reject a principle that allows us to take what he need not give. On this view, the person is not wronged and no wrong act was done. This would make it possible to retain the view that Scanlon's theory is about wronging while also being about doing wrong acts that we owe it to others not to do.

However, suppose the promisee could permissibly resist our taking his property given the size of his loss. Does this not suggest that he would be wronged if we took it? In a more dramatic case of this kind, suppose we have to torture an innocent bystander to stop a million people from being killed. Is the one tortured not wronged, and is it not a sign of this that he could permissibly resist our act despite the effects of that? If we could owe it to someone not to treat him in a certain way, even though we do the right act in so treating him, we could wrong him while doing a right act. Then it would not always be as a result of a wrong act that we wrong someone. Indeed, it might be wrong not to do what wrongs someone, A, because we would thereby fail to do an act that we owed it to others to do—and hence would wrong them, if we did not do the act that wrongs A.

If a wrong act is not a necessary condition of wronging, we must say that Scanlon's account of wrongness is really a partial account of wronging, dealing with wronging only when it involves a wrong act.

III. DERIVING MORAL PRINCIPLES IN CONTRACTUALIST REASONING

A. *Principles versus Rules*

In this section, I shall deal with various aspects of Scanlon's discussion (in his chapter 5) about how to find principles that no one could RR. He emphasizes that he is concerned with finding principles rather than rules. I shall suggest that, given how he uses those terms, his system may contrast with the aims of standard non-consequentialists (as I shall here call them).[21]

Scanlon contrasts rules with principles by describing the former as mechanical (that is, requiring no judgment to apply) and unable to help us to deal with some types of new cases. By contrast, principles help us to see the point of a certain practice. Once we see the point, we can exercise judgment in deciding, in an infinite variety of new cases, what reasons are relevant to whether an act of a certain type may be done consistently with the practice.

I have several concerns with the rule/principle distinction. First, is it true that once we understand the point of our practice prohibiting killing, we will be able to understand why it is impermissible to kill someone for his organs in order to help others survive (Transplant Case), but it is permissible to redirect a trolley away from killing five in a direction where it will kill one instead (Trolley Case)? I doubt it. Is it an exercise of judgment, based on understanding the point of prohibiting killing, that leads us to decide that we may kill in the Trolley Case but not in the Transplant Case? I doubt it. Second, are people very good at grasping principles independently of first considering many particular cases (which Scanlon thinks the principles will help us decide)? I doubt it. Consideration of cases can show us that our grasp of principles is often too coarse-grained to be correct. Further, I would expand on this point by arguing that standard nonconsequentialists try to use their intuitive judgments about many cases to uncover what I have (in chapter 5 and elsewhere in this book) called principles or doctrines but that on Scanlon's use of terms are more like *rules*. Only once they have a "rule" like the Doctrine of Productive Purity do they think that it is safe, in order to justify the rule and the judgment of individual cases, to try to understand the morally significant point—that is, in Scanlon's terminology, the principle—that lies behind the rule and the individual judgments.

I say that consideration of many cases leads to a rule on the basis of our discussion in chapter 5, where we deduced the Doctrine of Productive Purity. This doctrine is something that could be mechanically applied by a computer. However, the rule does not classify, in a coarse-grained way, a type of act, such as "killing," as impermissible. The rule can be subtle and fine-grained, which is not the same as being endlessly complex. For example, we may start off with the view that killing innocent people is wrong, but then decide that it is permissible to do so in the Trolley Case. We might then inch our way, via further cases, to what Scanlon would call a rule, for example, that it is prima facie permissible for greater good to cause lesser evil. Even a computer could use such a rule to check whether an act that leads to evil does so by first producing a greater good that then causes lesser evil. If so, the act is prima facie permissible; if not, it is ruled out. If we find counterinstances to *this* rule, we formulate a new rule. We do not just say that sometimes a principle (which remains constant) is appropriately respected in the breach. If a stable rule is uncovered, we try to find the moral significance of the rule. For example, why may greater good cause lesser evil but lesser evil may not cause greater good? The answer to this question should yield the underlying principle. If there is no principle that seems morally significant underlying this rule, it might be rejected and an error theory used to explain the intuitive judgments about cases. I believe that the standard nonconsequentialists' approach is more likely to produce correct results than is the attempt to begin by grasping what Scanlon calls principles.

B. Reasons for Rejection: "How" Factors and the Reliance on Standard Nonconsequentialism

Reasons for rejecting a principle in Scanlon's theory should be offered (hypothetically) to others, and one must consider whether others would have even stronger reasons for refusing to reject the principle. Scanlon emphasizes that, in his contractualism, because we are always thinking of justifying our behavior to others, we always consider many generic points of view besides our own when considering principles, including those of people who would actually find themselves in bad situations if the principle were rejected. Hence, there is no need for a Rawlsian veil of ignorance whose function is to force us to identify with others. (Some think this occurs by way of the possibility that we might have been in their position.)[22] Therefore, his approach lets us justify to a person a principle of mutual aid without our having to point out that she personally might need aid at some point.

Reasons for rejecting a principle must pertain to the widespread presence of acts that it would permit or disallow and to the effects of the principle as a standing element in a moral system. An example of the latter is the assurance it provides or the preparation it requires of us, even if no one ever acts in accord with it. We *cannot* present as a reason for rejecting a principle that the acts it licenses are wrong, because in Scanlon's theory wrongness is only a property an act has once any principles licensing it are shown to be reasonably rejectable. However, moral considerations other than wrongness (or rightness), such as unfairness, can be given as a reason for rejection. Hence, Scanlon is not trying to derive wrongness from only nonmoral considerations (rationality, narrowly construed); he derives one aspect of M1 from other M1 moral considerations as well as from nonmoral ones, such as effects on well-being, which may also be used as a reason for rejection.

An objection to a principle must make reference to a complaint of an *individual* either on her own behalf or on behalf of another individual. (This is the Individualist Restriction that we first discussed in chapter 2.) This rules out the aggregation of many small complaints across many individuals so that together they can be stronger than a large complaint had by one other individual. Further, Scanlon says, there is *no threshold complaint* (p. 196), such that when someone raises it, a principle gets rejected, and we need not consider the complaints of others to not having the principle. (For example, there might be no burden that is so great that it would always provide a sufficient ground to reject some principle, because someone else may have an even stronger ground against rejecting the principle, provided by an even greater burden.) Yet, it should be noted that in considering particular principles, Scanlon does not seem to take the no-threshold-complaint principle very seriously. For example, he says that having to give certain forms of aid, or the requirement that we be strictly impartial in making decisions in our personal lives, would be too intrusive for agents, and that settles the question of whether to have principles demanding these sorts of actions (pp. 224–25). If he really accepts the no-threshold principle, would he not consider the complaints of those who would suffer with the rejection of these principles? That is, while *as agents* they too might find these principles intrusive, suffering that cost might be overall in their interest given how much they would suffer if the aid were not present or impartiality were not required. Is it possible that one could better explain some of the particular results for which he argues if his contractualism did involve a threshold complaint?

The importance of this for judging the theory is whether, when the no-threshold-complaint element is taken seriously, contractualism will yield very non-standard results. Would Scanlon think that this showed the contractualist theory to be incorrect or, rather, commonsense morality to be incorrect?

An additional way to explain the particular results he derives is by hypothe-sizing that he allows complaints to focus on *how* costs to people come about. For example, when considering the limits of well-being as a ground for rejection, I think we can best account for his results by attributing to Scanlon the view that we can reasonably be concerned not only with absolute or relative levels of well being, but also with *how* they come about. In his Shipwreck Case (p. 196), A and B are drowning and A has managed to get to the one life jacket. Each will die without it and survive if he has it. May each equally raise a complaint to each of the following principles: (1) a finder should be allowed to keep the life jacket, and (2) someone in B's situation is permitted to try to take it away? (After all, B will die if he cannot get the life jacket, and A will die if he cannot keep it.) What Scanlon actually says is that each may not equally raise a complaint, for A may have worked hard to get the life jacket, and that is relevant to his getting to keep it. But suppose that A did not work hard; the life jacket floated to him. I suspect that Scanlon would think that the fact that A would die because someone interfered with what he already has, whereas B would simply be left to die and not be interfered with, is relevant. If so, he would be relying on the distinction between a certain level of well-being being the result of harming someone rather than the result of not improving someone's situation.

Consider his other examples: the Transmitter Room Case (p. 235) and the use of some people as guinea pigs in experiments that will yield a drug to save others (p. 208). In the Transmitter Room Case, we must decide whether to save a workman from severe pain that would last a quarter of an hour and that is caused by an accident in the transmitter room or to continue transmission of a soccer match to millions. Scanlon interprets this as a case where we would have to deliberately leave someone to suffer in order not to disturb our delivering a small benefit to each of many others, and he thinks doing so is impermissible. He distinguishes doing this from, first, treating people as guinea pig by deliberately leaving (or even causing) them to suffer because suffering is a means to (rather than a side-effect of) helping others to avoid death (also impermissible) and, second, causing someone's suffering as a foreseen side effect of acting to produce a significant benefit to each of many people (which he thinks is often permissible).

It may also be that if someone's death will come about if we do not aid, the high cost to us of aiding functions as a *threshold* complaint in Scanlon's system. By contrast, if we would *cause* someone's paralysis in the course of doing something in order to prevent our own death, the high cost to us of not doing this act might not be a threshold complaint. In other words, a cost can be a threshold relative to aiding but not relative to not harming.

I take his view of cases as evidence that Scanlon helps himself to many distinctions that are, at least, analogous to the distinctions between intending versus foreseeing harm, harming as a means versus as a side effect, and harming versus not-aiding.

While I am here primarily interested in showing that Scanlon emphasizes *how* levels of well-being come about, it also worth noting that he sometimes misdescribes the distinction present in the cases he presents, and this weakens his arguments. For example, in his Transmitter Room Case, the workman's suffering seems to be *caused* by the transmitting machinery that brings the small benefit to each of many people. Hence, if we continue the transmission rather than stop to help the workman, we would be *causing* the suffering in one person in order to benefit many people. This contrasts with a case in which the cause of the workman's pain is unrelated to the cause of the transmission (for example, a bear is sitting on him), but helping him requires us to stop doing what keeps the transmission going. This is a case in which we would let him suffer (but do not cause his suffering) rather than stop benefiting many people.

Scanlon thinks that his Transmitter Room Case shows that we should not aggregate small benefits to each of many people and weigh the total benefit against the big cost to one person. But since his case also involves us causing suffering to someone, it is possible, for all he says, that it is only because we would do this to the workman as a side effect of benefiting others that we should not benefit the many. For ordinarily such actions are ruled out by nonconsequentialists on the ground that, very roughly, not-harming takes priority over benefiting. Indeed, suppose that many people watching the game are in as much pain as the person in the transmitter room would be if we don't help him, and we can help them relieve their pain if we continue transmitting. Here there are not many small benefits aggregated against one big pain, but many large benefits each of which is equal to the benefit we would bring to the workman. Yet it still would not be permissible to continue transmitting when we then cause significant suffering to the person in the transmitter room.

Hence, to be useful for Scanlon's goal of showing that the aggregation of small benefits to many should not outweigh a great loss to one, we would have to imagine the Transmitter Room Case along the lines of my revised version of the case. That is, we have to choose between either (1) helping the person in the transmitter room who has been injured independently of any machinery we use to transmit the game (e.g., a bear is sitting on him), thereby interfering with our continuing to transmit the game, or (2) continuing to transmit the game, providing small benefits to people not already in great pain, and leaving the man to suffer. If it is true that in this case we should help the man, this would support the view that small benefits to people not badly off do not override preventing something very bad to someone else. And unlike what is true when the machinery we use to transmit is what harms the man in the room, it will also be true that if many of the viewers are suffering as much as the man in the transmitter room and by transmitting we could help them as much as we could help the man, we should *not* help him if helping implies that we cannot transmit.[23]

Standard nonconsequentialists spend a lot of time trying to defend the moral relevance of the intending versus foreseeing, means versus side effect, and harming versus not-aiding distinctions (or other distinctions such as those in the Doctrine of Productive Purity that have similar results for cases) from consequentialist criticism. One would have liked to see how Scanlon's contractualism could help to justify the moral relevance of these "how" factors, that is, show why contractors would reject principles that did not take account of *how* costs and benefits come about. But he does not do this. Instead, his contractualism just seems to take the distinctions for granted. Indeed, he seems to think that contractualism is, in part, justified because it provides an arena where these (assumed) morally relevant factors can be considered (for a related point, see his p. 238). That is, it does not exclude consideration of them and simply focus on the size of a burden—he rejects welfarist contractualism (p. 243)—for if it did, it would not be a correct moral theory. Much of standard nonconsequentialism is not only *not* being justified by Scanlon, it is being assumed to be correct.

It seems to me, given how much Scanlonian contractors, in deciding on principles, rely on factors whose moral significance standard nonconsequentialism tries to justify (or replace with justified factors) that there is a great deal of overlap between how contractualism generates principles and how standard nonconsequentialism does. Many of the steps in the argumentative path internal to contractualism and in standard nonconsequentialism overlap, though they must begin at different points in the path. Here are the steps for the standard nonconsequentialist: She (1) begins with the intuitive judgment that an act is wrong, (2) locates factors that may account for this judgment (for example, well-being affected, "how" factors), and (3) then tries to explain why these factors really do matter morally. The argument internal to contractualism cannot begin at (1), because the judgment that an act is wrong is the conclusion of its argument. It seems to begin at a new step, (4), in which at least some factors picked out at step (2) above, *minus* their characterization as what makes an act wrong, are used by contractors to RR a principle. The contractors moving to (3) would strengthen their view that certain factors are reasons to reject a principle. However, it is possible that Scanlon thinks that (4)—the fact that a consideration would serve as a reason to RR a principle—just is the answer (sought in [3]) to why the factors pointed to in (2) are morally relevant. The standard nonconsequentialist would not be satisfied with the replacement of (3) by (4), and would perhaps find (4) no explanation at all of why factors in (2) really matter. In any case, from (4), reasoning internal to contractualism reaches (5)—that an act is wrong. This final step just is the standard nonconsequentialist's initial step (1). However, as a conclusion, (5) may be held with greater certainty than (1) was by the standard nonconsequentialist prior to her engaging in steps (2) and (3).

While one may not use the judgment that an act is wrong as a reason to RR a principle, Scanlon seems to judge the adequacy of the contractualist system as a whole by considering whether its internal steps lead to the *right* answers, that is, to the conclusion that certain acts and not others are wrong. The certainty that *these* are the right answers and so can serve as bench marks by which to judge the adequacy of contractualism must be provided in some other way. Is that other way not just standard nonconsequentialism? If so, contractualism must be important for some reason other than that it is necessary to provide knowledge of what principles or acts are right and wrong.

C. Reasons for Rejection: Probability?

Now let us consider other particular reasons for rejecting principles in Scanlon's system. Scanlon claims that if someone were to be harmed under a certain principle, the fact that this principle would have a low probability of leading to harm *does not reduce* the person's complaint against the principle. Scanlon believes that the probability of harm is just a "stand-in" for a consideration that *can* reduce the complaint of someone who would be harmed, namely, whether care will be taken to avoid the harm. People who are harmed can complain if reasonable care was not taken to avoid the harm.

It certainly seems true that the fact that the probability of harm is small should not always reduce a complaint. For example, suppose that we deliberately inject someone with a chemical that has a low probability of killing him. If his death occurs, it was easy to avoid; we just had to not inject the person. Hence, he can complain. But is probability of harm always a stand-in for absence of reasonable care?

If the cost of reducing the probability of death goes up, because we must forgo various valuable activities that cause death, Scanlon thinks that it would be unreasonable to expect us to reduce the probability. Refusing to give up the activities is not failure to take reasonable care. Hence, he claims, a person harmed in such a scenario has no ground for complaint against principles allowing us to engage in these activities. I emphasize that Scanlon is thinking of *causing* harm when he says this. This helps to make this part of his view implausible to me, for it seems to sanction engaging in activities that have extremely high probabilities (even certainty) of causing harm to someone, if it would be "intrusive" to have to avoid these valuable activities. This is one of the places where Scanlon's official thesis of a no-threshold complaint seems to be forgotten, for it is also very intrusive to be killed. In this case, I think, the high probability of death has weight in itself as a reason not to act.

Scanlon emphasizes the high cost that can come from not engaging in activities. But he does not seem to include among these costs the opportunity costs that come from easily avoiding an act that would cause harm. For example, in my version of a guinea pig case, it is easy enough to *avoid* the act that cuts off someone's leg. The cost comes in our being unable to develop a serum from the leg in order to save a life or perhaps in our inability to engage in many activities that require that we have the serum. The fact that Scanlon does not deal with both *avoidance costs* and *opportunity costs* suggests that it is not really *cost* per se that is playing an important role in his determining if we have taken reasonable care and in his differentiating when we should and when we need not avoid acts that have a high probability of harming others. Rather, it seems that the intention/foresight or means/side-effect distinction (or some distinction playing a similar role) pertaining to costs imposed on others is doing the work. For he discusses cases where we may refuse to pay the cost of giving up activities that we *foresee* will cause harm to others as a *side effect*, but opportunity costs that are incurred if we fail to harm others as a *means* to some useful end do not support our refusal to refrain from the harmful act. This is not a cost-of-taking-care consideration per se, as there are costs in both situations. It is what I call a "how" factor. That is, *how* costs to us and to others come about seems to be important.

D. Reasons for Rejection: Priority to the Worst Off?

Scanlon rejects the idea that the complaint of those who will be worst off is always the strongest complaint in contractualism. He thinks that Rawls's emphasis on priority to the worst off is due to (a) the assumption that each cooperating member of a social system is entitled to an equal share of benefit from it, and any move away from equality must be justified to those worst off, and (b) the fact that the social system we design is what *causes* the worst off to be the worst off. The implication of this is that for Scanlon there is no general background assumption in morality, in general, that people are entitled to equal shares of such things as resources or welfare or to absolute priority for relief if they are the worst off.

In particular, Scanlon argues that priority to the worst off is inappropriate as a ground for rejecting principles of no-harm and assurance of personal property. He is opposed to recognizing a general exception to rules, such as fidelity to promises, whenever this would benefit the worst off. However, he also thinks that if we understand the point of wanting assurance (in personal property and otherwise), we also can see when exceptions would be appropriate. He thinks that the most likely context for the appropriateness of giving priority to the worst off is when we distribute a good. Even here, he says, it may be that we mistake the principle of priority to the worst off for the principle of providing the biggest benefit, because we usually satisfy the latter when we help the worst off.

He illustrates this possibility in connection with two specific principles of aid that he says we could not RR. The first is the Rescue Principle, which involves helping at moderate cost those who will be very badly off. The second is the Helpfulness Principle, which involves helping those not very badly off when aid is easy. He claims that while the Rescue Principle takes priority over the Helpfulness Principle, this is not necessarily due to a priority of helping the worst off per se, as it also provides a bigger benefit to someone, for example, to save his life than to give someone else directions on the highway.

Scanlon's suggestion that it is the size of the benefit rather than how badly off someone is that does much work could be supported by cases where helpfulness produces a very large benefit and rescue produces a small benefit. For example, imagine that we could either raise a middle-class person to millionaire status easily by giving some business advice or rescue someone from death for a few extra minutes of life. Would we then still think that Rescue takes precedence over Helpfulness?

Still, Scanlon is willing to concede that when we hold the size of the benefit constant, or sometimes even when the bigger benefit would go to the better-off person, we ought to help someone just because he would be worse off if we do not help. The Pain Case he uses to prove this point involves a choice between either helping A avoid two months of pain or helping B avoid one month of pain, when B but not A will go on to suffer five additional years of pain (p. 227). However, he constrains the dimensions on which one is worst off that are relevant to the decision to favor the worst off. For example, he rejects the view (which he attributes to Thomas Nagel)[24] that we should consider how someone's life will have gone from birth to death overall if we do not help him avoid the month of pain.

Scanlon does not clearly distinguish the following views that tell us how to compare individuals: (1) from birth to death on all dimensions, (2) from birth to death on a particular dimension that constitutes a particular separate sphere (to use Walzer's term),[25] such as health. The second view would consider it irrelevant that someone had a bad education and was very poor, in deciding who will be worse off for purposes of getting a scarce kidney. But it would not ignore how bad someone's health overall will have been in his life overall, if he does not get the kidney. However, Scanlon would, I believe, also reject distributing a good by evaluating who will be worst off from birth to death on a dimension as general as health.

Rather, Scanlon's Priority Rule (as I shall call it) for comparing individuals to find the relevantly worst-off person seems to be as follows:[26] The person must (a) be worst off *in a way* that the good we are distributing can do something about (pp. 227–28), and (b) be worst off to *a degree* that puts him in the class where the Rescue Principle applies rather than merely the Helpfulness Principle (p. 228).[27] From the example he gives, I believe that "a way...we...can do something about" in clause (a) is narrowly construed. So, if we are able to relieve pain, it must be in the pain way that someone is worst off.

But will Scanlon allow birth-to-death quantities of pain that someone will have suffered to be relevant to determining who is worst off? If A suffered much pain ten years ago but B did not, should that be relevant in deciding whom to help to avoid pain now? Though his Pain Case involves only pain that will come in the future in B's case, even if Scanlon rejects birth-to-death pain as relevant, he need not be committed to all and only future pain being relevant. For example, he might consider it irrelevant that B, but not A, will suffer only five months of pain ten years down the road, and he might consider relevant only five months of pain if B had just gone through it and now faced an additional month. I suspect that to express what he believes, Scanlon should add to his Priority Rule (as I described it above) a clause containing (what I would call) a Continuity Condition: (c) The person must be worst off because of a condition sufficiently similar to and continuous (either in past or future) with the problem with which we can help.

How does his Priority Rule so amended compare with the following view, which I have defended elsewhere?[28] (A) If someone is worst off in health and in a very bad condition in an absolute sense, and we can provide some significant benefit, this outweighs any size benefit to those who are significantly better off. (B) If the worst-off person (i) is not significantly worse off in health than the better-off person, or (ii) is not in a very bad condition in absolute terms, only assign multiplicative factors by which to multiply the benefit we can expect to produce in the worst off, to give extra weight to his case. (C) At high levels of absolute well-being, we do not assign any multiplicative factors. In this proposal, my characterization of worst off makes relevant (1) how one fared from birth to death, (2) on a broad dimension, such as health. These last two factors are the first thing Scanlon would reject, according to my analysis of his view. But consider a version of his Pain Case, in which B will soon lose an arm instead of suffering five more years of pain. I find it hard to believe that this might not be relevant in deciding whether to save B from a month of pain or A from two months. After all, when someone is going to have to deal with a new handicap, should he also have to deal with pain? I think that at least the rejection of factor (2) in Scanlon's Priority Rule is problematic.

A further difference between the view I defended and Scanlon's is that he nowhere commits himself to (A), that because someone is worst off and his condition is at a very low absolute level, a significant benefit to him can outweigh *any* benefit to someone who is significantly better off. Scanlon's case only allows two months' relief of pain to be trumped by one month to the worst-off person. From this alone, we do not know what else he would think is allowed; whether five month's pain relief in A is trumped by one month to B. Component (C) in my view, however, dovetails with his view that being worst off in a way that only puts one in the class of people needing help, rather than rescue, does not imply that one gets priority. In such cases no one is in a bad state in absolute terms.

However, what I have described as his Priority Rule is not the whole story of Scanlon's views on helping the worst off. He also says (p. 227) that *if* one had a duty to improve people's well-being overall—rather than just to rescue and help— then "all aspects of welfare would be in the same category." I take this to mean that condition (a) in the Priority Rule is weakened, and that all of an agent's duties can be relevant to deciding how to fulfill one particular duty. Presumably, the same would hold true if there were duties to promote selected categories of people's welfare overall. For example, if doctors have duties to promote all aspects of health in addition to pain relief, should not Scanlon's remark imply that doctors must consider overall health in choosing between candidates for pain relief assistance? This implies giving pain relief to someone who will be worst off because he will lose an arm rather than to someone who will not. Or if we have duties to improve economic well-being, health, and education, why should we not give health care first to those to whom we are unable to give the economic and educational benefits to which they are entitled?

Some might argue that the latter policy is appropriate at the macro level when deciding on the allocation of social resources, but not at the micro level when administering medical care. Perhaps this is because the individual agent in the medical context does not have all of these duties (though, arguably, social workers do). But could we also argue for separate (health, education, etc.) spheres at the micro level by rejecting Scanlon's (apparent) view that all of an agent's duties to provide for another can be relevant to deciding how to fulfill one particular duty? I am suggesting that at the micro level the fact that we have a duty to improve someone's situation in one sphere does not always make this duty relevant when deciding how to fulfill another duty to improve his situation in a different sphere.

But it is also important to note that *not* having a duty to improve someone's situation overall does not necessarily make consideration of his situation overall irrelevant in deciding how we distribute a good, and not having a general duty to help those who are worst off does not necessarily make consideration of who is worst off irrelevant to deciding how we distribute a good. It would be mistaken to think that just because I do not have a duty to make someone rich, the fact that he is not rich cannot be relevant (even if it does not generate a duty) in deciding how I treat him relative to others who are rich. Some of what Scanlon says about the unimportance of giving priority to those who are worst off in general may be due to an implicit reliance on an improper argument for irrelevance based on the absence of a duty.

Finally, notice that in all of the cases that Scanlon presents in which priority to the worst off is right, our aid is *not* efficacious in making the person not be the worst off. (We can only relieve a month of B's five years of pain.) Cases where the aid did have that big of an impact might give rise to the suspicion that it is the bigger benefit—*not* helping the worst off—that is important. But what if a bigger benefit would result from our aid, though the benefit does not deal with the type of problem with which the aid is directly concerned? Scanlon does not discuss such cases. For example, if we save C one month's pain, he can also go to work and rise out of severe poverty from which he should be rescued. If we save D one month's pain, this is all we accomplish, as D is not in poverty. Is the bigger benefit that would help the economically worst off relevant in the context of distributing the pain killer? Scanlon's Priority Rule, I believe, alone does not rule out producing the bigger benefit. This is because the good we are distributing can do something about his poverty and he is much the worst off in that respect. Yet it should sometimes be irrelevant to our choice of whom to help that we are able to produce such a bigger benefit when we help the worst-off person. I suspect that what motivates consideration of how badly off someone is only in the way that the good we are distributing can do something about ([a] of Scanlon's Priority Rule) actually supports the view that the bigger benefit we produce should be bigger in the way that the good we are distributing can *directly* do something about (i.e., relieve pain). This implies that we may help C or D. To yield this result, however, (a) in the Priority Rule should be revised. It is not enough that someone is worst off in a way that the good we are distributing *can do something about*, because by aiding C our good *can* also (indirectly) do something about his poverty. Scanlon probably believes that a person must be worst off in a way that the good we are distributing can *directly* do something about.

E. Reasons for Rejection: Aggregation?

Should contractualism allow one to reject a principle on the ground that (over time, at least) more people will suffer a certain loss if it is adopted than will if another principle is adopted?[29] For example, should we have a principle that tells us to save five people on one island from death rather than one person on another island when we cannot do both? Or should we have a principle that tells us to toss a coin in this case in order to decide whom we will rescue, giving everyone an equal chance? No individual among the five will suffer a greater loss than the one will, and the Individualist Restriction only allows for complaints on behalf of individuals. If the number who will suffer a loss is to count in rejecting principles, it must be because an *individual* in the larger group can complain if numbers are not allowed to count.

To show that someone in the larger group will have a complaint if numbers do not count, Scanlon uses what he calls the Tiebreaker Argument (p. 232).[30] It is based on the idea that we should have a principle that tells us to save the greater number (all else being equal), but not because we thereby produce the greatest amount of good. Rather, we should do so because what each person is owed is to have his presence fully taken account of, and this implies that what each is owed is to be weighed against an equal and opposite person. When this happens, the weight of one person on one side is met by the weight of one person on the other. In the larger group, there will be at least one person whose weight is not met by anyone on the other side. He can complain if his presence makes no difference. Further, since the weight of those in the smaller group has been completely taken account of by being used to balance out an equal and opposite member in the larger group, no one there should have a complaint if the presence of someone in the larger group *is* taken account of by making him a tiebreaker. Hence, we should save the greater number.

Notice that, on this account, no one of those in the larger group whose presence *is* balanced by individuals in the smaller group has a complaint if we do not save the greater number. *Only an individual who is not balanced out can complain.* Those balanced out on his side are, I would say, the *beneficiaries* of his successful complaint.

If this is correct, Scanlon's Individualist Restriction should (I suggest) be understood as implying: (1) Several individuals' complaints together cannot create a tie with another individual's complaint; (2) but individuals' complaints may be evaluated in the context of how the complaint of another individual relates to them; and (3) an individual's complaint may be evaluated in the context of other individuals' complaints.[31]

Scanlon clearly enunciates (1). However, I believe that his presentation conceals (2) and (3). This is because he emphasizes comparing the complaints of individuals, and this suggests comparing each individual's complaint with every other individual's complaint in isolation from their context. For example, suppose we can save either A's life or B's life but not both, and also save C's leg only if we save B. If we compare on an individual basis, in isolation from context, the potential loss of every individual, then losing a leg pales before losing life and would be irrelevant to what we should do. By contrast, Scanlon could (correctly, I think) treat the leg as a tiebreaker. Scanlon's theory also does not direct mere pairwise comparison of complaints in isolation from context when it takes account of how B's complaint relates to A's *dynamically*. That is, when C is also present with B, B's tie with A is resolved by balancing A with B rather than by tossing a coin between A and B. Further, C's complaint is an individual (versus group) complaint in sense (1), but not in the sense of the significance it would have in isolation when pairwise compared (where it pales beside a life). Rather, C's complaint is considered in a context where (i) A ties B, and (ii) B would be saved if C is. (Option [ii] is missing if A ties B, but C is on an island *alone*. Here the tie between A and B would not imply that C's leg should be saved, rather than A's or B's life.)[32]

While I agree with the Tiebreaker Argument so understood (as going beyond pairwise comparison in isolation), I believe that the way Scanlon presents it may be overly simple. I also do not support the strict individual-complaint model that Scanlon does. Furthermore, I think that there may be things one should say in connection with the Tiebreaker Argument that Scanlon's Individualist Restriction will make it difficult to say. Consider the last point first. As the number of people in the larger group who outnumber those in the smaller group increases, there is a *greater* wrong done if we do not save the greater number. In other words, there is more cause for complaint against a principle that does not allow saving the greater number as the numbers increase on one side. But there seems to be no individual complaint that can capture this problem, because each unbalanced-out individual's complaint is no worse than any other unbalanced-out individual's complaint, and how is it possible, just given the Tiebreaker Argument, to aggregate these complaints? Is it only from some point of view outside that of any individual that we can see the situation getting morally worse as more complaints are present?[33]

Perhaps defenders of the Tiebreaker Argument and the Individualist Restriction might respond to this complaint by simply repeating the Tiebreaker Argument at a higher level. That is, suppose that the Tiebreaker Argument says that we should save two people instead of one other person when we cannot save everyone. Then to compare (a) a case in which two people can complain if one person is saved instead of three with (b) a case in which one person can complain if one person is saved instead of two, balance the *two complaining* individuals against the *one complaining* individual. One complaining individual from the group of three is a tiebreaker in this balancing. Hence we should *first* go to prevent only one being saved in case (a), where three confront one, before we go to prevent only one being saved in case (b), where two confront one. This is, it might be said, what it amounts to say that there is a greater wrong in saving the smaller group as the numbers increase in the larger group. How great a wrong would occur in a particular case X is a function of how many intervening cases of increasingly unbalanced choices X would dominate if we had to decide which wrong to prevent first.

Now consider the view that Scanlon's presentation of the Tiebreaker Argument is overly simple because it raises what, I think, is a problematic implication that should be blocked, but that Scanlon does not consider. Suppose that we have a choice between saving A's life or saving B's life *and* curing C's sore throat. There is a tie between A and B, but I think that it would be wrong to take C's sore throat as a tiebreaker. Rather, it is what I call an irrelevant good in this context.[34] Yet C might say that A's weight has been fully accounted for in balancing out B, so how can A complain if C is a tiebreaker? If A *can* appropriately complain, this indicates that giving equal chances is appropriate in more contexts than Scanlon's Tiebreaker Argument allows for.

I have said that some goods are irrelevant as tiebreakers in some contexts. It is of some significance to distinguish different types of irrelevant goods or evils. Scanlon speaks of differences in how badly off someone will be (on a particular dimension) that are irrelevant to the "moral category" in which someone falls for purposes of forming a tie with another person. So one need not face exactly the same loss as someone else to be in a tie with her for aid, according to Scanlon. For example, if A stands to lose five fingers and B four and one-half fingers, they could form a tie. (This implies that "tiemaker" is not transitive, for it could be the case that A was in the same category as B, B in the same category as C, but C not in the same category as A.) However, I believe, something that might be irrelevant to what moral category one is in for tiemaking purposes could be relevant as a tie-breaker when it represents the loss to someone else who would break a tie between two others who are in the same moral category. On my view,[35] whether a loss (or gain) is *concentrated* in someone who will lose (or gain) something else rather than, by contrast, *distributed* to another person might make a difference to its moral relevance. For example, if A needs to be cured of being blind, deaf, and paralyzed in one leg, and B needs to be cured only of being blind and deaf, the paralyzed leg might not interfere with tossing a fair coin to choose whether we cure A or B. This is because both stand to gain the benefits it is reasonable to care most about, and each is not indifferent as to whether he or another gets the benefits. But suppose that A would be no worse off than B and only if we helped B could we also prevent C's leg from being paralyzed. In the latter case, I think that the leg could well be a tiebreaker, for we are helping an additional person, affecting significantly another life, rather than concentrating more benefits in someone who already stands to benefit greatly.

Notice that this case shows that the importance of affecting an additional person is not reducible to the importance of helping the worst-off person. For if C has a paralyzed leg, he is no worse off then A would be with a paralyzed leg, and C would not become the worst-off person if we compared him with A, once A had received his benefits of a cure for blindness and deafness but not a cure for paralysis. It is also hard to believe that the importance of affecting an additional person is due to our producing more good if we distribute the benefits. There would not be diminishing marginal utility if A got the paralyzed-leg cure just because he would be prevented from also being deaf and blind. And we might imagine another case in which the benefit to C is *less* than relief from a paralyzed leg but still significant enough to serve as a tiebreaker between A and B, even though A's relief from a paralyzed leg in addition to relief from blindness and deafness would not distinguish between him and B for purposes of tossing a coin to decide between them.[36] Hence, benefiting more people can be an independent, positive factor in an allocation decision, even when the total amount of benefit we produce over the greater number is not as great as the benefit we could produce in a single person.

There are more problems for the Tiebreaker Argument due to, I think, Scanlon's deemphasis of priority to the worst off (discussed in section IID above). These problems bear on whether the strict individual complaint model is correct.

Derek Parfit suggests that we consider cases like the following in which A, B, and C will die if they are not helped, but A will live for twenty years if he is saved while B and C will each live for twelve years if they are saved.[37] We can either save A or the group of B and C. Parfit argues that since A will be as badly off as B if he is not helped, but we could give him a much bigger benefit, there is no tie between A and B on Scanlon's view. Because of this, C cannot serve as a tiebreaker. Hence, Scanlon's view implies that we should save A. And this will be true, no matter how many others we add to the side of B and C, though the others face death and would get the same benefit as B and C would, that is, significantly less than the benefit A can get. Parfit argues that this implication of Scanlon's view—that we should give a great benefit to one person rather than a much greater total benefit, in significant amounts per person, to people each of whom would be as badly off as the single person—conflicts with all plausible principles of distributive justice.

Given the way that Scanlon describes his own view, he may well be subject to Parfit's criticism. However, if Scanlon put more emphasis on priority to the worst off, he could avoid the criticism. One way of reasoning about Parfit's type of case (described in detail in chapter 2) is as follows: It helps to think what we would do if the good we could give A were divisible. A and B are tied with respect to how badly off they will be and, if the good is divisible, with respect to a benefit of living up to twelve years. There are two ways to break the tie. Either vertically (as I call it), by giving A another benefit of eight years more, or horizontally (as I call it), by considering that there is another person, C, who will be as badly off as A and B if not helped and who will benefit to the level of twelve years of life. If we give greater weight to the horizontal dimension, it could be because it is *more important to help another person who will be as badly off as the others* (so long as he is helped significantly) than it is to provide someone (such as B, who would already get twelve years) with even more benefit. However, because C would get twelve years and A would only get an additional eight years, it is possible that we would favor C because we produce a bigger additional benefit. To rule out this factor, we could modify the case so that we could either give A twenty years or give B twelve years and C *eight* years. If we still give greater weight to the horizontal dimension, this would, I think, be because it is more important to break the tie by helping significantly someone else who would be as badly off as the others if not helped. (I call this argument the Balancing Argument II.)[38] In the actual case, of course, we cannot divide the benefit to A in this way, but the reasoning we have just considered suggests that we could virtually (i.e., imaginatively) divide the benefit and break the "virtual tie" between A and B at twelve years, by helping C (i.e., we break the tie horizontally). This is the method of virtual divisibility. (We would also thereby affect more people as well, and I have argued above that this may be a positive independent factor, at least when the additional people are no better off than the single person in whom benefits could be concentrated.)

If this were the correct way to decide what to do about Parfit's type of case, it suggests that Scanlon should give greater priority to helping the worst off than he seems to think. Giving more priority to the worst off leads one to the conclusion, based on Parfit's type of case, that at least sometimes it is more important to give smaller benefits to a greater number of people than to provide a bigger benefit to one person, so long as they will all be equally badly off if not helped. Put in the language of individual complaints, C will have the biggest complaint if improving A beyond twelve years had priority over C's being saved from death to live twelve years, given that B would also be saved to live twelve years.[39]

This also bears on the point that Scanlon tries to make in the Transmitter Room Case. As we noted above (n. 23), Scanlon seems to be assuming that none of the people watching the match is already in as bad shape as the person in the transmitter room. That is, he may be assuming that they are not people who are in great pain and that they each receive a small bit of relief from that pain when watching the match. The point here is that we must be careful when we consider providing small rather than great benefits to consider the independent question of the baseline at which recipients are or to which they would fall. If they are all at the same low baseline, the number of small benefits may aggregate to override providing a bigger benefit to one person.[40]

So far, not much revision to Scanlon's views is necessary for him to deal with Parfit's type of case. But there is a bigger problem, one that strikes at his Individualist Restriction.[41] Suppose that some great additional benefit to D (thirty years of life) if he is saved *should* override saving E and F to live two years each. Yet as we increase the number beyond two people who can be saved to live for two years, does not the reason to save the person who will have the much greater benefit get weaker? I think it does. But this cannot be because any one individual person in the larger group can say that it is more important to break a virtual tie (in how badly off people would be and in the degree of benefit people would get) by helping another person who would be as badly off if not helped. For D and E are tied for only two years of life, and D's additional benefit of twenty-eight years should probably trump a two-year benefit to any other individual, taking one individual at a time. It seems that it is only the combined number of these people that is doing the work.

It is, of course, possible to say that each person who will gain two years of life helps create a tie *between the group* and D by narrowing the gap between the benefit D will get and the *aggregated benefit* to the group. Then, at a point where the *additional* benefit that D would get is small enough, it can be outweighed by helping even to a lesser degree another person in the group who will be as badly off if not helped. At that point, that person in the group will, on his own, have the greatest complaint if he is not helped. But such an analysis just makes clear how it is permissible for a *group*, not an *individual*, to create a tie when each member would be as badly off as D. This conflicts with Scanlon's claim that groups cannot be used to create ties, that ties must first come from weighing individuals against individuals. It also supports Parfit's claim that it is not the aggregation of small benefits over many individuals per se that is problematic, but rather doing so when these people would not be as badly off if not benefited as another individual we could help. It supports the view that it is the failure to give priority to the worst off that is problematic, not the aggregation of small benefits.

Scanlon also considers some cases where there is no tie between individuals because one person is in a different moral category from another, in the sense that he will not be even nearly as badly off if he is not helped. (The test for whether A and B are in different moral categories should be whether on their own we would toss a coin to choose between A and B. So, for example, if A will die and B will be partially paralyzed, we would *not* toss a coin, but would choose to help A assuming a significant benefit is possible.) Moral categories that are different may nevertheless be what he calls "relevant to" each other. For example, total paralysis is, he thinks, a different moral category from death and yet it is relevant to death. This sense of relevance is important not merely in deciding what is a tiebreaker. For, in my view, a category that is not relevant *to* death in Scanlon's sense (for example, paralysis in one leg) could be relevant as a tiebreaker between two people who will die. (Hence, our discussion has now revealed that three senses of "relevant" are at play—relevant as a tie-breaker, relevant to whether one is in a different moral category, and relevant to a moral category.)

Scanlon suggests that his contractualist system might allow that if many people will suffer fates that are relevant to a worse fate, we may help the larger number instead of someone who will suffer the worse fate (on the continuing assumption that everyone could be benefited so that he completely avoids his bad fate). (Indeed, this may just be the operational definition of his notion of "relevant to.") He thinks that it is possible that an *individual* who will suffer the less bad relevant fate can complain if this is not done. But it is not clear how this could be so, unless, for example, one of several people who can be completely saved from quadriplegia complains if *his* fate is not determinative, once a group of many other people who can be saved from quadriplegia have *together* created a tie with one person who would die if not helped. Only this is a tie he can break.

I too have argued[42] that some significant bad fates, which, when present in one person, would not lead us to toss a coin with a worse-off individual, should, when enough individuals each face such a fate, lead us to save them rather than the worst-off person. I also noted, however, that the fact that we should do this has different import from the straightforward cases where we balance equals (or individuals between whom there is an irrelevant difference) against each other. As evidence for this, I noted that even if we should save many from quadriplegia while *letting* someone else die, we should *not* redirect a trolley headed toward causing many quadriplegias when it will then go down another track and *kill* someone else. By contrast, we should save many people from death while letting one die *and* also redirect a trolley headed toward killing many people when it will then go down a track and kill someone else. I claimed that the role of the killing/letting die distinction in these cases helps us to see that there is a distinction to be drawn between the idea of true *equivalents* (for example, one life versus one life) and the idea of *costs*. For example, many people becoming totally paralyzed may be a cost that we are not willing to pay, or involve a loss of goods we are not willing to forgo, in order to save a life. Nevertheless, it is not an equivalent from the moral point of view to someone's death. Perhaps such a distinction might be of use in Scanlon's contractualism, though I am not sure exactly how.

Finally, in connection with interpersonal aggregation, the willingness to save many from fates that are relevant to the worse fates of a few raises the problem of a downward spiral. For a headache (x) is not relevant to death (y), but there will be some fate (z) worse than a headache to which it is relevant, and so we should prevent a greater number from suffering x rather than prevent fewer from suffering z. The same will be true of z and some worse fate l, and by steps back to death. So, if transitivity holds:

$$y < n_1(w)$$
$$n_1(w) < n_2(l)$$
$$n_2(l) < n_3(z)$$
$$n_3(z) < n_4(x)$$
$$\overline{y < n_4(x).}$$

This yields the dreaded conclusion that enormous numbers of people, each of whom has only a headache, should be saved from their headaches rather than save one person (to a long life) who faces death.[43]

A way to stop the downward spiral (as I argued in more detail in chapter 9) is to make the qualitative dimension (i.e., whether the less bad fate is of a type "relevant to" [as Scanlon would say] the worse fate) have a veto over the quantitative dimension. But this also implies that whom we choose to save can vary with the alternative choices we have. So if we could prevent (i) death in one person, or (ii) many quadriplegias, or (iii) even more paraplegias, it is possible that we should prevent many quadriplegias. But if only a choice between the latter two options is available, it is possible that we should prevent the greater number of paraplegias. This is because in a context where a life is at stake, saving someone from paraplegia is not appropriate (because paraplegia is not relevant to death). Hence in this context, saving the paraplegics gets eliminated as an available course of conduct. Because of this, once we choose to leave one person to die in order to save many from quadriplegia (even when he has already died), we are not irrational if we do not instead save an even greater number from paraplegia; that option has been eliminated by its comparison with death. By contrast, in the second context, where no one's life is at stake, if paraplegia is relevant to quadriplegia, preventing a great many paraplegias instead of preventing many quadriplegias could be chosen.

Allowing our choice to be influenced by the alternatives available raises the specter of violating Arrow's Principle of the Independence of Irrelevant Alternatives. For example, suppose many quadriplegics know that they will be abandoned in order to treat a far greater number of paraplegics. To avoid this result, they may reposition themselves in a context where several people are also dying. Even though we should not act on the new option to save the dying people, this option that is irrelevant to action will alter our decision to save the paraplegics. Hence our decision is not independent of an irrelevant alternative. I do not find this result worrisome, as there are many other cases where we can account for the rationality of apparently violating the Principle of the Independence of Irrelevant Alternatives. For example, consider the famous case invented by the philosopher Sidney Morgenhesse to show why the principle is *correct*: I choose to have tuna on rye rather than on wheat bread. Then the waiter tells me that I can also choose white bread, and this leads me to change my choice to wheat. This decision seems bizarre. However, I believe that it could be rational in a particular context: Suppose there is a conflict between producers of rye and white bread, and when I come to know that these two are competing options, I never want to select one over the other, but choose wheat instead.[44]

Scanlon believes that the permissibility of aggregating many small losses intrapersonally, that is over one individual's lifetime, contrasts with the impermissibility of aggregating small losses over many individuals, and that such intrapersonal (versus interpersonal) aggregation can often explain the permissibility of acting in ways that cause harm to others.[45] He appeals to this point when he contrasts his Transmitter Room Case (in which we should save one worker much pain though it deprives each of many others [better off than the worker] of a small benefit) with our willingness to build a transmitter to broadcast entertainment to millions although we foresee that the construction will involve a worker's death (call this the Transmitter Building Case). Presumably, he means that in the Transmitter Room Case, no individual viewer will lose much if we interfere with one match, but if we do not build a transmitter, an individual will be inconvenienced on many occasions in his life. But we might wonder how even accumulated inconvenience in one life can come to outweigh (or even be relevant to) death to someone else?

Suppose that we revise his Transmitter Room Case so that it is more like the Transmitter Building Case with respect to the loss to a worker and to his voluntary assumption of risk for the sake of having a job, as well as to the *intra*personal costs to viewers. Hence, suppose that if we help the worker in the room when he would otherwise die of an accident due to transmitting, the transmitter will permanently cease working, and we do not have the resources to build a new one. Similarly, let us create a Revised Transmitter Building Case, in which a worker building the transmitter has fallen but is not yet dead. Should we abandon him because reaching him requires that we not protect from destruction a cable (that we cannot rebuild) necessary for transmission? Suppose it is more morally problematic to abandon workers in these revised cases than to operate or build the transmitter when we foresee that an accident will occur when we can no longer prevent death. Then it is not the greater importance of intrapersonal aggregation in the life of any single viewer that is making the crucial difference to what we should do. It may be the fact that there is an identifiable victim or the factor of *how* the loss to the worker and the costs to the viewers come about that is crucial.

To see how the cost to viewers comes about, consider that in the Transmitter Room cases and the Revised Transmitter Building Case, we would pay a cost down the line (forgoing some good) if we save a worker *in a way* that is in itself nearly costless. In the original Transmitter Building Case, if we did not build the transmitter, we would also forgo some good (the means to which causes a death), but not because we go and do something else to save a life in a way that is in itself nearly costless. In the original Transmitter Building Case, we would prevent the death by forgoing the means to a good; in the Transmitter Room Cases and the Revised Transmitter Building Case, we prevent death by a procedure that in itself is nearly costless but that *entails* forgoing a good. Is this a distinction to which it is worth attending in a moral system? Is it a distinction contractors should use to distinguish principles they reject from ones they accept?

IV. CONCLUSION

I have considered how Scanlon offers a metaethical theory about wrongness and wronging, a normative theory about how to value people and decide on principles of morality, and suggestions about the details of reasoning when deciding on such principles. The depth and sweep of his accomplishment are undeniable. Yet, I believe, he relies on, without justifying through contractualist methodology, many nonconsequentialist distinctions. The tasks undertaken in earlier chapters in this book, of isolating the correct distinctions and considering how to justify them, and the methods used to do this do not seem to be superseded by contractualism.

NOTES

For help on earlier versions of this chapter, I am grateful to Derek Parfit, Thomas Scanlon, David Enoch, Ryan Preston, Nomy Arpaly, members of the Department of Philosophy at the University of Colorado, and the editors of *Mind*.

1. This chapter is a revision of my article of the same name in *Mind* III (2002): 323–54.

2. T. M. Scanlon, "Contractualism and Utilitarianism," in *Utilitarianism and Beyond*, ed. Amartya Sen and Bernard Williams (Cambridge: Cambridge University Press, 1982).

3. T. M. Scanlon, *What We Owe to Each Other* (Cambridge, MA: Harvard University Press, 1998), p. 4. Hereafter, references to this book will be made in the text by citing pages in parentheses. Scanlon now apparently thinks that there being *no* nonrejectable principle that permits the act (which is what the second formulation implies) is crucial. The first formulation implies that an act is wrong if it is contrary to one nonrejectable principle, even if it were permitted by other nonrejectable principles. The second, more recent, formulation is weaker, because it allows that an act is not wrong if one nonrejectable principle does not permit it but another does. (Only if a system of principles in which one principle permits what another principle rules out is internally incoherent could the two formulations be extensionally equivalent.) Another difference between the first and second formulations is that the first makes explicit reference to individuals ("no one") whereas the second speaks of "people." Hence, the first makes explicit Scanlon's view that a nonrejectable principle is one that no *one* could reject, whereas the second does not commit itself to this. For it is logically possible for *people* to be reasonable in not rejecting a principle, even though some*one* among them could reasonably reject it. Given Scanlon's actual commitment to an Individualist Restriction on the rejection of principles, his earlier formulation may better reflect this aspect of his views.

4. This does not mean that an act is wrong if someone's actual reasons for doing it could not be licensed. There can be a good reason to do an act, in virtue of the act's properties, and so the act can be justified, even if a particular agent does not make the good reason his reason.

5. See especially the distinction in Scanlon, *What We Owe to Each Other*, p. 391, n. 21, between what makes an act wrong and what it is for an act to be wrong.

6. In his discussion of the scope of M1, Scanlon even includes creatures who lack all judgment-sensitive attitudes, for example, severely mentally retarded humans. Their inclusion in M1 might require us to also amend a focus on whether we could even hypothetically justify our act to others (as well as on whether others could RR). He includes them because he says they are related to "us." But rational Martians would presumably be included in M1, so should not their retarded members then be included in M1 because they are related to rational Martians? This would mean that some nonrational members in the scope of M1 would not be related to us, if "us" means humans, but would be related to us if "us" means rational beings.

7. He here follows Elizabeth Anderson in her *Value in Ethics and in Economics* (Cambridge, MA: Harvard University Press, 1993).

8. Notice that the reasons someone has to go on living might not only derive from the value of his life, but from his concern for the effect of his not living on the value of others lives. Also, Scanlon seems to allow that if a person *wants* to go on living, though he has no reason to (want to) go on living, we should not interfere. This would make one's desire a reason for *others*, even though Scanlon argues (in his chapter on reasons) that one's desire alone gives to *oneself* no reason to pursue the object of one's desire. He does not, I think, explain how to reconcile this asymmetry in the role of desires.

9. Kant, however, might speak in terms of principles to which they could reasonably consent rather than those they could not RR.

10. For help in clarification of issues discussed in the two paragraphs above, I am grateful to correspondence from Scanlon.

11. I argued for such a view in my "Physician-Assisted Suicide, the Doctrine of Double Effect, and the Ground of Value," *Ethics* 109 (1999): 586–605.

12. Again, on this distinction, see Scanlon, *What We Owe to Each Other*, p. 391, n. 21.

13. This brings out the fact that Scanlon introduces a metalevel of owing. That is, we not only owe specific acts to people, but we also owe it to them (somewhere down the line) to consider whether they could RR something.

14. Nonpaternalist theories take it as a mark of respect for persons to count their rejection of something, without necessarily endorsing or thinking about their reasons for rejection. But Scanlon only considers *reasonable* rejections as worthy of being heeded. Hence, we must endorse the reasonableness of others' reasons before we give moral weight to their rejections in this context.

15. Notice that just attending to reasons does not exclude attending to reasons that pertain to the effects on one person at a time.

16. This is in addition to the distinction between "wronging" and "harming," which draws attention to the fact that one can be wronged without being harmed (as in paternalistic acts) or harmed without being wronged because it is not wrong to harm someone sometimes.

17. I have discussed this in chapter 8.

18. Scanlon restricts the reasons for rejecting principles to the principles' implications for individual persons (as we shall see below). Hence he may deny that persons could reject (for an animal's sake) principles allowing ill treatment of animals. This conclusion may seem odd, as we could complain on behalf of each animal, not a group.

19. In chapters 7 and 8, I argued that one could wrong someone in the course of doing a right act. Below, I will reconsider this issue in relation to Scanlon's theory.

20. When I mistreat animals, I cannot justify my conduct to anyone, but I do not owe anyone the possibility of a justification and I do not owe anyone that I not mistreat animals. If I harm Jones by taking his organs without his consent in order to help Ann, I wrong him. I also cannot justify my behavior to Ann, and she could RR it, but, nevertheless, it seems that I do not wrong her nor owe it to her not to take Jones's organs. (David Boonin

suggested this example.) Hence, if we assume that only wrong acts can wrong when I do an unjustifiable act, I only wrong the person (Jones) the effect on whom makes the act wrong.

21. *Standard nonconsequentialism* is just the nonconsequentialism I have been describing in other parts of this book.

22. Oddly, Scanlon does not repeat in *What We Owe to Each Other* his earlier criticism (in "Contractualism and Utilitarianism") of this common interpretation of the veil of ignorance.

23. Other objections to Scanlon's opposition to aggregating small benefits or harms have been raised in chapter 2 and will be revisited below. In particular, what should we do when the audience watching the soccer match is already in as much pain as the workman (with the bear on him), but transmitting only helps each of many a small bit, but we can help the workman a great deal if we do that instead? Should the aggregate of many small benefits outweigh the single big benefit in this case?

24. Thomas Nagel, "Equality," in his *Mortal Questions* (New York: Cambridge University Press, 1979).

25. Michael Walzer, *Spheres of Justice: A Defense of Pluralism and Equality* (New York: Basic, 1983).

26. He does not explicitly say this. I am constructing the rule from what he says.

27. Condition (b) applies to *B* in Scanlon's Pain Case, presumably, because someone can be considered as needing rescue (from five years of pain) even if we are unable to provide help sufficient to completely rescue him. Scanlon's Priority Rule implies that when people we would aid fall under the Helpfulness Principle, we need not give the worst off priority.

28. See my *Morality, Mortality*, vol. 1 (Oxford: Oxford University Press, 1993), and chapter 1, this volume.

29. Parts of this section repeat in briefer form some material presented in chapter 2, for the sake of presenting a unified discussion of Scanlon's theory.

30. He says that it is similar to what I call the Balancing Argument. For more on this, see chapters 1 and 2.

31. I first noted the presence of (3) in Scanlon's view in *Morality, Mortality*, vol. 1.

32. For more detailed discussion of this Three Islands Case and Scanlon's Individualist Restriction see chapter 2.

33. I pointed to a related issue in chapter 1 when discussing the Argument for Best Outcomes.

34. For more on irrelevant goods and the Principle of Irrelevant Goods, see my *Morality, Mortality*, vol. 1, and chapters 1 and 2 in this volume.

35. Discussed along with the issue of irrelevant goods in *Morality, Mortality*, vol. 1, and in chapters 1 and 2 in this volume.

36. The suggestion that affecting additional persons may have independent significance may conflict in a minor way with some parts of my argument about whether it is morally permissible for an individual to receive multiple organ transplants over the course of time. See my discussion of this issue in the last section of *Morality, Mortality*, vol. 1.

37. In Derek Parfit, "Climbing the Mountain" (unpublished), and "Justifiability to Each Person" in *Ratio* 16(4) 2003, pp. 368–390.

38. I call it Balancing Argument II because, like my Balancing Argument for counting numbers of people, it assumes that we achieve the same good whether we give *A* twelve years or *B* twelve years when we cannot do both. More detailed discussion of this argument and the method of virtual divisibility (described briefly in what follows) was given in chapter 2.

39. In chapter 2, I discuss problems with, and different interpretations of, the method of virtual divisibility. Scanlon might respond to Parfit's objection in another way: *B*'s equal potential loss of life and his significant potential gain make his situation "relevant to" *A*'s

situation for purposes of creating a tie. I shall describe this approach below, though I think that it is not the best way to go in this case.

40. Larry Temkin, however, argues (in unpublished work) that even if the baselines of all the people are the same, benefiting each of millions very slightly does not aggregate so as to override providing a much bigger gain (total relief) to the man in the transmitter room, who is as badly off. Indeed, he claims that even if the baseline of the many people in the audience is lower than that of the man in the transmitter room (i.e., they are suffering more), giving each of them very small benefits by transmitting does not outweigh giving the single man the much bigger benefit of totally relieving his bad pain. His most radical claim is that we could decide to give a much bigger benefit to one person rather than very small benefits to many people without even considering what the comparative baselines are. These are much stronger claims than the one that Scanlon originally seemed to be making with the Transmitter Room Case, namely, that small benefits to people not as badly off cannot outweigh a big benefit of totally preventing a big loss to someone who would be very much worse off than the others if he suffered that loss. Scanlon may, however, accept Temkin's first two conclusions, as he seems to believe that an individual's complaint is based not only on how badly off he will be but on how much better off he could be. All of Temkin's claims still leave unanswered the question of whether small benefits to many people who are not badly off should, intuitively even if not contractualistically (to coin an adverb), outweigh helping a person who is very badly off just a small bit (e.g., reducing his pain slightly).

41. Also discussed in chapter 2.

42. In *Morality, Mortality*, vol. 1.

43. I emphasize that each small benefit will go to people who are not also facing death.

44. For more on this and its relation to intransitivity, see my *Morality, Mortality*, vol. 2.

45. In making this claim he assumes a normal lifespan, as we know it, for an individual. I suggest that he might not think that intrapersonal aggregation was very important if there were much more time within a life and between the costly incidents. So a million headaches, one each year, over the course of a million-year lifespan may well count morally for less than 20,000 headaches, 1,000 per year distributed over twenty people. Hence, the significance of intrapersonal aggregation is not independent of the *distribution* within the life, I believe.

BIBLIOGRAPHY

Anderson, Elizabeth. *Value in Ethics and Economics*. Cambridge, MA: Harvard University Press, 1993.

Anscombe, Elizabeth. *Intention*. Oxford: Blackwell, 1957.

———. "Who Is Wronged?" *Oxford Review* 5 (1967): 16–17.

Audi, Robert, ed. *Cambridge Dictionary of Philosophy,* s.v. "Doctrine of Double Effect." Cambridge: Cambridge University Press, 1995.

Battin, Margaret. "Euthanasia: The Fundamental Issues." In *The Least Worst Death*. New York: Oxford University Press, 1993.

Bennett, Jonathan. "Morality and Consequences." In *The Tanner Lectures on Human Values,* vol. 2. Edited by S. McMurrin. Salt Lake City: University of Utah Press, 1981.

Bratman, Michael. *Intention, Plans, and Practical Reason*. Cambridge, MA: Harvard University Press, 1987.

Brock, Dan. "Aggregating Costs and Benefits." *Philosophy and Phenomenological Research* 51 (1998): 963–67.

———. "Voluntary Active Euthanasia." In *Life and Death*. New York: Cambridge University Press, 1993.

Brody, Baruch. "Religion and Bioethics." In *A Companion to Bioethics*. Edited by Helga Kuhse and Peter Singer. Oxford: Blackwell Publishers, 1998.

Broome, John. "All Goods Are Relevant." In *Summary Measures of Population Health*. Edited by Christopher J. L. Murray, et al. Geneva: WHO Publication, 2002.

———. "Normative Requirements." Paper presented at Conference on Moral Theory and its Applications, Le Lavandou, France, June, 1999.

Darwall, Stephen L. "Agent-Centered Restrictions from the Inside Out." *Philosophical Studies* 50 (1986): 291–319.

Davis, Ann. "The Doctrine of Double Effect: Problems of Interpretation." In *Ethics: Problems and Principles*. Edited by J. Fischer and M. Ravissa. Fort Worth, TX: Harcourt Brace Jovanovich, 1992.

———. "The Priority of Avoiding Harm." In *Killing and Letting Die*. Edited by B. Steinbock. Englewood Cliffs, NJ: Prentice-Hall, 1980.

Dworkin, Ronald. Introduction to "The Philosophers' Brief to the U.S. Supreme Court." *New York Review of Books* 44 (1997): 41–47.

———. *Life's Dominion: An Argument about Abortion, Euthanasia, and Individual Freedom*. New York: Knopf, 1993.

———. "Rights as Trumps." In *Theories of Rights*. Edited by Jeremy Waldron. Oxford: Oxford University Press, 1984.

Enoch, David. "A Right to Violate One's Duty." *Law and Philosophy* 21 (2002): 355–84.

Feinberg, Joel. "Action and Responsibility." In *Doing and Deserving*. Princeton, NJ: Princeton University Press, 1970.

———. *Harm to Others*. New York: Oxford University Press, 1984.

———. "The Nature and Value of Rights." *Journal of Value Inquiry* 4 (1970): 263–67.

———. "Sua Culpa." In *Doing and Deserving*. Princeton, NJ: Princeton University Press, 1970.

———. "Voluntary Euthanasia and the Inalienable Right to Life." *Philosophy & Public Affairs* 7 (1978): 113.

Flory, James H., and Philip Kitcher. "Global Health and the Scientific Research Agenda." *Philosophy & Public Affairs* 32 (2004): 36–66.

Foot, Philippa. "Euthanasia." *Philosophy & Public Affairs* 6 (1977): 85–112.

———. "Killing and Letting Die." In *Abortion, Moral and Legal Perspectives*. Edited by Jay Garfield and Patricia Hennessey. Amherst: University of Massachusetts Press, 1984.

———. "The Problem of Abortion and the Doctrine of Double Effect." In *Virtues and Vices and Other Essays*. Berkeley: University of California Press, 1978.

Fried, Charles. *Right and Wrong*. Cambridge, MA: Harvard University Press, 1978.

Gert, Bernard. *Morality: Its Nature and Justification*. New York: Oxford University Press, 1998.

Gewirth, Alan. "Are All Rights Positive?" *Philosophy & Public Affairs* 30 (2001): 321–33.

Hare, R. M. *Moral Thinking*. New York: Oxford University Press, 1981.

Hart, H. L. A. "Bentham on Legal Rights." In *Oxford Essays in Jurisprudence: Second Series*. Edited by A. W. B. Simpson. Oxford: Oxford University Press, 1973.

Hill, Thomas E., Jr. "Moral Purity and the Lesser Evil." In *Autonomy and Self-Respect*. Cambridge: Cambridge University Press, 1991.

Hohfeld, W. N. *Fundamental Legal Conceptions*. New Haven, CT: Yale University Press, 1923.

Holmes, Stephen, and Cass Sunstein. *The Cost of Rights: Why Liberty Depends on Taxes*. New York: W. W. Norton, 2000.

Horowitz, Tamara. "Philosophical Intuitions and Psychological Theory." Paper presented at the Rethinking Intuition Conference, Notre Dame University, South Bend, Indiana, April 1996. Published in *Ethics* 108 (1998): 367–85.

Igneski, Violetta. "Distance, Determinacy, and the Duty to Aid: A Reply to Kamm." *Law and Philosophy* 20 (2001): 605–16.

Kadish, Sanford, and Stephen Schulhofer. *The Criminal Law and Its Processes*. 4th ed. Boston: Little, Brown, 1995.

Kagan, Shelly. "The Additive Fallacy." *Ethics* 90 (1988): 5–31.

———. *The Limits of Morality*. New York: Oxford University Press, 1989.

Kahneman, Daniel. "The Cognitive Psychology of Consequences and Moral Intuition." The Tanner Lecture in Human Values, University of Michigan, Ann Arbor, Michigan, November 1994.

Kahneman, Daniel, and Amos Tversky. "Prospect Theory: An Analysis of Decisions under Risk." *Econometrics* 47 (1974): 263–91.

Kamm, F. M. "Aggregation and Two Moral Methods," *Utilitas* 17 (March 2005): 1–23.

———. "Baselines and Compensation." *San Diego Law Review* 40 (2003): 1367–86.

———. "The Choice between People, 'Common Sense' Morality, and Doctors." *Bioethics* 1 (1987): 255–71.

———. Comment on "Accentuate the Negative: Moral Theory, Avoiding Harms, and Pursuing Ideals." In *Rationality, Rules, and Ideals: Critical Essays on Bernard Gert's Moral Theory.* Edited by Walter Sinnott-Armstrong and Robert Audi. Lanham, Maryland: Rowman & Littlefield, 2002.

———. "Conflicts of Rights: Typology, Methodology, and Nonconsequentialism." *Legal Theory* 7 (2001): 239–54.

———. *Creation and Abortion.* New York: Oxford University Press, 1992.

———. "Deciding Whom to Help, Health-Adjusted Life Years and Disabilities," in *Public Health, Ethics, and Equity*, ed. S. Anand, F. Peter, and A. Sen, pp. 225–242. Oxford: Oxford University Press, 2004.

———. "Disability, Discrimination, and Irrelevant goods" (unpublished).

———. "The Doctrine of Triple Effect and Why a Rational Agent Need Not Intend the Means to His End," in *Proceedings of the Aristotelian Society*, supplement 74 (2000): 21–39.

———. "Does Distance Matter Morally to the Duty to Rescue?" *Law and Philosophy* 19 (2000): 665–81.

———. "Equal Treatment and Equal Chances." *Philosophy and Public Affairs* 14 (1985): 177–94.

———. "Failures of Just War Theory." *Ethics* 114 (2004): 650–92.

———. "Faminine Ethics: The Problem of Distance in Morality and Singer's Ethical Theory." In *Singer and His Critics.* Edited by D. Jamieson. Oxford: Blackwell Publishing, 1999.

———. "Genes, Justice, and Obligations to Future People." *Social Philosophy & Policy* 19 (2002): 360–88.

———. "Grouping and the Imposition of Loss." *Utilitas* 10 (1998): 292.

———. "Harming, Not Aiding, and Positive Rights." *Philosophy & Public Affairs* 15 (1986): 3–32.

———. "Harming Some to Save Others." *Philosophical Studies* 57 (1989): 227–60.

———. "Harming Some to Save Others from the Nazis." In *Moral Philosophy and the Holocaust.* Hants, UK: Ashgate, 2003.

———. "Harming Some to Save Others from the Nazis." Revised version (unpublished).

———. "Health and Equity." In *Summary Measures of Population Health.* Edited by Christopher J. L. Murray et al. Geneva: WHO Publication, 2002.

———. "The Insanity Defense, Innocent Threats, and Limited Alternatives." *Criminal Justice Ethics* 6 (1987): 61–76.

———. "Justifications for Killing Noncombatants in War." *Midwest Studies in Philosophy* 24 (2000): 219–28.

———. "Killing and Letting Die: Methodological and Substantive Issues." *Pacific Philosophical Quarterly* 64 (1983): 297–312.

———. "Moral Improvisation and New Obligations" Forthcoming in *NOMOS XLIX, Moral Universalism and Pluralism*, edited by M. Williams and H. Richardson. New York: New York University Press, 2007.

———. "Moral Intuitions, Cognitive Psychology, and the Harming/Not-Aiding Distinction." *Ethics* 108 (1998): 463–88.

———. "Moral Status and Personal Identity: Clones, Embryos, and Future Generations." *Social Philosophy & Policy* 22 (2005): 283–307.

———. "Moral Status and Rights beyond Interests." Paper presented at the Conference on Moral Status at Santa Clara University, Santa Clara, California, April 2002.

———. *Morality, Mortality, Vol. I: Death and Whom to Save From It.* New York: Oxford University Press, 1993.

———. *Morality, Mortality, Vol. II: Rights, Duties, and Status.* New York: Oxford University Press, 1996.

———. "The New Problem of Distance." In *The Ethics of Assistance: Morality, Affluence, and the Distant Needy.* Edited by D. Chatterjee. Cambridge: Cambridge University Press, 2004.

———. "Nonconsequentialism." In *The Blackwell Guide to Ethical Theory.* Edited by H. LaFollette. Malden, MA: Blackwell, 2000.

———. "Nonconsequentialism, the Person as an End-in-Itself, and the Significance of Status." *Philosophy & Public Affairs* 21 (1992): 354–89.

———. "Owing, Justifying, and Rejecting." *Mind* 111 (2002): 323–54.

———. "Physician Assisted Suicide, Euthanasia, and Intending Death." In *Physician Assisted Suicide: Expanding the Debate.* Edited by M. Battin, R. Rhodes, and A. Silvers. New York: Routledge, 1998.

———. "Physician-Assisted Suicide, the Doctrine of Double Effect, and the Ground of Value." *Ethics* 109 (1999): 586–605.

———. "Rationality and Morality: A Discussion of Samuel Scheffler's *Human Morality.*" *Nous* 29 (1995): 544–55.

———. "Rescue and Harm: A Discussion of Peter Unger's *Living High and Letting Die.*" *Legal Theory* 5 (1999): 1–44.

———. "Rescuing Ivan Ilych: How We Live and How We Die." *Ethics* 113 (2003): 202–33.

———. "Responsibility and Collaboration." *Philosophy & Public Affairs* 28 (1999): 169–204.

———. Review of *Living High and Letting Die* by Peter Unger. *Philosophical Review* 108 (1999): 300–305.

———. Review of *Morality and Action,* by Warren Quinn. *Journal of Philosophy* 93 (1996): 578–84.

———. "A Right to Choose Death?" *Boston Review* 22 (1997): 20–23. Also appeared in Tom L. Beauchamp and LeRoy Walters, eds. *Contemporary Issues in Bioethics.* 6th ed. Belmont, CA: Wadsworth, 2003.

———. "Rights." In *The Oxford Handbook of Jurisprudence & Philosophy of Law.* Edited by J. Coleman and S. Shapiro. Oxford: Oxford University Press, 2002.

———. "Ronald Dworkin on Abortion and Physician-Assisted Suicide." In *Dworkin and His Critics.* Edited by J. Burley. Malden, MA: Blackwell, 2004.

———. "Terrorism and Several Moral Distinctions." *Legal Theory,* 12 (2006): 19–69.

———. "Supererogation and Obligation." *Journal of Philosophy* 82 (1985): 118–38.

———. "Towards the Essence of Nonconsequentialism." In *Fact and Value: Essays on Ethics and Metaphysics for Judith Jarvis Thomson.* Edited by Alex Byrne, Robert Stalnaker, and Ralph Wedgwood. Cambridge, MA: MIT Press, 2001.

———. "Why a Rational Agent Need Not Intend the Means to His End." In *From Liberal Values to Democratic Transition: Essays in Honor of Janos Kis,* ed. R. W. Dworkin, pp. 15–27 (Budapest: Central European University Press, 2004).

———. "Why Is Death Worse Than Pre-Natal Nonexistence." *Pacific Philosophical Quarterly* 60 (1988): 161–64.

Kant, Immanuel. *Fundamental Principles of the Metaphysic of Morals.* Translated by T. K. Abbott. New York: Prometheus, 1990.

———. *On the Old Saw: That May Be Right in Theory, But It Won't Work in Practice.* Translated by E. B. Ashton. Philadelphia: University of Pennsylvania Press, 1974.

Kaplow, Louis, and Steven Shavell. *Fairness versus Human Welfare.* Cambridge, MA: Harvard University Press, 2002.

Kitcher, Philip, "Global Health and the Scientific Research Agenda," *Philosophy & Public Affairs* 32 (winter 2004): pp. 36–65.

Korsgaard, Christine. "The Normativity of Instrumental Reason." In *Ethics and Practical Reason.* Edited by G. Cullity and B. Gaut. New York: Oxford University Press, 1997.

———. "The Right to Lie: Kant on Dealing with Evil." *Philosophy & Public Affairs* 15 (1986): 325–49.

———. "Two Distinctions in Goodness." *Philosophical Review* 2 (1983): 169–95.

Lewis, David. Review of *Living High and Letting Die*, by Peter Unger. *Eureka Street* 6 (1996).

Lippert-Rasmussen, Kasper. "Moral Status and the Impermissibility of Minimizing Violations." *Philosophy & Public Affairs* 25 (1996): 333–51.

MacLean, Douglas. "Accentuate the Negative: Moral Theory, Avoiding Harms, and Pursuing Ideals." In *Rationality, Rules, and Ideals: Critical Essays on Bernard Gert's Moral Theory.* Edited by Walter Sinnott-Armstrong and Robert Audi. Lanham, MD: Rowman & Littlefield, 2002.

McGinn, Colin. "Saint Elsewhere." *New Republic*, October 14, 1996.

McKerlie, Dennis. "Priority and Time." *Canadian Journal of Philosophy* 27 (1997): 287–309.

Miller, Richard. "International Justice and Biological Interconnectedness." Paper presented at Pacific APA, San Francisco, California, March 26–30, 2003.

Murphy, Liam. "The Demands of Beneficence." *Philosophy & Public Affairs* 22 (1993): 267–92.

———. "Institutions and the Demands of Justice." *Philosophy & Public Affairs* 27 (1998): 251–91.

Nagel, Thomas. "Equality." In *Mortal Questions.* Cambridge: Cambridge University Press, 1979.

———. *Equality and Partiality.* New York: Oxford University Press, 1991.

———. "Personal Rights and Public Space." *Philosophy & Public Affairs* 24 (1995): 83–107.

———. *The View from Nowhere.* New York: Oxford University Press, 1986.

Nozick, Robert. *Anarchy, State, and Utopia.* New York: Basic Books, 1974.

———. *The Nature of Rationality.* Princeton, NJ: Princeton University Press, 1993.

Nussbaum, Martha. "Philanthropic Twaddle." *London Review of Books* 19 (1997).

Otsuka, Michael. "Scanlon and the Claims of the Many versus the One." *Analysis* 60 (2000): 288–93.

———. "Skepticism about Saving the Greater Number." *Philosophy & Public Affairs* 32 (2004): 413–26.

Parfit, Derek. "Justifiability to Each Person." *Ratio* 16(4) (2003): 368–390.

———. "Innumerate Ethics." *Philosophy and Public Affairs* 7 (1978): 285–301.

———. "Justifiability to Each Person." *Ratio* 16 (2003): 368.

———. *Reasons and Persons.* Part I. New York: Oxford University Press, 1984.

———. *Climbing the Mountain* (unpublished manuscript).

Quinn, Warren. "Actions, Intentions, and Consequences: The Doctrine of Double Effect." In *Morality and Action.* Cambridge: Cambridge University Press, 1994.

———. *Morality and Action.* New York: Cambridge University Press, 1994.

Rachels, James. "Active and Passive Euthanasia." *New England Journal of Medicine* 292 (1975): 78–80.

Rawls, John. *A Theory of Justice.* Cambridge, MA: Belknap Press, 1971.

Raz, Joseph. *The Morality of Freedom.* Oxford: Oxford University Press, 1986.

———. "Rights and Individual Well-Being." In *Ethics in the Public Domain*. New York: Oxford University Press, 1994.

Ross, W. O. *The Right and the good*. Oxford: Clarendon Press, 1930.

Scanlon, Thomas. "Contractualism and Utilitarianism." In *Utilitarianism and Beyond*. Edited by Amartya Sen and Bernard Williams. Cambridge: Cambridge University Press, 1982: 103–128.

———. "Intention and Permissibility, I." *Proceedings of the Aristotelian Society*. Suppl. 74 (2000): 301–17.

———. "Means and Ends." (unpublished).

———. "Moral Assessment and the Agent's Point of View" (unpublished).

———. *What We Owe to Each Other*. Cambridge, MA: Harvard University Press, 1998.

Scheffler, Samuel. *Human Morality*. New York: Oxford University Press, 1993.

———. "Individual Responsibility in a Global Age." *Social Theory and Practice* 21 (1995): 219–36.

———. *The Rejection of Consequentialism*. Oxford: Oxford University Press, 1982.

Schmidtz, David. "Islands in a Sea of Obligation: The Nature and Limits of the Duty of Rescue." *Law and Philosophy* 19 (2000): 683–705.

Sen, Amartya. "Rights and Agency." In *Consequentialism and Its Critics*, edited by Samuel Scheffler. Oxford: Oxford University Press, 1988. Originally published in *Philosophy & Public Affairs* 11 (1982): 3–39.

Shiffrin, S. "Wrongful Life, Procreative Responsibility, and the Significance of Harm." *Legal Theory* 5 (1999): 117–48.

Singer, Peter. "Double Jeopardy and the Use of QALYs in Health Care Allocation," reprinted in *Unsanctifying Human Life*. Edited by Helga Kuhse. Oxford: Blackwell, 2002.

———. "Famine, Affluence, and Morality." In *World Hunger and Moral Obligation*. Edited by William Aiken and Hugh LaFollette. Englewood Cliffs, NJ: Prentice-Hall, 1977.

———. "Intuitions and Ethical Theory." Paper presented at the James Rachels Memorial Conference, University of Alabama, Birmingham, Alabama, Sept. 26, 2004.

———. *Practical Ethics*. 2nd ed. Cambridge: Cambridge University Press, 1993.

———. "Shopping at the Genetic Supermarket" [online]. Available at http://utilitarian.net/singer/by/2003----.htm.

Slote, Michael. *Goods and Virtues*. Oxford: Oxford University Press, 1983.

Sunstein, Cass. "Probability Neglect: Emotions, Worst Cases, and Law." *Yale Law Journal* 112 (2002): 61–107.

Taurek, John. "Should the Numbers Count?" *Philosophy & Public Affairs* 6 (1977): 293–316.

Temkin, Larry. "A Continuum Argument for Intransitivity." *Philosophy & Public Affairs* 25 (1996): 175–210.

Thomson, Judith Jarvis. "Killing, Letting Die, and the Trolley Problem." *The Monist* 59 (1976): 204–17.

———. "Physician Assisted Suicide: Two Moral Arguments." *Ethics* 109 (1999): 497–518.

———. *The Realm of Rights*. Cambridge, MA: Harvard University Press, 1990.

———. "Ruminations on Rights." In *Rights, Restitution, and Risk: Essays in Moral Theory*. Edited by W. A. Parent. Cambridge, MA: Harvard University Press, 1986.

———. "Self-Defense." *Philosophy & Public Affairs* 20 (1991): 283–310.

———. "The Trolley Problem." In *Rights, Restitution, and Risk: Essays in Moral Theory*, edited by W. A. Parent. Cambridge, MA: Harvard University Press, 1986. Originally published in *Yale Law Journal* 94 (1985): 1395–1415.

Unger, Peter. *Living High and Letting Die*. New York: Oxford University Press, 1996.

Velleman, David. "A Right of Self-Termination?" *Ethics* 109 (1999): 606–28.

————. "Well-Being and Time." *Pacific Philosophical Quarterly* 72 (1991): 48–77.

Waldron, Jeremy. "Introduction." In *Theories of Rights*. Edited by Jeremy Waldron. Oxford: Oxford University Press, 1984.

————. "Rights in Conflict." In *Liberal Rights*. Cambridge: Cambridge University Press, 1993.

Walzer, Michael. *Just and Unjust Wars*. New York: Basic Books, 1977.

————. "Political Action: The Problem of Dirty Hands." *Philosophy & Public Affairs* 73 (1973): 160–80.

————. *Spheres of Justice: A Defense of Pluralism and Equality*. New York: Basic Books, 1983.

Williams, Bernard. "A Critique of Utilitarianism." In *Utilitarianism: For and Against*. Edited by J. J. C. Smart and Bernard Williams. Cambridge: Cambridge University Press, 1973.

————. "Ethical Consistency." In *Problems of the Self*. Cambridge: Cambridge University Press, 1973, pp. 166–86.

————. "Moral Luck." In his *Moral Luck*. Cambridge: Cambridge University Press, 1981.

————. *Morality: An Introduction to Ethics*. New York: Harper and Row, 1972.

————. "Utilitarianism and Moral Self-Indulgence." In his *Moral Luck*.

Williams, Glanville. *Criminal Law: The General Part*. London: Stevens Sons, 1961.

Wolf, Susan. "Above and Below the Line of Duty." *Philosophical Topics* 14 (1986): 131–48.

————. "Moral Saints." *Journal of Philosophy* 79 (1982): 419–39.

INDEX

abortion, 408

accidents, 361

accountability, 311–22, 325. *See also* responsibility

Account Case, 372–73, 392

acting, "because of" versus "in order to," 92, 94–95, 100–104, 106–9, 112, 115–16, 118–21, 132, 134, 136, 157. *See also* Doctrine of Triple Effect

actions, 27–28, 124, 269; and intentions, 84–85, 121; justification of, 129, 457–58, 462–63, 466–67, 470, 488; moral significance of, 11–12, 30–31; and omissions, 18, 78–79, 84; permissibility of, 178, 231; reasons for, 52, 100, 120, 126, 137, 237; required versus optional, 389–90; for the sake of entities, 228–30; supererogatory, 14, 45, 85, 178, 260–61, 282, 301, 363, 367, 388–91, 397; wrong, 455–56, 461, 466, 473, 487

actors, substitute, 312

aesthetics, 404–5, 419

affirmative action, 448

agency, 252–53, 278, 407; eliminative, 89–90; opportunistic, 89–90; positive, 79, 81, 86–88; rational, 136, 177

agent-focus, 20, 252, 388

Agent Near Threat Case, 369–70

agent neutrality, 251, 268; and conflicts of rights, 262–63, 270–71, 287–89

agent regret, 325–26, 328, 341–42

agent relativity, 26–27, 146, 251–53; and conflicts of rights, 262, 264–65, 287–88

agents, 27–29, 161, 312–13

aggregation, 55, 250, 351, 408, 416, 472, 480, 484; of benefits/gains and losses, 35, 36, 483, 486, 489–90; intrapersonal, 37; and rescue, 48–51; of rights, 297–98

aid, 31–33, 37–38, 46, 380, 470; international, 193, 214, 408; principles governing, 414–18, 420; rights to, 263, 297; withholding/cessation of, 18–19, 42, 87–89, 152. *See also* under duties

aiding, 17–18, 20, 30, 53–54, 260, 351, 355, 358, 361, 383, 385, 387, 451, 453, 471. *See also* saving lives aims. *See* goals

allocation. *See* distribution

allocation fallacy, 68, 73

Already Sick Case, 179

altruism, 45

Ambulance Case, 30, 274–75, 284

amnesia, 403

animals: interests of, 246, 405–6; moral
  status of, 229, 232, 255; treatment of, 228,
  280, 410–11, 464–65, 467, 488

Anscombe, Elizabeth, 51–52, 55, 74

Argument for Best Outcomes, 32, 51, 55

Argument from Duress, 318

Argument from Necessity, 318

Art Works Case, 28, 268

artworks, 28, 228–29, 255, 268, 312–13, 407

Asian Flu Case, 424–25, 432, 434, 446

attitudes: judgment-sensitive, 232, 457–58,
  463–64, 466–68, 488; toward the past and
  the future, 442–45, 449

authority, 82–83, 232, 278, 320, 433, 438;
  illegitimate, 309, 318; over oneself, 87,
  120, 247

autonomy, 16, 87, 312

Bad Man Case, 132–33, 178

balancing, 59, 62–64, 67, 70, 72

Balancing Argument, 33–34, 53–58, 60–61,
  64–65, 70, 72, 489

Balancing Argument II, 66–67, 70,
  482, 489

Bankcard Case, 211

Bathtub Cases, 17

beauty, 28

behavior, 455–56, 463. *See also* actions

beliefs, 161

beneficence, 13, 334–35, 361–62

benefits, 66–68, 72, 180, 200, 211, 223,
  234–35, 408, 429, 472–73, 475, 477–78;
  distribution of, 423, 481–83, 489–90; and
  rights, 242–43. *See also* gains

Bennett, Jonathan, 91, 95–96, 117

Bentham, Jeremy, 242, 244, 277

biological warfare, 331

blame, 217, 311

Blinder View, 58–59, 75–76

Bob's Bugatti Case, 212–14

bodyguard example, 260–61, 263, 265,
  295–96, 457

bombing, 21–22, 24–25, 107–9, 117, 119, 125,
  143, 159–60, 172–75, 187, 444

Bratman, Michael, 96–97, 99, 124

Bridge Case, 143

bridging resemblance, 198

Brock, Dan, 46, 335

Brody, Baruch, 128

Broome, John, 126–27

burdens, 413, 423, 470, 473

Bystander Case, 92–93, 119, 123, 306, 314–15, 337

bystanders, innocent, 168, 183, 203, 207, 211,
  221, 259, 315, 336

capacities, 229, 233, 235

Captain Cases, 309–31, 336

Car Case, 22, 131–32, 136, 147, 181, 433–34

cases, judgments about, 5, 14, 191–92, 195, 424,
  426–28, 438–39, 444–45, 469

categorical imperative, 12–13, 41, 43, 459

causal chains, 159, 162, 330

causal effects, 25, 186, 204–5; producing
  versus sustaining, 137–38, 155–58, 161, 164

causality (causal relations), 111–12, 160, 260

changes, 423, 437

character traits, 402–3, 410

charity, 361

chemical warfare, 331

children, 213–14, 245, 266, 359; death of,
  108–9, 143–44, 160, 174–75, 177, 281–82,
  325–26, 415; and intelligence, 233–34; and
  tax policy, 439–41, 448

choice: moral, 234–35; and rights, 242–43

Choice Test, 265, 282, 292, 365, 376

civilization, 49

claims, 243, 459; and rights, 237, 239, 241

coercion, 415

coherentism, 427

collaboration, 308–10, 317, 323, 332,
  337–38, 340

commitments, 111

comparison, pairwise, 48, 50, 57–61, 64–65,
  71–72, 249–50, 416, 479–80

compensation, 200, 234, 240, 276, 311, 326,
  426, 443–45

competence, of patients, 333

complaints, 470–71, 474–75, 479–81, 490

Component Case, 158, 161–62, 166, 186–87

concentration camps, 170

confrontation, 165

conscientiousness, moral, 402

consciousness, 229, 235

consent, 13, 176, 219–20, 224, 234, 307, 310

consequences, 335, 423

consequentialism, 27, 35, 40, 220, 248, 252, 254, 309, 313, 424–25; act and rule, 11, 306, 319, 336; critiques of, 16, 329–30; impartial, 402–3; maximizing, 408, 410

conservatism, 436–37

considerations, 462, 470; aesthetic versus moral, 404–5, 419

Consistency Argument, 33, 53

constraints, 14, 17, 28, 31, 170, 173, 191, 193, 231, 239, 268–69, 305; agent-focused, 20; nonabsolute, 21, 30; victim-focused, 20. *See also* side-constraints

consumerism, 415–16

Context-Aware View, 58, 64, 75

contractarianism, 33, 407. *See also* contractualism

contractualism, 7, 55–57, 129, 455–56, 460, 462–63, 471, 473–74, 478, 484

cooperation, 380

costs, 215, 231, 341, 390, 473–74, 484, 486–87; and the duty to aid, 194, 348–49, 354, 360–61, 366, 383, 391, 471

Counterfactual Test, 22, 25, 95–96, 124

criticism, 311

Crossroads Case, 141, 151

death, 120–21, 189, 192, 234, 407, 449, 451, 474, 485; of children, 108–9, 143–44, 160, 174–75, 177, 281–82, 325–26, 415

decision making, 428, 446

decision theory, 423

defense, of others, 246

Delivery Case, 431–32

deontology, 30, 172, 280, 423; paradox of, 26, 28; threshold, 169–70, 231

dependents, 213–14

desert, 246, 323, 407

Desire Satisfaction Theory of Goodness, 461, 463

desires (preferences), 237, 250, 254, 405; satisfaction of, 278–79, 402, 461, 463

determinateness, moral, 381–85

difference principle, 362

dignity, 230

dirty hands, 313

disabled, the, 408–10, 448

dispositions, 138

disrespect, 88–89

distance, and duties to aid, 193–94, 212, 345–56, 359–61, 363–66, 368–81, 385–86, 388–91

Distant Owner Case, 372, 374, 392

distribution: of goods/benefits, 249–50, 423, 475–76, 478, 481–83, 489–90; of organs, 57; of resources, 37–39, 47, 57, 68–70, 362, 408, 477. *See also* justice, distributive

disutility, 441

doctors, 477; and assisted suicide, 333–35

Doctrine of Doing and Allowing (DDA), 78–79, 81, 86–87, 89

Doctrine of Double Effect (DDE), 21–24, 43, 78, 90, 100–101, 107–9, 124–25, 128, 131–35, 148, 159–62, 174, 176–77; and the Trolley Case, 92–94; and the greater good, 115–18; Warren Quinn on, 82–91

Doctrine of Initial Justification (DIJ), 159–61, 163–64, 186–87

Doctrine of Productive Purity (DPP), 164–65, 167, 169–71, 469, 473; application of, 173–76

Doctrine of Triple Effect (DTE), 23, 43, 92–93, 118–22, 132–36, 148, 156–59, 162, 185; problems with, 136–38. *See also* acting, "because of" versus "in order to"

Door Case, 357–58, 366

double effect. *See* Doctrine of Double Effect

Double Track Case, 112–15, 136–37, 178–79, 185

downstream theory, 138, 152–54

Driver, Julia, 337

drowning, 79, 194, 213, 250, 347–48, 350, 352, 356, 363, 428, 444

duress, 318–19, 341

duties, 13, 215, 230, 233, 241, 276, 342, 477; agent-neutral and agent-relative, 26–27, 29, 252; to aid others, 46, 82, 193–94, 244, 261, 281, 345–50, 357–63, 368–70, 374–75, 382–88, 415, 434, 478; avoidance of, 355, 358; directed and nondirected, 230, 239, 241–42, 244–45; to harm oneself and others, 195–96, 209, 213–16, 219–20, 262; not to harm, 23–24, 326, 386–88, 434; perfect and imperfect, 13, 384; prima facie, 14, 23; pro tanto, 384–85; and rights, 42, 237, 239–42, 262, 266, 269, 277–78, 286, 465

Dworkin, Ronald, 228, 250, 267, 282–83

education, 213, 277
Education Fund Case, 213
effects, 124, 128, 137–38, 157, 228
Effort Test, 265, 282
egoism, 387
embryos, 228–30, 233–36, 255–56, 279
emergencies, 231, 361
end states, 423–25, 436–37, 448
Endowment Effect, 430, 442, 444
ends, 104–5, 110–12, 117, 126, 131, 228.
    See also goals
Enoch, David, 277
entities, moral status of, 227, 229, 231–35, 247,
    255–56, 407
entitlements, 236, 244, 414, 429,
    438, 447
Envelope Case, 210, 212–13, 217–19, 223,
    360–61, 366
equality, 244, 246, 443; and chance for rescue,
    52–53, 58–59, 62
equalization, of cases, 265, 347, 349, 427–30;
    cross-definitional, 19
Equivalence Thesis, 17
error theory, 192
ethics, medical, 331–35
euthanasia, 309, 333–35, 411
events, 442
evil, 43, 102, 126, 128, 144, 148, 151, 162, 177,
    481; causal role of, 93–95, 152, 156; colla-
    boration with, 308–10, 317, 323, 332, 337,
    340; greater, 170, 183; intending, 21, 102–3,
    127, 131, 133, 135, 138, 157; justification of,
    162, 164, 167, 176, 184, 187; lesser, 24–25,
    104, 107, 116, 118, 132, 138–43, 147–55, 159,
    164–65, 172, 179–82, 185–86, 204–5, 209,
    259, 318, 322, 330, 333, 469; as a means,
    151–52, 160–61, 165, 170–73, 181, 189, 472;
    permissible, 92–93, 153, 158; probable
    necessity of, 160–61; reducing/preventing,
    450–54
evolutionary history, 418
Extra Push Case, 97–99, 103, 125, 134

fairness, 33–34, 37, 39, 219, 249, 349, 404, 409,
    425, 428–29, 435, 443; and aid/rescue, 51, 53,
    55, 62, 68, 362, 415
family, 223, 416
famine relief, 214, 217–18, 347, 349, 362–63,
    408, 415, 417

Far Alone Case, 348–52, 356–57, 359–60,
    384, 391
Far Costless Case, 348–49, 353,
    360, 383
Far Many Case, 348
Feinberg, Joel, 239, 278, 338, 432
Finkelstein, Claire, 339
Five-Dollar Case, 256–57
Foot, Philippa, 22, 24, 423, 433
force, use of, 415
foreseeing, versus intending, 21–24, 80,
    87–88, 91, 93, 102–3, 108, 118, 121, 131,
    133, 282–83, 472–75
framing effects, 424–25, 427, 431–33, 436,
    438–39, 445
freedom, 451; of movement, 238; of religion,
    248; of speech, 238, 245–48, 264, 266,
    271–72, 282, 284
friendship, 405
futility thinking, 363
future, attitudes toward, 442–45, 449

gains, 423–25, 427, 429–32, 434, 436–38,
    446; concentrated versus distributed, 35,
    481; denied, 428, 433; and losses, 34–35.
    See also benefits
Gap Question, 462, 464, 466–67
Gas Case, 22, 24, 177, 182
Gauguin, 342
George's Case, 331–33, 343
Gert, Bernard, 450–54
Gewirth, Alan, 301
Goal Test, 265, 293
goals (aims), 95, 99, 101, 124, 137, 157; evil,
    332–33; and intentions, 106, 108–9, 124; and
    means, 104–7; personal, 30, 301, 402. See
    also ends
God, 464
Gonzalez Case, 307, 314, 337
good, 461–63; common, 245; greater, 24–26,
    30–31, 44, 55, 93, 115, 128, 132–33, 138, 140,
    142–44, 147–51, 153–56, 159, 161–63, 165,
    170, 173, 175, 179–81, 184–89, 204–5, 209,
    249, 252–53, 256, 259–61, 292, 322, 330, 469;
    impartial, 15–16; individual/personal, 247,
    261, 461; maximization of, 11–12, 14–15, 33,
    39–40, 248, 261, 306, 316, 318, 402–3, 417,
    455; promotion of, 22, 238, 241, 254, 451;
    theories of, 461–63

goods: distribution of, 249–50, 475–76, 478; divisible, 66, 68, 70; loss of, 451–52; magnitude of, 77; relevant and irrelevant, 34–35, 62, 64, 481
government, 296, 301, 348, 362, 440–41
Grand Canyon, 230
gratitude, 13
Grau, Christopher, 339
Gresham's Law, 329, 343
Griffin, James, 278
Grocery Store Case, 426, 439, 443
grouping, projective, 195–96, 198–203, 207–8, 210–13
Guinea Pig Case, 83–84

Hall, Timothy, 434, 447–48
Hand Case, 409–10
happiness, 402
Hare, Richard, 401
Harel, Alon, 282
harm, 166, 200, 209, 234, 254, 325, 327, 474; duty not to, 14, 23–24, 28; intending versus foreseeing, 21–23, 82–83, 86–87, 91, 98; permissible, 24–26, 28, 44, 122, 130–31, 138, 147, 153, 158, 164, 170–71, 174, 180, 186, 195, 197, 201–4, 219, 253; preventing/reducing, 212, 235, 332, 340, 386, 411; and property losses, 193–94
harming, 20, 30, 196, 451, 488; versus not-aiding, 17–21, 23, 131–32, 138, 151, 164, 191, 213–14, 347, 410–11, 421–25, 427–28, 430–38, 447, 450, 453–54, 472; oneself and others, 195–96, 209, 213–16, 219–20, 262
Hart, H. L. A., 241–43
headaches, 36–37, 54, 485, 490
health, 476–77
health care, 38, 296, 300, 420–21, 424–25
Helpfulness Principle, 475–76, 489
heroism, moral, 413
Hobbes, Thomas, 240, 450–53
Hohfeld, W. N., 239–41
Holmes, Stephen, 301
Horizontal Test of Stringency, 257
Horowitz, Tamara, 434, 438, 445–46
House Case, 109, 111
"how" factors, 470–75
human nature, 247

ideals, 451–53
Igneski, Violetta, 381–85

immigration, 405
immunities, 241
impartiality, 32–35, 49–51, 54, 61, 64, 74, 389, 402–5, 409–11, 470–71
inconsistency, 220–21
inconvenience, 456
indebtedness, 178–79
independence, 82, 416
Indeterminate Rescue Case, 383
Individualist Restriction (IR), 55–57, 59, 67, 69, 470, 479–80, 483, 487
individuals, 82
infanticide, 408
infants, 232–33, 359
initiation, 319–20, 322, 340
injustice, 444
innocents, death of, 176. See also bystanders, innocent; threats, innocent
institutions, 296
instrumental rationality, 91–92, 104–5, 110–12, 121
integrity, 308–9, 314, 329–30
Integrity Objection, 308–9, 329–30
intelligence, 68, 233–34, 236, 406
intending, 43, 79–81, 84, 116–17, 159, 177, 280; versus foreseeing, 21–24, 80, 87–88, 91, 93, 102–3, 118, 121, 131, 133, 282–83, 472–75
intentions, 82–83, 92, 95–96, 98, 187; and aims/goals, 106, 108–9, 124; and the greater good, 115–16; and moral permissibility, 13, 80, 82–83, 85, 132–33, 178; and rationality, 104–12; varieties of, 95, 101–4, 108–9, 124–25
interests, 234, 243, 254, 267, 333, 405, 407; aggregation of, 33, 55; of others, 16, 27; personal, 271, 273, 339, 387; promotion of, 248–49, 253, 407; and rights, 244–48, 257–64, 286, 289–91, 293–95, 297; satisfaction of, 278–79, 407–8, 420
interference, 451–53
intuitions, 14–15, 17, 24, 191–95, 198–99, 214, 216, 220, 357, 417–18, 422–27, 434–36; about proximity/distance, 346, 352, 359–60, 368, 379, 381, 388; changing, 201, 203, 221; reasonableness of, 438–45; and side effects, 22; structure of, 8. See also judgments, intuitive

inviolability, 26, 28–29, 253–56, 258, 270–71, 280, 416, 424, 436
irrationality, 444

Jim and the Indians example, 305–14, 335, 339–40, 343; variations of, 309–31, 336
Joe Case, 381–82
Joint Venture Case, 211
judgments: case-based, 5, 14, 191–92, 195, 424, 426–28, 438–39, 444–45, 469; comparative, 219; considered, 14–15; intuitive, 17, 24, 138, 145, 188, 190–91, 197, 199, 213, 359, 379, 417–18, 422, 427, 444, 469, 473; and numbers of people affected, 49–56, 60–61, 65, 67, 69–74; and values, 217–18
just war theory, 21, 176
justice, 33, 362; distributive, 37, 39, 351, 361–62, 424; and rescue, 51, 53, 55
justification: of actions, 129, 457–58, 462–63; of evil, 162, 164, 167, 176, 184, 187; of moral principles, 456–57

Kahneman, Daniel, 422–32, 434–39, 441–42, 444, 446, 448
Kant, Immanuel, 13, 112, 126, 224, 342, 488; on the categorical imperative, 12, 41, 43, 459
Kaplow, Louis, 278–79
Keeping Busy Case, 211–13
killing, 27–29, 79, 140, 215, 252, 280, 311–12, 341, 462; impermissible, 270, 291–92, 469; versus letting die, 17–21, 23, 28, 42–43, 258, 411–14, 420–21, 484; as a means, 173, 189; permissible, 170–71, 195, 197, 202, 220, 257, 259, 269, 291–92, 294, 306–8, 310–11, 323, 327, 411, 453, 469; responsibility for, 314–16, 318, 336–37
Knee Damage Cases, 430, 432, 436, 439, 442–44
knowledge, 405
Korsgaard, Christine, 92, 110–12, 228

Landslide Case, 139, 182
law, 121, 238–39, 281, 301, 340–41
Lazy Susan Case, 24, 123, 142–43, 152, 168–69, 180, 182, 203–4
Legs Case, 34–35, 41, 53–54, 61, 63–64, 77
Lesser-Loss-Card Case, 207–9, 222

letting die, versus killing, 17–21, 23, 28, 42–43, 258, 411–14, 420–21, 484
Lewis, David, 222
liberties, 240–41
life, 39, 451, 453; good, 234, 409–10; meaningful, 402–3, 405, 407, 414; right to, 20, 38, 238, 248, 258, 260, 275, 279, 286, 292; value of, 36–37, 228, 233, 441–42, 458–61, 488
life expectancy, 38–39, 68–69, 490
life support, 18–19, 411–12
Loop Case, 25, 92–96, 98–105, 107–9, 112–13, 115, 117–18, 121–24, 126, 133–34, 136–38, 154–57, 177–79, 183
loss/no-gain distinction, 424–25, 427, 429–38, 444–45, 447–48, 453
losses, 205, 210, 213, 290, 423–25, 427, 429–32, 436–38, 443–46, 452, 454; aggregation of, 255, 257; concentrated versus distributed, 35, 481; and gains, 34–35; imposed, 428, 433; prevention of, 209, 219–20, 434–35, 453; of property, 193–95, 213, 223, 468
lying, 13, 342, 404

Massacre Case, 22, 117
maximin principle, 408, 419, 437
McGinn, Colin, 223
means, 131, 140, 147–50, 175, 209, 473–75; and ends, 104–5, 110–12, 117, 126; evil as a, 151–52, 160–61, 165, 170–73, 181, 189, 472; of providing aid, 369–78, 392, 396
Means Near Threat Case, 371
Means Near to Means Case, 375
Means Near Victim Case, 370–71
medical care, 38, 296, 300, 420–21, 424–25
memories, 441–43
mercy, 333
Method of Virtual Divisibility, 66–71, 73, 77, 482
Mill, John Stuart, 283
Miller, Richard, 397
Million Dollar Case, 236
Miracle Case, 155
Missile Case, 184
Modal Condition, 143–44, 159–60
Model Penal Code, 340–41
money, 371, 391
moral luck, 341
moral permissibility, 26, 28, 45, 86, 98, 117, 135, 143, 160, 164, 200, 205, 227, 312, 425, 434;

and intention, 13, 80, 82–83, 85, 132–33, 178; secondary, 169–73

moral principles, 56–57, 176, 191, 417, 426–27, 455–56, 459–61, 467, 469, 473, 487; derivation of, 5, 14–15; reasons for rejecting, 461, 470, 474–75, 478–79, 488

moral purity, 313; hyper, 313–14, 322

moral significance, 198, 379, 407, 414–17

moral status, 29–30, 82, 227–32, 234, 253–56, 270–71, 417

moral theory, 423, 425, 427, 439

moral worth, 228, 230, 247, 254, 270–71, 425

morality, 29, 82, 402, 404, 407, 456; common/ ordinary, 219–20, 450, 452–54, 471; goals of, 410, 450–51; scope of, 456–57

Morganhesse, Sidney, 485–86

motivation, 402, 411, 462

Multiple Option Case, 290

Munitions and Civilians Case, 108

Munitions Grief Case, 23, 119

murder, 341. See also killing

Murphy, Liam, 362, 391

Nagel, Thomas: on the Doctrine of Double Effect, 83, 177; on harms/losses, 4–5, 251, 387, 448, 476; on the moral point of view, 404, 420

narrative structures, 442

Near Alone Case, 348, 350–52, 356–57, 359–60, 362, 374, 384, 391

Near Costless Case, 348

Near/Far Case, 350–51, 365

Near Many Case, 348

Near to Victim's Means Case, 374

necessity, 160–61, 318

needs, 37–38, 356–58

negativism, 220

negligence, 341

Nervous Visitor Case, 355, 358

noncausal flipside, 140–42, 147, 149–56, 163, 165, 183–84, 186–88

nonconsequentialism, 7, 21, 59, 92, 132, 140, 142, 219–20, 260, 292, 306, 388, 423–25, 435, 473; and agent relativity, 27, 252; and the categorical imperative, 12–13; and constraints, 17, 231; definition/meaning of, 11–12, 14; and duties, 23, 31–32, 34, 37–38,

40; and harming, 328, 436; and intuitions, 191–92, 469; methodology of, 14–15, 190–91; and permissible/impermissible killing, 306–9; and rights, 248–49

Noncrossroad Case, 151

nonexistence, 449

noninterference, 239–40, 247, 258, 286, 465

norms, social, 218–19. See also rules

Nozick, Robert, 139, 280, 423, 445, 447

numbers, and moral judgments, 49–56, 60–61, 65, 67, 69–74

Nussbaum, Martha, 223

objections, moral, 219–20

Objective List Theory of the Good, 463

objectivity, 74

Olson, Kristi, 56, 125, 342

omissions, 18, 21, 78–79, 84

option acts, 326–27

options, 387

organ transplantation, 23–24, 57, 119–20, 131–32, 294–95, 307, 388

Organs Case, 307

Otsuka, Michael, 48, 58, 60, 70–73, 75, 77

outcomes, 37–38, 45, 51, 55–56, 251, 311, 408, 444, 455; producing versus sustaining, 137–38, 155–58, 161, 164

outrage, moral, 192

Overseas Case, 347, 360

owing, 230, 232, 235, 239, 276, 406, 456, 459, 463–64, 467–68, 488

Oxfam, 217–19, 362–63

pain, 120–21, 234–35, 406–7, 411, 441–44, 463–65, 472, 489–90; future and past, 443, 476; relief of, 129, 477

Pain Case, 120–21, 476–77, 489

pairwise comparison, 48, 50, 57–61, 64–65, 71–72, 249–50, 416, 479–80

paralysis, 36, 70, 158, 290, 295–96, 298, 312, 481, 484–85

parents, 245, 266, 415

Pareto optimality, 32, 45, 51, 61, 306, 336, 358

Parfit, Derek, 65–67; on aiding others, 15, 408, 482–83; on attitudes toward the past and the future, 443, 449; on rational irrationality, 419; on treating as means, 40–41; on the Trolley Case, 188

Party Case, 95–96, 102–3, 121, 178
past, attitudes toward, 443–45, 449
patients, 333–35
Peak-and-End Rule, 441–42
permissibility. *See* moral permissibility
Permissibility of Elimination Test, 358
persons, 26, 59, 233, 238; moral status/value of,
    29, 232, 254, 460–61; respect for, 17, 34,
    87–89, 230, 256, 464, 488; separateness of,
    20, 54–55, 59, 198, 200, 433, 453–54; sub-
    ordination of, 145–46, 165–67; substitut-
    ability of, 51, 59–60
perspectives: ex ante, 272–75; partial and im-
    partial, 387, 389–90, 403, 409. *See also*
    points of view
Pill Distribution Case, 71–74, 77
pleasure, 405–7, 451–53
points of view, 34–35, 55, 74, 461; moral, 65,
    403–5. *See also* perspectives
police protection, 267, 296
Pond Case, 347–49, 360–61, 364
poor, the, 383, 389, 439–41, 448. *See also*
    worst-off, the
pornography, 251
potential, 229
powers, 241, 243
practices, 469
preferences (desires), 237, 250, 254, 405;
    satisfaction of, 278–79, 402, 461, 463
prejudice, 405, 426
prerogatives, moral, 15–17, 31, 241, 386–87
Prevented Return Case, 122
prices, 428–29
Priest Case, 270
Principle of Alternate Reason, 135
Principle of Contextual Interaction, 17, 45,
    348, 412
Principle of Ethical Integrity (PEI), 209, 211,
    214–16, 223
Principle of Instrumental Rationality, 104,
    110–11
Principle of Irrelevant Goods, 34, 38, 290, 409
Principle of Irrelevant Need, 38
Principle of Irrelevant Rights, 289–90
Principle of Permissible Harm (PPH), 24–26,
    28, 30, 44–45, 186, 188, 204–5
Principle of Secondary Permissibility (PSP),
    26, 170–73, 183, 189, 221–22, 283, 324;
    Extension of, 171, 189

Principle of Secondary Wrong, 172
Principle of the Independence of Irrelevant
    Alternatives, 485
principles. *See* moral principles
priority to the worst-off, 38, 66, 475, 482
Priority Rule, 476–78, 489
privileges, 240
Prize Party Case, 102, 121–22, 179
Problem of Distance in Morality (PDM),
    345–46, 352, 368–69, 372; New, 376–77,
    379, 383
Problem of Interpersonal Allocation with
    Intrapersonal Aggregation, 37
projects, 16, 330, 387
promises, 30, 231, 388–89, 456, 468
properties: of actions, 19–21, 461–62; intrinsic
    and extrinsic, 228–30, 233, 411–14
property, losses of, 193–95, 213, 223, 468
property rights, 231, 244, 429
proportionality, 128
Prospect Theory, 422–25, 427, 430, 432–33,
    437
Protective Shield Case, 167
protophysics, 202–3, 221
proximity, and the duty to aid, 194, 346–47,
    352, 354, 358–59, 361, 365, 368, 370, 377,
    380–81, 385–86
psychology, cognitive, 422, 427
punishment, 178, 246, 279, 311, 316, 323–24,
    340, 407; capital, 224, 238
Push-Three Case, 201–2

quality of life, 39
Quinn, Warren, 78–82, 133, 135; on agency,
    89–90; on the Doctrine of Double Effect,
    82–91; on intending evil, 102–4

Rachels, James, 17
Rational Desire Theory of the Good, 462
rationality, 86, 126–27, 136, 177, 419, 426, 458,
    460–61; false, 444; instrumental, 91–92,
    104–5, 110–12, 121; and intentions, 104–12;
    and moral status, 232–33
Rawls, John, 361, 424, 475
Raz, Joseph, 244–47, 257–58, 277, 419
Reach Case, 352–54
reasoning: deontological, 172; about harms,
    190–91; practical, 110–12, 116, 126–27, 464;
    theoretical, 126–27

reasons: for action, 52, 91, 95, 100, 102, 120, 126, 232, 237, 313, 456–57, 459, 462; agent-focused, 388; exclusionary, 237, 248; heteronomous, 460; kinds of, 419–20; prima facie, 237; primary and secondary, 102, 137; for rejecting moral principles, 461, 470, 474–75, 478–79, 488

Rebellious Utilitarian Case, 218–19

reciprocity, 274

recognition, 356–57

redistribution, 362

redundancy effect, 466

reflection: case-specific, 191, 193, 214; general, 191–92, 203, 214; sociological, 219

reflective equilibrium, 5, 188, 426

regret: agent, 325–26, 328, 341–42; cause, 341

Rehnquist, William, 121

relations: causal and noncausal, 141, 144, 149, 158, 160, 167; doctor-patient, 335

relationships, personal, 389, 402, 414

relevance, 34–35, 62, 481, 484–85

rescue, 18, 80, 98–99, 125, 131, 154, 166, 361–62, 381–85, 475. *See also* saving lives

Rescue Cases, 80, 86, 120, 134

Rescue Principle, 475–76

Rescue Test, 98–101

Rescue Variants, 80–81, 98

research, 35–36, 46, 331–35

resemblance, bridging, 198

residue, negative, 328–29

resistance, 231, 236, 240

resources, distribution of, 37–39, 47, 57, 68–70, 362, 408, 477

respect, 246, 407; for persons, 17, 34, 87–89, 230, 256, 464, 488

responsibility, 27, 327, 330, 336, 341, 389, 407; and consequences, 314–17, 320, 322, 324–25, 330, 334–35, 338–39; and distance, 380–81, 386; and medical ethics, 331–35; negative, 305–6, 308, 310, 330, 411; positive, 309, 311–15, 317–25, 327, 329, 334–35, 338

responsiveness, 319–20, 322, 340

retardation, 232, 235, 406, 488

retirement fund, 212

rich, the, 439–41, 448

rights, 28–29, 167, 232–38, 241, 246, 249, 284, 438; beneficiary theory of, 242–43; choice theory of, 242–43; conflicts among, 248–49, 262–64, 268, 272, 285–98; and

duties, 42, 237, 239–42, 262, 266, 269, 277–78, 286, 465; to free speech, 38, 238; and the greater good, 249–50; holders of, 230, 238, 242, 247, 255–56; human, 238, 240, 249, 278; inalienable, 243, 273–74; infringement of, 231–32, 240, 257, 272, 465; interest theory of, 244–48, 257–58, 260, 270; and interests, 260–62, 286, 291, 293–95; and inviolability, 26, 28–29; irrelevant, 289–90; kinds of, 239–41; legal, 238–39, 301; to life, 20, 38, 238, 248, 258, 260, 275, 279, 286, 292; mixed, 287, 289, 296; moral, 238–39, 301; and owing, 464–66; positive and negative, 14, 249, 262–64, 267–71, 281–82, 285–94, 296–301, 346, 386, 388, 390, 416, 424, 430; to property, 231, 244, 429; stringency of, 249–50, 256–57, 261, 263–66, 281, 290, 292, 424; as trumps, 240, 250, 267; of victims, 168, 370; violation/transgression of, 26, 30, 124, 240, 251, 253, 259, 263, 265, 267–72, 279–80, 284–85, 289–90, 292, 294, 296; welfare, 296, 301

rights-consequentialism, 251–52

risks, 36, 38, 423, 446, 486; of death, 273–74

Road Cases, 18

Ross, W. D., 12–14, 23

Rube Goldberg devices, 150

rules, 402–3, 410–11, 426, 453–54, 468–69

sacrifice, 15–16, 29–31, 45, 215–16, 249, 254–55, 272–74, 319–20, 337, 355, 416–17, 424

salience, 191, 193–94, 346, 356–59, 363, 366

satisficing, 40

saveability, 254–55

saving lives, 18, 32–35, 39, 56, 60–65, 128–29, 141, 145, 162, 175, 177, 193, 195, 214, 248, 257–62, 272, 275, 288, 293–95, 328, 381–82, 389–90, 409, 416–17, 434, 446, 468, 480, 485; and aggregation, 48–51; of children, 79, 415

Scanlon, Thomas, 73, 77, 178, 276, 284, 339, 406–7; on aiding, 476–83, 485–86, 489–90; on contractualism, 7, 55–57, 129, 471–73, 484; on moral authority, 120; on moral status, 232–35; on owing, 464–67; on rules/principles, 469–70, 473–75, 488; on the Tiebreaker Argument, 59, 61–63, 65, 67, 69; on treating people as means, 41; on wrongness, 455–64, 466, 468, 470, 487

Scarce Resources Case, 83–85, 90

scarcity, 32, 38, 83–85, 90
Scheffler, Samuel, 241, 387, 389, 404, 420
Schelling, Thomas, 439
Schelling's Tax Case, 439–40, 448
Schweitzer, Albert, 367
Second Trolley Redirection Case, 202
Secondary Transplant Case, 119–20, 129
Sedan Case, 360, 366
self, future, 407
self-concern, 327
self-consciousness, 406–8, 457
self-defense, 21, 286
self-government, 232, 457–59
self-interest, 16, 307, 319, 355, 359, 402
self-sacrifice, 15–16, 31, 45, 215–16, 273
semantics, context-sensitive, 216–17, 219
Sen, Amartya, 27
Sending-Back Case, 167
sentience, 229, 235, 405, 407
separateness of persons, 20, 54–55, 59, 198, 200, 433, 453–54
separation, projective, 195–96, 200–203, 210, 212
Shavell, Steven, 278–79
Shiffrin, Seana, 234–35
Shipwreck Case, 471
side-constraints, 251–52, 410
side effects, 21–24, 109–10, 112, 115–19, 159–62, 166, 473–75
Singer, Peter, 347, 366, 445; ethical theory of, 401–3, 407–10; on killing and letting die, 411–14; on the moral point of view, 403–6; on principles governing aid, 414–18, 420
slavery, 41, 273, 408
Snow Shovel Cases, 428–29, 435
sobjectivity, 34–36, 39, 50
Socrates, 283
solicitation, 315–16
Sore Throat Case, 34, 61–64, 76
sorites structure, 200
sovereignty, 120, 248, 258–59
speciesism, 406
Splash Case, 132, 136, 147–48, 181
Standard Claim, 368–70, 377
Standard Implication, 368, 388–91
Standard View, 368–70
standards, 218–19
starvation, 18, 193–94, 415–17
state of nature, 453
states of affairs, 12, 27, 32

states of mind, 27–28, 135, 138, 156–57, 161, 268–69
status quo, 428–30, 438, 442
Store Case, 99–100
Stradivarius Case, 355, 358
Strangemind, 207–12, 222–23
strangers: aid to, 193–95, 212–13, 345–46, 360, 363, 387; harms to, 210–11
structural equivalents, 154–57, 162–63, 184, 186, 188
subordination, 145–46, 165–67
substitution, 145–46, 165, 167, 170
suffering, 192–93, 413–14, 443, 460, 471–72, 476; prevention/relief of, 333, 408, 416
suicide, assisted, 283, 309, 333–35
Sunstein, Cass, 301
supererogatory acts, 14, 45, 85, 178, 260–61, 282, 301, 363, 367, 388–91, 397
susceptibility, 113–14, 221
Switches and Skates Case, 196–97, 198–99, 202, 204–5, 207–8, 221

Tactical Bombing Case, 21–22, 175, 187, 444
Taurek, John, 32, 48–51, 54, 56–57
tax policy, 439–41, 448
Temkin, Larry, 490
temporally various cases, 377–79
Terminate Aid Case, 18–19
Terror Bombing Case, 21–22, 175
terrorism, 173–75
theft, 217–18, 389, 429
third parties, 169, 242–43
Thompson, Michael, 280
Thomson, Judith Jarvis, 42, 117, 255, 339; on the Doctrine of Double Effect, 159–60; on duties, 239–40; on rights, 240, 250–51, 263, 276–77, 279, 281–82, 284; on the Trolley Case, 91–92, 94, 122–23, 133
threats, 18–19, 166, 179–80, 185, 281, 324, 369, 378; innocent, 139–40, 168–69, 341; near and far, 369–70, 376–77, 381, 384, 392, 395–96; redirection of, 94–95, 113–14, 118, 122, 132, 134, 141–45, 151, 154, 165–68, 195, 197, 201–2, 205–12, 214–16, 223, 290, 306; susceptibility to, 113–14
Threats Incorporated Cases, 179
Three Islands Case, 60, 63
Tiebreaker Argument, 56–65, 72, 479–81
ties, breaking, 56–65, 72, 479–81, 481–84

time, and duties to aid, 353, 377–78
To-Be-Victim Case, 370
toleration, of harm to oneself, 209–10, 213
tools, 166
torture, 236, 238, 264–67, 283, 468
Track Trolley Case, 94, 180–81, 187
Tractor Case, 137–38, 156–57, 163–64, 179, 185, 187
transitivity, 266, 298, 485
Transmitter Building Case, 486
Transmitter Room Case, 471–72, 483, 486, 490
Transplant Case, 23–24, 44, 122–23, 131–32, 165, 469
treatment: of animals, 228, 488; of persons, 204, 227, 246, 253, 258, 361, 404, 459–60; as mere means, 12–13, 40–41, 89, 123, 172
Tree Trolley Case, 113–15, 144–45, 147, 221
trees, value of, 228
Trilemma Case, 214–15
triple effect. See Doctrine of Triple Effect
Trolley Case, 14, 23–25, 31, 41–44, 49, 79, 96–97, 112–13, 131–32, 139–42, 146, 149–52, 160–61, 168, 201, 204, 206, 215, 231, 259, 418, 438, 469; Judith Jarvis Thomson on, 91–92, 94, 122–23, 133; Peter Unger on, 195–200; and rights conflicts, 288–90
Trolley-Organs Case, 158
Trolley Tool Case, 166
truth: moral, 192, 218, 220; universal, 266
Tumble Case, 139
Tversky, Amos, 422–23, 425, 427–32, 434–39, 444, 446, 448
Two Diseases Case, 274
Two Loop Case, 97
Two Plants Case, 121, 129
Two-Step Case, 113–14

Unger, Peter, 183, 299, 356–57, 372–74, 416, 421; on duties to aid, 207–11, 213–14, 216, 219, 223, 360–63, 388–89; ethical method of, 191–93, 204; on intuitive judgments, 190–91, 220; on projective grouping, 201–3; on property losses, 193–94; on semantics, 216–20; on the Trolley Case, 195–200
UNICEF Card Case, 207–9
Unified Theory, 87, 89
Unintended Greater Good Case, 115–16, 118
universalizability, 426

urgency, 37, 382–83
utilitarianism, 218–19, 250, 280, 330, 408
utility, 267, 422–23, 436, 441–42, 444; marginal, 437, 448; maximization of, 230, 409, 439; and rights, 240

Vacco v. Quill, 121
Valuable Means Near Agent Case, 370
value, 12, 29, 69, 228; instrumental, 228–29; intrinsic, 228, 230; of life/persons, 36–37, 228, 233, 441–42, 458–61, 488
values, 193, 203, 210, 251; primary, 191–92, 217–19; secondary, 217–19
Van Case, 141
Veer Case, 148
veil of ignorance, 29, 33, 408–9, 470
Velleman, David, 279
victim-focus, 20, 252, 388
victims, 20, 27–28, 42, 168–69, 317, 392, 395–96, 431; distant, 374; potential, 216, 252
voting, 313
vulnerability, 19

Wagon Case, 94–95
Waldron, Jeremy, 264, 266–68, 271–72, 281, 283, 288
Walzer, Michael, 125, 313, 476
war, 21, 125, 176
warfare, chemical/biological, 331
wealth, 362, 415, 448
well-being (welfare), 234, 243–45, 247–48, 255, 258, 404, 437, 461, 464, 470–73, 477
Wiggle-the-Bridge Case, 162, 181–82
Williams, Bernard, 6, 305–10, 313, 325–32, 337, 339, 342–43
willing, 111–12, 224, 232
Wolf, Susan, 404
work, 402
World War II, 170
Worse-than-Dead Case, 163, 188
worst-off, the, 408, 436, 475–78, 481–82, 484, 489
wrong, secondary, 172–73
wronging, 230–32, 235, 239–40, 244, 276, 466–68, 488
wrongness, 126, 455–64, 466–68, 470, 487

Yacht Case, 372–73, 392
Yard Case, 202